URBAN LIFE AND SOCIETY

Harry Gold

**Professor Emeritus,
Oakland University**

Upper Saddle River, New Jersey 07458

Library of Congress Cataloging-in-Publication Data

Gold, Harry
    Urban life and society / Harry Gold.
      p. m.
    Includes bibliographical references.
    ISBN 0–13–021605–4
    1. Sociology, Urban.   2. Cities and towns. I. Title.

HT111.G575 2002
307.76—dc21   2001019912

AVP, Publisher: Nancy Roberts
Senior acquisitions editor: Chris DeJohn
Editorial assistant: Christina Scalia
Executive managing editor: Ann Marie McCarthy
Production liaison: Fran Russello
Editorial/production supervision: Russell Jones (Pine Tree Composition)
Prepress and manufacturing buyer: Mary Ann Gloriande
Cover art director: Jayne Conte
Cover designer: Bruce Kenselaar
Cover image illustrator: Brian Yarvin/Photo Researchers, Inc.
AVP, Director of marketing: Beth Gillett Mejia

This book was set in 10/12 Times Roman by Pine Tree Composition, Inc.,
and was printed and bound by Hamilton Printing Company.
The cover was printed by Phoenix Color Corp.

 © 2002 by Pearson Education Inc.
Upper Saddle River, New Jersey 07458

Printed in the United States of America

10 9 8 7 6 5 4 3 2 1

ISBN 0-13-021605-4

Pearson Education Ltd., *London*
Pearson Education Australia Pty. Ltd., *Sydney*
Pearson Education Singapore, Pte. Ltd.
Pearson Education North Asia Ltd., *Hong Kong*
Pearson Education Canada, Ltd., *Toronto*
Pearson Educación de Mexico, S.A. de C.V.
Pearson Education—Japan, *Tokyo*
Pearson Education Malaysia, Pte. Ltd.
Pearson Education, *Upper Saddle River, New Jersey*

CONTENTS

III   URBAN SOCIAL INSTITUTIONS   145

12   Urban Crime   260
by Kevin Early

13   Problems of Racial and Ethnic Minorities in Urban America   279

PREFACE

This book was first undertaken as a revision of an earlier work, *The Sociology of Urban Life* (1982). However, the large amount of time that has since elapsed, along with the vast changes that have occurred in the urban world, in the field of urban sociology, and in my own thinking on this subject, has led to this fresh new book. While some of the more basic and valid materials from the original book have been retained, particularly in the early chapters on the long history of urban development up to the middle of the twentieth century, the rest of the book has been revised, updated, and rewritten. Several previous chapters have been reorganized, reformulated, or dropped, and one completely new chapter has been added. Equally significant, updated materials from the perspectives of the *"new urban sociology,"* or *"political economy"* have also been added. This is reflected most directly in the two separate chapters on urban economic institutions and political institutions. Rather than being confined to just these two chapters, and segregated from other parts of the book, materials on the new urban sociology and political economy are also integrated into many other chapters, where they are most relevant.

The overall goal of this book is to provide a more comprehensive view of the broad field of urban sociology through a more balanced approach, providing exposure to all of the major theoretical perspectives that have, over time, defined the field's core concepts, as well as the ever changing boundaries. The author of such an approach is sometimes tempted to present an eclectic assortment of topics, in the hope that nothing significant will be left out. On the other hand, there is an equally compelling temptation to provide a more limited and focused perspective, with the risk that the greater selectivity of materials will provide a far less comprehensive overview of the field than usually called for by "survey" type courses common to urban sociology.

This book attempts to avoid the extremes suggested above. Of necessity, urban sociology remains a highly speculative and interpretive field, requiring the synthesis of a vast assortment of theories, concepts, data, and research findings. But such a synthesis ideally must provide a workable balance between focus and breadth, and between extreme eclecticism and rigid systemization. Hopefully, this balance has been achieved by the introduction to six major perspectives as the book's guiding frame of reference. They include: 1) the social change perspective; 2) the ecological perspective; 3) the social structure perspective; 4) the cultural (and social-psychological) perspective; 5) the social problems perspective; and 6) the social policy perspective. In turn, these perspectives are presented in the context of past, present, and projected future urban development, and with a concern for the quality of life in cities, suburbs, and metropolitan areas. The above perspectives are implied or assumed throughout the book rather than spelled out in every instance, but they are defined and explained in more detail in the introductory chapter.

Somewhat unique to this book (as part of the social structure perspective) are separate chapters on urban social institutions, including contemporary economic, political, welfare, and educational institutions, which developed in response to the demands and expectations of modern urban civilization. On the other hand, the survival of traditional social institutions, such as religion and the family, which are preurban in their origins, is often severely challenged by modern urbanization, and, as a result, these institutions have become significantly modified in urban societies. These two rapidly changing urban institutions are discussed in some detail in a separate chapter.

While urban sociology had traditionally focused entirely on cities, and more recently on the wider range of cities, suburbs, and metropolitan areas, it is now widely recognized that all parts of entire societies, such as American society, are indirectly, if not directly, affected by the process of urbanization. Thus, it is entirely appropriate to focus on urban societies, as well as on the more traditional topics of urban sociology, as does this book; hence the title, *Urban Life and Society.*

Finally, in addition to a guiding frame of reference, a wide variety of other student needs were taken into account in writing this book. These include an appropriate reading level, clarity of presentation, logical organization, sufficient explanation and illustration, and the need to maintain a high level of interest. But for potential instructors, the author has relied on his strong belief, based on many years of experience teaching courses in urban sociology and on reactions to his earlier book on the subject, that most instructors will prefer to supply their own anecdotes and experiences in presenting and explaining course materials to their students. Therefore, this book does not pretend to "teach," in place of the teacher's own inputs. Having prepared a very comprehensive and wide range of topics for this book, the author also understands that many, if not most instructors, will not attempt to assign or cover the entire book in a single course. On the positive side, however, the breadth of this book will hopefully provide instructors with some flexibility in choosing which topics they wish to cover.

Harry Gold
Professor Emeritus
Oakland University

ACKNOWLEDGMENTS

I wish to acknowledge some of the many persons who wittingly or unwittingly contributed to the making of this book. First are the many former teachers who first helped shape my interest and knowledge of the many theoretical and empirical dimensions of urban society— most notably, H. Warren Dunham, Albert J. Mayer, Albert J. Reiss, Amos Hawley, Donald Marsh, and Mel Ravitz. Colleagues who read portions of the manuscript and made many valuable suggestions include Gary Shepherd, Gordon Shepherd, David Maines, Leon Warshay, Richard Stamps, and Kevin Early. Colleagues who earlier read portions of *The Sociology of Urban Life,* upon whch this current book is partially based, include Robert Gutman, David Popenoe, Melvin Webber, William Faunce, and the late Donald I. Warren.

W. C. Dutton, Jr., Charles Blessing, John T. Howard, Robert Hoover, Robert Capenter, Bernard Frieden, Norbert Gorwick, and Robert Marans were among former colleagues, teachers, or employers in the field of urban planning who helped sensitize me to some of the aspects of urban planning as a social movement, as a function of local government, and as a policy making and applied profession.

Special thanks go to Jacqueline Scherer and Donald Levin, each of whom had written several chapters for the latter book, and whose previous contributions are liberally cited in the present volume. For the current volume, I am deeply indebted to Leon and Diana Warshay, who contributed chapter 11 on Urban Patterns of Social Stratification, and to Kevin Early, who contributed chapter 12 on Urban Crime. Needless to say, I alone accept full responsibility for the contents and any shortcomings of these chapters, as well as the remaining part of this book, which I have exclusively authored.

I am extremely grateful to John Chillingworth, former acquisitions editor of Prentice Hall, whose confidence in this project helped get it underway, and to his successor, Chris DeJohn, who diligently nursed it to fruition. Christina Scalia was most helpful in patiently assisting me to learn and apply twenty-first century methods and techniques for preparing the manuscript for publication, and in this, she was a great crutch! Robert J. S. Ross, Clark University, Corey Dolgan, Worcester State College, Richard Goe, Kansas State University, and Akbar Mahdi, Ohio Weslyan University were also most helpful in providing succinct, insightful, and timely reviews for all parts of the manuscript. Finally, I am most grateful to my wife, Patricia, who proofread the manuscript, helped prepare the index, and was supportive in many other ways too numerous to mention.

Part I

INTRODUCTION AND EARLY URBANIZATION

1

URBAN SOCIOLOGY
AS A FIELD OF STUDY

During the twentieth century, America has changed from a predominantly rural society to one in which a great majority of its population now lives in urban areas. This transformation had such far-reaching effects on the American way of life that near the beginning of the twenty-first century its significance has still not been totally comprehended by most Americans. Recent popular concern with the nature and quality of urban life seems to have been aroused by the turmoil of the 1960s through the 1990s, when a series of urban crises claimed national attention, and many Americans began pressing for answers to questions about the nature and causes of urban problems and about the future of American cities.

What the student of urban sociology soon learns, however, is that the so-called current urban crisis is the product of a vast and complex evolutionary, or perhaps revolutionary, social process that has been continuously unfolding for many centuries. The student may also soon learn that urban sociology is a field of study and research going back nearly a century, long before it assumed its current popularity. Therefore, before spelling out the major perspectives of this book, the first part of this introductory chapter begins with a brief review of the historical development of urban sociology as a field of study. Such a review should further help the student appreciate the intellectual development of this diverse, complex, and challenging field, as well as preparing the student for the rationale for the entire book, which follows this brief history.

THE GERMAN AND CHICAGO SCHOOLS
OF URBAN SOCIOLOGY

Although there are individual exceptions, the classic writers who began and stimulated the serious analysis of urban life from sociological perspectives fall primarily into two major schools. The first developed in Germany and was centered in Heidelberg and Berlin. Its members were a remarkable group of scholars who produced a series of essays and books during the first quarter of the twentieth century, many of which remain influential to this day. The second school is commonly referred to as the "Chicago School" because its leading members were on the faculty of the University of Chicago. The ideas of the Chicago School, which were produced primarily in the period between the First and Second World Wars, also still pervade much of the writing of contemporary urban sociologists.

The German School

One of the early sociological efforts to understand the modern urban community was Max Weber's *The City* (1958) , originally published in 1905. In this work, Weber viewed the city as a total systemic unit of human life, distinguished by a complex order of social actions, social relations, and social institutions. To constitute an urban community, a human settlement has to consist of at least the following features: a fortification; a market; a complex legal system, including a court and a body of autonomous law; and an elected political administration. Weber's concept of the city is best understood in the context of the term "cosmopolitan." A cosmopolitan human settlement is one in which diverse individuals and lifestyles can exist in the same community. To Weber, this definition is synonymous with the nature of the city itself: the city is that social form which permits the greatest degree of individuality and uniqueness in each occurrence or event produced within its boundaries. The city, then, represents much more than a single style of life. It is a constellation of social structures that can produce a multitude of lifestyles and encourage continuous social change.

Weber's work on the city is most valuable for the way in which it focuses the attention of urbanization as a fundamental process of social change and as a unique historical pattern. In this sense, the city represents a distinct and limited pattern of human life that could only appear under special conditions and at a certain time in history. To Weber, the ideal conditions conducive to the emergence of urban life were first produced in preindustrial Europe, which was characterized by the development and influence of rationality.

In opposition to traditional action—which emphasizes what is handed down from the past—cities of Western civilization emphasize rational action, which involves the calculated use of resources for the achievement of specified goals in the most economic way possible. Within this framework, Weber's work was comparative in that it recognized a great variety of forms of city life to be found in preindustrial Western societies as well as in non-Western societies.

Nevertheless, the Western city, as Weber saw it, was going through a transformation that raised serious questions as to its capacity to survive in its present form. The urban community had lost, or was losing, its legal and political autonomy to the larger and more powerful nation-state, the urban citizenry was no longer united by a common purpose, and the internal structure of the city was approaching a state of decay. For Weber, the end of the modern Western city, as he knew it, appeared to be in sight.

The work of another German theorist, Oswald Spengler (1928), differed from Weber in that Spengler believed that different states of city development were indicative of the development of civilization as a whole in Western culture, and that the stages of growth in both were cyclical in nature. He believed that city cultures throughout history have had a clear pattern of growth and decay, and that the cities of his own time were a cancer. He saw them sapping off the sources of vitality and energy that were more characteristics of earlier periods of urban development when cities and their surrounding countryside were of more equal strength and influence.

In his major work, he prophesized that the large metropolitan centers of his day would meet the fate of ancient Rome, modern cities would be destroyed by wars or other disasters, and civilized urban society would revert to a more barbaric form of preurban agricultural life. Then, the whole cycle of urban growth would reinstitute itself, civilized life would return, again become overripe at the point where the city overpowers the countryside, and would once again collapse.

A major contribution of both Spengler and Weber was to postulate that a particular cluster of traits or characteristics is associated with each stage of urban growth, and that the cluster of hypothetical characteristics they identify represents the pure or "ideal" type for that stage of development. Thus, their work was an early effort to classify types of communities along dimensions such as age, size, function, or complexity of structure.

An even earlier effort to develop a typology of urban development was that of another German theorist, Ferdinand Tonnies (Nottridge, 1972). Tonnies's typology was spelled out in a book published in 1917 entitled *Gemeinschaft and Gesellschaft*. The title has no precise equivalent in English but can be roughly translated into the terms "community" and "society." For Tonnies, these two concepts are opposites, and all human social relationships can be seen as divided between these two different types. *Gemeinschaft* relationships are found in the relationships within family and kinship groups and between physically close friends or neighbors who live or work together with close understanding and cooperation. The impression created by Tonnies is that these relationships represent "natural will," are deep, warm, and satisfying, and are most characteristic of small rural or agricultural communities. In contrast, *Gesellschaft* relationships are more impersonal, are bonded by formal contract rather than natural will, and tend to separate individuals and groups from one another by creating isolation, tension, and conflict. These relationships, it is implied, are characteristic of modern city life. And as the urbanization process expands, *Gesellschaft* relationships will grow more dominant and will eventually displace *Gemeinschaft* relationships.

The German social theorist whose work probably had the most direct influence on the thinking of early urban sociologists in the United States was Georg Simmel, who was a friend and younger colleague of Weber. Simmel's work on the effect of urbanization was similar to that of Weber and the others reviewed earlier in that he utilized an "ideal type" method of analysis to describe the form that cities take. But Simmel differed from the others by emphasizing the psychological rather than the structural aspects of urban life. In his classic article, *"The Metropolis and Mental Life" (1950),* Simmel speculated that the size, density, and complexity of urban life would produce distinct personality traits and distinct patterns of human interaction, as city dwellers attempt to defend themselves from the excess of psychic or nervous stimulation Simmel thought to be characteristic of life in large cities. Because of exposure to constant shifts in internal and external situations in their daily round of life, city dwellers find it difficult to maintain an integrated personality, and the quality of interpersonal relationships in urban settings fails to ensure consistency of behavior. Urban dwellers seek to protect themselves from the resulting state of overstimulation by seeking anonymity, by adopting an attitude of sophistication, or by masking their feeling with a blaze or "cool" posture in response to psychic overload. The result is that calculated expediency and the rationale of efficiency takes the place of feelings as the basis for personal relationships in the city.

Simmel was unsure whether these changes in the characteristic modes of human interaction resulting from urbanization would lead to dispirited alienation or would liberate the urbanite for a more civilized and uplifting kind of human freedom. The great subtlety of Simmel's thinking at this early point in the development of ideas about urban life was that he did not foreclose the possibility of either or both of the outcomes, and that he was willing to leave open for further exploration the potential for both good and evil that the giant and impersonal metropolis of his and later times might ultimately serve. Such exploration still goes on in modern urban sociology, because the issues raised by Simmel are still not satisfactorily resolved (Warren, 1973). Some of the materials included in this volume continue to confront the issues that Simmel originally posed.

The Chicago School

In the United States, the field of urban sociology was first widely recognized as a special subarea of sociology during the 1920s, and it was in 1925 that the annual meetings of the American Sociological Society were devoted almost exclusively to papers in the field of urban sociology (Burgess and Bogue, 1964). Actually, the development of urban sociology in the United States had been most strongly influenced by the work of a group of scholars affiliated with the University of Chicago during a period beginning about 1915 to about the middle of the twentieth century. Some of the greatest intellectual achievements of this group were accomplished in the 1920s and 1930s, establishing some of the main topical concerns of urban sociology, many of which are still highly relevant today. The most significant figures associated with the Chicago School were Robert Park, Ernest Burgess, Louis Wirth, and Robert Redfield. Although these men were strongly influenced by the German School, their work shifted to development of urban sociology in different directions. For example, the field of human ecology also evolved at the University of Chicago, becoming a subfield of sociology in its own right and sometimes viewed by its proponents as an alternative approach to the entire field of urban sociology. First, however, we shall consider the main contributions of the Chicago School.

The origins of the Chicago school can be traced back to an article by Robert Park entitled "The City: Suggestions for the Investigation of Human Behavior in the Urban Environment," published in 1916 (Burgess and Bogue, 1964). Formally a journalist, Park had turned to sociology as a result of his fascination with many aspects of the social, economic, and political life of the city of Chicago. During his lifetime, that city had gone through a period of remarkable social changes, such as a very rapid population increase due to immigrants of many different ethnic and cultural backgrounds coming to the city in wave after wave. This growth was accompanied by noticeable social problems, such as the creation of overcrowded slum housing conditions, increased crime, municipal corruption, unemployment, and ethnic exploitation and segregation.

Originally, Park approached these problems in the "muckraking" and reformist tradition of Lincoln Steffens and the whole school of journalism that he represented. Much of the earliest urban research of Park and his followers involved the discovery and reporting to the public that the feelings and sentiments of those living in the newly forming ethnic slums were in reality very different from those imputed to them by the larger public, which had by that time already formed strong prejudices and patterns of discrimination toward the newcomers (Burgess and Bogue, 1964). Quite often, Park and the other social scientists at the University of Chicago defended the immigrant groups publicly and spoke out for tolerance, understanding, and sympathy. When Park discovered that such efforts did not always lead to constructive change, his reformer or social work orientation gave way to an ambition to understand more fully the social and economic forces at work in the city and their effect on the social and personal organization of those who worked there.

By the early 1920s, this shift toward a more scientific analysis of city life led to the creation of a program of sociological field research, using the city as a laboratory for scientific study. The University of Chicago sociologists, with the assistance of their students, first undertook the task of discovering the physical plan of the city. They made maps showing the spatial distribution of all kinds of land uses and all kinds of social problems such as juvenile delinquency, mental illness, and prostitution. These were followed by maps showing the spacial distribution of local facilities such as movie theaters, dance halls, rooming houses, and brothels. Soon their students began making maps of any social data that could be plotted. Several classics that emerged from these early student field studies include *The Hobo,* by Nels Anderson; *The Gold Coast and the Slum,* by Harvey Zorbaugh; *Vice in Chicago* by Walter Reckless; and *The Gang*, by Frederick Thrasher (Burgess and Bogue, 1964).

The research of this period was based on the assumption that the city had a characteristic social organization and a way of life that differentiated it from rural communities. Further, the city was composed of "natural areas," each having its own distinctive physical features, social institutions, or subcultures based on differences of income, occupation, ethnic background, religion, race, or other salient social characteristics. Park never tired of pointing out how this process of differentiation conditioned almost every aspect of urban social life, and that the spatial segregation and differentiation of land uses and of groups of people were physical manifestations of social, psychological, and economic forces at work in the city as a whole. Thus, one finds in Park's work an important unification of ecological and cultural themes that have been essential to a more fully developed multiperspective approach for understanding the complexities of modern urban communities (see Maines, Bridger, and Ulmer, 1996).

Louis Wirth, whose book *The Ghetto* has also become a classic, was a major figure in the Chicago School. He had absorbed many of the ideas of Park and Simmel, and although his work was not as original, he perhaps went further in systematizing, detailing, and extending urban theory. His article "Urbanism as a Way of Life" was an influential contribution in that it helped to further define the boundaries of urban sociology as a field of study. Wirth (1938) viewed the shift from a rural to a predominantly urban society as producing a profound change in virtually every phase of human life. Although the city is the product of evolutionary rather than instantaneous growth and does not wipe out completely the previously dominant modes of folk society, he believed that the city nevertheless does produce a distinctive mode of life. He perceived city life as the opposite of life in preurban folk communities.

The skyline of Manhattan

Wirth defined the city as a "relatively large, dense, and permanent settlement of socially heterogeneous individuals." It was the task of urban sociologists to discover the forms of social action and social organization that typically emerged in settlements of this kind. Wirth hypothesized that, as the size, density, and heterogeneity of city populations increased, the character of social relationships and social organization would also change. For example, the occupational division of labor would become more elaborate and complex, and the bonds between residents would grow weaker and more impersonal, superficial, and transitory. Urban dwellers would become more rational, sophisticated, and anonymous; their lives would be lived at a faster pace; and their contacts would be physically closer but more superficial. Interest groups would multiply, producing a conflict of loyalties for urban dwellers who, at the same time, would become more geographically and socially mobile.

Wirth suffered from the underlying pessimism about city life that afflicted many of the other German and Chicago sociologists, in the sense that he saw personal disorganization, mental breakdown, delinquency, crime, corruption, and social disorder as products of the "rootlessness" of growing urbanization. It has been difficult to test the validity of Wirth's observations about urban life, and many of them have been challenged by more contemporary social scientists, as is reflected in later chapters of this volume. Yet Wirth's work still serves as a useful point of departure for much current urban research and theory, and as a useful way to focus on current urban issues for the serious student of urban life.

Robert Redfield (1947) was an anthropologist (also of the Chicago school) who had done much fieldwork among villages and other rural communities in Mexico. His work broadened that of his colleagues by showing how their view of the modern city were based on their assumptions about life in nonurban, or "folk," societies. By combining analysis of the internal characteristics of cities, in the Chicago tradition, with the analysis of broader forces of social change and development emphasized by the German school, Redfield demonstrated how the difference between urban and folk societies was related to the evolution of urban forms. Redfield's main variables in showing change from folk society to urban society were the increase in cultural disorganization, the increase in secularization, and the increase in individualization. In effect Redfield created a scale having at one end an "ideal type" with all the essential characteristics of a folk society and, at the other end, urban society. This concept has come to be referred to as the *folk-urban continuum* and has been widely quoted in the urban sociology literature (Hatt and Reiss, 1957). Redfield used this concept as the basis for an elaborate description of what happens to people as they become more urbanized. To Redfield, the move from folk to urban society was a process with a definite beginning and a definite end with various stages in between, through which cities might pass while evolving.

Of course, many of the theories and conclusions of the earlier contributors to the development of urban sociology have been expanded upon, updated, revised, or discarded by subsequent generations of urban scholars, and many of their concerns will be reintroduced and reexamined in more detail in the chapters to follow, in the light of more recent thinking and research. But this early work reviewed here was most influential in shaping the direction and topical concerns of much contemporary urban sociology.

THE NEW URBAN SOCIOLOGY

In reaction to urban ecology, which was an important offspring of the Chicago school, and which continues to dominate the field of urban sociology to this day, an alternative approach began to emerge in the last several decades of the twentieth century. Loosely labeled *The New Urban Sociology*, its proponents seek to reject the conventional wisdom of the ecological approach and other dimensions of urban sociology that had evolved from the Chicago and German schools and replace it with what they claim is a more valid approach.

However, the "new" urban sociology is not completely new. For example, many of the ideas of the new urban sociology are based on the work of nineteenth century or early twentieth century theorists such as Karl Marx, Frederich Engels, and Georg Simmel, or can be found in the work of leading urban ecologists of the mid-twentieth century, such as Amos Hawley and R. D. McKenzie (Hawley, 1981). Also, a recent edition of a leading sociology textbook (Palen, 1992) had added a chapter on the new urban sociology, but it appeared almost as a postscript and its approach was not visibly incorporated into the remaining body of the text. A still later edition of the same book (Palen, 1997) drops the heading "new urban sociology" altogether and substitutes the term "urban political economy," as perhaps a more accurate label for this alternative approach.

Nor has the new urban sociology completely supplanted more traditionally established approaches. For example, another recent book, entitled *The New Urban Sociology* (Gottdiener, 1994), presumes a new urban sociology perspective, but it too failed to significantly supplant preexisting models of urban sociology, including a well-established, urban ecology–based sociospatial approach, upon which the author significantly relied throughout this book.

Thus, it is probably more accurate to think of the new urban sociology as a useful addition to, rather than as a replacement for, preexisting approaches to urban sociology. In this context, the new urban sociology is of value in broadening the field by incorporating new variables, or by placing greater emphasis on preexisting ones, and therefore merits further discussion here.

Although not a totally unified school of thought, there are a number of common themes that run through the new urban sociology. One of these is that social conflict between competing interest or status groups is a ubiquitous social process. When applied to urban communities, such a process involves the struggle for control over community land uses, community physical or social resources, and the community's social, economic, or political institutions, leading to continuous changes to the community's social structure and physical layout. It is the task of the urban sociologist, according to the proponents of this school of thought, to identify these competing groups, to identify the systems of power governing the conflict between them (that is, the systems of dominance and subordination within which they compete), and to link these causative forces to the resultant sociospatial structure of urban communities (see Smith, 1979; Smith and Timberlake, 1997; Gottdiener; 1994).

A second major theme identifies capitalism as a dominant system of power dominating the development of modern urban-industrial communities. It also considers the interplay between capitalistic economic and political systems and the ways in which they interact, cooperatively or competitively, to increase, distribute, or redistribute community wealth and resources among community groups and across spatial subareas of the community. Usually, from the perspective of the new urban sociology, an undesirable biproduct of capitalism is an increase in economic inequality between competing segments of the community (see Bradshaw and Wallace, 1996; Logan and Molotch, 1987; Hutchinson, 1993; Lefebvre, 1991).

The new urban sociologists also legitimately argue that cities or metropolitan communities, which were once dominated by local, regional, and even national economic forces, are now increasingly controlled and shaped by the worldwide system of an emerging global economy. A growing body of literature, for example, treats the power exercised by giant international corporations on the economic, political, and social life of cities, as well as the nations that contain them (Sassen, 1991, 1994; King, 1990; Ross and Trachte, 1990). In the United States, large global corporations affect virtually all aspects of American domestic and foreign economic and political policy. Thus, economic cycles, business investment, employment and unemployment, domestic and foreign investment, education, health and welfare, the environment, public opinion and the mass media, electoral processes, and , of course, a whole range of urban processes are seen as shaped by global corporate activities (Gold, 1990).

Even though integrated global capitalism undeniably brings technological and economic progress, the new urban sociologists, as well as many other critics, also focus on the more disastrous effects of economic globalism. William Greider (1997) argues that new features of global capitalism will bring unparalleled inequality and exploitation in the wealthiest countries, as well as the poorest, as worldwide competition drags wages down in advanced nations toward those of the poorest countries. As poor nations race to get into the global economic "game" and rich ones innovate to stay ahead, the world is flooded with overproduction, which is sure to bring major plant closings and massive unemployment. And the severe dislocations and potentially inhumane treatment of the economically displaced workers, which Greider concludes are part of a global recipe for social "meltdown" and social disaster, are most likely to have greatest impact in the large cities or metropolitan regions of the world, rich and poor alike.

One of the most interesting aspects of the new urban sociology are the attempts to establish causal relationships between broad macroeconomic trends, such as the emergence of a world system or the growth of global capitalism, with a host of urban social problems at the more microsociological level of the local urban community or neighborhood, such as poverty, residential racial or ethnic segregation and conflict, crime, unemployment, transportation, poor housing, local educational problems, and so forth. But as the first version of this present volume has previously pointed out, "The relationship between a very broad and general social process such as urbanization and the much more concentrated examples of social problems such as those that are commonly classified within the framework of social disorganization, deviant behavior, or value conflict are very difficult to observe directly, and there is a very complex and indirect chain of events by which these two levels of social behavior can be said to be even remotely connected" (Gold, 1982). The same can be said about the broad social and economic forces focused on by the new urban sociology and their causal relationships to localized urban phenomena. Nevertheless, there is a growing body of theory and empirical research that attempts to establish these relationships, and a number of the more promising efforts are cited in this volume wherever they are most relevant.

ALTERNATE PERSPECTIVES FOR URBAN SOCIOLOGY

Our review of the historical development of urban sociology reminds us that the boundaries and core concerns of the field have been in a continuous state of flux and growth during this development, and many sociologists are no longer certain that it makes sense to treat urban sociology as a distinct subspecialty set apart from general sociology. Because of the diversity and complexity of the subject matter, the content of existing books about urban sociology differs widely, and when one looks at the existing body of urban sociology literature, the current boundaries of the field are not readily apparent.

Over the past thirty or forty years, the growing interest of legislators, government officials, journalists and the mass media, community leaders, private foundations, research centers, and the general public has resulted in a tremendous increase in the volume of urban research and writing. Millions of dollars have been poured into studies of virtually all aspects of urban life: population trends, changing patterns of residential and social mobility, poverty, inequality, housing, transportation and communications problems, race and ethnic relations, civil disorder, crime, city-suburban relationships, changing land use patterns, urban sprawl, municipal taxation and service delivery problems, pollution and other environmental problems, change in lifestyles and values—the list of urban related topics is virtually endless.

The field of urban sociology has, in fact, grown so broad in its scope and in its over-lapping concerns with topics associated with other disciplines, as well as with other sub-specialties of sociology, that some scholars have begun to doubt whether urban sociology really does have a clear focus of its own (Gutman and Popenoe, 1970). Very often, urban sociology courses and textbooks consist of a wide assortment of topics that do not seem to be connected to one another in any theoretically meaning sort of way. Much of the writing, for example, relegates the urban community to a background context within which particular kinds of problems are considered or certain types of social processes are played out, while at the same time the urban community itself is not the prime object of investigation. On the other hand, some courses or texts have become unduly restrictive in their focus to provide a more rigorous or systematic frame of reference for urban sociology. Thus, they may focus exclusively on ecology, social psychology, social stratification, the new urban sociology, demography, sociospatial patterns, or social problems at the expense of other equally important approaches or themes.

The perspective of this book is that the field of urban sociology is so complex and diversified that it cannot be completely understood from any single approach or frame of reference. What is needed is a multidimensional approach that can provide the student with a variety of perspectives to demonstrate the relationships between many kinds of urban concepts, theory, and data, and to clarify their meaning and significance without at the same time oversimplifying the unavoidable complexities of the phenomena involved. Also, the author of a volume such as this is sometimes tempted to present an eclectic assortment of topics in the hope that nothing significant will be left out. On the other hand, there is the equally compelling temptation to provide a more limited and focused perspective, as suggested earlier, with the risk that the greater selectivity of materials will provide a far less comprehensive overview of the field of urban sociology than is called for by its very nature. This volume attempts to avoid these extremes. Of necessity, urban sociology remains a highly speculative and interpretive field, requiring the synthesis of a vast assortment of theories, concepts, and research findings. But such synthesis must provide a workable balance between focus and breadth, and between extreme eclecticism and rigid systemization. This book attempts to meet this objective by the introduction of six major perspectives as the book's guiding frame of reference. Building on the development of the field of urban sociology so far, as it has been described in this chapter, these six perspectives include (1) the *social change* perspective; (2) the *ecology* perspective; (3) the *culture* perspective; (4) the *social structure* perspective; (5) the *social problems* perspective; and (6) the *social policy* perspective. A brief overview and explanation of each of these alternate perspectives is in order:

The Social Change Perspective

Urban communities, like most social phenomena, are ever-changing entities. They may grow or decline, they may rearrange themselves internally, or their essential character may change over time. One cannot discuss present-day urban communities and urban life without asking such questions as: How did these communities get to be the way they are? What are the existing forces likely to produce change? or What are these communities going to be like in the foreseeable future? Urban life as we know it is a relatively recent historical development, and there is no reason to believe that the urban community of tomorrow will be identical to the urban community of today. Because social change is ubiquitous to all social life, any effort to describe and explain current social realities is extremely difficult; and by the time existing social patterns, which have been observed through social research, can be analyzed and communicated by publication of the results (a process that in itself is continuously being radically realtered), the original social patterns may have been significantly altered.

To say that social change is ubiquitous is almost to say nothing, if the changes are not widespread or far-reaching in their consequences. The rhetoric of social change is currently in fashion, but if the concept of social change is widely and equally applied to all manner or conditions or is flagrantly abused, it may cease to have meaning or significance (Chirot, 1994).

For our purpose, the most significant social change process is *urbanization.* Urbanization refers to the processes by which (1) the very first cities in human history begin to emerge and develop in previously rural areas; (2) rural populations begin to move to cities; (3) urban communities continue to grow larger and to absorb an ever-increasing portion of a society's or region's population; (4) the behavioral patterns of migrants to cities are transformed to conform to those that are characteristic of groups in the cities; (5) as cities grow larger, their structure and form become more complex and elaborately differentiated; and, finally, (6) urbanization transforms the nature of the entire society in which it occurs. Thus, wherever urbanization takes place, it ultimately produces a radical transformation in the structure of the containing society.

The process of urbanization has been uneven throughout recorded history, moving slowly or not at all in some periods, accelerating rapidly in other periods, and declining in still others. In more recent periods, urbanization has occurred so rapidly that it has assumed truly *revolutionary* proportions. Lest this be considered an exaggeration, it is important to identify the manner in which the concept of revolutionary change is being introduced here. Social revolutions involve nothing less than changes that drastically alter the structure of the entire society in which they take place. Thus, the industrial revolution, the democratic revolution, the urban revolution, and so on are all examples of radical transformations of the basic social patterns of the societies in which they occur. Urbanization can further be described as revolutionary according to the following characteristics suggested by C. P. Wolf (1976) in his analysis of the structure of social revolutions:

A. *Suddenness.* The most rapid changes in the process of urbanization have taken place in the nineteenth and twentieth centuries, and the appropriate time dimensions within which the revolutionary characteristics of urbanization can be observed must often be counted in centuries and, at the very least, in decades. This may not seem to be very sudden to observers with a short sense of time, but against the total history of the human species, which has evolved over millions of years (less than a fraction of one percent of human existence has occurred within the context of urban civilization), the adjective "revolutionary" is indeed appropriate.

Bustling pedestrian scene in mid-Manhattan

B. *Acceleration.* If suddenness of change does not appear as revolutionary to some, drastic changes in the *rate* of change can be so considered. Again, as much of the work in this book emphasizes, the rate of urbanization accelerated dramatically in the nineteenth century and throughout the entire twentieth century. In fact, the acceleration has been so rapid that urban experts during the twenty-first century will most certainly continue to measure and assess its characteristics and consequences (Chirot, 1994), as this volume does also.

C. *Irreversibility.* A revolution can be defined as a relatively sudden set of changes that yield a state of affairs from which to return to the situation just before that revolution is "virtually impossible." This applies aptly to urbanization, for even though exceptions to the general rule occurred in earlier states of urbanization, no society in the modern world has returned to a preurban state after having become highly urbanized. This is especially true wherever urbanization and industrialization have occurred simultaneously.

D. *Discontinuity.* Revolutionary changes are not usually smooth and continuous, but rather they create deep breaches in the continuity of the change process. New social arrangements and patterns occur that are often dramatically and completely alien to those that have previously prevailed. Thus, social revolutions may create upheavals and dislocations that disrupt people's habitual patterns of routinized behavior and require them to learn completely new ways of thinking and doing. Of course much social strain, stress, and conflict may be created, which constitute the basis for some of the additional perspectives to follow.

The Ecology Perspective

At the most general level, ecology is concerned with the processes and forms of people's adjustments to their physical environment. The urban community (both its natural and its "man-made" spatial dimensions) is one major form that adjustment takes. More specifically, the study of territorially based spatial systems created by human endeavor, of which the urban community is the prime example, has come to be known as *urban ecology.* Although there is a broad and rich scholarly tradition of urban ecology with deep roots in the Chicago School of urban ecology, Otis Dudley Duncan (1961) has perhaps gone furthest in viewing the urban community as an *ecosystem.* The concept of the ecosystem developed by Duncan identifies four major classes of variables as the major elements of the ecosystem and specifies their relationships to one another and to the ecosystem as a whole. Duncan's four classes of variables include (1) population, (2) environment, (3) technology, and (4) social organization. This concept of the ecosystem is useful for illustration of not only how each of these four classes of variables interacts with and contains implications for the others, but it also helps us to understand the interrelatedness of urban life in a far more general way. The discussion to follow illustrates the main dimensions of the variables that comprise the ecosystem (population, environment, and technology are considered here). The fourth variable, social organization, is only briefly mentioned because it is discussed in much greater detail later under the heading *social structure.*

Population.   One of the most significant characteristics of any urban community is the size of its population. For example, a community of 10,000 people differs markedly in almost all respects from a community of 100,000 people, and a community of 100,000 people differs tremendously from a community of 1 million or more people, and so on. The size of a community's population may tell a good deal about its containing environment, its technology, or its social organization. In turn, the environment, technology, and social organization of a community may each or conjointly set limits on the size of its population. The relationships between population size and the other variables of the ecosystem are considered in more detail in later chapters.

The density, distribution, and rates of growth or decline of an urban population are additional population characteristics that affect and are affected by the other components of the ecosystem, as are also socioeconomic and age or gender characteristics. Rapid changes in any of the above characteristics of a community's population are surefire indications that significant changes are also taking place in its technology, social organization, or both. Of course, when rates of population change are so rapid that other components of the ecosystem are unable to keep pace with the changes, then a problematic form of ecological imbalance may be created, which ultimately may alter such population changes.

Environment.   The natural environment, including such elements as natural resources, topography, soil conditions, climate, and waterways, has always had an important bearing on the location in which cities originate and grow. In turn, these same geographic features may set ultimate limits on the size and density of the population in any given urban region. But in the process of accommodating to the local environment, an urban population may apply its technological, cultural, and social organization to modify the environment or its effects. Thus, hills may be leveled, canals dug, rivers diverted, swamps filled, foliage planted, fields irrigated, soil fertilized, roads built, and buildings heated and air conditioned. The very existence of a population in a given geographic area and the resultant artificial spatial distribution of land uses that are derived from that population's daily activities become as much a part of the urban dweller's environment as the natural features mentioned above.

In most cases, the more advanced technology and social structure are, the less limiting are the constraints imposed by the local physical environment. Thus, people are able to use modern technology to build new urban communities in previously uninhabited or geographically inhospitable regions, and to make these areas more directly accessible to established urban centers by new forms of transportation and communications, such as air, rail, or auto, and satellites, telephones, cable, or computers. Successful examples might include Soviet cities built in remote areas of Arctic Siberia, new towns built in the arid Negev Desert of Israel, or the new capital city of Brazil, Brazilia, built in the remote Amazon River basin.

For a number of years, urban ecologists had neglected the natural environment as a topic of concern, and urban sociologists have been criticized for failing to deal adequately with the interrelationships between the physical environment and social factors. However, concerns about the depletion of natural resources and of the ozone level and the pollution of air, land, and water by urban populations have recently become much more widespread. As a result, new questions again are being raised about the potential constraints to future urban growth and sprawl because of the increasingly evident undesirable effects on the natural environment.

Technology.   The earliest cities could emerge only after technological improvements in agriculture made it possible to produce large enough surpluses in food supplies to support confirm populations. Since the beginning of urban life, successive waves of technological development have enabled significant changes in the size, physical structure, and social structure of urban communities. It is no accident that the revolutionary growth in the size of cities and of the urban population since the beginning of the nineteenth century in Europe and North America paralleled the technological advances in manufacturing, transportation, communications, and economic organization brought about by the industrial revolution.

The metropolitan trend during this century toward the decentralization of city populations into sprawling suburbs and the redistribution of many industrial and commercial activities over an ever-expanding land area surrounding central cities has been greatly influenced by modern scientific and technological advances, especially in the areas of transportation and communications. The extensive use of the automobile has eliminated the necessity of locating the place of work and residence in close proximity. Thus, those who were first able to afford the use of the private automobile were among the first urbanites to resettle on a large scale in suburban residential enclaves. Shopping centers, factories, and other business establishments were able to decentralize as they lessened their dependence on waterways, railroads, and an adjacent labor supply. The telephone, the motor truck, and the automobile made them readily accessible to their suppliers, their customers, and their employees at almost any location within the metropolitan complex. Of course, this expansion was also facilitated by the ready availability of low-cost water, energy, and fuel supplies. As these become depleted or exorbitantly expensive, it is entirely possible that further urban growth and decentralization could be sharply curtailed.

The Culture Perspective

The general pattern of decentralization is also probably both the source and product of changing *values*, such as industry's desire for more space, more attractive living conditions for its managers and employees, and an increasing emphasis on visible symbols of status, such as may be afforded by such amenities as green open space and landscaping, pleasingly visible architecture, and adequate parking facilities. Of course, from the perspective of the new urban sociology, all of the *values* would be subsumed under the even more general value of the desire for greater profits! A growing focus on the availability of increased leisure time and the most effective means for utilizing it is also one of the significant *cultural* manifestations of the technological advances of the twentieth century. Thus, we have introduced the basic sociologically related concepts of culture and values to the perspectives selected to provide a frame of reference for the topics explored in this book.

Generally, the principal components of culture include *values*, *norms*, *sanctions*, and *symbols*. Values are ideas shared by people about what is good and bad, right and wrong, desirable and undesirable. Values are general ideas that shape the ideals and goals of a community's or society's culture. Norms refer to expectations of how people are expected to act, think, or feel in specific social situations. These may be written, in the form of laws, but mostly they are not written down but are widely understood and practiced by members of a society as part of its culture. Sanctions are the means through which a society culturally enforces its norms. Sanctions may be positive, in the forms of rewards for behaving "properly," or negative, in the form of punishment for behaving improperly. A symbol is anything that meaningfully represents something else. For example, an American flag may stand for patriotism, a swastika may stand for a dangerous enemy or patriotism (depending on the cultures in which they are displayed), a red light means stop, a green light means go, a thumbs-up gesture may be a sign of approval, thumbs down a sign of disapproval, or a pair of golden arches may indicate a remarkably standardized hamburger, no matter which community, region, or country found in. Symbols may be material, as in the case of most of the examples just listed, which are material objects of one sort or another, or they may be nonmaterial or abstract, such as languages, beliefs, or traditions.

The point being made here is that both material and nonmaterial culture are integral components of the physical structure and social life of all human communities, including all urban communities, which is a fact sometimes neglected in some alternate perspectives for urban sociology. But because large urban communities and the urban societies which contain them are extremely complex and contain a broad diversity of peoples from differing cultural backgrounds, it is important to think of large urban communities as containing a wide variety of different *subcultures* within a larger overarching urban culture. Each subculture may have its own ethnic, racial, or religious heritage, or may be differentiated from other subcultures on the bases of social class, occupational background, educational level, lifestyle, neighborhood or subcommunity, age, gender, marital status, political values, sexual preferences, or any other characteristic which differentiates it in some significant way from the larger containing culture and from other differing subcultures. Spatially adjacent subcultures may be seen as living in cooperation and harmony with one another, or they may be viewed as engaged in competition with one another, engaged in a constant struggle for access to or control of vital community resources. Which of these two views is most accurate depends, of course, on either the intellectual perspective of the observer, or on the available empirical evidence, in each case. These are still matters of debate among urban scholars of differing persuasions and are considered in more detail in numerous parts of this book.

The Social Structure Perspective

The social structure perspective deals with identifying and explaining the basic patterns of urban life that have evolved as a direct result of urbanization. Sociology as a discipline has probably made its largest contribution to this dimension of the urbanization process. The social structure of the modern urban community can be said to include a huge and complex network of individuals, groups, bureaucratic structures, and social institutions. This network is further differentiated into a complex division of labor, which, in turn, is overridden by a hierarchically stratified system of social class, status, and power. The basic units of social structure can be ranked from the smallest and most simple, to the largest and most elaborate.

The Individual. The individual person is the most basic unit of urban social structure and can best be described in terms of individual patterns of personality organization and individual lifestyles or patterns of behavior that are believed to have evolved in response to the conditions of urban life. For example, much of the early literature in urban sociology was based on the idea that the city produces distinct personality and behavioral characteristics that set urbanites apart from their rural counterparts. More recent writing on urban personality and lifestyle has been more dynamic and has described mechanisms for coping with or adjusting to the urban setting, or on the techniques of urban "survival" (Lofland, 1973). The concern with the individual also brings into focus many sociocultural dimensions, such as the positive or negative attitudes, values, beliefs, perceptions, and symbolic attachments that have come to be associated with urban life.

Primary Groups. These consist of small and intimate face to face groups, such as the family, couples, or intimate friendship groups. Of course, such groups are preurban in their origins and structure. Many scholars have speculated that as urban communities become larger and more elaborate, primary groups would be swallowed up or destroyed, and that all that would remain would be the segmented, impersonal, or dehumanized relationships thought to be characteristic of larger and more bureaucratic structures (Popenoe, 1970). Yet primary groups have remained a viable part of urban social structure. Although they appear to be necessary carryovers from rural societies, their form and functions have changed in response to modern urban conditions. Such change remains a focal point of much contemporary urban sociological research.

Neighborhoods and Social Networks.   Urban neighborhoods fall into the middle range of urban social structure, in terms of size and complexity. They are larger and more complex than primary groups, but are more informal and less complex than larger scale bureaucratic organizations. Sociologists do not entirely agree on the significance of local neighborhoods for providing social bonds, arenas of social participation, and order to urban life at the local level, and there is a great deal of research and speculation on this topic. However, recognition is growing that neighborhoods are an inherent part of the social fabric of modern urban communities and that a grasp of the social processes at work at this level of urban social structure is critical to a more complete understanding of urban life.

The same can be said of social networks, which are much more amorphous patterns of interaction than neighborhoods, as they are not necessarily tied to specific geographic locations. They also remain at a somewhat more primitive stage of classification and explanation in the sociological literature. Yet social networks are coming to be recognized as more important and universal than heretofore realized. The growing body of theory and research on the nature and functions of social networks should therefore be considered in any comprehensive description or analysis or urban social structure.

Collective Behavior.   Also at the intermediate level of urban social structure are the most transitory and diffuse patterns of social interaction, which may be referred to under the general heading of *collective behavior,* for want of a better term. This includes the everyday patterns of social interaction that routinely occurs in public and semipublic places, such as streets, sidewalks, parks, plazas, public buildings, theaters, meeting halls, stadiums, auditoriums, and other public gathering places. This public behavior sometimes takes the form of crowds, mobs, assemblies, audiences, spectators, or routine person-to-person encounters between strangers. Parodoxically, these kinds of encounters may be among the most frightening, as well as the most pleasurable aspects of urban living, and thus, they must be better described and explained, as some of the research reported in this book attempts to do.

Voluntary Associations.   Much has been said about the very high rates of participation in voluntary associations in contemporary urban America. Much has also been theorized about their structural characteristics and functions. For now it is enough to say that voluntary associations are also at the middle or intermediate level of urban social structure, and that they serve functions that are not adequately met at any other level of urban social structure. For example, they serve expressive functions for urbanites that are not met at either the primary group level or at the more formal and impersonal bureaucratic levels of community organization. More importantly, from our perspective here, they serve instrumental functions, such as providing the means for community groups to "fight city hall" by creating new blends of both primary group and bureaucratic forms of organization for this and other political purposes. From a *new urban sociology* perspective, voluntary associations are among the many interest groups that compete for the power to control decision-making processes within and among urban communities.

Bureaucracy.   Most large-scale and complex governmental and industrial organization in the modern world can be characterized as bureaucratic in structure. Typically, bureaucratic organizations consist of an elaborate network of specialized roles or positions organized into a hierarchical division of labor. Each position has a definite sphere of competence, with specified task obligations, and a specified degree of authority or power. The table of organization for bureaucracies typically defines the scope and limits of their functions, and such organizations are usually bound by a written body of rules that governs the behavior of its members.

The main significance of bureaucracy in the modern urban setting is that goods and services essential to the urbanite's well-being are increasingly available only in a bureaucratic context. In the popular mind, this trend is undesirable, because bureaucracies are often viewed as difficult to understand, difficult to utilize effectively, and are highly impersonal and unresponsive to individual needs. The bureaucratic mentality is the object of much popular contempt and ridicule, and little has more political appeal than promises to eliminate bureaucratic "red tape" and costs. Yet, bureaucracy remains a very real element in the daily lives of most urbanites, and it is doubtful that large modern urban communities could continue to exist without some form of bureaucratic organization. Therefore the study of the forms and effects of bureaucracy remains essential to those who wish to understand the social structure of urban society.

Social Institutions.   These are the largest and most abstract modes of social organization within the urban community. In the most general sense, social institutions consist of widely accepted patterns of behavior and expectations that evolve or are created as long-term solutions to the recognized needs of a community or society. Such basic institutions as the family or religion are, of course, preurban in their origins. Although their forms and functions may have changed drastically as a result of rapid urbanization, they continue to serve at least some of the recognized needs of modern urban communities. However, many social critics question the degree to which institutions such as these have the capacity to respond effectively to the changing demands and opportunities of urban living, and their very survival is sometimes viewed as doubtful.

Likewise, economic and political institutions are continually faced with the challenge of responding effectively to the ever-changing conditions of urban life. In addition, a host of more recent social institutions, such as mass communications, compulsory education, public welfare, commercialized leisure, and urban planning, have rapidly and dramatically emerged since the beginning of the industrial revolution. Institutional change may in fact be the key to the kind of revolutionary social changes that were earlier described as a product of rapid urbanization.

Alvin Boskoff (1970) has identified the main characteristics of social institutions: (1) they serve a specialized function or need; (2) they provide a set of guiding values that translate needs into specific objective or goals; (3) they consist of a cluster of social roles and skills, which translate ultimate goals into specific duties and responsibilities for individuals; (4) they produce the development of a coordinated network of social roles through the formation of social groups of one form or another (primary groups, voluntary associations, or bureaucracy); (5) they involve the participation of the entire community in this network of values, roles, and groups; and (6) the values and roles of dominant social institutions are internalized by a substantial portion of the population. So defined, social institutions clearly are the most inclusive and extensive level of social organization that we have identified so far, and much of the description and interpretation of contemporary urban life is at this level of analysis throughout the book.

Major urban social institutions have, over the years, been acquiring a greatly extended radius of influence and control, in terms of geography and population. Because they tend to be the practical source of both stability and social change in modern urban communities, they are central to our understanding of current urban problems and of the many efforts to solve them. As social institutions proliferate, as they have in the modern urban-industrial age, newer problems of institutional conflict and power appear as some institutions become dominant over others. For example, from the perspective of the new urban sociology, it is quite clear that economic institutions, such as global capitalism and the free market economy have dominated much of the world's urban growth and development over much of the twentieth century. And, as later chapters of this book make clear, these have significantly effected the nature of other urban institutions, such as the family, education, religion, and mass communications.

For the individual, and for many groups, the conflicts of divided and contradictory institutional obligations, loyalties, and identities are resultant new kinds of problems. On the whole, social institutions appear to represent groping trial and error adjustments to the complexities of urban living, and the survival and well-being of modern urban civilization are to a large extent dependent on how successful urban social institutions respond to the challenges confronting them.

Stratification and Power.   Virtually all sociologists view almost all human communities as highly stratified. That is, they are characterized by unequal distribution of wealth and income, social status, and power or influence among their inhabitants. This is no less true for urban communities, where the gap between the rich and the poor or the weak and the powerful may be enormous and highly visible. Thus, systems of stratified wealth and power can be seen as part of the social structure of every urban community, and as overriding all of the other layers of social structure just identified. In turn, local stratification systems may be directly affected or modified by larger systems of power and wealth at the national and global levels. This last point, in fact, illustrates one of the key assumptions of the new urban sociology perspective, as it has been described earlier.

However, systems of power and stratification may be very complex and often difficult to measure. They can also vary greatly from community to community and from society to society. Thus, sociologists often disagree about the exact form or shape that stratification systems take in given communities or societies, and they also disagree in the extent to which they influence the development of other important aspects of local urban communities (Gold, 1990). For example, one important school of thought views stratification and power as highly concentrated in the hands of a narrow and monolithic group of individuals, families, or giant corporations (the *elite* approach), whereas another school of thought views power and wealth as widely dispersed among a large number of competing interest groups (the *pluralist* approach). Unfortunately, the existing empirical research on these competing images of community power and stratification does not lead to clear conclusions on one side of the issue or another, and evidence can be found that supports arguments on both sides of the issue.

It is not our purpose here to choose among pluralist or elitist theories of community power and stratification structure. Rather, the point is to make it clear that stratification and power systems do have significant impact on urban social structure in ways that will be enumerated in a variety of ways throughout this book.

The Social Problem Perspective

In one way or another, almost all contemporary social problems have been associated with the process of urbanization. Thus, a diverse set of problems such as those relating to crime, mental illness, broken family life, inadequate housing, poverty, unemployment, social class conflict, racial and ethnic segregation and conflict, drug addiction, air and water pollution, and a host of other problems are often grouped together under the ominous title of the "urban crisis." This tendency has been so pronounced in recent times that the temptation often arises to treat such problems as synonymous with the city itself. But to do so is misleading, because the city is much more than a simple compilation of its recognized social problems. To describe cities in terms of their problems alone is akin to trying to describe human beings in terms of their diseases!

Neither is it accurate to suggest that urbanization alone is the main cause of most contemporary social problems. The relationship between a very broad and general social process such as urbanization and the much more concrete examples of social problems such as those just listed is very difficult to observe directly, and the chain of events by which these two levels of social behavior can be said to be even remotely connected is complex and indirect. Nevertheless the city and the metropolis are the settings in which many social problems have developed or intensified, and to understand these problems in their urban context is extremely important.

A variety of current "urban" social problems will be discussed throughout this book, and several chapters are devoted exclusively to some of the most widely recognized urban problems. This book does not intend, however, to deal with every possible aspect of the problems selected for inclusion, but mainly with those that are pertinent to their urban origins or settings. After all, this book is not designed as a text for a social problems course, and it will not duplicate the many excellent social problems textbooks currently available. In a book such as this, with its focus on urbanization and its impact, it is important to explain what it is about crime, poverty, unemployment, racial and ethnic conflict and segregation, dysfunctional family life, or mental illness that make these problems urban in character. All these problems have a long history and were prevalent in preurban societies, but they take on different forms and meanings in an urban society, and the urban sociologist has the added burden of identifying the theoretical or causal links between urbanization and the many "pathologies" commonly associated with modern urban life. This book attempts to identify these linkages wherever possible and appropriate.

In introducing a social problems perspective, a note of caution is in order. It is much too easy to approach social problems in overly simplistic terms. To avoid this, the following characteristics of social problems must be taken into account:

First, not everybody shares the same views as to what the problems are, who suffers the most as a result of the problems, or the degree to which they represent crises proportions. Banfield (1974), for example, suggested that what many urban experts refer to as an urban crisis is really not that at all but merely represents the observers' state of mind! Whether widely recognized social problems represent mainly the perceptual problems of the observer or objective reality raises philosophical issues which are beyond the scope of this book. However, individuals occupying different social positions in the social structure will tend to see problems differently and will be affected by them in different kinds of ways. For example, the affluent suburban dweller may see the problems of poor housing or urban poverty much differently than the unemployed inhabitant of an inner city slum. For all of the urban social problems discussed in this book, people's opinions and perceptions of their extent and consequences differ greatly.

Second, social scientists have not been conspicuously successful in identifying the main causes of major social problems, and a wide range of competing theories prevails at any given time among social scientists to explain the existence of any given social problem. For example, crime may be variously explained as the result of rapid urbanization, broken families, spiritual breakdown, inadequate socialization, the competitive free enterprise system and global capitalism, economic inequality, blocked opportunity structure, poverty, poor housing, unemployment, peer group relations in the youth culture, the impact of the mass media, class conflict, poor law enforcement, judicial permissiveness, individual genetic or biological traits, mental illness, or any number of other hypothetical causes. However, sociologists almost universally agree that for any given problem, *no one best explanation may exist.* The causes are multidimensional and will vary for different groups or individuals under different sets of circumstances.

Finally, opinions vary tremendously on what, if anything, should be done to solve recognized social problems. Just as there may be no one best explanation for the existence of certain problems, there also may be no one best solution. Efforts to solve problems for some groups may in fact create new problems for others. Indeed, consensus on what to do about solving social problems is rarely, if ever, possible in highly complex and diversified urban industrial communities, with their many competing interest and pressure groups. Nevertheless, the quest for solutions to urban problems continues to occupy the time, skill, and energies of many concerned individuals and groups at many levels of urban America and deserve careful consideration here.

The Social Policy Perspective

The notion that problems ought to and can be solved or minimized is closely related to acknowledgment that problems exist. Indeed, the relationship between the recognition of a problem and the desire or ability to solve it is a long acknowledged aspect of many common sociological definitions of a social problem (Gold and Scarpitti, 1967; Horton et al., all editions through 1997). For the urban problems reviewed in this book, an impressively wide variety of groups and organizations—at the local, state, and national levels, as well as in both the public and private sectors of our society—have been attempting to propose or initiate polices and programs designed to change or ameliorate those urban problems that have caused the most public concern. These planned interventions represent a bewildering diversity of approaches of varying promise, about which both the student and teacher of urban sociology must have some knowledge to assess their significance. Planned interventions are rapidly becoming a part of the social fabric of urban communities, and thus they become an integral part of the data and ideas upon which the understanding of modern urban life is based.

Many approaches and policies for urban problem solving are too recent in origin or too untried to have yet demonstrated their effectiveness. Many of them generate considerable controversy among those who are directly affected, among the public at large, among public officials, as well as those who are involved as professionals in urban service occupations. These controversies are often related to some very basic value conflicts about the way in which American democracy is expected or ought to work.

For example, do we blame the environment or the "system" and forgive the person for the existence of major urban problems, or do we put the onus on the individual? Do we treat problems through institutional change or individually by client or case? Do we use a few universal schemes or do we opt for pluralistic efforts by separate social agencies? Are national or international measures the proper vehicle or are local community efforts more valid? Do we favor militancy, conflict, and confrontation, or more conciliatory and cooperative tactics ("civility," in the case of post–1996 election congressional and presidential rhetoric!)? Do we need the input of additional professional experts, or should public opinion, no matter how well or poorly informed, be the basis for public policy decisions? Should the disadvantaged segments of urban society be helped with direct assistance, or is it better to stimulate the more "productive" segments of the society, with the hope that a "trickle down" process will ultimately help the needy? In American society, with its traditional strong emphasis on private enterprise, the question of who should attempt to bring about desired social change is always present. Is it the function of government to initiate, support, or operate programs designed to alleviate urban problem conditions? Or should these tasks be left to private groups or to the free play of the marketplace?

Most of the questions raised above have been played out in American politics over at least the last four decades of the twentieth century. For the most part, they represent strong ideological differences between liberal and conservative positions on the American political spectrum. Because of these controversies and value conflicts, most of which remain unresolved and are likely to remain unresolved into the first decades of the twenty-first century, the establishment and carrying out of an effective national urban policy for the United States has been an exceedingly complex and difficult, if not impossible, goal.

Moreover, despite efforts to guide social change through planned intervention, most social change, as we have described it in the other perspectives for this book, continues to proceed in unplanned or unanticipated ways. For example, changes in attitudes; lifestyles; consumer choices and preferences; patterns of family living; religious, political, or economic institutions; or changes in the ecosystem still appear to be largely beyond the guidance or control of consciously planned intervention by institutional planners at this stage of history, no matter how great the efforts in these directions.

Nevertheless, urban and social planning are coming to the forefront as potentially important sources of future social change and have already had some impact in some existing local urban communities. Such efforts at planned social change in urban communities are alluded to in many parts of this book. In particular, an entire chapter is devoted to some of the accomplishments, potentialities, and limitations of urban planning in the United States, as it has been practiced so far, and another chapter more speculatively focuses on some of the implications of social policy for the foreseeable urban future.

THE QUALITY OF URBAN LIFE

Overriding and relating to all six of the perspectives we have just introduced and discussed is a more general concern with the quality of urban life in contemporary American urban society. The quality of life, of course, is a relatively impressionistic and subjective concept, meaning different things to different people. In the past few decades, social scientists have attempted to measure objectively the quality of urban life through a variety of quantifiable social indicators and sample surveys, and some of these quantitative measures are cited in various parts of the book.

Our own use of the concept of quality of life, however, is more subjective and speculative, and has to do with our desire to develop a more humanistic interpretation of what it is about urban living that creates positive satisfaction and a sense of well-being for some, dissatisfaction for others, and a desire to escape completely from the urban environment for still others. Hundreds of social observers and "urbanologists" have speculated for many years about the quality of urban life, and we claim no originality in this regard. But what we have attempted to do is to tie such speculation to the major perspectives upon which this book is built, and to further tie them to some of the accumulated wisdom and knowledge developed by urban sociologists over nearly the past century or so.

Sociology, of course is not the only field to have contributed to our understanding of the quality of urban life, and it is necessary to borrow data and ideas from other academic disciplines or fields of urban professional practice. History, archeology, anthropology, geography, economics, political science, public administration, psychiatry, law, journalism, architecture, social work, criminal justice, civil engineering, and urban planning have all made significant contributions to understanding and coming to grips with modern urban life. Insights and knowledge from these fields will be utilized in this volume whenever appropriate or feasible. But it should be understood that this is primarily a work based on the accumulated contributions of experts who have called themselves or have been identified primarily as urban sociologists.

THE PLAN OF THE BOOK

Part I traces the development and evolution of cities from their pre-Christian origins to the beginning of the twentieth century. Chapter 2 provides a brief sociohistorical outline of urbanization up to the beginning of the industrial revolution in Europe. Only by reviewing preindustrial urban development in these earlier periods of history can one full appreciate the significance of modern urban-industrial communities and understand how they got to be the way they are. Chapter 3 begins with a discussion of the forces leading to the industrial revolution in Europe and the impact of industrialization on urban growth and development. It then proceeds to review the industrialization and urbanization process in nineteenth-century America. At this point in the book, except for a closing chapter on world urbanization and occasional international comparisons, the remaining parts focus primarily on more recent patterns of urbanization and urban life in North America.

Part II describes and analyzes the basic forms of urban existence that have emerged in the twentieth century and continue to the beginning of the twenty-first century. Chapter 4 identifies the revolutionary forms of *metropolitan* development and decentralization that have made the burgeoning suburbs as important, in terms of population size, as cities in the contemporary urban scene. This chapter also reviews many of the major theories of metropolitan structure and internal processes, and it deals with some of the attempts to classify the many component parts of the modern metropolis, such as cities, suburbs, natural areas, slums, or other spatially differentiated parts of increasingly complex metropolitan communities. Chapter 5 discusses middle-range levels of urban social organization, such as the structure and functions of social neighborhoods, social networks, and voluntary associations. Chapter 6 reviews some social-psychological aspects of the impact of urban social organization of individual personality and mental health; some cultural and symbolic aspects of urban life; and a discussion of urban collective behavior (or every day aspects of face-to-face interaction in urban settings).

Part III focuses on the recent history of current trends, and problems associated with the impact of urbanization and industrialization on some of the major social institutions of contemporary urban America. Chapter 7 analyzes modern urban-industrial economic institutions, such as capitalism, globalism, the free market, and the characteristics of the urban-industrial labor force.

These have become the dominant urban institutions in the modern era, and they modify and shape in significant ways all of the other social institutions identified below, which become subordinate to capitalism and the market economy. Chapter 8 deals with the political institutions of modern urban communities, including formal governmental structures and policies, as well as informal power structures and informal decision-making processes at the urban community level. More and more, urban political institutions are seen as crucial to efforts to solve urban problems and to help shape the future direction of urban development. It is also true that national and international political and economic forces also increasingly effect local political processes, and these are taken into account as well. Formal educational and welfare systems are among the most recently institutionalized features of modern American urban communities, and they are discussed in Chapter 9. These two institutions are often at the heart of major controversies surrounding what, if anything, can and should be done to ease the social and economic stresses of urban living and what can be done to better prepare individuals with the appropriate skills, knowledge, attitudes, and resources for successfully coping with urban living. These two institutions are increasingly responsible for attempts to improve the quality of life in urban societies, and their successes and failures are most important to consider in this context. Chapter 10 closes Part III with an analysis of two social institutions that are preurban in their origins—the family and organized religion—which have changed drastically in the modern urban-industrial context, and which have reeled under the impact of changes to all of the other urban institutions identified earlier, and to which the family and organized religion have become increasingly subordinate. As a result, the continued survival and well-being of traditional forms of family and religious life are being severely challenged in the modern urban world.

Part IV considers some of the most persistent and pressing social problems of urban America. Chapter 11 deals with the large gap between the wealthiest and poorest subcommunities within America's metropolitan areas and focuses on urban poverty as a byproduct of modern urban-industrial economic development. The spatial segregation of the poor from wealthier segments of the urban community, which are in themselves almost equally segregated, remains one of the paradoxes of modern American urban society, and generates much stress, controversy, and conflict. Chapter 12 explores the causes, extent, and consequences of various forms of crime, violence, and aberrant behavior in urban communities and considers the nature of the criminal justice system as a form of urban social control. Various proposals and policies designed to reduce urban crime and violence are discussed and evaluated, as is the *fear* of crime as a problem that has consequences probably as far reaching as the real incidence of crime itself. Chapter 13 deals with the problems of racial and ethnic minorities in urban America. Past trends, current realities, and controversies regarding public policy as a solution to problems of racial and ethnic conflict, segregation, or discrimination are discussed, with the greatest attention given to black Americans in large northern cities.

Part V deals with urban planning, social policy and the future of urban life. Chapter 14 provides a broad overview of the historical development, goals, and current realities of urban planning in America as an approach to improving the quality of urban communities by controlling or minimizing the most undesirable features. Urban planning is identified as a social movement, a legitimate function of urban government, and as a technical profession. Some of the accomplishments, potentialities, and limitations of urban planning in such controversial areas as urban renewal and housing, the development of new towns, transportation planning, and metropolitan or regional planning is discussed, as well as some aspects of urban planning as a professional career. Chapter 15 speculates on the future of urban America and considers some controversial policy alternatives that are expected to have considerable impact on the future of urban life. The survival of urban communities as we now know them may very well depend on the choices that are made. Chapter 16 closes the book with a brief comparative overview of world urbanization in the industrialized and wealthier parts of the world, as well as in the so-called "undeveloped" nations. The problems caused by rapid rates of growth in the Western world pale in comparison to those in large parts of Asia, Africa, and Latin America.

A FINAL NOTE

The six major perspectives around which the contents of the remaining parts of this book are loosely organized and do not apply uniformly or equally to every chapter, nor are they explicitly spelled out in every instance. For some of the topics in the book, two or more of the perspectives may be more appropriate and given greater emphasis than others. The main point is that each of the six perspectives has been presented in this introductory chapter as a useful frame of reference for making sense out of the vast array of concepts, theory, and data presented throughout the book.

SELECTED BIBLIOGRAPHY

BANFIELD, EDWARD C. *The Unheavenly City Revisited.* Boston: Little Brown, 1974.

BERRY, BRIAN J. L. *The Human Consequences of Urbanization.* New York: St. Martin's Press, 1974.

BOSKOFF, ALVIN. *The Sociology of Urban Regions,* 2d ed. New York: Appleton Century Crofts, 1970.

BRADSHAW, YORK, and MICHAEL WALLACE. *Global Inequalities.* Thousand Oaks, CA: Pine Forge Press, 1996.

BURGESS, ERNEST W., and DONALD J. BOGUE, eds. *Contributions to Urban Sociology.* Chicago: University of Chicago Press, 1964.

CHIROT, DANIEL. *How Societies Change.* Thousand Oaks, CA: Pine Forge Press, 1994.

DUNCAN, O. D. "From Social System to Ecosystem." *Sociological Inquiry* 31 (spring 1961).

GOLD, HARRY. "Political Sociology: A Developing Field." *CHOICE* 27 (February. 1990): 916–923.

GOLD, HARRY, and FRANK SCARPITTI, eds. *Combatting Social Problems: Techniques of Intervention.* New York: Holt, Rinehart & Winston, 1967.

GOTTDIENER, MARK. *The New Urban Sociology.* New York: McGraw-Hill, 1994.

GREIDER, WILLIAM. *One World, Ready or Not: The Manic Logic of Global Capitalism.* New York: Simon & Shuster, 1997.

GUTMAN, ROBERT, and DAVID POPENOE, eds. *Neighborhood, City, and Metropolis.* New York: Random House, 1970.

HATT, PAUL, and ALBERT REISS (eds.). *Cities and Society.* Glencoe, IL: Free Press, 1957.

HAWLEY, AMOS H. *Urban Society,* 2d ed. New York: John Wiley, 1981.

HORTON, PAUL B., et al. *The Sociology of Social Problems,* 12th ed. New York: Prentice-Hall, 1997.

HUTCHINSON, RAY, ed. *Research in Urban Sociology.* Greenwich, CT: JAI Press, 1993.

KING, ANTHONY. *Global Cities: Post-Imperialism and the Internationalization of London.* London: Routledge, 1990.

LEFEBVRE, HENRI. *The Production of Space.* Oxford: Blackwell, 1991.

LOGAN, JOHN, and HARVEY MOLOTCH. *Urban Fortunes: The Political Economy of Place.* Berkeley: University of California Press, 1987.

LOFLAND, LYN H. *A World of Strangers.* New York: Basic Books, 1973.

MAINES, DAVID R., JEFFREY C. BRIDGER, and JEFFERY T. ULMER. "Mythical Facts and Park's Pragmatism: On Predecessor-Selection and Theorizing in Human Ecology." *Sociological Quarterly* 37, no. 3 (1996).

NOTTRIDGE, HAROLD E. *The Sociology of Urban Living.* London and Boston: Routledge & Kegan Paul, 1972.

PALEN, J. JOHN. *The Urban World,* 4th ed. New York: McGraw Hill, 1992.

POPENOE, DAVID. *The Urban-Industrial Frontier.* New Brunswick, NJ: Rutgers University Press, 1970.

REDFIELD, ROBERT. "The Folk Society." *American Journal of Sociology* 52 (January 1947): 293–308.

ROSS, ROBERT, and KENT TRACHTE. *Global Capitalism: The New Leviathan.* Albany: State University of New York Press, 1990.

SASSEN, SASKIA. *The Global City: New York, London, Tokyo.* Princeton, NJ: Princeton University Press, 1991.

———. *Cities in a World Economy.* Thousand Oaks, CA: Pine Forge Press, 1994.

SIMMEL, GEORG. "The Metropolis and Mental Life." In *Sociology of Georg Simmel.* Translated by Kurt Wolff. New York: Free Press, 1950.

SMITH, DAVID A., and MICHAEL F. TIMBERLAKE. "The New Urban Sociology." In J. John Palen, *The Urban World,* 4th ed. New York: McGraw-Hill, 1992.

———. "Urban Poliltical Economy." In J. John Palen, *The Urban World,* 5th ed. New York: McGraw-Hill, 1997.

SMITH, MICHAEL P. *The City and Social Theory.* New York: St. Martins Press, 1979.

SPENGLER, OSWALD. *The Decline of the West.* Vol. II. Translated by C. F. Atkinson. New York: Knopf, 1928.

THOMLINSON, RALPH. *Urban Structure.* New York: Random House, 1969.

WARREN, ROLAND L. *Perspectives on the American Community,* 2d ed. Skokie, IL: Rand McNally, 1973.

WIRTH, LOUIS. "Urbanism as a Way of Life." *American Journal of Sociology* 44 (July 1938): 3–24.

WOLF, C. P. "The Structure of Societal Revolutions." In *Social Change: Explorations, Diagnoses, and Conjectures,* George K. Zollschan and Walter Hirsch (eds.). New York: John Wiley, 1976.

2

THE ORIGINS AND EARLY DEVELOPMENT OF CITIES

When and where the human species first appeared on earth is not exactly certain and remains a matter of much controversy. Estimates place the date anywhere between one or two hundred thousand years ago and even more than a million years ago, depending on which conception of the nature of the human species is preferred. Current archeological and DNA findings may soon extend the estimated date ever further back in time (see Wenke, 1980; Jurmain et al., 1997; Wolpoff and Caspari, 1997). Nevertheless, estimates are more certain that the urban community as a form of human settlement did not develop until about 5,500 or 6,500 years ago, with the first cities of any consequence appearing sometime between 3500 and 4500 B.C. (Whitehouse, 1977).

What is most significant about the above estimates for our purposes is that they remind us that urban life has existed during only a tiny fraction of the history of humankind, encompassing perhaps less than 1 percent of human beings' total existence as a species. It took a very slowly developing but remarkable transformation of human ways of life to produce the conditions that made the first cities possible, and one cannot overestimate how revolutionary were the changes necessary to support as many as several thousand people in permanent year-round settlements. Since this change occurred, the process of urbanization has been associated with continuous modifications in the conditions of human beings.

This chapter reviews some of the developments of the preurban era that made the emergence of cities possible. It provides a brief sociohistorical outline of urbanization from the earliest cities of antiquity to the beginning of the industrial revolution in Europe, when the rates of urban growth began to take off at unprecedented speed. Only by reviewing preindustrial urban development can one fully appreciate the significance of modern urban-industrial communities and how they got to be the way they are.

It is difficult to know, of course, with any high degree of precision or certainty the exact nature of the earliest cities and urban life. What we do know comes largely from the work of archeologists and historians, who are constantly enlarging our knowledge with each new discovery of early urban sites and with each new find of ancient artifacts or documents. Modern techniques of excavating and interpreting such finds are improving so rapidly that it is almost impossible for the nonspecialist to stay abreast of such advances.

Also, rather than presenting a strictly chronological description of discrete historical events, our purpose is to portray as broadly as possible what the conditions of early urban life must have been like, in terms of population, environment, technology, and social structure. Also, we attempt to identify those forces working at various points in time that made each succeeding stage of urban development in preindustrial cities possible.

PREURBAN NOMADS AND THE FIRST PREURBAN PERMANENT SETTLEMENTS

Prior to the emergence of the first permanent year-round settlements, people lived in nomadic hunting and food-gathering bands, wandering from place to place in search of sustenance, without any permanent place of habitation. Although climatic and environmental limitations on food supplies were an important barrier to permanent settlement in early human history, equally significant was the lack of adequate technological development and social organization. Not until people discovered the techniques of plant cultivation and the further development of agriculture, as represented by the domestication of animals; the development of the animal-drawn plow; the development of all kinds of tools (axes, fishing nets, etc.); the development of specialized skills, such as weaving and pottery making; and improvements in the techniques of fertilization and irrigation, did the first permanent towns and villages develop (Trigger, 1973).

Of course, these human inventions did not appear overnight and were thousands of years in the making. They seem to have first developed about twelve thousand years ago in an elongated, semitropical zone reaching from central Asia through southeastern Asia and into northern Africa, where, with the discovery of plant cultivation, formerly nomadic hunting and food-gathering tribes drifted into permanent settlement in fertile river valleys and became increasingly dependent on cereal foods (Trigger, 1973).

In particular, the so-called Fertile Crescent region—which includes what is now Lebanon, Jordan, Syria, Israel, and parts of Iraq and Iran—is where the first year-round settlements were likely located. The village farming community of Jarmo, located in the Fertile Crescent, is one of the earliest known examples (Braidwood and Willie, 1962). It is believed that approximately 150 people lived at Jarmo at a population density of approximately twenty-seven people per square mile. Such density seems extremely low compared with the densities of modern American cities. But in contrast to earlier hunting and gathering societies in which at least one square mile was required to support a single individual, such concentration of population was a major achievement. There is evidence that the inhabitants of Jarmo learned to domesticate goats, dogs, and possibly sheep. They grew barley and wheat, but they were still not able to supply all of their food needs in these ways. Thus, they still continued to engage in hunting and gathering for their livelihood.

Jarmo was inhabited from about 7000 B.C. to about 6500 B.C. Although it appears that its technology advanced during this period, as evidenced by stone tools, weaving, and pottery at the excavation site, it is not known for certain why Jarmo or many similar agricultural settlements, which emerged and spread throughout surrounding regions over the next several thousand years, failed to grow or survive. One of the most common explanations is that these earliest permanent settlements were easy prey to the marauding bands of nomads still occupying the regions in which they developed. In fact, a chronic state of warfare between the settled areas and the encircling nomadic groups probably existed for thousands of years (Hawley, 1981), but other possible causes, such as disease, famine, or internal strife, cannot be ruled out.

Paradoxically, the recurring needs for defense produced some of the most important innovations associated with the development of somewhat large and complex human settlements more accurately described as towns or cities. For example, defense requirements necessitated a development of organization beyond what was required for just the day-to-day food requirements. A military establishment with a clear-cut division of labor and a centralized command structure was created. A storable food surplus was required to maintain food supplies during periods of siege. This, in turn, required a system of taxation, initially applied against the agricultural product of the inhabitants, along with the organizational ability to enforce and administer the collection and distribution of the surpluses. Related developments in weapon making, record keeping, and administration thus became necessary. The construction of fortified places in which settlers could gather for mutual protection was one of the important physical manifestations of the need for defense, and often such fortresses are among the most visible excavated remains of settlements of this period. Even with these precautions, many of the early fortress settlements were overcome by force and perished (Hawley, 1981).

Those who successfully served as military chieftains in settlements that were able to survive probably emerged as rulers with broad power over the entire community. Such power often was passed from father to son over succeeding generations. A class structure appeared, based on a ruling family and a supporting cadre of functionaries superimposed on a large peasant class (Sjoberg, 1976). This social pattern is suggested by the archeological remains of palaces, royal tombs and granaries, military garrisons, and the like, which are common to many of the earliest known permanent settlements.

THE FIRST CITIES: THE PREHISTORIC CLASSICAL PERIOD

The actual time and place at which the first cities of any consequence appeared are of some dispute, depending on what one defines as the essential characteristics of cities. Gordon Childe (1946) has provided a useful point of departure by identifying a list of characteristics which he describes as essential to what can be described as *cities*. Accordingly, he argues that all of the cities of the first classical urban revolution contained at least some combination of the following features:

1. Permanent year-round settlements in dense population aggregations
2. A labor force of specialized *non*agricultural occupations
3. A system of taxation and capital accumulation
4. Monumental public buildings (temples, palaces)

5. A ruling class
6. A written language, with established techniques of writing
7. The acquisition of predictive sciences—arithmetic, geometry, and astronomy
8. A pattern of artistic expression
9. A system of negotiated exchange (trade)
10. Residence in place of kinship as the basis for membership in the community

Although not all of the early cities share these features to the same degree or in the same combination, what is important is that Childe's list of essential characteristics of the first cities represents a most significant transformation from what had previously existed into what has been commonly referred to as the beginning of recorded human civilization.

MESOPOTAMIAN CITIES

The communities having what Childe (1946) has described as the characteristics of cities first appeared in Mesopotamia around 4000 B.C. to 3500 B.C. (McAdams, 1973). Forms of city life became well developed during the next thousand years or so, after which they began to decline. Some of the early cities were Ur, Eridu, Erech, Ubaid, Nippur, Lagash, Babylon, and Nineveh. Jericho, on the left bank of the Jordan River, also probably emerged during this same period (Hawley, 1981; McAdams, 1973).

Ur is believed to have been the largest of the known Mesopotamian cities (Childe, 1946). The excavated walls of Ur enclosed about 220 acres of land, and the city is estimated to have had a population of about 24,000 people. Other Mesopotamian towns contained populations of up to about 20,000 people. By today's standards, these cities would be considered nothing more than small towns or villages. But Ur, with all its temples, canals, and harbors, was ten times the size of the earlier Neolithic agricultural villages, and must have been awesome in its time. McAdams (1973) estimates that even the largest cities of this period contained no more than 3 or 4 percent of all of the people of the regions in which they were located. Agriculture as then practiced still required forty or fifty agricultural workers to supply sufficient food surpluses to support a single nonagricultural city dweller. Thus, the size of cities was (and still is) limited by how much food surplus could be produced, stored, and distributed by the available agricultural technology.

The description of Ur by its chief excavator, Sir Leonard Woolley (1952), tells us much about the physical and social structure of the typical Mesopotamian city. At the center of the town was a fortress that housed monastaries, convents, and granaries. The surrounding area may have been as much for protection against the local people as against organized assaults from outsiders. Hawley (1981) suggests that the town's ruling classes were conquerors who had enslaved the local residents and built their wealth on the strength of exorbitant taxation of the peasantry. The artisans, the scribes, the domestic servants, and other retainers of the ruling class lived immediately beyond the inner fortress walls but were enclosed by the outer walls of the city. Within the outer wall, there were sufficient gardens and pasture lands to enable the town to withstand a siege by its enemies. The streets were narrow and meandered like animal trails. Housing, which rose to

Archeological excavations at Ur; one of the earliest known cities in human history

two or three floors, was dense and congested. Each house was built around an inner court, with blank walls facing the street for defense purposes.

Ur was located at the confluence of the Tigris and Euphrates Rivers, and like other Mesopotamian cities, engaged in some intercity and interregional trade. The marketplace was not located within the city walls but was outside, adjacent to the river harbor. At first, trade was reluctantly accepted as a necessary evil, and traders and merchants were accorded marginal and inferior social status. The amount of internal trade was negligible, because most of the residents of the town furnished their own material requirements from their farmlands and manors and had no special reason to buy or sell among themselves. Nevertheless, as agricultural surpluses began to be commonplace, trade became the most acceptable way of disposing of these surpluses. Eventually, successful trading activity came to be a desired end in itself, and trade already had become fairly extensive throughout the cities of the Mesopotamian region as early as 3000–2500 B.C. (McAdams, 1973).

Even though life in most Mesopotamian towns was ordinarily lived at a bare subsistence level, it must not be forgotten that warfare and conquest were often the means of enriching the town coffers. Thus, when a victorious king returned from forays rich with the spoils of war, he liberally distributed wealth to encourage the cultivation of learning and the creation of great works of art, such as sculpture, architecture, painting, and drama (Oppenheim, 1964). These periods of affluence, learning, and artistic creativity, were probably sporadic and infrequent in the history of any one town. Nevertheless, the occasional plunder of war also enabled the Mesopotamian towns to make remarkable cultural advances of the kind listed by Childe. Writing and record keeping; systems of numbers;

mathematical and astronomical calculations; systems for keeping time; law and administrative procedures; and many other elements of urban civilization all had their origins in Mesopotamian cities (Childe, 1946).

Given this description, Weber's (1962) definition of the classical city as a "fusion of fortress and marketplace" seems reasonable. Other scholars go further than Weber by also underscoring the importance of complex, universal religions as a functional characteristic of the earliest cities. Boscoff (1970), for example, describes the first urban wave (4500 B.C. to 500 A.D.) as built on the triumvirate of *defense, worship,* and *commerce.* Normally, the priesthood shared power with the military officials, and, in some circumstances, the emergence of a priest-king was the product of a political-religious fusion among ruling families. Early urban communities were characterized by a bewildering variety of local cults, rituals, and gods; in general, each city was an isolated religious island.

By the time that Mesopotamian cities had declined, for reasons that are not entirely certain, urban civilization had begun developing in other parts of the world. For example, urban societies had developed in the Indus River Valley of what is now West Pakistan and in the Yellow River Valley of China by about 2500 B.C. (see Pusalker, 1951; Eberhard, 1955–1956). In the Western Hemisphere, two urban civilizations, the Mayan of Central Mexico and the Incas in the Central Andes, had developed by about 1000 B.C. Although not certain, these seem to have developed independently from those emanating from the Middle East (McAdams, 1966). Even though all of the above urban civilizations were different from one another in many important respects, they all exhibited in some degree most of the essential characteristics of urban life enumerated by Childe.

EGYPTIAN CITIES

The cities of ancient Egypt probably represent the most direct diffusion of Mesopotamian culture and civilization. The first Egyptian cities appeared about 3300 B.C. and were remarkable for perpetuating a civilization with relatively few major changes for several thousand years (Clark and Piggot, 1965). Ancient Egyptian cities such as Memphis and Thebes were ruled by pharaohs who served in the dual role of god-king. The pharaoh was the head of a bureaucratic civil service structure that was quite elaborate and centralized for its time. He had at his service literate clerks or scribes who were trained in hieroglyphic writing and who used papyrus (paper) and ink, which were invented by the Egyptians. The bureaucracy had the power and skill to conduct an annual census of the population, collect taxes, and maintain a system of courts to enforce the laws of the ruling class. The Egyptians developed skills in medical sciences, such as anatomy, surgery, and pharmacy, and they invented a calendar similar to the one we use today. Notable examples of sculpture, painting, and architecture were also produced by full-time artisans and craftsmen who were in service to the pharaohs.

In some instances, the power of the pharaohs was so great that they were able to create completely new cities to reflect their own tastes and values. For example, the Pharaoh Ikhnaton (or Amenhotep the IV) of the eighteenth dynasty of the New Kingdom of ancient Egypt became dissatisfied with the existing religious, political, and cultural conditions that existed in the capital of Thebes when he assumed power around 1400 B.C. (White, 1949). Within a few short years, he built an entirely new city, which he called Akhetaton, and which he made the new capital of the Egyptian Empire. Under Ikhnaton's personal guidance, the city flourished, creating new forms of religion, philosophy, art, and architecture that were thought to be many centuries ahead of their time. Many observers, for example, believe that the monotheistic religious philosophy, which later became the basis for the Judaic-Christian religions, can be traced directly to the original religious thought of Ikhnaton (Freud, 1957; White, 1949; Breasted, 1912).

Even though Ikhnaton's reign lasted less than twenty-five years and the city of Akhetaton was abandoned shortly after his death, late nineteenth-century excavations have provided a fascinating picture of what the city must have been like in its prime (see Steindorff and Seele, 1942). Resting on the west bank of the Nile on the plain of Amarna, the city was approximately two miles long and one-half mile wide. On the hills surrounding the city, burial places were laid out for high officials and favorites of the pharaoh, and more substantial rock-hewn tombs for the royal family were located in a more secure and remote desert valley some distance farther. In the city itself, at least five temples were built and dedicated to Aton, the sun god, the symbol of the pharaoh's new religion. The principal temple of Aton was physically connected to the royal palace and consisted of a series of open courts and halls, connected by pylons, in which altars were set up to receive sacrificial religious offerings. The main palace had a large balcony across its facade which the pharaoh had laid out for himself and upon which his family would show themselves to the populace assembled in the large court in front of the palace. The private rooms of the palace were furnished with the "utmost splendor" and included paintings and mosaics of gaily colored stones; the columns, walls, and pavements were decorated with the "most splendid collar effects imaginable."

In the southern section of the city, the pharaoh had laid out for himself and his family a large pleasure garden with artificial pools, flower beds, groves of trees, a summer pavilion, a small temple, and numerous guardhouses. The interior rooms were also adorned with gaily colored columns and pavements painted with pictures of flowers, flying birds, and animals characteristic of the region. An important part of the city was occupied by the villas of the high officials and administrators of Ikhnaton's regime. These were elaborate establishments, consisting of administrative buildings, stables, and storehouses, along with gardens and luxurious dwellings. All of them were designed according to the same plan. The walls of the houses were decorated with reliefs depicting the royal family, usually at worship in the presence of a sun disk representing Aton.

As was usually the case in Egyptian cities of this period, the slaves and workers who were engaged in the miserable work of hewing rock tombs, maintaining cemeteries, and other menial activities resided in tiny, congested houses in a more crowded district of the city, separated and isolated from the residences, temples, and palaces of the ruling class by its own enclosure walls. Thus, even the early classical cities of antiquity were characterized by a highly stratified social class structure and a correspondingly stratified physical spatial pattern.

CITIES OF ANCIENT GREECE

The cities of classic Greek and Roman civilizations are often considered the high points of ancient civilization, and modern societies are still in awe of their splendid cultural and technological achievements. Yet it must be remembered that most of the great Greek and Roman cities were nothing more than small towns by contemporary urban standards. For example, ancient Athens at its peak occupied less than one square mile, or fewer than 612 acres of land. This is less than half of the size of the college campus at which this chapter is being written! Athens may have achieved a population as large as 150,000 people, but many scholars consider this estimate inflated and more indicative of the population of the entire city-state than of the city proper. Hawley (1981) is skeptical that cities such as Athens could have supported much more than 30,000 or 35,000 people in nonagricultural occupations, given the state of agricultural technology and land fertility at that time and place. Hawley also estimates that the normal reach of those cities' activities probably did not exceed a radial distance of three to ten miles.

By the fifth century B.C., Athens had become the metropolitan center of a well-organized city-state and a widespread trade network. Athens had turned to the sea for trade, for it was blessed with fine harbors. The city was filled with a growing number of merchants, craftsmen, sailors, and emissaries from other lands. Athenians could legitimately boast of the cosmopolitan character of the city and its hospitality to traders and other friendly foreigners in its midst. Residents of the city were able to enjoy the products of other countries, as well as their own. The expanding volume of trade made the introduction of coinage necessary for an efficient marketplace, and the Greeks were among the first people to develop the use of money as a widely accepted system of exchange (Hopkins, 1978). Hawley (1981) suggests that the use of money in place of the older system of payment in kind or the exchange of a service for a service had the effect of sharpening the difference between social classes. The lack of money by those not fortunate enough to adapt to the new monetary system had the effect of divesting them of their lands, their personal property, and perhaps even their freedom.

Except for the elites, Athens residents lived in conditions of overcrowding and squalor. Municipal services were poor and limited. Although the Greeks invented the concept of democracy, the rights of citizenship for most residents were limited to the right to worship at civic shrines. Citizenship was also limited to a small portion of the total population of the city-state. Because Athens was essentially a religious community, the lack of citizenship imposed strict limits on an individual's participation in public life. Yet the concept of citizenship in a city-state was a great achievement in social organization, for it enabled various families, clans, and tribes to band together in larger aggregates than previously possible for mutual aid and protection. To a certain extent, these functions benefited noncitizen residents as well. Without such innovations, Athens probably could not have become more than an agricultural village (Hopkins, 1978).

The physical structure of Athens was similar to other Greek city-states. For defense purposes the major city walls were built around a fortified hill called an acropolis. The acropolis was also the site of major temples. All the other major buildings, including those that served as a marketplace or meeting place, were located within the walls. The housing for the wealthiest and most privileged citizens was within the walls, but all other housing was densely clustered immediately beyond. Most of the streets of Athens outside the temple area were nothing more than unpaved winding lanes. However, Piraeus, Athen's port city, did have a more efficient grid street pattern in which the streets intersected at right angles and at regular intervals.

ROME AND THE ROMAN EMPIRE

The largest city of the ancient period was, of course, Rome. Estimates of its peak population have run as high as 1.2 million people. Again, this probably errs on the high side, according to other reliable sources, and may have included people who did not actually reside within the city. For the city proper, the maximum population size more likely was between 250,000 and 350,000 people (Russell, 1958). Such figures are difficult to confirm, but assuming that they are reasonably accurate, it is fascinating to consider that the cradle of the great Roman civilization at its peak was no larger than "medium" size American cities, such as Davenport, Iowa, or Lexington, Kentucky (Savageau and Boyer, 1993).

The city gained greater importance than ever before with the rise of the Roman Empire, which stretched all the way to Northern and Western Europe to the West and through the Middle East and Asia Minor to the East. No previous civilization was so extensively urbanized or was as successfully able to exploit the countryside in favor of city interests. The riches of the empire were drawn into the city through military conquest, tax collections, and exploitation of its colonies, farms, quarries, and mines (Braudel, 1978).

Rome was a crowded congested city. Almost one-third of the space enclosed within the Aurelian Wall was devoted to streets, warehouses, the Campus Martius, and other public uses (Russell, 1958). The clutter visible in the remains of the Roman Forum is clear evidence of further congestion. The roads were crowded with hucksters and business stalls and with residents on their daily trips to marketplaces. There was an extensive economic division of labor within and between crafts, such as tailoring, potting, or shoe making, and such specialists clustered on streets devoted to and named after each respective trade. The city was consumption oriented, and commerce was the dominant daily activity. Most of the artisans and businessmen were organized into guilds through which they sought to monopolize their trades. Commerce was shored up by a supporting cadre of moneylenders, teamsters, warehousemen, bookkeepers, and others (Hopkins, 1978).

Rome had excellent examples of municipal planning, but they did not extend beyond the center of the city. Although impressive public squares and public baths were provided, they were only for use by more affluent citizens and were not accessible to the great bulk of the population who were massed in squalid tenements reached only by a maze of narrow, crooked lanes. The magnificent main roads that connected the center of the city with its periphery were intended mainly as military thoroughfares or for ceremonial processions. As the city grew, the outer walls were torn down and rebuilt to include buildings that had developed on its outer rim. The city received its water supply from an extensive system of impressively engineered aqueducts, some of which still stand, and had an elaborately developed sewer system, at least in the more privileged residential areas.

Ruins of an ancient Greco-Roman settlement

Although Rome depended on imports from its hinterland, it also exported its innovations in engineering, law, and government. Its strong influence was felt in such provincial Roman cities as Paris, Vienna, Cologne, and London, all of which were laid out in rectangular grid patterns similar to the standard Roman military encampments, which they originally were. All the cities displayed their common Roman origins in their forums, coliseums, public baths, and other municipal buildings (Hopkins, 1978). Not to be overlooked were the splendid cities of the Byzantine Eastern Roman Empire, such as Constantinople, which are discussed in another context in the next section.

THE DECLINE OF CLASSIC CITIES: THE EMERGENCE OF THE FEUDAL SYSTEM

The provincial cities of the Roman Empire began to decline during the fourth century A.D., and the fifth century marked the effective fall of the Roman empire. Urban life, which had flourished in Europe and other parts of the empire, virtually disappeared, with few notable exceptions, as towns and cities were obliterated or reduced to agricultural villages (Gibbon, 1965). Even the city of Rome lost most of its population, with only about 20,000 people remaining to live among its ruins. For approximately 600 years thereafter, there was little or no evidence of any flourishing city life in most of Western Europe. This period, which was dominated by the decline of classical cities and civilizations and by the emergence of the feudal system, has been euphemistically referred to by many as the "Dark Ages" (Boskoff, 1970).

Actually, the feudal system that dominated Europe from about the fifth to the tenth century A.D. had many characteristics. The settlement pattern comprised a multiplicity of small villages of no more than several hundred people each, among which were interspersed castles, monasteries, burgs, and ecclesiastical towns. Europe under feudalism was a patchwork of small domains, each of which was isolated from all others, and each of which was jealously guarded from external intrusions by local feudal lords (some of whom may have been descended from former Roman military officers). The lords offered local peasants protection from outside raiders, demanding in return their serfdom.

Removed from outside influences, a rigid hereditary class structure emerged in which every person has an assigned place and status (Pirrene, 1939; Sjoberg, 1976). At the top was the family of a military overlord who controlled the land in each locality. The lands were subdivided among warrior vassals who subdivided their land allotments still further among lesser warrior vassals. At the bottom of the class structure were the serfs, whose condition of servitude was virtually slavery. During military conflicts, each stratum was obliged to support the next higher stratum. The ecclesiastic church was an overriding institution, and church representative and monastic orders frequently collaborated or competed with secular rulers for control of the secular order. Scholars refer to feudal societies as static, parochial, and ultraconservative in social structure (Hawley, 1981; Sjoberg, 1976).

The prevailing economy was subsistence agriculture. The townspeople, as well as the agriculturists, lived from the land. Virtually no market for foodstuffs existed, and food surpluses were rarely transported more than a few miles. Famines were recurrent, and people lived or died by what was produced in their own localities. Even the feudal lords often found it necessary to travel among their estates for sustenance, staying at each estate until the local food was consumed. Communications were poor, and the movement of surpluses from adjacent areas was almost impossible.

Journeys over the existing highways were extremely hazardous, and few travelers ventured far without groups of armed guards for protection from roving bands of robbers (the legends of "Robin Hood" would be a case in point). Even a journey of less than a hundred miles might fall under many different and probably hostile sovereignties, each with different rules, regulations, laws, weights, measures, and money. At every boundary, tolls had to be paid and fees extorted from the traveling merchants. All this served to maintain the insularity and isolation of each locality (Heilbroner, 1962).

The feudal system in Europe prior to the tenth century clearly was characterized by declining urban growth. Cities were losing population, commerce was severely restricted, and the towns became "festering sores rather than cases of responsible community life" (Boskoff, 1970, p. 20). Towns had lost most of their urban functions and were shadows of their former selves, often surviving as little more than fortresses or ecclesiastic centers, rather than as true cities. Yet they were an important historical prelude to the urban revival that followed.

Still, a few itinerant traders began to brave the dangers of travel to bring silks, linens, dyes, perfumes, and other luxury goods from the Near and Far East to those who could afford to buy them. Seasonal or annual fairs held outside the walls of the local towns were usually where traveling merchants displayed their wares or acquired additional merchandise to sell in a neighboring district. In turn, the fairs were exciting and festive occasions which afforded relief from the simple, self-sufficient routines of the townspeople, as well as an opportunity to barter the products of their own labor (Pirrene, 1939).

THE RISE OF THE MEDIEVAL TOWN IN EUROPE

The revival of urban growth following the feudal order required a major stimulus, one that could produce dramatic new waves of urban growth and activity. The impetus most likely came from the rather sudden resurgence of trade stimulated by the medieval religious Crusades. Trade was never entirely absent from the European scene during the "Dark Ages," and it seems to have grown slowly along with slow increases in population, improvements in the food supplies, and the development of rural handicrafts. The relatively slow growth of trade was dramatically accelerated in the eleventh century.

As the crusaders assaulted the Moslem world, they ended the isolation of Europe from the Byzantine East. During the Crusades, they carried with them a demand for European goods for which they paid with the bounties of war. When the crusaders returned from the Byzantine Empire, enriched with newly acquired wealth from plundered Byzantine cities, they brought back into feudal Europe highly expanded tastes for the consumer goods and luxuries of the East. They also introduced Europe to new ideas about the uses of money, technology, and alternative styles of living (Braudel, 1978).

It should be pointed out that the crusaders had also rediscovered the city of Constantinople, which, in spite of the decline of the Roman Empire, had continued to grow and thrive. According to Gibbon (1965), the population of Constantinople numbered at least 400,000 people at the time of the Crusades. The city was also blessed by great wealth, magnificent public buildings, great artistic achievements, exemplary civic institutions, and a very cosmopolitan culture, and it undoubtedly contributed to the wealth of material goods and cultural innovations brought back to Europe by the crusaders.

Feudal Europe was receptive to the goods and coins carried by the crusader turned merchant, but was not well prepared for the new notions of freedom, lack of commitment to the established order, and sophistication and wealth of the traders, who became fair

Medieval walled city and castle

game for anyone who could prey on them. Trade was still a hazardous, low-status occupation and was often received with contempt, suspicion, discrimination, and sometimes outright violence by feudal society. Nevertheless trade expanded rapidly from the tenth century onward (Rorig, 1967).

With the rapid expansion of trade, along with accompanying improvements in agriculture, the population of towns increased and city life expanded rapidly. Many new towns appeared almost spontaneously, and older towns on suitable transportation and trade routes experienced rapid revival. Heilbroner (1962) estimates that nearly one thousand new towns were added to the settlement pattern of medieval Europe during the twelfth century and immediately thereafter.

The merchant settlements that had previously developed outside of town walls were often annexed to the towns during this period. They were later surrounded by their own walls, which were attached to those surrounding the towns. Adding to the growth of existing towns, these annexed merchant settlements, called *faubergs,* were an early example of what we now call *suburbs.* The merchants gained new status as they came to be appreciated for the added economic value they brought to their towns. The feudal lords who benefited from new sources of monetary income began to take the merchants under their sponsorship and protection, and soon some of the wealthiest merchant "princes" became closely allied with the ruling classes (Herlihy, 1978).

For the most part, however, the merchants were becoming a respected and powerful middle class who sought to ensure favorable economic positions by demanding and receiving political safeguards from the ruling feudal authorities. The demands of the merchants included personal freedom to come and go as they pleased, to live where they wished, and to have wives and children emancipated from bondage to the whims of the nobles and ecclesiastic lords (Hughes, 1978).

The merchants, of course, were most interested in the right to unrestricted free trade, but in the course of gaining this privilege, a number of other economic, political, and legal innovations were initiated, leading to the emergence of a new set of municipal institutions that further freed the merchants and other townspeople from the rigid controls of the feudal order.

The right to own and sell private property and land was established, as was the right to establish urban courts for settling commercial disputes. The latter helped to eliminate the tediously overlapping claims of numerous jurisdictions and the irrelevant complexities of many archaic laws. As civic order became a problem, the merchant classes developed and legalized local police systems, as well as uniform and rationalized penal codes. The merchants freed themselves from the multiplicity of fees and tolls previously imposed by the lords and ecclesiastic authorities and won the right to levy their own excise and income taxes to pay for community services. Most important, they won the right to self-governance, as represented by municipal charters and by an elected city council as the key administrative body of the towns (Braudel, 1978).

The merchants, along with money changers, innkeepers, weavers, metalsmiths, and other artisans constituted a new social class known as the *bourgeoisie.* This new class was the forerunner of the development of a market economy characterized by free trade, the rise of capitalism, and the emergence of the so-called middle classes of contemporary urban-industrial societies, which were the antithesis of the feudal ruling classes. Under the guidance of the bourgeoisie, a political climate was created which was well described by a then current German expression that translates into English as "city air makes men free."

What we now call the university was an interesting innovation first institutionalized in city settings during the twelfth and thirteenth centuries. The first universities or colleges were informal organizations of individuals proficient in the scholarly areas of law, theology, and medicine. The status of the early universities was quite marginal. They were housed in ramshackle buildings, and their assets consisted of a few precious manuscripts and "a motley assemblage of variously ill-prepared students . . . learning was personal, barely dignified" (Boskoff, 1970). Despite numerous difficulties, the church, the merchants, and the ruling classes gradually came to accept and sometime even subsidize the universities, because they were expected to satisfy the increasing demand for skills in law, medicine, and a growing variety of professional service occupations that were becoming increasingly necessary for people living in an urban environment.

THE PHYSICAL AND SPATIAL STRUCTURE OF MEDIEVAL CITIES

During the medieval period, only a small handful of cities, such as Paris, Florence, Venice, and Milan, approached a population size of 100,000 (Braudel, 1978). Most were much smaller, hardly more than villages by contemporary standards. As was the case in earlier settlements, the wall remained an important element of the physical structure of medieval towns. The thick walls, with their watchtowers and external moats, defined the available living space and provide a rough outline of the physical patterns of the cities. When the population increased, the walls were torn down, and new city walls were built farther out.

Sometimes the resulting open space was used to construct ring roads or boulevards, such as the notable boulevards that ringed Vienna or Paris. Except for the main thoroughfares, which led directly from the town center to the town walls, the streets were narrow and winding and were densely lined with buildings that overarched or overhung the narrow streets. Streets and districts came to be differentiated by trades and crafts. The members of each occupation tended to cluster their residences and shops for mutual support and promotion of common interests. A trade or craft was a family concern, and the residence was not separated from the workplace.

The two main focal points of the community were the cathedral, which represented the religious side of community life, and the palace, which represented community political life. The cathedral often stood beside a main gate in the town wall next to a large open space or plaza, the setting for religious festivals and gatherings. The political center was marked by the palace of the reigning royal family. Residences of other members of the ruling class were gathered closely around the palace. The poorer and more underprivileged members of the community were relegated to the outer edges of the town and sometimes beyond its walls. It is interesting to compare this pattern with that of contemporary American cities, in which just the opposite takes place: the poor live near the center in "inner cities," whereas the middle and upper classes, with some exceptions, tend to live at the periphery or in suburbs. Actually, most of the cities of the world today still tend to follow the medieval pattern of spatial distribution of the various socioeconomic strata, with cities in the United States remaining the notable exception. This is an important distinction that is discussed in more detail in later chapters.

THE DECLINE OF THE MEDIEVAL CITY

Congestion and the lack of sanitary facilities made the medieval city a malodorous place. Sewage was dumped into streets, and the remains of slaughtered animals were allowed to rot where they were dropped. Streets were unpaved, and water purification was an unknown skill. Consequently, garbage accumulated in large heaps and puddles, serving as food and a breeding ground for rats and other vermin. Mortality rates were extremely high, as various plagues attacked the urban population. For example, the Black Death alone decimated at least one-fourth of the entire population of Europe in the first three years of this plague, between 1348 and 1350, and nearly one-third of the population of Europe succumbed to the disease during the fourteenth century (Hawley, 1981). The number of people in cities was so depleted that many of the cities were not able to continue functioning as viable social units. Havoc was intensified by people fleeing from areas where the plague was in full course and by people in other localities bitterly trying to shunt aside the flood of refugees. Trade was disrupted, organized community life was imperiled, and, in general, urban growth was drastically cut back during the fourteen century. It took more than a century for Europe to replace the population lost to the plagues, and the rural-based feudal system by that time had begun to disintegrate under the onslaught, never to regain its former prominence.

CITIES OF THE RENAISSANCE

By the fifteenth century, city life began to revive and urban populations began to grow again throughout Europe. By this time, new cultural, social and economic forces were set in motion that were eventually to lead to the industrial revolution, and to a growth in urban life so remarkable that in time it was to become the predominant mode of human existence in many parts of the modern world. The Renaissance (a term usually applied to the intellectual movement based on a revival of learning and art that marked this transitional period of history) began in Italian cities, such as Florence and Venice.

Contemporaneous with this new spirit of learning were the invention of printing, new methods of paper making, the explorations to discover new trade routes to the Far East, and the struggle for greater religious freedom under the Protestant Reformation. Among the most famous figures of the Italian Renaissance were Leonardo da Vinci and Michelangelo. Leonardo's interests ranged from painting, sculpture, and architecture to music, engineering, and all of the sciences then known. Michelangelo, nearly as versatile, produced masterpieces in painting, sculpture, and architecture, as well as distinguished poetry. The Renaissance movement was symbolized by the monumental architecture and decorative sculpture that dominated the private dwellings, as well as the public buildings of Florence, Venice, and, ultimately, Rome, which also experienced a significant revival during this period.

During the fifteenth and sixteenth centuries, the Renaissance movement spread to Northern and Western Europe, affecting many cities in countries such as Spain, France, Germany, the Netherlands, and England, although it took on slightly different forms in each of these countries in terms of the decorative art, sculpture, and architecture of principal cities such as Paris, Amsterdam, or London. Of course, the artistic and other intellectual achievements of the Renaissance were underwritten by wealth from the flourishing expansion of trade and exploration across larger portions of the known world. All this was an essential prelude to the urban-industrial revolution, which we explore in the next chapter.

First, however, one more important point should be made about the urbanization process. Not all of the social and technological changes associated with rapid urbanization have been accepted to the same degree or at the same rate of speed by all people exposed to these changes. Thus, at any given time, one can find individuals or groups of people who resist such changes and who do not represent the dominant modes of adjustment to the most advanced stages of urbanization in the regions in which they reside. For example, nomadic ways of life continued to persist in the Middle East long after cities became the center of Middle Eastern civilizations. Groups such as the Bedouins still continued to pursue their nomadic tradition of rearing sheep and camels in the deserts of the Middle East well into the twentieth century—in the same regions in which some of the earliest permanent year-round settlements and subsequent cities had first appeared (Kay, 1978).

Likewise, even in the most modern of urban communities, not all residents have adopted modern urban lifestyles, and every urban community contains people whose lives are still attuned to an earlier mode of existence. This "cultural lag"—or gap between technological advances and the resultant adjustments of customs, beliefs, and social practices—creates social strains in rapidly changing urban environments. Such strains are at the heart of many of the social problems associated with urban living that are explored in more detail throughout this book.

SELECTED BIBLIOGRAPHY

BOSKOFF, ALVIN. *The Sociology of Urban Regions,* 2d ed. New York: Appleton-Century-Crofts, 1970.

BRAIDWOOD, ROBERT, and GORDON WILLIE, eds. *Courses toward Urban Life.* Chicago: Alpine, 1962.

BRAUDEL, FERNANDO. "Pre-Modern Towns." In *The Early Modern Town,* Peter Clark (ed.). London: Longmont, 1978.

BREASTED, J. H. *The Development of Religion and Thought in Ancient Egypt.* New York: 1912.

CHILDE, GORDON. *What Happened in History.* London: Penguin, 1946.

CLARK, GRAHAM, and STUART PIGGOT, eds. *Prehistoric Societies.* New York: Knopf, 1965.

EBERHARD, WOLFRAM. "Data of the Structure of the Chinese City in the Pre-Industrial Period." *Economic Development and Cultural Change* 4 (1955–1956).

FREUD, SIGMUND. *Moses and Monotheism.* New York: Vintage, 1957.

GIBBON, EDWARD. *The Decline and Fall of the Roman Empire.* New York: Dell, 1965.

HAWLEY, AMOS. *Urban Society,* 2d ed. New York: Wiley, 1981.

HEILBRONER, ROBERT. *The Making of Economic Society.* Englewood Cliffs, NJ: Prentice-Hall, 1962.

HERLIHY, DAVID. "The Distribution of Wealth in a Renaissance Community: Florence, 1427." In *Towns in Societies: Essays in Economic History and Historical Sociology,* Philip Abrams and E. A. Wrigley (eds.). London: Cambridge University Press, 1978.

HOPKINS, KEITH. "Economic Growth and Towns in Ancient Antiquity." In *Towns and Societies: Essays in Economic History and Historical Sociology,* Philip Abrams and E. A. Wrigley (eds.). London: Cambridge University Press, 1978.

HUGHES, DIANE O. "Urban Growth and Family Structure in Medievel Genoa." In *Towns and Societies: Essays in Economic History and Historical Sociology,* Philip Abrams and E. A. Wrigley (eds.). London: Cambridge University Press, 1978.

JURMAIN, ROBERT, et al. *Introduction to Physical Anthropology,* 7th ed. Belmont, CA: West-Wadsworth, 1997.

KAY, SHIRLEY. *The Bedouin.* New York: Crane and Russak, 1978.

MCADAMS, ROBERT. *The Evolution of Urban Society: Early Mesopotamia and Prehispanic Mexico.* Chicago: Aldine, 1966.

———. "Patterns of Urbanization in Early Southern Mesopotamia." In *Urban Settlements: The Process of Urbanization in Archeological Settlements,* Ruth Tringham (ed.). Andover MA: Warner Modular Publications, 1973.

OPPENHEIM, LEO A. *Ancient Mesopotamia: Portrait of a Dead Civilization.* Chicago: University of Chicago Press, 1964.

PIRENNE, HENRY. *Medieval Cities.* Princeton, NJ: Princeton University Press, 1939.

PULSALKER, A. D. "The Indus Valley Civilization." In *The Vedic Age,* R. C. Mahumdar (ed.). Bombay: Bharatiya Vidya Bhaven, 1951.

RORIG, FRITZ. *The Medieval Town.* Berkeley: University of California Press, 1967.

RUSSELL, J. C. *Late Ancient and Medieval Population.* Philadelphia: American Philosophical Society, 1958.

SAVAGEAU, DAVID, and RICHARD BOYER. *Placed Rated Almanac.* New York: Macmillan, 1993.

SJOBERG, GIDEON. "The Nature of the Pre-Industrial City." In *Prehistoric Societies,* Graham Clark and Stuart Piggot (eds.). New York: Knopf. 1965.

STEINDORFF, GEORGE, and K. C. SEELE. *When Egypt Ruled the East.* Chicago: University of Chicago Press, 1942.

TRIGGER, BRUCE. "Determinants of Growth in Pre-Industrial Societies." In *Man, Settlement, and Urbanism,* Peter Ucko, Ruth Tringham, and G. W. Dimbleby (eds.). Cambridge: Shenkman, 1972.

WEBER, MAX. *The City.* New York: Collier, 1962.

WENKE, ROBERT J. *Patterns in Prehistory.* New York: Oxford University Press, 1980.

WHITE, LESLIE A. *The Science of Culture.* New York: Grove Press, 1949.

WHITEHOUSE, RUTH. *The First Cities.* New York: Dutton, 1977.

WOLPOFF, MILFRED, and RACHEL CASPARI. *Race and Human Evolution.* New York: Simon and Shuster, 1997.

WOOLLEY, LEONARD. *Ur of the Chaldees.* London: Penguin, 1952.

3

THE IMPACT OF THE INDUSTRIAL REVOLUTION ON CITY LIFE

The nineteenth century has been widely characterized as the age of the industrial revolution. The nineteenth century has also been aptly described as the period in which the proliferation and growth of cities reach explosive proportions. These two trends have been so intertwined that the concept of the *urban-industrial revolution* is often used to describe the unprecedented transformation in human society that took place during this period. So many of the patterns and problems of modern urban life are the consequences of the nineteenth-century industrial revolution that we must begin with an analysis of this development as a basis for understanding the major themes of the remaining portion of this book. Actually, the industrial revolution was the product of a diversity of social, economic, and technological changes that began in Europe about the fifteenth century. These changes combined in such a way during the nineteenth century in Europe and North America as to make rapid industrialization inevitable.

THE MARKET ECONOMY

Perhaps the most important prerequisite to industrialization was the emergence of a market economy. A market economy is one in which the process of exchanging goods and services is based on an impersonal and standardized monetary system. In modern industrial societies, this feature of the market economy is so institutionalized that it is taken for granted (see Yergin and Stanislaw, 1998, for an excellent discussion of the powerful momentum markets have had on twentieth-century economic growth). In a preindustrial society in which a market economy had not yet emerged, trade was conducted by bartering, a ritual involving much haggling over the value of the respective goods to be exchanged. Of course, such a system was time-consuming and inefficient, and it limited the volume of commodities that could be exchanged in any given time period. Also, the residents of such a society would have been shocked to learn that many services, which were to them too sacred or personal to have monetary value, such as buying food or drink in a restaurant, getting a bed in a hotel or motel, paying nurses to take care of us when we are sick, or paying a counselor for marital or sexual advice, are impersonally bought and sold on the open market in contemporary industrial societies. Yet, these and thousands of other examples of "rampant consumerism" had already begun to emerge in the European Renaissance cities of the fifteenth century, as a handful of superrich merchants and princes began flaunting their wealth and worldly possessions in a manner not seen in Europe since the fall of the Roman Empire (Jardine, 1996).

From the perspective of the new urban sociology, the commercialization of land and labor are among the most significant characteristics of a market economy. The idea that land was no longer a sacred trust, to be maintained and transmitted by families from one generation to another, but was a commodity to be sold to the highest bidder, or to be used for the most efficient or monetarily profitable purpose, would have been considered repugnant and strongly resisted by most feudal landlords (Heilbroner, 1962). Yet the impersonal and routinized sale of real estate, and the resultant frequent change in land use, are important characteristics of modern urban-industrial communities (see Lefebvre, 1991; Feagin, 1983; Gottdiener, 1994).

Likewise, the emergence of a market economy requires that, to participate in the market for goods and services, one must have cash at his or her disposal. In the preindustrial medieval economy, at least 60 or 70 percent of the actual working population labored as serfs without anything resembling full payment in money (Heilbroner, 1962). With the emergence of a market economy, however, no longer was labor part of an explicit social relationship in which one person (serf or apprentice) worked for another (lord or guildmaster) in return for lodgings and other nonmonetary subsistence. Labor now became a commodity, to be exchanged for the best monetary reward, in the form of the wages it could bring. The substitution of an impersonal wage system for the reciprocal obligations and responsibilities between serf or apprentice and lord or guildmaster also undermined some of the stability and security workers experienced under the feudal system and placed them at the mercy of whims and fluctuations in the labor market. Thus, the greater risk of unemployment was introduced as one of the more problematic characteristics of the market economy. This problem is discussed in more detail later in this chapter.

THE RISE OF CAPITALISM

One of the ideas basic to capitalism is private ownership of the means of production, and their operation for profit by private entrepreneurs competing in a free and open market. In the modern western world, it would be difficult to overestimate the impact of the profit motive as an inducement to industrialize or the importance of capital investment as an underlying prerequisite to industrialization. Sociological perspectives on capitalism have tended to emphasize the *culture* of capitalism, which involves mainly the values and beliefs that sustain and reflect the economic organization of capitalism as it developed in Europe and North America. For example, Max Weber (1930) has pointed out how certain values that emerged as features of the Protestant Reformation in Europe about the seventeenth century were conducive to the expansion of capitalism and economic rationality. High value is placed on an active rather than a contemplative life, unremitting labor is considered both a moral virtue and a moral obligation, and the individual who engages in highly productive labor is asserted to have found favor in the eyes of God. Thus, success, profits, and wealth are virtues. They are vices only if they lead to idleness and dissipation.

Although Weber did not attempt to prove a causal relationship between Protestantism and the rise of capitalism, the Protestant outlook undoubtedly was a powerful motivation for productive work and did historically coincide with the expansion of technology and production associated with the industrial revolution. However, the increase in secularism and growing faith in science that arose during the same period should not be minimized. Neither, should the same desires for wealth and profits that also have arisen in non-Protestant societies around the world, such as Japan or China be minimized. Wilensky and Lebeaux (1958) have attributed the values of American capitalism to the rational, acquisitive, self-interested individuals and groups who subscribe to the following beliefs:

1. Those who work hard and have ability will be rewarded with success (this includes not only economic wealth, but also power and prestige—along with the lifestyles that these permit).
2. Success is the reward of virtue: virtue will bring success. Failure (if it is not a temporary way station to success) is a sin and reveals a lack of virtue.
3. When the lazy, incompetent, and unvirtuous attain success, it is merely a matter of luck; it could happen to anybody, but it does not happen very often.
4. The test of reward should be the ability to contribute to the productive and other purposes of free enterprise. There should be unequal reward for unequal talents and unequal contributions.

Whether these still are, or should be, the dominant economic values in American society is still a matter of considerable ideological controversy and debate, but there is little doubt that they provided much of the incentive to industrialize in America during the nineteenth century, along with the revolutionary growth in American cities during that same time period.

NATIONALISM, COLONIALISM, AND IMPERIALISM

Between the fifteenth and nineteenth centuries in Europe, one tumultuous change of particular importance for the progress of industrialization was the movement toward political unification and the rise of the nation-states. This led to greater centralization of government controls of city and country alike as elaborate administrative bureaucracies arose, partly in response to the need or desire to promote and regulate economic growth in expanded trading areas (Hawley, 1981).

One consequence of this trend was increased growth in the political capitals of the emerging nation-states. Thus, cities such as Paris, London, Warsaw, Moscow, Lisbon, Vienna, and Copenhagen had attained populations of one hundred thousand or more by the middle of the seventeenth century. In turn, the resultant urban growth itself became the basis for expanded trade.

The expansion of trade in the European nation-states encouraged Europeans to search farther and farther for new markets and riches. The explorations of Columbus, Magellan, Marco Polo, and other exploratory expeditions were for this purpose. They also eventually established colonies for this purpose in Africa, Southern Asia, Latin America, and North America from the fifteenth century onward. This was made possible in part by some of the technological advances in transportation and navigation, as well as by their superior military technology. Once the large colonial empires were established, it was no accident that centers of these empires became the focal points for greater industrialization and urbanization, such as the growth of London, Manchester, and Birmlngham as popu-latlon and industrial centers for the British Empire.

THE MACHINE AND THE FACTORY
SYSTEM OF PRODUCTION

All of these forces combined during the latter part of the eighteenth century to make the introduction of the factory system of production both desirable and feasible. The substitu-tion of steam-powered machinery for inanimate sources of energy, previously supplied by humans in the form of tools or as extensions of their own limbs, was the earliest and most significant direct manifestation of the industrial revolution. The factory system of produc-tion, utilizing steam-driven machinery, first emerged in England in the 1780s in the textile industry, as machines were gradually substituted for hand tools in the related processes of spinning and weaving cotton and woolen fabrics.

Until the factory appeared, the household was the scene of nearly all industrial labor. In England, the dominant means of production just prior to the industrial revolution was the "cottage" or "putting out" system, in which an employer owns the raw materials and gives them out to various craft workers who produce finished products through processes carried out in their homes (Smelser, 1959). The worker then returns the goods to the employer, and, if they are not yet finished, the employer passes them on to other workers, who also engage in various craft processes at home. The employer is a capitalist in the sense of owning the materials during the processes of production and advancing wages to the workers.

As this system expanded, the employer eventually owned the tools or other equip-ment used during production. In many instances, the employer owned the cottages used by the workers, which were rented to them completely equipped for both production and family living. This cottage systen brought a number of workers under a moderate degree of supervision and direction by their employers, but on the whole the system did little to standardize the nature of industrial work. The rates and efficiency of productlon differed vastly from employer to employer and from cottage to cottage, because each worker still had a large degree of control over the pace and style of his or her work, as was the case in earlier stages of craft production (Usher, 1920).

What the factory system did was to bring large numbers of workers together under the same roof in buildings devoted solely to their work and under the direct surveillance and control of the employers. Increasingly, the pace of work became regulated by the re-quirements of the power-driven machinery, restricting much of the freedom that the worker enjoyed under the putting-out system. Workers at first resisted the organization of work in the factories, and a central problem for the new industrialists was to attract labor to their factories, especially when the factory system of production became very profitable and the demand for industrial manpower had greatly expanded. Because much of the factory work required far less skill than the crafts it replaced, the problem was essentially how to get rural, peasant people off the farms and into city-based industries (Wilensky and Lebeaux, 1958).

In the earliest days of the industrial revolution, coercion often played the main role in labor recruitment, with people being virtually pushed into factory work as much as they were voluntarily attracted by the great opportunity before them. In England, the enclosure movement, which culminated in the eighteenth and early nineteenth centuries, is an example of such coercion. The commercialization of land and property made the landed aristocracy, increasingly squeezed for cash, begin to see their estates as sources of monetary revenue. Aided by acts of Parliament (which was partial to commercial and industrial interests during that period), they began consolidating small strips of peasant-occupied grazing land into larger units to produce cash-producing crops for a growing city market. As the common grazing fields, which the peasants had previously shared with the owners for their mutual subsistence, were enclosed, the peasant tenants found it increasingly difficult to support themselves and were gradually pushed off the land (Heilbroner, 1962).

The enclosure process provided a powerful force for the destruction of the medieval village and its communal ties. By dispossessing the peasant, it created a new kind of landless labor force, without traditional forms of nonmonetary subsistence. Under the English Poor Laws of the early nineteenth century, the many destitute people wandering about the country were thrust into the workhouse if they did not take jobs voluntarily, and anyone who left a job without his employer's written permission was subjected to the same treatment. Thus, the peasants were compelled to find work for wages wherever it might be available—most likely in the growing industrial cities of London, Manchester, Birmingham, Sheffield, and Liverpool .

At the beginning of the nineteenth century, England was the most urbanized society in Europe. Using a minimum population size of twenty thousand to designate urban places, the population of Europe was less than 5 percent urban in 1800. At that date, England and Wales had a population that was 17 percent urban. Urban growth accelerated dramatically in England during each decade of the nineteenth century and had doubled by the middle of the century. By the last decade of the century, more than one-half of the English population lived in cities of twenty thousand or more people. As Table 3.1 illustrates, urbanization also increased throughout much of the European continent during the nineteenth century, but at a slower rate than in England.

The growth in the number of larger cities, with a population of one hundred thousand or more, is also a useful index of urbanization. In Europe, only twenty-three cities had a population of one hundred thousand or larger in 1800, but by the end of the century 143 cities were in this category. Although the total population of Europe slightly more than doubled during the nineteenth century, the population of the larger European cities of one hundred thousand or more increased tenfold during the same period (Hawley, 1981). The early European industrial cities, although producing much in the way of new wealth, were characterized by overcrowding and unbelievably poor sanitary conditions. Diseases

Table 3.1 Proportions of Total Populations in Cities of 20,000 or More Inhabitants (Selected Countries and Dates)*

YEAR*	ENGLAND-WALES	HOLLAND	GERMANY	BELGIUM	ITALY	AUSTRIA	HUNGARY	SWEDEN	FRANCE
1800–01	16.9%	—	—	—	4.4%	3.6%	2.3%	3.0%	3.9%
1810–11	18.1	—	—	—	—	—	—	—	—
1820–21	20.8	—	—	1.3%	—	—	—	—	—
1830–31	25.0	20.1%	—	—	—	—	—	—	4.5
1840–41	28.9	—	—	—	—	4.2	—	—	—
1850–51	35.0	21.7	—	5.2	6.0	—	—	—	6.0
1860–61	38.2	—	12.5%	—	—	—	4.6	3.4	—
1870–71	42.0	—	18.1	—	—	9.6	—	—	6.7
1880–81	48.0	—	—	—	—	—	—	—	—
1890–91	53.6	31.3	21.9	13.2	13.3	12.0	11.2	10.8	9.1

*Dates are approximate.

Source: A.F. Weber, *The Growth of Cities in the Nineteenth Century,* Columbia University Press, 1899, pp. 47–119.

and epidemics were common and mortality rates were high. Social critics have portrayed these cities as devoid of beauty, without parks or pure water supplies, public lighting or drainage, because such amenities were considered frivolous by the early industrialists. Discussing the slums, poverty, cruelty, and misery, the Hammonds (1925) have described the early English factory towns in these terms:

> The towns had their profitable smoke, their profitable disorder, their profitable igno-
> rance, their profitable despair. . . . The new factories and the new furnaces were like
> the Pyramids, telling of man's enslavement, rather than of his power; casting their
> long shadow over the society that took such pride in them.

A series of reforms began to take place in England around the middle of the nineteenth century that ameliorated some of the worst of the conditions, and urban-industrial cities continued to grow and thrive throughout England and the rest of Europe. But by this time the main thrust of urban growth had begun to shift to North America.

PREINDUSTRIAL URBAN GROWTH IN AMERICA

Except for the Aztec, Mayan, and Incan civilizations of Mesoamerica, which were centered in densely populated communities, no indigenous cities existed in North America when the first European colonists began to arrive. The new towns created by the early settlers led rather than followed the settlement of the rest of the country. The earliest centers to extend beyond village proportions were ports and trade centers such as New York, Philadelphia, Boston, Baltimore, and Charleston. Early town growth was slow, and as late as 1790 (the year the first U.S. census was taken), the five cities listed were the only ones in the United States with populations of more than ten thousand people. In all, only twenty-four towns or cities in the United States had more than 2,500 people, and at that date no city in the United States had yet achieved a population as large as fifty thousand. Only 5 percent of the total population of 3,929,000 lived in towns or cities (Table 3.2).

During the first several decades of the nineteenth century, the number of new towns and the urban population slowly increased as commerce continued to accelerate and as a steady stream of European immigrants settled in the existing cities or set up new communities in the expanding Western and Southern territories (Table 3.2 illustrates the population growth of principal American cities between 1790 and 1830). By then, New York had become the largest, with just less than a quarter of a million inhabitants. New York and Philadelphia were the only two cities with a population or more than one hundred thousand people, and just under 9 percent of the total population lived in cities or towns.

The urbanization process in America began to move faster in the period from 1830 to the beginning of the Civil War. As the national population increased and migration to the West accelerated, the need for new and larger cities grew still more rapidly. Part of the urban increase resulted from a new flux of immigrants who settle in the established cities of the northeast as well as in the new western cities. The pattern of urban growth in America during this period differed from that in Great Britain in that it was still being spurred by commercial rather than industrial development (McKelvey, 1973). In turn, the enormous growth of trade and the expansion of trading areas were facilitated by major innova-

Table 3.2 Populations of Principal U.S. Cities, 1790 to 1830*

CITIES	1790	1800	1810	1820	1830
New York	33,131	60,515	96,373	123,706	202,589
Suburbs			4,402	7,175	39,689
Totals			100,775	130,881	242,278
Philadelphia	28,522	41,220	53,722	63,802	80,462
Suburbs	15,574	20,339	33,581	45,007	80,809
Totals	44,096	61,559	87,303	108,809	161,271
Boston	18,320	24,937	33,787	43,298	61,392
Suburbs			4,959	10,726	18,104
Totals			38,746	54,024	85,568
Baltimore	13,503	26,514	46,555	62,738	80,620
New Orleans		9,000	17,242	27,176	46,082
Cincinnati		750	2,540	9,642	24,831
Charleston	16,359	18,924	24,711	24,780	30,289
Albany	3,498	5,349	9,356	12,630	24,209
Washington		3,210	8,208	13,247	18,826
Providence	6,380	7,614	10,071	11,767	16,833
Pittsburgh	376	1,565	4,768	7,248	15,369
Richmond	3,761	5,737	9,735	12,067	16,060
Salem	7,917	9,457	12,613	12,731	13,895
Portland	2,239	3,704	7,169	8,581	12,598
Troy		4,926	3,895	5,264	11,856
New Haven	4,487	4,049	5,772	7,147	10,180
Louisville	200	359	1,357	4,012	10,341
Newark			5,008	6,507	10,953
Total of Urban Residents	202,000	322,000	525,000	693,000	1,127,000
Number of Towns over 2500	24	33	46	61	90
Percent Urban	5.1	6.1	7.3	7.2	8.8
Total U.S. Population	3,929,000	5,308,000	7,240,000	9,638,000	12,806,000

*U.S. Census Office, *Seventh Census: 1850* (Washington, D.C.: U.S. Government Printing Office, 1951), p. liii; U.S. Bureau of the Census, *Thirteenth Census: 1910* (Washington, D.C.: U.S. Government Printing Office, 1911), *Population,* I, p. 80; U.S. Bureau of the Census, *Seventeenth Census: 1950* (Washington, D.C.: U.S. Government Printing Office, 1951), I, U.S. Summary, Table 15.

tions in land and water transportation. The steamship came into general use, first on river and coastal routes, then in transoceanic service. The adoption of steam-driven trains as a principal means of land travel advanced rapidly as the railways began to provide a continentwide transportation network linking the hinterlands to the existing urban centers. Overland trips that had been measured in days and weeks now could be accomplished in a matter of hours. The invention of the telegraph also speeded the flow of trade by making possible more closely timed buying and selling transactions over larger and larger territories.

By 1860 the principal outlines of the urban settlement pattern east of the Mississippi had been completed, and most of the present larger cities in that region now having a population of one hundred thousand or more were already established. West of the Mississippi, St. Louis and San Francisco had already become urban centers. Still, New York

Table 3.3   Populations of Principal U.S. Cities, 1830 to 1860*

CITIES	1830	1840	1850	1860
New York	202,589	312,700	515,500	813,600
Philadelphia	161,271	220,400	340,000	565,529
Brooklyn	15,396	36,230	96,838	266,660
Baltimore	80,620	102,300	169,600	212,418
Boston	61,392	93,380	136,880	177,840
New Orleans	46,082	102,190	116,375	168,675
Cincinnati	24,831	46,338	115,435	161,044
St. Louis	5,852	14,470	77,860	160,773
Chicago		4,470	29,963	109,260
Buffalo	8,653	18,213	42,260	81,130
Newark	10,953	17,290	38,890	71,940
Louisville	10,340	21,210	43,194	68,033
Albany	24,209	33,721	50,763	62,367
Washington	18,826	23,364	40,001	61,122
San Francisco			34,776	56,802
Providence	16,833	23,171	41,573	50,666
Pittsburgh	15,369	21,115	46,601	49,221
Rochester	9,207	20,191	36,403	48,204
Detroit	2,222	9,012	21,019	45,619
Milwaukee		1,712	20,061	45,246
Cleveland	1,076	6,071	17,034	43,417
Total of Urban Residents	1,127,000	1,845,000	3,543,700	6,216,500
Number of Towns over 2500	90	131	236	392
Percent Urban	8.8	10.8	15.3	19.8
Total U.S. Population	12,866,000	17,069,000	23,191,800	31,433,300

*Derived from U.S. Censuses in 1850, 1860, and 1910 (Washington, D.C.: U.S. Government Printing Office).

(including the borough of Brooklyn) was the first and only American city to have produced a population of more than a million by that date, and the greatest spurt in city growth was yet to come. Table 3.3 illustrates the growth of American cities from 1830 to 1860. Although urban growth as a portion of the total U.S. population had more than doubled during this period, less than 20 percent of the population resided in cities in 1860, and it was still too soon to refer to the United States as an urban society.

THE INDUSTRIAL REVOLUTION IN AMERICA

The full force of the industrial revolution finally reached America in the 1860s. Because it followed the industrial revolution in England by more than a half-century, it was no longer a new phenomenon, and American cities already possessed the essential ingredients for rapid industrialization. Economic historians are divided as to whether the Civil War promoted or hindered industrialization (McKelvey, 1973), but northern industrialists did begin producing steel, coal, and woolen goods at faster rates to gain from the inflated profits stimulated by the demands of war. The return of hundreds of thousands of men from military service also helped generate new demands for facilities and services. The nation's net income from manufacturing increased 77 percent during the 1860s, placing it ahead of all industrial nations for the first time (McKelvey, 1973). Expanded rates of productivity in cities that were rapidly becoming manufacturing centers, such as Scranton, Jersey City, Cleveland, Indianapolis, Newark, Milwaukee, Rochester, Cincinnati, Buffalo, and Pittsburgh, contributed to urban growth as immigrants flocked to these cities and others in search of the new economic opportunities promised by the potential of industrial work.

Growth was by no means confined to the manufacturing cities, because other cities also began to take on more specialized functions, complementary to those of manufacturing. Thus, many cities became centers of trade, administration, education, or recreation and leisure, and they too shared in the tremendous population expansion of the latter part of the nineteenth century (Hawley, 1981).

The U.S. population mushroomed from 31 million in 1860 to 92 million in 1910, with most of the increase going to the cities. Until the 1880s, much of the growth was provided by Irish, German, or Scandinavian immigrants, most of whom were skilled and literate. They were able to take advantage of the Homestead Act and become farmers. Beginning in the 1880s, migration shifted from northern and western Europe to southern and eastern Europe, becoming mostly Italian, Greek, Croat, Czech, Slovak, Slovene, Polish, Hungarian, Rumanian, and Russian by nationality (Wilensky and Lebeaux, 1958; Parrillo, 1997). Many of the newer immigrants were un-skilled peasants who came to the industrial cities and had to adjust simultaneously to urban and industrial ways of life. More will be said about this problem later.

As in England, the burgeoning manufacturing cities were often dirty, noisy, overcrowded, and congested with pollution-producing factories. They were certainly not attractive by today's standards, to say the least. Pittsburgh has often been pointed out as a prototype of the American industrial cities of the latter nineteenth century. A description written in 1834 vividly depicts the city:

> Pittsburgh is a smoky, dismal city at her best. At her worst, nothing darker, dingier or more dispiriting can be imagined. . . . The smoke from her dwellings, stores, factories, foundries and steamboats, uniting, settles in a cloud over the narrow valley in which she is built, until the very sun looks coppery through the sooty haze. . . . It has thirty-five miles of factories in daily operation, twisted up into a compact tangle, all belching smoke, all glowing with fire, all swarming with workmen, all echoing with the clank of machinery. . . . In a distance of thirty-five and one-half miles of streets, there are four hundred and seventy-eight manufactories of iron, steel, cotton, brass, oil, glass, copper and wood, occupying less than four hundred feet each. . . . These factories are so contiguous in their positions upon the various streets of the city, that if placed in a continuous row, they would reach thirty-five miles. (Glazier, 1884, pp. 332–334)

The demand for housing often greatly exceeded the supply, and the concentration of large numbers of people in relatively small land areas made itself felt in intolerable living conditions and repeated epidemics of major proportions in some cities. Buildings with no sanitary facilities beyond the privy and the gutter were being crowded together in such a

Table 3.4 Population of Cities That Reached 100,000 by 1910*

CITIES	1860	1870	1880	1890	1900	1910
Albany, N.Y.	62,367	69,422	90,758	94,923	94,151	100,253
Atlanta, Ga.	9,554	21,789	37,409	65,533	89,872	154,839
Baltimore, Md.	212,418	267,354	332,313	434,439	508,957	558,485
Birmingham, Ala.			3,086	26,178	38,415	132,685
Boston, Mass.	177,840	250,526	362,839	448,477	560,892	670,585
Bridgeport, Conn.[1]	13,299[1]	18,969	27,643	48,866	70,996	102,054
Buffalo, N.Y.	81,129	117,714	155,134	255,664	352,387	423,715
Cambridge, Mass.	26,060	39,634	52,669	70,028	91,886	104,839
Chicago, Ill.	109,260	298,997	503,185	1,099,850	1,698,575	2,185,283
Cincinnati, Ohio	161,044	216,239	255,139	296,908	325,902	363,591
Cleveland, Ohio	43,417	92,829	160,146	261,353	381,768	560,663
Columbus, Ohio	18,554	31,274	51,647	88,150	125,560	181,511
Dayton, Ohio	20,081	30,473	38,678	61,220	85,333	116,577
Denver, Colo.		4,759	35,629	106,713	133,859	213,381
Detroit, Mich.	45,619	79,577	116,340	205,876	285,704	465,766
Fall River, Mass.	14,026	26,766	48,961	74,398	104,863	119,295
Grand Rapids, Mich.	8,085	16,507	32,016	60,278	87,565	112,571
Indianapolis, Ind.	18,611	48,244	75,056	105,436	169,164	233,650
Jersey City, N.J.	29,226	82,546	120,722	163,003	206,433	267,779
Kansas City, Mo.	4,418	32,260	55,785	132,716	163,752	248,381
Los Angeles, Cal.	4,385	5,728	11,183	50,395	102,479	319,198
Louisville, Ky.	68,033	100,753	123,758	161,129	204,731	223,928
Lowell, Mass.	36,827	40,928	59,475	77,696	94,969	106,294
Memphis, Tenn.	22,623	40,226	33,592	64,495	102,320	131,105
Milwaukee, Wis.	45,246	71,440	115,587	204,468	285,315	373,857
Minneapolis, Minn.	2,564	13,066	46,887	164,738	202,718	301,408
Nashville, Tenn.	16,988	25,865	43,350	76,168	80,865	110,364
New Haven, Conn.	39,267[1]	50,840[1]	62,882[1]	81,298	108,027	113,605
New Orleans, La.	168,675	191,418	216,090	242,039	287,104	339,075
New York, N.Y.[2]	1,174,779	1,478,103	1,911,698	2,507,414	3,437,202	4,766,883
Manhattan Borough	813,669	942,292	1,164,673	1,441,216	1,850,093	2,331,542
Bronx Borough	23,593	37,393	51,980	88,908	200,507	430,980
Brooklyn Borough	279,122	419,921	599,495	838,547	1,166,582	1,634,351
Queens Borough	32,903	45,468	56,559	87,050	152,999	284,041
Richmond Borough	25,492	33,029	38,991	51,693	67,021	85,969
Newark, N.J.	71,941	105,059	136,508	181,830	246,070	347,469
Oakland, Cal.	1,543	10,500	34,555	48,682	66,960	150,174
Omaha, Nebr.	1,883	16,083	30,518	140,452	102,555	124,096
Paterson, N.J.	19,586	33,579	51,031	78,347	105,171	125,600
Philadelphia, Pa.	565,529	674,022	847,170	1,046,964	1,293,697	1,549,008
Pittsburgh, Pa.[3]	77,923	139,256	235,071	343,904	451,512	533,905
Portland, Oreg.	2,874	8,293	17,577	46,385	90,426	207,214
Providence, R.I.	50,666	68,904	104,857	132,146	175,597	224,326
Richmond, Va.	37,910	51,038	63,600	81,388	85,050	127,628
Rochester, N.Y.	48,204	62,386	89,366	133,896	162,608	218,149
St. Louis, Mo.	160,773	310,864	350,518	451,770	575,238	687,029
St. Paul, Minn.	10,401	20,030	41,473	133,156	163,065	214,744
San Francisco, Cal.	56,802	149,473	233,959	298,997	342,782	416,912

(*continued*)

Table 3.4   (*Continued*)

CITIES	1860	1870	1880	1890	1900	1910
Scranton, Pa.	9,223	35,092	45,850	75,215	102,026	129,867
Seattle, Wash.		1,107	3,533	42,837	80,671	237,194
Spokane, Wash.				19,922	36,848	104,402
Syracuse, N.Y.	28,119	43,051	51,792	88,143	108,374	137,249
Toledo, Ohio	13,768	31,584	50,137	81,434	131,822	168,497
Washington, D.C.[4]	61,122	109,199	177,624	230,392	278,718	331,069
Worcester, Mass.	24,960	41,105	58,291	84,655	118,421	145,986

[1]Population of town; town and city not returned separately.
[2]Population of New York and its boroughs as now constituted.
[3]Includes population of Allegheny as follows: 1900, 129,896; 1890, 105,287; 1880, 78,682; 1870, 53,180; 1860, 28,702; 1850, 21,262; 1840, 10,089; and 1830, 2,801.
[4]Population as returned from 1880 to 1910 is for the District of Columbia, with which the city is now coextensive.
*U.S. Bureau of the Census, *Thirteenth Census: 1910* (Washington, D.C.: Government Printing Office, 1913), I, p. 80.

way as to leave many dwellings virtually without light and air. In New York, for example, a law prohibiting the building of residential rooms without windows was not passed until 1879 (Gold, 1965).

None of the large cities made adequate public provision for disposal of sewage until late in the nineteenth century, and even in 1900 Philadelphia and St. Louis had twice as much street mileage as sewer mileage. In the same year, Baltimore, New Orleans, and other cities were still relying on open gutters for drainage. Frequently, cities were prompted to construct sewer systems only by social catastrophe. Memphis, for example,

Immigrants, tenements, and shops crowd Hester Street in late nineteenth century New York

did not take this step until after the city had been practically depopulated by a yellow fever epidemic in 1879 (Gold, 1965).

In many other ways, a large gap existed between the needs of a growing urban population and the capacity or willingness of the local urban municipalities to supply solutions to those needs. At the beginning of the industrial revolution, municipal fire and police departments had not yet become fully institutionalized as legitimate ongoing functions of local government, and these services were still sometimes being offered by volunteers, or to private subscribers, by profit-oriented private companies. With few notable exceptions, many industrial cities were devoid of public parks or playgrounds until very late in the nineteenth century.

POVERTY, UNEMPLOYMENT, AND INDUSTRIAL UNREST

In the early days of the industrial revolution, the workers' job security was often precarious. This was partly because most manufacturing industries were concentrated in large numbers of rather small family owned and managed units engaged in fierce competition with one another, making the owner's lot precarious as well. In addition, the fortunes of business were subjected to wide fluctuations between various booms and depressions that were probably more severe than those in modern regulated economies. Thus, despite relatively high wages, industrial workers were often faced with long periods of unemployment and with much work and residential dislocation, because they moved frequently from firm to firm, industry to industry, and city to city. Because the provision of financial aid through public welfare or unemployment insurance was an idea whose time had not yet come, the unemployed were left to the whims and limitations of church supported and other private charities, or just as likely were left to their own meager resources for subsistence.

There is some evidence that many of the immigrants who came to the cities in search of wage labor were never successful in this endeavor and became vagabonds, vagrants, hoboes, or beggars (Glaab, 1963). Others survived through marginal economic activities, such as rag-picking and bone-gathering. A New York State report of 1857, based on a survey of slum areas in Manhattan and Brooklyn, describes one such group:

> "Rag-pickers' Paradise" is inhabited entirely by Germans, who dwell in small rooms in almost fabulous gregariousness. . . . We were told of a colony of three hundred of these people, who occupied a single basement, living on offal and scraps, . . . their means of livelihood, degraded as it is, is exceedingly precarious, especially in severe winters, when snow storms, covering the ground, hide the rags, shreds of paper, etc., on the sale of which they subsist. In such seasons the children are sent out to sweep crossings or beg, and many of the most adroit practitioners on public charity are found among these urchins, who are generally marked by a precocity and cunning, which render them, too often, adepts in vice at the tenderest ages. . . . The colonies sally out at daybreak with their baskets and pokers, disperse to their respective precincts, and pursue their work with more or less success throughout the day. On their return, the baskets, bags and carts are emptied into a common heap. Then, from the bones and

scraps of meat, certain portions are selected wherewith to prepare soups. The rags are separated from bones and sorted, washed and dried . . . after which rags and bones are sold—the former to adjacent shopkeepers who live by the traffic, at about two cents per pound, and the latter for thirty cents per bushel.

When it is recollected that the process of washing filthy rags, collected from the gutters, sinks, hospital yards, and every vile locality imaginable, is conducted in the single apartment used for cooking, eating, sleeping, and general living purposes, by the tenants (sometimes a dozen in one room) . . . and where to these horrible practices are superadded the personal filth, stagnant water, fixed air, and confined, dark and damp holes, all characteristic of the tenant-house system, . . . it is no wonder that these unfortunate people are yearly decimated; it is not strange that the cholera and other epidemics have, as we are told, made frightful havoc among them in past years (Glaab, 1963, pp. 277–278).

This kind of poverty, plus other newly emerging insecurities of industrial life—the new dependence on the employer, the obsolescence and dilution of skills, the difficult adaptation to factory discipline, the new insecurity of old age—added to a long period of labor unrest and protest in the latter part of the nineteenth century. The decade of the 1880s, for example, produced a near-revolutionary upheaval. Following the accelerated tempo of industrialization and several periods of depression, wage cuts, and unemployment, labor protest began to sweep the land. This involved the skilled and unskilled, women and men, the native-born and the foreign-born in a rush to organize into labor unions. General strikes, sympathy strikes, consumer boycotts, and working-class political movements became the order of the day. Reactive employer associations were quickly formed and countered in kind with lockouts, blacklists, armed guards, and detectives

Immigrant mother and her children

(Wilensky and Lebeaux, 1958). This was also the time of the famous bomb explosion on Haymarket Square, which touched off a period of hysteria and police terror in Chicago, which was, incidentally, one of the fastest growing cities in America during the same decade (Miller, 1996).

During this period many rural and small-town Americans began to see the cities as a serious menace to their concept of civilization. This was in part based on a native-born, Anglo-Saxon, Protestant, puritan reaction to the somewhat more permissive lifestyles and values of the immigrants from predominantly Catholic European countries. Thus, the saloon and the resulting intemperance were frequently cited, along with the growing inequities in the class structure, as an unfortunate and dangerous byproduct of urbanization and industrialization. Josiah Strong (1885, pp. 128–138), an influential reformist Congregationalist minister of the day, stated what he saw at that time as the "dangers" of the city:

> Socialism not only centers in the city, but is almost confined to it; and the materials of its growth are multiplied with the growth of the city. Here is heaped the social dynamite; here roughs, gamblers, thieves, robbers, lawless and desperate men of all sorts, congregate; men who are ready on any pretext to raise riots for the purpose of destruction and plunder; here gather foreigners and wage-workers; here skepticism and irreligion abound; here inequality is the greatest and most obvious, and the contrast between opulence and penury the most striking; here is suffering the sorest.

Strong and other critics seriously questioned whether the existing social, economic, and political institutions could survive the revolutionary forces they saw operating in American cities at that time (Glaab, 1963). The ferment of labor and radical movements of this period provided impetus for reform and social welfare. Many of these reforms were ultimately achieved early in the next century, with the enactment of factory codes requiring proper ventilation and sanitary appliances, workers' compensation laws, bars on contract labor, child labor laws, the shortening of the work day, and many other reforms that culminated in the New Deal days of the 1930s. These reforms must be seen in the context of late nineteenth century urban-industrial unrest, agitation, and protest, epitomized by the social stresses and strains of the 1880s.

TECHNOLOGICAL INNOVATION

In spite of the many social strains, a large number of technological innovations developed in the nineteenth century which enabled cities to grow still larger and more populated. Until the horse-drawn railway made its appearance early in the century, city transportation was largely pedestrian. This limited the spread of settlement, as factories, commercial establishments, and the homes of workers all had to be within walking distance of one another. Whenever cities expanded beyond this scope, it was as a series of adjacent cells rather than as a unified whole (Hawley, 1981). The horse-drawn railways permitted a wider spread of settlement, along with a greater differentiation and specialization of such land use activities as manufacturing, commerce, and residency. Hawley views the emergence of a central business district serving an entire large city as related to this improvement in the means of transportation. The advent of the electrified street railway later in the century made possible an even greater concentration of people at a given place in a smaller amount of time, widening the spread of settlement more than ever.

The growing importance and concentration of the central business district was facilitated by the addition of iron and steel frame construction in architecture, which allowed the construction of high-rise buildings, some rising to eight and ten stories in cities such as Chicago, New York, and St. Louis in the 1860s and 1870s (McKelvey, 1973). The successful development of a safe and reasonably fast passenger elevator encouraged the effort to build even taller buildings, and by the close of the century the skyscraper had become a dramatic and indelible feature of the skylines of both Chicago and New York, a pattern that has since been emulated in countless American and world cities.

The telephone, invented in the 1870s, won such immediate favor that numerous cities soon had telephone lines in operation. The great benefits it provided by speeding communications were partially matched by the application of electricity to street lighting and finally for indoor use with the development of the incandescent electric light bulb. As well as providing still greater opportunities for industrial development, the telephone and the electric light found immediate use in the expanding department stores that were appearing in the downtown sections of the largest cities, and these developments of course helped to transform the shopping habits of many urbanites (McKelvey, 1973). Still another invention of this period that helped to create an urgent demand for skyscrapers and a greater concentration of office workers in the downtown areas was the typewriter, which, along with the telephone, greatly expanded the volume of communications in commerce and industry. Thus, innovations such as these enabled the city centers to expand vertically, as well as horizontally (Rybeszynski, 1995).

Working replica of early trolley car

SOCIAL INNOVATION

So far we have described nineteenth-century industrialization primarily in terms of major economic, technological, and physical changes in the form and content of city life. But social changes were equally significant. For example, many of the older body of rules, procedures, and understandings, which guided the commonplace behavior of preindustrial village residents as they pursued their everyday needs, were no longer adequate to the exigencies of urban life. Older institutional arrangements had to be overhauled, and new institutions had to be created to accommodate the new forces at work.

Many of the resultant social innovations that took place in American cities arose because the growing cities were becoming populated mainly by European-born and native-born rural migrants who were encountering the complexities of city life for the first time. They had no knowledge of how to live in the new context or of the demands that would be placed on them. The skills necessary for successful accommodation were not easy to acquire, and this process often took a generation or more. Nevertheless, the trial-and-error efforts of the immigrants in forging a new urban life did help produce a number of innovations, many of which have survived to thrive in contemporary urban society.

Some of the most significant social innovations came from structural changes in the family. The specific causes, forms, and consequences of these changes are too complex to be considered in detail here and are examined more extensively in a later chapter. One important change was a direct result of migration and the conditions under which it took place. The literature on immigration is filled with examples of extended families and even of almost entire villages leaving the old country or rural areas and arriving intact to begin a new life in the city (Handlin, 1951). For the most part, however, the larger family units dissolved at the points of departure, as characterized in the musical play *Fiddler on the Roof.* The main pattern was one of younger members migrating as married couples or unattached individuals, leaving their older relatives behind. Migration tends to be selective of young people; thus, the population of the rapidly growing industrial cities came to be made up preponderantly of persons in the fifteen to thirty-five age bracket (Hawley, 1981).

For the first time, many of these young people were left to their own wits and resources, free from the surveillance, controls, or guidance of the older members of their families and villages. Even the children living with immigrant parents discovered that many of the family customs and traditions were not adequate guides for coping with the demands or opportunities of urban-industrial life. For example, the tradition of passing occupational roles from father to son withered as it was discovered that the father's agricultural background and limited knowledge of the more specialized industrial, commercial, and professional occupations were not helpful. The increased separation of work and residence helped to increase the gap between the generations, as did other extrafamilial institutions such as compulsory education. Traditional forms of "love control" such as the dowry system, arranged marriages, and chaperonage likewise withered under the onslaught of city life.

One interesting innovation to come out of this set of circumstances was the youth-oriented immigrant settlement house. Initially staffed by middle- and upper-class volunteers, these organizations were the forerunners of the various public and privately sponsored social agencies and their full-time professionally trained staffs which are now a well-institutionalized feature of urban society. Hull House in Chicago was an early and prime example. Jane Addams, a founder of Hull House, was a notable reformer well ahead of her time and active in various movements to improve the quality of life in the immigrant slums. She was an acute observer of young people as they moved about the streets of the city pursuing their newfound urban interests. Of particular concern to her was what she saw as the lack of adequate community-sponsored recreational facilities for young working people, who were being exploited in this area by the dispensers of commercialized leisure. In a book published shortly after the turn of the century, this is how she described the problems of the city's youth:

> In the medieval city the knights held their tourneys, the guilds their pageants, the people their dances, and the church made festival for its most cherished saints with gay street processions. . . . Only in the modern city have men concluded that it is no longer necessary for the municipality to provide for the insatiable desire for play. . . . A further difficulty lies in the fact that industrialism has gathered together multitudes of eager young creatures from all quarters of the earth as a labor supply for the countless factories and workshops, upon which the industrial city is based. Never before in civilization have such numbers of young girls been suddenly released from the protection of home and permitted to walk unattended upon city streets and to work under alien roofs. . . . Never before have such numbers of young boys earned money independently of the family life, and felt themselves free to spend it as they chose in the midst of vice deliberately disguised as pleasure. . . .
>
> In every city arise "gin palaces" in which alcohol is dispensed, not only to allay thirst, but ostensibly to stimulate gaiety, it is sold really in order to empty pockets. Huge dance halls are opened to which hundreds of young people are attracted, many of whom stand wistfully outside a roped circle, for it requires five cents to procure within it for five minutes the sense of allurement and intoxication which is sold in lieu of innocent pleasure. We see thousands of girls walking up and down the streets on a pleasant evening with no chance to catch a sight of pleasure even through a lighted window save as these lurid places provide it. Apparently the modern city sees in these girls only two possibilities, both of them commercial: first a chance to utilize by day their new and labor power in its factories and shops, and then another chance in the evening to extract from them their petty wages by pandering to their love of pleasure. . . .
>
> One of the most pathetic sights in the public dance halls of Chicago is the number of young men, obviously honest young fellows from the country, who stand about mainly hoping to make the acquaintance of some "nice girl." They look eagerly up and down the rows of girls, many of whom are drawn to the hall by the same keen desire for pleasure and social intercourse which the lonely young men themselves feel. Perhaps never before have the pleasures of the young and mature become so definitely separated as in the modern city (Addams, 1910, pp. 3–21).

As sympathetic and enlightened as Jane Addams was for the times, the quoted passages reflect turn of the century upper-middle-class values in equating commercialized recreation with vice and sin. But from the modern sociological perspective of functionalism, implicit in these descriptions of the saloons and dance halls is that an important need or want was being fulfilled, and that these establishments were the forerunners of a significant urban institution of commercialized leisure. Out of the same set of circumstances, one can see the rise of professional athletics (the first professional baseball clubs, all of them in urban-industrial cities, were first franchised before the turn of the century, and professional prizefighting had already become a popular urban sport), vaudeville and the musical stage, the motion picture, jazz and popular music, radio and the phonograph. All these were forms of popular entertainment created to satisfy the tastes and needs of the same youthful urban masses described by Jane Addams. Although some of these forms of popular entertainment may have originated to satisfy creative or artistic urges as well, the most successful of them proved to be highly profitable to their providers and were the basis for a multimillion-dollar popular entertainment industry.

To a degree, one can also see organized crime syndicates in American cities arising from the same set of circumstances, as some members of various immigrant groups one after another became involved in the marginal and sometimes illegal business of satisfying wants that were otherwise taboo or suppressed by the conventional puritan morality of the day, such as gambling, alcohol, drugs, prostitution, and pornography (Bell, 1953; Cohen, 1998). It is no accident that the leading prizefighters, ball players, singers, movie actors, comedians, and organized crime figures often came from the same family, neighborhood, or immigrant group and intermingled socially as they rapidly climbed the ladder of success that these new and expanding urban industries provided. The life of the late Frank Sinatra is a good illustration of this last point. In some cases, the same individuals have moved freely across the boundaries of professional sports, show business, and organized crime in the process of pursuing a popular and readily available vision of "making it big" in American society.

By the first decade of the twentieth century, all of the main features of an urban-industrial civilization were in place and intact. In 1910, fifty American cities had a population of 100,000 or more people. New York City had a population of nearly 5 million people, and Chicago, demonstrating phenomenal growth, increased its population twentyfold in half a century: from 109,260 in 1860 to 2,185,283 in 1910. (Table 3.4 illustrates population growth in the fifty largest American cities from 1860 to 1910.) Approximately 46 percent of the nation's 92 million people lived in cities in 1910, compared with less than 20 percent in 1860.

The nation had not yet fully accepted or assimilated the significance of the changes that had been taking place, but reform movements were underway to minimize some of the more undesirable features that the urban-industrial revolution had wrought, mainly in the areas of housing, sanitation, public health, recreation, zoning and planning, education, social service, and municipal government. These are considered in greater detail in later chapters.

By this time, the first social-scientific studies of urban life had begun to appear. Adna Weber's (1899) *The Growth of Cities in the Nineteenth Century* and the field studies reported in the Hull House Papers, which go back to 1895 (Burgess and Bogue, 1964), were among the most significant of the early efforts at objective empirical analysis of urban life and forms. Similar work had been going on in New York City and in other cities that had undertaken social surveys or investigations of slums. The first formal studies of the city by professional sociologists began in the decade of World War I, as previously discussed in Chapter 1. These efforts were in welcome and refreshing contrast to the more biased and impressionistic forms of observation that had prevailed earlier. As Ernest Burgess, one of the key figures in the development of urban sociology, has suggested: "Although he was not there first, the sociologist made a big difference in urban research. It was sociology that emphasized science and the importance of understanding social problems in terms of the processes and forces that produce them" (Burgess and Bogue, 1964, p. 4).

SELECTED BIBLIOGRAPHY

ADDAMS, JANE. *The Spirit of Youth and the City Streets.* New York, 1910. (Cf. Glaab, 1963.)

BELL, DANIEL. "Crime as an American Way of Life." *Antioch Review* 13 (summer 1953): 131–154.

BURGESS, ERNEST W., and DONALD J. BOGUE, eds. *Contributions to Urban Sociology.* Chicago: University of Chicago Press, 1964.

COHEN, RICHARD. *Tough Jews: Fathers, Sons and Gangster Dreams.* New York: Simon and Shuster, 1998.

FEAGIN, JOE. *The Urban Real Estate Game.* Englewood Cliffs, NJ: Prentice-Hall, 1983.

GLAAB, CHARLES N. *The American City: A Documentary History.* Homewood, IL: Dorsey Press, 1963.

GLAZIER, WILLARD. *Peculiarities of American Cities.* Philadelphia, 1884. (Cf. Glaab, 1963.)

GOLD, HARRY. "The Professionalization of Urban Planning." Ph.D. dissertation, University of Michigan, 1965.

GOTTDIENER, MARK. *The New Urban Sociology.* New York: McGraw Hill, 1994.

HAMMOND, JOHN L., and BARBARA HAMMOND. *The Rise of Modern Industry,* 2d ed. London: Methuen & Co., 1925.

HANDLIN, OSCAR. *The Uprooted.* Boston: Little, Brown, 1951.

HAWLEY, AMOS H. *Urban Society.* New York: Ronald Press, 1981.

HEILBRONER, ROBERT L. *The Making of Economic Society.* Englewood Cliffs, NJ: Prentice-Hall, 1962.

JARDINE, LISA. *Worldly Goods: A New History of the Renaissance.* New York: Nan A. Talese/Doubleday, 1996.

LEFEBVRE, HENRY. *The Production of Space.* Oxford: Blackwell, 1991.

MCKELVEY, BLAKE. *The Urbanization of America: 1860–1915.* New Brunswick, NJ: Rutgers University Press, 1963.

———. *American Urbanization: A Comparative History.* Glenview, IL: Scott, Foresman, 1973.

MILLER, DONALD L. *City of the Century: The Epic of Chicago and the Making of America.* New York: Simon & Schuster, 1996.

PARRILLO, VINCENT N. *Strangers to These Shores,* 5th ed. Boston: Allyn & Bacon, 1997.

RYBCZYNSKI, WITOLD. *City Life.* New York: Simon & Schuster, 1995

SMELSER, NEIL. *Social Change in the Industrial Revolution: An Application of Theory to the British Cotton Industry.* Chicago: University of Chicago Press, 1959.

STRONG, JOSIAH. *Our Country: Its Possible Future and Its Present Crisis.* New York, 1885. (Cf. Glaab, 1963.)

THERNSTROM, STEPHAN, and RICHARD SENNETT, eds. *Nineteenth Century Cities: Essays in the New Urban History.* New Haven, CT: Yale University Press, 1969.

USHER, ABBOTT PAYSON. *The Industrial History of England.* Boston: Houghton Mifflin, 1920.

WEBER, A. F. *The Growth of Cities in the Nineteenth Century.* New York: Macmillan, 1899.

WEBER, MAX. *The Protestant Ethic and the Spirit of Capitalism.* Translated by T. Parsons. London: George Allen & Unwin, 1930.

WILENSKY, HAROLD L., and CHARLES N. LEBEAUX. *Industrial Society and Social Welfare.* New York: Russell Sage, 1958.

YERGIN, DANIEL, and JOSEPH STANISLAW. *The Commanding Heights: The Battle between Government and the Marketplace That Is Remaking the Modern World.* New York: Simon & Shuster, 1998.

Part II

Basic Forms of Urban Life in the Modern Metropolis

4

THE METROPOLITAN REVOLUTION: CITIES AND SUBURBS

Until the twentieth century, the city was the dominant form of urban development. Throughout recorded history, the distinction between city and country was a clear one, because cities were seen as self-contained entities with easily recognizable boundaries. Although such compact and densely settled cities and towns still exist, the appearance and growth of the metropolis and its eventual dominance of the national landscape is the principal theme of American urban development during the last three-quarters of the twentieth century. Like nineteenth-century urbanization, the process of twentieth-century metropolitanization has been so rapid that there has been a cultural lag in public awareness of and response to what is happening. This partially explains the urban crises of the late twentieth century. Americans had become part of a predominantly metropolitan society even before they had become fully aware that they were members of a society that was no longer rural but largely urban.

Simply put, a *metropolitan* community contains and consists of a large city and its surrounding suburbs. Sometimes the spatial pattern of a metropolitan community can be described as a central city surrounded by a suburban ring of development. Of course, the cities came first, and the surrounding suburbs mostly were a product of the dispersion of population from the central city into the surrounding countryside (although preexisting villages and small towns ouside of the city's boundaries also were often engulfed by and absorbed into the larger metropolitan complex).

HISTORICAL FACTORS LEADING TO METROPOLITAN GROWTH

The industrial revolution, which brought large numbers of rural and foreign migrants to American cities in the latter part of the nineteenth century, had persisted well into the early part of the twentieth century. By 1920 more than one-half of the U.S. population lived in urban areas. Until that time, most of the growth had been concentrated in the largest cities, which had been growing in numbers and density, and this trend had produced serious problems of overcrowding in residential, industrial, commercial, and public facilities. The health and sanitation problems created by the concentration of large numbers of people in relatively small land areas often made living conditions impossible. In effect, the big cities were bursting their seams.

Also creating problems was the uncontrolled competition for scarce urban space, which often led to the incompatible uses of adjacent parcels of land, represented by the intrusion of unsightly, noisy, and congestion producing commercial and industrial activities into residential areas and an ever more intensive utilization of the land, without regard for such consequences as increased pressures on already overburdened transportation, sewage, water, and utility systems, recreation facilities, and so on. Residential areas tended to deteriorate and become dilapidated in the expectation by many landowners that eventually such properties would succumb to the inevitable pressures of more intensive and economically more productive industrial and commercial uses. In fact, much slum clearance supposedly undertaken for the benefit of the affected slum dwellers actually hastened the conversion of residential areas into nonresidential uses (Gans, 1962; see also chapter 14).

What happened in this process was that residential land values became so high that many middle-income city families were either forced to live in substandard housing at excessive cost or were forced to leave the central cities in order to find suitable housing within a reasonable price range. Of course, the housing problem became even more difficult for the many low-income and minority groups caught in the squeeze between high-cost substandard housing in the central cities and the social barriers that excluded them from the suburban housing market (see chapter 13). For these groups the overcrowded slums were the only available alternative (see the discussion of slums later in this chapter).

In contrast to the plight of the city dweller, the migration of those who have moved to outlying suburban areas is a much larger and more significant trend toward decentralization of the growing urban population. This has produced a metropolitan pattern of urban settlement. Recent metropolitan development not only represents a decentralization of the residential population, but also includes a redistribution of many industrial, commercial, and cultural activities over an ever-expanding land area surrounding the central cities.

This trend has been greatly facilitated by scientific and technological advances of this century, especially in the areas of transportation and communications. The extensive use of the automobile has eliminated the necessity of locating the place of work and residence in close proximity. Thus, those who were first able to afford private automobiles were among the first urbanites in large numbers to resettle in suburban residential enclaves, well separated from the more hectic, noisy, or other unpleasant aspects of the central business district or factory (earlier suburbs of more limited population were built along rail commuter lines).

Shopping centers, factories, and other business establishments were able to decentralize as they lessened their dependence on waterways, railroads, and an adjacent labor supply. The telephone, the motor truck, and the automobile made them readily accessible to their suppliers, their customers, and their employees at almost any location within the metropolitan complex. More recently, helicopters increasingly have been used to provide

Commuter freeway in Chicago

this same service. Much of the industrial and commercial decentralization thus made possible was probably a response to the larger quantities of cheaper land in outlying suburban fringes. However, this general pattern of dispersion and decentralization is also the result of changing values, such as industry's desire for more space, more attractive living conditions for its executives and employees, and an increasing emphasis on visible symbols of status such as may be afforded by the availability of green open space, pleasingly visible architecture and landscaping, and adequate parking facilities.

THE EXTENT OF METROPOLITANIZATION

Identifying the boundaries or assessing the extent of metropolitan growth and development is difficult because the term is rather imprecise and because there are no standard agreed-upon definitions of what is metropolitan. Some descriptions, for example, portrayed the sprawl of metropolitan growth in these commonly recognizable but impressionistic visual terms:

> Seen from above, the modern city edges imperceptibly out of its setting. There are not clear boundaries. Just now the white trace of the superhighway passes through cultivated fields, now it is lost in an asphalt maze of streets and buildings. As one drives in from the airport or looks out from the train window, clumps of suburban housing, industrial complexes, and occasional green spaces pass by; it is hard to tell where the city begins and the country ends. (Handlin and Burchard, 1963, p. 1)

In recent decades, the most useful definitions and estimates have been those developed by the United States Office of Management and Budget (OMB), and used most often by the U.S. Bureau of the Census. Over the decades, beginning in 1949, the metropolitan concept has been redesignated from time to time by these official governmental agencies, using terms ranging from "metropolitan area," "standard metropolitan area," "standard metropolitan statistical area," and, finally, beginning in 1983, *metropolitan statistical area*" (*New York Times Almanac 2000,* 1999, p. 257).

Metropolitan statistical areas (MSAs) are based on measures which provide a more accurate reflection of how many people actually live in a metropolitan area than do city population figures alone. For example, the city of Boston had just 558,934 people in 1996, making it the twentieth largest city in the United States. But the Boston MSA, which includes suburbs spreading from New Hampshire to Rhode Island, was the seventh largest metropolitan area in the country in 1996, with a total population of 5.6 million people living within a one-hour commuting time from the central city. An MSA is defined as an urban area that includes at least one city with 50,000 or more residents and a total population of at least 100,000 people. An MSA also includes the county in which the central city is located, plus any adjacent counties in which at last 50 percent of the population is classified as having certain urban characteristics, such as daily commuting to the central county of the MSA, or minimum residential density standards (*Statistical Abstract of the United States,* 1999; see Phillips, 1996, pp. 150–155, for a more detailed discussion of this definition and its limitations). In New England, MSAs are defined in terms of cities and towns, rather than counties.

The idea that the twentieth century can best be characterized in the United States as one of tremendous metropolitan growth can be easily illustrated. In 1900, only sixty-one urban centers qualified as metropolitan areas. These contained a total of about 23.6 million people, comprising 31 percent of the total U.S. population. By midcentury the number of metropolitan areas had grown to 191, housing a total of approximately 89 million people who represented 58.8 percent of the total U.S. population (Gold, 1982). According to the 1990 Census, the U.S. population living in MSAs totaled 192.7 million people, more than twice the 1950 number, and the number of MSAs had grown to 274.

Metropolitan growth has generally consisted of the movement of people and activities from the center of urban concentrations outward. However, this should not be construed to mean that such dispersion is randomly devouring raw land, because metropolian development in the United States is highly concentrated within specific regions of the country, with vast portions of the total land area still relatively undeveloped or unpopulated. For example, the *New York Times Almanac 2000* reported that although the 274 MSAs were home to more than 75 percent of all Americans in 1990, they occupied only about 16 percent of the country's land area. In summary, at the latest available count, there were approximately 211.9 million Americans, or nearly 80 percent of the entire U.S. population, living in 274 MSAs occupying about 704 thousand square miles of land in 1996 (*Statistical Abstract of the United States,* 1999). By 1997 there were 47 MSAs with populations of one or more million people, including eight MSAs with 5 million or more people. The New York metropolitan area, with nearly 20 million persons, and the Los Angeles metropolitan area, with 15.6 million people, are by far the two largest metropolitan areas in the United States.

One important consequence of metropolitanization is that it tends to blur traditional rural-urban differences, particularly in the rural areas immediately adjacent to the metro-

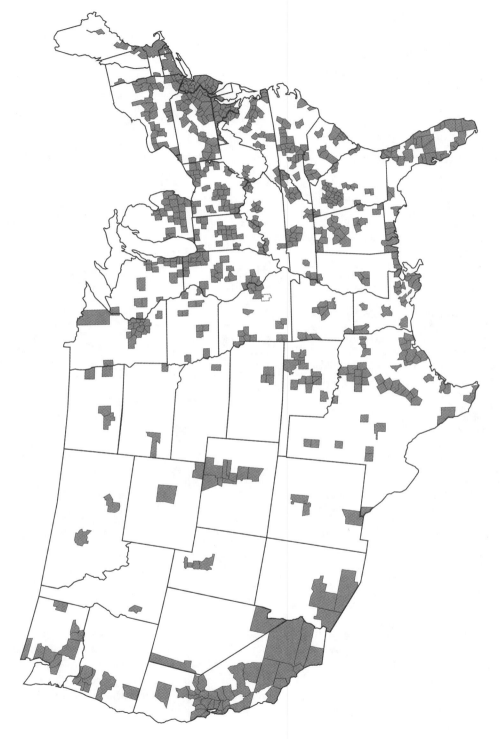

Figure 4.1 Metropolitan areas (CMSAs, and MSAs) 1990

Table 4.1 Population Change in the Top 25 Metropolitan Statistical Areas, 1990-96

Note that since the 1990 Census, the Census Bureau has changed the boundaries of several dozen metropolitan statistical areas, merging some areas within others and separating some areas out of larger MSAs. For example, Washington, D.C. and Baltimore, Md. are now considered one consolidated metropolitan statistical area rather than two. As a result, population statistics before and after 1990 are not directly comparable for more than 75 MSAs.

METROPOLITAN STATISTICAL AREA	POPULATION		CHANGE, 1990-96	
	1990	1996	NUMBER	PERCENT
1. New York-Northern New Jersey-Long Island, N. Y.-N. J.- Conn.- Pa. CMSA	19,549,649	19,938,492	388,843	2.0%
2. Los Angeles-Riverside-Orange County, Calif. CMSA	14,531,529	15,495,155	963,626	6.6
3. Chicago-Gary-Kenosha, Ill.-Ind.-Wis. CMSA	8,239,820	8,599,774	359,954	4.4
4. Washington-Baltimore, D.C.-Md.-Va.-W.Va. CMSA	6,726,395	7,164,519	438,124	6.5
5. San Francisco-Oakland-San Jose, Calif. CMSA	6,249,881	6,605,428	355,547	5.7
6. Pphiladelphia-Wilmington-Atlantic City, Pa.-N.J.-Del.-Md. CMSA	5,893,019	5,973,463	80,444	1.4
7. Boston-Worcester-Lawrence, Mass.-N.H.-Maine-Conn. CMSA	5,455,403	5,563,475	108,072	2.0
8. Detroit-Ann Arbor-Flint, Mich. CMSA	5,187,171	5,284,171	97,000	1.9
9. Dallas-Fort Worth, Texas CMSA	4,037,282	4,574,561	537,279	13.3
10. Houston-Galveston-Brazoria, Texas CMSA	3,731,029	4,253,428	522,399	14.0
11. Atlanta, Ga. MSA	2,959,500	3,541,230	581,730	19.7
12. Miami-Fort Lauderdale, Fla. CMSA	3,192,725	3,514,403	321,678	10.1
13. Seattle-Tacoma-Bremerton, Wash. CMSA	2,970,300	3,320,829	350,529	11.8
14. Cleveland-Akron, Ohio CMSA	2,859,644	2,913,430	53,786	1.9
15. Minneapolis-St. Paul, Minn.-Wis. MSA	2,538,776	2,765,116	226,340	8.9
16. Phoenix-Mesa, Ariz. MSA	2,238,498	2,746,703	508,205	22.7
17. San Diego, Calif. MSA	2,498,016	2,655,463	157,447	6.3
18. St. Louis, Mo.-Ill. MSA	2,492,348	2,548,238	55,890	2.2
19. Pittsburgh, Pa. MSA	2,394,811	2,379,411	-15,400	-0.6
20. Denver-Boulder-Greeley, Colo. CMSA	1,980,140	2,277,401	297,261	15.0
21. Tampa-St. Petersburgh-Clearwater, Fla. MSA	2,067,959	2,199,231	131,272	6.3
22. Portland-Salem, Oreg.-Wash. CMSA	1,793,476	2,078,357	284,881	15.9
23. Cincinnati-Hamilton, Ohio-Ky.-Ind. CMSA	1,817,569	1,920,931	103,362	5.7
24. Kansas City, Mo.-Kans. MSA	1,582,874	1,690,343	107,469	6.8
25. Milwaukee-Racine, Wis. CMSA	1,607,183	1,642,658	35,475	2.2

Source: Statistical Abstract of the United States. 1999

politan centers. As metropolitanization gathers momentum, it reaches out to link and absorb formerly rural areas on the periphery of the metropolis. In the last several decades, population growth rates of rural communities and villages within a fifty-mile radius of metropolitan areas was more than twice that of similar places at greater distances from metropolitan areas. No longer are the rural areas of America primarily agricultural. Rural residents are increasingly being employed in a wide range of nonagricultural occupations.

In 1990, although only 23 percent of the nation's population was still classified as rural by the U.S. Census Bureau, five out of every six people were nonfarmers. In no state in the entire continental United States was the majority of the rural population still engaged in farming on a full-time basis (Phillips, 1996).

The Time-Distance Factor

A two-way flow of migration between urban and rural places is now commonplace, as is daily commuting between metropolitan areas and their surrounding rural areas. The latter is particularly feasible for those with immediate access to the interstate highways and beltways that now connect many metropolitan areas with their rural fringes and that considerably shorten the time for such commuting trips (assuming no major traffic tie-ups!).

Changes in the time-distance factor serve as a useful index to the ways in which modern time-saving means of transportation have furthered the expansion of the radius and frequency of interaction between metropolitan areas and their hinterlands. The distance that can be traveled in sixty minutes provides a reasonable basis for illustration. Before the arrival of the automobile, the sixty-minute radius of cities seldom exceeded six miles. The automobile extended the one-hour travel distance to approximately twenty-five miles. With the advent of freeways and other highway system improvements, the sixty-minute commuting distance to major places of recreation and employment has risen to approximately thirty-five miles in most metropolitan areas. In those parts of the United States where metropolitan areas are relatively close together, almost all of the rural population is now within this sixty-minute time-distance. Approximately 95 percent of the country's population, both rural and urban, now lives within the daily commuting field of the central city of a metropolitan area (National Research Council, 1975, p. 10).

The farm population of the United States has diminished to less than 5 percent of the total. Farming has also become more of a business enterprise and has declined markedly as a distinctly rural way of life. Widespread ownership of automobiles, telephones, radios, satellite or cable television, and computer-based systems of communications by farm people, along with greater access to other mass media sources, have given rural residents access to the same information, attitudes, and opinions available to urbanites. In almost every sphere of their lives, the residents of rural areas, with few exceptions, are now served by urban-type institutions. Therefore, whether a person resides in a rural or a metropolitan area is less and less a useful basis for identifying distinctive patterns of behavior. More and more it becomes reasonable to speak of the United States as an urban society in which a shared urban culture is the predominant pattern. Of course, regional variations in lifestyles and other behavioral patterns continue to exist, but they are probably less significant than those related to such characteristics as socioeconomic status, age, occupation, education, or ethnic background. Such variations all occur within the framework of an encompassing urban civilization of which they are an integral part (see chapter 6).

THE ANATOMY OF THE METROPOLIS

The growth of the metropolitan community involves the spatial redistribution of population and land use activities, as the central cities expand outward from their centers. This growth process also helps to produce a complex sociogeographic division of labor among the component parts of the metropolitan community. Each part or subarea of the community becomes clearly differentiated from the other parts, in terms of its population, physical, economic, or cultural characteristics. In turn, a complex network of interdependencies is created as each part or subarea develops its own specialized functions essential to the needs of the entire community.

These concepts are among the basic assumptions of the ecological approach to urban analysis, which entails understanding how these component parts are organized and coordinated into a recognizable and integrated ecological entity, in response to the more general patterns of metropolitan growth and dispersion. Much of the classic urban ecological research and theory has been devoted to the task of mapping and analyzing the spatial, functional, and symbiotic relationships among the component parts of the modern metropolis.

To date, no completely acceptable standardized nomenclature has evolved for delineating and classifying local areas within the metropolitan community, and this has proved to be a difficult task for the professional urbanologist, as well as the nonspecialist. Thus, concepts such as "central city," "suburb," "local community," "neighborhood," "slum," "inner city," "urban fringe," "gray area," "satellite," or "ghetto" are so imprecise that they often mean different things to different people. Nevertheless, some attempts at classification do stand out, and a review of some of them is in order here.

Burgess's Concentric Zone Theory

First advanced in the early 1920s, Burgess's concentric zone theory is widely regarded as one of the classic statements of urban growth and differentiation. Ernest Burgess (1925) saw growth and differentiation of metropolitan areas in the United States as occurring in gradually extended concentric zones, each characterized by a typical pattern of land use. These zones were produced as the result of expansion outward from the central business district.

The *central business district* (CBD) is the first or inner zone, comprising skyscrapers, department stores, hotels, and other forms of retailing, light manufacturing, or commercialized leisure. The second zone, which surrounds the central business district, is called the *zone of transition* because it is subject to change caused by enroaching business and industrial land uses expanding beyond the CBD. This zone is described by Burgess as a mixture of residential and nonresidential uses. The residents tend to be a heterogeneous assortment of low-income groups, immigrants, and unconventional types or social outcasts, such as prostitutes, addicts, or criminals, interspersed with some high-income groups living in luxurious "Gold Coast"–style apartments. Zone three is the *zone of workingmen's homes,* occupied mainly by second-generation immigrant

Elevated view of the Gold Coast District of downtown Chicago

blue-collar workers, who are higher in socioeconomic status than most of the zone of transition dwellers, but who are still not fully assimilated into the middle class. The fourth zone is the *zone of middle-class dwellers*, comprised of mainly professional people, small business persons, managerial types, and other white-collar workers. The fifth zone, the *commuter's zone,* is the area consisting of suburbs or satellite cities on the outer periphery of the metropolitan area's central city. In the larger metropolitan areas, this zone may form a ring from thirty to sixty miles beyond the CBD. Burgess's title for this zone implies an efficient transportation network allowing city workers to arrive daily from and escape nightly to "bedroom" communities beyond the political boundaries of the central city.

Burgess did not insist that his theory was empirically accurate as a physical description of any given city, and he recognized that physical barriers, such as hills, rivers, lakes, or transportation lines, could produce variations from his model. Rather, the concentric zone theory is an idealized concept designed to identify in dynamic terms general processes of city growth and differentiation over time, with minor variations, in most modern industrial cities in the United States.

Hoyt's Sector Theory

Homer Hoyt (1939) developed the sector theory as an outgrowth of a study of 142 American cities conducted during the depression years. Hoyt hypothesized that instead of forming concentric zones around the center of the city, the city tends to grow in sectors along the major transportation arteries outward from the center, creating a pattern akin to an octopus with tentacles extending in various directions, or in the shape of a multipointed star. Hoyt assumed that most residential, commercial, and industrial development of urban areas was distributed in a definite pattern within these sectors. He viewed the location and movement of various socioeconomic levels of the residential population as the key factor in patterning urban growth. As the cities grow in population, the upper-income groups move outward along a particular street or transportation line, so that upper-income residential areas tend to be located on the outer edges of the sector. In turn, lower-income groups tend to inherit or invade the aging and frequently deteriorating portions of the sector that have been or are being thus abandoned.

The theory is similar to the concentric zone theory in that the socioeconomic status of the population varies from low to high as one moves from the center of the city to the periphery, the main difference being that this occurs in sectors shaped like the cut of a pie radiating outward from the center rather than within concentric zones encircling the center of the city. A more detailed summary of Hoyt's sector theory includes the following elements: (1) industrial areas do not develop in a circle around the CBD but also follow transportation lines, such as railroads, waterways, or highways; and (2) upper-class residential areas first emerge near retail or administrative centers, and tend to follow established commuter routes toward desirable residential sites on scenic high grounds or along scenic lakes, rivers, forests, or parkways. They also tend to grow in the direction of open and undeveloped countryside rather than toward areas restricted by preexisting developed areas or natural barriers.

Harris's and Ullman's Multiple-Nuclei Theory

Harris and Ullman (1945) argue that cities developed around a series of centers serving a variety of different functions and located at several points within their boundaries, rather than producing a single center at the heart of the city. Thus, cities may develop retail centers, wholesale centers, residential centers, and the like, each representing the concentration of a specific activity at a particular location that may be best suited for that activity. They argue that multiple centers develop as a result of the following four factors: (1) certain activities require specialized facilities, such as water, sewerage, parking, or accessibility, and they tend to concentrate in the vicinity of these facilities, wherever they may be; (2) similar activities benefit from locations close to one another, and they group together for mutual advantages, as in the cases of high-fashion retail shops, law offices, or the headquarters of financial institutions; (3) certain unlike activities may be incompatible or disadvantageous to one another—for example, locating a glue factory in the middle of a prime residential area would be considered highly offensive to the citizens of such an area and probably would be forbidden by local zoning codes; and (4) for many activities, such as storage facilities or warehousing, land in the CBD or other choice locations may be too expensive or may not be sufficiently advantageous to warrant the costs of competing with other potential users for the use of such locations.

The multiple nuclei theory does not specify a particular pattern for the distribution of centers within the urban area, but implies instead that each city develops its own

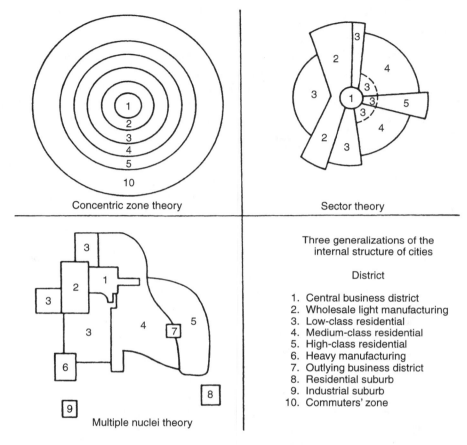

Concentric zone theory

Sector theory

Multiple nuclei theory

Three generalizations of the internal structure of cities

District

1. Central business district
2. Wholesale light manufacturing
3. Low-class residential
4. Medium-class residential
5. High-class residential
6. Heavy manufacturing
7. Outlying business district
8. Residential suburb
9. Industrial suburb
10. Commuters' zone

Figure 4.2   Classic theories of metropolitan growth and structure (C. D. Harris and Edward L. Ullman, *Annals,* 242, November 1945, 7–17).

special pattern as a result of its unique historical circumstances. Thus, there is no typical way in which multiple centers arrange themselves in relationship to one another.

A Critique of the Classic Theories of Growth

All three of the classic theories just discussed have been widely accepted by social scientists, but not without considerable criticism. Most of the criticism centers on the assumption that these theories were intended as literal generalized descriptions of the spatial patterning of cities. The multiple-nuclei theory, which does not specify concrete patterns, escapes this particular criticism. But empirical examination of particular cities that do not seem to fit any of these theoretical schemes, especially the concentric zone theory and to a lesser extent the sector theory, is often cited to cast doubt on their accuracy or validity.

For example, Firey (1947, pp. 41–68) found both the concentric zone and sector theories inadequate for the city of Boston.

Davie (1937, pp. 133–161) conducted a detailed study of New Haven, Connecticut, and examined land-use maps for twenty other cities. He found considerable heterogeneity within zones and many irregularities of pattern and concluded that the idea of a symmetrical distribution of land uses in concentric rings was overly simple. Caplow's (1952, pp. 544–549) findings in Paris and a study of Budapest by Beynon (1943, pp. 256–275) are examples of studies of European cities that have found exceptions to the concentric zone pattern of development.

Hawley (1981, p. 101) concludes that criticisms like these have been provoked by a too literal interpretation of the zonal hypothesis, and much of the objection might have been obviated had it been conceived of in more general terms as an ideal typology of growth rather than as a concrete descriptive model. Moreover, empirical studies have supported the concentric zone theory. Blumenfeld's (1949, pp. 209–212) examination of Philadelphia strongly confirmed the dominance of the concentric zone pattern in that city, although he found only three main zones rather than five. Schnore and Jones (1969) have found that a rough approximation of Burgess's model does apply to older and larger American industrial cities, primarily in the Midwest and Northeast.

In an important word on this subject, Berry and Kasarda (1977, p. 90) suggest that if the concentric, sector, and multiple-nuclei schemes, as illustrated in Figure 4.2, are conjointly overlaid on the land-use and population maps of any city, they reveal weblike patterns of neighborhoods whose social, physical, and economic patterns exhibit both concentric and axial dimensions. Thus, they conclude the three classic principles of internal structure of cities are "independent, additive descriptions of the social and economic character of neighborhoods in relation to each other and to the whole."

Perhaps the most valid criticism of the classic ecological theories is that they are unidimensional in the characteristics assumed to be distributed within the metropolitan complex. More recent ecological theory and research are based on the assumption of a multiplicity of characteristics, each of which may be spatially distributed somewhat differently than the others. Some of these more advanced ecological attempts to describe the characteristics and functions of subareas within the metropolis are described below, but whatever the criticisms of the concentric zone theory, the sector theory, or the multiple-nuclei theory, they are still widely cited in the current sociological literature on urbanization, and they constitute a useful introduction and point of departure for more refined and detailed urban analysis.

Social Area Analysis

Social area analysis is a technique for describing and assessing the spatial distribution of many key variables that allegedly delineate significant subareas or social areas of the urban community. The objective is to classify and compare small sections of the metropolitan community on the basis of their main social attributes. The basic units for analysis are census tracts. These are areas of approximately 4,000 persons, drawn up by the U.S. Census Bureau for the purpose of providing census data for relatively small and compact segments of the urban population. Most of the larger metropolitan areas are composed of at least several hundred census tracts. The concept and techniques of social area analysis were originated by Shevky and Bell (1955), using census data from the Los Angeles and San Francisco Standard Metropolitan Statistical Areas. Shevky and Bell identified what they concluded were the three main dimensions of urban society and used available census data to construct the following indexes:

1. *Social Rank.* This represents the socioeconomic status of an area, as measured by its occupational and educational levels.
2. *Urbanization.* Shevky and Bell (1955) define urbanization in terms of the family structure of an area. This measure is derived from the fertility rates of women, the proportion of gainfully employed women, and the percentage of the area housing in single-family dwelling units.
3. *Segregation.* This index is based on the ecological or spatial separation of racial and ethnic groups.

These indexes make it possible to provide a social profile for each census tract of the metropolitan area and to compare their relative standing for each of the three major social dimensions just described. For example, one tract might be high in social rank and segregation but low in urbanization, another tract might be high in segregation and urbanization but low in social rank, and so on.

The proponents of social area analysis (Bell, 1959) argue that the approach is useful to social scientists because it provides a simple and systematic method for delineating urban neighborhoods and communities having different social characteristics. In addition to facilitating comparative studies of the social areas of different cities at one point in time, changes within a given area over time can also be systematically examined by this approach. The approach can be used to examine the relationship between social rank, urbanization, or segregation, and an almost unlimited variety of measurable phenomena, such as crime rates, rates of mental illness, voting or religious behavior, lifestyles, and property values.

Social area analysis, like the theories preceding it, is not without its detractors. Some critics (Duncan, 1955; Hawley and Duncan, 1957; Van Arsdol et al., 1958) viewed the approach as lacking both an adequate theoretical rationale and sufficient empirical utility. For example, no clear theoretical relationship is specified between the basic concepts of social rank, urbanization, and segregation, and the particular census tract variables used in constructing the index. Likewise, it is argued, there is no particular advantage in using these social area indexes instead of individual census measures, which may give considerably better results. In fact, these critiques imply that the indexes are nothing more than arbitrary groupings of variables without a clear-cut rationale for their selection. Nevertheless, social area analysis was a useful step in systematically measuring the multidimensionality of the modern urban community, and it helped to pave the way for more sophisticated and elaborate methods of urban research.

Factorial Ecology

Rees (1970) has suggested that the use of many more variables detailing the socioeconomic characteristics of census tract populations constitutes a logical expansion of social area analysis. Through the more sophisticated methods of factor analysis, the fundamental patterns of variations in the data can be isolated, whether they conform to the main dimensions of social area analysis. "Factorial ecology" is the term now used to characterize studies applying factor analysis to ecological study. In this sense, factorial ecology is a more sophisticated elaboration and outgrowth of the social area analysis approach.

One of the major results of factorial ecology has been the comparison of preindustrial urban ecological systems with those found in modern industrial communities, such as comparisons between Chicago and Calcutta (Berry, 1971; Rees, 1972) designed to show what common spatial structural characteristics occur in cities in different parts of the world. But there have been other major studies of single cities based on factorial ecology (Smith, 1973, pp. 40–44). Rees's (1970) study of Chicago is one of the best illustrations of factor analysis of an American city. Rees compiled data based on fifty-seven socioeconomic and demographic variables for 222 subareas of the Chicago SMSA and performed a factor analysis. The first factor represented socioeconomic status, as measured by occupation, education, and income. The second factor dealt with stages in the life cycle and was based on family size, age, and housing type. The third factor comprised race and resources, as indicated by census tract measures of blacks as a percentage of total population, and the proportion of the total census tract population in low-status employment, with low incomes, and living in substandard housing. These three factors taken alone accounted for 45.1 percent of the variance in the original fifty-seven variables. What is significant here is that Rees's study of Chicago, as well as other factorial studies of American cities (Berry and Kasarda, 1977, p. 123), have succeeded in isolating and reinforcing the importance of the social area indices originally proposed by Shevky—socioeconomic status, family status, and ethnic status. Berry and Kasarda also conclude that there is some fit of each of these three dimensions with the essential features of the classic spatial models previously discussed.

The Social Indicators Movement

Both factorial ecology and social area analysis have been criticized for relying almost exclusively on the content of census reports for their data. Smith (1973, p. 43) has identified one major omission in all of these studies: an adequate representation of social pathologies or social problems of urban centers, which are not directly available in census reports. Thus some of the important conditions of human existence that may also be spatially differentiated are not included in these approaches. Smith argues for the need to tackle the problem of area variations in "social well-being" within urban centers, in the context of whether socially undesirable conditions are getting better or worse over time. This can be done by combining some of the techniques developed in the factorial ecology approach with sets of data that more accurately and fully reflect social well-being or the quality of life than do the contents of census reports, for example, measures of physical and mental health, crime and violence, delinquency, child abuse, drug addiction, alcoholism, dependency, suicide, life expectancy, and the like.

The gradual recognition of this situation has led in recent years to what has been referred to as the "social indicators movement" (Smith, 1973, p. 52). Alternatively described as "social accounting," "social reporting," or "monitoring social change," social indicators measure conditions as they vary in space and time. Social indicators may apply to nations, states, or regions, but their inter- and intracity applications are what concern us here.

One key illustration of the application of intracity social indicators research is a study of Tampa, Florida (Smith and Gray,1972). In this study, forty-seven variables were assembled to measure the spatial distribution of six major criteria of social well-being within the city: (1) economic status; (2) environment; (3) health; (4) education; (5) social disorganization; and (6) participation and equality. The forty-seven variables are listed in Table 4.2. In contrast to earlier efforts at social area analysis, most of the variables were provided from local sources rather than from U.S. Census reports. The data illustrated in Table 4.2 embody many important conditions having a bearing on the quality of individual life and provide a useful measure of the general concept of social well-being.

Table 4.2   Criteria of Social Well-Being and Variables Used in Tampa Study

CRITERIA AND VARIABLES		
I ECONOMIC STATUS		
i) *Income*		
1 Income per capita ($) of persons 14 and over 1970	+	(1)
2 Families with income less than $3000 (%) 1970	–	(1)
3 Families with income over $10,000 (%) 1970	+	(1)
4 Persons in families below poverty level (%) 1970	–	(1)
ii) *Employment*		
5 Unemployed persons (% total workforce) 1970	–	(1)
6 Persons aged 16-24 working less than 40 weeks (%) 1969	–	(1)
7 White-collar workers (%) 1970	+	(1)
8 Blue-collar workers (%) 1970	–	(1)
iii) *Welfare*		
9 Families on AFDC program (%) Oct. 1971	–	(2)
10 Persons aged 65 and over on Old Age Assistance (%) Oct. 1971	–	(2)
II ENVIRONMENT		
i) *Housing*		
11 Average value of owner-occupied units ($) 1970	+	(1)
12 Owner-occupied units valued less than $10,000 (%) 1970	–	(1)
13 Average monthly rental of rented units ($) 1970	+	(1)
14 Rented units with monthly rentals less than $60 (%) 1970	–	(1)
15 Units with complete plumbing facilities (%) 1970	+	(1)
16 Deteriorating and dilapidated houses (%) 1971	–	(3)
ii) *Streets and Sewers*		
17 Streets needing reconstruction (% of total length) 1971	–	(4)
18 Streets needing scarification and resurfacing (% of total length) 1971	–	(4)
19 Sanitary sewer deficiencies (% of total area) 1971	–	(5)
20 Storm sewer deficiencies (% of total area) 1970	–	(4)
iii) *Air Pollution*		
21 Maximum monthly dustfall (tons/sq. mile) 1969	–	(6)
22 Average suspended particulates (μgm/m^3/day) 1969	–	(6)
23 Maximum monthly sulfation (mg SO$_3$/100 cm^2/day) 1969	–	(6)
iv) *Open Space*		
24 Area lacking park and recreation facilities (%) 1971	–	(7)

(continued)

Table 4.2   Criteria of Social Well-Being and Variables Used in Tampa Study (*continued*)

CRITERIA AND VARIABLES

III HEALTH		
i) *General Mortality*		
25 Infant deaths (per 1000 live births) 1970	−	(8)
26 Death rate (per 10,000 persons 65 and over) 1970	−	(8)
ii) *Chronic Diseases*		
27 Cancer deaths (per 100,000 population) 1970	−	(8)
28 Stroke deaths (per 100,000 population) 1970	−	(8)
29 Heart disease deaths (per 100,000 population) 1970	−	(8)
30 New active tuberculosis cases (per 10,000 population 1970	−	(8)
IV EDUCATION		
i) *Duration*		
31 Persons aged 18-24 with 4 or more years high school or college (%) 1970	+	(1)
32 Persons over 25 with 8 years or less school (%) 1970	−	(1)
33 Persons over 25 with 4 years high school (%) 1970	+	(1)
34 Persons over 25 with 4 years college (%) 1970	+	(1)
V SOCIAL DISORGANIZATION		
i) *Personal Pathologies*		
35 Narcotic violations arrests (per 10,000 residents) 1971	−	(9)
36 Venereal disease cases (per 10,000 population) 1970	−	(8)
ii) *Family Breakdown*		
37 Families with children, having husband and wife present (%) 1970	+	(1)
38 Persons separated or divorced (% ever married) 1970	−	(1)
iii) *Overcrowding*		
39 Dwellings with more than 1.0 persons per room (%) 1970	−	(1)
iv) *Public Order and Safety*		
40 Criminal violation arrests (per 1000 residents) 1971	−	(9)
41 Juvenile delinquency arrests (per 10,000 residents) 1971	−	(9)
42 Accidental deaths (per 100,000 population) 1970	−	(8)
v) *Delinquency*		
43 Juvenile delinquency arrests by residentcy (per 10,000 population) 1971	−	(9)
VI PARTICIPATION AND EQUALITY		
i) *Democratic Participaton*		
44 Registered voters (% population 18 and over) 1971	+	(10)
45 Eligible voters voting in mayoral election (%) 1971	+	(10)
ii) *Equality*		
46 Racial distribution index 1970	−	(1)
47 Income distribution index 1970	−	(1)

Sources of Data: (1) *1970 Census of Population and Housing.* (2) Division of Family Services, State of Florida. (3) Hillsborough County Planning Commission. (4) Department of Public Works, City of Tampa. (5) Sanitary Sewers Department, City of Tampa. (6) Hillsborough County Pollution Control Commission. (7) Metropoltian Development Agency, City of Tampa. (8) Hillsborough County Health Department. (9) Police Department, City of Tampa. (10) Supervisor of Elections, City of Tampa.

Figure 4.3 illustrates the general spatial patterning of social well-being in Tampa, as indicated by combining the results for all of the variables listed in Table 4.2. The darkly shaded areas are those poorest in the general indicators of well-being. They appear to be concentrated around the central business district and within the innermost parts of the northeastern sector of the city, whereas the "better" areas tend to occupy the opposite

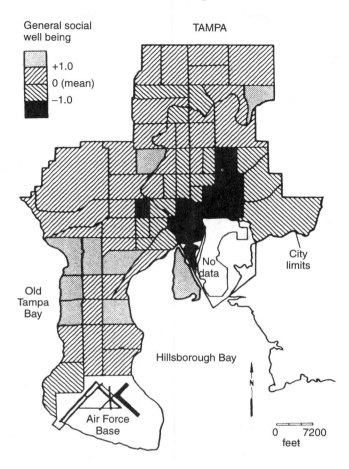

Figure 4.3   Standard scores on a general indicator of social well-being, based on data on all 47 variables listed in Table 4.2. (David M. Smith, *The Geography of Social Well-Being in the United States: An Introduction to Territorial Social Indicators,* New York: McGraw-Hill, 1973, p. 126).

sector. Relatively poor conditions are also found in isolated census tracts in the extreme northern and southern parts of the city.

Not coincidentally, the areas indicating the worst conditions had at the time of this study already been designated as the target of various public projects aimed at permanently raising the socioeconomic and physical living standards of the most deprived population groups of the city.

Smith (1973) argues that one basic advantage to mapping social indicators in this way is that one can achieve a more humanistic view of the internal differentiation of cities. This may lead to the examination of the basic mechanisms of urban systems that give rise to the extreme disparities in the quality of life in the different areas of American metropolitan centers.

One of the shortcomings of this approach, as is also the case with the other attempts to identify the component parts of the urban community previously discussed, is that such study can become an end in itself, without enough concern for the kind of direct social action aimed at improving the unsatisfactory conditions that the social indicators movement has the potential for precisely identifying (Plessas and Fein, 1971, pp. 43–44). The eventual usefulness of the social indicators movement depends on the ability and willingness of urban planners, policy makers, and the general public to incorporate valid measures of social well-being into programs of direct social action designed to improve the quality of life in urban communities.

IDENTIFYING LOCAL AREAS IN THE METROPOLIS: THE "SLUM" AS A SPECIAL CASE

In contrast to scientific efforts to classify subareas of the metropolis, lay descriptions and definitions tend to be imprecise and impressionistic. For example, the primarily suburban students in a large urban sociology course taught by me were recently asked to define the essential characteristics of an urban slum and to identify those parts of the nearby city of Detroit that best represented their concept of it. The responses were vague on both counts. Many of the perceptions had to do with the physical condition of the housing, whereas others focused on the social characteristics of the residents. At one extreme, some students labeled the entire city a slum; at the other, some were unwilling to consider any part of the city a slum. Within these extremes, the responses were varied.

The variations in perception were as great among those who claimed to know the city well, as among those who were only remotely familiar with the city. The responses were only slightly less varied when these same students were asked to identify and describe the "inner city." Yet these students strongly agreed that the slums represented a serious social problem about which something should be done. The most common response was that massive slum clearance was the only realistic solution. When asked to define the criteria by which areas would be designated as slums for the purpose of slum clearance, the students' responses were again imprecise, impressionistic, and widely varied.

On the surface, social area analysis, factorial ecology, or social indicator analysis would seem to provide a more rational and precise method for identifying areas for the purposes of planned social and economic changes such as slum clearance or urban renewal. To a certain extent, some large American cities already have applied techniques similar to these to systematically classify local subareas for conservation, rehabilitation, or massive demolition. To devise a reasonable set of objective measures upon which to build an empirical description of an urban residential slum is relatively simple, although tedious. Such an index might very well be based on the number of dwelling units within an area in dilapidated condition, the degree of overcrowding within housing units, the degree of absentee ownership of local dwelling units, the age of housing in a neighborhood, rental value, and so on. It is even possible to construct an index of the characteristics of slum dwellers, based on income, employment, or a wide variety of other available indicators of social well-being.

Such measures lack one important ingredient, which has to do with the attitudes and values of the residents. If the residents of a given area do not consider it to be a slum or even an undesirable place to live, to impose such a label might not always be fair or wise. The West End of Boston is a case in point. This area was designated a slum by city officials several decades ago and scheduled for massive rebuilding. This required the massive relocation of its then current residents. What was overlooked was that this was a cohesive and stable ethnic community to which its residents were strongly tied by sentiment and tradition (Gans, 1962). Subsequent studies of those who were involuntarily relocated to other parts of the community indicated that there was much psychological suffering and a profound sense of loss as a result of this displacement from what was to them a good community that satisfactorily met most of their real and perceived needs (Fried, 1963; see also chapter 14).

What has often happened is that when such areas have been targeted for slum clearance, city officials have been bombarded with resistance from the residents of such areas who do not consider their own neighborhood to be a slum or to need such drastic treatment as massive demolition. Obviously, in these cases, a large discrepancy in the perception of what constitutes a slum exists between the city officials on the one hand and the residents on the other. In disputes like these, the question of whose perception and judgment should prevail often becomes an emotionally charged political issue that is difficult to resolve to the satisfaction of the competing interest groups involved.

Thus, efforts to identify areas as slums should include measures of the attitudes and sentiments of their dwellers, in addition to more formal measures of physical condition or socioeconomic status. It seems reasonable to apply this label only to those areas considered undesirable places to live *by their own inhabitants,* as well as by outsiders.

A TYPOLOGY OF SLUMS

Actually, those areas of the city stereotypically regarded as slums by outsiders contain a great diversity of social groups and perform a wide variety of functions for the metropolitan community as a whole. Some of the more easily recognized slum subcultures and the functions they perform can be identified as follows.

Urban Villages

These include immigrant groups who settle in distinct areas of the city and who carry on the peasant life of their native communities. These areas are characterized by traditional family structures, local institutions such as ethnic churches, newspapers, social service agencies, restaurants, and commercial establishments. Ethnic groups in these areas may form a strong identification with the local neighborhood and its institutions, which in turn may serve as a source of stability, cohesiveness, and social control for that group. They supply a stable labor supply for the metropolitan labor market, and may become identified with particular occupations, depending on their skills, previous experience, and the opportunities currently available. Urban villages may provide a source of cultural diversity for the larger community with their ethnic restaurants and food shops, arts and crafts, and social customs. One of the most important functions of urban villages in American cities is that because they have been the port of entry for millions of impoverished and dispossessed migrants from rural areas or other lands, they enhance socialization and assimilation for these people as they become accustomed to their new urban environment.

Skid Row

The inhabitants of these areas tend to be "skidders" or failures from other walks of life, such as chronic alcoholics, drug addicts, or vagrants. They usually are older, unattached, isolated males—the so-called "homeless men" of an earlier period of sociological literature (Burgess and Bogue, 1964). Rooming houses, flop houses, and transient hotels are the principal kinds of housing for these inhabitants, and the local institutions include social service agencies such as the Salvation Army, pawnshops, saloons, employment agencies, and the police.

These areas function to segregate their inhabitants from other parts of the community where they usually are not tolerated. But contrary to the lay image of the residents of these areas as "bums," they are often an important source of day labor for the central business district as janitors and maintenance workers, restaurant workers, street cleaners, and the like. One can see large lines of skid row inhabitants in front of local employment agencies looking for day work, and many local businesses depend on them for certain types of work. In a more morbid sense, the skid row areas may also serve as a kind of burial ground where their homeless and aging population awaits death.

Young Adults

Slum areas of large American cities are inundated with many kinds of young people: students at metropolitan universities, colleges, and specialized trade schools, divorcees, childless newlyweds, unmarried couples, or young singles who have left their parents' homes to begin life on their own or to locate near their work. Such areas may serve as stepping-stones to social mobility for young people beginning careers in urban occupations. Although their residence may be temporary, many local institutions cater to their needs, including movie theaters, discotheques, coffee shops, dating bureaus, parks, bars, and other meeting or gathering places. In turn, many young suburban adults also congregate in these areas for the active social life they create.

Nonconformists

Bohemian, beatnik, hippy, and gay are labels that have been intermittently used to describe avant-garde or nonconforming innovative behavior. Predominantly young adults, such groups have often congregated in inner city areas such as Greenwich Village, Haight-Ashbury, Yorkville, or the Left Bank of Paris. These areas provide escape from the controls or constraints of the conventional middle classes and an opportunity to experiment with new forms of expression in music, poetry, drama, literature, painting, filmmaking, fashion, politics, lifestyles, or sexual behavior. Very often, the cultural innovations created in these settings pave the way for ultimate general acceptance by the larger society, and their creators have sometimes become mass media celebrities (Andy Warhol, Allen Ginsberg, Timothy Leary, for example). Thus, such areas are a source of cultural diversity for the larger society and may afford many individuals a release from the constraints and frustrations of more conventional lifestyles.

The "Underworld"

Pornography, prostitution, gambling, drug distribution, and other "vices" tend to be concentrated in slum areas, where they are offered by a variety of underworld professionals, hustlers, or exploiters. Usually unattached individuals, they may or may not reside in the areas in which they operate. In some cities, special districts are set aside for these activities to prevent them from spreading to other areas where they are unwanted by the residents. Such areas may serve as a tourist attraction and a boost to the local economy, often attracting conventions and visitors from outside the metropolitan area. They also may provide an occasional outlet or escape from the frustrations and constraints experienced by the residents of local middle-class areas (who at the same time may work hard to keep such activities out of their own neighborhoods!).

The Ghetto

These areas provide homes for those who are not permitted to live anywhere else in the local community. Traditionally, this concept of *ghetto* applied to the involuntarily segregated Jewish communities of central and northern Europe of the preindustrial period. In the United States, the term has been increasingly applied to segregated black communities, in which the segregation was also historically involuntary, and to Spanish-American, Asian-American, and many other ethnic communities, whether such segregation is entirely involuntary. Of course, residential segregation by race, ethnicity, or by socioeconomic status and lifestyle characteristics raises many issues of significant importance in the field of urban sociology and is considered in much greater detail in remaining chapters of this book.

Other Groups

Finally, slum areas may be desirable to other groups who have none of the characteristics just described simply because of their convenience to the central business district or other centrally located activities. Or they may serve as a convenient meeting place for strangers who wish to carry on all sorts of activities with a maximum of privacy and a minimum of surveillance.

The main point in this discussion of urban slums is that to make simple generalizations about the characteristics of local areas of a metropolitan community is not easy. They tend to be more diversified, heterogeneous, and complex than commonly supposed.

Most current popular stereotypes or images of subareas of the modern metropolis, such as the so-called "slums" are often inaccurate, oversimplified, and unwarranted.

CITIES AND SUBURBS: A COMPARATIVE VIEW

Of all the efforts to classify the component parts of the modern metropolitan area, none are as significant or widespread as the efforts to compare the central cities of metropolitan areas with their suburban "rings" or "belts." Some of the reasons for this particular concern are obvious. Although the traditional past concerns of urban sociologists had focused on the city, most of the large cities in the United States had matured by the period immediately following World War II and had begun to experience rapidly declining growth rates. Between 1950 and 1980, many of these cities had in fact begun to lose population. The 1990 Census has revealed an additional loss in the central city population as a portion of the total U.S. population, as well as a net loss in the total number of Americans living in the central cities of SMSAs.

In contrast, almost all urban growth in the United States in the past several decades has been in the suburbs. During the 1960s the suburbs surpassed the cities as the predominant form of urban development, as the total population of the suburbs became larger than that of the cities they surround for the first time in recorded history. Schwartz (1976, p. vii) estimated that there were then over 13 million more people in the suburban rings than in the cities they surround, and that this gap promises to widen. Thus, suburbanization represents the newest form of urbanization, but, more importantly, it is widely considered to be a distinct form of urbanization representing a sharp departure from the earlier development of the cities from which they have expanded.

If, in fact, cities and suburbs are distinctly different forms of human settlement, then twentieth-century suburbanization was as revolutionary a change as was the urban-industrial revolution of the nineteenth century, with as great a potential for transforming the entire character of American society. It is in this context that city-suburban comparisons are highly significant.

Sociological comparisons of cities and suburbs generally have been made at several levels. The first has to do with ecological comparisons, which focus on differences or similarities in physical land-use patterns, or which attempt to identify the economic function each area serves for the larger containing metropolitan community. The second focuses on differences or similarities in the demographic characteristics of the populations of cities and suburbs, such as socioeconomic status, household formation, and race and ethnicity. The third area of comparison has to do with differences or similarities in attitudes, lifestyles, or social behavior. The following discussion focuses on all three of these levels of comparison.

The Suburban "Myth"

In contrast to the diversity, complexity, and heterogeneity of cities, much of the earlier literature on suburbs (see Kramer, 1972; Schwartz, 1976) described them impressionistically as "bedroom communities" or "dormitories" for managerial or professional-level

Table 4.3 Twenty-four Most Populated U.S. Cities, 1960-1990

CITY	POPULATION, 1990	POPULATION, 1980	POPULATION, 1970	POPULATION, 1960	PERCENTAGE OF CHANGE, 1980-1990	PERCENTAGE OF CHANGE, 1970-1980	PERCENTAGE OF CHANGE, 1960-1970
New York City, NY	7,322,564	7,071,639	7,894,862	7,781,984	3.5	-10.4	1.5
Los Angeles, CA	3,485,398	2,966,850	2,816,061	2,479,015	17.5	5.6	13.6
Chicago, IL	2,783,726	3,005,072	3,366,957	3,550,404	-7.4	-10.1	-5.2
Houston, TX	1,630,553	1,595,138	1,232,802	938,219	2.2	29.3	31.4
Philadelphia, PA	1,585,577	1,688,210	1,948,609	2,002,512	-6.1	-13.4	-2.7
San Diego, CA	1,110,549	875,538	696,769	573,224	26.8	25.7	21.6
Detroit, MI	1,027,974	1,203,339	1,511,482	1,670,144	-14.6	-20.5	-9.5
Dallas, TX	1,006,877	904,078	844,401	679,684	11.4	11.3	24.2
Phoenix, AZ	983,403	789,704	581,562	439,170	24.5	35.3	32.4
San Antonio, TX	935,933	785,880	654,153	587,718	19.1	20.2	11.3
San Jose, CA	782,248	629,442	445,779	204,196	24.3	36.7	118.3
Baltimore, MD	736,327	785,795	645,153	587,718	-6.3	-13.0	-3.5
Indianapolis, IN	731,327	700,807	744,624	476,258	4.4	-4.9	56.3
San Francisco, CA	723,959	678,974	715,674	740,316	6.6	-5.2	3.3
Jacksonville, FL	635,230	540,920	528,865	201,030	17.4	21.7	163.1
Columbus, OH	632,910	564,871	539,677	471,316	12.0	4.6	14.5
Milwaukee, WI	628,088	636,212	717,099	741,324	-1.3	-11.3	-3.3
Memphis, TN	610,337	646,356	623,350	497,524	-5.6	3.5	25.3
Washington, DC	606,900	638,333	756,510	763,956	-4.9	-15.7	-1.0
Boston, MA	574,283	562,944	641,071	697,197	2.0	-12.2	-8.1
Seattle, WA	516,259	493,846	530,831	557,087	4.5	-7.0	4.7
El Paso, TX	515,342	425,259	322,261	276,687	21.2	32.0	16.5
Cleveland, OH	505,616	573,822	750,903	876,050	-11.9	-23.6	-14.3
New Orleans, LA	496,938	557,515	593,471	627,525	-10.9	-5.9	-5.4

Source: *Census of Population and Housing, 1990.* U.S. Department of Commerce, Bureau of the Census, Summary Tape, File 1C (CD-Rom); *Census of Population, Characteristics of the Population, Number of Inhabitants,* U.S. U.S. Department of Commerce, Bureau of the Census, Summary, Table 27; *1970 Census of Population, Characteristics of Population, Number Inhabitants,* U.S. U.S. Department of Commerce, Bureau of the Census, Table 28.

male white-collar workers who commuted daily to and from their place of employment in the central city. In this literature the suburbs were hotbeds of fertility in the sense that child rearing was among their most important functions, the suburban housewife remaining at home to fulfill this function while her spouse was away at work.

Physically the suburbs were viewed as serving primarily a residential function for middle-class or higher-level families who could afford the perceived advantages of single-family homes on large, well-landscaped lots segregated from the noise, overcrowding, congestion, pollution, and other perceived disadvantages of living in the city. Thus, they were distinguished from the central cities by the more homogeneous socioeconomic status and the familial or child-rearing status of their residents. Some of the literature had focused on zoning restrictions and other efforts by suburban residents to protect the uniqueness of their communities from encroachment by urban types of land-use development, such as factories, commercial areas, multiunit apartment house developments, or lower status or racially different populations.

Another common theme was the homogeneity of the population in conforming to common values and behavior. "The suburb," said Riesman (1957, p. 134), "is like a fraternity house at a small college . . . in which like-mindedness reverts upon itself as the potentially various selves in each of us do not get evoked or recognized." Whyte (1956) described the suburbs as the proving ground for a new social ethic—a mind-set emphasizing teamwork in place of individuality—which had been nurtured among the young executives of the large corporations who inhabited the mass-produced postwar suburbs such as Park Forest, Illinois, or Drexelbrook, Pennsylvania. He detected in these suburbs a unique and unparalleled similarity in the lives of their inhabitants.

Yet much of the current reevaluation of the suburbs calls into serious question these early images of the suburbs as homogeneous and distinct from the cities upon which they depend. Critics in recent years have labeled the above notions of suburbia "the suburban myth." Out of a series of studies (see Kramer, 1972; Schwartz, 1976) came the realization by many social scientists that suburbia is a dynamic setting, its social institutional, and demographic structure becoming more diverse, complex, and urban than previously realized. Kramer (1972), for example, argued that to employ the term "suburb" to suggest a single type of place, or to imply that there is an overarching pattern of suburban social organization is to greatly overgeneralize. Thus, as a descriptive sociological term, suburb has little meaning.

Schnore (1972) has found that many significant differences exist between the socioeconomic status of central city and suburban populations but that no one type of city-suburban differential applies to all metropolitan areas. He has identified several major types of patterns according to income differentials. The most common type is that in which the highest and lowest income groups are overrepresented in the central city and the middle-income group is overrepresented in the suburbs. The next most frequent type is that in which high-income groups are suburbanized and low-income groups are concentrated in the central city. But another type has high-income groups concentrated in the central city while low-income groups reside in the suburbs. Using years of education completed as a criterion, Schnore identified at least six types of differences between cities and suburbs, again supporting the notion that there is no one single pattern of differences between cities and suburbs. Schnore suggests that the size and the age of the metropolitan community are major factors producing different types of city-suburban differentials. Studies of working-class suburbs (Berger, 1971), low-income black suburbs (Kramer, 1972), and new mass-produced suburban communities such as Levittown, New Jersey (Gans, 1967), also challenge the traditional suburban myth with their findings that do not conform to the stereotype of a homogeneous and undifferentiated middle-class suburban population.

To date, there has been no really adequate effort to systematically classify the many diverse types of suburban development. The most basic attempt is that of Schnore (1963, pp. 77–86), who distinguished two main types of suburbs—employing and residential. Employing suburbs are highly industrialized, providing a large portion of their working population with jobs in the local community. Residential suburbs are those containing relatively few industrial or commercial activities, which therefore have a resident working population that must commute to workplaces outside the local suburb. Comparing these two types of suburbs in the New York SMSA by using census data, Schnore found that employing suburbs had a higher percentage of foreign-born, nonwhite, and aged residents than residential suburbs, and were more likely to be losing population or growing at a slower rate of increase. Conversely, residential suburbs were higher in socioeconomic status, with a larger percent of their populations in white-collar occupations, with more formal education, and with higher incomes than residents of employing suburbs. Also, the inhabitants of residential suburbs were more likely to occupy their own single-family housing units of a newer vintage than those of the employing suburbs. Schnore also identified a third, intermediate type of suburb, containing elements of both the employing and residential.

Pollster Louis Harris (*Time*, March 15, 1971, pp. 14–20) has used a typology limited to residential suburbs, which is based on whether the suburb is expanding or has reached its peak in growth, as well as in socioeconomic status. The types are (1) affluent bedroom; (2) affluent settled; (3) low income growing; and (4) low income stagnant. Thorns (1972) has developed a typology for suburbs in the United States and England based on social class, whether the suburb was planned in its development, and the distinction between residential and industrial suburbs suggested by Schnore. This typology lists the following types of suburbs: (1) middle-class planned residential; (2) working-class planned residential; (3) middle-class unplanned residential; (4) working-class unplanned residential; (5) middle-class planned industrial; (6) working-class planned industrial; (7) middle-class unplanned industrial; and (8) working-class unplanned industrial. Boskoff (1970, pp. 113–119) has developed a six-part typology: (1) the traditional upper-class suburb; (2) the identity-conscious suburb; (3) the mass-produced suburb; (4) the suburban slum; (5) the stable variegated suburb; and (6) the industrial suburb.

These typologies are incomplete and their usefulness obscure, but they all acknowledge the growing disparity and complexity of modern suburban development. An important question raised here is that in view of an increase in the heterogeneity of suburban life and forms, are some of the traditional distinctions between cities and suburbs beginning to disappear? To put it another way, are the suburbs beginning to be more and more like the cities from which they sprang?

Are the Suburbs More and More Like Cities?

There is no doubt that the suburbs have been "invaded" in recent decades by a large influx of citylike facilities and amenities: shopping centers, which often exceed central city department stores in the volume of business they do and in the variety of merchandise they carry, a wide variety of ethnic shops, restaurants, and social services; cultural facilities such as civic centers, concert halls, movie theaters, art galleries and museums; bars and nightclubs; athletic clubs and stadiums, hospitals and clinics; high-rise office buildings and hotels; and multiunit housing developments, such as apartment houses, row houses, and condominiums. Also on the increase in the suburbs is the portion of the population living in household units other than families with young children. These include single adults, childless couples, the divorced, and the aged. For many suburbanites, frequent trips to the central city for employment or urban goods or services are no longer necessary, for they are now to be found conveniently near home in the suburbs.

Social problems traditionally associated with large cities have also invaded the suburbs: traffic congestion, air pollution, rising crime rates, deteriorating housing in some of the aging suburban nieghborhoods, and poverty and unemployment. According to a HUD newsletter, the number of poor suburban residents, began to increase at a more rapid rate than did the central city poor during the 1960–1970 decade. It is fair to conclude that suburbia no longer affords, if it ever did, complete escape from the conditions of city life that many Americans have long sought.

All of these characteristics certainly suggest that citylike features and characteristics now common to many suburbs do in fact blur many city suburban differences, and thus much of the sociological analysis of urban life in the following chapters of this book applies equally to suburbs as well as to cities. It can also be suggested that a new form of urban development has begun to appear in the suburbs which has many of the characteristics of the traditional central cities and "downtowns" of metropolitan areas, yet is significantly different from these earlier urban forms. For want of a better term, the label *edge city* has been applied to this new hybrid form of city-suburban development by Joel Garreau (1992).

Edge Cities

The significance of the concept of *edge city* can be illustrated by a quote from the forward from the book of the same title (Garreau, 1992).

Most of us now spend our entire lives in and around these Edge Cities, yet we barely recognize them for what they are. That's because they look nothing like the old downtowns: they meet none of our preconceptions of what constitutes a city. Our new Edge Cities are tied together not by locomotives and subways, but by freeways, jetways, and jogging paths. Their characteristic monument is not a horse-mounted hero in the square, but an atrium shielding trees perpetually in leaf at the cores of our corporate headquarters, fitness centers, and shopping plazas. Our new urban centers are marked not by the penthouses of the old urban rich, or the tenements of the old urban poor, but by the celebrated single family–home with grass all around. For the rise of the Edge City reflects us moving our jobs—our means of creating wealth, the very essence of

Atrium of a fairly typical suburban shopping mall

our urbanism—out to where we've been living and shopping for two generations. The wonder is these places, these curious new urban cores, were villages or corn stubble just thirty years ago.

Edge cities are now relatively common, and Garreau tentatively identifies approximately 120 that are already established in approximately forty metropolitan areas in the United States. He also asserts that a nearly equal number are in the emergent stages of development, and that edge cities can also be found in other parts of the world such as Canada or Europe.

Garreau specifically defines an edge city as any place that:

1. Has 5 million square feet or more of leasable office space. This is an area larger than the old downtowns of Memphis Tennessee, or Minneapolis.

2. Has 600,000 square feet or more of leasable retail space. This is the equivalent of a good-size mall containing at least three nationally famous department stores and eighty to one hundred specialty shops.

3. Has more jobs than residential bedrooms. People head toward this kind of place at the beginning of the workday, not away from it.

4. Is perceived as one place, with usually an official or unofficial name that is used or recognized by the population of the local metropolis. It is a place that "has it all" from jobs, to shopping, to entertainment.

5. Was nothing like a city as recently as three decades ago. In other words, this is a brand-new form of urban development.

Because of its newness and fast—almost revolutionary—rate of development, Garreau is ambivalently both optimistic and pessimistic, with respect to its ultimate impact on future urban civilization, for the edge city not only appears on the edge of existing urban developments, but "puts people on edge. It gives them the creeps." (Garreau, 1992, p. xxii). This view is supported by the historian, Robert Fishman (1988), who argues that all new city forms appear to be chaotic in their early stages, and whose following quote of Charles Dickens on London in 1848 is endorsed by Garreau as the best one-sentence description of an edge city to date: "There were a hundred thousand shapes and substances of incompleteness, wildly mingled out of their places, upside down, burrowing in the earth, aspiring in the earth, moldering in the waster, and unintelligible as any dream" (Fishman, 1988).

We have included this discussion of edge cities in support of the argument that cities and suburbs are becoming more and more alike. But important differences between cities and suburbs certainly do continue to exist. Schwartz (1976, pp. 333–339) argues that in spite of the many criticisms and contrary evidence, the so-called suburban myth does contain a persistent degree of accuracy. For example, most suburbs continue to remain racially segregated white enclaves, while urban blacks remain largely in segregated communities within the central cities. Almost all economic expansion in the last several decades has taken place in the suburbs, while the economies of many large central cities have significantly declined. Even though the variations in the economic status of both city and suburban populations are great, overall differences between the general economic well-being of city dwellers and suburbanites still remain. Finally, but not the least important, many traditional stereotypes and misconceptions have created a climate of conflict between many large cities and their suburban rings. Mutual antagonisms, prejudices, fear, and mistrust often inhibit cooperative solutions to the problems that afflict cities and suburbs alike. Some of these problems are addressed more fully in later chapters.

MEGALOPOLIS: POSTMETROPOLITAN URBAN DEVELOPMENT

This entire chapter has been devoted to the emergence of metropolitan patterns of urban development, the implications of which are not yet fully understood. In the last half of the twentieth century, a new and larger supermetropolitan form has emerged and is just beginning to be recognized. This newer form involves the overlapping and penetration of previously separate metropolitan areas. This overlapping creates a continuous band of urban and suburban development, stretching for hundreds of miles in some regions. These expanded, supermetropolitan areas are sometimes referred to as "conurbations," or more commonly "megalopolis." Originally a classic Greek concept, the term megalopolis was applied by Gottman (1961) to a region of the northeastern seaboard that extends about 600 miles from southern New Hampshire to northern Virginia and extends up to 100 miles inland from the Atlantic shore to the foothills of the Appalachian mountains. Sometimes called "BosWash," this megalopolis encompasses all of Massachusetts, Rhode Island, Connecticut, New Jersey, Delaware, and the District of Columbia, as well as large sections of Maryland, New York, and Pennsylvania. It includes approximately one-fifth of the entire U.S. population. Another megalopolis can be identified as emerging in the Great Lakes region, stretching from Milwaukee through the Chicago metropolitan area across northern Indiana, northern Ohio, and southern Michigan, encompassing Detroit, Flint, Toledo, Cleveland, Akron, and possibly Pittsburgh. Still a third megalopolis stretches along the West Coast from San Diego to San Francisco.

It is difficult for the average person to grasp the concept of megalopolis or personally to identify with this type of development in any significant way. The need to understand more fully and to come to grips with megalopolis as a new dominant force in American society was first suggested in these passages by Gottman (1961, pp. 5–16):

> The old distinctions between rural and urban do not apply here any more. . . . In the area, then, we must abandon the idea of the city as a tightly settled and organized unit in which people, activities, and riches are crowded into a very small area clearly separated from its non urban surroundings. Every city in this region spreads out far and wide around its original nucleus; it grows amidst an irregularly colloidal mixture of rural and suburban landscapes; it melts on broad fronts with other mixtures, of somewhat similar though different texture, belonging to the suburban neighborhoods of other cities. . . . This region serves thus as a laboratory in which we may study the new evolution reshaping both the meaning of our traditional vocabulary and the whole material structure of our way of life. . . . So great are the consequences of the general evolution heralded by the present rise and complexity of Megalopolis that any analysis of this region's problems often gives one the feeling of looking at the dawn of a new stage in human civilizatio. . . . Indeed, the area may be considered the cradle of a new order in the organization of inhabited space. . . . Megalopolis stands indeed at the threshold of a new way of life, and upon solution of its problems will rest civilization's ability to survive.

One of the best empirical studies attempting to understand the megalopolis, in terms of its leadership or political power structure, is Delbert Miller's *Leadership and Power in the Bos-Wash Megalopolis* (1975). This study emphasized the complexities of the economic, social, and political structure of the Bos-Wash region and led the author to pluralistic conclusions about the nature and distribution of power in a megalopolis. To date, very little systematic scientific analysis of megalopolis has been attempted, and this phenomenon needs further exploration and explanation.

SELECTED BIBLIOGRAPHY

BELL, WENDELL. "Social Areas: Typology of Urban Neighborhoods." In *Community Structure and Analysis,* Marvin Sussman (ed.). New York: Thomas Y. Crowell, 1959, pp. 61–92.

BERGER, BENNETT M. *Working Class Suburb.* Berkeley: University of California Press, 1971.

BERRY, BRIAN J. "Comparative Factorial Ecology." Supplement to *Economic Geography* 2 (1971).

_____, and JOHN D. KASARDA. *Contemporary Urban Ecology.* New York: Macmillan, 1977.

BEYNON, ERDMAN D. "Budapest: An Ecological Study." *Geographic Review* 33 (1943): 256–275.

BLUMENFELD, HANS. "On the Concentric-Circle Theory of Urban Growth." *Land Economics* 25 (1949): 209–212.

BOLLENS, JOHN C., AND HENRY J. SCHMANDT. *The Metropolis: Its People, Politics, and Economic Life,* 3d ed. New York: Harper & Row, 1975.

BOSKOFF, ALVIN. *The Sociology of Urban Regions,* 2d ed. New York: Appleton-Century-Crofts, 1970.

BURGESS, ERNEST W. "The Growth of the City." In *The City,* Robert E. Park, Ernest W. Burgess, and Roderick D. McKenzie (eds.). Chicago: University of Chicago Press, 1925.

———, and DONALD J. BOGUE, eds. *Contributions of Urban Sociology.* Chicago: University of Chicago Press, 1964.

CAPLOW, THEODORE. "Urban Structure in France." *American Sociological Review* 17 (1952): 544–549.

DAVIE, MAURICE. "The Patterns of Urban Growth." In *Studies in the Social Sciences,* G.P. Murdock (ed.). New Haven, CT: Yale University Press, 1937.

DUNCAN, OTIS DUDLEY. "Review of Social Area Analysis." *American Journal of Sociology* 61 (1955): 84–85.

FIREY, WALTER. *Land Use in Central Boston.* Cambridge: Harvard University Press, 1947.

FISHMAN, ROBERT. *Urban Utopias in the Twentieth Century.* Cambridge: MIT Press, 1988.

FRIED, MARC. "Grieving for a Lost Home." In *The Urban Condition,* Leonard J. Duhl (ed.). New York: Basic Books, 1963.

GANS, HERBERT. *The Urban Villagers.* New York: Free Press, 1962.

———. *The Levittowners.* New York: Vintage Books, 1967.

GARREAU, JOE. *Edge City: Life on the New Frontier.* New York: Anchor Books, 1992.

GOLD, HARRY. *Sociology of Urban Life.* Englewood Cliffs, NJ: Prentice Hall, 1982.

GOTTMAN, JEAN. *Megalopolis: The Urbanized Northeastern Seaboard of the United States.* New York: Twentieth Century Fund, 1961.

HANDLIN, OSCAR, and JOHN BURCHARD. *The Historian and the City.* Cambridge: Harvard University Press, 1963.

HARRIS, CHAUNCY, and EDWARD ULLMAN. "The Nature of Cities." *Annals of the American Acadamy of Political and Social Science* 242 (1945): 7–17.

HAWLEY, AMOS. *Urban Society: An Ecological Approach.* New York: Wiley, 1980.

———, and OTIS DUDLEY DUNCAN. "Social Area Analysis: A Critical Appraisal." *Land Economics* 33 (1957): 337–345.

HOYT, HOMER. "The Structure and Growth of Residential Neighborhoods in American Cities." Washington, DC: U.S. Federal Housing Administration, U.S Printing Office, 1939.

KRAMER, JOHN, ed. *North American Suburbs: Politics, Diversity, and Change.* Berkeley, CA: Glendessary Press, 1972.

MILLER, DELBERT. *Leadership and Power in the Bos-Wash Megalopolis.* New York: Wiley, 1975.

National Research Council. *Toward an Understanding of Metropolitan America.* San Francisco: Canfield Press, 1975.

New York Times 2000 Almanac. New York: Penguin Reference Books, 1999.

PHILLIPS, E. BARBARA. *City Lights: Urban-Suburban Life in the Global Society,* 2d ed. Oxford University Press, 1996.

PLESSAS, D. J., and R. FEIN. "An Evaluation of Social Indicators." *Journal of the American Institute of Planners* 38 (1971): 43–51.

REES, P. H. "Concepts of Social Place: Toward an Urban Social Geography." In *Geographic Perspectives on Urban Systems,* Brian J. Berry and F. Horton (eds.). Englewood Cliffs, NJ: Prentice-Hall, 1970.

———. "Problems of Classifying Subareas within Cities." In *City Classification Handbook,* Brian J. Berry (ed.). New York: John Wiley, 1972.

RIESMAN, DAVID. "The Suburban Dislocation." *Annals of the American Acadamy of Politial and Social Science* 314 (1957): 123–146.

SCHNORE, LEO F. "The Socioeconomic Status of Cities and Suburbs." *American Sociological Review* 28 (1963): 76–86.

———. *Class and Race in Cities and Suburbs.* New York: Markham, 1972.

———, and JOY K. JONES. "The Evolution of City-Suburban Types in the Course of a Decade," *Urban Affairs Quarterly* 4 (1969): 421–422.

SCHWARTZ, BARRY, ed. *The Changing Face of the Suburbs.* Chicago: University of Chicago Press, 1976.

SHEVKY, ESHREF, and WENDELL BELL. *Social Area Analysis.* Palo Alto, CA: Stanford University Press, 1955.

SMITH, DAVID M. *The Geography of Social Well-Being in the United States: An Introduction to Territorial Social Indicators.* New York: McGraw-Hill, 1973.

———, and R. J. GRAY. "Social Indicators for Tampa, Florida." Urban Studies Bureau, University of Florida, 1972. Mimeographed.

Statistical Abstract of the United States: The National Data Book, 119th ed. Washington DC: U.S. Department of Commerce, October, 1999.

THORNS, DAVID C. *Suburbia.* London: MacGibbon & Dee, 1972.

VAN ARSDOL, MAURICE, SANTO CAMILLERI, and CALVIN SCHMIDT. "The Generality of Urban Social Area Indexes." *American Sociological Review* 23 (1958) 277–284.

WHYTE, WILLIAM H. Jr. *The Organization Man.* New York: Anchor Books, 1956.

5

NEIGHBORHOODS, NETWORKS, AND ASSOCIATIONS

Early sociological observations concerning the social organization of urban communities tended to emphasize either social disorganization or the lack of adequate organization. A widely accepted "theory of social disorganization" fed on the apparent evidences of disorganization in urban slums and other urban subareas. There was the primary group, as represented by the family and closely knit peer groups; on the other hand, there were the increasingly bureaucratic large-scale institutions of modern urban society, such as the modern corporation or nation-state. What was missing, according to this perspective, was the adequate organization of communal life that lies between these two extremes—the local neighborhoods, social bonds, or formal associations that were thought to provide meaning, purpose, and order to life at the local level. Popenoe (1969, p. ix) has stated this general perspective succinctly:

> The modern citizen finds a limited sense of personal and communal identity and meaning around his immediate family, peers, and private interests (such as his occupation): similarly he is "plugged in" fairly well to his nation-state—indeed this is the only group in modern times, aside from his family, for which an individual is prepared to give his life (although this social fact seems presently to be on the decline). There is a profound lack of feelings of general identity and sense of community in the middle range, however, between the levels of family-occupation-corporation and nation-state. There are too few social ties and concerns bonding together the variety of social groups and individuals at the local and regional levels. A man's private and family concerns are too narrow and limited, his national concerns too abstract and depersonalized, to generate a strong commitment to the general welfare in the arena of the urban-industrial community.

The modern urban community, it has now been established, is a highly intricate social, ecological, and economic organization. Its social structure includes all of the simpler forms of social organization, such as the family (see chapter 7), and the more complex forms, such as those having bureaucratic characteristics. However, it also includes a varied web of social organization at the middle range of size and complexity. These middle-range elements, sometimes lumped together under the general rubric of "community" or "primary group," are an inherent part of the social fabric of modern urban communities, and recognition is growing that a grasp of the social processes at work at these levels of urban social organization is critical to the more complete understanding of urban social structure.

As Wilensky and Lebeaux (1958, p. 136) note, "a lively primary group life survives in the urban area, and primary controls are effective over wide segments of the population. The alleged anonymity, depersonalization, and rootlessness of city life may be the exception rather than the rule."

Some of the middle-range forms of social organization, such as the neighborhood or friendship groups, are of course preindustrial in their origins, but they continue to survive in modified forms in the modern era. Others, such as voluntary associations, have evolved more recently in the context of urban-industrial development. Still others, such as social networks, have always existed but remain amorphous and at a primitive stage of classification and explanation in the sociological literature on urbanization. The shape and characteristics of all of them are still subjectively identified, and some urban sociologists of an ecological bent are prone to minimize their significance. Nevertheless, we intend to review some of these concepts and supporting research materials in this chapter, because they do have much bearing on the quality of life in urban areas.

THE URBAN NEIGHBORHOOD

The first problem encountered in any effort to synthesize present knowledge about the urban neighborhood is the existence of varied and inconsistent definitions of the term "neighborhood." Glass (1948, pp. 150–170) recognized this problem when she presented two alternative definitions. The first describes the neighborhood as "a distinct territorial group, distinct by virtue of the specific physical characteristics of the area and the specific social characteristics of its inhabitants." This historically popular conception, as advanced by Park and his followers, assumed that, as particular kinds of individuals clustered together in metropolitan areas, they produced unplanned "natural areas." In a more recent example of this approach, Abrahamson (1976, pp. 154–160) seems to reject the more amorphous social psychological definitions of the neighborhood in favor of designating physically well-defined census tracts as neighborhoods, in the manner of social area analysis (see chapter 4).

Glass's second definition describes the neighborhood as "a territorial group, the members of which meet on common ground within their own area for primary group social activities and for organized and spontaneous social contacts." Carpenter (1933, p. 357) had earlier provided a more elaborate version of this second conception:

> The most distinctive characteristics of a neighborhood are its relations with a local area sufficiently compact to permit frequent and intimate association and the emergence of such association of sufficient homogeneity and unity to permit a primary or

face-to-face social grouping endowed with a strong sense of self-consciousness and capable of influencing the behavior of its several constituents.

Other problems with the concept of neighborhood arise from efforts to precisely delimit neighborhood boundaries. Some observers (see Mann, 1965; Hawley, 1981), particularly community planners, sometimes equate the boundaries of neighborhoods with those of local schools. For example, the radius around an elementary school within which elementary students reasonably can be expected to walk to and from school may be one such approximation. Ross (1962) suggested that the boundaries of commonly recognized and commonly labeled subcommunities, such as Beacon Hill or the Back Bay areas of Boston, are appropriate determinants of neighborhood units. Caplow and Foreman (1950, pp. 357–366) employed as a working definition of neighborhoods in Minneapolis "a family dwelling unit and the ten family dwelling units most accessible to it." Suttles (1972) identified the typical city block as one useful frame of reference for neighborhood analysis, and the parochial ethnic group was identified as another. Clearly, there is no commonly agreed-upon definition of a neighborhood or the appropriate boundaries of neighborhood units. Keller (1968, pp. 91–92) has suggested that four approaches may have been used most predominantly by social scientists in both theoretical and applied studies of the urban neighborhood. These four approaches are summarized as follows:

A. **The Ecological Neighborhood Approach**. From this perspective, a neighborhood is a physically delimited area having an ecological position in a larger area and particular physical characteristics arising from natural geographic conditions and from a particular configuration of land uses. Natural areas, such as skid rows, waterfront areas, cultural centers, or red light districts are apt illustrations of this conception of neighborhood.

B. **The Neighborhood Resources Approach**. This approach focuses on the specific physical resources of an area, such as stores, housing, schools clubs, and offices, which may suggest the special functional role that the neighborhood serves for its own residents. Of course, resources in a given neighborhood may also be used by outsiders who do not reside in the local area, and such outside use of the neighborhood for recreational, business, or cultural purposes may contribute heavily to the general character of the neighborhood.

C. **The Symbolic Neighborhood**. This approach views a neighborhood as representing certain values both for the residents and for the larger community. Thus, a neighborhood may evoke value-laden images such as social solidarity, political cohesion, lawlessness, ethnic or religious compatibility, or prestige of its residents, as well as the aesthetic quality (cleanliness, quiet, or beauty) of its physical features. What is important here are the meanings that a neighborhood evokes in the minds of the resident or nonresident observers, whether such symbols are based on "objective reality."

D. **The Subcultural Neighborhood**. The history of the social, economic, and ecological factors operating in a given neighborhood tend to give that neighborhood its own special cultural atmosphere, which may persist over a long period of time. Once the cultural characteristics of an area become well established, they usually persist over decades, despite the turnover of individuals residing there. For example, a well-established ethnic neighborhood may retain its essential ethnic character generation after generation. Likewise, a middle-class suburb or a highly transient skid row area may each have a history

Chinese New Year celebration in the Chinatown of a large American city

that produces a collective quality of life persisting over decades and that is not necessarily modified by individual variations in the actions of its residents.

The problems of definition aside, the most crucial questions for those professionally interested in the analysis of neighborhoods have been along these lines:

1. What are the useful social functions of the neighborhood; for its inhabitants on the one hand, and for the larger containing community on the other?
2. What are the particular mechanisms or social processes through which the functions of the neighborhood are achieved or maintained?
3. What are some of the internal or external forces that maintain sound and viable neighborhoods, and what are some of the forces that threaten their disintegration?
4. What are some of the significant variations among different types of neighborhoods, with respect to their structural characteristics, social processes, or functions?
5. What is the future prospect for the urban neighborhood, in terms of growth, stability, or decline?
6. What, if anything, can or ought to be done in the way of deliberate social planning to improve urban neighborhoods as effective units of social participation or social action?

THE FUNCTIONS OF NEIGHBORHOODS

The urban neighborhood in the modern metropolitan complex can be seen as fulfilling many functions not necessarily served at other levels of urban social organization. Warren (1977) identifies at least six major functional roles for the neighborhood: (1) as an arena for interaction; (2) as a center for interpersonal influence; (3) as a source of mutual aid; (4) as a base for formal and informal organizations; (5) as a reference group; and (6) as a status arena.

The Neighborhood as an Arena for Interaction

This function has to do with the informal interchanges of physically proximate residents within the neighborhood as a whole. Warren makes a useful distinction between these neighborhoodwide patterns of interaction and those more narrowly limited to next-door neighbors or close friendship groups. They may include casual greetings or visits with those members of the neighborhood with whom one does not necessarily have a close or intimate relationship. These exchanges imply an attitude of cordiality or neighborliness. This provides the individual with a sense of belonging to the neighborhood and mitigates some of the depersonalizing influences commonly ascribed to the urban environment.

The Neighborhood as a Center for Interpersonal Influence

Face-to-face contacts with neighbors may provide a means of defining the norms of child rearing, education, or socioeconomic aspirations that the larger society generates. Forms of social influence, such as ostracism rewards based on social acceptance and the attendant definitions of conforming or deviant behavior, can take place in more detail in the neighborhood than in the more diffuse institutions of the larger community. This is particularly true when neighborhood interaction is frequent and intense. In a "two-step flow of communication," local opinion leaders who are exposed to the mass media and other extraterritorial influences pass along these influences to those in the population who are relatively isolated from them. The transmitting or filtering role of local opinion leaders provides mechanisms for integrating the individual into the larger society and for preventing the breakdown of local norms; the neighborhood opinion leaders may provide at the local level the selective integration of values disseminated from the larger community.

The Neighborhood as a Source of Mutual Aid

Studies have documented the extent to which exchange of help between those living in close proximity in urban areas is a frequent and important activity. The rapid response of neighbors is essential when such aid is not available from other sources, such as relatives or formal organizations. Despite the proliferation of social service agencies (see chapter 12), such bureaucratic organizations often lack the ability to respond promptly and flexibly to many emergencies (for example, approximately 75 percent of all disaster rescues are made by neighbors). A study of fatherless families found that mutual aid was extensive for employed mothers, and that minor exchanges—borrowing or lending groceries or small amounts of money, baby-sitting, or shopping—were frequent for both husbandless and married mothers. Only 16 percent did not report such exchanges. The local neighborhood's role as a center for mutual aid may take the form of protection against outside intrusions, as well as serve as a substitute for external support. Thus, refusing to

The street serves as a playground in a crowded multiethnic urban neighborhood

give information to authorities or to aid institutions viewed as alien to local neighborhood values is important protection for the values of local residents. When there is a sudden disaster, for example, or when the cost of seeking resources outside the neighborhood is excessive, or when protection from external social institutions alien to the local area is involved (some observers see this as a negative or divisive function), mutual aid may play a significant role for many urban families.

The Neighborhood as a Base for Formal and Informal Organizations

Many voluntary associations (discussed in more detail later in this chapter) are organized at the neighborhood level. They may compete with other social units in the neighborhood or they may link the neighborhood to the larger community by promoting the participation of local residents. Neighborhoods are often characterized by frequent population turnover and local voluntary associations often speed the assimilation of newcomers into the neighborhood. Depending on the character of such organizations, they need not conflict with other neighborhood social units, such as the family, or prevent individuals from forming close ties with neighbors more informally. If a neighborhood can integrate individuals quickly through voluntary associations, rapid population turnover need not produce a lack of neighborhood cohesion. Under some circumstances, local associations provide a means for mobilizing people to engage in efforts at social change. By defining what otherwise might be a diffuse sense of dissatisfaction felt by local groups, neighborhood organizations may stimulate rather than retard participation in social movements.

The Neighborhood as a Reference Group

Although many studies suggest that informal and formal contacts are more extensive in most urban neighborhoods than commonly supposed, the fact that many neighbor contacts are ephemeral and low in intensity suggests that the influence exerted by neighbors is often subjective. Implied in the term "reference group" is that many individuals may be guided and changed in their behavior and values by what they understand to be the values of a perceived social entity. In this way, people's self-images may be shaped by what they think others think of them. The social climate of a neighborhood may lead individuals to seek out others who agree with them and thereby reinforce the attitudes they already hold. Merely believing that a majority of one's neighbors agree with one may have the same effect.

The Neighborhood as a Status Arena

Perhaps the least explored function of the neighborhood is its importance as a status-conferring entity. Status symbolism, in terms of both the housing or prestige of a given neighborhood, may be valued by outsiders, but insiders may use such symbols to protect themselves against insidious status comparisons by outsiders. The neighborhood may act as a mirror of personal achievement and well-being by screening out definitions of class or status that are irrelevant at the local level and by providing an area within which status claims derived from the larger society are "cashed in" in terms of housing quality, lifestyle, or other highly visible symbols of social status. As status centers, neighborhoods enable local opinion leaders to act as agents of status bestowal or appraisal for the entire neighborhood, particularly when positive status is not forthcoming from the larger community.

Using these six functional categories in a sample of twenty-eight local black neighborhoods in the Detroit area, Warren (1975) found that these neighborhoods fulfilled various combinations of the functions for their residents. In addition, a comparison of white and black neighborhoods also supported the notion that the functions were fulfilled in white neighborhoods, but in different combinations than in the black neighborhoods.

TYPES OF NEIGHBORHOODS

Not all urban neighborhoods are equally effective in fulfilling the functions just described, nor do all of the residents of the most cohesive neighborhoods participate in the interactional activities characteristic of their particular neighborhood. For, as Fischer (1976, p. 121) suggests, the fate of social relations in general does not depend on the fate of neighborly relations. In answer to the rhetorical challenge "Who needs neighborhoods?" he suggests that some persons certainly do, but many also seem to do well without them.

Some studies support the notion that patterns of participation in neighborhood activities vary widely from one kind of neighborhood to another. For example, Fava (1959) has found that suburban residents in the New York metropolitan area exhibited a higher degree of neighboring than did inner city residents. In the suburban areas, activities such as informal interaction between neighbors, entertaining, and collective efforts at problem solving took place more frequently than they did in the inner city neighborhoods. Another body of literature supports the theory that the neighborhood is more likely to be meaningful as an arena of participation for lower-income groups for whom limited education, ethnic dissimilarity, minority group status, or poverty limit the opportunities for participation in the larger community (Hawley, 1981, pp. 194–197). Those groups with greater resources or statuses are better able to spread their radius of interaction over a wider range of the metropolitan area and therefore need not submit to the limited choices in the immediate neighborhood or to dependence on their neighbors for social contacts.

To account for some of these kinds of differences in neighborhoods and patterns of neighborhood participation, some observers have attempted to develop typologies, which take into account different patterns of neighborhood social organization and different patterns of residents' orientation toward neighbors and neighborhoods. Borrowing concepts from the work of Warren (1977), Suttles (1972), Dentler (1968), Shostak (1969), Litwak and Fellin (1968), and others, we have identified several types of neighborhoods as representing a reasonable composite of the most salient types of local neighborhoods in the modern American metropolis:

The Integral Neighborhood

This type of neighborhood represents the ideal for those who see stable, well-organized local neighborhoods maintaining strong integrative links to the larger communities of which they are a part as essential to the well-being of urban communities. In this type of neighborhood, people are extremely cohesive, they know each other reasonably well, they frequently interact with one another, and they belong to many local organizations, such as block clubs, community councils, PTAs, and other locally oriented voluntary associations. In all, these are extremely active neighborhoods with much face-to-face interaction and participation in the organized activities of the local area.

The residents of such neighborhoods also actively support the norms and values of the larger community and participate actively in its affairs. Behavioral indicators, such as voting in elections and maintaining contact with the political institutions of the larger community, indicate some of the external links to the larger communities, as do memberships in informal groups or formal voluntary associations that are not in the local neighborhood. Thus, the integral neighborhood is not only a very cohesive center of local activity, but it is also a cosmopolitan center as well. The integral neighborhood is most effective in mobilizing both local and external resources when it attempts to solve local problems or responds to challenges caused by changes taking place in the larger community. This neighborhood type has been well illustrated in Whyte's (1956) study of Park Forest and in Seeley, Sim, and Loosley's (1956) study of Crestwood Heights. Both these communities were middle- or upper-middle-income suburban communities, which are among the most likely candidates to become integral neighborhoods; some big city neighborhoods with more heterogeneous socioeconomic characteristics also appear to have taken on the characteristics of integral neighborhoods.

The Anomic Neighborhood

With respect to the amount of social cohesion, the anomic neighborhood is at the opposite end of the scale from the integral neighborhood. It is the most completely disorganized and atomized type of residential area described in the earlier body of sociological literature. It lacks established patterns of participation in community affairs and a common identification with either the local area or the larger community. Such settings usually reflect mass apathy and lack of involvement in any form of collective action (Warren, 1977).

Estrangement from the values of the larger community manifests itself in nonvoting and indifference to the goals of the larger community. The anomic neighborhood would be least likely to influence, mobilize, or alter the values of its residents through any efforts at social control or planned social intervention. The very absence of social organization might suggest the emergence of values defined as deviant by the larger community, but the more reasonable hypothesis is that residents of the anomic neighborhood are not engaged in active resistance to the values of the larger society as a result of alienation, but are rather displaying passive behavior of a diffused nature (Warren, 1977). As suggested at the beginning of this chapter, this type of neighborhood occurs less frequently than commonly supposed in the traditional conventional wisdom. At least some anomic neighborhoods may be found in urban communities, but they are the exception rather than the modal type of urban neighborhood in the American metropolis.

An important variation of the anomic neighborhood is the transitory, or stepping-stone, neighborhood, in which the residents keep to themselves, avoid local entanglements, or fail to participate in or identify with the local community. In this case, the motives for noninvolvement may be that, because of strong economic or status aspirations, the members of a given family must devote their energies to working, getting more education or training, and a variety of self-improvement efforts. Such commitments usually mean that both husband and wife and their working or school-age children simply have little time, energy, interest, or opportunity for participating in neighborhood activities. According to Warren (1977), this may help to explain the low rates of participation in some working-class, blue-collar suburbs, where the strong desire to work up and out of such areas may lead the residents to view strong neighborhood links and activities as a threat or barrier to their aspirations.

The Defended Neighborhood

Suttles (1972) has resurrected the concept of the defended neighborhood from the earlier work of Park and Burgess and their followers. The concept identifies neighborhoods in which the residents seal themselves off from outside intrusions through the efforts of well-organized gangs, restrictive convenants, sharply defined and enforced boundaries, or by a forbidding reputation. The most obvious earmark of the defended neighborhood is street corner gangs claiming their "turf" and warding off strangers or anyone else not a proper member of the neighborhood (Anderson, 1990). It is here that one finds vigilante community groups, militant neighborhood conservation groups, a high incidence of uniformed doormen or security guards, and the frequent use of door buzzers and television monitors. According to Suttles (1972, p. 245), these defensive tactics indicate the "general apprehension of inner city dwellers, rich and poor alike, and the necessity for each of them to bound off discrete areas within which he can feel safe and secure."

The defended neighborhood is not necessarily delineated by the physical features of the area, but rather by "cognitive maps" that the residents form in their own minds for describing not only what their own and other areas of the city are like but also what they think they ought to be like. Suttles (1972) argues that these cognitive maps, which may be shared by the residents of a given neighborhood, serve a useful function because they are part of the social control apparatus of urban areas and are of special importance in regulating spatial movement to avoid conflicts between antagonistic groups. Cognitive maps of a neighborhood provide a set of social categories for differentiating between those people with whom one can or cannot safely associate and for defining the concrete groupings within which certain levels of social contact and social cohesion are based. The basis for such cognitive differentiation may be ethnicity, race, socioeconomic level, lifestyle, or the like.

Historically, defended neighborhoods have tended to be concentrated in the central cities of the large metropolis and to consist primarily of lower-income groups. These are the areas where ethnic and racial cleavages are the most apparent (see chapter 13 for a more extended discussion of these problems) and where population density and transiency are the highest. These residents have the greatest need for a set of cognitive guidelines by which they can safely navigate within their own residential areas. As Suttles (1972, pp. 244–245) states, "It is here that the defended neighborhood should have its greatest appeal and serve best to mollify the imagined or real dangers which exist in the inner city."

Empirical illustrations of what can be described as defended neighborhoods are boundless. Zorbough's *The Gold Coast and the Slum,* Whyte's *Street Corner Society,* Gans's *Urban Villagers,* Thrasher's *The Gang,* and Suttles's own more recent studies of the Near West Side of Chicago (1968) are all excellent descriptions of defended neighborhoods in the inner areas of big cities. But some studies of stable blue-collar working-class suburbs have also identified characteristics similar to those associated with Suttles's concept of defended neighborhoods (see Shostak, 1969; Berger, 1960).

One structural characteristic of defended neighborhoods is that a certain amount of social cohesion ensues when residents must band together from time to time in joint actions to protect the neighborhood from what they consider to be undesirable intrusions or changes. These may consist of the actions of outside agents of the community, such as politicians, industrialists, realtors, or city planners, who threaten to change the physical character of a neighborhood. The residential "invasion" of a neighborhood by outside groups of differing ethnic, racial, socioeconomic, or behavioral characteristics also may be seen as threatening or resisted by neighborhood groups. For example, the movement of hippies, gays, prostitutes, cults, or therapeutic groups (such as Synanon) into stable low-income working-class neighborhoods is often met with fierce organized resistance by local neighborhood groups organized for this purpose.

Another more subtle characteristic of defended neighborhoods is that the residents may share secrets and myths stemming from the gossip and rumors of informal interaction. Such half-truths and bits and pieces of information may add up to a sort of subculture shared by the residents and may give them a common identity. Their views of their own neighborhood and of the outside world may not correspond to the views of the officials of the larger community or to that of outsiders in general, and their behavior and attitudes may appear to be deviant or nonconforming to outsiders. This characteristic reinforces the cohesion and differentiation of the defended neighborhood and its isolation from the larger community.

The Contrived Neighborhood

With the advent of city planning, urban renewal, public housing, and expanding markets for housing in the suburbs, a relatively new form of neighborhood has now appeared—mass-scale housing developments that are created and built in the same architectural mold virtually overnight. Public housing projects, apartment and condominium complexes, and suburban single-family housing subdivisions are among the best examples. The most striking feature of these "planned" neighborhoods is the relatively extreme homogeneity of both its physical characteristics and the socioeconomic status of its residents. Residential homogeneity is almost assured because the screening of new occupants is centralized in the hands of a single realtor, developer, or manager.

The cultural uniformity of the residents tends to make these areas even more segregated than defended neighborhoods. Although racial or ethnic segregation in these newer developments may not be acceptable policy or permitted by law, one can now find entire developments restricted to child-rearing families, singles, childless couples, or retirees of the same general socioeconomic levels. The contrived or artificial neighborhood has easily distinguishable boundaries, which are reinforced by its unified architectural design and a single source of development. These neighborhoods also have a ready-made name and image usually created by the developers, which is adopted as the official name of the area by the residents. Such designations may be a source of pride, as in the case of prestigious subdivisions, or a source of deprecation, such as the case of some low-income public housing projects in areas commonly referred to as slums.

Suttles (1972) describes the contrived neighborhood as a variation of the defended neighborhood in the functions it serves for its residents. The main difference, however, is the extreme specialization and homogeneity in the social characteristics of the residents. Also, when the contrived neighborhood selects residents with cosmopolitan lifestyles (see chapter 6 for a description of cosmopolitan lifestyles), it may take on the social characteristics of the integral neighborhood. In other words, the residents may form strong bonds to both the local neighborhood and the larger containing community. Gans's (1967) study of Levittown is a good illustration of a relatively cosmopolitan contrived neighborhood. Many observers have described virtually all suburbs as specialized contrived neighborhoods, but this clearly is not the case and is but another example of the suburban myth described in chapter 4. The extremely specialized contrived neighborhood is still not clearly identified in the sociological literature, and its significance is still

not clearly understood. Much more research needs to be done on the nature and significance of specialized contrived communities.

The Neighborhood as a Staging Area

Much of what goes on in many local neighborhoods is not necessarily initiated by
local residents but is rather the product of the interplay of groups and interests with a
much larger base in the surrounding city or, indeed, in the national society. Thus, certain
kinds of neighborhoods often become the staging area for national dramas, in which local
residents play only secondary roles. Neighborhoods likely to become staging areas for the
activities of outside interest groups are likely to be seen by these outsiders as in the midst
of crises such as poverty, crime, or social unrest which, if left unchecked, could have an
undesirable effect on the entire containing community. Thus, such neighborhoods are
likely to become the staging areas for action by municipal, federal, or private social agencies bent on altering the character of the local neighborhood through planned intervention.

The concept of the neighborhood as a staging area was introduced by Dentler
(1968) in his analysis of Ocean Hill–Brownsville, a troubled neighborhood in the New
York City borough of Brooklyn. Dentler had identified organized helping professions in
the fields of health, education, labor unions, industrial corporations, political parties,
municipal bureaucracies, and private foundations as all having a high stake in producing
changes in this neighborhood through various strategies of planned intervention. The
local neighborhood thus becomes a stage upon which these outside interest groups engage
in a contest to act out their complex strategies in cooperation, competition, or conflict
with one another. Dentler argued that the neighborhood as such a staging area is something less than a cohesive or viable community.

In addition to the "colonization of the underclass," Dentler (1968) suggested that
another incentive for neighborhoods to become staging areas is economic. Subcommunities that have an aging or declining industrial or commercial base, or are declining in their
capacity to provide a tax revenue base, may be targeted for industrial or commercial redevelopment by powerful industrial, commercial, or governmental interest groups outside
the local neighborhood. In either of these cases, the residents, no matter how great their
efforts may be to control the destiny of their own community, may find those efforts
blocked by larger forces over which they have no control, or they may discover that their
efforts are caught up in larger contests that may distort or destroy any real possibility of
local control. Yet Dentler held out the hope that the conflicts that frequently occur as
neighborhoods become staging areas could also have the side effect of strengthening residents' interest and participation in the affairs of their neighborhood, as is apparently what
eventually happened in Ocean Hill–Brownsville.

WHO NEEDS NEIGHBORHOODS?

The review of different kinds of neighborhoods fails to establish that the local neighborhood is a well-organized social entity in all cases, or that it is a powerful influence in the
lives of all urbanites. As easy-to-use transportation facilities, such as the automobile or

mass transit, or communications facilities such as the telephone and internet have become more available to urbanites, many have become increasingly liberated from the close ties and constraints of the local neighborhood. As Wellman (1977, pp. 221–223) observed:

> It is fruitless to concentrate on the neighborhood as the fundamental area of personal relations. Too many people are moving beyond its confines for too many personal relationships. Being concerned only with developing neighborhood interaction works against having the liberating effects of being able to select one's own intimates and acquaintances from a metropolis-wide pool of applicants. Neighborly relations must be seen in perspective as only one special aspect of urban personal ties. . . . a concentration on neighborhoods as the central basis of personal relationships has become anachronistic and is doomed to failure.

It is also true that many examples of successful neighborhoods can be found on the urban scene and that they continue to serve useful and necessary functions for their residents and often for the larger community. To some social observers, the integral or the defended neighborhood still remains the epitome of the ideal community, and some have a strong ideological commitment to preserve and strengthen the neighborhood as a unit of social action. Warren (1977), for example, argues that well-organized neighborhoods can positively contribute to social change in the following three ways:

1. Neighborhoods can provide an appropriate program unit for governmental and private efforts at planned social intervention.
2. Given the high rate of built-in social change in a mass, industrial, bureaucratic society, neighborhood primary groups may be able to respond to conditions of urban life more flexibly and effectively than formal organizations.
3. Neighborhood organizations can play a major role in clarifying and defining the solutions to urban problems by clearly differentiating among problems with a local focus that are amenable to solution by local self-help and self-determination and those problems that clearly require wider bases of mobilization and collective action.

Warren advocated a strong community organization movement aimed at converting individual needs and interests into a collective source of influence and to mobilize people at the neighborhood level to bring about effective change. To further this aim, Warren has coauthored the *Neighborhood Organizers Handbook* (Warren and Warren, 1976), designed to train both professionals and volunteers in the techniques of community organization, which has become a significant subspecialty within the social work profession (see chapter 9).

Many successful instances exist of neighborhoods that have been helped by innovations in community organization, but whether such efforts can successfully protect or improve local neighborhoods in the face of the larger community and societal forces threatening to alter them or minimize their significance remains to be convincingly demonstrated. In the next section, we discuss patterns of social interaction in the urban community that may in fact be replacing the neighborhood as an object of concern among social scientists.

SOCIAL NETWORKS

It is increasingly clear that many urbanites maintain informal social contacts in a wide variety of settings that do not conform to the boundaries of primary groups and territorial-based neighborhoods on the one hand, or large-scale formal organizations on the other. Thus, one may develop informal social relationships on the basis of friendship, common occupation or social class, old school ties, or common leisure-time pursuits or hobbies.

Wellman (1977) argues that many kinds of personal relationships in the city have become "despatialized." His research in Toronto's East York area, for example, found that a city-dweller's intimates (relatives, friends, and acquaintances) live all over the entire city. Few people to whom the city-dweller felt close actually lived in the same neighborhood. The large majority lived in other parts of metropolitan Toronto or outside of the metropolitan area.

Fischer (1977) suggests that each individual in the urban community is the center of a web of social bonds that radiates outward to the people one knows intimately, those one knows well, those one knows casually, and to the larger community beyond. These kinds of social bonds are increasingly coming to be called *social networks*. Fischer suggests that to understand the individual in the larger urban community, it is increasingly necessary to understand the fine mesh of social relations between the person and the society.

The concept of social networks is not restricted to the boundaries of the urban community. Even the most seemingly formal institutions, such as large bureaucratic organizations, are in many ways the framework within which social networks of personal ties are developed. In another example of the nonterritorial character of social networks, the election of Bill Clinton as president brought mass media attention to the hundreds, perhaps thousands of his close personal contacts around the country (and around the world!), commonly referred to as the "Friends of Bill." Another recent example would be rapidly growing networks of people who communicate regularly with people all over the world through the Internet, e-mail, and Web services of their personal computers, which would have been almost unimaginable before the 1990s. A small but growing number of sociologists and anthropologists have identified the concept of social networks in urban settings as a promising new area of theory and research for better understanding the total fabric of modern urban life. Scherer (1972, p. 115) described social network analysis as "an exciting and stimulating possible means of understanding human relationships in situations where the usual social structures are not observed and contacts appear scattered and diffused." The concept of social network arises in part from the work of Elizabeth Bott (1971), who initially defined a social network as a social configuration in which some, but not all, of the component external units maintain relationships with one another. She further used the term "close knit" to describe a social network in which many of the people a person knows tend to reach consensus on norms, exert consistent informal pressure on one another to conform to the norms, to keep in touch with one another, and, if need be, to help one another.

This form of social network is also found in Liebow's (1967) study of street corner groups in a low-income neighborhood, and in the work of Scherer (1972, pp. 111–113), who mapped the social networks of a group of fifty-two nonresidential students of a technological college in central London. Scherer's study found many variations and differences in the range of contacts and the number and depth of the relationships that were identified. Scherer's finding, along with the question of how close knit the networks were, implies that social networks may vary widely in such characteristics as their size, duration of membership, or the content, frequency, and intensity of contact.

Lauman (1973, pp. 114–115) has distinguished "loose knit" or "radial" networks from close-knit networks as those in which the persons involved have little need for uniform opinions and are likely to have relatively low affective involvement and commitment to their relations with one another, because their common interests and concerns are likely to be more specialized and more severely circumscribed close-knit networks. He implied that although loose-knit networks will share less intimate information than close-knit ones, they are more significant in contemporary urban society because they are more flexible and more adaptive to the demands of a continuously changing society whose members are likely to be geographically and socially mobile.

Granovetter (1973) identified networks based on relatively weak social ties, such as those based on marginal social contacts, sporadic or accidental contacts with former coworkers, old college friends, or people who get together several times a year at conferences or conventions. Journalist Vance Packard (1972) suggested that even sports or hobby enthusiasts can form these "weak" networks that may be meaningful to them over the years, even if the network members live hundreds of miles apart. Although such weak social ties may be amorphous and transitory, it can be argued that they form an integral part of the fabric of modern urban life.

Warren (1977) added to the still evolving typology of informal social networks by identifying "proximity anchored helping networks" as those that emerge in response to specific problems the people in a given area may face. This type of network may provide the mechanisms for solving local problems that are not supplied by any other type of urban social organization. He suggested that this type of network may become the basis for more permanent and institutionalized patterns of social organization, such as block clubs, community councils, or other types of voluntary associations. Thus, social networks can be viewed as linked to neighborhoods and other territorial-based subunits of the urban community and as serving the same kinds of functions. This is only one special application of the social network concept, and social networks can be identified at all levels of the social organization of urban communities, including nonterritorial forms of urban social organization.

APPLICATIONS OF SOCIAL NETWORK ANALYSIS

The analysis of urban social networks is sociologically significant for several reasons. First, social networks can be seen as extremely useful for the individual by providing a diversity of social contacts from which one can choose those that best accomplish one's desires and goals. Second, social networks may be seen as providing the thread that holds the urban community together as a social system. The analysis of social networks can offer descriptions of the urban system's structure and function. Third, social network analysis provides the means by which traditional assumptions about the nature of urban social life can be more adequately tested and perhaps challenged. For example, the traditional view that urban life is highly disorganized, atomistic, or lacking social bonds has been brought into much doubt and criticism by studies of social networks.

One of the most significant findings of network research is growing appreciation of the role social networks play in providing informal communications and informational systems that link individuals not to one another but to other networks and to the larger containing community (Wigand, 1977). Eames and Goode (1977, p. 242) suggest that cities ultimately be viewed as "a network of networks," whereby identifiable social networks coalesce into more formal groups and institutions and ultimately the entire urban structure. Studies of mass communications identified a two-step flow of information that works this way: a few opinion leaders obtain information or messages about products and adopt points of view about issues reported in the mass media; they influence others who have come to respect their judgment. This model of communications can be extended to include the possibility that through a wide web of separate but overlapping social networks, such information or messages ultimately becomes widely diffused throughout an entire community.

In such ways, such innovations as changing fashions of dress, self-health measures (diets or the use of drugs), patterns of voting, patterns of leisure-time activities, or the patterns of migration by ethnic groups become widely diffused among large segments of the urban population. These may be a direct result of the informal mechanisms for communicating information and ideas supplied by a widespread participation in networks. For example, in one classic study of the diffusion of medical innovations in several cities, Coleman (1966) found that doctors who were friends and professional associates of other physicians were more likely to prescribe a new drug earlier than doctors who were somewhat isolated from their colleagues, but that through more loosely constructed communications channels, the use of the new drug eventually spread to increasingly wider circles of physicians.

Likewise, some anthropologists have used network analysis to examine the process of migration to urban societies and found that social networks were very important in mitigating the more traumatic aspects of rural to urban migration (Eames and Goode, 1977; Fischer, 1977). What happens is that many migrants travel to cities where they already have kin or friends who may have transmitted information in advance as to what to expect in the city. Upon arrival, the migrant is assisted by the associates in his or her network, who provide help in finding housing and jobs and may introduce him or her to more people. The migrant's social network then expands as he or she adds new members, such as fellow workers, neighbors, and those who are met casually in shopping places, public eating places, or places of recreation. In these ways, the migrants are assimilated into networks involving mutual aid, exchange of goods and services, and diffusions of ideas and information, as well as emotional support and sociability for its own sake. Social networks also serve similar functions for already urbanized individuals or families making city-to-city, city-to-suburb, or suburb-to-city moves.

It seems reasonable to conclude this very brief discussion of informal social networks in the urban community by suggesting that while they are among the most diffuse and impressionistically identified forms of urban social organization, they may be the initial stages of newer institutionalized patterns of nonterritorial urban life. For example, Barber (2000) has asserted that social networks may be the backbone of a newly emerging form of civil society which has risen on a global level in opposition to the more commercial aspects of world globalization (see also the epilogue to chapter 16), whereas Orum (2001, pp. 225–226) has recently identified social networks as an integral requirement of citizen participation in the political power structures of American urban communities. In the context of more traditional social theory, Macionis and Parrillo (2001, p. 187) remind us that social networks, along with neighborhoods and other forms of informal or casual social interaction, continue to flourish in large urban social structures, even into the twenty-first century, as characteristic examples of Tonnies's earlier concept of *gemeinschaft* (see chapter 1).

VOLUNTARY ASSOCIATIONS

Voluntary associations are those more or less formally organized groups whose membership is by choice. They are the most structured of the middle-range forms of social organization considered in this chapter. Any time two or more persons identify a common interest that cannot be satisfactorily pursued individually or through preexisting forms of social organization, including those previously discussed in this chapter, the potential arises for the creation of a voluntary association. Social clubs, special interest groups, hobby groups, occupational associations and unions, political committees, and the like are well-known examples. The modern urban community is sprinkled with thousands of such groups, which have become increasingly important components of urban social organization. The 17,000 nationally or regionally organized associations listed in the *Encyclopedia of Associations* (1972) are probably a small fraction of the total number. Voluntary associations have been particularly characteristic of American urban life since its earliest manifestations. For example, de Tocqueville, a notably perceptive observer of the American scene, wrote as early as 1831:

> In no country in the world has the principle of association been more successfully used or applied to a greater multitude of objects than in America. Besides the permanent associations which are established by law . . . a vast number of others are formed and maintained by the agency of private individuals. (de Tocqueville, 1946, p. 106)

Voluntary associations may vary greatly in size and jurisdiction, ranging from small neighborhood units consisting of a relatively small handful of members residing in close proximity, to large, nationally organized units with thousands of members and with many local chapters or branches in all regions of the country. The Boy Scouts, League of Women Voters, American Red Cross, The National Rifle Association, or the AFL-CIO are examples of the latter. They may also vary in the complexity of their organizational structures, with some producing elaborate hierarchies or divisions of labor and elaborate formal rules or constitutions, whereas others appear to be rather haphazardly and informally organized. In general, voluntary associations can be viewed as an intermediate type of social organization, more formally organized than primary groups but less formal than highly bureaucratized organizations. They are experimental blends of both types of social organization, neither of which has been judged as entirely adequate by itself to provide the range and quality of organization deemed necessary for coping with the complexities of urban living. Thus they supplement but do not displace primary groups and highly formalized bureaucratic institutions.

Much speculation has arisen on the motives for participation in voluntary associations. For example, they may offer warmth and friendship, particularly when such needs are not satisfactorily supplied by primary groups. They may serve as a source of personal identification, as illustrated by the uniforms, emblems, or titles associated with fraternal orders, lodges, or social clubs. They may provide enhanced social status or upward mobility to status-conscious individuals who may consider the prestige of an association as an inducement to join, or they may provide social contacts with persons who are in a position to supply jobs, services, recognition and visibility, or other rewards. Members may join to protect a common vested interest or to apply pressure against outsiders to produce desired social change.

One important distinction among voluntary associations identifies *expressive* associations as providing their members regular opportunities for self-expression, creativity, or diversion in some special field of interest or hobby that can be commonly shared. *Instrumental* associations, on the other hand, are created to accomplish specific objectives within the larger community, through lobbying, political contributions, demonstrations, public relations campaigns, and other techniques of persuasion that can roughly be labeled as political in character. Thus voluntary associations at the local or national levels may spring up to promote or to block a specific piece of proposed legislation or public policy, to promote a specific moral cause, to protect or enhance the character of a local community or neighborhood, to protect taxpayers' or property owners' interests, or to further the interests of a specific social institution, such as education, religion, corporations, industry, or health care. For example, the traditional cliché "You can't fight city hall" is

A citizen represents a local voluntary association at a public town meeting

more often than not countered by the actions of well-organized voluntary associations designed to do just that! (See chapter 8.) To the extent that instrumental voluntary associations are often the basis for a successful social movement (Orum, 2001), they must be counted among the most significant sources of (or barriers to) planned or unplanned social change in urban-industrial societies.

PARTICIPATION IN VOLUNTARY ASSOCIATIONS

Although voluntary associations are widely distributed throughout the United States, this does not guarantee that all urbanites will necessarily become joiners. Extensive research on rates of participation in voluntary associations provides increasing evidence that membership in voluntary associations has not been equally available or attractive to all of the urban subgroups. One of the most important variables determining who participates in voluntary associations appears to be social class. Available studies generally indicate that people with high income and occupational status tend to participate more extensively in associations than individuals of lower socioeconomic status. Although the results of studies undertaken in different communities at different times show slightly different patterns, the general pattern is one in which well over one-half of those with middle- or upper-class status participate in some degree in voluntary associations, and significantly less than one-half of those with lower or working-class status participate. Among those who do participate, the number of associations with which they are affiliated also rises in direct relationship to socioeconomic status.

What is not clear in the literature on neighborhoods, networks, and associations is the relative importance of each to the urbanite, and the degree to which each can serve as a reasonably satisfactory substitute for the others in providing a sense of belonging to the larger community or providing a sense of having a voice in its decision-making processes (as implied earlier in this chapter, neighborhoods, networks, and voluntary associations may or may not coexist to serve mutually complementary or supportive functions). But it is far more certain that those individuals who have no ties to either neighborhoods, social networks, or voluntary associations are the most likely to conform to the traditional sociological image of the personal isolation, loneliness, powerlessness, and depersonalization depicted in the earlier urban literature (see chapters 1 and 6).

SELECTED BIBLIOGRAPHY

ABRAHAMSON, MARK. *Urban Sociology.* Englewood Cliffs, NJ: Prentice-Hall, 1976.

ANDERSON, E. *Streetwise: Race, Class and Change in an Urban Community.* Chicago: University of Chicago Press, 1990.

BARBER, BENJAMIN R. "Globalizing Democracy." *The American Prospect* September 11, 2000, pp. 16–19.

BERGER, BENNETT. *Working Class Suburbs.* Berkeley: University of Calitornia Press, 1960.

BOSKOFF, ALVIN. *The Sociology of Urban Regions,* 2d ed. New York: Appleton-Century-Croft, 1970.

BOTT, ELIZABETH. *Family and Social Networks,* 2d ed. New York: Free Press, 1971.

CAPLOW, T., and R. FOREMAN, "Neighborhood Interaction in a Homogeneous Community." *American Sociological Review* 15 (June 1950): 357–366.

CARPENTER, N. "Neighborhoods." In *Encyclopaedia of the Social Sciences,* p. 357. New York: Macmillan 1933.

COLEMAN, JAMES S., et al. *Medical Innovation.* Indianapolis, IN: Bobbs-Merrill, 1966.

DENTLER, ROBERT A. "Brownsville: Community or Staging Area?" *Center Forum,* November 13, 1968, pp. 12–14.

DE TOCQUEVLLLE, ALEX. *Democracy in America,* vol. II, New York: Knopf, 1946.

EAMES, E., and J. G. GOODE. *Anthropology of the City.* Englewood Cliffs, NJ: Prentice-Hall, 1977.

FAVA, SYLVIA F. "Contrasts in Neighboring." In *The Suburban Community,* W. M. Dobriner (ed.), pp. 122–130. New York: Putnam, 1959.

FISCHER, CLAUDE S. *The Urban Experience.* New York: Harcourt Brace Jovanovich, 1976.

————, et al. *Networks and Places.* New York: Free Press, 1977.

GANS, HERBERT. *The Levittowners.* New York: Vintage Books, 1967.

GLASS, RUTH. *The Social Background of a Plan.* London, 1948.

GRANOVETTER, MARK S. "The Strength of Weak Ties." *American Journal of Sociology* 79 (May 1973): 1360–1379.

HAWLEY, AMOS H. *Urban Society.* New York: John Wiley, 1981.

KELLER, SUZAN. *The Urban Neighborhood.* New York: Random House, 1968.

LAUMAN, E. O. *Bonds of Pluralism.* New York: John Wiley, 1973.

LIEBOW, ELLIOTT. *Talley's Corner.* Boston: Little, Brown, 1967.

LITWAK, E. and P. FELLIN. "The Neighborhood in Urban American Society." *Social Work* 13 (July 7, 1968): 72–79.

MACIONIS, JOHN J. A. and VINCENT N. PARRILLO. *Cities and Urban Life,* 2d ed. Upper Saddle River, NJ: Prentice Hall, 2001.

MANN, PETER. *An Approach to Urban Sociology.* New York: Humanities Press, 1965.

ORUM, ANTHONY M. *Introduction to Political Sociology,* 4th ed. Upper Saddle River, NJ: Prentice Hall, 2001.

PACKARD, VANCE. *A Nation of Strangers.* New York: McKay, 1972.

POPENOE, DAVID, ed. *The Urban-Industrial Frontier.* New Brunswick, NJ: Rutgers University Press, 1969.

ROSS, H. L. "The Local Community: A Survey Approach." *American Sociological Review* 27 (February 1962): 75–84.

SCHERER, JACQUELINE. *Contemporary Community: Illusion or Reality?* London: Tavistock, 1972.

SEELEY, J. R., A. R. SIM, and E. W. LOOSLEY, *Crestwood Heights.* New York: Basic Books, 1956.

SHOSTAK, ARTHUR. *Blue Collar Life.* New York: Random House, 1969.

SUTTLES, GERALD D. *The Social Order of the Slum.* Chicago: University of Chicago Press, 1968.

————. *The Social Construction of Communities.* Chicago: University of Chicago Press, 1972.

WARREN, DONALD I. *Black Neighborhoods.* Ann Arbor: University of Michigan Press, 1975.

————. "Neighborhoods in Urban Areas." In *New Perspectives on the American Community,* 3d ed., Roland L. Warren (ed.). Skokie, IL: Rand McNally, 1977.

————, and Rochelle B. Warren. *The Neighborhood Organizer's Handbook.* Notre-Dame, IN: University of Notre Dame Press, 1976.

WELLMAN, BARRY. "Who Needs Neighborhoods" In *New Perspectives on the American Community,* 3d ed., Roland L. Warrren (ed.). Skokie, IL: Rand McNally, 1977.

WHYTE, WILLIAM H. Jr. *The Organization Man.* New York: Simon & Schuster, 1956.

WIGAND, ROLF T. "Communication Network Analysis in Urban Development." In *Urban Communication,* W. E. Arnold and Jerry L. Buley (eds.). Cambridge, MA: Winthrop, 1977.

WILENSKY, H. L., and CHARLES N. LEBEAUX. *Industrial Society and Social Welfare.* New York: Russell Sage, 1958.

6

SOCIAL-PSYCHOLOGICAL AND CULTURAL DIMENSIONS OF URBAN LIFE

Social psychological and cultural dimensions of urbanization often have been treated as residual or derivative components of urban social systems. As such, they have often been cursorily examined or neglected altogether in many ecologically or "new urban sociology" treatments of urban sociology (see Schwab, 1992; Gottdiener, 1994). Compared with other urban sociology topics, little systematic effort has been made to detail the social psychology of urban life, even though much of the early theorizing about urbanization focused on questions of social psychological or cultural significance, and much contemporary field research has been conducted in this area.

Yet our understanding of the fabric of life in an urban context is not complete without some consideration of how individuals experience or give meaning to their lives as urbanites, and how they interact with others within a context of commonly shared meanings and symbols on the one hand, or within a context of a diversified range of attitudes, values, and perceptions on the other. This chapter is devoted to a review of social psychological and cultural topics, such as the impact of urbanization on individual personality structure, urban lifestyles, everyday patterns of interaction in public places, and the symbols and imagery of urban life. Our position is that, far from being residual or derivative components, these dimensions of urban social systems contribute as heavily to an understanding of the quality of urban life as do the other components of urban ecosystems—population, environment, technology, and social organization.

THE IMPACT OF URBANIZATION ON PERSONALITY AND MENTAL HEALTH

One of the questions that has long intrigued social scientists and other observers of the urban scene is whether the impact of urbanization is powerful enough to produce distinct differences between the personality characteristics of urban and nonurban dwellers. To the extent that human personality is shaped by sociocultural influences of all sorts and is not exclusively a product of physiological or biological factors, it seems reasonable to conclude that the urban environment constitutes one such major sociocultural influence. Wirth (1938) and Simmel (1950) are the best-known examples of sociologists who used this kind of deductive reasoning to postulate ideas about the personality characteristics that were believed to derive from the conditions of urban living, as they saw them. For the most part, they saw the city as highly disorganizing and disruptive for the individual, creating a wide variety of psychological pathologies. They hypothesized that friction, irritation, nervous tension, and personal frustration would increase in response to the greater size, density, and heterogeneity of the urban population and the more rapid tempos of urban life. Wirth, for example, argued that "personal disorganization, mental breakdown, suicide, delinquency, crime, corruption, and disorder might be expected under these circumstances to be more prevalent in the urban than the rural community" (1938, p. 162). Such reasoning for a long time has been the conventional wisdom of urban sociology, although usually the early proponents had not backed their conclusions with empirical analysis. More recent empirical research, as reviewed in the following section, has cast doubt on the validity of the theory that urban dwellers are any more prone to mental illness

Traffic accidents are among common sources of stress in urban settings

than rural dwellers, and the findings point to other sociocultural variables as potentially more significant than rural or urban residence as causative factors.

Classifying and Measuring Mental Illness

Modern psychiatry has not been conspicuously successful in the classification of mental illness, and there are now literally hundreds of differing diagnostic categories. But the major categories of mental illness recognized by psychiatry are still the *psychoses,* which entail a gross derangement of mental processes and inability to evaluate external reality correctly; the *neuroses,* which entail impairment of functioning, often confined to a segment of behavior, but with no sharp break with reality; *psychosomatic disorders,* which produce very real organic symptoms and malfunctions caused to a large extent by psychological processes; *mental retardation,* which entails a defect in intellectual functioning such that the person is not capable of performing normal mental tasks appropriate to age and environment; and *senility,* or mental disorders of old age.

Many contemporary psychiatrists and psychologists, on the other hand, are more likely to focus attention on situational factors which are stress producing and on the individual's capacity for "coping" successfully with stress (see Seligman, 1997; Strack, Argyle, and Schwartz, 1991). Also, coping with or "surviving" in an urban environment have become popular psychological themes in the mass media. An increasing number of mental health professionals and therapists have taken up these themes in their work with patients, particularly those therapists who identify with the community mental health movement.

Instruments for measuring rates of mental illness in a population have been equally varied, and different indicators produce different results. One of the most frequently used measures of the incidence of mental illness has been hospitalization or confinement to a facility for the mentally ill. Using this approach, Goldhamer and Marshall (1962) computed the rate of admission to hospitals for psychosis in the state of Massachusetts between 1840 and 1940. They reasoned that because that particular time period was a century of greatly increasing urbanization, mental health rates should also have risen accordingly. Their findings at first glance seemed to support this conclusion, as rates of admission for psychosis more than doubled over this period, from 41 per 100,000 in 1840 to about 85 per 100,000 in 1941. However, controlling for age, Goldhamer and Marshall found that for those between twenty and fifty years of age there was no significant change in admission rates during the entire century studied, and that only persons over fifty experienced higher admission rates. This difference probably is accounted for by the fact that it was easier for rural and farm people to care for the older mentally ill members of their families at home than it is for city people living in less spacious or in isolated accommodations. Thus, the findings of this study did not support the theory that mental illness has increased with greater urbanization.

In another classic study using rates of hospitalization as an index, Faris and Dunham (1939) plotted the residential distribution of all patients admitted to public and private mental hospitals from the city of Chicago and computed rates of hospital admission for various diagnostic categories of mental illness. Although no urban-rural comparisons were made, the study did demonstrate the significant fact that hospitalized mental illness was not randomly distributed through the city. Highest rates were found near the center of the city, in areas of high population mobility and low socioeconomic status. Conversely the lowest rates were from the stable residential areas of higher socioeconomic status.

There are major shortcomings of hospitalization as an indicator of mental illness which apply to the kind of studies cited above. Hospitalization rates are inadequate unless all mentally ill members of the population have roughly an equal chance of being hospitalized or confined. To the extent that rates of hospitalization can be influenced by such factors as closeness or accessibility to a mental hospital, the availability of bed space in such facilities, differences in tolerance for symptoms of mental illness among subgroups of the population, or by the existence of alternatives to hospitalization, hospitalization rates will be poor indicators of the true rate of mental illness in a population. Gibbs (1962) compared rates of mental hospitalization with some noninstitutional indicators of the amount of psychopathology in the population, using data from the forty-eight continental states. Using such measures as deaths from mental disorder, deaths from suicide, deaths from duodenal ulcer, deaths from alcoholism, and the number of homicide victims under four years of age as indicators of psychopathology in the population, he found that rates of mental hospitalization were not closely related to noninstitutional indicators.

Other studies of community mental health have been based on sample surveys, in which the respondents are asked to assess their own personality adjustment. In some cases the results are then coded and rated by professionals skilled enough to classify the findings in psychiatric or psychological terms. One of the most thorough surveys of personal adjustment using this approach was reported by Gurin, Verroff, and Feld (1960). Researchers from the University of Michigan Survey Research Center interviewed a large national sample of adults who were representative of the total population in terms of sex, income, education, occupation, and place of residence. Nearly 25 percent of those interviewed had at one time in their lives felt sufficiently troubled to need help, mainly in the areas of marriage, parenthood, work, and personal psychological problems. Feelings of general dissatisfaction were widespread among the respondents and showed no consistent relationship to place of residence, urban or rural. Differences by place of residence were fewer than those based on education, income, and sex. In effect, the survey found no greater symptoms of poor mental health among the residents of metropolitan areas than among those residing in the less urbanized areas of the United States.

The Leightons (1957) surveyed a rural county and found that over half of the population had at some time or other exhibited psychoneurotic symptoms and that 77 percent reported having had psychosomatic disorders to a significant degree. A study of the Hutterites, a closely knit religious sect residing primarily in the nonindustrial, nonurban parts of the Midwest, indicated a sufficient rate of psychoses and other untreated types of mental illness to challenge further the conventional view that people living in stable, self-contained rural communities are less likely to experience symptoms of mental illness than those living in larger urban communities (Eaton and Weil, 1955). Likewise, Lewis's (1951) study of a small Mexican agricultural village found considerable evidence of violence, cruelty, suffering, and strife both within the village and in its relations with other villages. Far from being harmonious and free of stress, the residents of such rural communities may be subject to as great a degree of anxiety and personal adjustment problems as those residing in urban areas. Studies of the incidence of schizophrenia among primitive people living in preliterate and tribal societies (see Demareth, 1955; Lin, 1959) indicate that the serious psychoses are widely prevalent in such preurban societies, contrary to common belief.

Clearly there is no simple yes-or-no answer to the very complex questions as to whether modern urban civilization has led to an increase in the amount of mental illness in the population. The research results to date do not support such a conclusion, but the possibility cannot yet be completely discounted. In general, the amount of mental illness in any society or population will depend upon the genetic composition of the population, the prevalence of certain types of trauma or pathogenic processes in early family life, the kinds of stresses to which adults are exposed late in life, cultural definitions of mental illness, and the exercise of potential social controls, which may limit the development of symptoms. The relative weights and particular forms of causative factors, and the degree to which the various urban and non-urban environments are contributing factors have not yet been conclusively established.

Variations in Mental Health within Metropolitan Areas

Although the data comparing mental illness in urban areas with that in rural areas are inconclusive, it is far more certain that within metropolitan areas, mental disorders are not evenly distributed and vary widely from subarea to subarea or group to group. Also, the distribution of particular types of mental disorders, such as the psychoses, neuroses, and psychosomatic disorders, is widely varied.

Social class appears to be one of the most important factors related to variations in rates of mental illness. The Midtown Manhattan Study (Srole, 1975) was one of the more notable attempts to assess the relationship between mental health and social class. In this study approximately 1,700 white adult residents of mid-Manhattan between the ages of twenty and fifty-nine were randomly selected for interviews in their homes. The interviewers asked questions about depression, immaturity, psychosomatic illness, and so on.

Two psychiatrists, from whom information that might identify the socioeconomic class of the respondents was withheld to prevent possible class biases from influencing the results, independently rated the number and severity of the reported psychological symptoms and placed each person into one of four mental health categories: well, mild symptom formation, moderate symptom formation, and psychologically impaired. The well group had no significant symptoms, whereas the impaired group had symptoms of mental illness severe enough to handicap them greatly in coping with everyday life. The mild and moderate groups were between these two extremes: they indicated some degree of psychological difficulty, but they were able nevertheless to carry on their adult activities successfully.

The results did not demonstrate a relationship between mental health and such variables as immigrant generation status, national origins, religious identity, or urban-rural origins. The age of the respondents and their marital status was only moderately correlated with the mental health ratings. But of all the variables, *social class* was by far the best predictor of mental health and mental illness. In the lowest socioeconomic stratum of the sample, only 4.6 percent of the respondents were rated as well or free of symptoms, in contrast to the 30 percent of the highest socioeconomic stratum who were symptom free.

Although only 12.5 percent of the highest socioeconomic stratum was rated as psychologically impaired, nearly half (47.3 percent) of the lowest stratum was classified as impaired. Thus the members of the lowest status group were four times more likely to be severely impaired psychologically than the highest status group, and were six times less likely to significantly escape the symptoms of mental illness and enter the "well" category. Later follow-up studies by Srole (1980) concluded even more strongly that urban living did not adversely affect mental health and that socioeconomic status was a far more significant factor.

Another earlier major study demonstrating a strong relationship between social class and mental illness was conducted in New Haven, Connecticut, by Hollingshead and Redlich (1958). The study was based on data for at least 98 percent of the residents who were receiving psychiatric care at the time of the survey. This included not only those who were hospitalized but also those who were receiving outpatient care from private practitioners and clinics. Dividing the community into five social classes, the study found that the prevalence of treated pyschosis was more than three times greater in the lowest class than in the highest class. Also, once a lowest-class patient is diagnosed as psychotic and committed to a mental health hospital, that patient tends to remain hospitalized nearly twice as long as patients in the highest social class. For neurosis, the relationship to social class was just the reverse, with higher rates positively associated with higher social status.

LIFESTYLE AND ADJUSTMENT TO URBAN LIVING

The question of what it is about lower-class status in an urban environment that produces a negative impact on mental health, in contrast to higher-status groups that seem more successfully to escape the most debilitating impact, cries for a reasonable explanation. One possible explanation comes from the new urban sociology, which implies that the urban poor are powerless victims of harsh economic forces imposed by wealthier and more powerful groups in the form of capitalistic and free market policies (Bradshaw and Wallace, 1996).

Another, perhaps more fruitful and direct approach lies with the concept of *lifestyle*. Lifestyles abound among various urban groupings, some of which bear at least some relationship to social class. If any particular urban style of life can be seen as a means of accomodation to the conditions of urban life, or as an adjustment to ease the stresses and strains of urban living, then it can also be argued that some ways of life provide a better fit than others to the demands of urban living. From this perspective, the problems lie not so much with the particular conditions of the urban environment as with the way in which groups of people adjust or accommodate to this environment (Parducci, 1995).

Gans (1968) has earlier presented a discussion of five urban ways of life, based mainly on social class and on stages of the family and life cycle, which suggests how analysis of lifestyles may provide clues to the quality of adjustment to urban life. The first lifestyle is that of the *cosmopolites*. Cosmopolites include those who consciously choose to reside in an urban environment to participate in the cultural activities the city has to offer, which are highly important to them. They occupy varying socioeconomic levels, but tend to be intellectuals and professionals, or are artistically inclined.

The *unmarried and childless* constitute a second lifestyle grouping. Such groups tend to cluster in apartment house areas that also provide an active night life, such as singles bars and other places of entertainment. These groups participate actively in the varied activities of the city. Their residence in the city may be transitory, however, as many of them move to single-family housing in the suburbs when and if they enter the child-rearing stages of their life cycle.

The third major lifestyle is that of *ethnic villagers* (see chapter 4 for a discussion of this lifestyle in another context). Ethnic villagers are immigrant or migrant groups who attempt to carry on in urban enclaves the peasant life of their native regions. They create their own close-knit social structures, which help cushion or isolate them from what they consider to be the harmful effects of the city, including other competing ethnic or racial groups whom they may attempt to prevent from encroaching on their "own" neighborhoods.

The fourth group, the *deprived,* are those who are in the city largely because of the handicaps of extreme poverty, emotional problems, or racial discrimination, which leave them with no alternatives but to remain in deteriorating housing or blighted neighborhoods in the worst areas of the central cities.

The final group, the *trapped and the downwardly mobile,* consists of those who cannot afford to move when a neighborhood changes for the worse and those who can no longer compete economically for good housing, such as retirees on fixed pensions or widows who have lost the income of a breadwinner. Such groups may suffer a visible loss of status and well-being as their situations grow worse with the changing circumstances of their environment.

Of the five lifestyles suggested by Gans, only the last two represent the types of social and personality disorganization that traditionally have been associated with urban living. The deprived and the trapped or downwardly mobile are subjected to stresses and strains for which they may not have the psychic or material resources to cope successfully. Under such circumstances, it is no wonder that such groups represent a large segment of the lowest socioeconomic levels that usually have the highest mental illness rates in the cities.

The ethnic villagers are often protected from the disorganizing effects of urban life. But under rapidly changing circumstances, such as are caused by the encroachments of urban renewal or invading external groups that may rapidly change the character of their neighborhood, even the ethnic villagers may be dramatically subjected to new stresses or strains beyond their control. Thus, whether the ethnic villagers do, in fact, produce a style of life ideally suited to the conditions of urban living remains circumstantially problematic.

The urban singles have received a good deal of attention from the mass media in recent years. Singles bars with their nightly crowds of unattached young people looking for companionship, "one night stands," or short-term affairs without long-term commitments, and large singles-only apartment complexes that function in ways similar to a resort hotel are part of the popular image of a supposedly fun and carefree "swinging" lifestyle. Even though sociological documentation is somewhat scanty for this group, there is no certain reason to suspect that such a lifestyle is particularly conducive to satisfactory adjustment to city life or to superior personality integration in the urban context.

On the other hand, neither is there clear evidence that young singles are more prone to serious personality disorders than other lifestyle segments of the urban population. Palen (1975, pp. 125–126) describes the lifestyles of singles as more humdrum in reality than popular images suggest. For example, most of the young singles are faced with the everyday problems of making a living, finding a decent place to live, making friends, eventually finding a suitable mate, and so on. Hardly social or economic radicals, they are in Palen's view "trying to achieve essentially middle class material goals without being able to rely on many of the usual institutional supports for their activities."

A study by Starr and Carns (1973) of singles in their early and midtwenties who were working in Chicago indicated that most singles do not live in singles apartment complexes and that such groups had no community roots in the housing areas or neighborhoods in which they resided. In addition, the singles bars that were often frequented did not necessarily serve as satisfactory substitutes for an active community involvement, and interest in frequenting such places would drop off rapidly after six months or so, or by the time the respondents began to reach their late twenties. For most working singles, the workplace is a more effective site for meeting people and forming relationships than places of residence or places of entertainment. At any rate, the question of the degree to which Gans's unmarried and childless category cushions its members from disorganizing aspects of urban life remains largely unanswered, except that the detachment of the singles from undesirable commitments or obligations probably does protect them from some of the kinds of problems experienced by the "deprived" or the "trapped."

The cosmopolitans have received the least attention in the sociological literature on urban lifestyles. This is unfortunate, for it is among this group that one must look in order to satisfactorily answer the question, Is a truly urban lifestyle emerging? One can argue that problems of community or personality disorganization are most commonly associated with those urban groups with the least urbanized lifestyles. On the other hand, those groups that have made a satisfactory adjustment to urban life, are attuned to its opportunities and demands, and actively partake in the unique activities the city has to offer tend to be ignored as objects of inquiry because they are not at the core of commonly perceived social problems. A more extended discussion of cosmopolitan lifestyles is therefore in order.

COSMOPOLITAN LIFESTYLE AS AN URBAN "IDEAL TYPE"

Just as Wirth (1938) and Simmel (1950) had earlier postulated a set of traits or characteristics that would provide a composite view of the urban personality as an "ideal type," so we intend here to postulate a set of characteristics or traits representing our view of an ideal type model of a cosmopolitan lifestyle. In contrast to the views of Wirth, however, our model does not assume that personality pathology or disorder is the inevitable product of urban living. It asserts instead that under certain circumstances an urban lifestyle can be perceived that provides a "best fit" with the conditions and demands of urban living, and that is positive in the sense that it maximizes the pleasures and satisfactions of urban living. At the same time, this model of a cosmopolitan lifestyle protects the individual from undesirable distortions of his or her personality in the process. What we are trying to do is to identify those lifestyle characteristics or traits most likely to be associated with good mental health in the metropolitan setting. Although such a model is still largely speculative, we shall cite some of the arguments that seem to reinforce it.

The cosmopolitan lifestyle we present here is not representative of the majority of people currently residing in urban areas. In fact, most current urban dwellers probably are not fully attuned to or satisfied with the conditions of urban living that they now experience and would prefer to live in another kind of environment (see the concluding section on public opinion). Most urban dwellers have not yet accommodated themselves to urban living by the adaptation of lifestyles which in our view provide the best fit or accommodation to living in metropolitan communities. Instead it is useful to think of the cosmopolitan lifestyle as a potential about which we can find a number of examples from among limited segments of the urban population. The following elements comprise our model of the cosmopolitan lifestyle.

Knowledgeability

A wide knowledge of the urban community and its resources is an essential characteristic of this lifestyle, if one is to benefit fully from urban life. One must know what cultural, economic, and service facilities are available and be able to use them. For example, if one wishes to pursue a career in an urban environment, one must be familiar with many of the occupations making up an urban labor force, be familiar with the qualifications or training necessary for any given occupation, know where to apply for such positions or for the opportunity to train for them, and know the most effective routes to arrive at a given work site at the most reasonable cost of time, money, and distance. If one wishes to enjoy cultural and social activities, one must know what is available, the time and place, and the criteria for admission. Finding a good doctor, dentist, counselor, attorney, auto mechanic, hairdresser, or other dispensers of desired professional services, and knowing where to find other people with similar interests or with whom one may wish to associate are further examples of the need to be knowledgeable of the urban environment in order to successfully live a cosmopolitan lifestyle.

Such knowledge can be acquired in two ways. The first involves completing some period of formal education and becoming literate enough to use formal informational systems, such as libraries, newspapers and magazines, directories, maps, printed instructions, and, increasingly, computers and automated telephone systems. The inability to use telephone directories, read instructions on application forms, follow printed instructions, or to read signs or maps can be highly frustrating and discouraging to the functionally illiterate, and the need for a relatively high level of literacy to function effectively in an urban environment has long been widely recognized.

The second source of such knowledge comes through experience with living in an urban environment. Thus, those who have been born and reared in an urban environment or are descendants of urban dwellers are more likely to have the appropriate kinds of knowledge than those who are recent migrants from nonurban environments. Through experience, urban dwellers may acquire a kind of "street wisdom" enabling them to accurately judge potential rewards or dangers and to avoid situations their experience tells them may be undesirable.

Skill

The old adage "practice makes perfect" applies here. One must develop skills in using urban resources, such as knowing how to find places or ask for directions; getting on or off escalators, elevators, subway cars, and buses; filling out questionnaires and forms; communicating with others in situations where exchanges of information are necessary, and dealing with bureaucratic functionaries to receive desired services.

Skill and knowledgeability are closely connected because the skills necessary for successful urban living can best be acquired through various combinations of experience and formal education. In many large cities, the public schools have begun to facilitate this process through such devices as field trips, apprenticeships, and other skill-oriented forms of training (see chapter 9 on education and welfare). Lofland (1973, pp. 158–159), in a somewhat different vein, views the appropriate knowledge and skills as a prerequisite for having fun or adventure in the urban setting, characterizing such experiences as exhilarating or exciting for sophisticated urbanites. As she remarks, they "sometimes find it enjoyable to seek out a little danger, to court a little fear, to engender a little anxiety. They sometimes find it enjoyable, that is, to go adventuring."

Tolerance

To the extent that urban communities contain diverse peoples with unlike social characteristics and behavior patterns, successful accommodation to urban living would seem to require a high degree of tolerance and flexibility. Becker and Horowitz (1972), in writing of the high degree of tolerance shown for "deviance" in the city of San Francisco, identify a "culture of civility" which they believe to be relatively uncommon in many other American cities. An implicit "live and let live" kind of social contract exists where "straights" do not become outraged by "freaks," and the latter have a greater degree of freedom for engaging in their preferred lifestyles, provided they do not go beyond certain implicit but agreed-upon boundaries. As the city becomes widely known for allowing certain kinds of deviants or eccentrics to live with a degree of acceptance and a minimum of harassment, it continues to attract more of these unconventional types, who, in a mutual display of tolerance for one another, tend to increase the overall tolerance levels of the city as a whole. Karp, Stone, and Yoels (1977) suggest that Becker and Horowitz's model of civility in San Francisco is too static and does not take into account the possibility that tolerance sometimes disintegrates when ultra lifestyle groups begin to test the limits of a community's tolerance by pushing their deviance to unacceptable extremes. Fischer (1971, pp. 847–856) qualifies the relationship between urbanization and the amount of tolerance for such groups as racial or ethnic minorities by suggesting that tolerance for diversity is probably more a byproduct of the social characteristics of the residents of a given community than it is of community size.

Our purpose here, however, has not been to demonstrate the association between tolerance and urbanization, but rather to suggest that some degree of moral relativity and tolerance for diversity may protect individuals from the kinds of strains and frustrations experienced by those who are more rigidly intolerant and prejudiced as they attempt to deal with a wide range of people who might be unacceptable to them because of their own prejudices, but with whom they are unable to avoid contact in a highly diversified urban environment. Any form of bigotry based on race, ethnicity, religion, gender or sexual preferences, socioeconomic status, or any other kind of lifestyle would, of course, definitely *not* conform to the model of a cosmopolitan lifestyle being suggested here. Whether or not a high degree of tolerance is actually a widespread reality in the current urban scene, it is a necessary and reasonable characteristic of an "idealized" cosmopolitan life style.

A sense of humor about the many inconsistencies, paradoxes, and dilemmas of urban living certainly eases the adjustment process, and we include this characteristic as a component of a tolerant and flexible cosmopolitan attitude. It is no accident that professional comedians are among the top celebrities of the mass media world of entertainment and are often admired as individuals who are helpful in relieving the stresses of urban living through their comedy. Even elected political figures sometimes successfully finesse politically embarrasing situations with highly selective humorous remarks or self-parodies, as was frequently the case with both the Republican and Democratic presidential canditates during the 2000 presidential election period!

Self-awareness

The urbanite is daily confronted with a bewildering variety of choices and is constantly bombarded with one form of persuasion or another, be it demands on time, energy, or income. Some observers have described the conflict of making choices from the bewildering assortment of urban alternatives as somewhat akin to the conflict of choosing what to eat in a well-stocked cafeteria! In this case, the range and variety of choices available to the individual probably does increase with the size of the community. To make intelligent choices, the individual must be aware of his or her own abilities, limitations, likes and dislikes, and needs. One must be aware of how one's own needs can best be satisfied and be able to make the appropriate choices from among the competing alternatives. One must be able to take on satisfying relationships and activities as well as to abandon those that are detrimental to one's own well-being. Also, the ability to "travel light," not excessively burdened by the obligations of property or tradition, in order to pursue one's own interests, might very well constitute a component of a cosmopolitan lifestyle. Thus a "take it or leave it" attitude toward people or things potentially can supply a degree of freedom and mobility for those who are most in tune with the wide range of opportunities afforded in an urban environment.

Meaningful Work Roles

Having an occupational role that is meaningful, prestigious, and visible in the urban context may be among the more important dimensions of a cosmopolitan lifestyle, particularly in an urban-industrial society. A blacksmith, snake charmer, or horse trader may be accorded very little social standing by urbanites, but an attorney, television talk show host, disk jockey, journalist, actor, musician, social worker, physician, police officer, or public official may be recognized as being in an occupation that makes a useful or interesting contribution to the quality of urban life. Such areas as politics and government, science, education, the professions, business management, the arts, social and health services, and popular entertainment would meet our criteria for inclusion here as a component of a cosmopolitan lifestyle. Although many of the workers in these areas have above average incomes, the amount of money earned at an occupation is not the prime consideration here (even though having an adequate income would certainly be necessary). The sense that one is engaged in work that is pertinent to the interests of the community, however, can provide a better sense of belonging to and participating in the urban community than an occupation having no apparent link to what is widely perceived to be important. (See chapter 7 on urban economic institutions for further analysis of urban work roles and the urban labor force.)

Positive, Appreciative Attitudes

Finally, liking the urban environment, its crowds, its physical development, its facilities, its amenities, and its resources, and having a positive attitude toward participating in the cultural activities of the urban community are essential ingredients of a cosmopolitan lifestyle. This dimension comes closest to what Gans had in mind when he first suggested the idea that a cosmopolitan lifestyle goes further than most in cushioning the individual from the harshest, most unpleasant, and most disorganizing aspects of urban living. One interesting example of this aspect is the delight with which many urbanites enjoy "people-watching" or "rubbing elbows" in crowded and busy urban settings. New York's Greenwich Village, Central Park, and Rockefeller Plaza are examples that immediately come to mind. In the suburbs, one can see the newer enclosed shopping malls serving this same function for many of their users.

Although we are not asserting that a cosmopolitan lifestyle, as we have described it, is representative of the populations now residing in urban settings, nevertheless many of the components of such a lifestyle are relatively commonplace. One can find many examples of the attitudes and behavior associated with a cosmopolitan lifestyle being considered desirable goals. Cosmopolitan attitudes and behavior are implicit in the programs of public school systems and institutions of higher learning; they are integrated into the child-rearing practice of many urbanites, and countless examples can be found among mass media heroes and celebrities, television talk show hosts and news commentators, and elected officials. Widely known figures such as Bill Cosby, Robin Williams, Peter Jennings, Ted Koppel, Woody Allen, Colin Powell, ex-President Clinton, Barbara Walters, Gore Vidal, Oprah Winfrey, Brian Lamb, Kathy Lee Gifford, Whoopie Goldberg, Wolf Blitzer, the late John Kennedy Jr. and other various members of the Kennedy family are among those that have occurred to the author's students as they attempted to associate the concept of a cosmopolitan lifestyle with examples commonly visible in the mass media.

We wish to make it clear that it is not our intention to assert any claims of moral superiority for a cosmopolitan lifestyle in comparison to other alternatives; such judgments are best left to the reader. We do believe, however, that a concern for the mental health and well-being of persons residing in urban settings should lead to further investigations of the relationship between lifestyle and personality adjustment in the context of specific social and physical urban environments. Although such investigations in the field of urban sociology are not as currently frequent as one would like, the fields of psychology and psychiatry have recently begun to focus on the more positive aspects of personality and lifestyle, and on the social contexts in which a more satisfying psychology of "happiness," "joy," or "creativity" can be observed. For example, a recent biography of the late Eric Erikson, a prominent psychoanalyst, notes that he tried to do something that Sigmund Freud failed to do, which was to offer a psychoanalytically based portrait of "human happiness." In this way, Erikson challenged psychoanalysis to create a more positive vision of the potential for the psyche to achieve a state of full energy and good health (Friedman, 1999). Further, Martin Seligman, the 1998 president of the American Psychological Association, has called for a more positive psychology of "joy" that would use rigorous scientific methods to study questions relating to psychological "strengths" of ordinary people for dealing with everyday aspects of life, with respect to such central lifestyle concerns as love, work, and play (*New York Times,* April 28, 1998, p. B10). And a growing body of research in this direction appears to be supportive of the validity of our model of an "ideal type" of cosmopolitan urban lifestyle developed in this chapter (see Seligman, 1997; Parducci, 1995; Csikszentmihalyi, 1996; Strack, Argyle, and Schwartz, 1991; and Argyle, 1987).

EVERYDAY BEHAVIOR IN PUBLIC PLACES

Some of the most transitory and diffuse patterns of urban social organization can be referred to under the general heading of *collective behavior*, for want of a better term. This includes the kind of behavior that occurs in public and semipublic places, such as streets, sidewalks, parks, plazas, public buildings, theaters, meeting halls, and other gathering places. This public behavior sometimes takes the form of crowds, mobs, assemblies, audiences, or spectators. What is important here is that such patterns of collective behavior generally involve person-to-person encounters between strangers (see Lofland, 1998). The sheer volume of such potential interaction between strangers in a large city is illustrated by Whyte (1974), who has estimated that on one short city block on New York City's Lexington Avenue—between 57th and 58th streets—some 38,000 people pass by on an average weekday.

Ever since the earlier writing of Simmel (1950), who believed the everyday tempo of city life significantly affects the social psychology of urbanites, many observers have tended to couch the everyday interaction of strangers in public urban places in highly negative terms. For example, they have often been described as uncivilized, insensitive, indifferent, uncaring, or blasé, if not downright rude or aggressive. One widely shared negative image has been restated by anthropologist Edward Hall (1969, p. 174): "Virtually everything about American cities today . . . drives men apart, alienating them from each other. The recent and shocking instances in which people have been beaten and even murdered while their neighbors looked on without even picking up a phone indicates how far this trend toward alienation has progressed."

Open and flagrant examples of pilfering and looting that sometimes takes place during natural disasters such as floods or during technological breakdowns, such as electric power blackouts, further feed the image of everyday city life as potentially chaotic and disorganized.

The problem with these images, however valid they may be in some instances, is that they do not adequately explain how everyday city life is possible in any form. Millions upon millions of urbanites manage to go about their daily business of living in a routinized pattern with a minimum of disruption. This, in spite of the negative factors, suggests that there may be some degree of order to the process, no matter how fragile it may appear. In the last two decades or so, a number of scholars have begun to readdress themselves to the interaction patterns of everyday public behavior to discover whether order or regularity underlies such behavior, and whether such behavior has meaning that can be made sense of by the participants (or at least by objective social observers). Much of this work has emanated from the followers of Goffman (1963, p. 4), who has suggested that the informal rules of conduct in streets and other public places where people commonly gather should be the object of inquiry if one wishes to understand fully the most diffuse forms of social organization that constitute everyday urban behavior.

Lofland (1971, 1998) maintains that public ordered life between strangers is possible because urbanites successfully have created what she calls a workable social contract or a public "social bargain." This is based on the need recognized by urbanites that they must protect one another so that all can carry on the business of living. According to Karp, Stone, and Yoels (1977, p. 110), this social bargain demands that persons cooperate with one another enough to ensure some intelligibility and order in their everyday lives, while seeking at the same time to keep their involvement with one another at a manageable minimum. Urbanites must take others into account at the same time that they seek to protect their personal privacy. They are required to strike a balance between involvement, indifference, and cooperation with one another as they seek to minimize involvement and maximize social order. At a more concrete level, the empirical question they put forth is, "What are the types of normative conventions followed by city persons that maximize intelligibility and predictability in their relations with others while simultaneously maximizing their own sense of privacy in public?" (Karp, Stone, and Yoel, 1977, p. 113).

Some research by Wolff (1973), based on close, careful observations in natural settings, nicely demonstrates how everyday urban life is ordered along the lines just suggested. He studied pedestrian behavior on 42nd Street in Manhattan, and was able to show through a series of videotape pictures that a number of consistent patterns of accommodation were made by the supposedly autonomous strangers in the streets, which demonstrated a high degree of cooperation among them. These patterns have been summarized as follows:

1. Step-and-slide pattern. As persons pass one another, there is a "slight angling of the body, a turning of the shoulder, and an almost imperceptible slide step—a sort of step and slide." The interpretation here is that pedestrians cooperate with one another by twisting their bodies so as to minimize the amount of physical contact.

2. The head-over-the-shoulder pattern. Pedestrians maintain a head over the shoulder relationship with persons walking less than five feet in front of them to see what is occurring ahead, while at the same time avoiding stumbling onto the feet of the persons in front.

3. The spread effect. This involves persons walking in the same direction distributing themselves over the fullest width that the sidewalks will allow. Presumably, this maximizes the efficiency of movement.

4. Detouring. This occurs when a person forced to detour around another person returns to the original path once the detour has been accomplished.

5. Avoiding perceptual objects. People tend to treat perceptually distinct parts of the sidewalk surfaces, such as grating, as obstructions to be avoided whenever possible.

6. Monitoring. Persons tend continually to monitor the immediate environment in order to avoid collisions, as well as to evaluate the potential behavior of others. They scan the faces of persons coming from the opposite direction and turn or stop in response to out of the ordinary facial expressions that may signal some unusual situation to be monitored.

Karp (1973) has studied the behavior of people in Times Square pornographic bookstores and movie theaters, supposedly the epitome of an anonymous inner city area. He found that the people, who were engaged in somewhat unconventional behavior, were nevertheless concerned with being defined as "proper" by total strangers in their immediate vicinity and would adjust their behavior accordingly. They would attempt to hide, obscure, or shield their interest in buying or using pornographic materials from those strangers who might be around them before entering a pornographic bookstore or theater. Once inside, the normative structure seemed to demand a careful avoidance of either eye or physical contact with other customers. Karp concluded that the persons in this semipublic urban setting were involved in a highly structured social situation in which the norms of privacy were highly standardized and readily understood by the participants.

Lofland (1971, p. 226) has suggested that people will use a variety of ways to protect their self-esteem when in the presence of strangers in public places. She states that "if a person is to exist as a social being . . . there must be some minimal guarantees that in interaction with others he will receive the affirmation and confirmation of himself as a 'right.'" She mentions the following as major techniques or devices used by persons in public places to protect their self-images under the scrutiny of strangers:

1. Checking for readiness—persons will check their appearance, making sure that their hair is in place, zippers are zipped, and so on, before entering a potential encounter situation.

2. Taking a reading—this involves stopping to take stock of the social setting before entering it.

3. Reaching a position—once having decided on the spot or the point they wish to occupy, persons tend to make a direct approach to that spot in as inconspicuous a way as possible in order to avoid remaining under the social spotlight longer than is absolutely necessary.

Karp, Stone, and Yoels (1977, pp. 112–113) interpret some of these regularities of encounters in public places by suggesting that society provides a baseline of knowledge in the form of rules or norms which provide a shared meaning to the participants, in spite of slight variations of meaning from person to person or situation to situation: "Without this commonsense sharing of knowledge, social order would be impossible. Such social knowledge is extremely far-reaching, encompassing literally thousands of social conventions." However, they also recognize that the meaning of any social act is situationally specific, and that knowledge must be continually reevaluated as one moves from one social setting to another.

The Impact of Public Spaces

Another body of literature focuses on the fact that different cities will produce markedly different patterns among strangers in such public spaces as streets, sidewalks, or parks. Cities differ in their attitudes to the suitability of using the streets for walking, "people-watching," or other similarly pleasurable participation in the public life of the community. Detroiters, for example, many of whom view their own central business district as unsafe for pedestrian activity, will often comment on the pleasant, safe, and pleasurable ambiance of street life of nearby Toronto. Goffman (1963, p. 200) and others have compared the ambiance of public streets in Paris with those in England and the United States. He refers to the greater "looseness" of the streets of Paris, where one can eat from a loaf of bread while walking to and from work or become heatedly involved in a passionate conversation. These variations in patterns are often accompanied by varying images of different cities as enjoyable places in which to live or visit. Speaking of Paris, Hall (1969, p. 175) observes: "Paris is known as a city in which the outdoors has been made attractive to people and where it is not only possible but pleasurable to stretch one's legs, breathe, sniff the air, and take in the people and the city . . . It is noteworthy that the little streets and alleys too narrow to accept most vehicles not only provide variety but are a constant reminder that Paris is for people."

Observers such as Jane Jacobs (1961) and William H. Whyte (1989) focus on those areas within cities that are widely known to provide a diversity of activities, which draw people to them for differing degrees of contact, excitement, or enjoyment with many other people similarly attracted. Boston's North End, Greenwich Village and the midtown areas of New York City, San Francisco's Fisherman's Wharf, or the Yorkville area of Toronto are among such places. Jacobs suggests that the density and diversity of such areas, as well as the effective use of space, are the basis for an active, interesting street life, and she criticizes much of current city planning for not taking these aspects of urban design into account (see chapter 13). Whyte calls for the creation of parks and plazas having an abundance of movable seating placed in the areas of highest activity or where those using them can conveniently view interesting activities or objects. Widened sidewalks for greater pedestrian access and comfort, pleasant landscaping, and the availability of food vendors are some of the amenities advocated by Whyte (1989) as ways of enhancing the quality of those areas of highest pedestrian activity.

Whyte's observations of such areas in midtown Manhattan over a four-year period showed an increase in the number of persons using open spaces and parks, more street entertainers and more people eating outdoors or having impromptu street conferences. As his article concludes, "schmoozing, smootching, noshing, ogling are getting better all the time. The Central City is alive and well" (1974, p. 30). Somewhat along the lines of Whyte and others, Mitchell Duneier has more recently focused on a long term study of secondhand book peddlers who operate on the streets of certain sections

Street vendors add to the spice of life on city streets.

of Greenwich Village in lower Manhattan and concluded that they were assets to a "vibrant, vital city." He presents the itinerant booksellers' routine interactions with potential and actual customers as integral to a healthy neighborhood (see chapter 5), and they provide extra sets of eyes that keep the street safe while providing "book-crazed New Yorkers with inexpensive reading materials." In a city with strong racial and social class divisions, he observes that the sidewalk book tables draw a wide cross section of browsers and readers, "fostering interaction between people who might never otherwise mix" (Duneier, 2000).

The value of such observations is that they also may help to explain why many city areas are perceived negatively as depersonalized, lonely, or potentially dangerous; they can be explained by the absence of characteristics or amenities such as those just described. Thus, there may be some lessons here for the design or redesign of many urban spaces in large metropolitan communities that are now perceived to lack such positive qualities

Karp, Stone, and Yoels, upon whose work this section has drawn heavily, provide an apt conclusion for our brief discussion of the social organization of everyday urban life:

> The city can be a humane, personal place. If we agree upon the value of creating even more humane cities, we must understand the normative demands of public interaction. We must understand the limitations and potentialities of public city life. To do that, we must not casually take at face value the readily accessible and commonly expressed images of city life promoted by the mass media and frequently sustained by our most distinguished literary and philosophical figures. If our conceptualizations of the urban

environment become too rigid (or too narrow), we severely restrict the range of possible experiences that urban residents may undergo. (1977, p. 127)

THE CULTURAL SYMBOLISM AND IMAGERY OF URBAN LIFE

To develop a completely objective, value-free view of urban communities and urban life is probably impossible, for people's attitudes to them are strongly subjective. The modern city is an object of hatred for many people, but it is also a love object to many others. Still others may have more ambivalent, love-hate sentiments toward the city. The modern city may be perceived or valued in an extremely wide variety of ways, including the following:

> As a feast—a place of novelty and excitement, of fashion and style, of ideas and artifacts, a center of sumptuous consumption, of diversity and delight. As a den of iniquity—a place where vice and crime abound, and political corruption rides high.

> As a fountainhead of service—a place where health and wealth, the arts and sciences, the educational and welfare services reach their highest levels. As a center of loneliness—a place where man is depersonalized, anonymous, alone, rootless, afraid, uniquely separated from his fellow men. (Wilensky and Lebeaux, 1958, p. 116)

Gist and Fava (1979, p. 573) suggest that it is important to describe what is known of the sentiments and symbols attached to cities, if only to avoid possible attitudinal biases that may color research on urban life. Moreover, such imagery can have real consequences on policy decisions concerning the urban community. For example, if the city is seen as so evil, decayed, or anachronistic that it is beyond salvation, then it may be neglected or abandoned as an object of further investment or planned social intervention. On the other hand, if it is seen as totally satisfactory in its present condition, then the perception very well might be that no further social intervention, other than perhaps the free play of "natural" market forces, is necessary. According to this perspective, the city can easily deal with its own contingencies without help from external agencies (see Banfield, 1974; Greer, 1962; Downs, 1976; Caputo, 1976). Perceptions between these two extremes, which are the most reasonable from our point of view, are more likely to be that urban communities are worth preserving, but that in many cases they need massive intervention and social guidance if they are to remain workable and livable.

Many popular images of the city and attitudes toward urban life have been commonly expressed in the mass media, public opinion surveys, popular music, literature, and films. Our purpose here is briefly to summarize some of the main dimensions of these popular sentiments. Of course, social scientists have produced their own images of urban life, but these have been the major focus of other parts of this book.

Popular Music

The folklorist Botkin (1954) has found that American cities possess a folklore that has grown up around landmarks, streets, and neighborhoods expressed in the form of folk, jazz, or popular music. Much of it also expresses a positive attachment for urban sights and sounds, or a longing for a city or place left behind by a geographically mobile wanderer. The music of the late jazz composer and conductor Duke Ellington, for example, includes many compositions expressing positive affection for his adopted hometown of Harlem, as illustrated by such titles as "Drop Me Off in Harlem," "Harlem Upbeat," "Echoes of Harlem," "Harlem Speaks," "Heart of Harlem," "A Tone Parallel to Harlem," or "Harlem Airshaft" (Ellington, 1973). He has fondly said of the latter:

> So much goes on in a Harlem air shaft. You hear fights, you smell dinner, you hear people making love. You hear intimate gossip floating down. You hear the radio. An air shaft is one great big loudspeaker. You see your neighbor's laundry. You hear the janitor's dogs. The man upstairs aerial falls down and breaks your window. You smell coffee. A wonderful thing that smell. An air shaft has got every contrast. One guy is cooking dried fish and rice and another guy's got a great big turkey. You hear people praying, fighting, snoring. Jitterbugs are jumping up and down always over you, never below you. (Smithsonian, 1973)

New York City has long been the object of affection by a multitude of composers and songwriters, and Nancy Groce (1999), an ethnomusicologist, in a book entitled *New York: Songs of the City,* has identified almost one thousand songs about New York spanning a period of about three centuries, including those by popular twentieth-century composers, such as Rodgers and Hart, George M. Cohan, Irving Berlin, George and Ira Gershwin, Cole Porter, Vernon Duke, Leonard Bernstein, and Betty Comden and Adolph Green. A very brief review of this book by Eric P. Nash (*New York Times Book Review,* August 29, 1999) suggests that another volume "cries out" to be written about end of the twentieth-century New York music "from doo-wop to Brill Building pop and hip-hop."

The other side of the coin is expressed in the city blues, such as the St. Louis, Kansas City, Beale Street, or Memphis blues, which cry out about being down and out, lonely, or abandoned by a loved one in the "cold, impersonal" city. Popular songs such as "I Left My Heart in San Francisco," "Give My Regards to Broadway," "I'll Take Manhattan," "Moon over Miami," "I Love Paris," or "Chicago, My Kind of Town," all express a sentimental desire to return to an urban scene associated with pleasant memories of one sort or another (Charosh, 1968). It has also been suggested that much of the country and western music that has recently become popular, particularly in the cities of the South, Southwest, and the industrial North, attracts an audience of "urban hillbillies" for whom the themes of much contemporary country western music probably remind them of the problems they faced in their recent urban migration (Wilgus, 1971).

One thing that is interesting about popular, folk, or jazz music with an urban theme is that it invariably focuses on the city or on specific subareas of the city. But so far none of it deals with the larger types of metropolitan complexes discussed in chapter 4. Evidently the larger metropolitan unit is too large, too new, too abstract, too impersonal, or too amorphous to have yet taken its place as an object of sentimental identification. We have yet to hear popular expressions of attachment to these larger units in hypothetical song titles such as "I Left My Heart in the San Francisco Metropolitan Statistical Area" or "Give My Regards to the Bos-Wash Megalopolis!"

The City in Popular Literature

The novel and contemporary feature films are two important sources of urban symbolism. In them the city may simply be a setting in which the plot unfolds or it may be an important part of the story line itself. Early in the nineteenth century, a body of literature already existed that depicted an American city as a backdrop for heartless commercialism, poverty, crime and evil, loneliness, and personal defeat. The works of Melville, Hawthorne, and Poe, for example, portray the city as a source of nightmares and other frightening personal experiences. Around the turn of the century, the burgeoning industrial cities of the Northeast and Midwest were viewed with distaste by popular authors such as Upton Sinclair, Frank Norris, and Theodore Dreiser. Prominent social critics such as Jane Addams and Joshua Strong wrote of the city in nonfictional terms with equal distaste (see chapter 3).

In the 1930s and 1940s, John Marquand's novels involving upper-class Bostonians (*The Late George Apley*) or transplants from rigidly stratified small towns to the more open social class structure of big cities (*Point of No Return, H. M. Pulham, Esq.*) provided a satirical view of the class structure of New England towns, large and small, while Meyer Levin's *The Old Bunch* and James T. Farrell's *Studs Lonigan* vividly portrayed peer group relations among the adolescents and young adults of Chicago's well-defined hyphenated American ethnic subcommunities. F. Scott Fitzgerald portrayed the naiveté of Midwesterners transplanted into the more cynical and worldly urban East (*The Great Gatsby*), and much of John O'Hara's work (*Appointment in Samara, Rage to Live, Butterfield Eight, Ten North Frederick*) often contrasted Manhattan with his semifictional hometown of Gibbsville, Pennsylvania, from which financially able natives would occasionally escape to carry on nefarious activities in the anonymous big city.

In the 1950s, Saul Bellow's semiautobiographical *The Adventures of Augie March* evoked a vivid sense of Chicago as the environmental setting in which a young man comes of age. Mordecai Richter's *The Adventures of Duddy Kravits* used the city of Montreal in much the same way in his similarly titled novel. The city as Armageddon has been another theme of some novels, with Nathaniel West's *The Day of the Locust* a case in point. In this work, Los Angeles is the setting in which a set of unrelated circumstances eventually comes together in such a way as to produce senseless mass violence and self-destruction among hordes of people crowded in the streets at the premier of a Hollywood movie. Doris Lessing's *Memoirs of a Survivor* projects the ultimate collapse and destruction of the fabric of urban life in response to a breakdown in the ecological order upon which the survival of the city depends. Similar themes are repeated in countless popular science fiction works.

Tom Wolfe, in the 1980s, wrote *Bonfire of the Vanities,* a searing and satirical portrait of a New York City sharply divided by social class, race, ethnicity, corrupt municipal politics, and cynical opportunism by the local press, all of which come into play as a result of a tragic traffic incident involving an elite, WASP, "master of the universe" securities dealer and a young, downtrodden, male black. More recently, Fernanda Eberstadt has provided in *When the Sons of Heaven Meet the Daughters of the Earth* (1997) a "worldly, perception and good natured" portrait of the "glittering, overheated" art world of New

York in the late 1980s, as experienced by her principal characters, wealthy, middle-aged patrons of the arts and the struggling artists, whom they discover and take under their wings. In contrast to most of the works mentioned, this author appears to love the city of which she writes.

The City in Films

Many of the above novels also have been re-created as motion pictures, and the motion picture medium has been most effective in borrowing materials from novels, short stories, and the theater for plot materials. But it has created original material of its own as well. Although not always attuned to the artistic intent of the authors of these sources, the film medium does have the added advantages of sight and sound. Films provide a more realistic and intense sense of the cityscapes and scenes in which the plot action takes place. Such settings are often created in a film studio, but more and more films are produced on location in the appropriate city or cities. One common film cliché is to begin by zooming in on the skyline of the film's city setting to create a more authentic sense of place of the story's locale. The skyscrapers of New York; the hills, bridges, and bays of San Francisco; and the streets of Los Angeles have probably been used most often for this effect in American films. What is important is the idea that popular movies, whatever the sources of their plots, are a rich and diversified source of urban imagery. For many film-goers, films shot on location in such cities as Los Angeles, New York, Chicago, San Francisco, Boston, Miami, Honolulu, Seattle, or Denver are their only direct contact with such places and may be one of the most important influences on their impressions of these places. Television tends to use these same locales for their urban-based series or specials and thus may have a similar positive or negative impact on the viewer.

The city as a major theme in movies goes back to the early days of the silent picture. Fritz Lang's *Metropolis* portrayed a futuristic industrial city in which a captive working class is controlled and manipulated by a small but powerful elite. Ritualism, mechanization, and depersonalization dominate the social life of Lang's fictitious city. Charlie Chaplin's *Modern Times* painted an equally gloomy picture of the modern industrial city, although of course this was done with comic overtones. In *City Lights,* a cheerier and more sophisticated film by Chaplin, two lonely strangers befriend each other in the unfriendly, hectic, and busy urban setting of which they are a part, and each manages to come to grips with the problems of city living in his and her own way.

In the depression years of the 1930s, the city became a setting for organized crime in many popular films, such as *Scarface, Public Enemy, Little Caesar,* or *Dead End.* In these films, poverty was commonly viewed as a major cause of crime, but equally important was the theme of immigrant groups attempting to win the fame and fortune that were not available to them through more legitimate means. Thus, actors such as James Cagney, Edward G. Robinson, Paul Muni, and George Raft became closely identified in the public's mind with Irish, German, Italian, Jewish, Greek, or other ethnic groups, all of which have produced their share of film gangsters. The role of organized crime as a source of assimilation and upward mobility for immigrant groups attempting to establish themselves in the context of American cities has for several decades been a persistent theme in films, with *City for Conquest* and *House of Strangers* excellent examples from the 1940s. *On the Waterfront* and *Asphalt Jungle* carried this theme into the 1950s, *The Godfather* and *The Sting* continued the theme into the 1970s, and another example, *Only in America,* appeared in the 1980s.

In a recent book entitled *Somewhere in the Night: Film Noir and the American City*, the author, Nicholas Christopher (1997), has watched more than 350 films which illustrate film noir, which he describes as a way of looking at the world, as a "dark mirror reflecting the dark underside of American urban life." In a perceptive review of the book, Michiko Kakutani (*New York Times,* March 28, 1997) writes:

> Mr. Christopher . . . argues that film noir mythologized the American city as a kind of modern-day Babylon, a Darwinian jungle where crime pays, and killers, con men and extortionists prey on the vulnerable and weak. Even its titles underscore its urban bias: *The Naked City, The Captive City, While the City Sleeps, The City That Never Sleeps, Side Street, One-Way Street, The Street With No Name, Scarlet Street,* and *Street of Chance.* . . . Such movies turn the labyrinthine streets and office corridors of the city into a metaphor for the psychological mazes their heroes travel in search of self-knowledge, and in doing so, create a potent image of the modern American metropolis as a forbidding (and alluring) den of iniquity and sin. The noir city is a place devoid of the small-town consolations of neighborliness and compassion, a place where misfits and malcontents lead lives of sullen desperation, eager to use whatever means necessary to get their crack at the American dream.

The pain and dislocation of urban renewal was illustrated in *Harry and Tonto,* which portrays an elderly retiree who is forcibly and involuntarily evicted from his New York City apartment and is forced to seek housing for himself and his cat elsewhere. *Miracle on 34th Street,* a popular Christmas season rerun, deals with the cynicism and secularism of New Yorkers of all types, as they refuse to believe in the "reality" of Santa Claus, who appears in the guise of a department store Santa Claus in an annual Christmas parade (Santa can now be most likely found in suburban malls during the Christmas season!). *Midnight Cowboy* and *The Pawnbroker* illustrated again the alleged anonymity, depersonalization, and exploitation of urban life, although the former did allow the possibility that chance meetings between strangers can lead to enduring friendships among individuals of disparate backgrounds.

The paradoxes and pitfalls of urban living often have a comic twist, and these have been vividly portrayed in Neal Simon's, *The Out of Towners.* In this film, a couple from the Midwest on a job-seeking trip to New York City find themselves without a hotel room due to overbooking. They encounter every conceivable frustration as they are robbed, mugged, chased, cheated, or led astray by a variety of big city characters. Their final decision not to accept a job placement in New York because of their traumatic experience was no doubt representative of the attitude of countless viewers. Woody Allen's *Annie Hall* humorously contrasts the lifestyle of a dyed-in-the-wool New Yorker with his small town girlfriend. It also satirically compares the "in" lifestyles of "hip" New Yorkers to that of Los Angelites. *New York, New York* was based on the chance encounter between a jazz musician and a girl he attempts to pick up in a public dance hall. This film parodies film musicals, which in themselves often present various impressions of urban life. *On the*

Town, for example, follows the antics of three sailors on leave in a big city, whereas *Guys and Dolls* features a wide variety of the colorful Runyonesque hustlers and gamblers who inhabit Broadway. This film presents these lifestyles in contrast with that of a fundamentalist Salvation Army worker who seeks to mend their "sinful" ways. In a more serious way, Leonard Bernstein's *West Side Story* tells the tragic story of a "rumble" between two youthful, rival urban gangs attempting to control their respective turfs in a big city slum.

Although the films, literature, and popular music discussed are not a random or exhaustive selection, they illustrate the wide diversity of impressions of urban living, both positive and negative that have been presented in countless ways during the twentieth century.

PUBLIC OPINION

One means of measuring the attitudes of the general public and, more specifically, the residents of urban communities toward the communities in which they reside has been through sample public opinion surveys. For example, some of these polls have asked people to indicate the size of type of community in which, ideally, they would prefer to live. A number of these polls seem to suggest that a large majority of people would prefer to live in the country or small towns and suburbs rather than in large cities. One Gallup survey found only 13 percent of the respondents preferring city living to suburbs, small towns, or farms, and the U.S. Commission on Population Growth found only 14 percent choosing large cities over smaller cities, towns, or the countryside. These results point to a rather strong antiurban bias, even though a substantial majority of the U.S. population continues to reside in urban areas.

Although most people indicated they were generally satisfied with the quality of life in the communities in which they lived, another Gallup poll found that the residents of metropolitan communities of a million or more population were slightly less satisfied than the residents of places of less than 2,500 persons: 83 percent of the residents in the smaller areas expressed satisfaction, compared with 71 percent in the larger areas.

That many big city residents would prefer to live in smaller communities but do not choose to do so would seem to suggest that attitude surveys are not necessarily a reliable predictor of actual behavior. A more reasonable explanation, however, is that many people are reluctant urban dwellers who feel they have no real choice because of occupational ties to the metropolitan labor force or other economic circumstances that prevent their moving to less urbanized areas.

Some surveys have pinpointed dissatisfaction with particular aspects of urban living rather than total disillusionment. For example, Fischer has reported the results of several studies suggesting that distrust of other people tends to increase with community size. The same report also showed that anxiety about crime increases with city size. Only 14 percent of rural respondents felt that it was unsafe to walk outside at night, whereas 57 percent of the respondents who resided in the center cities of large metropolitan areas felt that it was unsafe (Fischer, 1976). Likewise big city residents are more than twice as likely as rural residents to think it is important to lock their doors when they leave home (Marans and Rodgers, 1975).

Although the balance of public opinion tends to swing toward negative views of urban living, such views are not universally shared and a significant minority of Americans are prourban. Some studies suggest that those who are highly educated, employed in professional and white-collar occupations, the young or elderly, or childless couples are interested in the cultural activities of the city, tend to have positive attitudes toward city living, and are more likely to already be living in urban environments (Mazie and Rawlings, 1972).

A more recent *New York Times* poll (*New York Times,* March 12, 1997) found New Yorkers more upbeat about their city than they had been in nearly a decade. The poll pointed to a "relative hopefulness" taking hold in parts of the city, and half the people surveyed said that even if they had the option to move away, they would not leave New York. Sixty-three percent responded that life in the city has gotten better in the past four years, 59 percent said that the city's economy was good, 81 percent believed that the city was as safe or safer than four years earlier, and 54 percent agreed that the police were doing a good or excellent job. However, less than half of the respondents believed that the schools were the same or better than they were four years earlier, and only 35% thought that race relations in the city were good.

In general, the same survey also found that attitudes about the city were sharply divided by social class, race, and gender, with blacks and Hispanics much less positive and hopeful than whites on all of the discussed survey items, and women slightly less positive and hopeful than men. Thus, the upbeat view of the city is driven by respondents who are white, male, and are of upper middle or upper socioeconomic status (reported household incomes of $30,000–$50,000 and over $50,000).

The urbanites most positive about life in large cities, as reported in the two studies, tend to be the cosmopolites discussed in an earlier part of this chapter. To the extent that current demographic trends point to an increase in the portion of the total population expected to have such social characteristics, such as greater literacy, urban experience, and earning potential, it seems reasonable to speculate that an increase in cosmopolitan lifestyles among the urban population could eventually lead to more positive attitudes toward urban living than is now the case. Certainly some real or perceived improvements in the conditions of urban living that are now deemed unsatisfactory—such as a decrease in crime, better educational opportunities, greater economic equality, and an improvement in race relations— would probably serve to enhance this prospect (see later chapters on these topics).

SELECTED BIBLIOGRAPHY

ARGYLE, M. *The Psychology of Happiness.* Oxford: Oxford University Press, 1987.

BANFIELD, EDWARD C. *The Unheavenly City Revisited.* Boston: Little, Brown, 1974.

BECKER, HOWARD, and IRVING L. HOROWITZ. *Culture and Civility in San Francisco.* New Brunswick, NJ: Transaction Books, 1972.

BOTKIN, B. A., ed. *Sidewalks of America.* New York: Bobbs-Merrill, 1954.

BRADSHAW, YORK, and MICHAEL WALLACE, *Global Inequalities.* Thousand Oaks, CA: Pine Forge Press, 1996.

CAPUTO, DAVID A. *Urban America: The Policy Alternatives.* San Francisco, CA: W. H. Freeman and Company Publishers, 1976.

CHAROSH, PAUL. "The Home Song." In *Urbanism in World Perspective,* Sylvia F. Fava (ed.). New York: Thomas Y. Crowell, 1968.

CHRISTOPHER, NICHOLAS. *Somewhere in the Night: Film Noir and the American City.* New York: Free Press, 1997.

CSIKSZENTMIHALYI, MIHALY. *Creativity: Flow and the Psychology of Discovery and Invention.* New York: Harper Collins, 1996.

DEMARETH, N. J. "Schizophrenia among Primitives." In *Mental Health and Mental Disorder,* Arnold Rose (ed.). New York: W. W. Norton & Co., 1955.

DOUGLAS, JACK. *Understanding Every Day Life.* Chicago: Aldine, 1970.

DOWNS, ANTHONY. *Urban Problems and Prospects,* 2d ed. Skokie, IL: Rand McNally, 1976.

DUNEIER, MITCHELL. *Sidewalk.* New York: Farrar, Straus & Giroux, 2000.

EATON, J., and R. WEII. *Culture and Mental Disorders.* New York: Free Press, 1955.

ELLINGTON, EDWARD K. *Music Is My Mistress.* Garden City, NY: Doubleday, 1973.

FARIS, ROBERT, and H. WARREN DUNHAM. *Mental Disorders in Urban Areas.* Chicago: University of Chicago Press, 1939.

FISCHER, CLAUDE S. "A Research Note on Urbanism and Tolerance." *American Journal of Sociology* 76 (March 1971): 847–856.

———. *The Urban Experience.* New York: Harcourt Brace Jovanovich, 1976.

FRIEDMAN, LAWRENCE J. *Identity's Architect: A Biography of Eric H. Erikson.* New York: Scribner, 1999.

GANS, HERBERT J. "Urbanism and Suburbanism as Ways of Life." In *Urbanism in World Perspective,* Sylvia F. Fava (ed.). New York: Thomas Y. Crowell, 1968.

GIBBS, JACK P. "Rates of Mental Hospitalization." *American Sociological Review* 27 (1962).

GIST, NOEL P., and SYLVIA FAVA. *Urban Society.* New York: Thomas Y. Crowell, 1979.

GOFFMAN, ERVING. *Behavior in Public Places.* New York: Free Press, 1963.

GOLDHAMER, HERBERT, and ANDREW W MARSHALL. *Psychosis and Civilization.* New York: Free Press, 1962.

GOTTDIENER, MARK. *The New Urban Sociology.* New York: McGraw-Hill, 1994.

GREER, SCOTT. *The Emerging City.* New York: Free Press, 1962.

GROCE, NANCY. *New York: Songs of the City.* New York: Billboard/Watson-Guptill, 1999.

GURIN, G., J. VERROFF, and S. FELD. *Americans View Their Mental Health.* Ann Arbor: University of Michigan Survey Research Center, 1960.

HALL, EDWARD T. *The Hidden Dimension.* Garden City, NY: Doubleday, 1969.

HOLLINGSHEAD, AUGUST B., and FREDERICK REDLICH. *Social Class and Mental Illness.* New York: John Wiley, 1958.

JACOBS, JANE. *The Death and Life of Great American Cities.* New York: Random House, 1961.

KARP, DAVID A. "Hiding in Pornographic Bookstores: A Reconsideration of the Nature of Urban Anonymity." *Urban Life and Culture* 4 (January 1973): 427–451.

———, GREGORY P. STONE, and WILLIAM C. YOELS. *Being Urban: A Social Psychological View of City Life.* Lexington, MA: Heath, 1977.

LEIGHTON, A. H. et al., eds. *Explorations in Social Psychiatry.* New York: Basic Books, 1957.

LEWIS, OSCAR. *Life in a Mexican Village: Tepoztlan Restudied.* Urbana: University of Illinois Press, 1951.

LIN, SUNG-YI. "Effects of Urbanization on Mental Health." *International Social Science Journal* 11 (1959): 24–33.

LOFLAND, LYN. "Self Management in Public Settings: Part 1." *Urban Life and Culture* I (April 1971): 93–117.

———. *A World of Strangers.* New York: Basic Books, 1973.

———. *The Public Realm: Exploring the City's Quintessential Social Territory.* Hawthorne, NY: Aldine de Gruyter, 1998.

MARANS, R. W., and W. RODGERS. "Toward an Understanding of Community Satisfaction." In *Metropolitan American in Contemporary Perspective,* Amos Hawley and V. Rock (eds.). New York: Halstead, 1975.

MAZIE, S. M., and S. RAWLINGS eds. *Population, Distribution, and Policy.* Washington, DC: U.S. Government Printing Office, 1972.

PALEN, J. JOHN. *The Urban World.* New York: McGraw-Hill, 1975.

PARDUCCI, ALLEN. *Happiness, Pleasure, and Judgment: The Contextual Theory and Its Applications.* Mahwah, NJ: Lawrence Erlbaum Associates, 1995.

SCHWAB, WILLIAM A. *The Sociology of Cities.* Englewood Cliffs, NJ: Prentice-Hall, 1992.

SIMMEL, GEORG. "The Metropolis and Mental Life." In *The Sociology of Georg Simmel,* Kurt H. Wolff (ed.). New York: Free Press, 1950.

SELIGMAN, MARTIN E. P. *The Optimistic Child.* Boston: Houghton Mifflin, 1995.

———. *Finding Flow: The Psychology of Engagement with Everyday Life.* New York: Basic Books, 1997.

Smithsonian Collection of Classic Jazz (from record guidebook). Washington, DC: Smithsonian Institution, 1973.

SROLE, LEO et al. *Mental Health in the Metropolis,* rev. ed. New York: Harper & Row, 1975.

———. "Mental Health in New York." *The Sciences* 20: 16–29, 1980.

STARR, JOYCE R., and DONALD E. CARNS. "Singles and the City: Notes on Urban Adaptation." In *Cities in Change,* John Walton and Donald E. Carns (ed.). Boston: Allyn & Bacon, 1973.

STRACK F., M. ARGYLE, and N. SCHWARTZ eds. *Subjective Well-being.* Oxford: Pergamon, 1991.

WHYTE, WILLIAM H. "The Best Street Life in the World." *New York Magazine* 15 (1974): 26–33.

———, *The City: Rediscovering Its Center.* New York: Doubleday, 1989.

WILENSKY, HAROLD L., and CHARLES N. LEBEAUX, *Industrial Society and Social Welfare.* New York: Russell Sage, 1958.

WILGUS, D. K. "Country Western Music and the Urban Hillbilly." In *The Urban Experience and Folk Tradition,* A. Parades and E. J. Steckert (eds.). Austin: University of Texas Press, 1971.

WIRTH, LOUIS. "Urbanism as a Way of Life." *American Journal of Sociology* 44 (July 1938): 1–24.

WOLFF, MICHAEL. "Notes on the Behavior of Pedestrians." In *People in Places: The Sociology of the Familiar,* Arnold Birenbaum and Edward Sagarin (eds.). New York: Praeger, 1973.

Part III

Urban Social Institutions

7

URBAN ECONOMIC INSTITUTIONS

In preindustrial societies, the family, religion, the state, and the military were usually the dominant social institutions, and most preindustrial urban communities were organized mainly around these institutions. Of course, all human communities also have been organized around some kind of basic economic activities, which provide the necessary economic means for survival. But in preindustrial urban communities, such economic activities often have been incorporated into the kinship system, the church, or the sustaining political body. As such, the economy has not necessarily been regarded as a separate entity with its own set of institutional characteristics. In modern urban-industrial societies, the economy not only becomes a separate institution in its own right, but it also becomes the dominant institution. Thus, commercial buildings, such as skyscrapers or office buildings, factories, and department stores or shopping centers tend to be the dominant visible symbols of modern urban-industrial communities, whereas palaces, fortresses, and cathedrals or temples dominate the skylines of preindustrial cities. The economy of modern urban communities is so powerful a force that it has the capacity to alter the forms and processes of other institutions rather than the other way around.

Also, according to the perspective of the *new urban sociology,* the modern urban economy has become global in character (Smith and Timberlake, 1997; Hodson and Sullivan, 1995; Sassen, 1991). Thus, although this chapter mainly reviews some of the characteristics of economic institutions in urban America, the impact of global urban economics is also highlighted. The emphasis is on the processes of production, distribution, and consumption in the urban marketplace, on the impact of economic processes on urban real estate and land uses, and on the urban world of work.

The dominant form of ownership of productive organizations in the early days of the industrial revolution was small individually or family owned proprietorships and partnerships. Although such small businesses are still prevalent in modern urban-industrial communities, much of the productive capacity is now concentrated in much larger units of organization. These larger units, usually corporations, are created by pooling and coordinating the resources, facilities, and skills of many previously competing smaller firms or establishments into an autonomous and impersonal system, which legally separates ownership from the management of such enterprises. The greater efficiency and profit potential of corporations are such that they tend to be always expanding, spreading their influence and control over ever-wider sectors of the urban economy.

In the United States, the growing concentration of industrial power in the hands of a relatively small handful of corporations had become of widespread concern even before the turn of this century. The Sherman Antitrust Act was passed in 1890 and the Clayton Act in 1914 as efforts by the federal government to prevent the monopolization of manufacturing activities. In spite of these and other efforts, however, the concentration of ownership of industry has continued to grow. By the beginning of World War II, less than one-twentieth of the total number of corporations owned 93 percent of the corporate assets in the fields of transportation and public utilities. In manufacturing, less than 2 percent of the corporations owned 66 percent of the assets. Even in the construction industry and in agriculture, which still tend to be strongly competitive, a few multimillion dollar corporations owned over one-fourth of the total corporate assets. Today, one, two, three, or four giant corporations control well over half of the total market in well over a dozen separate major industrial areas in the United States.

This tendency toward "bigness" and concentration of ownership extends not only into manufacturing, but also into transportation, distribution, and communications industries as well. For example, changing technology and the advantages of large-scale operations have dramatically reduced the number of daily newspapers from the 1909 figure of about 2,600 serving a population of 90 million people, to 1,750 daily papers for a population of 241 million people by 1990 (Horton, et al., 1997). By that time, daily newspaper competition had disappeared from all but less than twenty cities in the United States, and there were thirty-one states in which no city had competing daily papers. Similar concentrations of ownership and control have more recently developed in newer industries, such as cable television and the computer field. At the time of this writing, the Intel Corporation was supplying more than 80 percent of the Pentium processors used for currently manufactured personal computers, whereas Microsoft, which already supplied its Windows operating system and related software for more than 80 percent of personal computers currently on the market, had just acquired a significant financial interest in its principal rival, Apple Computers (*Detroit Free Press,* September 11, 1997, pp. 1–2F).

A large number of critics (see Gold, 1990) describe how large corporations effect virtually all aspects of American politics, including domestic and foreign policy. Thus, economic cycles, business investment (and disinvestment), employment and unemployment, education, health care, the environment, public opinion and the mass media, and even electoral processes are seen as molded or shaped by corporate activities. Of course, the creation of new activities, such as factories, office buildings, or shopping centers create significant land-use changes and resultant changes in the real estate market and land-use values in the urban areas in which they take place. But corporate decisions to downsize, relocate, or abandon existing economic enterprises in given urban localities may have equally powerful effects on the economy of local urban communities, which are often devastating in terms of poverty, unemployment, and urban dislocation or decay (Bluestone and Harrison, 1982; Hodson and Sullivan, 1995; Tausky, 1996, Kuttner, 1997).

MULTINATIONAL CORPORATIONS
IN A GLOBAL ECONOMY

Some of the most recent theoretical insights in the study of economic development from a sociological perspective have been incorporated into *world system theory* (Wallerstein, 1984). This theory is based on the view that the world economy is and for a long time has been an *integrated* economic system. Further, the theory focuses on the stability of the world system and its continuing unequal relationships of inequality between "core" and "peripheral" or dependent nations. The first elements of an integrated world economy emerged in the seventeenth century with the development of world-scale colonial empires by imperial nations such as the Netherlands, Spain, and England (for a further discussion of the impact of this development on the urban-industrial revolution, see chapter 3). In turn, the movement of capital from nation to nation and continent to continent also creates a large-scale migration of people between nations and continents and from the perspective of urban sociology from rural to urban communities or from city to city (Portes, Castells, and Benton, 1989).

The modern world economy, in fact, tends to be controlled by *multinational corporations* rather than nations or national empires. A multinational corporation is one that operates in many countries. Increasingly, the pattern is one where the headquarters of a corporation is headquartered in one of the wealthier industrially advanced nations with existing plants located in a variety of other established industrial nations, while newer plants are scattered in less economically developed nations, where labor costs are much lower (see Dicken, 1992). Thus, corporations headquartered in large cities, mainly in the United States, Japan, Germany, or France, may produce products assembled in or using parts manufactured in Canada, Denmark, Norway, Spain, Italy, Austria, Australia, Poland, Brazil, Mexico, Korea, countries of Southeast Asia, and many other parts of the world. Reflecting this new reality, the Ford Focus, for example, is now designed, manufactured, and marketed as a "world car" rather than as a vehicle associated with any particular country, and General Motors planned to build new assembly plants in Brazil, Argentina, Mexico, Poland, India, Thailand, Indonesia, and China between 1995 and into the next decade (*New York Times,* October 26, 1997, Section 3, p. 1.).

The immense power exercised by multinational corporations is compounded by the fact that such power is concentrated in the hands of the leaders of a relatively small number of worldwide corporations. By 1985, for example, over 80 percent of the assets of the Western world were controlled by the two hundred largest world corporations (Hodson and Sullivan, 1995). The urban centers from which the world economy is managed are the headquarters of huge international corporations located in such cities as New York, London, Tokyo, Paris, or Detroit, which in turn can best be described as global cities.

The top executives of the largest multinational corporations often make decisions that have greater impact on the daily lives of the residents of many countries than do those of government authorities, such as presidents, prime ministers, or legislators. Nevertheless, the leaders of such corporations often place corporate interests above loyalty to the countries in which they are located. As the leader of one such corporation is quoted as once having put it, "I have long dreamed of buying an island owned by no nation and of establishing the World Headquarters of the Dow Company on the truly neutral ground of such an island, beholden to no nation or society" (Barnet and Muller, 1974, p. 56). Critics put it quite another way by arguing that the multinational corporations not only operate in disregard of the countries in which they operate, but also actively subvert national policies when it is in their interests to do so (see Greider, 1997).

As multinational corporations operate increasingly in the context of a world economic system, the pattern that emerges is one of massive movements of capital resources (banks, factories, offices, warehouses, raw materials and manufactured products, distribution centers, retail and wholesale outlets, research centers and laboratories, and skilled workers, such as managers, scientists, engineers, and other highly specialized technicians) from country to country, region to region, and city to city. According to world systems theory and the new urban sociology, such movements do not occur randomly but tend to be distributed in a hierarchical and global "division of labor" consisting of *core, peripheral,* and *semiperipheral* nations and cities (Wallerstein, 1984; Smith & Timberlake 1997).

Core nations tend to be the wealthiest and most economically developed, such as the United States, the countries of Northern Europe, or Japan, whereas the peripheral nations include the relatively poorer nations characteristic of major parts of Africa, Asia, and Latin America. Semiperipheral nations are, of course, midway between these two extremes, with some of them beginning to move toward the core as they become more economically advanced and produce world cities, such as Bangkok, Mexico City, or Sao Paulo. The core, semiperipheral, and peripheral nations are thus hierarchically coordinated or "integrated," with wealth and power generally moving toward the core nations and cities, which in turn, "farm out" many of their work activities to the less costly (in terms of wages, land and material costs, etc.) peripheral nations. Such a pattern also tends to maintain or widen the gap that already exists between the wealthier and poorer nations.

THE LOCAL ECONOMY OF CITIES

The discussion so far has focused on the economics of a global system, from the perspectives of the *new urban sociology.* We now turn to economic processes in the context of local urban communities. Of course, in the modern world no individual city or metropolitan area has a completely self-sufficient economy, not only because of the emergence of a global economy, but also because no city or metropolis can produce all that is consumed by its inhabitants, and no local urban economy produces goods and services for strictly local consumption. Consequently the economy of any urban community must in some way be linked in exchange relationships with economic units external to it and over which local economic functionaries can have little or no control. The economy of any urban community thus consists of three essential components: (1) *the export sector,* consisting of those activities primarily oriented toward the export of goods and service to other communities and social entities; (2) *the import sector,* consisting of the goods and services which must be obtained from external producers for local consumption; and (3) *the local sector,* consisting of those activities primarily oriented toward production, distribution, and consumption within the local community.

The relative importance of each of the above sectors for the growth and viability of a city's economy is debatable. Even though export activities bring new wealth into the community's economy, the industries in the export sector cannot adequately thrive without adequate support from locally oriented activities. The more mature and elaborate the local economy, and the greater its ability to produce for local consumption, the less it will need to rely on imports (the one major exception is of course reliance on foodstuffs, which are produced in rural areas). In turn, the lesser the reliance on imports, the greater will be the degree of economic self-sufficiency and autonomy for the local community. However, this latter point cannot be carried to its logical extreme in modern metropolitan economies because complete economic self-sufficiency is probably impossible in such communities. For this reason, Hawley (1950) much earlier correctly labeled all modern urban-industrial communities as "dependent" communities, as opposed to the "independent" communities of the early preindustrial era. At any rate, no such completely self-sufficient local community has yet been identified in the modern world.

In numerous instances, export and import sectors interact in such a way as to produce cities that are relatively specialized in their overall functions. Such cities often develop visibly identifiable and often oversimplified images with respect to their principal functions. Thus, Las Vegas, Nevada; Atlantic City, New Jersey; and Monte Carlo became known as gambling and entertainment communities, and Ann Arbor, Princeton, and Chapel Hill became university towns. Detroit and Pittsburgh are widely labeled as manufacturing cities, Chicago serves as a trade and transportation hub, and Los Angeles became an entertainment (movies and television) center. Seattle, Portland, San Diego, and Boston are port cities, and numerous cities in Florida and Arizona are known as resort or retirement communities. In spite of the relatively high degree of functional specialization in these kinds of cities, their local sectors remain relatively diversified to meet the everyday needs of their residents, as would be the case in any other city of comparable size.

Finally, although we have described the world economy as highly stratified, so too are local economies, often with enormous gaps between the richest and poorest residents even in the worlds' wealthiest and largest world cities. Such urban inequalities in wealth, status, and power are discussed in much greater detail in chapter 11 and other chapters to follow.

INSTITUTIONAL INNOVATIONS IN URBAN ECONOMIES: PRODUCTION, DISTRIBUTION, AND CONSUMPTION

Along with the growth of modern corporations and urban populations, the complexity and size of the market for manufactured goods has increased enormously. The variety of wants among urbanites who have the purchasing power to pursue these wants in the urban marketplace is almost beyond estimation. As a result, it becomes increasingly difficult for producers accurately to calculate consumer demands and to plan the development of new products or to plan future production schedules to meet anticipated future sales. At first glance this would seem to suggest that modern business enterprise faces greater risks in the marketplace than in preindustrial economies, in which the relationship between the producer and consumer is at a much more personal and intimate level. Yet modern urban industry is no longer attuned to the rigors of competition in the classical sense (see chapter 3), but exhibits instead a comprehensive effort to reduce risk taking. In response to the complexities and uncertainties of the urban marketplace, a number of corporate innovations are designed to produce more efficient and controllable relationships between the production and purchase or consumption of manufactured products. These innovations, which are now relatively institutionalized include:

1. Market Research. Modern industry sponsors a good deal of sample survey research and/or focus group research to measure consumers' preferences, wants, and anticipated future purchases of an extremely wide variety of products, from pantyhose or toothpaste to homes, automobiles, major appliances, computers, videos, clothing, food products—the list is virtually endless. Such research may also pretest the appeal of newly developed products to a sample of potential users. Market research not only identifies the potential size of the market for a given product but often will also precisely identify which specific segments of the population are also most likely to purchase the product. Thus "demographics," a set of techniques for differentiating the population according to such variables as purchasing power, income, place of residence (often in areas as small as telephone area codes or postal zip codes in the 1980s and 1990s), age, gender, lifestyle, or level of education, is often used in market research to identify target groups of likely consumers.

2. Product Diversification. To minimize the risk of promoting obsolete products of overdependence on the success of a limited range of products, modern industry attempts to diversify its product or model lineup to satisfy multiple tastes and preferences. For example, the auto industry has moved from the position in which a given firm would produce only one or two basic models (the Model "T" available only in black from the Ford Motor Co. is an example of concentration on a single product line in the early days of the auto industry), to the present format of offering a relatively wide range of models to suit the varied preferences of a wide assortment of consumer groups. Auto manufacturers now offer two- and four-door sedans, sport coupes, station wagons, vans, utility vehicles, and pickup trucks in a wide variety of sizes and weights, colors, and price ranges, with a wide variety of available options, such as transmission types, radios, cassette or CD players, trim, seat fabrics, and so on. In the personal computer industry, Dell and Gateway have gained an impressive share of the mail order computer market by allowing their customers to customize features and options, and by mid 1997, Compaq and other competitors had also begun to offer such diversification to their customers through their established retail outlets. Thus, when contemporary manufacturers miscalculate the demand for any single product model, they are able to more quickly shift their productive resources to other products and models to minimize their potential losses.

3. Standardization. Paradoxically, the ever-increasing diversity of goods offered in the urban marketplace often confuses and discourages the consumer, particularly about products that are too new or unknown to inspire confidence in their quality. Therefore, many manufacturers or distributors will emphasize and promote the "name brand" of their products as standards of quality and reliability. Likewise corporations offer a standardized corporate "logo" as symbols of corporate standards. The intent is that the consumer will come to rely on standardized name brands or logos as at least an indication that the manufacturers "stand behind" their products and have sufficient resources to honor warranties and supply necessary repairs or parts. Often, simply the comfortable familiarity with a product or brand name will induce the consumer to purchase a particular brand, as against the uncertainty of purchasing an unlabeled product. In the fast food industry, for example, the golden arch of McDonald's is assurance (for better or worse!) of a uniform quality hamburger, no matter in what neighborhood, city, region, or nation it is purchased and eaten. The process of standardization has spread so widely through modern urban society that George Ritzer (1996) has decried the trend in a book apply entitled *The McDonaldization of Society.*

Ritzer and others have rightly described all these trends in modern urban economies as somewhat manipulative of the average person as a potential consumer. Of course the other side of the coin is that the modern urban consumer grows ever more sophisticated and discriminating in selecting from among the competing products and services. In this task, the consumer is now often aided by a growing number of consumer-oriented interest groups and product-testing organizations. Among the best known of these is the Consumers Union, which publishes the monthly *Consumer Reports* of objectively tested competing products and services, such as cameras, tape and CD players, appliances, dehumidifiers and humidifiers, clocks, autos, bedding, processed foods, or television sets, comparing their design, usability, durability, or safety. Increasingly, in the late 1990s, services such as insurance and annuities, health care, or financial and investment planning and management are also objectively evaluated as they become more and more standardized or controlled by large national or multinational corporations.

4. Advertising and Public Relations. To the extent that urban economies depend on maintaining high rates of consumption, mass media advertising has become a ubiquitous force in the everyday life of urbanites, as producers attempt to create and maintain a high degree of demand for their products through the constant display of highly visible advertising messages. Through television, radio, magazines, newspapers, circulars, mailings, and, increasingly, the Internet and telemarketing, advertising invades the homes of nearly every urbanite on a daily basis. Leaving home provides no escape, as the urbanite is met with lighted signs and posters and billboards along highways, on auto radios, in store fronts, and in buses and trains. Even the sky may present advertising messages carried by aircraft, the Goodyear Blimp being a notable example.

A more subtle form of advertising is institutional public relations. In this format, large corporations do not attempt to sell their products directly, but instead attempt to create a generally favorable public image of their corporate enterprises and activities. For example, DuPont makes better things for better living, a giant oil or chemical producer focuses on its efforts to preserve or enhance the environment or raise the general standard of living, Archer-Daniel-Midland feeds the world, and lumber-producing corporations are dedicated to preserving our forests, if such institutional public relations advertising is to be believed. The many millions of dollars spent yearly on direct advertising or institutional public relations attest to the efficacy of advertising or public relations to generate or maintain consumer confidence and demand.

5. Consumer Credit. Whereas the earliest phases of the industrial revolution were in part made possible by the emergence of standardized monetary and wage labor systems, which place disposable cash in the hands of workers, modern urban economies are sustained to an ever-increasing degree by the widespread use of consumer credit. Systems of consumer credit allow people to purchase goods for which they do not presently have sufficient cash on hand and to pay later through an agreed-upon number of installment payments. The use of consumer credit was originally limited to such high-cost purchases as homes, automobiles, large appliances, and furniture. Now credit is widely used for purchasing every conceivable product or service currently available in the urban marketplace. One additional convenience to the customer is the ability to shop or travel without carrying substantial amounts of cash, carrying instead an assortment of credit, debit, or ATM cards that are almost universally negotiable.

That the consumer pays dearly for the use of such credit does not seem to be a deterrent. Far from the values of thrift, savings, and investment that accompanied the early days of capitalism and industrialization (see chapter 3), today's values promote indebtedness as healthy for the economy (and as enriching for the lender or creditor!). Government planners and business managers despair when consumers attempt to reduce their indebtedness or to save rather than spend their current and anticipated income. Indeed, the failure to raise consumption through the liberal use of consumer credit now almost seems un-American to many business leaders in the current urban scene. On the other hand, to be denied credit as a poor risk may be as stigmatizing today as to have been labeled "idle" or "lazy" earlier in the twentieth century. At the very least, the individual who does not have consumer credit at his or her disposal may be seriously disadvantaged in the everyday aspects of modern urban living.

In many ways, the characteristics of modern urban economic institutions so pervade urban culture that all other urban social institutions are altered to conform to the new exigencies. One can even now find that some aspects of modern religion and formal education have been bent to the demands of the urban economy and have adapted some of the same forms of survival that are analogous to those used by corporations. For example, schools and churches now conduct market research studies to identify relevant target populations; diversify their product in response to the segmentation of their constituents' (customers') wants (schools diversify their curricula, and churches provide religious and social activities for such diverse groups as young people, the aged, married couples, or divorcees and singles); advertise their services of in local urban media, such as television, radio, or newspapers; and offer the option of installment or credit card payments for tuition fees or charitable contributions. In these and many other ways, to be discussed in later chapters, the values and practices of the corporate economy have invaded nearly all aspects of urban living.

THE URBAN WORLD OF WORK AND THE OCCUPATIONAL DIVISION OF LABOR

Of all the changes brought about by the urban-industrial revolution, none are more significant than changes in the nature of work in modern urban-industrial societies. The emergence of the corporate bureaucracy and other related technological and organizational trends has produced a highly complex and rapidly changing division of labor and an increasingly more elaborate degree of specialization among the jobs available in the urban labor market. Adam Smith was able to point out that in the early days of the industrial revolution a division of labor for making a product as simple as a straight pin was so specialized that one worker would draw out the wire, another would straighten it, a third would cut it, a fourth would grind a point at one end of it, a fifth would grind the other end, and two or three others would do the necessary tasks to make the head of the pin. In the meatpacking industry, according to Wilensky and Lebeaux (1958), one could specialize as a "large stock scalper," "belly shaver," "crotchbuster," "gut snatcher," "gut sorter," "snout puller," "ear cutter," "eyelid remover," stomach washer," "hindleg toenail puller," "frontleg toenail puller," and "oxtail washer."

No one knows for certain how many such specialized occupations exist in the modern labor force. The latest (1991) edition of the *Dictionary of Occupational Titles* lists and describes more than 22,000 distinguishable occupations, but others estimate there are probably many more that are too new to have yet been classified. It is interesting to compare this estimate with efforts by the U.S. Census Bureau to itemize a complete list of occupations just a century and a half ago. In 1850, only 323 different occupations could be identified, just a small fraction of the current number of the available occupational specialties.

The enormous proliferation of occupations in the United States is by no means confined to manufacturing industries but has occurred in the entire occupational hierarchy. Such specialization has divided fields such as dentistry, medicine, social work, law, and the academic disciplines, as well as clerical, sales, and administrative work, into countless subspecialties. Even in the field of sociology, it is now impossible for any one individual to master the entire discipline, and the latest *Guide to Graduate Departments* published by the American Sociological Association identifies more than 100 subspecialties within the field.

Among the consequences of this elaborate division of labor in the urban world is the fact that individuals entering the labor market are confronted with a bewildering variety of occupation choices. Further, no one individual will have intimate knowledge of more than a handful of the many choices available. Because most occupational roles are thus "invisible" to the average person, once an individual has chosen an occupation, that occupational role will most likely be obscure to most people with whom one comes in contact. Recent studies of occupational prestige, for example, have generally indicated that most respondents cannot properly identify the kind of work associated with as many as fifty to one hundred different occupations with any degree of accuracy (Tausky, 1996).

THE CHANGING OCCUPATIONAL COMPOSITION OF THE URBAN LABOR FORCE

Enormous shifts have taken place in the kinds of occupations pursued by American workers throughout the entire twentieth century, as a result of the social, economic, geographic, and technological changes produced by urbanization and industrialization. Table 7.1 details the major changes in the eleven major occupational categories of the labor force from 1900 to 1995, with projections estimated to 2005.

Table 7.1   Occupational Distribution of the U.S. Labor Force, 1900–1995 (in percent)

OCCUPATIONAL CATEGORY	1900	1950	1960	1970	1980	1995	2005*
White-collar workers	**17%**	**37%**	**43%**	**48%**	**52%**	**58%**	**57.4%**
Professional and technical	4	9	11	14	16	18	19.3
Managers and officials	6	9	11	11	11	13	10.3
Clerical workers	3	12	15	17	19	15	17.2
Sales workers	4	7	6	6	6	12	10.6
Blue-collar workers	**36**	**41**	**37**	**35**	**32**	**25**	**22.6**
Foreman and skilled workers	10	14	13	13	13	11	10.4
Semiskilled workers	13	20	18	18	14	10	8.6
Nonfarm laborers	13	7	6	4	5	4	3.6
Service workers	**9**	**11**	**12**	**12**	**13**	**14**	**17.0**
Private household workers	5	3	3	2	1	1	2.0
Other service workers	4	8	9	10	12	13	15.0
Farm workers	**38**	**11**	**8**	**4**	**3**	**3**	**3.0**
Farmers and farm managers	20	7	4	2	2	1	1.0
Farm laborers and foreman	18	4	4	2	1	2	2.0

*U.S. Census Medium Projections (Hodson and Sullivan, 1995).
Sources: Data for 1900 and 1950, U. S. Bureau of the Census, *Historical Statistics of the United States, Colonial Times to 1970,* Bicentennial Edition (Washington, DC, 1975), Part 2, p. 139; for 1960, 1970, *Statistical Abstract of the United States: 1973,* p. 230; and for 1980 and 1995, U.S. Department of Labor, Bureau of Labor Statistics, *Employment and Earnings,* June 1980, p. 35, and March 1995, p. 27.

Perhaps the most striking change in the American labor force is the remarkable decline in the number of people who work on farms or in farm-related activities. In Table 7.1 we see that farmers, farm managers, and farm laborers or foremen have dropped from 38 percent of the labor force in 1900 to about 3 percent in 1995, and are expected to continue to decline to about 2.5 percent in 2005. This decline illustrates the degree to which America has moved from being an agrarian society to being an urban society in which the vast bulk of the labor force is employed in nonagricultural urban work. In the following sections, we discuss in some detail the major occupational trends in urban or nonfarm segments of the labor force.

WHITE-COLLAR WORKERS

Clerical workers and those in related occupations amounted to only 3 percent of the labor force in 1900. Since then, until the 1980s, the increase in numbers and proportions of clerical workers had exceeded all other categories of workers, having increased sixfold to about 19 percent of the labor force by 1980. Although the rate of increase had fallen somewhat by 1995, this class of occupations is expected to be among the fastest growing into the beginning decade of the twenty-first century (Hodson and Sullivan, 1995).

The largest single group within the clerical workforce is composed of secretaries and stenographers; together with typist and stenographers, they now number well above the 3 million mark. Increasing more rapidly since the 1980s, of course, are electronic computer operators, as well as clerical workers operating other office machines, such as copiers, fax machines, scanners, printers, and the like. For example, it is estimated that computer and peripheral computer equipment operators were among the twenty most rapidly growing occupations between 1984 and 1995, increasing by about 46 percent during that period (Tausky, 1996).

Aside from technological advances, a major reason for the massive growth in clerical work throughout the twentieth century is the proliferation of large-scale bureaucracies in both industry and government. Such large-scale bureaucracies require innumerable clerical workers to handle the paperwork that is their lifeblood. In addition to increasing the numbers of people employed in this category, bureaucratization has also radically altered the nature of white-collar work. Whereas white-collar clerical work formerly brought with it a higher status than blue collar work, the growing "factory" life structure of many bureaucracies has reduced the status of much white-collar clerical work by making it virtually indistinguishable from blue-collar factory work, in terms of the way it is managed and controlled (Ritzer, 1996), and in terms of the wage stagnation of the 1990s. It is expected that the demand for clerical workers will continue well into the twenty-first century, as bureaucratic and technological changes continue to expand occupational opportunities in the clerical categories (see Table 7.1).

Professional and technical workers have increased from 4 percent of the labor force in 1900 to 18 percent in 1995. Taken together (and a significant proportion does work together), professional and clerical personnel now account for about one out of every three workers in the United States.

The increasing need for professional and highly trained technical expertise in urban societies has led to the expansion of professional and technical careers such as teaching at all levels; engineers and draftsmen; the health fields, including physicians, nurses, and nurses aides, dentists and dental technicians, pharmacists, veterinarians, dietitians, nutritionists, medical and nuclear medical technicians; and the scientists' group, including physicists, mathematicians, chemists, biologists, geologists, metallurgists, astronomers, and paleontologists. In the so-called helping professions, therapists, counselors, social workers, human resource development (personnel) workers, psychologists, and librarians are members of growing occupations, and in government and business, accountants and auditors, city planners, economists, and computer programmers are on the list of expanded occupations, as are lawyers, architects, and the clergy.

Because the professional and technical fields are so varied, no single factor can fully explain the growth of the many different kinds of occupations in this category. Likewise, the use of the concept *profession* to describe many of the occupations in this category is somewhat misleading, for sociologists may have something quite different in mind when assessing the question of whether a given occupation has earned professional status other than from the far more arbitrary criteria used by government agencies for classifying labor force statistics into occupational categories. Professionalization is a process in urban societies that has significance in its own right, independent of the problems of labor force classification schemes (see Friedson, 1998, for classic sociological definitions of the term profession).

Nevertheless, several factors leading to growth of professional and technical occupations can be tentatively identified. For example, the increased wealth and sophistication of the urban consumer has led to an increased demand for the services of professional occupations, such as psychiatrists, psychologist, marriage or sex counselor, tax accountant, financial planner, divorce lawyer, architect, and interior decorator, and many mass media publications or broadcasts advise their readers or viewers as to the desirability of employing these and other professions to help solve their problems. The helping professions themselves attempt to generate increased demands for their services by informing the public of their alleged value. In these and many other ways, the urban public is increasingly dependent on a growing core of professional workers. In turn, the professions have become among the most attractive career alternatives to a growing number of young people who have the necessary prerequisites, namely, the appropriate amount and type of higher education. Thus the increase in the number of professional workers in the United States is directly related to the increased portions of the population seeking the sort of credentials provided by colleges and universities, which is simply another characteristic of modern urban-industrial economies.

Another factor is the growth of professional and technical occupations related to the growing demands for highly trained people to handle the increasingly sophisticated technology, machinery, or knowledge base of advanced urban civilizations. Almost by definition the professions most affected by technological changes are those of scientists, as virtually all technological changes are now derived from basic and applied scientific research. In turn each new scientific discovery that leads to scientific change raises a host of new scientific questions (effects on health, safety, the environment, or climate) that require still more scientific research. As both a cause and a result of technological change, the number of doctorates in science multiplied enormously throughout the twentieth century, and it has been estimated that well over half of the scientists who have ever lived are alive today.

Professional firefighting has emerged as just one of many essential urban occupations

In a similar way, growth in engineering and related technological fields have also proceeded at a rapid rate, creating not only an increase in the total number of engineers (over 2 million in 1995), but also an increase in the number of engineering specialties, such as civil, mining, metallurgical, mechanical, electrical, chemical, aeronautical and space, automotive, nuclear, and medical. In fact, many new kinds of technical occupations now exist that were not even heard of just a few decades ago. For example, the occupation of computer programmer is now very common, but it was not even listed in the 1949 edition of the *Dictionary of Occupational Titles.*

Proprietors and managers is the name of an occupational category composed of two quite distinct groups insofar as employment trends are concerned. About 75 percent of the category is made up of salaried managers and officials of business enterprises, and their numbers have been increasing substantially as they have become prime workers in the corporate economy. Part of the growth has been a result of the creation of many new types of managerial occupations over the past several decades. A good example is the manager of computer services, an important kind of new position in industry, government, and medical service facilities, such as hospital and clinics. In a similar way, a substantial number of traditional management positions have been modified by social and technological change. The manager of the accounting department in many organizations has been forced to deal with and manage many new kinds of technologically advanced electronic data processing services and therefore has been forced to learn the theory and functioning of electronic computers, as the managers of customer service departments also have been forced to deal with a variety of new electronic communications systems. The managers of personnel (human resource development) departments have been forced to deal with a wide range of new demands imposed by workers or by government policy with respect to pension plans, health insurance plans, and other "fringe" benefits, worker's compensation laws, and affirmative action programs and other civil rights issues. As a result, many new occupational subspecialties within the ranks of human resource development workers have been created over the past several decades to deal with new urban workplace contingencies such as these.

The remaining 25 percent of the proprietors and managers category is composed of the independent proprietors of small businesses—gas stations, grocery or convenience stores, and retail specialty stores of all kinds—which have been condescendingly referred to at times as "mom and pop" stores. Also in this category are small machine shops and manufacturing facilities, beauty and barber shops, restaurants, and repair or maintenance facilities that are individually or family owned and operated. In spite of the fact that at one time, to be self-employed in these ways was at the heart of what it meant to be "middle class," the number of these small businesses had declined rapidly in recent decades. Although to be self-employed in one's own business may still be a part of the American dream, to start up such a business is very risky and is subject to a relatively high rate of failure. This decline is largely due to the long-run shift from these largely local businesses to larger and more competitive corporate-type business organizations, such as national chain stores, restaurants, and service organizations. As a result, there has been a relatively steady decline of total employment in the proprietors segment of this category, and expected rapid growth in the managerial segment is not expected to be sufficient to offset the losses in the proprietary segment by the year 2005 (Table 7.1).

Sales workers represent the final category of the white-collar segment of the labor force. More than 50 percent of all sales workers are employed in retail outlets of one kind or another. Also included, however, are real estate agents, insurance agents, telemarketers, manufacturers' representatives, and the like. This segment of the labor force had just about kept pace with the growth in overall employment during this century, maintaining a relatively constant 6 percent of total overall employment over the four or five decades preceding 1980. Although this portion just about doubled between 1980 and 1995, projections indicate another slight decline in the portion of the labor force in sales work by the year 2005. To a certain extent, the shift in retailing toward large branches of chain stores with their growing dependence on self-service and check-out counters has somewhat depersonalized sales transactions and limited the potential growth in the number of retail salespersons in favor of cashiers, security guards and store detectives, stock handlers, price markers, and inventory clerks, and other personnel who are included in other more rapidly growing segments of the labor force.

BLUE-COLLAR WORKERS

Blue-collar work is classified by the skill levels associated with the jobs in this category. At the top of the skill ladder among blue-collar workers are *craftsmen*. This group is a varied one and includes tool and die makers, auto mechanics, locomotive engineers, bakers, typesetters, foremen, instrument repairers, and a range of construction skills, including carpenters, plumbers, electricians, bricklayers, masons, and painters. The skilled worker category generally implies a period of prescribed training or apprenticeship anywhere from several months to several years as a prerequisite to full skilled status. Back in 1900, there were six recognized skilled trades—engravers, locomotive engineers, brick masons, blacksmiths, metal molders, and shoemakers—which together represented 20 percent of all the skilled craftsmen. In the late 1990s, they represented less than 4 percent of that group. In 1900 another six skilled trades—carpenters, mechanics and repair persons, cranemen and stationary engineers, plumbers, electricians, and telephone line workers—together represented less than 40 percent of the skilled blue-collar workers. Now they include over 70 percent (including cable installers and repairers). Thus, within this group, quite different trends of growth or decline of employment opportunities have developed; overall the group has been very gradually declining each decade since the 1930s, and it projected to do so into the first decade of the twenty-first century.

Nevertheless, skilled craftspersons are the elite of the blue-collar workers, and their income often exceeds that of many white-collar workers. In terms of income or prestige, in fact, social scientists often have difficulties in deciding to classify these workers as lower- or working-class, or as having achieved middle-class status. At any rate, a substantial portion of skilled blue-collar workers now reside in suburban communities that are generally characterized as middle-class (see chapter 4).

The *semiskilled* operative groups make up the largest segment of the blue-collar labor force. It is typified by the operator of a production machine of a factory. Such specialties are semiskilled in the sense that it may take several days or weeks of supervision to train a worker to use and maintain such a machine properly. Another important semiskilled operative group comprises the workers who make their living as drivers or delivery persons, including long-distance truck drivers, taxicab and bus drivers, and those who deliver such products as retail packages, laundry and dry cleaning, or a wide variety of foodstuffs. This portion of the labor force grew rapidly in the first half of the twentieth century, as the result of the mechanization of industry and the growth of the automobile and truck as the principal means of transportation. This growth was largely at the expense of unskilled work, which was often upgraded to the to the semiskilled level as the machine began to displace unskilled manual labor. It has declined rapidly, by about 50 percent since 1950, and is expected to continue to decline well past the year 2000. This is due in part to the increased efficiency of production because of innovations in engineering, science, and management, which have raised the productivity of the American industrial worker, but, increasingly, it is also due to downsizing by corporations seeking still greater efficiency and increased profitability.

At least part of the reasons for increased productivity and efficiency has been the mechanization of control over the production process, commonly referred to as *automation*. There has always been a great deal of controversy regarding the eventual effects of automation. Those who view the effects as positive, in eventually creating more jobs and more wealth, tend to see these effects as long-run rather than short-run gains. On the other hand, those who view automation with alarm are equally concerned with its more immediate consequences: mainly those that will affect the current labor force and perhaps the children of the current generation. Because the impact of rapid technological change has already taken its toll among significant numbers of workers whose skills have been rendered obsolete or whose jobs have been seriously altered or eliminated, automation and related technological changes tend to generate feelings of insecurity among both semiskilled and unskilled workers.

At the beginning of the twentieth century, *unskilled laborers* constituted the largest segment of the blue-collar labor force (13 percent). Unskilled manual jobs were the ticket of entry into the urban economy for millions of migrants from domestic and foreign rural regions. Literacy was not an imperative for obtaining these widely available unskilled jobs, and they could be learned in minutes, hours, or days.

In fact, most unskilled workers at the turn of the century were functionally illiterate: They usually had no formal education beyond the fourth grade level. Even as recently as 1950, 10 percent of the labor force was still functionally illiterate, and more than half (54 percent) never went beyond elementary school. For all these reasons, opportunities to obtain employment as an unskilled blue-collar worker have been steadily shrinking over every decade of the twentieth century, compared with other segments of the urban labor force. Unskilled workers constituted only about 4 percent of total employment in 1995, and opportunities to find this kind of work are expected to continue declining into the foreseeable future.

Among this segment of the labor force, functional illiteracy and unemployment have remained consistently the highest in recent decade. The largest unemployed pool of unskilled workers in American society now tends to be concentrated in large American cities, where it is now most difficult to gain accessibility to other segments of the labor force because these have become more decentralized (see chapter 4). And it is also in these same cities that available educational resources are the most inadequate for the task of training more literate and skilled workers (see chapter 10) to meet the rapid changing job opportunities and demands of the urban labor market. This is widely perceived as one of the most important urban social problems to American life. Current newcomers to urban living can no longer expect to rely on unskilled manual labor as a way to obtain secure positions in the urban labor market.

HOW CHANGES IN THE URBAN LABOR MARKET TAKE PLACE

In the previous sections, shifts from agricultural occupations, from manual labor to skilled blue-collar occupations, and from all other categories to the professions (where higher education becomes the intervening variable) were described as among the major changes occurring in the urban labor market during the twentieth century. Some of these shifts have been gradual, but others have been abrupt and dramatic, producing sharp imbalances between the supply and demand for certain skills at any given time. Thus, in recent decades there were critical shortages of workers in some professional and scientific areas, while at the same time, there were surpluses in other areas. For example, nursing and public school teaching moved from shortage occupations to surplus occupations virtually overnight. Rapid and continuous changes in the occupational composition of the labor force are, in fact, ubiquitous in all modern urban societies. The questions that the resultant frequent imbalances in the supply and demand for labor raise are (1) How do shifts in the labor force take place? (2) What are the mechanisms through which segments of the population move from one part of the labor force to another? and (3) What is likely to happen to individual workers who are displaced from one segment of the labor force as they attempt to find employment or new career opportunities in other occupational areas?

BASIC ASSUMPTIONS OF A FREE LABOR MARKET

In American urban society the assumption is usually made that people make job changes within the framework of a free or laissez-faire labor market. The basic assumptions of a free labor market are well known to nearly everybody. They have also traditionally formed the foundation of the work of labor economists. These common assumptions can be restated as follows:

1. All individuals are free to seek the work of their choice.
2. Individual occupational choices are rational. They are based on the maximization of individual self-interests and involve the selection of the best occupational arrangement from among the various opportunities available.
3. All individuals are free to compete for the most desirable occupational opportunities, and all available jobs are open to free competition.
4. All individuals will compete for the most desirable positions (those offering the greatest material or psychic rewards), and the most skilled and motivated competitors will win the most desirable jobs or positions.

5. The incentives for occupational competition—the rewards—are primarily economic. These consist of the wages, salaries, or earnings available in exchange for one's work.

In effect, the free urban labor market is supposed to work something like this: as each individual finds his or her own occupational level or niche, the needs and the requirements of the society are somehow met. The free urban labor market is expected to ensure that there will always be an appropriate distribution of skills throughout the entire labor market, and that, therefore, society's needs for labor are best met through the free play of the labor market. In a free labor market, it is anticipated, the labor force will automatically adjust itself to the needs for labor existing at any given time, preventing serious imbalances between the supply and demand for workers.

BARRIERS TO CAREER CHANGES IN THE URBAN LABOR MARKET

In actuality, although the illustrated model of a free labor market is useful for conceptual purposes, it is not an entirely accurate representation of reality. One would be hardpressed to find empirical examples of a completely open labor market, even in a free society such as the United States. Relatively high rates of unemployment in periods of relatively high general prosperity in recent decades testify to the existence of forces that make it difficult if not impossible for many workers to readily shift from one occupational category to another. Even in the late 1990s, with official unemployment rates as low as 4.6 percent, there were still 6.2 million Americans officially unemployed, with an additional 3.9 million working part time because full-time work was unavailable (*New York Times,* December 6, 1997, p. B3).

There are, in fact, many barriers or impediments to the free movement of workers from one segment of the labor market to another, and such movements do not take place "automatically." These barriers may affect not only unskilled workers but many highly skilled specialists as well. It is possible to tentatively identify what some of these barriers are. Some of them are the personal characteristics or attitudes that the workers themselves bring into the labor market, but in order not to entirely "blame the victims," it is equally important to point out that many of the important barriers are routinely imposed by employers in their recruitment and selection of workers, or in other more indirect ways to be discussed later.

Barriers Imposed by Workers Themselves

Workers may resist shifting occupations when such shifts also require geographic mobility or a willingness to relocate. Although the number of people who migrate in any given year is quite high (more than 40 million people move their place of residence each year), a majority of the working population resists such moves. Professional and technical personnel are the only workers whose migration rates are greater than 50 percent over a five-year period, whereas many others, such as clerical workers, service workers, and skilled and unskilled blue-collar workers, have a migration rate of less than 30 percent during the same time frame.

Age is an important factor affecting the willingness or ability of workers to migrate from region to another to secure or advance their employment prospects. Young workers between ages twenty and twenty-nine have the highest rates of migration. Thereafter the migration rates drop off sharply during each decade from thirty to sixty-five years of age. Clearly the older worker may have more at stake or more invested in resisting geographic moves as a route to job or career changes, such as family, friendship, or real estate ties.

It is also clear that the geographic preferences of workers who migrate does not necessarily coincide with the availability of job opportunities. For example, sun belt cities, such as Atlanta, Austin, or Los Vegas, and coastal cities, such as Boston, New York, Miami, Los Angeles, San Francisco, or Seattle, continue to attract migrants in numbers well beyond their capacity to be absorbed easily into the local labor markets, whereas communities considered undesirable places to live may have difficulties in attracting enough workers to fill available positions (*Detroit Free Press,* December 5, 1997, p. F1).

A lack of knowledge of available opportunities, common to urban residents, may restrict movement in the highly diversified and complex urban labor market, and many newer kinds of occupations tend to be invisible to potential recruits. Thus, the process of looking for work or choosing a career may be one of the most difficult and troubling tasks faced by urban dwellers. The task is also made more difficult because many job opportunities are not publicly announced or advertised to the general public and are filled instead

Emergency medical services are vital to public health and safety in urban settings

through word of mouth or personal contacts. It is my personal observation that even many graduating college seniors do not have the slightest notion of how to go about seeking employment or getting useful information about job or career prospects. This suggests that the lack of such information is by no means limited to unskilled or poorly trained individuals, although these latter groups usually experience far more difficulty in obtaining secure employment.

Workers may have skills so specialized that they are not readily transferable to new areas. For example, automotive engineers cannot readily transfer to other engineering specialties without expensive and lengthy retraining, and attorneys cannot become physicians or physicians cannot readily become sociologists, for the same reasons. A modern urban economy's labor market is highly segmented, with very limited or restricted movement from one segment to another. In some cases, organized groups, such as professional societies or unions, may limit access to specific occupations through such devices as licensure, registration, certification, or by prescribed lengthy periods of internship or apprenticeship. Many potential seekers of new career opportunities often resist such barriers, because of general resistance to change, or, more likely, an unwilling to incur lengthy and expensive retraining, because of fears of risky or uncertain outcomes. Finally, studies of occupational prestige and occupational socialization reveal that people may also have many different levels of motivation or aspiration, inasmuch as, contrary to the traditional economic model reviewed earlier in this part of the chapter, not everyone necessarily wishes to compete for the most rewarding or prestigious positions available or has the resources to do so.

Barriers Imposed by Employers

Employers, in setting up criteria of any kind for the recruitment and selection of workers, are, in effect, at the same time establishing barriers that may exclude certain segments of the labor force from consideration as prospective employers. Of course, consciously or not, this serves as a barrier to free movement in the labor market for the job seekers so excluded. Many such barriers are legitimate in that they pertain directly to the skills required to perform the jobs that are available. But employees may also consciously or not introduce biases or procedures into the recruiting process that may be incidental to the task of finding individuals who are best qualified to perform the necessary work tasks. Such practices run contrary to the expectations of the free labor market. The most invidious biases, of course, are those having to do with racial, ethnic, religious, gender, or age discrimination. Such forms of discrimination are now generally forbidden by a large body of civil rights legislation passed in the 1960s, and by presidential orders banning discrimination in federal employment and in the armed services, in private firms working under contract with the federal government, and almost all other activities of the executive branch of the federal government (see Gold and Scarpitti, 1967). Despite such legislation and executive department actions, forms of discrimination still continue to exist, as acknowledged by virtually every leading social problems textbook in the country (see Curran and Renzetti, 1996; Horton, Leslie, Larson, and Horton, 1997; Henslin, 1996; Eitzen and Zinn, 1997; and Kornblum and Julian, 1992, as typical examples). The Equal Employment Opportunity Commission recently found that out of 106,000 discrimination claims resolved in the 1996–1997 fiscal year, 11 percent had merit, and the plaintiffs received a total of $178 million in damages. More specifically, studies done in the early 1990s by the Urban Institute found that whites were offered jobs 15 percent more often then equally qualified blacks and 52 percent more often than Hispanics. The Fair Employment Council found that whites received job interviews 22 percent more often than equally qualified blacks (*New York Times,* December 7, 1997, p. 22). More will be said about this and other forms of urban inequality in later chapters.

There are many other biases and forms of discrimination in the workplace beyond those mentioned earlier, which are not forbidden by law, but which are nevertheless also relatively widespread. For example, some employers may engage in the kind of recruiting where having attended the "right" schools or colleges, coming from the "right" families or social circles, or having the "appropriate" social values or gender preferences are substituted for skill as a criterion for selection. There may also be biases about physical characteristics, such as height, weight, physical attractiveness, hairstyle, style of dress, and speech mannerisms.

Earlier in this chapter, the growing practice of employers in a global economy moving jobs from community to community or country to country while at the same time drastically downsizing the size of their workforce was discussed, and this too directly affects the employment prospects of workers so displaced.

In response to all of these kinds of difficulties for workers who need to move about freely and flexibly in complex and rapidly changing urban labor markets, modern urban societies have evolved a number of innovative institutional devices. These include the development of public employment agencies, public systems of unemployment compensation, private employment and outplacement agencies, private career counseling services and public vocational guidance services (often in public schools), university placement services and job fairs, detailed governmental studies and projections of labor market trends, public and private affirmative action programs, and mass media dessemination of occupational information and publication of employers want ads. In turn, all these activities have helped to create a number of newer occupational specialties, such as employment interviewers and counselors, job development specialists, job trainers, affirmative action investigators, and human resource development workers.

ORGANIC SOLIDARITY AND ECOLOGICAL DEPENDENCE IN THE URBAN LABOR MARKET

In his early seminal work *The Division of Labor in Society,* Emile Durkheim (1947) saw preindustrial societies as characterized by what he called "mechanical solidarity," in which social unity stemmed from the fact that everyone did essentially the same kind of work. As the nature of work becomes more differentiated and specialized with the more complex division of labor in modern urban industrial societies, mechanical solidarity becomes gradually displaced by what he called "organic solidarity." Organic solidarity refers to the social integration of society based on the recognition that individuals in highly specialized occupational roles are highly dependent on other individuals in other highly specialized but unlike roles to supply goods and services that they cannot supply themselves. In modern ecological terms, the interdependent interactions among individuals who occupy specialized roles that are different from one another are called "symbiotic" relationships (Hawley, 1950).

Durkheim (1947) argued that organic solidarity requires an ethical or moral system that emphasizes the need for a high degree of conscious cooperation and understanding among unlike segments of the labor force. However, Durkheim recognized that organic solidarity did not come about automatically, and that social integration of societies characterized by an increasing division of labor was threatened by the following possibilities: (1) anomie, or a sense of normlessness or isolation, may increase with the division of labor; (2) individuals may be reluctantly forced to perform tasks that are not in line with their character or to conform with a division of labor that might not be of their own choosing; and (3) the division of labor may be so minute that any given work task does not seem to be meaningful or relevant. Yet the degree of interdependence among all segments of the modern urban industrial labor force is so great the entire economic system may be seriously disrupted when any one group of highly specialized workers, for whatever reason, withholds its services from the labor market.

Thus, in recent decades, work stoppages by workers such as UPS drivers, transportation workers, air traffic controllers, firefighters, police officers, bus drivers, dairy workers, school teachers (and even college professors!), nurses and other health workers, social service workers, television performers or technicians, public sanitation workers, lithograph and press operators (employed by daily newspapers), telephone operators, supermarket cashiers, social service workers, and other urban service workers have threatened to disrupt the daily flow of activities that urbanites routinely depend on for their

Labor union strikes have become increasingly common among municipal workers, as illustrated by striking firefighters in Chicago

survival or well-being. Urbanites tend to take these services for granted until they are inconvenienced by strikes, walkouts, picketing, and other work stoppages by workers who might not always be visible, but who are nevertheless essential to the daily rhythm of the urban economy.

But when schools are closed because of dispute with teachers, daily newspapers are not printed or distributed, a house burns down with firefighters standing idly by, or someone is robbed while police officers are home with the "blue flu" due to labor problems, or when one cannot routinely shop at the local supermarket or send packages because delivery men are on strike and the shelves are bare, the typical urbanite will respond with frustration, anger, or miscomprehension at what is happening to him or her. In one recent example, approximately 5,400 workers went on strike in Philadelphia, shutting down a transit system that routinely provides bus, subway, and trolley service to approximately 435,000 people a day (*New York Times,* June 2, 1998, p. A14).

Urban workers increasingly have become formally organized as labor unions or are more willing to use strategies invented by labor unions to further their own occupational self-interests. Once thought to be characteristic only of production workers in industrial work organizations, labor unions are now common among all segments of the urban workforce, including white collar and professional workers. One can now find university professors, physician, nurses, and clergy organized into labor unions, although just a few decades ago it was widely believed that the values of such professionals would prevent their considering unionization as an acceptable alternative for furthering their occupational goals (Lipset, 1967). Even self-employed agricultural workers had not too long ago considered withholding from planting their crops as a national protest against prevailing federal agricultural policies, which illustrates the degree to which urban behavior patterns penetrate rural areas in a society that is highly urbanized (see chapter 4).

In the broadest sense, labor unions, trade unions, professional associations, and business associations may be described as *categoric* units of urban social organization. A categoric unit is one made up of members occupying a single status category who unite in a collective attempt to meet common external threats or to maintain the status quo: "Categoric units emerge only in those occupations that have been confronted by challenges, which, if unattended, might impair or eliminate the sustenance base of the individuals involved. These are usually the most highly skilled occupations which are often so specialized that the individuals committed to them cannot readily shift to other occupations. The medieval guild and modern professional associations are illustrative of highly developed categoric units" (Hawley, 1950). This trend can be seen quite clearly among public service workers in local government. Until the mid-1930s, municipal workers conceived of themselves primarily as "public servants" or as professional or quasiprofessional workers and had not yet begun to affiliate with labor unions. But by the 1960s, municipal unions such as the American Federation of State, County, and Municipal Employees had already become the fastest growing segment of the labor union movement, and now public employees are more than twice as likely to be members of unions than workers in the private sector.

Thus, whenever their occupational aspirations appear to be threatened or frustrated in any way, the members of an occupation collectively demand that their representative organization, be it a union, professional association, or trade association, provide a solution to the problem. Although the desire for higher income is always the "usual suspect" in American society, other motivations are equally or more important sources of concern. Very often the concern may be job security or advancement. In the case of occupational groups with aspirations for professional status, the relevant issues may often be based on demands for greater autonomy or increased control over the conditions of work. When lobbying, public relations, or attempts at negotiating solutions fail, strikes, work stoppages, picketing, and other devices pioneered by industrial unions to protect their interests have been increasingly used by municipal workers.

Power struggles between public employees' unions and city or county governments for which their members work are now a relatively common occurrence in American urban communities, and there is no end to these in immediate sight (Zax, 1989). Without debating the merits of the arguments on each side of the struggle, one can reasonably conclude that disruptive labor disputes are often a detriment to the solution of community-wide problems that require cooperative efforts by municipal officials and municipal workers, as well as by the public at large, whose support may be critical to each side in such disputes.

Although the potential of municipal employees to exercise power has been so recently recognized that it has been largely ignored in studies of community power structure, it is important to remember that the current emphasis on global urbanization, as reflected in the opening pages of this chapter, should not be viewed in an overly deterministic fashion, because local events, including the local power disputes discussed in the closing pages of this chapter, continue to be of considerable significance in their own right and continue to be discussed in remaining portions of this book.

SELECTED BIBLIOGRAPHY

BARNET, RICHARD J., and RONALD E. MULLER. *Global Reach: The Power of the Global Corporations.* New York: Simon and Shuster, 1974.

BLUESTONE, BARRY, and BENNETT HARRISON. *The Deindustrialization of America.* New York: Basic Books 1982.

CURRAN, DANIEL J., and CLAIRE M. RENZETTI. *Social Problems: Society in Crisis,* 4th ed. Boston: Allyn and Bacon, 1996.

DICKEN, PETER. *Global Shift,* 2d ed. New York: Guilford Press, 1992.

DURKHEIM, EMILE. *The Division of Labor in Society.* New York: Free Press, 1947.

EITZEN, D. STANLEY, and MAXINE B. ZINN. *Social Problems,* 7th ed. Boston: Allyn and Bacon, 1997.

FRIEDSON, ELLIOT. "Formal Knowledge, Power, and the Professions." In *Working in America: Continuity, Conflict, and Change,* Amy S. Wharton (ed.). Mountain View, CA: Mayfield, 1998.

GOLD, HARRY. "Political Sociology: A Developing Field." *Choice* 27, no. 6 (February 1990).

———, and FRANK SCARPITTI. *Combatting Social Problems: Techniques of Intervention.* New York: Holt, Rinehart and Winston, 1967.

GREIDER, WILLIAM. *One World, Ready or Not: The Manic Logic of Global Capitalism.* New York: Simon and Shuster, 1997.

HAWLEY, AMOS H. *Human Ecology.* New York: Ronald Press, 1950.

HENSLIN, JAMES M. *Social Problems,* 4th ed. Upper Saddle River, NJ: Prentice-Hall, 1996.

HODSON, RANDY, and TERESA A. SULLIVAN. *The Social Organization of Work,* 2d ed. Belmont, CA: Wadsworth, 1995.

HORTON, PAUL B., GERALD R. LESLIE, RICHARD F. LARSON, and ROBERT L. HORTON. *The Sociology of Social Problems,* 12th ed. Upper Saddle River, NJ: Prentice-Hall, 1997.

KORNBLUM, WILLIAM, and JOSEPH JULIAN. *Social Problems,* 7th ed. Englewood Cliffs, NJ: Prentice-Hall, 1992.

KUTTNER, ROBERT. *Everything for Sale: The Virtue and Limits of Markets.* New York: 20th Century Fund/Knopf, 1997.

LIPSET, SEYMOUR M. "White Collar Workers and Professionals: Their Attitudes and Behavior toward Unions." In *Readings in Industrial Sociology,* William A. Faunce (ed.). New York: Appleton-Century-Crofts, 1967.

PORTES, ALEJANDRO, MANUEL CASTELLS, and LAUREN BENTON, eds. *The Informal Economy: Studies in Advanced and Less Developed Countries.* Baltimore, MD: Johns Hopkins University Press, 1989.

RITZER, GEORGE. *The McDonaldization of Society: An Investigation into the Changing Character of Contemporary Social Life.* Rev. ed. Thousand Oaks, CA: Pine Forge Press, 1996.

SASSEN, SASKIA. *The Global City.* Princeton, NJ: University of Princeton Press, 1991.

SMITH, DAVID A., and MICHAEL F. TIMBERLAKE. "Urban Political Economy." In *The Urban World,* 5th ed., J. John Palen, (ed.). New York: McGraw-Hill, 1997.

TAUSKY, CURT. *Work and Society,* 2d ed. Itaska, IL: F. E. Peacock, 1996.

WALLERSTEIN, IMMANUEL. *The Politics of the World Economy.* Cambridge, U.K.: Cambridge University Press, 1984.

WILENSKY, HAROLD L., and CHARLES N. LEBEAUX, *Industrial Society and Social Welfare.* New York: Russell Sage, 1958.

ZAX, J. "Employment and Local Public Sector Unions." *Industrial Relations 28* no. 1 (1989): 21–31.

8

URBAN POLITICAL INSTITUTIONS

It is a common practice to include single chapters on the *urban political economy* in contemporary urban sociology texts (see Palen, 1997; Macionis & Parrillo, 1998). However, discussions of urban economic institutions and urban political institutions, no matter how much they appear to be intertwined, can be usefully separated into separate chapters for more detailed analytical purposes, as they have been here. Further, this chapter takes into account two major dimensions of urban politics. First, it deals with the nature of the *formal* or legitimate structure of local urban government and politics, which has been a traditional component of the academic fields of political science and public administration. Second, it focuses on the underlying *informal* social forces that give rise to the formal political processes of urban communities and societies that are among the recognized concerns of the emerging subfield of political sociology (see Gold, 1990).

FORMAL GOVERNMENTAL STRUCTURE AND POLICIES

The governance of American cities of the first half of the nineteenth century was much simpler than today because such cities were generally separated from one another by large expanses of rural or undeveloped land. They were also more autonomous and self-sufficient in their governmental structures. But the metropolitan areas of modern urban America are unique in that they are now characterized by a complex and bewildering variety of distinct forms of local governmental units. For example, the Chicago standard metropolitan area includes 6 counties, 49 townships, 10 towns, 30 cities, 110 villages, more than 400 school districts, and about 235 special tax districts. Moreover, it sprawls over two states, and it is further under the jurisdiction of countless federal government programs and policies. Even the much smaller Baltimore metropolitan area includes 23 local governments and six separate counties. Generally the greater the population of an urban area, the greater will be the number and complexity of local governmental units. And, of course, virtually all urban areas in the United States are impacted by the globalization of the world's economy (as discussed in chapter 7) .

Perhaps the most apparent effect of governmental fragmentation in a metropolitan area reflects the failure to deal with the interdependent nature of such areas. Metropolitanization has created demands requiring areawide action. For example, the need for police and fire protection, pollution controls, water and public utility resources, adequate housing, public transportation, health and welfare services, jobs, educational, and recreational needs are areawide and do not necessarily fit easily into the boundaries of local jurisdictions within the larger area. Studies of any large metropolitan area will reveal numerous service and fiscal inequities (see Miranda and Walzer, 1994).

As the more affluent citizens leave the central cities for the surrounding suburban communities, they are often replaced by low-income residential populations whose needs for all these services and resources put added strains of fiscal budgets just when the city's resources may be decreasing. In turn, many small suburban units often lack the fiscal and administrative resources to provide adequate services, especially when populations and land uses are rapidly expanding. Furthermore, the displacement of population from the central cities to the suburbs also tends to deprive the central cities of strong civic or political leaders. The same kinds of processes and problems keep reoccuring, of course, as newer suburbs or subdivisions at the fringes of metropolitan areas draw populations from the older, better established suburbs.

With many separate governmental units operating independently within an interdependent metropolitan area, a climate of political nonresponsibility tends to develop. In the absence of some central authority to speak or act for the larger area, no policy-making body is held accountable for metropolitan problems and for failure arising from governmental action or inaction. Hence, the diffusion of political responsibility and authority tends to act as a roadblock to coordinated problem-solving efforts (see Weisbrod and Worthy, 1997; Berry, Portney & Thomson, 1993; Clark, 1994).

This high degree of fragmentation within metropolitan areas is not only a confusing and inefficient arrangement, but also one that places great burdens on some segments of the population, while giving advantages to others. The central cities suffer the greatest disadvantages, because they are locked in and unable to benefit from the wealth that generally accompanies expansion at the periphery. For example, the older residential and business sections of the central cities may fall into disrepair as residents and business firms move to sites outside the central city, where taxes are generally lower, traffic is not as congested, and parking is less problematic. As each city's tax base declines, the per capita share of governmental costs increases and falls more heavily on those who remain. At the same time, the growth of incorporated suburban governmental units that surround the central cities may shut them off from the possibility of expansion through annexation.

LOCAL GOVERNMENT STRUCTURE

How local urban governments are organized and structured varies greatly in the United States. Differences exist in the degree of legal power and responsibility given to the various officials, governmental bodies, and other agencies that constitute the governmental complex. Differences also exist in how each of these political elements relate to one another in terms of legal superiority or subordination. An understanding of influence and decision making in urban communities requires more than just knowing the formal government structure of a city, but such knowledge is nevertheless important because it helps us understand the ultimate route through which power and influence are channeled in their mission to effect change.

Urban governments in the United States have been generally organized along one of the following patterns: (1) the mayor-council form, (2) the council manager form, (3) the commission form, or (4) the "boss-machine" form. Among the earliest manifestations of the mayor council form was the weak mayor–strong city council, which emerged in the last half of the nineteenth century, after the Civil War. A product of Jacksonian democracy, with its emphasis on government by the average citizen, this political philosophy welcomes the urban masses to share in the function of government, broadened the base of popular participation in elections, and ensured access to government by all without regard to special qualification or prior training. Rotation in office, popular election of numerous officials, and broad-based party organizations with its emphasis on the spoils system became standard features of local government. But the weak mayor–strong council structure that became the most typical form of city government in the post–Civil War era also provided the opportunities for enterprising politicians to manipulate municipal affairs to their own often selfish advantage. By fragmenting the power of city government, this structure created a "disjointed, leaderless, and uncoordinated local governmental monster with dispersed power centers in local legislatures and the distribution of influence among many independent administrative boards and commissions" (Shank and Conant, 1975, p. 18). This often led to corruption, patronage, and boss or machine rule (about which more will be said later), but it also led to the major Progressive-era reorganization plans that evolved roughly between 1890 and 1915 which attempted to remedy problems through the development of a strong mayor system. This was seen as a means of strengthening executive authority and centralizing control over city administration by creating a chief executive with powers of appointment and/or removal of key department heads. Under this system, the mayor would also have power to submit budget plans, propose legislation, transfer funds as needed, and exercise veto power over legislation passed by a city council.

Although the current mayor-council system still favors the strong mayor format, not all cities have adopted it, and one must really view the mayor council structure as existing along a continuum, with some cities operating toward the strong mayor pole and others are positioned more toward the strong council end. Detroit, New York, Philadelphia, Cleveland, Boston, and Baltimore are good examples of cities whose governmental structure tends to veer toward the strong mayor pole, and Seattle, Milwaukee, and Los Angeles more closely limit the authority of their mayors. But weak or strong, mayors often have little discretion over the expenditure of available city revenues. In San Francisco, for example, the mayor actually controls only about 30 percent of the city's budget. The rest has to be spent according to state or federal mandates, on programs such as health care or jails (Phillips, 1996).

The commission form of city government, unlike the mayor-council system, provides for the election of a small governing body whose members collectively make

The San Francisco city hall symbolizes the important role of local government in large cities

legislative policy and individually exercise executive functions over the various city departments. This approach has not been used in cities of over 500,000 people and is currently only being used in several large cities with a population of over 250,000 (Levin, 1982). While attracting a lot of interest when first started in Galveston, Texas, in 1901, following a major flood that left the city devastated, the commission system later became less popular as the council-manager form gained widespread support. The lack of a central focus of political leadership and the difficulty of reconciling the policy-making and administrative functions of local government have tended to make this plan unappealing to most large cities today. Almost every decade sees cities organized along this scheme adopting a different governing structure, and there have been practically no new adoptions of this form of local government during the last three-quarters of the twentieth century.

Big city machines, run by "bosses," were characteristic of most U.S. large cities at some time or another from shortly after the end of the Civil War until well into the latter part of the twentieth century. Today, they are remembered with nostalgia as having been "colorful" and somewhat romantic. Although they consisted of informal systems of influence or power that never appeared as part of the formal structure of local government, they were highly organized, functionally specific, and at least as well recognized and accepted as the official governmental units they supplemented. Merton (1968) has argued that machines came into existence because they fulfilled latent functions not served by other institutions, including the provision of personalized and humanized welfare for the poor, jobs and social mobility for ethnic newcomers and others lacking adequate opportunities for upward social and economic mobility, informal access to local governmental decision makers by big business interests, and protection for various illegal activities run by those excluded from legal opportunity structures. In short, the machines existed because they provided services that were not otherwise available through more formal government structures.

The immigrants that came to the United States in the latter third of the nineteenth century had settled for the most part in rapidly growing cities that had at the time powerful and expanding political machines, which gave them economic favors in exchange for political support. The political machines were decentralized among the various ethnic wards of the cities, and ward-level grievance machinery enabled the immigrants to make their voices heard and their power felt. The immigrants were also able to enter politics directly by joining the machines as ward "heelers" and in other positions. They exercised considerable influence over the construction of public buildings and roads in the cities, and they provided employment in construction jobs for their immigrant voters. Ethnic groups as public employees often were able to dominate one or more of the municipal services, such as the police and fire departments, municipal welfare departments, public transportation and sanitation departments, and sometimes even public school systems (Gold, 1982).

On the other hand, many critics saw the machines as undemocratic, corrupt, and greedy, guided by spoils and nepotism, and interested only in taking money from the local public treasury to feather their own nests. Out of such criticisms came the local government reform movement of the Progressive era, roughly beginning in the last part of the nineteenth century and continuing through the first quarter of the twentieth century. This movement attempted to make machine government much more difficult or unlikely, tried to make elected officials more accountable to voters, tried to make government less political and less tied to political parties, and tried to make city governments more businesslike (Phillips, 1996). To accomplish these goals, reformers introduced measures, such as direct primaries and nonpartisan elections (in which voters—not machines—selected candidates), provisions for referendum and recall elections, civil service merit systems for selecting public employees (free from nepotism or partisan considerations), and efforts at better education for both citizens and professional public administrators.

As efficient and widespread these kinds of reforms were (and continue to be), not all observers are equally enthralled with the results of the reform movement. For example, Samuel Hays (1964) contended that minorities, immigrants, and members of the lower classes would tend to be excluded from city politics by the upper-middle and upper-class WASP elites who tended to dominate the reform movement. Lineberry and Fowler (1967) conducted a study, which concluded that the more a city government was reformed, the less responsive it became to the needs of different racial and income group constituencies. Along these lines, I have previously written that as a result of the reform movement:

> [B]lacks were effectively removed from patronage jobs, political appointments based on recognition of blacks as a legitimate interest group, and were strongly underrepresented on the governing boards of vital city agencies. Interestingly, cities such as Chicago and New York, with some form of political machines with strong links to the

A big city Mayor gives a speech

ghetto wards still persisting into the late 1960s, were able to avoid the civil disturbances and riots that had occurred during that period in the black ghettos of many
other large American cities. While there are many other valid explanations for this
complex phenomenon, it is fair to conclude that the political officials in these two
cities were probably more skillful, better informed and more responsive to dealing
with grievances, unrest, and provocative incidents than cities without such machines,
such as Detroit, Cincinnati, or Tampa. (Gold, 1982)

COMPETITIVE GOVERNMENTS
AND ECONOMIC COMPETITION

During the 1980s and 1990s, local officials had become markedly more entrepreneurial in
their efforts to create economic development in their communities than at any other time
in the twentieth century. They had become increasingly innovative in the ways in which
they have been intervening in the private marketplace to assist the private sector in locating or building new businesses, creating jobs, and producing more revenues for their local
areas (Watson, 1995). The new competition that local communities and state governments
have waged to attract new economic developments to their areas, such as the new
Mercedes-Benz plant in Alabama, the new BMW plant in South Carolina, or the United
Airlines maintenance facility in Indianapolis, are on the increase and show no signs of
abating. The changing world economy has placed a premium on high-paying manufacturing, commercial, and government jobs, so state and local governments are willing to go to
great lengths to be competitive with other communities and states. Not incidentally, the

political benefits to the elected officials who land major projects appear to be large and provide incentives to mayors of governors to use local or state government resources to compete for economic development.

John Logan and Harvey Molotch (1988) have rightly argued that the interest in entrepreneurial growth in American cities goes beyond that of local elected officials and is inclusive of all people making up "urban growth coalitions" who are primarily interested in real estate as a commodity to be bought and sold. The individuals and organizations that are part of the "growth machine" are primarily interested in increasing the market value of land and paving the way for continued investment and land development. They further argue that the main backers of urban growth machines are primarily large corporate and individual property owners and institutions that provide financial and legal services to them, such as banks and savings institutions and other major investors in urban real estate. According to Douglas Watson (1995), although there has been some negative public reaction to the incentive packages offered by the elite coalitions of politicians and business leaders of various communities as they compete for major economic projects, there does not as yet appear to be sufficient public opposition to slow this process down.

Some urban theorists and researchers believe that Molotch, Watson, and others who see consciously directed urban growth as the principal, and perhaps the only, driver of urban decision-making processes are overly deterministic in their conclusions. For example, Clark and Goetz (1994) point to potentially successful efforts by organized citizen groups and political leaders to control, limit, or manage growth in a variety of local urban communities, and they further imply that an "antigrowth machine" has emerged as a counterforce to the prevailing growth machine hypothesis. Their own surveys of 179 American cities found that 26 percent of them had antigrowth movements and that many more had adopted growth-limiting policies. Analyzing various sources of antigrowth movement, Clark and Goetz found little support for the growth machine and progrowth regime hypotheses of Molotch and others. They conclude:

> Shifting to growth-limiting policies adopted by local governments, we find that the political mobilization-organized group's hypothesis is the most consistently supported: cities with more active organized groups opposing growth adopt more growth-limiting policies. Political entrepreneurs may supplement these antigrowth movements if they are elected as mayors or city council members. When antigrowth thus becomes the "establishment," the antigrowth movement may decline, but growth-limiting policies nevertheless continue in a more "institutionalized" manner. (Clark and Goetz, 1994, p. 137)

The antigrowth position of Clark and Goetz seemed to be supported by the results of the 1998 elections. The *New York Times* (November 11, 1998, p. A31) reported that the elections provided a clear mandate for elected officials to deal with unmanaged growth, commonly known as urban sprawl. For example, approximately two hundred state and local ballot initiatives related to urban sprawl were passed, including plans to preserve historical sites, parks, farmland and open space in Alabama, Arizona, Florida, Michigan, Minnesota, Oregon, and Rhode Island, as well as in locations as diverse as Douglas County, Colorado, and Cape Cod, Massachusetts. Further, urban growth restrictions were approved in seven California communities, and a constitutional amendment was passed in

New Jersey that commits up to $98 million annually for historic preservation and open-space conservation. In the same *New York Times* article, Richard Moe, president of the National Trust for Historic Preservation, concluded that Americans were increasingly "fed up with traffic congestion, strip malls, visual blight and loss of open space. It is also clear that voters will pay for sensible means of dealing with them. . . . Once limited to a relatively small but determined band of environmentalists, support for smart growth policies is now widespread among governors and local officials as well as the public."

Our own view of the arguments between proponents of growth machine theories and antigrowth machine theories comes closest to the *Socio-spatial Perspective* offered by Gottdiener, who offers what appears to be a reasonably accurate synthesis of the two competing models and goes somewhat beyond them. He aptly concludes:

> There is a rich complexity of people and interests involved in metropolitan growth and change which is captured neither by ecological or political economy perspectives, be-cause they ignore particular agents, nor by the growth machine approach, which re-duces conflict to a simple dichotomy of pro- and anti-growth factions. . . . For example, each community group may have its own interests which are manifested in local politics. They often join in coalitions. . . . Growth is not the result of single-minded efforts by some machine. Rather, development is a contentious process involv-ing many groups in society that push for a variety of forms: rapid growth, managed growth, no growth, and so on. Local social movements arise not just because of eco-nomic needs, but because of racial, religious, ethnic, and community interests con-cerned with the quality of life. . . . Local politics consists of the clashes between all these separate interests as they play themselves out . . . within the forum of local gov-ernment. (Gottdiener, 1994, pp. 143–144)

STATE POLITICS AND THE CITIES

Even though local governments and the states that contain them often share common in-terests, the relationships between state and local governments are often strained and much more complex than commonly realized. For example, state constitutions usually include enabling clauses which restrict the rights of cities and other local communities to exercise rights that are reserved for the states by the federal constitution. In addition, many mem-bers of state legislatures have traditionally been elected by their rural or small-town con-stituencies and have been hostile to meeting the needs of their more urbanized communities, such as the larger cities. Outstate legislators tended to dominate the mem-bership of at least one house of every state legislative body even among those states with large urban constituencies. This domination was possible because of various political de-vices that guaranteed rural representation according to patterns existing in the nineteenth century when rural populations did represent the majority. Fearful of losing this domina-tion in the face of the rapid growth of cities in the late nineteenth and twentieth centuries, reapportionment legislation was enacted that tended to ignore the significant population shifts that were taking place (Levin, 1982). As a result of this pattern, an overrepresenta-tion of rural and small town legislators existed who tended to share with their constituents a prejudicial "anti-big city mentality, as regarding their cities as sources of corruption, low morals and boss rule, and populated by alien people like Irish-Catholics, later, Italian and Eastern European Catholics and Jews, and still later, 'slum blacks.'" Furthermore, cities were negatively perceived as "the homes of intellectuals, free-thinkers, and radical types of all sorts" (Caraley, 1997, p. 71; see also Glaab, 1963). It is obvious that governing bodies characterized by these types of biases would unlikely be responsive to diverting statewide funds to meet urban demands, nor would they likely be willing to allow such urban groups to exercise power within state political structures proportionate to their numbers (Levin, 1982: Phillips, 1996).

Beginning in the early 1960s, a series of Supreme Court decisions established reapportionment of state legislative districts to reflect a "one person, one vote" doctrine with the expectation that this would work to guarantee representation proportionate to the reality of population location. Although proponents hoped that this would establish greater equity of big city representation in state legislatures, reapportionment has not, in fact, led to substantial strengthening of the political power of the large cities in state capitals but has tended, instead, to work to the political advantage of the suburbs. Given the rapid growth of the suburbs (see chapter 4), it was soon obvious that it was the suburbs, not the cities (some of which have actually been losing population), which have gained greater representation due to reapportionment. Because suburban political representatives often see the interests of their adjacent central cities as being much different than that of their suburban constituents, the central cities often lack the political support to pass legislation favorable to their interests. In fact, it is quite common that suburban and central city interests in large metropolitan areas diverge greatly along liberal-conservative lines. In recent decades it has become clear that suburban voters tend to feel disengaged from cities and are reluctant to fund public programs or policies designed to directly benefit cities and their residents (Phillips, 1996). Mike Davis (1993) has concluded that suburban and rural representatives in Congress form a conservative coalition to oppose any large federal investments in large cities, and that in recent presidential elections, large cities "have been demoted to the status of a scorned and impotent electoral periphery."

THE FEDERAL GOVERNMENT AND THE CITIES

Until the 1930s, the federal government had directed very little attention to the problems of individual American cities, but because of the pressing economic demands created by the Great Depression of that period, the Roosevelt administration created a variety of welfare, health, and housing programs under its New Deal political policies. Even though the legislation creating these programs was not directly aimed at urban based problems, they did have a great impact on the nation's cities because so many victims of the depression toward whom these programs were directed did live in the nation's cities. In that sense the early 1930s constituted a strong start in the evolution of the federal government's relationships with large cities.

Unable to assume direct responsibility for cities under the federal system as it was originally conceived under the constitution, the federal government had chosen instead to involve itself with such problem areas categorically, as in the case of housing, poverty, income maintenance, health, education, or crime. During the post–World War ll period

(1946–1960), the major emphasis was on the continuation of the welfare, health, and housing programs that began in the 1930s, with additional new emphasis on programs affecting education, transportation, and community development, all of which had a visible impact on American cities. The Housing Act of 1949 (signed by President Truman) was a particularly significant piece of legislation for urban America, because it established a continuing slum clearance and redevelopment program that turned out to be the forerunner of the controversial urban renewal programs which began developing in the mid to late 1950s.

Federal involvement in the cities during the 1950s might have been even greater if various congressional proposals, which would establish programs for area redevelopment, broaden social security benefits and unemployment compensation, establish medical care for the aged, or provide federal aid to education, water pollution control, public health facilities and the like, had been passed. This might have been more likely had there been a president less cautious and reluctant than Dwight Eisenhower (1952–1960), who was basically a conservative on domestic economic and social issues.

The changes in the political climate after 1960, with the election of John F. Kennedy and later the ascendancy of Lyndon Johnson to the presidency brought with them a strong resurgence of federally sponsored, urban-oriented programs. Responding to the urban political-interest groups that usually support Democratic politicians, and also motivated by the growing national awareness of the plight of the cities, these administrations were able to create grant programs in such areas as air pollution (1963), neighborhood youth corps (1964), equal employment opportunity (1964), community action (1964), aid for educationally deprived children (1964), solid waste disposal (1964), water and sewer programs (1965), law enforcement assistance (1965), and model cities (1966). In addition, many other programs were established under the rubric of "the war on poverty," as well as for a wide variety of health services, including Medicare and Medicaid. Although most of the programs were not directly labeled as part of an urban policy by the federal government, they have, for the most part, had their major impact in the large metropolitan areas of the country.

During the Nixon-Ford years, the national government began backing away from the direct grant approach in favor of the concept of revenue sharing, which would provide federal funds to the states and local governments to be used at their own discretion according to a complex formula that assigned various weights to such factors as population, local revenue-raising efforts, and per capita income. These policies tended to move public decision-making responsibilities away from Washington and seemed to be a way to ease out of the narrowly targeted categorical programs created in the 1960s, many of which were regarded as "alien, ineffective, or mischievous" by the Republican administrations (Gorham and Glazer, 1976, p. 13). Once the general concept of revenue sharing was adopted, the federal government began to play a less active role in the resolution of local urban problems. These policies gradually evolved into the "new federalism" of the 1980s during the so called Reagan revolution. One of the most significant results of these shifts in policy was to retarget federal funds for a wide variety of programs to the states, where, once again, the big cities were relatively powerless to exercise sufficient power over state governments which, as described in the previous section on the relationships between cities and state governments, were now increasingly dominated by the interests of their suburban constituencies and increasingly less sympathetic to the needs of the big cities. This trend continued through the 1990s, when, in spite of control of the White House by democrats from 1993 through the end of the decade (and the end of the 20th century), both houses of the congress and a majority of state governorships came under control of Republicans.

By this time it was more clear than ever that political power in the United States had shifted away from the cities toward the states and the suburbs and that the problems of cities, or the possibility of a national urban policy by the federal government, were off the screen of serious political attention or interest. At the very least, it is clear that the problems of American cities were barely mentioned in 1992 and 1996 presidential campaigns or debates by candidates of any of the major political parties. More and more the fate and well-being of American cities was being determined by local efforts, both public and private, and by the larger forces of the national and global marketplaces, with which many local urban communities are tenuously attempting to come to grips (see Clark, 1994, for an excellent compilation and evaluation of a variety of these efforts).

INFORMAL URBAN POWER STRUCTURES

Our discussion in this chapter began with descriptions of formal power structures represented by various levels of local, state, and national government that are "legitimate" in the sense that they are sanctioned by the electorate. On the other hand, sociologists tend to focus on "illegitimate" forms of power—more specifically those that are not formally sanctioned or are not embodied in the formal structure of political institutions, such as cities, metropolitan regions, states, or the federal government. Virtually all sociologists recognize that, contrary to traditional American "myths," such power is distributed unequally, whether at the local, state, or national levels (Gold, 1990). However, they disagree on the degree to which it is unequally dispersed or in whose hands it is most likely to be concentrated. Thus, there are competing conceptions on the nature and distribution of political power, which are very often divided into "elitist" and "pluralistic" schools of thought on the subject. While some of the competing conceptions of how power is distributed in local urban communities have already begun to be introduced in the earlier parts of this chapter (see Logan and Molotch, 1998; Clark and Goetz, 1994: Gottdiener, 1994). They are examined in more detail below.

Community Power Structure

The question that is frequently raised by urban sociologists is whether the formal governmental mechanisms really indicate how decisions regarding the governing of urban communities are made, or whether more important informal mechanisms are at work. A good deal of attention was paid to this question during the last half of the twentieth century, resulting in a large number of studies, which attempted to answer some of the following questions:

1. Are the power and influence structures operating in American urban communities monolithic in nature, or is there instead a series of competing power structures that tend to act as checks and balances against one another?

2. Which groups or individuals within the community actually wield power and in what fashion?

3. Are there differences in structure of power between small cities, large cities, and still larger and more complex metropolitan areas?

4. Is there any relationship between a city's power structure and that of regional and national or global power systems?

5. What effect do changes in local population patterns and other shifts in internal social structure have on local patterns of power?

Although there were comprehensive sociological studies of community social structure undertaken as early as the 1920s and 1930s (see Lynd and Lynd, 1929, 1937), *Community Power Structure* by Floyd Hunter (1953) was one of the first to focus exclusively and in extensive detail on the power structure of a large American urban community. Using an investigatory approach known as the "reputational" method, Hunter sought to identify individual leaders or groups ("crowds," in Hunter's terms) who exercised the greatest degree of power over decision making in Regional City (a pseudonym for Atlanta, Georgia). He did this by first assembling lists of known civic, governmental, and business leaders and then submitting this list to a panel of knowledgeable local "judges" who were asked to rate them according to their ability to influence vital community decisions. There was a high degree of consensus among the judges as to who the real power wielders were. Drawn mainly from business and industrial circles (the mayor was the only elected official among the top ten leaders), these leaders constituted, according to Hunter, a small, highly interrelated, and cohesive group in which the members were intimately known to one another. Preferring to remain anonymous, they remained behind the scenes, relying instead on government officials as "puppets" to carry out their wishes. Hunter (p. 24) concluded that these elites were "able to enforce their decisions by persuasion, intimidation, coercion, and if necessary, force." Hunter's elitist conception of community power became the model for a number of other community power structure studies over the years (see Lowry, 1965; Rose, 1967; Aiken and Mott, 1970; Hawley, 1981; Domhoff, 1983; Phillips, 1996), which essentially agreed with Hunter that decision making in local American urban communities operates in a monolithic system with power concentrated in the hands of ruling elites which, because of the dominant economic roles they play in the community, are able to wield dominant influence over local political processes. This school of thought has generally been referred to as the *elitist* model of local community power structure.

Of course, not all social scientists who have studied local community power structure agree with the conclusions of those adhering to the elitist model, and a number of them have hypothesized a competing *pluralistic* model. Foremost among these was Robert Dahl (1961), whose investigation of New Haven, Connecticut, came up with results dramatically different from those of Hunter's study. Using a different methodological approach, Dahl chose to analyze the resolution of various kinds of community issues to determine the dynamics involved the decision-making processes examined in New

Haven. Rather than relying on opinions of who the leaders were (as in the "reputational" methods employed by hunter), Dahl was more interested in studying the actual process of applying power in action. He first identified a group of 238 individuals who occupied visible positions of economic power, as well as other potential wielders of influence (such as elected officials and religious leaders) who had roles of central economic importance. Then, by looking at the specific community issues under investigation, he sought to identify those individuals or groups who actually played major roles in the decisions made. From this methodological approach, Dahl's findings were dramatically different from those of Hunter's study. He concluded that the top leaders were not a small, covert, and monolithic elite but were rather a somewhat broader coalition of individuals and groups from both the private and public sectors who, in combination, broadly reflected the varied interests and concerns of different segments of the community. As Dahl reported, "The economic notables, far from being a ruling group, are simply one of many groups out of which individuals sporadically emerge to influence the politics and acts of city officials" (p. 72). Many other observers have attempted to more specifically identify some of the many types of groups and organizations within urban communities that attempt to exercise influence over the decision-making processes of local government, including political parties, trade associations, professional societies, labor union locals or labor councils, community service organizations, parent-teacher associations, tenants rights groups, consumers rights groups, environmental protection organizations, organized religions, and, of course, organizations representing racial and ethnic groups. In fact, various racial and ethnic groups have become majorities in many large American cities and now exercise considerable political influence over local political institutions (much more will be said about this in later chapters). Finally, the local affiliates of such national organizations as the American Civil Liberties Union, the NAACP and Urban League, or the National Education Association may also on occasion become important players in local affairs.

Thus, as in the case of the elitist model of community power structure, the pluralist model also has had its own share of intellectual proponents (see Rose, 1967; Braungart, 1976; Polsby, 1980; Clark, 1994). The arguments and debates in favor of or critical of each of these models have been extensive and vigorous over the decades, but given the current states of knowledge of the distribution of power in American urban communities, the earlier tendency for the advocates of each model to project either the elitist or the pluralist model as generally applicable to all American cities now seems greatly oversimplified. Such projections were often influenced either by the methodology employed by the various research strategies and methodologies or by the ideological predilections of the researchers. In addition, the limited number of communities investigated by community power studies hardly constitute a random selection of American cities.

More realistically an understanding of the power structure of a particular city can only be understood in relation to that community's peculiar social, economic, demographic, and governmental characteristics. Each community is likely to possess certain characteristics that make it unique and imperfectly comparable to other communities. Further, it may not only be the presence of particular factors, but their combinations and interaction in a particular setting that may be most important in shaping the power structure of a given urban community.

To many current observers of the distribution of power in American urban communities, the issue of which theory of power, elitist or pluralist, is most accurate and generalizable has almost become moot and relatively less important because higher national levels of government and industry make more and more of the kinds of decisions that reduce local autonomy. As a result, the undertaking of local community power structure studies has significantly been reduced in recent decades and interest has been focused elsewhere. However, it is still this author's view that knowledge about the power structure of a given community is essential in understanding how and in what terms public policy in that community will be formulated and executed. For example, whether the creation of such policy corresponds to the democratic ideal of broad citizen participation in any given American urban community remains of vital concern, because many, if not most, local functions, resources, and actions still are of local origin and impact. And, of course, the kind of debates among proponents of *urban growth machine* and *antigrowth machine* theories, as discussed in earlier parts of this chapter, now seem to have modified or supplanted earlier arguments about the nature and distribution of the power structure of decision making in local urban communities (see Clark, 1994; Gottdiener, 1994; Phillips, 1996).

National Power Structure

Elitist Perspectives.   By far, the single most influential work on the power structure of the United States as a whole has been *The Power Elite* by C. Wright Mills (1956). In this book, Mills asserted what had become the basis of a body of elitist theories of how power is distributed in America. Beginning with Mills, the elitist approach stresses the following:

1. There is a great concentration of power among a relatively small handful of very wealthy families at the apex of the American power structure.
2. These elite families share common values and interests and form a cohesive class or group.
3. This power elite controls vastly disproportionate shares of the nation's wealth and controls decision making over vast portions of the nation's economic and political life.
4. Among the elite, decision making occurs behind closed doors and beyond the scrutiny of the general public. Power elites tend to be monolithic in their internal cohesiveness and conspiratorial in their strategies for maintaining or increasing their power.
5. Elected officials tend to be "puppets" of the elites—thus, they tend to be relatively powerless in their own right.
6. As a result, elections make very little difference for the decision-making process of the nation.
7. The masses tend to be powerless, relative to the elites.
8. The concentration of power as described is a very undemocratic force in American society.

Under the circumstances, there is little or nothing the masses can do to increase their voice in decision making short of massive protest or revolution. Thus, for the most part, they tend to remain passive and/or apathetic (Gold, 1990). The elitist perspective, as outlined earlier, has been perpetuated in works by William Domhoff (1983), Steven Lukes (1974), Leonard and Mark Silk (1980), Gabriel Kolko (1962), and Michael Parenti (1988).

The Pluralistic Perspective.   As in the case of studies of local community power structures discussed earlier, sociologists also strongly disagree as to how power, whether highly concentrated or widely dispersed, is actually distributed in the United States. In strong opposition to elitist models, the pluralistic school contends that power is widely dispersed across a broad spectrum of competing interest groups representing a large majority of the American population. Each competing group may have "veto power," in the sense that they may have the capacity to prevent rival groups with competing interests from achieving their own goals, in spite of the possibility that each group may not be powerful enough to further its own interests in every instance. Although some groups may be more powerful than others (elitist and pluralist theories alike agree that "big business" groups are among the most powerful in the United States), none is sufficiently powerful to monopolize the political decision-making structure, as elitist theorists contend. Thus, the pluralists assert that even though the power structure of the United States is not ideal, it does come closer to the democratic ideal than do the perceptions of power held by elitist theorists. For example, Arnold Rose (1967) has earlier argued that although the elitist approach is much too simplistic and ignores the complexity of the real world, the elitist model more tellingly tends to ignore the power exercised by formal political bodies and elected officials, often in opposition to the interests of organized economic elites. Although both elitist and pluralist both tend to ignore the relationships between national and local power structure, one of the best empirical studies of power in the context of a large sprawling supra metropolitan region is Delbert Miller's (1975) *Leadership and Power in the Bos-Wash Megalopolis.* Here the complexities of the economic, social, and political structure of this sprawling region lead the author to pluralistic conclusions about the nature and distribution of power.

Somewhat independent of the elitist-pluralist controversy, a growing body of literature treats the power exercised by giant corporations on the political life of nations. Some of the impact such corporate power may have on local communities has been discussed briefly in chapter 7, and it is true that the power exercised by national and international corporations, as described in chapter 7, closely resembles the elitist model of power, as we have identified it here. The focus on corporate power differs from elitist perspective only in that corporate power is more impersonal and driven more by deterministic market or economic forces, and less by individual, family, or group values. Corporate elites may be less conspiratorial, less dependent on inherited wealth or privilege, and less driven by personal desires to consciously exercise power than traditional elitists would suggest. Instead, the drive to increase profits is the overwhelming motivation of corporate activity— the exercise of political power is simply an inevitable byproduct. This view has been clearly articulated in works such as Phillip Blumberg's *The Megacorporation (1975),* Mark Green and John Berry's *The Challenge of Hidden Profits* (1985), Robert Heilbroner's *The Limits of American Capitalism, in the Name of Profits* (1966), and Edward Herman's *Corporate Control, Corporate Power* (1981).

In *The Anatomy of Power,* John Kenneth Galbraith (1983) begins to avoid some of the oversimplifications and polemics often associated with both sides of the elitist-pluralist controversies. He argues that power is highly concentrated, as the elitist theories suggest, but that it is spread among four or five giant interest groups rather than in a single, monolithic entity. These include big business, big government, big agriculture, big distribution, and big labor. Other nationwide entities, such as education, the mass media, or the health care industry, could easily be added to Galbraith's list without distorting his argument. Because the interests of each of these groups may in many cases be contrary to that of the others, the power of each of these giant interest groups may be balanced against the others in a system of "countervailing" power, which prevents any one of them from gaining a complete monopoly over key decision-making processes in the United States.

In a similar vein, more recent works on American power structure avoid the more simplistic conclusions of both elitist and pluralistic theories. For example, Thomas Dye (1995) concludes in a recent edition of his frequently revised book *Who's Running America* that "We do not yet have sufficient evidence to confirm or deny the major tenets of elitist or pluralistic perspectives. Our research on institutional elites produces evidence of both hierarchy and polyarchy in the nation's elite structure" (Dye, 1995, p. 249). Nevertheless, Dye still finds a relatively large concentration of power among the twelve largest institutional sectors of American society, which in turn are dominated by approximately 7300 top leadership positions. These top positions, taken together, control nearly 75 percent of the industrial assets of the nation, half of all assets in communications and utilities industries, over one-half of all U.S. banking assets, and over three-quarters of all insurance assets; and they direct Wall Street's largest investment firms. They control the television networks, the most influential news organizations, and major newspaper chains. They control nearly 40 percent of all the assets of private foundations and approximately two-thirds of all endowments for private universities. They direct the nation's largest and most influential law firms, as well as many of the nation's major civic and cultural organizations. They occupy key positions in the executive, legislative, and judicial branches of the federal government, and they occupy virtually all the top command positions in the Army, Navy, Air Force, and Marines (Dye, 1995, p. 5). But what Dye and most other students of the American power structure—whether of elitist, pluralist, or intermediate pursuasions—fail to explicitly deal with is the impact of national power structures on decision making in local urban communities, or, putting it another way, the relationships between national and local community power structures.

One major exception is William Domhoff (1998), who, in the latest edition of his long-standing work, *Who Rules America?: Power and Politics in the Year 2000,* tenuously begins to review these relationships. Having modified his earlier positions as an elitist theorist, Domhoff now sees the so-called national power elite as a coalition of the corporate community, major policy formation organizations, and the social upper class of the United States. Further, like Dye, he avoids direct identification with either the elitist or pluralist school with the assertion that his book "is situated between interest-group pluralism on the one hand and institutional elitism on the other" (Domhoff, 1998, p. 12).

What is more important, for the purposes of this discussion, is the relationship between the nationwide corporate community and the local urban growth coalitions that he sees at the center of power in American society. Borrowing the concept of *urban growth coalitions,* as developed by John Logan and Harvey Molotch (1988) and briefly discussed earlier in this chapter, Domhoff makes a valuable contribution by tentatively identifying the links between local urban power structures and national power structures. Local growth coalitions and the national corporate community, according to Domhoff, have much in common and often work together. The basis for cooperation between the corporate community and the local growth coalitions is based on the fact that the local coalitions must attract corporate investments to their areas in order to support their own growth ambitions. To do this, they try to satisfy the needs of the corporate community by providing them with the local physical infrastructure, municipal services, local labor markets, and political climate that the corporations find necessary or attractive. Further, the local growth coalitions continue to advance their own goals by taking advantage of corporate investments in their communities as a basis for attracting still more local developments, such as new government buildings, university campuses, and other civic amenities designed to attract more new residents, housing developments, and further growth activities which produce still more wealth for themselves and their local communities (Domhoff, 1998, pp. 59–60).

What helps move Domhoff further from the elitist camp and closer to Galbraith's theory of countervailing power is his recognition that the relations between local growth coalitions and national and international corporations can, under a variety of circumstances, be characterized by strain and conflict. He acknowledges that although corporations freely move their resources into a community if it suits their purposes, they can also move out if they find taxes, regulations, or wage levels too costly or restrictive. This ability to move also stimulates constant competition among rival urban communities for new capital investments, and this creates tensions between local growth coalitions and corporations, as well as the more obvious competition between urban growth machines themselves, as rival cities offer tax breaks, less restrictive regulations, or other "incentives" in order to induce corporations to add plants, offices, workers, or other corporate facilities to their communities. Domhoff also recognizes the more recent emergence of antigrowth coalitions which are created for the purpose of resisting the "collusion, between local growth coalitions and corporations to create what is viewed by anti-growth groups as undesirable development." Although the antigrowth groups add complexity to the tensions and conflicts between competing interest groups at the local levels, Domhoff is not as optimistic about the potential clout of the movement to prevent or control corporate-sponsored growth or development in local urban communities as some of the other observers discussed earlier in this chapter (Domhoff, 1998, pp. 60–61).

Finally, Domhoff's observations about the relationship between national power structures and the power structures of local urban communities are highly tentative and are subject to changing circumstances, although they are an important first step in theorizing about this relationship, which has usually been neglected by those who focus on the study of national political power, as well as by those who study political power in local urban communities. Also, more generally, the study of urban political economy has tended to focus on the economic side of this concept, while leaving ideas about the precise relationships between economic and political institutions in urban settings somewhat blurred and underformulated (see Smith and Timberlake, 1997, pp. 126–128; Macionis and Parrillo, 1998, pp. 209–212, for brief critiques of the political economy approach). In this volume, we have discussed urban economic and political institutions in separate chapters, with the hope that the readers will better grasp the complexities of the relationship between these two arenas of American urban life and will appreciate the need for greater development, clarification, and integration of these areas.

SELECTED BIBLIOGRAPHY

AIKEN, MICHAEL and MOTT, PAUL E. *The Structure of Community Power.* New York: Random House. 1970.

BERRY, JEFFREY M., KENT E. PORTNEY, and KEN THOMSON. *The Rebirth of Urban Democracy.* Washington, DC: Brookings Institute, 1993.

BLUMBERG, PHILLIP I. *The Megacorporation in American Society: The Scope of Corporate Power.* Englewood Cliffs, NJ: Prentice-Hall. 1975

BRAUNGART, RICHARD G., ed. *Society and Politics: Readings in Political Sociology.* Englewood Cliffs, NJ: Prentice-Hall, 1976.

CARALEY, DEMETRIOUS. *City Governments and Urban Problems.* Englewood Cliffs, NJ: Prentice-Hall 1977.

CLARK, TERRY N., ed. *Urban Innovation: Creative Strategies for Turbulent Times.* Thousand Oaks, CA: Sage Publications, 1994.

———, and EDWARD G. Goetz. "The Anti-Growth Machine: Can City Governments Control, Limit, or Manage Growth?" In *Urban Innovation: Creative Stategies for Turbulent Times,* Terry N. Clark (ed.). Thousand Oaks, CA: Sage Publications, 1994.

DAHL, ROBERT A. *Who Governs?* New Haven: Yale University Press. 1961

DAVIS, MIKE. "Who Killed L.A.?: The War against the Cities." *Crossroads* 32(1993): 2-19.

DOMHOFF, WILLIAM G. *Who Rules America Now?: A View for the 80's.* Englewood Cliffs, NJ: Prentice-Hall, 1983.

———. *Who Rules America?: Power and Politics in the Year 2000.* Mountain View, NJ: Mayfield, 1998.

DYE, THOMAS R. *Who's Running America: The Clinton Years.* Englewood Cliffs, NJ: Prentice-Hall, 1995.

GALBRAITH, JOHN KENNETH. *The Anatomy of Power.* New York: Houghton Mifflin, 1983.

GLAAB, CHARLES N. *The American City: A Documentary History.* Homewood IL: Dorsey, 1963.

GOLD, HARRY. *The Sociology of Urban Life.* Englewood Cliffs, NJ: Prentice-Hall, 1982.

———. "Political Sociology: A Developing Field" (Bibliographic Essay). *CHOICE* (Feb. 1990).

GORHAM, WILLIAM, and NATHAN GLAZER, eds. *The Urban Predicament.* Washington DC: The Urban Insitute, 1976.

GOTTDIENER, MARK. *The New Urban Sociology.* New York: McGraw-Hill, 1994.

GREEN, MARK, and JOHN F. BERRY, *The Challenge of Hidden Profits: Reducing Corporate Bureaucracy and Waste.* New York: W. Morrow, 1985.

HAWLEY, AMOS. *Urban Society: An Ecological Approach,* 2d ed. New York: John Wiley, 1981.

HAYS, SAMUEL P. "The Politics of Reform in Municipal Government in the Progressive Era." *Pacific Northwest Quarterly* 55(1964): 157–169.

HEILBRONER, ROBERT L. *The Limits of American Capitalism.* New York: Harper and Rowe, 1966.

HERMAN, EDWARD S. *Corporate Control, Corporate Power.* Cambridge, U.K.: Cambridge University Press, 1981.

HUNTER, FLOYD. *Community Power Structure.* Chapel Hill: University of North Carolina Press, 1953.

KOLKO, GABRIEL. *Wealth and Power in America: An Analysis of Social Class and Income Distribution.* Westport, CT: Praeger, 1962.

LEVIN, DONALD M. "Urban Political Institutions: Formal Governmental Structure and Policies." In Gold, *The Sociology of Urban Life,* Englewood Cliffs, NJ: Prentice-Hall, 1982.

LINEBERRY, ROBERT P., and EDMOND P. FOWLER. "Reformism and Public Policies in American Cities." *American Political Science Review.* 3 (1967):701–716.

LOGAN, JOHN R., and HARVEY MOLOTCH. *Urban Fortunes.* Berkeley: University of California Press, 1988.

LOWRY, RITCHIE P. *Who's Running This Town?* New York: Harper, 1965.

LUKES, STEVEN. *Power: A Radical View.* New York: MacMillan, 1974

LYND, ROBERT S., and HELEN M. LYND. *Middletown.* New York: Harcourt, Brace, and World, 1929.

———. *Middletown in Transition.* New York: Harcourt, Brace, and World, 1937.

MACIONIS, JOHN J., and VINCENT N. PARRILLO. *Cities and Urban Life.* Upper Saddle River, NJ: Prentice-Hall, 1998.

MERTON, ROBERT K. *Social Theory and Social Structure.* New York: Free Press, 1968.

MILLER, DELBERT C. *Leadership and Power in the Bos-Wash Megalopolis.* New York: John Wiley, 1975.

MILLS, C. WRIGHT. *The Power Elite.* New York: Oxford University Press, 1956.

MIRANDA, ROWAN A. and NORMAN WALZER. "Growth and Decline of City Government." In *Urban Innovations: Creative Strategies for Turbulent Times,* Terry N. Clark (ed.). Thousand Oaks, CA: Sage Publications, 1994.

PALEN, J. JOHN. *The Urban World,* 5th ed. New York: McGraw-Hill, 1997.

PARENTI, MICHAEL. *Democracy for the Few,* 5th ed. New York: St. Martins, 1988.

PHILLIPS, E. BARBARA. *City Lights; Urban-Suburban Life in the Global Society,* 2d ed. New York: Oxford University Press, 1996.

POLSBY, NELSON W. *Community Power and Political Theory,* 2d ed. New Haven: Yale University Press, 1980.

ROSE, ARNOLD M. *The Power Structure: Political Processes in American Society.* New York: Oxford University Press, 1967.

SHANK, ALAN, and RALPH CONANT. *Urban Perspectives.* Boston: Holbrook Press, 1975.

SILK, LEONARD, and MARK SILK. *The American Establishment.* New York: Basic Books, 1980.

SMITH, DAVID A. and MICHAEL F. TIMBERLAKE. "Urban Political Economy." In J. John Palen, *The Urban World,* 5th ed., New York: McGraw-Hill, 1997.

WATSON, DOUGLAS J. *The New Civil War: Government Competition for Economic Development.* Westport, CT: Praeger, 1995.

WEISBROD, BURTON A. and JAMES C. WORTHY, eds. *The New Urban Crises: Linking Research to Action.* Evanston, IL: Northwestern University Press, 1997.

9

WELFARE AND EDUCATION AS EMERGENT URBAN INSTITUTIONS

The quality of life in any urban area depends, to a large degree, on the functioning of social institutions concerned with the general welfare of the urban population. In the United States, two competing conceptions of social welfare seem to have been dominant throughout the twentieth century. The first of these is the *residual* concept, which holds that social welfare institutions should only come into play when the "normal" structures of the family and the urban-industrial market breaks down. The second, the *institutional* concept, sees welfare services as normal mainline functions of modern urban-industrial societies. These are the two concepts around which many past and present ideological and political battles over the appropriate amounts and types of welfare services have tended to focus. Thus, the competing values of economic individualism and free enterprise on the one hand, and the values of security, equality, and humanitarianism on the other, are among the conservative or liberal political choices that are from time to time faced by elected officials, welfare professionals and administrators, and the public at large, with respect to welfare policies and programs (Wilensky and Lebeaux, 1958).

The residual concept of social welfare was more predominant in the period preceding the Great Depression of 1929, and it was consistent with the more traditional American ideology of individual responsibility and self-help that dominated the first three decades of the twentieth century. But with the coming of the New Deal in the depression-ridden 1930s, the institutional notion of social welfare became dominant and persisted well into the last decade of the twentieth century, when it was largely modified in the direction of the previous conception by the Welfare Reform Act of 1996.

The institutional concept of social welfare that characterized the greater part of the last century can be characterized as an organized system of social services and agencies, designed to aid individuals and groups to attain "satisfying standards of life and health." It aimed at personal and social relationships which permit individuals the fullest development of their capacities and the promotion of their well-being in harmony with the greater needs of the urban community. Under this doctrine, all people are regarded as having needs that become legitimate claims against the attention and resources of the whole society.

Government and the private sector were both seen as channels to supply these needs, and they had vastly broadened their responsibilities during most of the last century. Under this conception, social welfare became accepted as a proper and legitimate function of modern urban society, and the inability of the individual to provide fully for him or herself or to meet all one's needs in family, work, and economic settings was considered a "normal" condition, along with the achievement of established institutional status by the appropriate helping social agencies. Now, at the beginning of the twenty-first century, both the earlier and later doctrines coexist in an ambiguous compromise of both sets of values, in an as not yet adequately tested or demonstrated set of new social policies and programs. More is discussed about these in later parts of this chapter.

THE CONCEPT OF PUBLIC WELFARE IN AMERICA

In many urban-industrial societies, social welfare is thought of as a social institution comprising all those policies and programs through which government guarantees a defined but minimum level of social services, income maintenance, and consumption rights according to criteria other than that which is prescribed by the "free" market economy. In the United States, welfare has largely been used to refer to income maintenance programs for specific categories of eligible recipients, including the poor, elderly, disabled, unemployed, or children. However, public support for such programs has often been uneven or controversial. Although some services, such as education and social security or veteran's benefits, have largely been accepted as "rights," others, such as those more commonly referred to as "welfare," have been strongly resisted by large segments of the U.S. population. Such resistance can be partially explained by a complex fusion of cultural, historical, and social attitudes. For example, puritanical attitudes toward work and leisure, the industrial revolution and the rise of capitalism, social class differences, and place of residence are among the many factors associated with significant American resistance to coordinated services or benefits as a right to which all citizens are entitled. When such benefits and services are considered to be a social good, they are more likely to become rights that are guaranteed by the provision and institutionalization of public resources. To the extent that such benefits and services are well established, recognized, and accepted as proper and necessary in a given society, and a significant portion of a society's wealth and energies are dedicated to maintaining these rights, then such a society can be referred to as a *welfare state.* Most European urban societies, of course, are more fully developed as welfare states and have been so for a much longer period of time than the United States (see Karger and Stoesz, 1994, pp. 409–415), where the resistance to such status has been much greater, as clearly evidenced by the welfare debates and reforms of the 1930s, 1960s, and late 1990s. Here a brief historical perspective is in order.

WELFARE IN THE COLONIAL PERIOD

The early American colonists brought with them English patterns of social services, and these patterns dominated welfare until the late nineteenth century. Two dimensions of the English tradition were critical: the belief that welfare was the responsibility of local communities rather than the national government; and an ideology of *scarcity,* which held that those at the bottom of the economic ladder could only be helped at the expense of those above them and that therefore all care or aid for the poor had to be as inexpensive and humiliating as possible. This scarcity ideology, which was reflected in the English Elizabethan poor laws of the seventeenth century, was generally accepted in the United States well into the early part of the twentieth century, when it was generally superseded by the ideology embodied in the New Deal policies of the 1930s and the Kennedy-Johnson "War on Poverty" policies of the 1960s (Gold and Scarpitti, 1967). However, the core of some conservative economic thought which emerged and became more predominant in the 1980s and into the 1990s appeared once again to be based on an ideology of scarcity. Therefore it is useful to reexamine the scarcity ideology underlying the poor laws as aptly summarized by sociologist Jessie Bernard as follows:

> Human nature is essentially bad, so that unless you make welfare as difficult and as humiliating as possible, people will just naturally take advantage of you. There must, therefore, be means tests of some sort or other; that is, poor people must prove their destitution and be willing to pay the price in humiliation, or even sacrifice of civil rights, if need be. Those receiving welfare must be kept below the level of self-supporting families because economy in the administration of funds is a prime consideration and the taxpayer must be protected against a potential horde of chiselers, or even the more worthy and deserving poor. He must be protected against the squandering of relief funds on swindlers; most people who need welfare are inferior or deserve this misfortune, therefore there should be no "coddling" of clients. Public welfare must be made as disagreeable, as punitive, and as unendurable as possible in order to reduce the numbers asking for it. Generosity would inevitably lead to abuse. Economy in the use of public funds, taken for granted as a good thing, demands that the natural tendency for people to take advantage of generosity be curbed. (Bernard, 1957, p. 28)

In almost complete contrast to the scarcity ideology of the poor laws, there is a much different ideology implicit in current welfare legislation, such as the welfare reform act of 1996. The currently prevailing ideology emphasizes instead the importance and even the necessity of maintaining individual family income through employment for all segments of the economy, including the welfare poor. Maintaining income in poor families through employment requirements is no longer viewed as merely charity, philanthropy, or even generosity. Instead, it has become defined as a basic functional prerequisite of an abundant society. If increasing production capacities are to have an outlet, there must be a population, including the poor, with an adequate income to buy the products that are offered. All segments of the economy, including the poor, must be put to work in income-producing jobs to produce the money to spend in order to keep the economy functioning properly. In other words, the poor must be removed from the welfare rolls and be put to work in productive jobs in order to maintain a healthy economy. Although this ideology of abundance may appear to be more humane, it is also based on assumptions that jobs providing adequate income for the poor are readily available and that the poor have the skills, training, and other requirements to fit the available positions. At the beginning of the twenty-first century, it is still not clear how well the above assumptions and expectations will be met, and considerable skepticism remains among critics of the current welfare system. More will be said about this following the continuation of our review of the evolution of welfare policies in urban America.

As a result of the emphasis on local responsibility and the worthiness or unworthiness of the poor, American villages and towns of the colonial period developed various strategies to deal with the needy. Those unable to work were often sent to "poor houses" or "almshouses." These were often unpleasant homes on farms where assistance was meager, and the idle or lazy were punished. Those considered more worthy, such as widows with small children, the old, and the ill or disabled were often supplied with provisions, bedding, or other necessities which would, if possible, allow them to remain in their own homes. In smaller towns unable to support the unworthy in institutions such as public almshouses, it was not uncommon for the town councils to auction off the poor to neighboring farmers, apprentice out children, place the poor in private homes at public expense, or send them to privately operated almshouses. It was widely believed that children should be part of a family unit and thus the practice of indenture became relatively widespread. By the end of the colonial period, the focus of responsibility for the poor began to shift from the towns to the colonies and, ultimately, the states (Scherer, 1982).

WELFARE IN THE NINETEENTH CENTURY

For the most part, the nineteenth century did not produce significant advances in public welfare or significantly broaden its scope. During the 1840s a brief reform era led to the establishment of state mental health hospitals after Dorethea Dix, a prominent human rights crusader, helped to arouse public indignation about the terrible conditions that existed for the mentally ill. The reform efforts were short-lived, however, because the traditional ways of thinking about welfare inherited from the English system and the poor laws still dominated the thoughts of the period. The Civil War also ushered in a new spurt in welfare-related activities. Families who had lost a breadwinner or who had a breadwinner return from the war permanently disabled could, of course, not be blamed for their misfortunes. As a response to these kinds of hardships, many local communities passed laws that raised funds for the disabled and needy and, in some instances, for the founding of homes for disabled soldiers.

Other welfare issues during the Civil War included the disease and filth in army camps and hospitals and the shortage of trained medical personnel. In response, a group of citizens (composed mainly of women) organized the U.S. Sanitary Commission in the 1860s, the first important national public health group. Working in the area of preventative health education, the Commission eventually became involved in a variety of direct and indirect ways of serving the health needs of soldiers (Karger and Stoesz, 1994). More significant was the creation of the Freedmen's Bureau in 1865. The bureau performed a variety of services designed to help African Americans make the transition from slavery to freedom. In addition to providing emergency relief services to former slaves, the Bureau also functioned as an African-American employment agency, a settlement agency, a health center that operated hospitals, an educational agency that encouraged the funding of African American colleges and provided financial aid, and, finally, as a legal agency that maintained courts in which civil and criminal cases involving African Americans were heard. The Freedmen's Bureau set an important precedent for federal involvement in a variety of social welfare services, but nevertheless these programs were all discontinued when the Bureau was dissolved by an act of Congress in 1872 (Trattner, 1974, p. 87).

During the latter part of the nineteenth century, the rapidly growing number of foreign-born immigrants migrating to the rapidly growing cities of the United States had become critical. The personal problems faced by many of these new residents often included overwhelming poverty, the inability to communicate in English, loneliness for a faraway homeland, separation from family members, frustration in adjusting to the rapid industrialization of the cities, unhealthy working conditions, poor education, and political powerlessness (see chapter 3 for a more detailed discussion of these conditions). At the same time, the philosophical theme of *Social Darwinism* had begun to emerge, which often was drawn upon to justify relatively harsh responses to the plight of the newcomers and other destitute urban populations.

The application of Darwin's theories of evolution to society and then applying them to laissez-faire principles of economics led to a problematic set of assumptions regarding the doctrine of "survival of the fittest." According to this doctrine, subsidizing

Jane Addams (1860–1935) was a founder of Hull House, an early immigrant settlement house in Chicago, and was an important pioneer in the development of social work as a profession

the poor allowed them to survive, thus circumventing the laws of nature. And because the poor reproduced more rapidly than the "more industrious" middle classes, society would subsidize its own demise due to the "fact" that the poor would eventually over-run society and bring down the general level of civilization. The Darwinists also maintained that if competition for resources was the governing principle of life, the poor would be impoverished because they could not compete. At the same time, the economic elites are entitled to their share of the pot because of their superior competitive abilities and "hereditary fitness." By subsidizing the poor and allowing them to reproduce, society artificially alters the laws of nature, and in so doing, weakens the gene pool. Finally, Social Darwinists believed that, although unfortunate, the poor must pay the price demanded by nature and be allowed to die out. Thus, it was assumed, according to these theories, that most forms of social welfare would thwart nature's plan of evolutionary progress toward higher forms of social life.

TWENTIETH-CENTURY PUBLIC WELFARE

A reaction to the extreme harshness that characterized Social Darwinism was reflected in the Progressive Movement that made an impact on social policy from about the late 1890s to about the beginning of World War I. The ethos of this movement centered on a belief that government should regulate the public good, a commitment to social justice, and a concern for the "common man." The resultant reforms included the development of the U.S. Children's Bureau, a workers' compensation law for certain federal employees, the establishment of the eight-hour day for workers on interstate railroads, and some restrictions on child labor employed in interstate commerce. In addition, many states passed laws protecting the rights of women workers in areas such as minimum wages, restricted working hours, and other conditions of work. One of the most interesting reforms to come out of this was the Settlement House Movement. Hull House, which was founded in Chicago by Jane Addams, was probably the best example (see chapter 3) and provided services to poor immigrants in helping them find work, obtain job skills, how to use community resources, and to improve their lives in many other ways. In an interesting byproduct, Jane Addams and the Hull House settlement staff laid the foundation for the development of a new occupational specialty: professional social work (see chapter 7). The economic boom period following World War I through the 1920s tended to diminish the liberal impulses of the Progressive era, and some of the welfare legislation was rolled back or rescinded.

WAVES OF CHANGE: THE NEW DEAL, THE NEW FRONTIER, AND THE GREAT SOCIETY

The Great Depression, which followed the stock market crash of 1929, led to massive unemployment and unrest throughout the United States. By 1932, employment reached a high of nearly 25 percent, and in the large industrial cities, the rates and numbers were even higher. For example, over six hundred thousand workers were jobless in Chicago and approximately 1 million in New York City. In Detroit and Cleveland, one-half of all workers were unemployed, and in Toledo, Ohio, the unemployment rate was 80 percent. Manufacturing output fell to 20 percent or less of its capacity, and factory wages for those still employed shrank to almost half of their previous levels. Several million people were roaming across the country in search of work; shanty towns had sprung up in most large cities to house the many newly homeless people; and soup lines became part of the urban landscape. Many cities attempted to provide relief to aid the victims of the depression, but most quickly ran out of funds for doing so. As a result more than one hundred cities had no funds left to appropriate for relief by 1932. For the first time, more people emigrated from the United States than migrated to it in the same year (although by then, the depression had reached world proportions).

When Franklin D. Roosevelt assumed the presidency in 1933, he faced a country increasingly divided between extremist political factions energized by the depression, an industrial system near collapse and facing violent forms of worker unrest, and the social class structure of the society near the breaking point. The Roosevelt administration moved quickly to try to alleviate suffering and unrest and to provide food, shelter, and clothing for the millions of unemployed workers. It did this through a series of policies and programs eventually labeled as the New Deal.

A brief summary of some of the key provisions of the New Deal is as follows:

1. The Federal Emergency Relief Administration, which distributed over $5.2 billion of emergency relief to states and local communities.
2. The National Recovery Act (NRA) which provided a comprehensive series of public works projects.
3. The Works Progress Administration (WPA), which employed workers to build dams, bridges, and other important public projects. WPA projects employed white- and blue-collar workers, as well as unskilled laborers, and produced roads, public parks, airports, schools, post offices, and various other public buildings. It also provided work opportunities through the Federal Writers' Project, the Federal Arts Project, and the Federal Theater Project.
4. The Civilian Conservation Corps (CCC) and the National Youth Administration (NYA) addressed the problems of unemployed young people by putting them to work replanting forests and helping with soil conservation projects (CCC) or by assisting them to obtain vocational, high school, or college training, along with part-time employment (NYA).
5. The Fair Labor Standards Act, which established a federal minimum wage, a maximum work week, and a provision for time-and-a-half pay for overtime work. This act also abolished child labor for those under sixteen.
6. The National Labor Relations Act, which guaranteed private-sector workers the right to bargain collectively, organize as labor unions, and strike.

One of the most significant, widely accepted, and long-lasting components of the New Deal was the Social Security Act of 1935. This included a national old age insurance system, federal grants to states for maternal and child welfare services, relief to dependent children, vocational rehabilitation for the handicapped, medical care for crippled children, aid to the blind, and a federal-state unemployment insurance system. Clearly, the social security program, along with the other programs listed earlier, gave the federal government a very strong and visible role in providing broad-based welfare services and, in effect, created the framework of the modern welfare state. Although many critics at the time accused the Roosevelt administration of socialistic or marxist intentions in creating the New Deal, modern observers were more inclined, in hindsight, to credit Roosevelt with having saved the capitalistic system and preserving American democracy through the bold antidepression policies and programs of the 1930s (Karger and Stoesz, 1994, p. 64). In spite of the New Deal programs and the subsequent periods of relative prosperity during the 1940s and 1950s, large pockets of poverty still remained, and it has been estimated that about 22 percent of the nation's population still lived below the poverty level in 1959 (Morris, 1986), even though attitudes toward the poor and programs to serve their needs had hardened during those two decades. Virtually no new welfare programs had been proposed, and the existing ones were in constant jeopardy. Many Americans actually believed that poverty had been eliminated for the most part, and many political leaders balked at the continuing need for the welfare programs. In the 1960s, there was a new focus on the problems of the poor and the need for solutions to eradicate or minimize poverty. One might conclude that the period from the end of World War II until the 1960s, when poverty all but disappeared from active concern and then suddenly reappeared, simply reflects the fact that during this relatively short period of time Americans had shifted their attention to problems of reestablishing a peace-time economy and establishing some sort of stable world order. At any rate, those Americans still experiencing poverty at the bottom of the economic ladder were no longer widely featured in the mass media or popular literature, as they were in the 1930s. More and more the popular heroes became middle class, and the "rat race" of Madison Avenue or "sex in the suburbs" became popular themes displacing the older emphasis on the trials and virtues of the poor. During this period, the fortunate majority had more and more assumed that almost every one was sharing the rapidly rising living standards, or that everyone was prospering as they themselves were as the result of good economic conditions.

As Michael Harrington put it in his popular book, *The Other America,* the millions of Americans who did not share this economic growth had become increasingly "invisible" to the prosperous majority. This invisibility resulted from the fact that the very poor had become, in a variety of ways, almost completely segregated from the rest of society. Poverty was off the "beaten path," confined largely to certain geographic regions or in the deteriorating slums of central cities, well isolated from the well-to-do suburbs where most middle-class families now lived. This spatial segregation had removed poverty from the living, emotional experience of millions upon millions of middle-class Americans. Living out in the rapidly growing suburbs, it was all too easy to assume an affluent society (Gold and Scarpitti, 1967, pp. 11–12).

It had been reported at the time that Harrington's book actually did impress President John. F. Kennedy of the needs for renewed federal action in combating poverty with its dramatic description of the magnitude and nature of the poverty problem (*Newsweek,* February 16, 1964), which were expressed in his proposals for a "New Frontier." After Kennedy's assassination in 1963, President Lyndon Johnson exploited the shock of the nation with the declaration of a "War on Poverty" which was a key component of his "Great Society" program designed to cure poverty in America. Driven by massive urban riots in African American communities and other forms of social unrest during the middle and late 1960s, Johnson's programs were aimed at empowering poor communities to arrest poverty and to increase economic opportunities within such communities.

The Great Society programs included Volunteers in Service to America—a domestic peace corps; Upward Bound, a program that encouraged poor and ghetto children to attend college; a Neighborhood Youth Corps for unemployed teenagers; Operation Head Start, a program that provided preschool training for lower-income children; special grants and loans to rural families and migrant workers; a comprehensive Community Action Program designed to mobilize community resources; the Legal Services Corporation; the Model Cities program; the Job Corps, a manpower program providing jobs for disadvantaged youths under twenty-one; the Economic Development Act of 1965, which provided states with grants and loans for public works and technical assistance; and the Economic Opportunity Act of 1964, which emphasized education and job training (see DiNitto and Dye, 1987).

Of course, in total these programs were very costly, and, along with the fact that the Vietnam War was underway at the same time that the War on Poverty policies were undertaken, many of them became financially unsustainable and unpopular with the public. Most of them were cut back or dismantled during the Nixon years. Despite the subsequent criticisms and lack of support for these programs, it should be remembered that during the Great Society period, the number of people living below the poverty line was cut almost in half, from about 25 percent in the early 1960s to around 12 percent by 1969 (Karger and Stoesz, 1994, p. 66). In other words, if the goals of these programs were designed to reduce the amount of poverty in America, they were remarkably successful, contrary to the collective memories of many subsequent reviewers!

Beginning in 1980, the campaign and governing philosophy of President Reagan was that federal government expenditures for public welfare should be significantly reduced and only be available to those who were "truly" needy and then only on a short-term basis. As a result, welfare expenditures dropped sharply for those receiving federal public assistance, and homelessness grew at rates that were unusual for a nondepression period. The income gap between the wealthy and poor began to widen (see chapter 11 on social stratification), and the levels of homelessness began to grow. The general economic conditions of the economy and the government were complicated by enormous budget and trade deficits which provided an additional rationale for curtailing the welfare functions of the federal government. The welfare policies of Reagan carried over to the Bush administration between 1989 and 1992. Although Bush emphasized the role private voluntary and philanthropic organizations played in helping the needy under the rubric of his call for "a thousand points of light," a rise in the numbers of those in poverty continued through his administration, along with an increase in unemployment, homelessness, and a 5 percent increase in the number of people on the Aid to Families with Dependent Children (AFDC) program. Even though Bush was admired for his foreign and Persian Gulf War policies, it was clear to many that his perceived lack of interest or involvement in domestic policy matters helped lead to his defeat by Bill Clinton in the 1992 presidential election.

WELFARE REFORM IN THE 1990s— "THE WAR AGAINST WELFARE"

By the 1990s, the need for adequate health care insurance had become a major political issue, and President Clinton had campaigned for a health care delivery system that would guarantee "universal" health care insurance for all Americans. Such a plan was presented to Congress, but in response to much opposition by organized-interest groups, such as those formed by the private health insurance industry and others opposed to the concept of universal national health care insurance, the legislation for the plan failed to be passed by Congress in 1994. To date, no similar effort has been made to reintroduce similar legislation, although it has been estimated that approximately 40 million Americans are still not covered by any form of health care insurance.

Clinton had also campaigned on a pledge to "reform welfare as we know it," and in this, he was much more successful, although the legislation which was eventually passed in 1996, and which he signed into law was not necessarily what he or the Democratic Party had intended. What had happened over the preceding decades is that the social problem of poverty had largely been redefined by public opinion as a problem of welfare rather than a problem of poverty (Horton et al., 1997, pp. 345–349). Images of the welfare poor as " lazy," "irresponsible," "promiscuous," or "chiselers and cheaters" were widely circulated and accepted as true, although they were mostly not backed up by careful examination and in spite of much careful research and scholarship to the contrary (Danziger and Gottschalk, 1995; Schiller, 1994; Bane and Ellwood, 1989). Thus, the "war on poverty" had turned against the poor and became the "war against welfare."

Because both Clinton and the Republican congress were under political pressure to "do something about the welfare *mess*" before the upcoming national elections, Congress passed and the president, in spite of some reservations, reluctantly signed the Welfare Reform Bill of 1996. In effect the bill drastically restricts the federal government's long-established role in providing a safety net for the welfare poor. More specifically, the bill provides for the following changes:

1. It completely abolishes a federal welfare "entitlement." No longer will being destitute, homeless, and hungry guarantee an individual or family a welfare check.
2. It turns the entire welfare program over to the individual states, along with block grants of funds to the states, which are then free to experiment with assistance programs.
3. With some exceptions, it sets a two-year limit to a single welfare stay, and a lifetime five-year limit for each client. (Horton et al., 1997, p. 349)

It is still to soon to assess the long-term effects of these changes in welfare law and policy, but preliminary estimates suggest that there have been both positive and negative impacts on those directly affected. For example, most studies suggest that welfare caseloads are down significantly since the new law took effect. One study has reported in mid-1999 that welfare caseloads have been cut nearly in half since peaking in 1994 (*New York Times,* August 23, 1999, p. A12). Similar results were cited by President Clinton during a tour of poverty stricken areas (*New York Times,* July 8, 1999, p. A25).

Although the new programs appear to be successful in getting people off of welfare, they do not appear to have done much to reduce poverty for those who have left the welfare rolls. In fact, for many, the welfare changes have made the very poorest worse off than they were before (*New York Times,* August 23, 1999, p. A2; January 19, 2000, p. A21; January 23, WK 3). There are a variety of reasons why people who have left the welfare rolls, voluntarily or involuntarily, are very often worse off: (1) they often lose re-lated benefits, such as food stamps or Medicaid; (2) those that find full-time work at mini-mum wages do not earn enough to raise them above the poverty line; (3) many people only work part-time because they cannot find full-time work, and many people who do find work are not necessarily employed year-round; and (4) many employed single mothers cannot find reliable or low-cost child care for their children. Perhaps from the perspective of urban sociology, one of the most significant facts about the welfare poor are that as welfare rolls shrink, they are increasingly concentrated in the inner-city neighborhoods of the nation's larger metropolitan areas, many of which the very good economic times of the 1990s did not reach. According to many local officials and welfare policy experts, welfare rolls are shrink-ing more slowly in big cities than in surrounding areas, and "the largest American cities are becoming home to a larger and larger share of the nation's welfare recipients" (*New York Times,* June 6, 1999, p. Y22). Part of the problem, according to this same *New York Times* article, is that "Three-fourths of the people on welfare live in inner cities, but two-thirds to three-fourths of all new jobs are being created outside these inner-city areas."

Compounding the problem for the big cities in meeting the needs of their poorest residents is that affordable housing for the working poor has become harder to find as the rising economy has raised the costs of rental housing to unprecedented levels in large cities. According to a 2000 report issued by the Department of Housing and Urban Devel-opment, over 5 million low-income families were paying more than half their income for housing, or living in dilapidated housing, worsening their living conditions since the start of economic expansion began in 1991 (*New York Times,* March 28, 2000, p. A18). Fur-ther impeding aid for the welfare poor, the block grants provided by the new welfare act go directly to the states, and there is no guarantee that the governors and state legislatures will provide this money to cities in proportions to their need, because, as has been sug-gested in chapter 8, there are often biases against the big cities in the capitals of many states. At the time of this writing, concern has been expressed by both the president and some members of Congress that the welfare reforms might be having some unintended consequences, such as a loss of Medicaid benefits (*Detroit Free Press,* April 8, 2000, p. A2), which will have to be corrected in the future in order to prevent possible greater harm to the recipients. Also under consideration at the end of the twentieth century were studies by the Census Bureau, the Office of Management and Budget, to determine whether the poverty line, as it is currently measured, should be raised to better reflect the actual cost of living for poor families in the United States, potentially making more fami-lies eligible for benefits than is the case under the present definitions of poverty and eligibility levels. For example, the poverty line set by the Census Bureau for a family of three for 1999 was $13,003 a year, yet a recent study by the University Center for Social and Urban Research at the University of Pittsburgh concluded that basic living wages should be at least $25,000 a year (*Detroit News,* October 24, 1999, p. 7A). Of course, such revisions may be many years away, if ever, and will probably depend more on the political and public opinion climate at the time than on the actual economic needs and well-being of the poor.

PRIVATE FORMS OF WELFARE
AND CHARITY IN URBAN SOCIETY

The discussion so far has mainly focused on public forms of welfare provided by various levels of government, but the private sector has also been a recognizable component of social welfare institutions, beginning early in the nineteenth century to the present. Residing largely in the nonprofit sector of the American economy, private forms of social welfare include individual philanthropy, trusts and foundations, religious organizations ("Faith-based institutions," in the rhetoric of the George W. Bush administration), charities, voluntary associations, organized associations of professional social service workers (social workers, counselors, psychologists, health workers, etc.), independent social service agencies, communitywide and bureaucratic social service federations, national social service associations, and incorporated national confederations, such as the United Way of America. Table 9.1 lists just a few of the many national social services organizations and their annual budgets, numbers of local affiliates, and the kinds of services they provide. Actually the private social service sector includes hundreds of thousands of separate organizations, many of which are not affiliated with national organizations like those listed in Table 9.1. Although it is difficult to provide a full inventory of these organizations, just those alone that received tax exempt status as social service agencies from the Internal Revenue Service numbered slightly more than five hundred sixty thousand in 1987 (Hodgkinson and Weitzman, 1986, p. 14).

Perhaps the most widely recognized private sector, nonprofit social service organizations within the large cities and metropolitan areas of the United States are the local federations of many separate organizations under the general rubric of United Way, United Fund, Community Chest, Red Feather, or similarly named metropolitan federations. The general purpose of these federations is to annually raise funds on a communitywide basis and then to allocate these funds locally to affiliated member agencies. In turn, the communitywide local United Way federations hold membership in the national United Way of America Confederation, headquartered in Washington, DC.

It is important to note that contrary to popular assumptions, the private social service sector is not primarily bankrolled by wealthy philanthropists and their foundations. Instead, they are funded, for the most part, by working- and middle-class voluntary contributors; for example, through the communitywide annual fund-raising drives by United Way, Community Chest Confederations, and the like. Originally, although wealthy philanthropists supported local charities and social services and served on their governing boards, the mid-

Table 9.1   Nonprofit Human Service Organizations, 1992

NAME	BUDGET ($ MILLIONS)	AFFILIATES	SERVICES	CURRENT ISSUES/GOALS
American Foundation for the Blind	15.5	5 regional offices	Education, rehabilitation, and socialization of the blind; public education about vision impairment	Enhance services to the multihandicapped; develop special services for the aged blind and blind Native Amerians; Braille literacy; enhance services to deaf/blind and handicapped children
American Red Cross	1.105	2,763 chapters; 277 armed forces stations; 56 regional blood centers	Disaster relief; blood donor program; water safety; first aid training	AIDS education; human tissue banks for transplantation
Arthritis Foundation	65.0	69 chapters and divisions	Health and exercise programs for those with arthritis; biomedical research on the causes and relief of arthritis	Establish a separate association for those with rheumatism; pilot a special program for children
Association for Retarded Citizens of the United States	5.26*	1,300 local groups; 46 state groups	Research, education, and prevention of retardation and physical handicaps	Bioengineering projects to aid the physically handicapped
Big Brothers/Big Sisters of America	3.8*	11 regional groups; 4 district groups	Providing adult guidance for children from single-parent households	Increase minority recruitment
Boy Scouts of America (1988)	49.7	413 councils	Leadership and citizenship training; drug and child abuse awareness	Enhance number of scouts and leaders; reduce costs of liability insurance
Boys Club of America	11.7*	1,100 club units	Leadership education, socialization of poor youth	Outreach to at-risk youth; delinquency prevention
Campfire Boys and Girls	3.5	240 local groups	Personal living skills and leadership development	Internal reorganization; develop enterprise dept.; enhance revenue and membership
Catholic Charities USA	1.46*	633 affiliates	Counseling; adoption; immigration; emergency support; housing	Economic justice; family life; shelter; hunger; health care

*National office only. (Source: *Encyclopedia of Associations, 1993, 27th Edition.* Annual reports of organizations.)

Table 9.1   Nonprofit Human Service Organizations, 1992 (*continued*)

NAME	BUDGET ($ MILLIONS)	AFFILIATES	SERVICES	CURRENT ISSUES/GOALS
Child Welfare League of America	6.5	5 regional groups	Abused children; adolescent pregnancy; child care; adoption services	Develop child day care; adolescent pregnancy prevention; parenting effectiveness education
Council of Jewish Federations	8.1*	200+ in North America	Services to families and the aged; community organization and planning; Jewish cultural development	Make up for decreased United Way funding; develop worldwide satellite transmissions; strengthen relationship with Israeli and North American Jewry and sense of Jewish identity
Family Service America	8.9*	200+ community agencies	Counseling and advocacy services to families	Expand services dealing with substance abuse and abuse in the family; internal organizational development
Girl Scouts of the U.S.A.	29.0	335 local groups	Leadership, education, and socialization of girls	Eliminate institutional racism; diversify funding; respond to council and community needs
Goodwill Industries of America	6.1*	179 members	Vocational rehabilitation for the disabled	Compensate for cuts in govt. funds; focus on hi-tech skills; respond to competition from retail firms
National Council on Alcoholism	17.0	186 local groups	Prevention of alcoholism; public education policy analysis	Include drugs other than alcohol in programs
Nation Easter Seal Society	301.0	150 affiliates in U.S.; 400 service centers	Home health care for the disabled; public education and advocacy of the disabled	Computer applications to assist the disabled; design to accommodate disabilities
National Mental Health Association	1.76*	550 state groups	Client and public policy advocacy for the emotionally disturbed; direct client support services; public education	Increase mental health services as a national priority

(*continued*)

Table 9.1   Nonprofit Human Service Organizations, 1992 (*continued*)

NAME	BUDGET ($ MILLIONS)	AFFILIATES	SERVICES	CURRENT ISSUES/GOALS
National Urban League	18.9	113 local groups	Advocating equality for minorities; public education; policy monitoring	Improve behavior of adolescent males; mobilize communities to fight crime
Planned Parenthood Federation of America	383.0	171 affiliates	Family planning; sex education in schools; abortion rights	Expand reproductive rights to underserved groups; respond to changes in health policy; review bioethical implications of new reproductive technology
The Salvation Army	5.3*	1,097 community centers	Homelessness; disaster relief; services to children and youth	Balance evangelism and social service
United Cerebral Palsy	6.5*	180 members	Rehabilitation of those with cerebral palsy and other severe disabilities; medical research on causes of cerebral palsy	Increase public education efforts, fund raising, biomedical research
USO (United Service Organization)	16.0	3 regional groups; 70 state groups	Fleet and airport centers; family support; cultural and recreational services	Make entertainment programs self-sufficient
Visiting Nurses Association of America	6.0	150 members	Home health services	Decrease cost of home health care to patients
Volunteers of America	3.4*	400 programs in 200 communities	Shelter and food for the disabled; employment training; community corrections	Literacy; child day care; at-risk youth
Young Men's Christian Association	1,432.0	2,069 local groups	Personal and social development; child care; community development	Obtain liability insurance; retain tax-exempt status
Young Women's Christian Association	11.2*	Over 4,000 locations in 400 communities	Developing potential of women; social and support services to women; advocacy of equality and justice	Develop non-partisan political training workshop

dle-class professionals and welfare planners who emerged to manage and staff these agencies eventually recognized that new sources of revenue to support their ever-expanding programs would have to be found. Moving to community fund-raising campaigns as the answer, it was recognized that these fund-raising campaigns would not succeed unless there was broad-ranged middle-class support. That is, if the controls over health and welfare activities remained entirely in the hands of the economic elites, it would be more difficult to gain the support of middle-class groups (see Weltford and Gallagher, 1987).

As a result of this shift toward middle-class support of the voluntary agencies, a new set of relationships between service agencies, the donors, and their clients seems to have emerged. For example, more services had been demanded and made available to middle-class groups (vocational counseling, marital and family counseling, preventative health and outpatient psychological and psychiatric services, etc.). Although some financial aid is still provided, it is generally not made available to the poorest segments of the community and is generally receding in importance. Instead, noneconomic services are provided, for which the working and middle classes are increasingly expected to pay. Thus, where the donors and clientele of private social service agencies formerly represented at least two distinct and somewhat socially distant social strata, they now, especially in suburban and other middle-class segments of metropolitan areas, represent to a large extent the *same* stratum of the urban social class structure (Odendahl, 1990).

This new relationship is partially reflected in the fund-raising strategies of the agencies that now operate in more middle-class settings. Such agencies often base their appeals for support on the likelihood that the donor, his or her family, or at least his or her immediate acquaintances, will probably at some time benefit directly from the services offered. For example, some of the recent health campaigns conducted in the mass media stress the high incidence of various illnesses and the likelihood that all persons or their families reached by these mass media messages, including the middle classes, of course, will somehow be affected by this high incidence of heart disease, cancer, Alzheimer's disease, muscular dystrophy, and other illnesses, whether directly or by contacts with family, friends, neighbors, and business associates or colleagues. In essence, these fund-raising campaigns, both at the national and local levels, merge the donors and clients into a single target group. Implicit in these campaigns is the stress on the "market" relationship between the health agencies and the "donor-client," a relationship based on a *reciprocity* of interests. This is, of course, counter to the traditional image of social welfare as charity or philanthropy. The question that remains, which has not been adequately answered to date, is what happens to the poorest segments of urban America previously served by voluntary agencies, which now cater increasingly to middle-class clientele, and who were more recently served by the public sector, until the much more restrictive Welfare Act of 1996 was adopted?

URBAN EDUCATION AND EDUCATIONAL OPPORTUNITIES

The process of transmitting the culture, technology, and skills of a society from one generation to the next has been recognized as a necessity throughout human history. It is only in recent times that this function has become sufficiently differentiated from the family and religious institutions so as to constitute a separate social institution in its own right. Today formal education has become a major feature of all urban-industrial societies, and its central importance as a social institution keeps growing by leaps and bounds.

The reasons for modern urban society's increasing reliance on a massive scale are varied, but there are at least five major societal needs that are served by modern urban educational systems. They include:

1. The need for a quick, efficient, and meaningful communications network among urban groups. Formal education provides the necessary tools—techniques, ideas, and acquired interests, all of which, of course, require minimum levels of literacy.

2. A formal educational system is necessary to transmit the skills of a vast and complex system of specialized occupations and vocations, upon which urban societies are increasingly dependent (see chapter 7). As a result of the increased division of labor, the family is no longer adequate to the difficult task of allocating occupational roles among members of modern urban societies.

3. Modern economies increasingly rely on the cultivation of expanding tastes and desires for consumer goods and service. Formal education on a large scale generally tends to expand the appetites and preferences of the mass consumers, which leads to continually higher living standards and increased productivity in urban industrial societies such as the United States.

4. Formal education provides the motives and values necessary to maintain and enhance the "non-economic civic and cultural amenities of modern urban communities, such as civic centers, libraries, museums and parks or recreational facilities" (this argument may be somewhat circular, because formal education may in fact provide the initial desires for such amenities).

5. Changes and innovations in the technological, economic, political, and social organization of complex urban-industrial societies are increasingly dependent of a core of managers, officials technicians, and professionals trained in and recruited from a highly developed educational system. (Gold and Scarpitti, 1967, p. 59)

Another important function of formal education in a pluralistic urban society such as ours is the transmission of skills and attitudes necessary for citizenship. In a democracy, this function is so obvious that it is often overlooked. Formal education provides the incentives and means for enriching intergroup living, for regulating intergroup competition and conflict, for minimizing potentialities for violence and disorder common to all large pluralistic societies, and for preserving democratic principles and procedures in the process. These are the kinds of functions formal education provides for society as a whole. But in our society, there is also the expectation that education will serve the individual needs of all citizens and social groups and will provide the opportunities to utilize their various talents and abilities to the fullest. Putting it another way, education is expected to provide everyone in the society with an equal opportunity for social, economic, and political advancement. As technology becomes more complex and sophisticated and social and economic life becomes more complex, formal education has virtually become the major source of social and economic mobility; conversely the lack of adequate formal education has become the major barrier to socioeconomic advancement or security for those who lack it. One might add, of course, that the achievement of a cosmopolitan lifestyle as providing the best fit to the conditions of modern urban living (according to the materials in chapter 6) was also based on the acquisition of a high level of formal education.

SOME EDUCATIONAL TRENDS

Universal or compulsory public education in the United States first became firmly established in about the middle of the nineteenth century, when in 1852 Massachusetts enacted the first compulsory attendance laws. By 1900, all of the states required children to attend school, usually until age sixteen. Thus universal and mandatory education had by then become the established norm (Curry, Jiobu, and Schwirian, 1999). As a result of the widespread belief in mass education, the American school system has grown to be the most extensive in the world. Approximately 50 percent of people ages three through thirty-four are enrolled in some type of school. Even though only 4 percent of the college-age population actually attended college at the beginning of the twentieth century, about 61 percent of all high school graduates now go on to college; and more than 16 million Americans annually are expected to enroll in an institution of higher education by 2003 (Bureau of the Census, 1994).

These trends mean that the American public has a growing faith in the utility—or the necessity—of formal education at all levels. This faith has been growing for an increasing variety of reasons, and it has been growing faster than the capacity of our educational system to keep itself abreast of all the resulting new demands. In fact, it must be concluded that many current concerns with the problems of education have to do with rapidly rising demands and expectations in a nation with rapid growth and accomplishment. Once expectations begin to rise in anticipation of major institutional change, they generally accelerate at a rate that exceeds the capacity of complex and unwieldy social institutions, such as formal education, to respond as quickly as desired. In other words, current social problems in education may be broadly defined as a case of a growing gap between social expectations and social reality. For example, only a decade or two ago, computer literacy was considered a novelty, confined to a relatively small number of computer "wonks," or to workers in a handful of occupational specialties which required such skill. Today computer literacy is considered almost a universal necessity, and the schools are struggling to provide, at great expense, the required equipment and training to as many students as possible. Thus many new expectations, demands, and requirements—in the face of many qualitative and quantitative improvements in the U.S. educational system—are at the heart of many contemporary concerns and controversies about education as a major social issue, as reflected by the fact that it had become one of the major issues of the 2000 presidential, congressional, and most local elections.

SOME SOCIAL PROBLEMS OF EDUCATION

Any analysis of a broad range of current urban social problems reveals that education is almost universally considered to be a strategic causal factor. For example, problems of poverty, unemployment, crime, and racial, ethnic, sex, or gender discrimination are routinely viewed as at least a partial result of unequal educational opportunities, as failure on the part of some groups to utilize existing educational opportunities to their fullest, or as a failure on the part of the schools to offer proper training, guidance, incentives, or controls (see Eitzen and Baca Zinn, 1997; Curry, Jiobu, and Schwirian, 1999; Feagin and Feagin, 1997; Kornblum and Julian, 1992; Horton et al., 1997). The relationship between poverty and education in the light of current trends is often illustrated in terms such as these: "Those who are unemployed for very long at this time are mainly the uneducated and untrained for whom there will *never again* be enough jobs to go around. In most cases, the boy or girl who leaves school early, fails to learn what has been taught there, or who has no good school to attend, will be condemned to a lifetime of low wages, periodic unemployment and relief check living" (Gold and Scarpitti, 1967).

Almost all of the personal pathologies or other forms of deviant behavior have been seen at least in part a result of "inadequate socialization." Because the schools play an increasingly significant and visible role in the socialization process, inadequate socialization is often viewed as a failure on the part of the schools to perform one of their expected functions. On the other hand, the faith that many Americans have in universal education is often based on the assumption that education can and should solve most of the major social problems. On the basis of having taught many large sections of social problems courses over a large number of years, I have observed that most of my students sincerely believed that more education was the major solution to the social problems covered in the courses.

Of course, formal education, or the lack of it, is neither the cause nor the cure-all of social problems that many people believe it to be, because formal education represents only one segment of American culture and society, having at best only a limited impact on the larger society. The educational system largely reflects the morals, values, aspirations, and confusion of the society of which it is an instrument. The schools by themselves cannot maintain values that are crumbling in the communities around them, for they are subject to the same forces that are constantly reshaping urban society. Nor can they cure social ills such as racial discrimination, crime and violence, or poverty, whose sources and remedies lie far beyond the scope of the schools.

Nevertheless the schools in America have come under widespread attack for a wide range of social problems, and for much of the general discontent in contemporary urban society, and they are at the center of many controversies regarding the nature of and potential solutions to social problems. Thus they are caught in the crossfire of attack generated by pressure groups representing almost every imaginable kind of interest. Among such groups are PTA and other parent groups; teachers and teachers' unions; other labor unions; taxpayers' associations; city councils and municipal finance committees; political, business, and commercial organizations; television; the press; local and state power elites; churches or religious groups; veterans' organizations; chambers of commerce; service clubs; fraternal organizations; farm organizations; welfare organizations; civil rights groups; ethnic, racial, and other minority groups; women's organizations, presidential candidates; governors and local politicians—the list is virtually endless.

What very often happens is that the crossfire of incompatible or competing goals and programs for the schools tend to cancel one another out and effectively neutralize many school districts, preventing them from moving boldly in any direction. For example, for every proposal to broaden the curriculum, there are counterdemands to restrict or narrow the program to "basics," such as the three Rs (reading, "riting," "rithmetic!"); for every demand to maintain separation of religion and the state, there are counterproposals to bring prayer into the public schools; for every proposal to add the teaching of evolution to the curriculum, there are demands to instead teach creationism (Feagin and Feagin, 1997, p. 216); for every request to add more serious or meaningful novels to the literature curriculum, there are an equal number of demands that controversial reading materials be censored; and for every group demanding that some sort of sex education be included, there are countergroups insisting that it be kept out. In particular, social science materials tend to be carefully screened and are often watered down lest they offend the political, ideological, or social sensibilities of some segments of the community. Under such conflicting pressures, school boards become politically sensitive and defensive and place teachers under greater surveillance and control in efforts to minimize outside pressure by critical pressure groups. Under such conflicting pressures, it is hardly any wonder that in many respects the American public schools fail to completely satisfy anybody!

Another related major issue facing the schools is a preoccupation with order and control. The desire for high levels of achievement and academic excellence are in normal circumstances also related to high levels of individuality and creativity. But in the public schools, with their sensitivity to public expectations and surveillance in areas such as those listed earlier, there is also the conflicting expectation that there will be high levels of discipline and conformity in the schools. In the light of several highly dramatized episodes of homicide in the public schools in the late nineties, plus an even more sensational instance of a homicide in a Michigan elementary school in 2000 involving six- or seven-year-old children as victims or perpetrator, these highly publicized incidents have only intensified the demands for greater social control over the public schools.

In their quest for order, according to sociologists Stanley Eitzen and Maxine Baca Zinn (1997), many schools require conformity in clothing and hairstyles (even President

Graffiti disfigures the facade of an urban public school

Clinton had recommended uniforms for the public schools), and conformity is demanded in "what to read, where to set the margins on . . . word processors, and how to give the answers teachers want." Among the resulting dilemmas and contradictions urban educational institutions face are the following:

1. Formal education encourages creativity but curbs the truly creative individuals out of fear they will disrupt society.
2. Formal education encourages an open mind but teaches dogma.
3. Formal education has the goal of turning out mature students but does not give them the freedom essential to foster maturity.
4. Formal education pays lip service to meeting individual needs of the students but in actuality encourages conformity at every turn.
5. Formal education has the goal of allowing all students to reach their potential, yet fosters the kinds of competition that continually causes some people to be labeled as failures.
6. Formal education is designed to allow people of the greatest talent to reach the top, but it differentially benefits certain categories of people regardless of their talent—-the middle- and upper-class students who happen to be white. (Eitzen and Baca Zinn, 1997, p. 397).

The last of the six dilemmas of American education raises the issue of inequality and discrimination in the public schools. Education is assumed by many people to be the great equalizer and is the process by which the poor and the disadvantaged minorities are given equal opportunity to climb the economic ladder and achieve the American Dream (see Maines, 2000, for an extended discussion of the American Dream). The reality is that the public schools are highly stratified along social class, racial, and ethnic lines, and that such stratification produces significant differences in educational outcomes. For example, in large, consolidated high schools with economically diverse student bodies, students from higher socioeconomic backgrounds are more likely to score higher on tests, graduate from high school, and go on to receive a college-level education than those from lower income or nonwhite minority backgrounds. Bowles and Gintis (1976) found that individuals in the lowest 10 percent in socioeconomic status will achieve an average of approximately five less years of formal education than individuals in the top 10 percent of the economic ladder. Tracking systems are also now commonplace. Students from higher-income backgrounds tend to be on an academic track, whereas those from a low-income background are more likely to be offered a vocational curriculum. High schools tend to vary in their relative emphasis on vocational or academic programs, with central city and rural schools emphasizing vocational education and predominantly white suburban schools emphasizing academic programs. In integrated schools, black and Hispanic students are three times as likely as whites to be placed in vocation education or special education programs (Feagin and Feagin, 1997, p. 197).

Even more significant are the great disparities in the spatial distribution of educational resources among the subareas of metropolitan communities, which tend to be segregated from one another on the basis of race and income, which in turn reflects the patterns of residential segregation in urban areas (see chapter 13). Again, students in affluent, predominantly white, suburban communities usually attend well-equipped schools which provide almost unlimited learning opportunities, whereas minority students in poor neighborhoods usually face larger classes and outdated books and equipment in aging and

An inner city school playground

deteriorating buildings in need of repair (Feagin and Feagin, 1997, p. 198). Funding disparities also help account for the differences in educational opportunities between poorer and wealthier school districts. For example, the highest spending school district in New York State spent over $32,000 per pupil, and the lowest spending district only spent a little over $5,000 per pupil (Karp, 1995, pp. 18–19). Likewise, the highest funded school districts in Texas spent over fifteen times more per pupil than the lowest funded districts; the highest funded district in California spent over seven times per pupil than did the poorest district; and in Massachusetts the ratio of spending in the highest funded district compared to spending in the lowest funded district was also more than seven to one (Karp, 1995, pp. 18–19). Clearly, as Feagin and Feagin (1997, p. 199) have put it: "The tracking systems and the radically different resources of central city, rural, and suburban schools are not random chance conditions but reflect the intent on the part of many white business and political leaders and school officials, at the national, state, and local levels, to structure schools according to the same class-race-gender framework that exists in the larger society. Inequality is still the norm in the United States." Although the assertion of *intent* may be questioned by some, the problematic results are nevertheless the same.

IMPROVING EDUCATIONAL OPPORTUNITIES IN URBAN AMERICA

It should not be concluded from the discussion so far that some innovation is nonexistent in American education today. Actually there have been many changes that have been continually underway in instructional techniques, teacher training and recruitment, curricula planning, facilities planning, school-community relations, school financing, educational resource allocations, and educational administration at all levels from preschool to higher education. In addition, there is a great deal of planning going on with respect to anticipating future educational needs. Amid all the educational conflicts, controversies, and intellectual ferment surrounding current education problems, one set of new standards reflecting some consensus, at least among educators, seems to have emerged. These new standards, which illustrate the major tasks facing public education today, can be summarized as follows: Start the child in school at an earlier age (preschool); keep him and her in school more months of the year in smaller classes; retain all who start school for at least twelve to fourteen years (longer, if possible); expect him and her to learn more and more during this period, in wider and wider areas of human experience and in new technologies, under the guidance of a teacher who has had more and better training (and who is better paid), and who is assisted by more and more specialists, who provide an ever-expanding range of services with access to more and more detailed personal records, based on more and more carefully validated test and performance criteria. In addition, current educational programs and policies are being implemented, in at least some urban communities in these three major areas: (1) improving and equalizing education opportunities for culturally deprived or racially restricted groups in low-income areas; (2) providing continuing education opportunities for adults whose education has been interrupted for a variety of social and economic reasons; and (3) extending the range of higher education opportunities to ever-growing numbers, and extending the range of services available to the larger urban society through higher educational institutions (see Epps, 1995; Macionis, 1999).

With respect to the latter, one of the most rapidly expanding forms of higher education in the larger metropolitan areas is extension programs offered by established universities in off-campus rented office buildings and other "nontraditional" sites primarily during evening and weekend hours for working adults, usually of nontraditional college age. For example, it was estimated as early as the 1960s that at least 30 million people were enrolled part-time in university extension or evening college courses (Gold and Scarpitti, 1967, p. 65). The reasons for this trend for adults past the conventional school age, who tend to be neglected in most discussions of urban educational problems, are simply that many of them have not previously acquired the appropriate skills, knowledge, or "credentials" for the increasingly complex roles they are expected or wish to play. As a result, many of them suffer consequences at least as acute for themselves, and nearly as costly to the larger society, as problems that faced a previous generation of teenage school "dropouts." As a result there has been a dramatic increase in recent decades in the number of adults who seek some kind of continuing adult education or retraining. Included are adults whose formal education was previously disrupted for economic, social, or personal reasons; adults whose occupational skills have become obsolete; adults who wish to advance their social or economic status; and, believe it or not, at least some adults for whom continuing education is a pleasurable "avocation!"

Finally, at the beginning of the twenty-first century, the social problems of public urban education will probably remain as serious, controversial, and highly charged as they were in the twentieth century. For example, have the public schools "failed," as their critics have charged, to provide adequate levels of education to students and therefore are undeserving of continued public financial support? If so, as many conservatives now argue, the solution lies in reduced financial support from taxpayers, with such support then being shifted to private schools (including those that are religiously sponsored) in the form of publicly financed "vouchers" paid to parents of children who make this choice. Or should the public schools continue to be supported and enriched with more and better teachers, smaller classes, better learning materials, and better building equipment and technology, with greater public investments in schools with the greatest needs, such as those in low-income and minority communities, as liberals tend to argue? These are among the issues that were being debated and fought out in the first presidential election of the twenty-first century.

SELECTED BIBLIOGRAPHY

BANE, MARY JO, and DAVID T. ELLWOOD. "One-Fifth of the Nation's Children: Why Are They Poor? *Science.* 245 (September 1989).

BERNARD, JESSIE. *Social Problems at Midcentury.* New York: Holt, Rinehart and Winston, 1957.

BOWLES, SAMUEL, and HERBERT GINTIS. *Schooling in Capitalist America: Educational Reform and the Contradiction of Economic Life.* New York: Basic Books, 1976.

CURRY, TIM, ROBERT JIOBU, and KENT SCHWIRIAN. *Sociology for the Twenty-First Century,* 2d ed. Upper Saddle River, NJ: Prentice-Hall, 1999.

DANZIGER, SHELDON, and PETER GOTTSCHALK. *America Unequal.* New York: Harvard University Press, 1995.

DiNITTO, DIANE M., and THOMAS R. DYE. *Social Welfare: Politics and Public Policy.* Englewood Cliffs, NJ: Prentice-Hall, 1987.

EITZEN, D. STANLEY, and MAXINE BACA ZINN. *Social Problems,* 7th ed. Boston: Allyn and Bacon, 1997.

EPPS, EDGAR G. "Race, Class, and Educational Opportunity: Trends in the Sociology of Education." *Sociological Forum.* 10, no. 4 (December 1995).

FEAGIN, JOE R., and CLAIRECE BOOHER FEAGIN. *Social Problems: A Critical Power-Conflict Perspective,* 5th ed. Upper Saddle River, NJ: Prentice-Hall, 1997.

GOLD, HARRY. *The Sociology of Urban Life.* Englewood Cliffs, NJ: Prentice-Hall, 1982.

———, and FRANK SCARPITTI. *Combatting Social Problems: Techniques of Intervention.* New York: Holt, Rinehart and Winston, 1967.

HARRINGTON, MICHAEL. *The Other America: Poverty in America.* Baltimore, MD: Penguin Books, 1963.

HODGKINSON, VIRGINIA, and WEITZMAN. *Dimensions of the Independent Sector.* Washington, DC: Independent Sector, 1986.

HOFSTADTER, RICHARD. *Social Darwinism in American Thought.* Boston: Beacon Press, 1959.

HORTON, PAUL B. et al. *The Sociology of Social Problems,* 12th ed. Upper Saddle River, NJ: Prentice-Hall, 1997.

KARGER, HOWARD JACOB, and DAVID STOESZ. *American Social Welfare Policy: A Pluralistic Approach,* 2d ed. White Plains, NY: Longman, 1994.

KARP, STAN. "Equity Suits Clog the Courts." *Rethinking Schools.* 9 (summer 1995).

KORNBLUM, WILLIAM, and JOSEPH JULIAN. *Social Problems,* 7th ed. Englewood Cliffs, NJ: Prentice-Hall, 1992.

MACIONIS, JOHN J. *Sociology,* 7th ed. Upper Saddle River, NJ: Prentice-Hall, 1999.

MAINES, DAVID R. "Thoughts on the American Dream and Its Future." *Oakland University Journal.* 1 (spring 2000): 88–95.

MORRIS, ROBERT. *Rethinking Social Welfare.* New York: Longman, 1986.

ODENDAHL, TERESA. *Charity Begins at Home.* New York: Basic Books, 1990.

SCHERER, JACQUELINE. "Welfare and Education as Emergent Institutions." In *Sociology of Urban Life,* Harry Gold (ed.), pp. 260–280. Englewood Cliffs, NJ: Prentice-Hall, 1982.

SCHILLER, BRADLEY. "Who Are the Working Poor?" *The Public Interest.* 155 (spring 1994).

SUMNER, WILLIAM GRAHAM. *Social Darwinism.* Englewood Cliffs, NJ: Prentice-Hall, 1963.

TRATTNER, WALTER. *From Poor Law to Welfare State.* New York: Free Press, 1974.

WELLFORD, W. HARRISON, and JANNE GALLAGHER. *The Role of Nonprofit Human Service Organizations.* Washington, DC: National Assembly of Voluntary Health and Social Welfare Organizations, 1987.

WILENSKY, HAROLD L., and CHARLES N. LEBEAUX. *Industrial Society and Social Welfare.* New York: Russell Sage Foundation, 1958.

10

THE IMPACT OF URBANIZATION ON RELIGION AND THE FAMILY

The family and organized religion are similar in that as social institutions, they both have preurban origins. Stark (1998, p. 383), for example, suggests that the Neanderthals had certain beliefs and practices that can be characterized as religious which go back at least 100,000 years. The first communities in recorded history having the characteristics of cities were described by their excavators (see chapter 2) as having monumental temples, monasteries, and convents at their centers, which were symbolic of the central role played by organized religion in these early cities, and the importance of complex, universal religions as central to early urban life has been long recognized by a variety of urban scholars (Boskoff, 1970; Weber, 1962; Sorokin, 1928).

In the case of the family, preurban nomadic communities consisted chiefly of extended kinship groups, in which virtually all members were related to one another by ancestry and birth, and the family remained firmly entrenched in a dominant position of the institutional structure of preindustrial urban society for many centuries. Indeed, the family, along with organized religion, was often characterized as a "sacred" institution because it was usually beyond question or criticism.

Ever since the urban-industrial revolution of the nineteenth century, however, both organized religion and the family have been going through many important organizational, cultural, and functional changes. No longer is either organized religion or the family among the dominant social institutions of modern urban industrial societies such as the United States. It was clear by the end of the twentieth century that the economy, which had long been a separate institution in its own right, has become the dominant institution. In fact, as stated in chapter 7, the economies of modern urban communities are so powerful a force that they have "the capacity to alter the forms and processes of other institutions rather than the other way around."

In this chapter both the family and organized religion are examined in their contemporary urban-industrial and postindustrial contexts and explained in terms of how they both, for better or worse, have adapted to some of the urban, economic, technological, social, and environmental changes of the late nineteenth and twentieth centuries. Also some of the newer alternative or "nontraditional" patterns of religious practice and expression and family living arrangements at the beginning of the twenty-first century are briefly explored.

RELIGION IN URBAN COMMUNITIES

Throughout most early urban history, organized religion was central to the cultural, economic, and political life of cities. For example, in the ancient Egyptian cities of Memphis and Thebes, the pharaohs held nearly absolute power in their dual role of god-king, and in some instances the power of the pharaohs was so great they were able to create completely new cities with new forms of religions to reflect their own tastes and values (see chapter 2). Likewise, ancient Athens was essentially a religious community in which citizenship was restricted to a small portion of the population, whose rights as citizens were limited to the right to worship at civic shrines. During the so-called "Dark Ages" of feudal Europe, the church was an overriding institution, and church officials and monastic orders frequently collaborated or competed with secular rulers for control of the social order (Hawley, 1971; Sjoberg, 1960). Cities during the medieval period continued to be characterized by strong religious controls over other institutions. For example, the schools were not separate from the established churches, and both political and legal institutions were legitimated by "official" religious bodies. Thus, laws and courts were guided by religious doctrine, and "to be tried as a heretic often meant torture and death" (Kornblum, 1997, p. 587). The religious orders were actively engaged in large-scale economic activity, owned much land and property, and often mounted their own armed forces.

Secularization

A combination of religious beliefs and practices may constitute a *sacred* institution, in the sense that such an institution is based in a belief of a supernatural force of some sort and a sense that such a belief is beyond question or criticism. Secular beliefs or practices, on the other hand, are based on "respect for values of utility rather than of sacredness alone, control of the environment rather than passive submission to it and, in some ways most importantly, concern with man's present welfare on this earth rather than his supposed immortal relation to the gods" (Nisbet, 1970, p. 388). Thus, when religious institutions become differentiated from the family, the economy, the state, public education, the mass media, and so forth, and organized religion loses some of its moral authority or control over these institutions, then it can be said that a process of *secularization* has taken place (Berger, 1967; Wilson, 1961).

In Western Europe, the Renaissance, the Enlightenment, and the emergence of the market economy and capitalism stimulated the differentiation of economic, social, cultural, and political institutions from established religious institutions. This process of differentiation was rapidly accelerated by the onslaught of the urban-industrial and metropolitan revolutions of the nineteenth and twentieth centuries (see chapters 3 and 4). Many aspects of these changes had already reached Colonial America by the time of the American Revolution, and they were subsequently reflected in the constitutional provision for the separation of church and state and in the establishment of public educational institutions separate from those connected with organized religion.

As the economy, science, and technology expanded in the context of rapid urban-industrial development, a growing number of social scientists and other observers began to predict a decline in the power and influence of organized religion; some of them went as far as to predict that religion would eventually decay and wither away under the onslaught of "modern" urban-industrial social forces. (See Sorokin, 1928, chapter 12, for an extended discussion of late nineteenth century and early twentieth century social thought on this topic.) However powerful the forces of secularization have been since the beginning of the urban industrial revolution, it is not accurate to suggest that it has led to the demise of organized religion. Even in extreme examples of societies which have consciously tried to eliminate organized religion, as was the case in the former Soviet Union, various forms of religious practices and beliefs continued to persist among a majority of the world's population (Stark, 1998, p. 387). Rather, most contemporary observers of religion agree that it has vastly changed in response to the rise of secular institutions and other conditions of modern urban living, and that it is continually modified in response to ever-changing challenges and opportunities (Macionis, 1999; Stark, 1998; Kornblum, 1997). Although its power and influence have somewhat waned, religion still continues to occupy a special place in the hearts and minds of large segments of urban populations in most parts of the urban world, including the United States, despite the fact that the forms of religious practices and beliefs have become extremely diversified, complex, and often controversial in urban settings

Religious Diversity in Urban Areas

A major characteristic of religious organization in urban America is the great diversity of separate religious groups. For example, within a fifteen-minute drive from the author's residence in metropolitan Detroit can be found Roman Catholic Churches; Baptist Churches; Methodist Churches; Lutheran Churches; Episcopalian Churches; Reformed, Presbyterian, and Congregational Churches; Mennonite Churches; Unitarian Churches; Quaker Churches; Mormon Churches and temples; Greek, Russian, Armenian, and Syrian Orthodox Churches; Reformed, Conservative, and Orthodox Jewish synagogues, Islamic centers, Buddhist temples, and Hindu temples. In the United States and Canada, there are more than two hundred separate Christian religious bodies alone, claiming approximately 159 million members, with another 10 million people as members of Jewish, Muslim, Buddhist, or other religions, sects, or cults (*New York Times 2000 Almanac,* 1999, pp. 414–419).

St. Patrick's Cathedral in midtown Manhattan contrasts with a modern office tower

A traditional sociological notion of religion was that religious identity and affiliation was an *ascribed* status, passed from generation to generation and, of course, expected to last throughout the entire life span of individuals. But in the modern urban setting, the large variety of organized religious bodies provide such a wide range of membership choices that there are the following consequences: first, large-scale organized religious groups actively compete to attract new members, while striving at the same time to maintain active participation and loyalty among established members; second, individuals, faced with an incredible number of choices among the many alternatives, are frequently tempted to "shop" around for the option that best suits their religious beliefs or personal needs and preferences. Individuals, in fact, may change their religious affiliations freely as they move out of, into, or between different religious entities as they seek the most satisfying alternatives. In these ways, a "market" situation is produced in which the "suppliers" or "producers" of religious services and experiences adopt techniques and procedures that were pioneered and used in the capitalistic, free enterprise sector of modern urban-industrial economies to attract loyal and reliable "customers" (Iannoccone, 1992; Sherkat and Wilson, 1995).

Urban Innovations in the Production, Distribution, and Consumption of Religious Behavior

In chapter 7, a model was developed to describe and explain a number of institutional innovations that have evolved in modern urban-industrial economies to minimize risk by producing more efficient and controllable relationships between the production and the purchase or consumption of manufactured products. It is my premise that this model clearly applies to religious organization and behavior in modern urban-industrial societies such as the United States, as follows:

1. Churches and related religious bodies now often conduct market research studies to identify the relevant target populations most likely to be receptive to organized efforts to attract them to the resources and offerings of a particular religious group or facility. Such research often relies on demographic variables, such as age, sex, income, lifestyle, social class, place of residence, or on sample survey research, which may provide information on values, religious preferences, and social or psychological preferences or needs, which could potentially be satisfied by religious organizations.

2. Recognizing that there may be a wide range of wants or needs among a diverse body of potential "consumers," religious bodies often diversify their "product" to satisfy diversified needs or preferences. Thus, they may offer services and activities to such diverse groups as young children or adolescents, teenagers, young adults, seniors, married couples and families, divorcees, singles or gays, and may offer counseling services of various types by various counseling professionals to those who want or need them. The Roman Catholic Church, in particular, attempts to appeal to a variety of ethnic groups by providing religious services in established urban ethnic communities in languages other than English, such as Italian, Polish, or Spanish.

3. Urban economies rely on a constant display of highly visible or audible advertising messages through television, radio, magazines, newspapers, circulars, mailings, and, increasingly, the Internet. Organized religion increasingly uses these same marketing outlets to reach present and potential new constituencies. In fact, television and radio have become the mainstays of many national or local ministries, some of which are totally dependent on them, having few or no members independent of those connected to them by the media alone. The television ministries of Oral Roberts, Pat Robertson, or Jim Bakker were recent examples that come to mind. With the advent of cable television, entire channels have been created that are solely devoted to the broadcast of religious messages and "commercials."

4. Finally, beyond the voluntary services provided by their members, most organized religious groups in urban societies are dependent on the voluntary and routine financial contributions of their members. Increasingly, they have adopted forms of consumer credit once limited to economic transactions. That is, they now accept contributions made through credit card payments or through installment plans similar to those offered for the purchase of commercial products and services. It is also important to note that in the United States, such contributions also fall under the heading of "charity" for federal income tax purposes. Thus, the federal government provides a strong economic incentive for religious contributions.

One of the best recent illustrations of the melding of commercial culture with that of organized religion has been provided by Diane Winston (1999) in a history of the rise of the Salvation Army in New York in the nineteenth century. Her reviewer writes:

> . . . the keys to the Army's history was its practice of plunging headlong into the emerging commercial culture of city life. This was true both literally—Salvationist

preachers routinely "invaded" dance halls, saloons, brothels and amusement arcades—and figuratively. The Army's newspaper, The War Cry, was self consciously modeled after the penny press of the day. The famous adman Bruce Barton helped develop its slogans . . . and the department store mogul John Wanamaker advised Salvationists on their retail enterprises (including a "Commander Day" sale). (Glenn, *New York Times Book Review,* May 30, 1999, p. 20)

In all these and many other ways, the values and practices of the corporate market economy have invaded the traditionally sacred religious institutions of urban America and nearly all other aspects of modern urban living (see Per and Olson, 2000; Phillips, 1998; and Stark and McCann, 1993, for alternative applications of market theory to the analysis of religious behavior).

Religious Conflict

The patterns of religious diversity in America are consistent with the tradition of religious freedom, which supports the idea that everyone is free to practice the religion of their choice (or not to practice any religion) in any legal manner in which they see fit. However, this same pattern of diversity sometimes leads to conflicts between competing sets of religious beliefs and practices, and it often appears that the greater the intensity of religious beliefs, the stronger will be the lack of tolerance for those with opposing religious or secular views. This tendency seems to be greater in rural or nonurban regions of the country, and conversely, it is in the large cities that one probably finds the highest levels of tolerance for religious diversity and experimentation. Yet some disagreements, arguments, and strains between the followers of dissimilar religious faiths tend to be commonplace and continuous in the United States, whether in the country, cities, or suburbs, as reflected in arguments about the teaching of religion or prayer in the public schools, abortion, appropriate sexual behavior, pornography, marriage and divorce, the teaching of theories of evolution or creationism (see chapter 9), the posting of the Ten Commandments in public places, homosexuality, and the morality of public officials or other highly visible "role models." The controversies about the legal proceedings and articles of impeachment directed against President Clinton in 1999, in part for his "improper" involvement with Monica Lewinsky, was an excellent example of how differences in religious and moral beliefs play themselves out in the public arena of American life. In this instance the findings of most public opinion polls reported in the *New York Times* and on CNN during that period tended to support the notion that people in the more urbanized areas of the country were more tolerant of the president's personal behavior than people in the more rural regions, with religious "fundamentalists" being the most intolerant as to beliefs about whether the president deserved to be impeached for his moral indiscretions.

To follow up on the last point made, the conflict among religious groups is further compounded by differences *within* religious groups, as well as *between* them. Within many religions and religious denominations, religious beliefs and practices can be placed on a continuum between dichotomies, such as "traditional-modern," "conservative-liberal," "fundamentalist-moderate," "controlling-permissive," "orthodox-reform," and so on. In more political terms, most of these dichotomies can be observed as products of "right-wing" and "left-wing" movements which may develop within any given religious group experiencing internal changes or external challenges. In other words, many of the kinds of conflicts that arise between different religious groups in a complex and changing urban environment may also produce similar controversies within given religious groups that challenge their cohesiveness or solidarity. For example, the role of women in the clergy; the role of religions in marrying people of "conflicting" religious backgrounds or of the same gender; the observance of religious rituals or holy days; the meaning, truth, or validity of sacred texts and testaments; the nature of the origins of the universe or of the human species; views about abortion, the proper way to rear children; or the appropriate relationships between religion and the state are all arenas in which fundamental disagreements have persisted within specific religious groups, as well as between them, in recent decades.

Some of the controversies mentioned are reflected in and intensified by a trend toward greater religious fundamentalism. According to Macionis (1999, p. 500), fundamentalism has made the greatest gains among some Protestant denominations, such as Southern Baptists and the "Christian Coalition," for example, but in other religions as well. In response to what they see as the growing influence of science and secularization and the erosion of the traditional family, fundamentalists defend what are seen by them as traditional values. As they see it, according to Macionis, "liberal churches are simply too tolerant of religious pluralism and too open to change."

Religious leaders of a fundamentalist persuasion have often found the urban scene threatening and hostile to traditional religious views (Marty, 1979; Sandeen, 1970). One response to this perceived threat was to emphasize "old-fashioned" values and strict adherence to dogmatic interpretations of religious beliefs. It was as if fundamental and dogmatic religious ideas could shield urban dwellers from the secular dangers of cosmopolitan life (Scherer, 1982, pp. 178–179). The famous Scopes "monkey" trial of 1921 and the threat to the biblical explanation of creation that had rallied fundamentalists groups against the teaching of Darwinian theories of evolution in a local high school and fears that science, social change, and urbanization would threaten traditional views have persisted to this day among some fundamentalist religious groups.

Out of such conflicts, one can also often anticipate and understand the bases for the emergence of many new denominations, splinter groups, sects, or cults, which frequently split off from previously established religions, and become part of the larger religious mosaic of urban life (see Shepherd and Shepherd, 2000, pp. 9–22 for a recent example). Sects tend to stress emotionalism and individual mystical experiences and tend toward fundamentalism rather than the kinds of intellectualism and more restrained emotionalism of the more establishment mainline churches. This helps to explain the recent movements away from established denominations—which tend to attract better educated members of higher social status—toward more fundamentalist churches, sects, or cults—which tend to attract members from more moderate social statuses (Macionis, 1999, p. 497; Kornblum, 1997, p. 526). One can point to still another pattern of religious behavior that involves people outside of established religious groups referred to as *unofficial religion* (Wilson, 1978). It is engaged in by people who purchase religious books and magazines, follow religious television, make religious pilgrimages, "or practice astrology, faith healing, transcendent meditation, occult arts and the like" (Kornblum, 1997, pp. 519–521) but who do not necessarily belong to organized churches. Not to be left out of this discussion, of course, are the small minority of individuals who abandon religious affiliations, religious practices, or religious beliefs altogether. And the beliefs or behavior of such individuals are more likely to be tolerated, ignored, or left alone (often willingly!) in big cities or metropolitan areas than elsewhere.

Religiosity

In spite of the emergence of a secular and religiously pluralistic and diverse urban America with its seemingly endless varieties of religious organization, behavior, conflict and social change, what appears to be rather constant is a relatively high level of *religiosity,* which refers to the nature and depth of one's religious beliefs and feelings. When directly asked, about 95 percent of Americans express a belief in a divine power of some sort (National Opinion Research Center, 1996, p. 33; *Washington Post National Weekly,* April 24, 2000, p. 34), and about 90 percent express a more specific belief in the existence of a god, and about 86 percent express certainty about a life after death (Kornblum, 1997, p. 521*).* A smaller percent, but still a majority (57 percent) of adults say they pray at least once a day. But only 30 percent say they attend religious services on a weekly or almost weekly basis (NORC, 1996, pp. 120–124). This finding suggests that there is not necessarily a strong correlation between religious beliefs and actual religious practices; rather beliefs relating to the existence of supernatural forces are much more ubiquitous in urban society than any universal pattern of religious organization or behavior designed to support such beliefs.

Some Alternative Forms of Religious Expression

Some sociological observers of religion have sought to separate the concepts of the terms "sacred" and "religion" from one another in order to provide new meanings and applications for each. For example, N. J. Demerath (2000, pp. 3–8) has suggested that although there surely are religious phenomena that have lost their power and are no longer sacred, there are just as surely sacred entities and symbols that have a compelling power without being religious. That is, to the extent that the concept *sacred* has generally been applied to supernatural phenomena of all kinds in the context of the study of religious behavior and beliefs, Demerath argues that the concept should be broadened to also encompass those kinds of secular phenomena which over time have come to exhibit various dimensions of supernaturalism as well.

One of Demerath's prime illustrations of a secular institution that has become sacred is that of *civil religion* in the United States. The concept of civil religion, as originally expounded by Robert Bellah (1967), is based on the premise that traditional religion is being supplanted by the emergence of a set of quasi-religious beliefs that link people to the nation-state in what amounts to a blend of profane and sacred concepts. As Curry, Jiobu, and Schwirian (1999, p. 369) have more recently illustrated the concept, the notion of patriotism in the United States is part of a civil religion because Americans are socialized to view their country as both good and sacred. They respond to their country with "awe, love, and obedience," and express these feelings by participating in rituals and worshipping symbols of the nation, such as national holidays like Thanksgiving and the Fourth of July. At these events, "stirring speeches are made and the national anthem is played. Sometimes the audience arises and sings the Star-spangled Banner or recites the Pledge of Allegiance, a vow that openly links the nation to religion with the phrase 'one nation under God.'" In addition, Americans generally consider the American flag as a sacred symbol, with many of them favoring a constitutional amendment that would make desecration of the flag a federal offense. And Curry, Jiobu, and Schwirian conclude that responses to rituals and symbols such as these tend to evoke emotions that are similar or identical to the kind of emotions evoked by religious services.

Demerath makes a persuasive case for a very expansive application of sacred status to a broader range of social institutions and collectivities, such as economic systems, political systems or movements, education, family and kinship institutions, an assortment of voluntary associations, and the like. Going further in identifying heretofore secular entities which exhibit sacred tendencies, he includes social movements, organizations, and subcommunities that are countercultural in the sense that they are outside the cultural and societal mainstream and sometimes stand in opposition to it. Some of the examples he provides of nonreligious countercultures, which nevertheless provide their participants with sacred meanings and symbols, include the Ku Klux Klan, Skinheads, Survivalists, and the Operation Rescue group, all on the right wing of the political spectrum. On the left, he includes radical wings of the civil rights movement, antinuclear activists, environmentalists, and supporters of feminist, gay, and lesbian causes.

Demerath does not stop here and still further asserts that "virtually every ascriptive distinction has the potential for generating sacred movements, including ethnicity, social class, age and gender." In a more specific urban context, movements often develop when personal identity is fused with forms of expression produced by the followers of mass media and popular culture figures, including groups such as "hippies, rappers, punk rockers, Deadheads, Trekkies"—or possibly followers of athletic teams such as the "bleacher bums" of the old Brooklyn Dodgers, the Cleveland Brown's "dogpound," or English soccer "hooligans" (Demerath, 2000, p. 7). The author of this book would add his own observation that mass media, political, popular music, motion picture, and other celebrities of urban societies often become "deified" by their followers and endowed with sacred qualities, especially when such individuals have suffered from an early or tragic death. Elvis Presley, James Dean, Marilyn Monroe (a sex "goddess"), John Lennon, Judy Garland, John F. Kennedy, and Princess Diana are among some of the figures who immediately come to mind. The religious or sacred symbolism attached to these figures are obvious, as their followers characterize them as "larger than life," attest to their immortality ("Elvis lives," etc.), conduct annual or periodic rituals in their memory, or sanctify their previous residences or tombs as "shrines." And in Woody Allen's movie, *Play it Again, Sam,* as one more example, the ghostlike figure of Humphrey Bogart, another highly "worshipped" film icon, comes back to life to haunt Woody as his "spiritual" advisor. To conclude this section, one can find numerous examples of sacred symbols, as they have been defined here, throughout the entire secular urban world, if one looks for them.

Some Functions of Religion in Urban Settings

The fact that religions or quasi-religions continues to exist, and in many instances, to thrive in modern urban societies in spite of secular forces working in an opposite direction, requires some explanation. To earlier sociologists, such as Emil Durkheim (1915), religious rituals were the affirmation of group existence and religious beliefs were the foundation of all social order. Religion provided the cultural glue of common values, understandings, and ideologies which brought people together. Durkheim adopted the term "collective conscience" to refer to group morality. Durkheim was, of course, applying a *functional* approach to explaining the persistence and central role of religion as a social phenomena, of which one of the main social purposes was to provide unity and cohesion to preurban-industrial communities. Although Durkheim's theory does not as adequately apply to large modern urban communities with a diversity of competing religious groups, modern sociologists have attempted to modify functional approaches to better explain existing social realities.

Modern functional theories attempt to examine urban religious institutions as the source of unity for particular groups rather than for a community or society as a whole (Scherer, 1982), for example, as centers of culture for different ethnic groups in American cities. Churches were a haven for people of one nationality in an ethnically differentiated society, providing places where religious beliefs and cultural traditions could be easily shared. A Polish-Catholic parish, a Russian-Jewish synagogue, or a German-Lutheran church are examples of the ties between religious and ethnic subcultures. Herberg (1955, p. 85) had earlier described an ethnic group as a "form of self identification and self-location" that is linked to religious affiliation. Greeley (1972, p. 115) further noted that "instead of Americans belonging to churches because they believe in religion, there may be a strong tendency to believe in religion because they belong to churches."

Thus, the sense of belonging to a clearly identifiable group may be an important motivation for religious affiliation within a large, heterogeneous, urban population for many people. Religiously similar ethnic groups can provide primary relationships in a complex impersonal world, meeting human needs for fellowship and coming together with others who share similar views on significant issues. The relative unity of the Cuban American exile community in Miami, over the recent (spring 2000) case of Elian Gonzales, in spite of apparently different views on the subject among larger American society, is an interesting example that comes to mind. Within this group, the rescue of Elian from imminent drowning was, of course, widely viewed in this subcommunity as a miracle with strongly religious overtones (see *New York Times* or other newspaper reports on this topic over an approximately two month period from early March to late April 2000).

Scherer (1982, pp. 180–181) concluded that a sense of belonging is recognized as one of the most important functions of church membership, and that churches are thereby "part of the web of affiliations that help to solidify the individual's social bearings." Other benefits of belonging to a religious group are said by Scherer to be psychological: "The church provides comfort in times of trouble, security in times of fear, and companionship in times of loneliness. This comfort theory of religion suggests that the primary function of religion in urban society may be the enrichment of individual lives rather than social groups. . . . One of the ways in which urban religious institutions differ from their rural counterparts is an emphasis on religion as a personal, voluntary, and private matter rather than as an issue of public policy."

Other sociologists see the function of organized religion as an instrument of social control and as a means to maintain order in otherwise disorderly communities or societies. Virtually all major religions claim authority over critical events in everyday life, such as births, marriages, death, reproduction, and child rearing. Religion provides both direction and control over how such events are to be interpreted and ritualized (Curry, Jiobu, and Schwirian, 1999, p. 364). Although governmental and political institutions have the power to punish people who violate norms or laws while they are alive, religions are able to exercise control over people's behavior by threatening eternal punishment in the hereafter. For example, the threat of eternal damnation or perpetual reincarnation into lower animal forms are among the ways that various organized religions have historically attempted to control the behavior of their members. Likewise, the appropriate behavior or observance of rituals, such as prayer or penance, will be viewed with favor and ultimately rewarded with promises of eternal bliss of some sort. At the time of this writing, some religious and political leaders were strongly arguing that copies of the Ten Commandments be posted in every classroom of the public schools in the United States in order to help maintain discipline and avoid the kind of deadly violence that had recently occurred in some schools, ranging from elementary to secondary levels, in various school districts around the country. It remains to be demonstrated whether such attempts at religious social control in these settings will ever be enacted or will prove to be effective. But it is not unusual to find a high degree of cooperation between religious and political leaders in the United States or other modern urban societies in efforts to influence the behavior of large urban populations.

Sociologists with a neomarxist or conflict perspective are more likely to view the functions of organized religion in a more negative light. Karl Marx, for example, claimed that religion serves ruling elites and perpetuates inequality by legitimizing the status quo and diverting people's attention from such inequality. He criticized religion as the "sigh of the oppressed creature, the sentiment of a heartless world, and the soul of soulless conditions" (1964, p. 27). Religion, according to Marx, is the "opium of the people" because it eases the suffering of the poor through prayer and ritual and deludes the masses into accepting their situation as divinely ordained rather than organizing themselves to radically change the existing social system. Other conflict theorists see that gender inequality is also a product of organized religion, "since virtually all the world's major religions reflect and encourage male dominance in social life" (Macionis, 1999, pp. 484–485). In the United States, slavery and the resultant forms of racism that dominated the deep South of the late nineteenth and early twentieth centuries were justified on religious grounds because they "converted heathens" to Christianity and were "willed by God" (Rose, 1966). Most churches across the country still remain racially segregated to this day.

Critics of conflict and marxist theory argue that although some elements of these theories reflect current social reality, there are important exceptions to Marx's claim that religion functions primarily to preserve the status quo. These critics point to the fact that religion can and often does lead to new ways of organizing societies, including new political and economic institutions and new lifestyles. One supporting example is *liberation theology,* started in the 1960s in Latin America by the Roman Catholic Church. This movement was a fusion of Christian principles with a form of political activism that was marxist in character (Macionis, 1999, p. 486; Berryman, 1984). It was designed to promote greater economic equality by helping people to liberate themselves from extreme poverty. During the same period, the civil rights revolution in the United States was strongly supported by many religious groups, many of whose clergymen, priests, or rabbis were often active participants in the protests, demonstrations, and marches of that period and were frequently vocal opponents of the status quo of racial discrimination and segregation. The role of Afro-American churches and the leadership of the Reverend Martin Luther King Jr. and other prominent black clergymen were, of course, central to many of the successes of the civil rights revolution and should not be overlooked (Garrow, 1988). Thus the question of whether organized religion inhibits or promotes social change and equality remains an open one, to which the answer probably varies with time, the particular circumstances, and the roles of specific religious groups, their members, and their leaders.

Spatial and Ecological Dimensions of Urban Religion

The churches and cathedrals of the Medieval and Renaissance periods were massive and ornate in structure, and to symbolize permanence, they were built to "last forever." Because religion played a much more central role in the life of the cities of these periods than in the cities of today, churches and cathedrals were located near the geographic center of the cities, where they towered over all other buildings (except perhaps, the palaces of the ruling elites with whom they shared power), and they were usually visible to and

A Pentecostal church in New York City is representative of the great diversity of religious groups in Urban America

within walking distance from all parts of the city (see chapter 2). Today these majestic cathedrals still are major attractions to tourists and religious pilgrims from all over the world, but as has already been suggested, the nature and influence of the religions practiced within their walls have changed drastically.

Although many equally impressive churches were built and still stand near the centers of large North American cities of the late nineteenth and early twentieth centuries, the rapidly changing population and migration patterns of the last half of the twentieth century have drastically changed the locations, architecture, and functions of churches of modern metropolitan communities. The migration of rural or foreign born groups, largely black or Hispanic, to the central cities (see chapter 12) and the movement of working- and middle-class whites to the continually growing suburban rings surrounding the central cities have created higher levels of geographic social mobility among all segments of the population and a great deal of spatial dislocation for established churches and their congregations. Where permanency and tradition were the norms for earlier churches, change and transience have become the norms for many churches in American metropolitan communities. As each ethnic or religious group residentially disperses from the inner cities to the outlying areas and builds new church buildings in the new residential areas, their older church buildings are sold off or are abandoned. Newcomers then occupy the old buildings and convert them to their own purposes.

In the inner city of Detroit, for example, no longer viable churches and synagogues have been sold off to incoming migrant groups or have been converted to other purposes (see Bridger and Maines, 1998). Many such buildings have been turned into theaters, recital halls, warehouses, party stores, and other nonreligious uses, or abandoned altogether. In successive waves of dispersal, Catholic, Jewish, and Protestant congregations have moved into neighborhoods farther from the center of the city and have built new churches and synagogues, only to later move still farther out into the suburbs, once again selling or abandoning these no longer viable religious buildings, and once again building still newer churches and synagogues in the more recently settled outlying suburban areas. This pattern of the spatial redistribution and turnover of religious congregations as the metropolitan expands outward from its center has been estimated to have reoccurred in the Detroit metropolitan area approximately four times in the last three-quarters of the twentieth century and is expected to continue into the foreseeable future. Overall this pattern of spatial redistribution and decentralization of churches and other religious structures very much has followed the growth pattern of Burgess's Concentric Zone Theory or Hoyt's Sector Theory described in chapter 4 under the heading, "Classic Theories of Metropolitan Growth and Structure."

The continuous geographic mobility of religious congregations has had a number of ecological consequences. For example, church architecture in the suburban rings of the metropolis has become simpler, more unassuming, relatively less expensive, more quickly built, and more replaceable or expendable than in the more permanent structures of the past. Such churches have also become more utilitarian and multipurpose to accommodate a wider range of religious and social activities. They now often include more offices to house larger and more diversified staffs, gymnasiums, recital halls, classrooms or playrooms, meeting rooms, and the like. And particularly in suburbs with little or no public transportation available, they require lots of space for parking!

This discussion of urban religious institutions concludes with the observation that they likely will continue to be transformed by ever-changing patterns of urbanization, and that they will continue to compete against more secularized and powerful urban institutions. No one denominational view will likely become powerful enough to represent diverse urban populations, and continuous religious experimentation will continue to support religious pluralism, with still more ambiguously blended forms of both sacred and secular belief and behavioral systems as among the likely outcomes. Urban religions will continue to be called upon to reinterpret daily life for those who have faith in a supernatural being, whereas other individuals will continue to look for meaning in more secular activities and settings.

THE URBAN FAMILY: CHANGE AND CONFLICT

The family is clearly the oldest and longest surviving of all human institutions. In pre-urban societies, in fact, the human community itself was virtually synonymous with the large extended family. Although the earliest cities of antiquity were the first human communities that were organized on a basis other than kinship relationships, the family remained firmly entrenched in the social traditions and authority structure of preindustrial urban societies for many centuries. Like religion, it was a "sacred" institution, in the sense that it was beyond questioning or open criticism. Although it took different forms in different societies, the family in preindustrial communities has usually been characterized as based on extended kinship or blood ties that, through lineage, connect several generations and various networks of related individuals under the same system of family controls and interdependencies, usually in the same household. The extended family conferred status and prestige, supplied individual members with occupational roles and duties, and arranged marriages at an early age for the youngest family members (Levin, 1982, p. 8.)

Like all of the other social institutions discussed in this part of the book, the greatest changes that have affected the forms and functions of the family coincided with and were the product of the urban industrial revolution. What emerged during the earliest periods of this transformation was the displacement of the extended family as the dominant form of family organization by the smaller and more mobile *nuclear family,* which consists of a husband, wife, and their immediate offspring. The nuclear family remained the dominant form of family organization well into the second half of the twentieth century, but in recent decades, it too has been threatened by the continuing forces of economic, technological, social, and cultural change. As a result, the survival of the family in its "conventional" nuclear form is in doubt at the beginning of the twenty-first century, and some gloomy prognosticators have already begun to predict its inevitable decline and disintegration. First , however, it is important to understand just what it was about the urban-industrial revolution that had such an important role in reducing the dominant position of the extended family.

It is important to remember that before industrialization, the family was the major unit of production, and most people worked in their homes as family units. With the emergence of the factory system of production (see chapter 3), men, and sometimes women and children, had to leave their homes to go to work in the factories. In this sense it was the journey to work that for the first time separated individuals from their homes and other family members on a daily basis. Most factories were located in growing industrial cities in growing industrial societies. This created a great deal of residential dislocation as rural families had to move to the cities or had to migrate to distant countries to find industrial work or seek better lives, and in most of the latter cases, the extended families dissolved at the points of departure (see the film or play *Fiddler on the Roof* for a vivid illustration of extended families dissolving, as each generation and each family member depart for different destinations). To the extent that fathers, and most likely their wives and their children, were often employed in different work settings, they no longer shared the same daily work routines and experiences. When child labor was eventually forbidden by law during reform periods in most advanced industrialized economies, children for the first time were no longer economic assets and instead became economic liabilities (Henslin, 1996, p. 393). To the extent that children thus became nonproductive and more expensive, there developed a strong rational on the part of many parents to drastically limit the number of children they wished to bring into the world. Adding to the desire for smaller families was also the greater demands for more formal education associated with the conditions of life in urban-industrial societies, and both the costs of such education and the resulting longer period of economic dependency of children on their parents made child rearing even more expensive. All these factors helped lower birthrates and the average size of urban families, as also did the competition for affordable living space in the increasingly dense and crowded urban-industrial centers.

As urbanization continued to grow, other institutions, such as those discussed in the previous three chapters, progressively began to strip the family of many of its previous functions, such as producing food, educating the young, providing recreation, and nursing the sick and the aged (Henslin, 1996, pp. 394–395). The reductions in these functions, along with technological and mechanical innovations (washing and drying machines, automatic dishwashers, electric clothes irons, vacuum cleaners, etc.) that reduced some of the time-consuming drudgery of many traditional household tasks, helped to modify the role of women in the family and increasingly placed them in the position of providers of emotional support for their husbands and children.

Industrialization and urbanization also brought greater equality between husbands and wives and between parents and their children. This did not occur without a great deal of resistance by males, who were reluctant to surrender their traditional positions of power within traditional family structures, and without the support of the feminist revolution of the latter part of the twentieth century. This struggle for family or gender dominance continues and has, in fact, received a great deal of continuing attention in recent decades by feminist scholars and other scholars of marxist or conflict persuasions (see Feagin and Feagin, 1997, pp. 145–160; Eitzen and Baca Zinn, 1997, p. 284; and Levin, 1982, p. 163). These struggles, along with the declining economic functions of the nuclear family, helped contribute to rising divorce rates in modern urban societies and are linked to some of the other changing family and marriage patterns to be described.

Changing Marriage and Courtship Patterns

Marriage in contemporary urban society has emerged as a social system separate from that of the traditional family, which exercised a great deal of control over marriage and courtship choices. Marriage was either arranged in terms of socioeconomic terms or came about through a relatively restricted courtship process. In the modern urban world, marriage does not depend on the stability of the extended family and its ties to property, location, and land. Marriage, instead, increasingly depends on the mutual attraction between individuals in the form of romantic love or on the anticipated compatibility or companionship of prospective mates. In urban America, the opportunities for meeting and choosing mates are not highly structured or institutionalized, and it often seems to many that the possibility that a single person will eventually meet a suitable mate happens primarily by "chance" or "luck." And of course this perception has been heightened by popular romantic movies or fiction. As Levin (1982) points out, the choice of a mate in the urban setting is not purely a random process. For example, proximity plays a role for many, whose mate selections are drawn from among family acquaintances, neighbors, church groups, fellow school or college students, or coworkers. For those for whom these contacts are unsuccessful, newer modes of meeting people of the opposite sex have emerged which more or less supplement these more traditional settings. For example, newspaper and magazine advertisements, dating bureaus, singles bars, discotheques, dance halls, and coed singles apartments, and on-line Web sites are all among the commercialized services that have entered the urban marketplace to meet this kind of need. For gays, about whom more will be said later, these same kinds of specialized services are also emerging and becoming more visible.

Given the pluralistic nature of urban society and the freedom of individuals to be exposed to varied subcultural influences, people are continually coming into contact with new interpretations of what marriage should be and what obligations, if any, the participants have toward each other. New patterns of mate selection emerge and new social and economic influences prevail that contribute to the ultimate decision as to who marries whom or who does not marry at all. Nurtured in a climate of individualism, egalitarianism, and personal fulfillment and given viability in a social system that has opened education opportunities to many, and where economic restrictions against the working woman have been greatly reduced, these new interpretations have altered the nature of the marriage relationship and have made it less stable and predictable than in traditional societies (Levin, 1982, pp. 162–163). Separation and divorce become more viable options when romantic or other expectations fail to be realized in the marital relationship.

Recent data demonstrate the declining status of marriage in the United States over the past several decades. For example, in 1970, 71.7 percent of all Americans over the age of 18 were married, but by 1998, the married portion of the population over 18 had shrunk to 59.7 percent. Likewise the portion of the U.S. population over 18 that was divorced more than tripled from 3.2 percent to 9.8 percent during the same time period (U.S. Bureau of the Census, *Marital Status and Living Arrangements,* March 1998). In addition, the number and percentage of adults who have never married also increased from 1960, accounting for nearly 24 percent of the adult population in 1998. In addition to getting married in fewer numbers, people are also getting married at a later age. In 1960, about 40 percent of all 19-year-old women were married, but by 1990 only 11 percent were. About 92 percent of all women were married before they reached age 30 in 1960, but by 1990, only 81 percent were. Further, between 1970 and 1990, the proportion of the 30- to 34-year-old cohort who had never married almost tripled, rising from 6 to 16 percent for women and from 9 to 27 percent for men. For those age 35 to 39, the proportion of those never married doubled over these same two decades (*New York Times 2000 Almanac,* 1999, p. 292).

Divorce rates also increased rapidly in the United States from 1960 to the mid-1990s and stabilized somewhat thereafter. But although the divorce rate has stabilized, the ratio of divorced persons to married persons (with spouse present) has climbed dramatically since 1970 , from 47 divorced persons per every 1,000 who were married, to nearly quadrupling to 175 per 1,000 married persons by 1998. In 1998, there were nearly 20 million divorced persons in the United States, nearly 10 percent of the entire adult population (*New York Times Almanac 2000,* 1999, p. 293). A related development has been an increasing number of single parent families. More than 27 percent of families with children were headed by a single parent in 1998, doubling from only 13 percent in 1970. The number of households headed by never married women with children also continues to grow. There was approximately a quarter-million of such households in 1990, but there were over 4 million of them in 1998. This is even larger than the approximately 3 million households headed by divorced women with children. One interesting related change has been the growth in the number of single parent homes headed by fathers. In 1998, they number 1.8 million, or 5 percent of all U.S. families (U.S. Bureau of the Census, Household and Family Characteristics, March 1998 [1999]). But a study reported from the General Social Survey by National Opinion Research Center (NORC) researchers at the University of Chicago provides the most direct and succinct finding about the declining status of the nuclear family in the United States. The survey found that the percentage of American households made up of married couples with children dropped to just 26 percent in 1998, down from 45 percent in the early 1970s, and as the director of this study concluded that such a family has now become the exception rather than the rule (*New York Times,* November 26, 1999, p. A22).

Two other significant studies, relying on similar bodies of census and other statistical data, have reached similar conclusions about declining marriage patterns. For example, the Rutgers University National Marriage Project found that the nation's marriage rate has dipped by 43 percent in the past four decades—from 87.5 marriages per 1,000 unmarried women in 1960 to 49.7 marriages in 1996—leaving it at its lowest point in recorded history (*Washington Post National Weekly,* July 19, 1999, p. 34). A study by a sociologist at the Institute for Social Research at the University of Michigan reports that the number of children who live in households headed by unmarried couples who live together is on the increase. According to this study, about 40 percent of all children will spend at least some time living with their mother and her unmarried partner, and less often, children will live with their unmarried father and his partner (*New York Times,* February 2000, p. D8). Even though the number of unmarried couples who live together with children is increasing, however, it is still not clear how this increase in cohabitation will affect the traditional role of marriage. This study, which also relies on sample survey data, further reports that 56 percent of all marriages between 1990 and 1994 were preceded by cohabitation, a great increase from the 10 percent of marriages preceded by cohabitation from 1965 to 1974. The same report also found that 55 percent of people who cohabitate end up marrying, but of these, 40 percent later divorce.

The authors of the Rutgers study conclude that marriage is no longer the presumed route from adolescence to adulthood and has lost much of its significance as a rite of passage. A coauthor, sociologist David Popenoe, expressed concern that the down trend away from marriage would continue, and that with the breakdown of the family, the "peer culture," which includes pop culture, has become a stronger force on the outlook of teenagers and that "nothing could be more anti-marriage than much of the popular culture" (*New York Times,* July 4, 1999, p. Y12). He asserts that teenagers express continuing belief in marriage as an abstract ideal but are negative in applying this ideal to themselves, in part because so many had seen or lived through divorces and did not have good examples of marriage to emulate. His coauthor Barbara Dafoe Whitehead concurs, "Young people today want successful marriages, but they are increasingly anxious and pessimistic about their chances for achieving that goal" (*Washington Post National Weekly,* July 12, 1999, p. 34). Perhaps the fact that the percentage of married people who reported being "very happy" in their marriages fell from 53.5 in 1973–1976 to 37.8 in 1996, as reported in this same study, also helps explain the pessimism about marriage afflicting so many of the offsprings of these marriages.

Parent-Child Conflicts in Urban America

Some of the alienation toward marriage and family living reported needs further explanation in the context of the urban settings in which it occurs. The task of being a parent in urban America is a complex and often ambiguous undertaking for many, frequently causing confusion and discouragement. Unlike traditional societies, where roles and expectations between parents and their children tended to be concrete and beyond questioning, urban parents are confronted with a bewildering number of often contradictory child rearing options and models (Levin, 1982, p. 164). The behavioral sciences (psychiatry, sociology, anthropology, and psychology, as well as the medical sciences) produced a large number of popular "child experts" after World War II who became "worshipped as the high priests of child rearing" (Pohlman, 1969), and American parents became increasingly dependent on the advice of these often self-appointed experts as to how to raise children. The problem was that this advice was often faddish, contradictory, and swung dramatically between polarized extremes over relatively short time spans. For example, the swings between sterner discipline and more permissiveness were often dramatic and confusing (and some of these kinds of shifts were common to public school education, as well). Skolnick (1973, p. 303) had concluded that "ironically, attention to the experts among middle-class people seems to raise anxiety rather than reduce it. Research on middle-class mothers . . . suggests that the more awareness a mother has of the child rearing literature, the more uncertain she feels that she is doing the right thing."

Increased leisure time and close physical proximity in the cities have also helped to contribute to the development of a more powerful youth peer group than existed in rural societies where most of the time of young people was absorbed by work on the farm. The associations formed within these groups often becomes translated into new norms of behavior and loyalties that challenge the power and influence of parents and produce conflicts that have come to be labeled as "the generation gap." (Levin, 1982, p. 165). The impersonality and anonymity of the city are conditions that may limit the parents' ability to be knowledgeable about their children's outside activities and behavior, and the pervasive nature of the mass media frequently portrays values that may not be in harmony with the values the parents would like their children to adopt.

Married Women Who Work

One of the greatest changes having a direct impact on the urban family has been the very rapid increase in the rate of participation of women in paid work outside the home. For example, although only 37.7 percent of women participated in the labor force in 1960, their levels of participation grew to 59.8 percent by 1998 (U.S. Bureau of Labor Statistics, Employment and Earnings, January 1999). Also, employed women as a percentage of the total civilian labor force jumped from about 33 percent in 1960, to about 46 percent in 1998 (*New York Times Almanac 2000,* 1999, p. 348), while the percentage of men in the labor force actually dropped slightly during the same thirty-eight-year period. Further, by 1997, 63 percent of married women with children under the age of six were employed for wages or salaries, as were 77 percent of married women with children between six and seventeen years of age (U.S. Bureau of the Census, 1997). The percentages of divorced women in the labor force who have children were even higher.

Although women have not yet gained parity with men with respect to earnings and employability, the gains that they have already made have created some ambiguities about the shifting roles of men and women in some marriages. In a "striking rewriting of the age-old compact between husbands and wives," Amy Goldstein (2000) has asserted that "the proportion of couples in which the woman is chief breadwinner has been increasing so markedly that nearly one in three working wives nationwide is now paid more than her husband, compared with fewer than one in five in 1980." The trend is particularly pro-nounced among the most highly educated women, nearly half of whom have incomes higher than their spouses, according to Goldstein, who reports that some 10.5 million American women who earned more than their husbands by 1998 were testing gender roles in ways "far more concrete than the feminist movement of a generation ago." She adds that, according to economists, sociologists, and couples themselves, wives' heightened wages have "unbalanced other aspects of the equation of marriages: housework and child care, economic power, egos and expectations." Although available data do not yet support the conclusion that marriages in which wives bring in the most income are significantly more likely to end in divorce than other marriages, Goldstein does report anecdotal evi-dence that divorce was in fact the outcome in some such marriages, and she identifies still other cases in which nontraditional financial disparities between husbands and wives have been a source of much tension, frustration, and anxiety. At any rate, two-earner families have become commonplace in urban America, as more and more breadwinners of both sexes routinely leave their households separately and in different directions in the daily journey to work. Although this does not necessarily break family ties in all cases, it may serve to create severe strains in the marital relationship. In suburbs where public trans-portation resources are limited, the two or more car family living in homes with two car or more garages has become common, and for many two-earner families, a necessity.

Single Parent Families, Grown Children Living at Home, and Grandparents

Among the changes that have taken place over the last several decades, one of the most revealing involves the increase in the number of children living with single parents. For example, only 12 percent of children lived with one parent in 1970, but that percentage has more than doubled to 28 percent (more than one out of every four) of all children under eighteen living in single-parent households by 1998 (*New York Times Almanac 2000,* 1999, p. 300). This increase reflects not only the rising divorce rate, but also a large increase in the number of children born to unwed mothers. Growing acceptance of this new reality is reflected in the findings of the Rutgers University National Marriage Project, which recently found that more than half (53 percent) of the teenage girls surveyed agreed that having a child out of wedlock is a "worthwhile lifestyle" (*Washington Post National Weekly,* July 12, 1999, p. 34).

One parent families, most of which are headed by a single mother, result from divorce, widowhood, or by the decision of an unmarried woman to have a child (Macionis, 1999, p. 473). Since 1990, about 20 percent of white children, 31 percent of Hispanic children, and more than half of all black children under age eighteen have lived with only one parent, usually the mother (*New York Times Almanac 2000,* 1999, p. 300). Although many of them are successful, single-parent families struggle with a wide array of economic, social, and emotional issues and often experience substantial economic instability and loss of income—more specifically, poverty. As Macionis (1999, p. 474), citing a large number of recent authoritative sources puts it, "On average, children growing up in a single-parent family start out poorer, get less schooling, and end up with lower incomes as adults. Such children are also more likely to be single parents themselves."

Given the trend toward marrying at an older age and the greater number of years of formal education or training required to gain financial independence, along with rising housing costs and stagnant wage levels for all but the very top economic strata, there has been a modest trend for young adults to continue living at home in their parent dwellings for a longer period of time. It is also increasingly common for those who had gone away to college or those who had entered the labor force for a period of time, to return to again live with their parent or parents. In 1970, 8 percent of young adults, age twenty-five to thirty-four years old, lived with their parents, but by 1987, that number had grown to just under 12 percent, where it has remained ever since (*New York Times Almanac 2000,* 1999, p. 300). Young women in this age bracket were only about one-half as likely to continue to live with their parents than men, probably because they are likely to marry at a younger age than men.

Although it is very rare in American urban society for three or more generations of the same family to live under the same roof as an extended family, this is most likely to happen in extremely poor families with limited housing resources, or extremely wealthy families living on large estates. But a total of approximately 4 million children did live with their grandparents in 1998. Of these, nearly 50 percent lived there with their mothers, about 6 percent lived there with their fathers, and about 12.6 percent lived with both their parents in their grandparents homes. The remaining 35.5 percent (approximately 1.4 million children) live with their grandparents with neither parent present (U.S. Bureau of the Census, *Marital Status and Living Arrangements,* March 1998).

The latter data suggest that not every dimension of the extended family has completely disappeared. Nevertheless, as life expectancies have gone up, the elderly in America tend to be healthier, live longer, and, in the case of the middle classes and higher, they also are likely to better off financially (often supported by pensions as well as social security). Although they do not necessarily desire to live in the same households with their adult children or grandchildren, many of them do choose to live near nearby where they can visit them frequently. But many do not, and one interesting trend has been the development of specialized for seniors only retirement communities, often with resort or country club amenities. Although these have appeared elsewhere, they tend to be concentrated in the sun belt regions of the country which attract large numbers of retirees from all parts of the country. Sun City and Sun City West, developed by the Del Webb Corporation in suburban Phoenix, is a prime example. Limited to active people fifty-five years of age or older, these communities are relatively self-contained, with their own shopping centers, hospitals and health care facilities, recreation areas, libraries, theaters, and the like. What they do lack, of course, are primary or secondary schools, because there are no school-age children as residents. And because the original Sun City is an independent incorporated community, there are no local school taxes for its residents. However, some local universities do occasionally offer courses for seniors on the premises. The Sun City concept has caught on, and there are now additional Sun City Developments near Tucson, in California, South Carolina, and still more planned for other states. As already suggested, similar types of specialized adult residential developments are now widespread and can be found in or near the major metropolitan areas all over the country.

Family Alternatives

It is obvious from the discussion so far that a majority of Americans do not live in nuclear family households, and that modern urban society is more accepting and permissive with respect to alternative modes of living which are increasingly available and provide individuals with more freedom to make either conventional or nonconventional choices.

Independent Living.   A growing number of people choose to or are forced by circumstances to live by themselves. According to recent census figures, about 26 million people or about 10 percent of the total population of the United States live alone (*New York Times Almanac 2000,* 1999, p. 298). The majority of these, according to Glick (1994) are between the ages of twenty-five to fifty-four years, and college educated. "They have dated recently and are in good health and are working for pay." One of the reasons that many young people live alone has been an increase in the age of marriage, which has already been discussed. Divorce is also one of the causes already discussed, as has been the increase in the life span, which leaves more people as widows or widowers. The fact that women have longer life expectancies than men accounts for the fact that more elderly women than men live alone.

It is also true that many people choose a single life in large metropolitan communities because they like the lifestyle or the anonymity. Living alone gives them fewer obligations, more privacy, and greater freedom to come and go as they please. Some may prefer more solitary activities, such as reading, whereas others may prefer more spontaneity than structured familylike relationships provide, or greater numbers of choices for such social activities as dating, partying, participation in voluntary associations, or other social networks. Many of these kinds of activities certainly fall within the framework of a *cosmopolitan* lifestyle, as described in chapter 6, and one should not exclude from the "joys of singlehood," for example, the growing number of people who are virtually addicted to networking on the Internet or other computer-related "obsessions."

Disco dances provide meeting places for urban singles

It should not be concluded from this discussion that all unrelated singles who prefer to live alone actually do so. Although reliable data for singles sharing living quarters as roommates with other singles, outside of cohabitation or sexual relationships with one another, is not readily available, this is certainly an option chosen by some as a convenient way of sharing expenses and household chores in relationships that are less demanding or binding than those of a sexual or familial nature. Such relationships for singles are not unlike that of college roommates, and in fact, for some may be a way of extending such dormitory-like friendship relationships beyond the college years.

Communal Living.   A commune is a small, self-supporting community voluntarily joined by groups of individuals committed to living together in a family-like environment, with members usually sharing duties, resources, and financing. Communal living is not necessarily an urban phenomenon, because people have been forming communes for thousands of years, usually in nonurban settings (Zablocki, 1980), and they have been relatively rare in urban settings. However, they do exist and do attract certain kinds of individuals from time to time for various reasons. According to Coleman and Cressey (1984, p.149), they are relatively easy to start in urban areas: "All that is needed is a house and a few interested people." The motives for such group living, however, are usually much more complex. Often the motivations are associated with new and nonconventional religious movements of one sort or another and have the characteristics of sects or cults (see Hamilton, 1995; Zablocki, 1980; Roberts, 1995; Stark and Bainbridge, 1997). Other motives may be secular in nature, but in almost all cases, idealism, ideology, or utopianism are also usually essential prerequisites. Stark (1998, p. 100) has suggested that the most prolific period of commune formations in U.S. history occurred in the late 1960s and early 1970s as an intrinsic part of the "hippie" drug culture of that time. Some of these communes were based on religious experimentation, some were based on radical political movements of the period, and some were simply created by the followers of popular rock musicians. But despite the diversity of motivation, Stark asserts that all of the communes were "attempts to get away from what members considered to be the materialist, aggressive values of 'straight' society. Each, in its own way, was attempting to create an egalitarian new culture, so much so that they began to . . . talk endlessly about breaking down the old norms." Most of these communes did not last very long, as is the case with most experiments in communal living in America, for a variety of reasons. However, one study of 143 communes created earlier in American history found that those based on religious ideologies were much more likely to survive for a much longer period of time than those based on political or secular ideologies (Stephen and Stephen, 1973). And Shepherd and Shepherd (2000), for example, have reported in detail on one relatively successful contemporary new religious movement with over 10,000 members living communally in more than 800 homes located in 88 different countries, which has been in existence for more than three decades. Thus, whatever the basis for the success or failure of experiments in communal living, such options continue as real alternatives to conventional nuclear family living for at least a small segment of the urban population.

Gay and Lesbian Couples. Because of the stigma, homophobia, and discrimination traditionally attached to homosexual relationships and because of the resultant felt needs by homosexual couples to keep their relationships secret, there have been no accurate census counts of homosexual families, nor is there much research about life in gay and lesbian households (Kornblum, 1997, p. 488). However, since the recent gay rights revolution, homosexuals have been more openly stating their sexual preferences and desires to live freely as gay and lesbian families, with all the same kinds of rights and protections accorded to traditional heterosexual family units. Progress in this direction has been slow, and most religious bodies still will not perform marriage services for gay and lesbian couples. Likewise the legal status of such marriages has not been recognized in most governmental jurisdictions within the United States.

However, there have recently been some important breakthroughs in some areas. For example, the Disney Corporation, long viewed as a defender of traditional family values, surprised many Americans by agreeing in 1995 that it would begin to provide spousal benefits, such as health insurance, pension rights, and the like, for its employees who were part of a same-sex relationship or marriage (Kornblum, 1997, p. 488). Further, several cities, including Seattle and San Francisco, have passed laws that permit gay or lesbian couples to publicly and legally declare that they are "domestic partners" with many of the same rights as any other married couples (Curry, Jiobu, and Schwirian, 1999, p. 309). It should be also noted that in these instances, full marriage status was not granted, and this still falls short of the goals of the gay rights movement.

A more substantial breakthrough was made within the reform movement of Judaism early in the year 2000, when it was announced that Reformed Jewish rabbis, who previously had been permitted to perform "commitment" ceremonies for Jewish gay and lesbian couples, would now be permitted to perform these rituals as full marriages, if the rabbis so choose. With the beginning of the twenty-first century, it now appears that a few Protestant clergy persons and Catholic priests have also begun to undertake similar kinds of commitment ceremonies for some gay or lesbian members of their congregations, although it is not yet clear whether such ceremonies will be fully approved or "blessed" with the full status of marriage by their respective denominations. The resistance to such change is still great.

More significantly, in the same year, Vermont was the first state to pass a law creating same-sex marriages in almost every respect but the name. The law created a sweeping marriagelike system that allows the state to confer on same-sex couples virtually all of the more than three thousand rights and responsibilities enjoyed by married couples, from health insurance benefits to inheritance rights (*New York Times,* April 26, 2000, p. A12). Couples seeking these civil unions must register with their town clerk and have the unions certified by a clergy member or justice of the peace. Likewise, gay partners seeking to dissolve such a union must go through a family court, just as married couples seeking a divorce do. It is still very questionable whether such unions will be recognized by other states or whether they will entitle the partners to federal benefits in the foreseeable future.

An interesting quasi or alternative marriage pattern worth mentioning here recently began in France as an effort to legalize gay unions, short of marriage. Passed in late 1999, a law that gives couples some of the benefits and responsibilities of marriage—but not all—has proven to be very popular, with almost fourteen thousand ceremonies performed in the first four months of the law's existence (*New York Times,* April 18, 2000, pp. A1 and A4). What is most surprising about the response to this new option is the fact that it has also proven to be almost as popular with heterosexual couples as well, who comprise an estimated 40 percent of those who have taken advantage of it. The same *New York Times* report says that although both gay and heterosexual couples are using the new law, they tend to see it differently. For gay couples, who have no alternative, the option is celebrated like a marriage: "The couples dress up, take pictures and have parties to mark the event." The heterosexual couples tend to see the union more as a trial run for a conventional marriage and "often don't even tell their parents."

A reasonable conclusion of this discussion about the changing nature of the family in urban societies is that although a shrinking proportion of modern urban populations participate in traditional forms of marriage and the family, most of the other alternatives are based on the desire of most people to live in households shared with other individuals, whether they are related to them by birth or marriage. This is as equally true for homosexuals as it is for heterosexuals. Although only about 26 percent of the American population still lives in nuclear family households, an even smaller portion live alone in single-person households. Alternatives to the traditional nuclear family and to traditional marriages, for better or worse, are becoming more and more acceptable to cosmopolitan urban dwellers.

SELECTED BIBLIOGRAPHY

BELLAH, ROBERT N. "Civil Religion in America." *Daedalus.* 96 (1967): 1–21.

BOSKOFF, ALVIN. *The Sociology of Urban Regions,* 2d. ed. New York: Appleton-Century-Crofts, 1970.

BERRYMAN, PHILLIP. *The Religious Roots of Rebelllion.* Maryknoll, NY: Orbis Books, 1984

BERGER, PETER. *The Sacred Canopy: Elements of a Sociological Theory of Religion.* New York: Doubleday, 1967.

BRIDGER, JEFFREY, and DAVID MAINES. "Narrative Structures and the Catholic Church Closings in Detroit." *Qualitative Sociology.* 21 (1998): 319–340.

COLEMAN, JAMES, and DONALD CRESSEY. *Social Problems.* 2d. ed. Cambridge: Harper & Row, 1984.

CURRY, TIM, ROBERT JIOBU, and KENT SCHWIRIAN. *Sociology for the Twenty-first Century,* 2d. ed. Upper Saddle River, NJ.: Prentice-Hall, 1999.

DEMERATH, N. J. "The Varieties of Sacred Experience: Finding the Sacred in a Secular Grove." *Journal for the Scientific Study of Religion.* 39 no. 1 (March 2000).

DURKHEIM, EMIL. *The Elementary Forms of Religious Life.* New York: Free Press, 1915.

EITZEN, D. STANLEY, and MAXINE BACA ZINN. *Social Problems,* 7th ed. Boston: Allyn and Bacon, 1997.

FEAGIN, JOE R., and CLAIRECE BOOHER FEAGIN. *Social Problems: A Critical Power-Conflict Perspective,* 5th ed. Upper Saddle River, NJ.: Prentice-Hall, 1997

GARROW, DAVID. *Bearing the Cross: Martin Luther King, Jr. and the Southern Leadership Conference.* New York: Vintage, 1988.

GLICK, PAUL. "Living Alone during Middle Adulthood." *Sociological Perspectives.* 37 (1994): 445–457.

GOLDSTEIN, AMY. "When Wives Bring Home More Bacon." *Washington Post National Weekly Edition,* March 6, 2000, p. 18.

GREELEY, ANDREW. *Unsecular Man: The Persistence of Religion.* New York: Delta, 1972.

HAMILTON, MALCOLM B. *The Sociology of Religion: Theoretical and Comparative Perspectives.* London and New York: Routledge, 1995.

HAWLEY, AMOS. *Urban Society.* New York: Ronald Press, 1971.

HENSLIN, JAMES M. *Social Problems,* 4th ed. Upper Saddle River, NJ: Prentice-Hall, 1996.

HERBERG, WILL. *Protestant, Catholic and Jew.* New York: Doubleday, 1955.

IANNOCCONE, LAWRENCE. "Religious Markets and the Economics of Religion." *Social Compass* 39 (1992): 123–131.

KORNBLUM, WILLIAM. *Sociology in a Changing World,* 4th ed. Fort Worth: Harcourt Brace, 1997.

LEVIN, DONALD M. "The Family in the Urban World." in Gold, Harry. *The Sociology of Urban Life,* Englewood Cliffs, NJ: Prentice-Hall, 1982.

MACIONIS, JOHN J. *Sociology,* 7th ed. Upper Saddle River, NJ: Prentice-Hall, 1999.

MARTY, MARTIN. *Righteous Empire: The Protestant Experience in America.* New York: Dial Press, 1979

MARX, KARL. *Selected Writings in Sociology and Social Philosophy.* Translated by T. M. Bottomore. New York: McGraw-Hill, 1964.

NISBET, ROBERT. *The Social Bond.* New York: Knopf, 1970.

PER, PAUL, and DANIEL V. A. OLSON. "Religious Market Share and Intensity of Church Involvement in Five Denominations." *Journal for the Scientific Study of Religion.* 39 no. 1 (March 2000).

PHILLIPS, RICK. "Religous Market Share and Mormon Church Activity." *Sociology of Religion.* 56 (1998).

POHLMAN, E. H. *Psychology of Birth Planning.* Cambridge, MA: Schenkman, 1969.

ROBERTS, KEITH A. *Religion in Sociological Perspective,* 3d ed. Belmon, CA: Wadsworth, 1995.

ROSE, ARNOLD. "Race and Ethnic Relations." In *Contemporary Social Problems,* 2nd ed., Robert K. Merton and Robert A. Nisbet (eds.). New York: Harcourt Brace and World, 1966.

SANDEEN, ERNEST. *The Roots of Fundamentalism.* Chicago: University of Chicago Press, 1970.

SCHERER, JACQUELINE. "Religion in the Urban Community," in *The Sociology of Urban Life,* Harry Gold (ed.). Englewood Cliffs: NJ: Prentice-Hall, 1982.

SHEPHERD, GORDON, and GARY SHEPHERD. "The Moral Career of a New Religious Movement." *Oakland Journal.* 1 (spring 2000).

SHERKAT, DAREEN, and JOHN WILSON. "Preference Constraints and Choices in Religious Markets: An Examination of Religious Switching and Apostasy." *Social Forces.* 73 (1995): 993–1026.

SJOBERG, GIDEON. *The Pre-Industrial City.* New York: Free Press, 1960.

SKOLNICK, ARLENE. *The Intimate Environment.* Boston: Little-Brown, 1973.

SOROKIN, PITIRIM. *Contemporary Sociological Theories.* New York: Harper and Brothers, 1928.

STARK, RODNEY, *Sociology,* 7th ed. Belmont, CA: Wadsworth, 1998.

STARK, RODNEY, and WILLIAM SIMS BAINBRIDGE. *Religion, Deviance, and Social Control.* New York: Routledge, 1997.

STARK, RODNEY, and JAMES C. MCCANN. "Market Forces and Catholic Committment: Exploring the New Paradigm." *Journal for the Scientific Study of Religion.* 32 (1993).

STEPHEN, KAREN H., and G. EDWARD STEPHEN. "Religion and the Survival of Utopian Communities." *Journal for the Scientific Study of Religion.* 12 (1973): 89–100.

WEBER, MAX. *The City.* New York: Collier, 1962.

WILSON, BRYAN. *Sects and Society.* Berkley: University of California Press, 1961.

WILSON, JOHN. *Religion in American Society.* Englewood Cliffs, NJ: Prentice Hall, 1978.

WINSTON, DIANE. *Red-Hot and Righteous: The Urban Religion of the Salvation Army.* Cambridge, MA: Harvard University Press, 1999.

ZABLOCKI, BENJAMIN. *Alienation and Charisma.* New York: Free Press, 1980.

Part IV

PERSISTENT URBAN SOCIAL PROBLEMS

11

URBAN PATTERNS OF
SOCIAL STRATIFICATION

Leon H. Warshay and Diana W. Warshay

A THEORETICAL FRAMEWORK FOR THE ANALYSIS OF URBAN STRATIFICATION

Inequality is built into social life—urban, suburban, rural, peasant, and folk—but the bases for inequality vary in terms of size and kind of community. Although a small village is likely to have an overall stratification system, usually based on a combination of class and status, larger communities exhibit both an overall, universal stratification system and multiple stratification systems that, as separate worlds or subuniverses, are usually unacquainted with or separated from one another. Hence, it is legitimate to ask whether, even within one society such as the United States, can one's rank(s) in, for example, New York City, validly be compared with rank(s) in Detroit, in Los Alamos, in Aspen, or in small towns or villages? The presence of multiple stratification systems in addition to a universal one increases the incidence of *status inconsistency*, particularly in urban areas. For example, a recent immigrant may have achieved a relatively substantial (economic) class level through occupational success but not yet acquired a comparable status—social prestige or honor.

What appear to be true about inequality and stratification, urban and other, are the following:

- All societies are stratified at least by age and gender.
- The closest to an equalitarian society or community is the band, such as a foraging group, where social attachments are fragile and shifting.
- An increase in a society's or community's economic surplus results in an unequal distribution of that surplus making for greater inequality such as a class or caste system.
- An increase in social complexity increases inequality.
- Different sizes and types of communities have differing bases of inequality.

What is usually considered the first comprehensive study of social stratification in America was that by W. Lloyd Warner and colleagues of Newburyport, Massachusetts, a city of 17,000, in the early 1930s. A six-class system (really a six-level status system) was presumably derived from their studies (Warner, Meeker, and Eells, 1949). It was said by Warner to apply to the United States as a whole, although he thought a five-class system would be more relevant as one went westward. Warner used both *objective* methods, such as income and occupation, and *reputational* methods, the prestige gained in the general community through membership in different ethnic groups and social clubs. Other studies of stratification have used these methods and also *subjective self-designation*, the class or status category that people assign to themselves (Cuber and Kenkel, 1954; Bendix and Lipset, 1966). Some urbanists have used approaches such as *social geography*, the spatial location and distribution of groups and how this changes over time, and *ethnography*, case studies of individual communities (Kleniewski, 1997).

THREE IDEOLOGICAL ORIENTATIONS FOR EXAMINING STRATIFICATION

Stratification can and should be analyzed and evaluated from various ideological orientations, each yielding its own explanation, methodology, and causation. Three ideological orientations—liberal, conservative, and radical—present a reasonable idea of the ideological range used in contemporary sociology. These are defined and then applied below in terms of their diverse approaches to urban stratification.

1. Liberalism: This ideological orientation is a centrist one. It emphasizes individualism, the individual as potential for good. Individual autonomy and rights are basic to liberalism. Liberals favor freedom and civil liberties and are generally opposed to censorship.

From the liberal standpoint, society in its macrosense is artificial, a creation of humans; hence, the suspicion of the power of institutions such as church and state and of traditional communal and familial manners and morals. However, the community can be improved through participation by individual citizens in the voluntary organizations of the civil society (see chapter 5).

Liberalism's social base is in the urban middle class, the home of reason, competition, freedom, and individualism. This is related to a central characteristic of liberalism, its secular bias toward the factual, empiricist, objective, detached, and value free. Bias and preconceptions are to be rejected, particularly those coming from tradition, community, authority, politics, and/or ideology. The rationality of business, of science, and of the intellect are to prevail.

2. Conservatism: Within this rightist ideology, tradition and heeding the lessons of the past are paramount. These lessons inhere in community, kinship, hierarchy, authority, religion, and a strong central value system. An organic view of society underlies this ideology, that society's vital functions are fulfilled by major institutions such as family and religion. Society, culturally integrated by means of basic values, is moving toward equilibrium and homeostasis. Such an outlook is most likely found in small towns, in traditional religions, in military castes, and where there are traditional classes such as the rural aristocracy and peasantry (see chapter 10).

Conservatism is antisecular, suspicious of both individualism and equalitarianism. The "reforms" arising from such standpoints are held to lead to unintended and/or unwanted consequences of industrialism and urbanism such as family breakdown, anomie, and suicide. Mottoes relevant to a conservative position would be: "Do not disturb a thing at rest," "If there is *no* need to do something, then there *is* the need *not* to do it," and "Those who ignore the past are condemned to repeat it."

3. Radicalism: This ideological standpoint is leftist. Radicals, such as marxists, hold that society is real and that it is a stratified system with the upper class controlling the means of production, as well as the major institutions. These institutions are condemned as artificial and alien. Radicals point to the contradictions and, therefore, the tensions between society's base (the forces of production and relations of production) and its superstructure (legal, political, and spiritual institutions). Hence, society is characterized by class struggle, latent or manifest, which will ultimately change it into a new and humane one (see chapters 7 and 8).

The social bases of radicalism are in the working classes, in some of the peasantry, and in other oppressed classes such as minorities and women. These are all regarded as marginal groups for whom current institutions such as family, religion, and the state are artificial and alien. Under certain historical and societal conditions, social classes and other exploited groups become politicized, thereby becoming active and often violent sources for major structural changes.

Comparisons among the Orientations

To liberals, individual freedom and competition are ultimate values. Such values are looked upon as dangerous by conservatives because they disrupt societal integration and as a sham by radicals because they provide a means for the upper class to maintain control. Thus, liberals are seen as radical by conservatives and as conservative by radicals. Community, not central for liberals, is central for both conservatives and radicals, communities of the past (tradition) for conservatives and community of the future (communism) for radicals.

A LIBERAL APPROACH TO STRATIFICATION

Despite class and status differences violating liberal values of opportunity and autonomy, liberals study inequality, but as objective fact, another liberal value. The measures of inequality are not purely urban although most of the class and status studies involved people who were urban or suburban residents. These measures, moreover, do reflect a society whose urban values have been spreading to rural areas through widespread mass media, travel, and the Internet.

Class Differences

The most evident measures of inequality, reflecting *class* more than *status*, reveal vast and increasing differences in income and wealth. Studies of *income* distribution in the United States show a large discrepancy between the top and bottom incomes. Studies of *wealth*, such as property and stocks and bonds, show an even larger discrepancy.

Discrepancy in *income* distribution is well illustrated by the following statistics. In 1987, the richest 20 percent of the population received 44 percent of the national income in contrast with the poorest 20 percent which received 5 percent (U.S. Bureau of the Census, 1987). In 1996, the richest 20 percent received 47 percent of the national income in contrast with the poorest 20 percent which received 4 percent (U.S. Bureau of the Census, 1998). Moreover, the income inequality has been increasing over a twenty-seven-year period, with the richest 20 percent receiving 41 percent in 1970 and 1980, 44 percent in 1990, and 47 percent in 1996; the comparable values for the poorest are 20 percent in 1970, 5 percent in 1980 and 1990, and 4 percent in 1996.

The discrepancy in *wealth* has been even greater than in income. In 1983, 79 percent of the nation's wealth was held by the richest 20 percent of the population contrasted with 6 percent of the wealth held by the poorest 20 percent (U.S. Bureau of the Census, 1983). If we omit people's primary residence from calculations of wealth, the discrepancy increases. Furthermore, wealth differences increase when one look at smaller portions of the richest. Of the richest 20 percent, the top 5 percent has become richer than the next 15 percent; within the top 5 percent, the top 1 percent has become richer than the next 4 percent; and within the top 1 percent, the top 0.25 percent has become richer than the remaining 0.75 percent (Krugman, 1995, p. A15). Overall, the differences in the distribution of the nation's wealth have been increasing: the top 5 percent received 16 percent in 1970, dropping to 15 percent in 1980, and rising to 17 percent in 1990 and to 20 percent in 1996.

Status Differences

One measure of status differences is urban-rural differences in occupational prestige. Rural occupations have been valued less by the American population than have urban occupations. Prestige ratings of ninety occupations in the United States from surveys conducted in March 1947 and June 1963 by the National Opinion Research Corporations using the North-Hatt scale (Bendix and Lipset, 1966) demonstrate the superior ranking of urban occupations:

> Of the three occupational titles that were clearly rural in that all required living on a farm, their occupational prestige rankings all fell below the median rank of 45.5 for the 90 occupational titles of the entire North-Hatt scale with lower scores signifying higher status. These three were "tenant farmer" with a rank of 51.5 in both the 1947 and the 1963 surveys, "farm hand" with 76 in 1947 and 83 in 1963, and "share cropper" with 87 in both years of the survey.

> Two other rural occupations had a rank above the median for the 90 occupational titles, "county agricultural agent" with a rank of 37.5 in 1947 and 39 in 1963 and "county judge" with 13 in 1947 and 14 in 1963; these are occupations which, although

located in rural areas, are professional and products of the literate urban culture of industrial society (see chapter 7).

Other Correlates of Class and Status

Both class and status are related not only to income and wealth but also to other measures of life chances such as unemployment, longevity, disease, happiness, and psychiatric condition, to measures of social disorganization such as divorce and crime and delinquency, to political attitudes and behavior, to general values and leisure activities, and to fertility and child rearing style (cf. Henslin 1999, pp. 76–77 and pp. 264–267; Gortmaker and Wise, 1997, pp. 156–159 and pp. 165–166; Williams and Collins, 1995, pp. 359–363 and pp. 380–381).

Much comparative data about health and other life chances between black and white urban residents are actually data about urban stratification given that most African Americans live in central cities and, on the average, are of lower status than are whites (cf. Williams and Collins 1995, pp. 363–364); in addition, the gap between blacks and whites in family income continues to increase (Karoly, 1993, in Williams and Collins, 1995, p. 360). Moreover, although "white flight" had been a familiar characteristic of many cities in recent decades, middle-class black flight has also been increasing, thereby further concentrating black poverty in central cities (Wilson, 1987), including a rising percentage of black children living in poverty (Hernandez, 1993, in Williams and Collins, 1995, p. 360; see also chapter 13).

Central city residence is also related to changing health behaviors, such as increased use of alcohol and tobacco, which raise the risk of disease and death (Williams and Collins, 1995, p. 363). Significant measures of the social circumstances of inner cities are increased infant mortality and reduced life expectancy (Williams and Collins, 1995, pp. 360–361). Life expectancy is clearly a sensitive and valid measure of social pathology, and infant mortality is "a legitimate indicator of underlying social conditions," such as poverty and low-education attainment (Gortmaker and Wise, 1997, pp. 156–157).

A CONSERVATIVE APPROACH TO STRATIFICATION

From the conservative orientation, inequality is both inevitable and beneficial. This is because stratification is deemed inherent in social life and intimately tied to social organization. Inequality is seen as a source of stability to society. Its presence arrests excessive competition, conflict, and ambiguity as long as the inequality is not extreme, when it becomes potentially disruptive. Inequality is functional in that it gives structure to society, integration to the community, and assigns different places in society to diverse individual talents. Inequality is therefore good for society, the community, and the individual according to the conservative ideology.

That inequality is beneficial to society is an expression of the "functional theory of stratification" (Davis and Moore, 1945). In this theory, society is perceived to have various "needs, " one of which is to fill certain *positions* in the occupational structure and elsewhere with qualified people. Society therefore offers *rewards* to those occupying these positions, and the rewards become rights, privileges, and/or perquisites for position occupants. That is, rank is a reward.

It then follows, for Davis and Moore, that the *rank* that a position holds in society is determined by:

1. The functional importance of that position to society, that is, the degree to which no other position can satisfactorily perform its duties and that other positions are dependent upon it and

2. The scarcity of the ability to perform that position's duties and/or the difficulty of the training required for that position.

For example, although janitors and garbage collectors are functionally important, even vital, to society, neither the ability nor the training to perform these tasks is scarce; consequently, the rewards for fulfilling those positions are meager.[1] Similarly, the rewards are insubstantial for such occupations as juggler and acrobat, positions which, although calling for scarce abilities or talents and long, intensive training, are not functionally important to society.[2] (See chapters 6 and 7.)

A RADICAL APPROACH TO STRATIFICATION

Radicals consider inequality unnatural and inhuman, resulting from the power of the upper classes, and a potential for revolutionary change. Inequality is condemned as exploitation. That is, a small class expropriates human resources for its own benefit, thereby exploiting others with less power. Stratification is based on economic power, whether directly conveyed economically or through other cultural forms such as political or religious institutions.

Therefore, class is domination, much of it intended and planned because the upper class, the most class conscious of all the classes, is the most aware of its interests and has the most control of the resources that give power and authority over other classes. Karl Marx argued that inequality in all societies is based on exploitation, whether of slave by master, of serf by lord, of worker by owner, of wife by husband, or of child by parent.

---

[1]The "conservative" functional theory of stratification sounds liberal in that it stresses competition, inequality as an outcome of competition, and money as a reward. Another aspect of this theory is the narrowness of its conception of reward which ignores or downplays esteem or honor as rewards such as esteem and honor as well as intrinsic rewards of the occupations such as self-fulfillment.

[2]A liberal answer to the functional theory of stratification has been presented by Melvin Tumin (1953). His argument is that class differences are not the results of competition but, rather, of previous resources. Status or rank limits competition by limiting access to training, education, and/or useful contacts, that is, to opportunity. Medical schools "unnecessarily" limit admission to certain people as do the high-status universities, thereby excluding the poor and the lower middle class who are not part of the right social circles and networks. Thus, the ablest people are not necessarily selected to fill the higher ranked positions. It then follows that class determines competition as much as competition determines class. It also follows that inequality, at least extreme inequality, is neither functional nor inevitable.

URBAN AND RURAL STRATIFICATION: DIFFERING SETTINGS AND BASES

Urban Stratification

Urban stratification is largely extracommunity, that is, its reference is to the whole society rather than just the local community. The basis for urban stratification is in a complex, societal, division of labor more closely related to the political economy of the greater society, especially economic and political institutions, often also to other institutions such as recreational and medical. In the urban setting, because everyone cannot know everyone else, urban residents rely upon signs to indicate another's rank in the stratification system. However, some of these signs are ambiguous due to the large number and diversity of urban areas, the high incidence of social and spatial mobility, and the number of transients. Although one can readily distinguish between people who are at the extremes of stratification in terms of a single social item such as house type, dress, speech, or position in an organization, each of these markers is less categorically definitive for distinguishing between adjacent strata, such as office supervisor and bookkeeper.

Moreover, because individuals often are ranked in terms of two or more hierarchies such as class and status, this requires people to recognize the meaning of certain *symbols*, whether local or more universal. Given the large number and diversity of urban occupations, one needs to infer the class or status of others through occupational indicators such as dress, implements, or accessories; organizational, political, and familial relational or network ties; other material indicators such as neighborhood and house; and more personal characteristics such as speech or manner, some of these changing over short time periods. At the same time, urban areas are more likely to contain some who are "out of it," almost "untouchables," who are unfamiliar with, unaware of, or uncaring about the relevant symbols of class and status.

Urban stratification is more tied to *class* than it is to status. The signs for class membership are material, the more obvious because the more universal, such as money and possessions. The signs for status, such as prestige, honor, and taste, are more contextual, more likely to be relevant to a particular social setting or population. Hence, class is more visible than status in the greater anonymity of urban life although urban stratification also involves status reputation that may have originated beyond the local community.

Urban stratification is tied to *social change* because change is built into its materialism, antitradition, competition, spatial mobility, large number of occupations, and new occupations. One major source of change is in the economic and political sectors of society. For example, in world cities such as New York, London, and Tokyo, their decline as manufacturing centers and subsequent growth as financial centers left financial occupations in a stronger position and paying the highest average salaries in all three cities (Sassen, 1991, p. 244).

Other major sources of urban social change are organizational, political, and familial. There is a greater role for politics and ideology, as found in social movements, audiences, masses, and public opinion, that is, in the elementary collective behavior in and around the highly organized aspects of urban life. There are also the more or less rapidly changing fashions and tastes that give some groups status or power over others. Given the relative anonymity of urban life, acquisition of economic resources and symbols are more important, and make a difference sooner, than where status partly rests on communal values. Changes in urban status based on prestige and honor take longer to occur

Rural Stratification

If rural is defined by smaller size and density, less isolation, and more insulation, then other characteristics relevant to stratification become apparent. One is a greater role for communal values and norms there than in urban areas, a greater influence of the traditional and interpersonal, including knowledge of others and of their familial and other networks. As is urban stratification, rural stratification is also tied to the political economy, but other, traditional, bases assume more importance. There is a greater role for status in the sense of honor and the role of family and kinship is central. This is more likely in a small town of a few hundred to a few thousand people that is not at the outskirts of a large city. It is certainly more likely in peasant communities and especially in folk communities such as isolated hamlets.

Class and power—economic, political, and legal—tend to have both local and universal bases, particularly for rural areas that are part of urban-industrial societies. However, the more universal bases for stratification have been increasing as rural life has been becoming more directly connected to the greater society, earlier with rise of newspapers, then with the railroad and the telephone, later with the coming of radio and television, more recently with computers, fax machines, and the Internet. As Robert Park might put it, the change has been from "culture" to "civilization" (1950, chapter 2). Hence, in addition to local, and "localite" bases for stratification, the more a rural community is part of the urbanized greater society, external symbols matter such as occupational, type of house and furnishings, organizational, and style of dress, some of these originating internationally (see chapter 4).

The more a rural area approaches the peasant and even folk model, the more likely are the different dimensions of stratification to become intertwined and even indistinguishable from one another. In such circumstances, societal wealth and economic and political power become less differentiated from the more communal sociocultural dimension of status, honor, and prestige, even education and culture, and also from the more societal political dimension of power, the power based on economics, government, or the military but affected by organizational ties and, certainly, by family ties. Hence, class and status tend to be commingled in rural communities (as well as peasant and folk communities), reflecting both the limited division of labor and also communal institutions such as familial and religious. Rural communities, compared with urban ones, have more enduring bases for class and, particularly, for status because of time and tradition. Moreover, personal bases for stratification increase as community size decreases. Therefore, change in class and status is slower in rural areas than in urban areas but may be massive if and when it occurs.

Suburban Stratification

By the end of the twentieth century, about half of Americans had come to live in suburban communities, 48 percent by 1990. That the earlier suburban communities in the United States were essentially white middle class created considerable class and status differences between urban and suburban communities. The American middle class had begun moving outward from the city as far back as the early years of the nineteenth century in America, unlike European city-suburb relations where middle-class cities surrounded by working class suburbs was often the pattern (cf. Glaab and Brown, 1976). In the United States, improved transportation and communication facilitated the outward movement of many citizens, and many corporations relocated their factories and warehouses to peripheries of cities and to suburbs so as to reduce the incidence of strikes, picketing, sabotage, and other forms of management-labor conflict. After World War II, this inclined the suburbs to support Republican candidates for political office (see chapter 8).

Moreover, with the industrialization of suburbs, suburbs were becoming the center of the American community and increasingly reflecting the diversity of American society. Class diversity first, and racial diversity eventually, increased with the outward migration of more city dwellers to the near suburbs and, soon, to the far suburbs. However, this was not class integration and was racial integration even less. Spatial separation of suburban class and, especially, race increased as suburbs were beginning to approach the class and racial concentration and segregation of society generally. Moreover, suburb-to-suburb commutes were increasing for travel to work and for other purposes such as shopping and visiting friends and relatives. Many suburbanites were increasingly and willingly becoming uninvolved with, and even unaware of, central cities (Baldassare, 1992, pp. 475, 482; see also chapter 13).

In summation, suburbs have gone through what appears a natural life history. They had developed from remote towns outside of cities, then to small communities for a few affluent commuters, then to centers of growing middle-class areas after World War II. During the last few decades of the twentieth century, suburbs have grown and become more industrialized and diversified in terms of class and ethnicity, thereby beginning to resemble the central cities. Suburbanites have thus begun to experience some of central cities' social problems, such as congestion and crime. In addition, many have had less access to affordable single-family housing, some having to move farther out from their place of work, and there has been a general diminution of the quality of community life (cf. Schwartz, 1976; Baldassare 1981, 1986, 1992, pp. 486–488; Cervero, 1986; see also chapters 4 and 12).

URBAN AND SUBURBAN STRATIFICATION: THREE SPATIAL AND ECOLOGICAL MODELS

Spatially and ecologically, the social-class distribution of urban and suburban residents, as measured by objective indices, tends to follow one or more of three models: the concentric zone, the sector, or the multiple nuclei (see chapter 4, for a different interpretation of these models).

Concentric Zone Model

The best known of the three models is the concentric zone, propounded by Ernest Burgess (1925). It describes a process of "invasion and succession" in all directions from the central business district outward, the class level tending to rise as one moves toward the outer zones in the outer reaches of cities and into suburbia. This means that the outward movement of the middle class from central cities has continued beyond those cities, enhancing the populations of many suburbs. The initial movement was to suburbs near the city and then, eventually, to suburbs farther out, earlier by the middle class and later by ethnic and other working classes, including minorities. The concentric zone model appears applicable to some older cities such as Chicago, but less to cities such as New York or Los Angeles, each of which is actually a complex of several cities in one.

Sector Model

The sector model of Homer Hoyt (1939), based on a study of 142 cities, emphasized growth from the center outward along major transportation routes; it appears more applicable to the diverse class distribution of suburbs. This model resembles the concentric zone model in its outward movement from a central business district, but this movement occurs within sectors, each sector following its own major transportation route such as highways, railroad lines, or rivers. Each sector uses the land in its own way, the whole pattern resembling slices of a pie. Examples that fit the sector model are Philadelphia and the class distributions of the Boston suburbs and California's Silicon Valley (Glaab and Brown, 1976, p. 141; Garreau, 1991, p. 311; Hoyt, 1939, p. 113; Kweit and Grisez, 1990, p. 32).

Multiple Nuclei Model

The multiple nuclei model of Chauncy Harris and Edward Ullman (1945) departs from the emphasis upon the outward movement of population of the Burgess and Hoyt models; instead its focus is the development of cities and suburbs into separate nuclei or centers, each with its own specialized land use. The suburbs thus may differ in whether they, as centers, specialize in one or more of the following functions: financial, retail, manufacturing, administrative, bedroom communities, and/or areas for the young or aged. Hence, the multiple nuclei model may best fit the growing function, and class and status, specialization and differentiation between and within many suburbs and even cities.

SOCIAL STRATIFICATION
IN URBAN NEIGHBORHOODS

Working-Class Neighborhoods

Working-class urbanites, whose occupations are semiskilled and skilled, face limited opportunities and may live in some degree of poverty. Their neighborhoods are characterized by homogeneity, mutual aid, and relative isolation from the rest of the city. Solidarity, based on necessity and low-spatial mobility and resting not only in class membership and, perhaps, occupation, is often enhanced by family, leisure pursuits, religion, ethnicity, and friends who live nearby. They attend local churches, shops, and taverns and take part in an active street life. They are likely to be socially conservative and to court and marry within the neighborhood (Keller, 1968, pp. 50–54; Kleniewski, 1997, pp. 197–198).

The isolation of working-class urbanites from the rest of the city is based on dissimilarity from the outside. They are less likely to use or participate in urban functions and events outside of the neighborhood, such as theaters and museums, but may attend rock concerts and sporting events. Working-class neighborhoods may fit the following models: Toennies's *gemeinschaft*, Simmel's concentric affiliation, Cooley's caste relations (the "heredity" principle, biological and cultural), Gans's urban villagers, and Granovetter's strong ties (cf. Toennies, 1887; Simmel, 1955, pp. 146–150, Cooley, 1909, chapter 18; Gans, 1962; Granovetter, 1973; see also chapter 5).

However, working-class neighborhoods have been declining with the increasing deindustrialization of the economy and with the suburbanization of industry. Some of these neighborhoods are becoming home to the poor, and others are being gentrified. Some members of the working class are consequently being drawn to emerging, but less cohesive, "working-class suburbs" in which they appear to continue their urban attitudes and weak associational practices.

Middle-Class Neighborhoods

The middle class is, by definition, more affluent with professional, semiprofessional, and business occupations; consequently, their need for mutual aid is lessened Their focus is on work and (largely nuclear) family, with leisure in the background. They differ from the working class in their greater selectivity in interaction with neighborhood and city and suburban Others, both individuals and organizations, depending on compatible taste and style. The middle-class competitive style makes for individuation rather than solidarity although their organizational skills incline members of the middle class to cooperate on specific local concerns and projects such as schools, recreational facilities, condition of the streets, and political issues (Keller, 1968, pp. 51–54, 153; Gans, 1967; Kleniewski, 1997, p. 197).

Herbert Gans wrote that, although middle-class people tend to be "object-oriented," this does not last as they soon or eventually settle down and become more person-oriented in new social circles which "share their characteristics and interests" (Gans, 1962, p. 258). Middle-class neighborhoods appear to fit the following models: Toennies's *gesellschaft*, Simmel's multiple group affiliation, Cooley's class (also multiple group) relations ("competition" principle), and Granovetter's weak ties (cf. Toennies, 1887; Simmel, 1955, pp. 150–154; Cooley, 1909, chapter 21; Granovetter, 1973).

Upper-Class Enclaves

The upper class, typified by earned or inherited wealth, is far less numerous and does not live in heterogeneous neighborhoods but in more or less homogenous enclaves such as Beacon Hill and Back Bay in Boston (Abrahamson, 1996, 23, pp. 28–29), with physical and social barriers that separate and protect their mansions from the homes and even mansions of others. This class, concerned with preserving class codes and traditions (cf. Keller, 1968, p. 153), does this by its members living very near one another in "the 'right' addresses where 'everybody' lives" (Baltzell in Kleniewski, 1997, p. 195). Upper-class people send their children to select private schools in the neighborhood or in other parts of the country and maintain close contacts with one another in neighborhood churches and clubs and by means of an intense social life.

Their "neighborhood" transcends the local area in that upper-class connections are often national and international, including family members and influential occupational, social, and cultural networks. Granovetter's strong ties fit the familial relations of this class and its relations with close friends, which approach primary group ties, and Granovetter's weak ties fit their large number of diverse economic, cultural, and political ties which reach beyond local, state, and national boundaries (Granovetter, 1973; see also chapter 5).

Lower-Class Neighborhoods

Lower-class neighborhoods are low-income neighborhoods such as slums and ghettos defined by poverty, unskilled labor, and unemployment. Unlike working-class neighborhoods, and some ethnic ones, lower-class neighborhoods are characterized by social disorganization; little control over their territory; weakened family life, both nuclear and extended; and separate social worlds for women and men. The basis for poverty is partly structural, resting in conditions such as changing technologies and loss of jobs to suburbs, thus isolating lower-class neighborhoods from economic opportunities. Also, residents of lower-class neighborhoods tend to be poorly educated and have fewer informal or formal social relationships and fewer weak ties that might open them to economic opportunities

Rundown housing in a low-income neighborhood in South Brooklyn

A homeless child naps on abandoned mattresses in a vacant lot in a slum neighborhood

(Granovetter, 1973, 1983). They are what Joseph T. Howell called "hard living" blue-collar families. The lower-class neighborhood is the model or pure type of a pseudo-community, characterized by social isolation and even anomie (Flanagan, 1995, pp. 266–269; Howell in Phillips, 1996, pp. 282–283; Kleniewski, 1997, pp. 198–200). Chapter 6 provides alternative bases for classification and interpretation.

THE EROSION OF CLASS-BASED URBAN NEIGHBORHOODS

It is not only lower-class neighborhoods that are characterized by disorganization and anomie; working-class and middle-class neighborhoods have been losing their cohesive character. The rapid growth of jobs and the general economic upturn in the United States at the end of the twentieth century has accelerated population movements, thereby weakening neighborhood cohesiveness, not only for the middle classes but also for the ethnic working classes. Working- and middle-class families moving to suburbs in search of better housing, better education for their children, better civic services, and amenities such as parks and streams and less pollution have also encountered increased traffic congestion and the invasion of neighborhoods by industry and strip malls that are not locally owned (Gurwitt, [1991] 1995). Eventually this has led to further population movements, albeit for a temporary respite.

The continuing movement to ever-newer suburbs has been weakening the sense of neighborhood and community in that it takes time for these to develop. Heterogeneity may discourage participation and local organization (Kweit and Grisez, 1990, p. 201). This weakening is particularly noticeable in ethnic neighborhoods, reducing their distinc-

Renovated housing in a gentrifying neighborhood

tive character. Such ethnic concentration appears in great decline for the foreseeable future, at least until the next heavy influx of working-class, and even middle-class, immigrants (see chapter 5 on neighborhoods).

URBAN STRATIFICATION BY GENDER, AGE, RACE, AND ETHNICITY

Gender

Historically, cities have tended to be divided into men's *social spaces*, the *public sphere* of the political economy and major institutions, and women's *social spaces*, the *private sphere* of family and community. Although in recent decades, women have been entering the public spheres of occupations in such large numbers so as to constitute half of the labor force, occupational barriers remain. Women continue to be segregated from men largely in low-status, female-dominated occupations such as clerk and secretary, with low pay and restricted opportunities for upward mobility (Phillips, 1996, p. 288).

One reason for the occupational discrimination against women is that they have usually been the ones integrating the social space of home with that of work. Because of home responsibilities, many women have limited themselves to jobs that have been not far from home or to those that are home-based; other women have increasingly become self-employed. This partly explains the lower median household income of white female householders, about $22,500, contrasted with that of white male householders, about $32,000. These figures are about one-third less for black women and Latinas (U.S. Bureau of the Census, 1996, pp. 2–4).

Age

Urban spatial segregation by age may be seen by the following: The young are underrepresented in areas of the city close to the central downtown, an area of light industry, childless couples, and the aged (Zone 2 in the Burgess concentric zone model of urban growth) and overrepresented in other parts of the urban area such as working-class and middle-class suburban districts. In contrast, the aged are dispersed relative to wealth, underrepresented in middle-class districts in cities and suburbs, and overrepresented in areas of the city close to the central downtown (Zone 2) and, like women, in low-paid occupations, in retirement communities, and in developments not amenable to children such as those characterized by small apartments and few play areas. In contrast with more traditional societies, including urban areas before World War II where several generations often lived under the same roof or nearby, many young people do not have frequent or intimate contact with the aged.

Race

African Americans.   African Americans first came to the American colonies from Africa in the early seventeenth century as indentured servants, but soon many others were forcibly brought over to be enslaved, largely in the American South. The Emancipation Proclamation of 1863, the Thirteenth, Fourteenth, and Fifteenth Amendments to the U.S. Constitution, and the post–Civil War Reconstruction only nominally improved the condition of the former slaves, and their condition often worsened. Within a few decades of the end of the Civil War, southern whites, through both legal and violent means, depressed the position of the former slaves into that of a semislave status. In the twentieth century, particularly during the two world wars and after World War II, southern blacks were attracted to jobs in northern cities and tended to live in crowded, segregated ghettoes.

Today, despite wars and depressions, migration of many blacks from the southern states to northern and western cities, and the civil rights movement of the 1950s and 1960s, racial segregation continues in urban America with most African Americans still lodged in the inner portions of cities and in a few black suburbs. With many industries having moved to the suburbs and, given inadequate public transportation systems, many blacks find it difficult to hold jobs, particularly better paying jobs. "White flight" from central cities continues to occur both in response to blacks moving into white city and near-suburb neighborhoods and because of the decline of the urban economy and urban institutions such as education and city government. Moreover, the increasing incidence of "black flight," that is, the African American middle class, to the suburbs has added to the plight of poor urban blacks. Toward the end of the twentieth century, blacks had begun to migrate to the south, but to southern urban rather than rural areas, thus they are as likely to migrate from north to south as from south to north (Massey and Denton, 1993; Palen, 1987, p. 222; see chapter 13).

The last third of the twentieth century has frustrated African American hopes for greater affluence and acceptance in American society. Even though the black education level has risen significantly, structural changes in the American economy such as deindustrialization have impeded commensurate returns. Likewise, the increase in African American political power has brought meager economic returns. Even though blacks have become significant voting blocs in urban areas, their heavy concentration in certain districts has restricted their influence. Moreover, although more cities have come under African American political rule, these have often occurred in cities that have been declining economically, such as Gary; Newark; Washington, DC; and Detroit (Wilson, 1978, 1987, 1996; Palen, 1987, pp. 215–225; Spates and Macionis, 1987, pp. 326–330; Massey and Denton, 1993; Phillips, 1996, pp. 240–242; see chapter 13).

Native Americans.   The history of the European invasion and occupation of the New World is one of death and destruction of about 90 percent of the American natives, both from slaughter at the hands of the European invaders and from European diseases to which the native peoples had not acquired immunity; their numbers had fallen to about 250,000 in 1890. Since that time, Native Americans have been moving from reservations into urban areas, largely in the Western United States. The Native American population had risen to almost 2 million in 1990, and was almost evenly divided between reservation and city.

Today, the position of the 545 federally recognized tribes, such as the Navajo, Cherokee, Sioux (Lakota-Oyate), Apache, and Hopi, is that of a poorly educated minority with high rates of births, unemployment, poverty, alcoholism, and suicide. Back and forth movement between reservation and city has hindered Native American upward mobility and organizing ability in general American society, as have values toward consensus and cooperation rather than toward competition. Recent efforts to raise Native American economic, educational, and political position, such as casinos and other economic enterprises, a tribal-controlled college in South Dakota, and political organizing such as the National Indian Youth Council and the American Indian Movement as well as court decisions, have improved the situation of some tribes and may eventually improve the situation generally for Native Americans (Sorkin ,1978; Palen, 1987, pp. 237–240; Spates and Macionis, 1987, 337–338; Flanagan, 1995, pp. 127–129; Phillips, 1996, pp. 239–240).

Asian Americans.   Following over a century of prejudice, discrimination, violent opposition, and exclusion, particularly against Chinese and Japanese in the western states, today's Asian Americans have done better than the average American in income and education. They have been increasingly able to leave the urban Chinatowns, Little Tokyos, and Koreatowns, but this has left many others behind in poor paying jobs and in poverty. Suffering less racial prejudice than blacks and with a different history, Asian American families have found it easier to assimilate, to use their technological skills, to socialize their young toward success, and to cooperate with other Asian Americans of the same ethnic background (Spates and Macionis, 1987, pp. 335–337; Palen, 1987, pp. 240–244; Flanagan, 1995, pp. 124–127; Phillips, 1996, pp. 242–245.

Ethnicity

Ethnicity is less related to urban segregation than it has been. Among the exceptions are immigrant areas such as Mexican, Puerto Rican, Dominican, and other Latinos. (See chapter 13). Among other exceptions are working-class neighborhoods dominated by an ethnic group such as Italian, Polish, and French Canadian. Also included are middle-class ethnic neighborhoods such as Irish, Jewish, German, and Asian and upper-class WASP enclaves.

CONCLUSION

At any level of social organization more complex than the band, stratification appears inevitable and, usually, based on more than one variable such as economic, political, cultural, territorial, or ethnic. As an ideologically contentious area, social class and other forms of stratification lend themselves to controversy about their origin, basis, function, and what to do about them. There is also the question of *comparability*, not only because different methods of measuring stratification sometimes yield different conceptions and results, but also because there is the real question of whether stratification is the same across urban, suburban, rural, peasant, and folk communities and in different urban communities throughout the world.

Urban stratification, a relatively late arrival in human history, introduces a noncommunal element to stratification in that the bases for classifying others go beyond the local community, a societal fact because not everyone can know everyone else. Urban residents, therefore, have to rely on signs that often originate outside the local setting, some of these ambiguous, and evaluate others in a changing and less certain social context. These signs may refer to diverse bases for class and status such as occupational category and group membership, whether traditional, formal, or informal. Moreover, urban areas, both city and suburb, are changing more rapidly than rural areas or peasant communities have been. Urban neighborhoods of whatever social class background have a life history that resembles, on a local and more circumscribed level, the business cycle and perhaps even the rise and fall of empires.

Urban society, the idea of community, and urban stratification as well appear to be changing rapidly with radical changes in communication and travel and their methods and technologies. Urban stratification is becoming globalized, going beyond the influence of industrial centers such as those of New York, London, and Tokyo (Sassen, 1991, chapter 1), the scope of the analysis needing to be greatly broadened. However, the basic principles of urban stratification, local and global, appear to remain. The population of the world, having reached an estimated 6 billion by the year 2000, is rushing toward 10 billion some time during the twenty-first century. Moreover, the world's largest cities and metropolitan areas are to be found more in Asia than in Europe and the Americas. Urban stratification has become world stratification, not only within urban areas but between them. However, students of social stratification, and of urban stratification, while studying inequality that is global, will probably still have to apply some of the familiar variables used by social scientists to study stratification. Among these variables are class and status, face-to-face relations and community, and indirect relations and societal and cross-societal relations. These will probably remain central to the analysis and understanding of stratification, urban and rural, local and global.

SELECTED BIBLIOGRAPHY

ABRAHAMSON, MARK. *Urban Enclaves: Identity and Place in America.* New York: St. Martin's Press, 1996.

BALDASSARE, MARK. *The Growth Dilemma: Residents' Views and Local Population Change in the United States.* Berkeley: University of California Press, 1981.

———. *Trouble in Paradise: The Suburban Transformation in America.* New York: Columbia University Press, 1986.

———. "Suburban Communities." *Annual Review of Sociology.* 18 (1992): 475–494.

BALTZELL, E. DIGBY. *Philadelphia Gentlemen: The Making of a National Upper Class.* New York: Free Press, 1958.

BENDIX, REINHARD, and SEYMOUR LIPSET, eds. *Class, Status, and Power,* 2d ed. New York: Free Press of Glencoe, 1966.

BURGESS, ERNEST W. "The Growth of the City: An Introduction to a Research Project." In *The City,* Robert E. Park, Ernest W. Burgess, and Roderick D. McKenzie (eds.). Chicago: University of Chicago Press, 1925.

CERVERO, ROBERT. *Suburban Gridlock.* New Brunswick, NJ: Urban Policy Research, 1986.

COOLEY, CHARLES. *Social Organization.* New York: Charles Scribner's Sons, 1909.

CUBER, JOHN F., and WILLIAM F. KENKEL. *Social Stratification in the United States.* New York: Appleton-Century-Crofts, 1954.

DAVIS, KINGSLEY, and WILBERT E. MOORE. "Some Principles of Stratification." *The American Sociological Review.* 10 (1945): 242–249.

FLANAGAN, WILLIAM G. *Urban Sociology: Images and Structure,* 2d ed. Boston: Allyn and Bacon, 1995.

GANS, HERBERT J. *The Urban Villagers.* New York: Free Press, 1962.

———. *The Levittowners.* New York: Vintage Books, 1967.

GARREAU, JOEL. *Edge City.* New York: Doubleday, 1991.

GLAAB, CHARLES N., and A. THEODORE BROWN. *A History of Urban America,* 2d ed. New York: Macmillan, 1976.

GORTMAKER, STEVEN L., and PAUL H. WISE. "The First Injustice: Socioeconomic Disparities, Health Services Technology, and Infant Mortality." *Annual Review of Sociology.* 23 (1997): 147–170.

GRANOVETTER, MARK. "The Strength of Weak Ties." *American Journal of Sociology.* 78 (1973): 1360–1380.

———."The Strength of Weak Ties: A Network Theory Revisited." In *Sociological Theory—1983,* Randall Collins (ed.), pp. 201–233. San Francisco: Jossey-Bass, 1983.

———. "A brief outlining of Network theory principles," p. ii in *Social Structures: A Network Approach,* Barry Wellman, and S. D. Berkowitz (eds.). Cambridge: Cambridge University Press, 1988.

GURWITT, ROB. "The Rule of the Absentocracy." In *Urban Society,* 7th ed., Fred Siegel (ed.), pp. 69–73. Guilford, CT: Sluice Dock, [1991] 1995.

HARRIS, CHAUNCY, and EDWARD ULLMAN. "The Nature of Cities." *Annals of the American Academy of Political and Social Science.* 242 (1945): 7–17.

HENSLIN, JAMES M. *Sociology,* 4th ed. Boston: Allyn and Bacon, 1999.

HOYT, HOMER. "The Structure and Growth of Residential Neighborhoods in American Cities." Washington, DC: U.S. Federal Housing Administration, U.S. Printing Office, 1939.

KELLER, SUZANNE. *The Urban Neighborhood: A Sociological Perspective.* New York: Random House, 1968.

KLENIEWSKI, NANCY. *Cities, Change, and Conflict: A Political Economy of Urban Life.* Belmont, CA: Wadsworth, 1997.

KRUGMAN, PAUL. *Development; Geography and Economic Theory.* Cambridge: MIT Press, 1995.

KWEIT, ROBERT W., and MARY GRISEZ. *People and Politics in Urban America.* Pacific Grove, CA: Brooks/Cole, 1990.

MASSEY, DOUGLAS S., and NANCY DENTON. *American Apartheid: Segregation and the Making of an Underclass.* Cambridge, MA: Harvard University Press, 1993.

PALEN, J. JOHN. *The Urban World,* 3d ed. New York: McGraw-Hill, 1987.

PARK, ROBERT E. *Race and Culture.* Everett C. Hughes et al. (eds.). Glencoe, IL: Free Press. 1950.

PHILLIPS, E. BARBARA. *City Lights: Urban-Suburban Life in the Global Society,* 2d ed. New York: Oxford, 1996..

SASSEN, SASKIA. *The Global City: New York, London, Tokyo.* Princeton, NJ: Princeton University Press, 1991.

SCHWARTZ, BARRY, ed. *The Changing Face of the Suburbs.* Chicago: University of Chicago Press, 1976.

SIMMEL, GEORG. *Conflict & the Web of Group-Affiliations,* Kurt H. Wolff and Reinhard Bendix (trans.). New York: Free Press of Glencoe, 1955.

SORKIN, ALAN L. *The Urban American Indian.* Lexington, MA: Lexington, 1978.

SPATES, JAMES L., and JOHN J. MACIONIS. *The Sociology of Cities.* Belmont, CA: Wadsworth, 1987.

TOENNIES, FERDINAND. *Community and Society* (Gemeinschaft und Gesellschaft), [1887], Charles P Loomis (trans. & ed.). East Lansing, MI: Michigan State University Press, 1957.

TUMIN, MELVIN M., Some "Principles of Stratification: a critical analysis" *American Sociological Review* 18: 387–93, 1953.

U.S. Bureau of the Census. *Income, Poverty, and Valuation of Noncash Benefits: 1994.* Current Population Reports, Series P-60, no. 189, April 1996.

———. *Share of Aggregate Income Received by Each Fifth and Top 5 Percent of Families: 1970 to 1996.* In *Statistical Abstract of the United States 1998*, Table 747, p. 473. Current Population Reports, P60-197, March 3, 1998.

WARNER, W. LLOYD, MARCHIA MEEKER, and KENNETH EELLS. *Social Class in America.* Chicago: Science Research Associates, 1949.

WILLIAMS, DAVID R., and CHIQUITA COLLINS. "U.S. Socioeconomic and Racial Differences in Health: Patterns and Explanations." *Annual Review of Sociology.* 21 (1995): 349–386.

WILSON, WILLIAM JULIUS. *The Declining Significance of Race: Blacks and Changing American Institutions.* Chicago: University of Chicago Press, 1978.

———. *The Truly Disadvantaged: The Inner City, The Underclass, and Public Policy.* Chicago: University of Chicago Press, 1987.

———. *When Work Disappears: The World of the New Urban Poor.* New York: Knopf, 1996.

12

URBAN CRIME

by Kevin Early

Any discussion of urban crime as a social problem must begin with an agreed-upon definition of the nature of the problem, for the idea of crime may mean different things to different people. For some, crime is defined in terms of its consequences, for example, loss of life or property or physical injury. Others confine crime to a legalistic definition, that is, crime is an "act or omission prohibited by law, by one who is held accountable by that law" (Champion, 1998, p. 33). Strictly speaking, any act that violates the law of the political jurisdiction in which it takes place and that is punishable by the political jurisdiction in a legally prescribed manner is a crime, no matter how innocent, innocuous, or abhorrent that act may appear to interested parties. Such an act is a crime whether an arrest or conviction has been made, or whether the act has been observed by legally reliable witnesses or reported to the police. This definition is objectively the most useable because it gives us the best basis for estimates of the actual amount of crime committed, independent of the subjective impressions of how extensive different people with different standards think crime is. Public perceptions of crime as a social problem may vary drastically from its actual incidence.

THE EXTENT OF CRIME IN AMERICA

When criminologists measure the incidence of crime in the United States, they rely upon data contained in the index to serious crimes. Developed in 1929, this index, referred to as the Uniform Crime Reports (UCR), is the most comprehensive source of official statistics on crime and apprehended offenders in the nation. The Federal Bureau of Investigation (FBI) distinguishes between two categories of offenses: Part I offenses and Part II offenses. Part I offenses, also known as index offenses, are crimes designated by the FBI as "most serious." Part I offenses consist of violent crimes (murder and nonnegligent manslaughter, robbery, aggravated assault, and forcible rape) and property crimes (burglary, larceny-theft, motor vehicle theft, and arson). Part II offenses are crimes designated by the FBI as "less serious." Part II offenses include simple assault, disorderly conduct, vagrancy, loitering violations, public drunkenness, gambling, prostitution, drug abuse violations, and several other offenses about which some but not all information is recorded. The UCR is a voluntary reporting system in which the FBI collects monthly data on crimes from more than 17,000 law enforcement agencies in the United States. The crime statistics are then compiled and published annually by the FBI in *Crime in the United States*. It should be noted that the UCR concentrates on measuring a limited number of well-defined crimes committed in the United States. Because the FBI makes a distinction between "more serious" and "less serious" crimes, several offenses (e.g., drug crimes, kidnapping, white-collar crimes, etc.) perceived as "serious" by the public are not included in the UCR. This, no doubt, is a major flaw in the way crime statistics are computed.

The UCR has several deficiencies in the way it defines and counts crime. Further, the process of gathering crime statistics does not give an accurate measure of the amount of crime actually committed. First, most crime is never reported to the police and therefore never appears in the official crime statistics. Citizens do not report all the crimes about which they have knowledge. Second, some crimes reported to the police are not officially recorded and included in crime statistics. Crimes do not become a part of the UCR crime statistics unless a citizen reports it to the police, and the police record it in the figures they send along to the FBI (Livingston, 1992, p. 61). Third, the conditions under which local police departments receive information about crime and officially report it may vary drastically. Fourth, in terms of detailed information, the FBI UCR focuses exclusively on Part I or "more serious" crimes. The offenses classified by the FBI as important are only a tiny segment of the total range of crimes. The UCR routinely omits information on crimes that are not in the index list or in the Part II list of crimes (e.g., white-collar and corporate crimes). Despite its shortcomings, the UCR has been an invaluable source of crime statistics since its inception. It describes trends and patterns in crime over time, records clearance rates, includes information about the proportion of crimes that are solved by the police, and contains information about arrestees.

Recorded crime rates certainly have increased dramatically since the 1960s, although in recent years the volume has begun to show a slight downward trend. But police efficiency and the methods of detection have also improved over the same period, as have techniques for reporting and recording crime, in response to official demands. Therefore, reported increases in crime may be due to these factors rather than to an actual increase in crime. Mass media reporting of crime has intensified, and this too may have a bearing on the public's greater willingness to report crime to the police. Arrest statistics indicate teenagers and young adults are more crime-prone, including serious predatory crimes, than other segments of the population. Juvenile arrests rates for violent crimes in 1998, although lower than those for adults, showed higher arrest rates involving burglary, larceny-theft, and motor vehicle theft than those for adults (UCR, 1998). Roughly 70 percent of all those arrested for index property offenses are under the age of twenty-five. If this is actually true, then the recent upsurge in the proportion of young people in the population would seem to support the notion that crime will increase across the teenage years, the years of high risk for index property offenses. But even more recent reductions in the birthrate would, by the same reasoning, suggest that crime should begin to level off and drop more sharply in the new century.

Criminologists are divided over whether crime actually is increasing. Some suspect that, even though recorded rates have been increasing, actual crime is not on the rise. According to them, American society has always been crime ridden and has always had a high degree of tolerance for lawlessness (Bell, 1960, p. 137). Thus, there is no reason to suspect that crime is any more widespread now than it has always been. Others, however, believe that there actually has been a substantial increase in the commission of crime and will point to what are to them logical reasons why this is so. There is as yet no consensus among social scientists on this question.

CRIME ON THE STREETS

Another difficulty in assessing crime as a social problem is that there are many different types of crime, each with different causes and consequences, and each of which differs in the degree to which the public perceives it to be serious enough to warrant drastic efforts at solution. For the most part, it is the so-called "street" crimes such as homicide, aggravated and simple assault, rape and sexual assault, and armed robbery that the public is most likely to identify as the crime problem. These kinds of crimes create sensational news coverage and are highly dramatized on television and radio broadcasts. Such reporting makes the amount of street crime seem vastly exaggerated to those who rely exclusively on the mass media for their information, no matter how extensive street crimes are in reality. As such, public concern with crime vacillates with media reporting. The greater the news coverage, the larger the proportion of citizens believing violent crime is the country's foremost problem.

Police officers questioning a suspect on a city sidewalk

The UCR estimates the rate of crime in a state-by-state crime analysis which includes the total volume of crime in a specific jurisdiction, over a particular period of time, controlling for the population of that jurisdiction. The crime rates are standardized to a base of every one hundred thousand inhabitants. As stated earlier, the UCR focuses primarily on the eight offenses designated by the FBI as index crimes. The most serious felonies are crimes against persons. Most major felonies, however, are crimes involving property, including burglary, larceny, motor vehicle theft, and arson. Index crimes are believed to be an indicator of the nation's crime experience because of their seriousness and frequency of occurrence.

Since the early 1960s, the overall volume of index crimes has increased, although in recent years the volume has been leveling off or even declining. Crime rates fluctuated between the mid-1970s and the 1990s; increasing 64 percent in the 1970s and 23 percent in the 1980s and remaining flat or downward in the 1990s (Crutchfield, 2000, p. 27). In 1997 there were an estimated 13.2 million Part I offenses reported, including 18,209 homicides, 96,120 forcible rapes, 497,950 robberies, 1,022,490 serious assaults, 2,461,100 burglaries, 7,725,500 larcenies, and 1,353,700 motor vehicle thefts (Inciardi, 2000, p. 63). Of the four violent index crimes, aggravated assault is the most common serious violent crime in the nation: 382 per 100,000 (UCR, 1998). Aggravated assault is the most frequently reported violent crime in the nation and has the largest percentage of arrests for all violent crimes (Table 12.1). Robbery, including assault to commit robbery as well as attempted robbery, comprised 24 percent of serious violent crimes in 1999, that is, 186.1 per 100,000 (UCR, 1998). Roughly three-fourths of those arrested for robbery live in urban centers, and approximately one-fourth of the arrests were made in suburban communities.

Assaults, robberies, burglaries, carjackings, and homicides are common enough to concern all urban and suburban residents. That most crimes occur in heavily populated metropolitan areas forms the basis of fear from both urban residents and those living in surrounding communities (Table 12.2). Those living in suburban areas often have an exaggerated sense of fear of urban centers and "feel safe in smaller metropolitan areas that may be more dangerous than some big cities" (Russell, 1995, pp. 22–31).

Table 12.1   Total Estimated Arrests for the United States, 1997

CRIME	NUMBER OF ARRESTS
Murder and nonnegligent manslaughter	12,226
Forcible rape	20,654
Robbery	90,146
Aggravated assault	349,818
Burglary	230,960
Larceny-theft	970,552
Arson	111,288
Violent crime	472,844
Property crime	1,325,793
Crime Index Total	1,798,637

Source: Crime in the United States, 1997, Federal Bureau of Investigation, 1998.

Table 12.2   Murder Rate of 50 Metropolitan Areas

RANK	METROPOLITAN AREA	RATE	RANK	METROPOLITAN AREA	RATE
1	New Orleans, LA	37.7	26	Monroe, LA	15.8
2	Shreveport-Bossier City, LA	25.8	27	Rocky Mount, NC	15.8
3	Jackson, MS	25.2	28	Washington, DC-MD-VA-WV	15.8
4	Jackson, TN	23.3	29	Galveston-Texas City, TX	15.5
5	New York, NY	23.2	30	Danville, VA	15.3
6	Memphis, TN	21.9	31	Jacksonville, FL	15.1
7	Fayetteville, NC	21.7	32	Vineland-Millville-Bridgeton, NJ	15.0
8	Los Angeles-Long Beach, CA	21.3	33	Montgomery, AL	14.9
9	Gary-Hammond, IN	20.2	34	Dallas, TX	14.6
10	Little Rock-North Little Rock, AR	20.1	35	Riverside-San Bernadino, CA	14.6
11	Alexandria, LA	19.8	36	Savannah, GA	14.6
12	Pine Bluff, AR	19.7	37	Anniston, AL	14.4
13	Birmingham, AL	19.3	38	Oakland, CA	14.4
14	Baton Rouge, LA	19.1	39	Florence, SC	14.2
15	Albany, GA	18.7	40	Laredo, TX	13.9
16	San Antonio, TX	18.6	41	Columbus, GA-AL	13.7
17	Miami, FL	18.1	42	Las Vegas, NV	13.1
18	Richmond-Petersburg, VA	17.4	43	Mobile, AL	13.0
19	Baltimore, MD	17.2	44	Gadsden, AL	12.9
20	Texarkana, TX-AR	17.1	45	Augusta-Aiken, GA–SC	12.8
21	Fresno, CA	16.9	46	Stockton-Lodi, CA	12.8
22	Charlotte, NC	16.6	47	Bakersfield, CA	12.5
23	Waco, TX	16.4	48	Flint, MI	12.4
24	Houston, TX	15.9	49	Atlanta, GA	12.2
25	Detroit, MI	15.8	50	Norfolk-Virginia Beach, VA	12.1

Source: Crime in the United States, 1993, Federal Bureau of Investigation, 1994.

Horton and Leslie (1974) aptly suggest that violent, dramatic street crime should not really be considered as the main crime problem. Instead, they conclude that the less dramatic and less publicized types of crime may be more costly and disruptive to the general public overall than the more widely feared violent street crimes:

> For every woman killed by a "sex fiend," several are slaughtered by their husbands; but the sex crimes attract more interest and arouse far greater anxiety. For every person murdered in calculated detective story fashion, dozens are killed by drunken and reckless drivers (negligent homicide, if it can be proved). For every dollar taken in armed robbery, hundreds or thousands are taken by gamblers, racketeers, and white-collar criminals. The corruption of police and government officials by organized and white-collar crime wreaks an injury to public life and public morals beside which the depredations of pickpockets, shoplifters and bank robbers are of minor importance. Yet these crimes rate the headlines. It would be only slightly exaggerated to say that the genuine social destructiveness and financial cost of a form of crime varies inversely with the publicity it receives and the public concern it arouses. (Horton and Leslie, 1974, p. 139)

Whatever the arguments of objective social scientists or statistics to the contrary, across the nation people are being held hostage by the fear of crime. In many urban centers, the fear of crime has discouraged people from using public transportation, streets, and accommodations. Fear is not confined to those living in the unstable, disadvantaged, lower-class neighborhoods of our inner-cities racked by street crime and urban violence. It transcends locale and socioeconomic status, extending to those living in affluent, suburban, middle-class neighborhoods, privately guarded residential areas, and rural communities. Despite the data that show that crime and violence have been declining in the last decade, there continues to be widespread fear on the part of the public that crime is one of the number one problems in the nation. Between 1993 and 1994, "the percentage of Americans ranking crime/violence as the nation's foremost problem jumped from 9% to 49%" (Chiricos, Hogan, and Gertz, 1997, pp. 107–129). This belief was confirmed in a 1993 Gallup Poll which reported that 50 percent of households own firearms and 18 percent have burglar alarms. A 1994 *Los Angeles Times* poll reported that 65 percent of Americans attributed their fear of crime to what they read or saw in the media. Twenty-one percent said the fear was based upon a victimization experience. Whatever the case, the FBI reports that crime rates are lower in 2000 than they were in the 1980s. A significant decrease in violent crime "has occurred in the country's largest cities, such as New York and Los Angeles (Table 12.3), but to the surprise of many observers, violent crime increased dramatically in many mid-size cities, such as Louisville, Nashville, and Cincinnati, where the number of murders increased by more than 50 percent" (Inciardi, 2000, p. 57). The public's persistent fear of crime is a result of the changing pattern of crime—in particular, the growth in juvenile violence, the increasing involvement of guns in crimes, increases in urban and suburban violence, and the belief that crime is connected to the illicit drug industry. The public has also been influenced by some crime experts who argue that crime is beginning to move into the suburbs and may be increasing there at a more rapid rate than in the inner cities. In fact, the same survey indicated that residents of small cities and rural areas were far more likely to report increased crime in their communities than were those living in the largest of medium-size cities.

Table 12.3   Percent Increase/Decrease for Select Cities, 1990–1997

METROPOLITAN AREA	MURDER RATE
Boston, Massachusetts	−70%
New York, New York	−66%
Los Angeles, California	−41%
Washington, DC	−36%
Atlanta, Georgia	−35%
Miami, Florida	−20%
Indianapolis, Indiana	+60%
Albuquerque, New Mexico	+44%
Durham, North Carolina	+43%
Jackson, Mississippi	+39%
Portland, Oregon	+39%
Phoenix, Arizona	+37%

Source: Crime in the United States, 1997, Federal Bureau of Investigation, 1998.

WHITE-COLLAR CRIME

White-collar crime was originally thought of as crime committed by business and professional persons, government, and other varieties of workers who in the course of their occupation violate the basic trust placed in them or act in unethical ways (Sutherland, 1949; Inciardi, 1997, p. 41). In current usage, the concept has been loosely broadened to include nearly all nonviolent crimes of personal enrichment committed by "respectable" persons having community standing and status. Thus, middle- or upper-class individuals or people in business who engage in income tax violations, bribery of public officials, embezzlement and various types of fraud, stock manipulation, price fixing, and misrepresentation in advertising would be committing white-collar crimes (as would also the public officials receiving the bribes).

The public does not become as aroused by these types of crimes because they probably do not see them as direct and immediate threats to their safety or security. Such acts nevertheless are criminal if they violate the criminal law. Although some authorities believe that such white-collar crimes as consumer fraud or antitrust violations are not as serious as street crimes, others believe that the extent and annual costs of white-collar crime is far greater than that from conventional crime of those crimes generally perceived of as "street crimes" (i.e., murder, rape, robbery, vehicular theft, battery, and larceny). Financial losses from white-collar crimes are in the billions of dollars each year. The Department of Justice has estimated the cost of white-collar and corporate crime to be close to $200 billion annually (Bureau of Justice Statistics, 1994).

Concern about crime is often popularly expressed in terms of "we," the good, respectable, law-abiding majority, versus "they," the bad,, disrespectable, law-violating minority. This view tends to see crime as caused by a small, antisocial, criminal "class." Those who hold this view often respond with disbelief when they discover that even corporations, prominent business leaders, or top government officials and law-enforcement personnel are themselves not above occasionally committing crimes, usually of the white-collar variety, when it suits their purposes. For example, John Mitchell, the attorney general of the United States from 1968 to 1972, was later convicted of a felony and sent to prison for criminal acts associated with the Watergate affair. More fortunate was former Vice President Spiro T. Agnew, who escaped indictment on fifty criminal charges, including accepting bribes while vice president, by pleading no contest to one minor charge of tax evasion. Former President Nixon, of course, escaped possible criminal indictment and conviction for Watergate-related offenses by resigning the presidency and by being pardoned by his successor. Yet all of these men were among the strongest advocates of strict law enforcement and had publicly criticized those who were "soft" on law violators or who favored "coddling" the "criminal class." This obvious double standard is not uncommon in the United States and is one of the reasons that it is so difficult to deal with crime as a social problem. Those who demand the suspension of traditional Bill of Rights protections afforded the so-called criminal class nevertheless are quick to demand these same rights for themselves when they are similarly suspected of violations of the criminal law.

At the other end of the spectrum, there have been a number of crimes against consumers involving manufactures and the sale of unsafe products. For example, in the 1970s

Ford Motor Company manufactured what was then most popular car of the decade: the Pinto. The Pinto was introduced to meet the demands of a growing economy and an international energy crisis. In short, the Pinto was relatively inexpensive and fuel efficient. However, a design flaw in the position of the fuel tank caused the vehicle to explode during low-impact rear-end collisions. Ford engineers estimated the cost to redesign the fuel tank at $11 per unit. This plan was rejected by Ford management who balanced the cost of a national recall with the amount Ford would have to pay out in civil lawsuits. As a result, several Pinto owners and passengers were seriously burned and killed in collisions. "Seven years after Ford started putting the unsafe cars on the market" the Pinto was recalled for fuel-tank modification (Mokhiber, 1988, pp. 373–382). In 1984 a class action suit was filed against A. H. Robbins Company, maker of the Dalkon Shield. The Dalkon Shield, an intrauterine contraceptive device (IUD) was used in the United States and Third World countries. Despite warnings from A. H. Robbins research and development laboratories that the IUD had dangerous, even fatal, side effects, Robbins kept the device on the market while concealing its harm from the millions of women around the world using it. Amidst pressure from the FDA and lawsuits from women around the country, the device was recalled.

The collapse of the savings and loan industry may be the costliest set of white-collar crimes in history (Pontell and Calavita, 1993, p. 380). Experts argue that the "financial losses incurred in the savings and loan crisis are in part the result of deliberate and widespread criminal activity" (Pontell and Calavita, 1993, p. 388).

At the lower level, a number of major cities have experienced the exposure of corruption within local police departments. In Los Angeles, Miami, and New York, "the number of police officers charged with selling drugs or involved with drug-related graft and extortion markedly increased during the 1980s and 1990s" (Inciardi, 1997, p. 108). Fourteen New York City police officers were recently indicted for extracting protection money from Harlem drug dealers. The officers were "assaulting dealers who failed to provide protection fees and [stole] hundreds of thousands of dollars in cash from the apartments and cars of other dealers" (Inciardi, 1997, p. 108). A recent indictment of an FBI agent for "accepting almost $1 million in bribes and skimming 42 kilos from a load of cocaine he helped seize" (Inciardi, 1997, p. 108) suggests that some officials of national law-enforcement and investigative agencies have been implicated in violations of the criminal law in the conduct of their official duties.

ORGANIZED CRIME

Organized crime is conducted by large, organized groups of criminals who operate in more or less clearly defined territories and maintain constant connections with law enforcement officials, without whose connivance such criminal organizations probably could not sustain themselves. Organized crime is distinguished from other types of crime by its hierarchical organizational structure, its dependence on the threat of force and violence to maintain a monopoly over its area of criminal activity, and its immunity from the law through the corruption of law enforcement officials. The activities of organized crime involve traditionally illicit services, such as gambling, trafficking in narcotics and other drugs, loan-sharking, prostitution, racketeering, commercialized vice, bootlegging, and disposing of stolen merchandise. "These activities are very lucrative because certain segments of the population are willing to pay high prices for illegal goods and services" (Meier, 1989, p. 212). More and more, organized crime is beginning to infiltrate legitimate businesses by reinvesting its illegal earnings into enterprises that it then attempts to manage or control. Hotels and motels, night clubs, restaurants, liquor and cigarette distributors, vending machine distributors, real estate syndicates, and linen supply services are businesses that have been infiltrated by organized crime in many large cities. Some labor unions and banks or loan agencies also are controlled by organized crime interests, which now attempt to profit from the less risky and violent areas of white-collar crime. Organized crime is big business and is estimated to cost the national economy about $100 billion or about 1.1 percent of the gross national product (Pace, 1991, p. 14).

The success of organized crime seems to rest on supplying illegal goods and services to supposedly honest, ordinary people who want and will gladly pay for them. Many people, for example, are eager to buy such stolen merchandise as autos, jewelry, bicycles, or television sets at bargain prices as long as they can expect to get away without being caught. Likewise, those who wish to gamble or use alcohol and drugs under illegal conditions are not deterred, especially if wholesale evasions of existing laws are widely condoned or tolerated by the general public, as well as by law enforcement officials.

The people who use the services of organized crime may themselves be engaging in what Horton and Leslie (1974, p. 142) refer to as institutionalized crime. This refers to criminal acts that are repeated so often that they become a part of the normal behavior of a group, yet are so perfectly rationalized that they are not defined as crime by those committing them. The compliance of otherwise honest law enforcement officials may also fall in this category, especially when they do not wish to be criticized for "harassing" the public by disrupting what they know to be widely accepted patterns of community behavior, no matter how criminal these may be according to the law.

CAREER CRIMINALS

Career criminals make a significant portion of their income from the commission of crime. Sutherland (1949) defined career criminals as individuals who do not use force or physical violence in their crimes and live solely by their wits and skills. Contemporary criminologists define career criminals as individuals who identify with a criminal subculture, who make the bulk of their living from crime, and who have highly developed skills that enable them to commit crimes with success. Career theft usually refers to nonviolent forms of criminal behavior that are undertaken with a high degree of finesse, for monetary gain, and minimal possibility of apprehension, such as safecracking, bank robbery, jewel theft, pickpocketing, burglary, shoplifting, forgery, extortion, and counterfeiting. Career criminals are sometimes referred to as "professionals," but perhaps the only work traits they share with well-established, legitimate professions such as medicine or law is that they are highly skilled and take great pride in their competence or craftsmanship. They tend to be contemptuous of amateur criminals, and they take pride in maintaining their reputation as professionals among others of their own "calling." Career criminals rarely get caught, for to do so brings humiliation because it implies incompetence. But if caught, the career criminal will use expert lawyers and a wide variety of legal devices designed to lessen the possibility of imprisonment. Incarceration rarely reforms career criminals because of their lifelong commitment to an illegitimate career. Imprisonment, if it does occur, is regarded as merely a temporary nuisance, inconvenience, or embarrassment. Although the professional career criminal frequently is portrayed in the mass media as a sympathetic and sometimes heroic figure, a very small fraction of all crimes committed involve professional career criminals.

URBANIZATION AND CRIME

Having briefly discussed several categories of crime that many experts contend are overall more damaging and costly than the types of street crimes routinely measured by the FBI Uniform Crime Reports, we must now come back to street crime because it is still the type of crime most closely linked in the public mind to city life and urbanization. So far we have not yet dealt with the question of the spatial distribution of street crime and the degree to which it is more characteristic of big cities or small towns and rural areas. Unfortunately, there is no clear-cut answer to this question because of the inadequacies of recorded crime statistics discussed previously.

The recorded data do clearly indicate that rates of violent crime known to the police are higher in urban areas and suburban areas than in rural areas. Urban residents showed higher victimization rates than suburban residents, who, in turn, had rates higher than rural residents. There was, however, relatively little difference in the rape/sexual assault and aggravated assault victimization rates of suburban and rural residents (Table 12.4). The 1997 FBI UCR indicated that the rates of serious crime were 29.2 per thousand population in rural areas, 36.3 per thousand in the suburbs, and 51.2 per thousand in urban areas. As with violent crimes, property crimes known to the police are higher in urban and suburban areas than in rural areas (Table 12.5).

Table 12.4   Rates of Violent Crime by Residence of Victims, 1997

					VICTIMIZATION PER 1,000 PERSONS 12 OR OLDER VIOLENT CRIMES			
						Assault		
Residence	Population	All	Rape/ Sexual Assault	Robbery	Total	Aggra- vated	Simple	Personal Theft
Urban	64,609,030	51.2	2.0	7.4	41.8	12.4	29.4	2.8
Suburban	108,671,050	36.3	1.2	3.4	31.7	6.9	24.8	1.3
Rural	46,559,030	29.2	1.1	2.1	26.0	7.3	18.8	0.7

Source: Crime in the United States, 1997, Federal Bureau of Investigation, 1998.

Table 12.5   Rates of Property Crime by Residence of Victims, 1997

Residence	Number of Households 1997	VICTIMIZATION PER 1,000 HOUSEHOLDS			
		Total	Burglary	Motor Vehicle Theft	Theft
Urban	31,912,480	309.9	56.5	20.1	233.3
Suburban	50,284,550	235.4	38.9	12.7	183.8
Rural	21,791,640	187.7	40.1	7.1	140.5

Source: Crime in the United States, 1997, Federal Bureau of Investigation, 1998.

Although street crime still is higher in cities than in suburban or rural areas, data from the 1997 UCR indicated that the homicide rate has been on a steady decline for the last five years and that it was decreasing more rapidly in cities than in other areas (Table 12.6). The Department of Justice attributed these improvements to better law enforcement.

Most experts conclude that the available data support the notion that "true" rate of crime is probably directly related to the degree of urbanization. After observing that crime rates rise consistently with city size, Wolfgang (1969) has suggested that the regularity and consistency of the data lead to the conclusion that "criminogenic" forces were probably greater in the city than in less urbanized areas. Palen (1992) has concluded that even with the serious biases and problems of obtaining reliable crime data, the national problem of crime is clearly an urban problem to a disproportionate degree. Gist and Fava (1974, p. 524) also conclude that even after allowing generously for inadequacies of incomplete data, the differences in crime rates between rural areas or small towns and the larger metropolitan areas are quite impressive.

However, not all observers are equally convinced that the actual rate of crime is clearly greater in the city than elsewhere. For example, Horton and Leslie (1974, p. 126) make the following qualifications:

> Cities show higher crime rates than rural areas, but it is probable that rural crime is less fully reported. The city also attracts people intending to commit crimes, as it provides more opportunities for crime and provides greater anonymity for those seeking an unconventional mode of life. But there is no evidence that country-reared persons are conspicuously less criminal than their city-reared compatriots.

Table 12.6   Murder Rate per 100,000 Population, 1993–1997

Urban Character	MURDER RATE PER 100,000 POPULATION				
	1993	1994	1995	1996	1997
Metropolitan cities	10.6	10.0	9.1	8.1	7.4
Smaller cities	5.3	4.8	4.7	4.5	4.2
Rural counties	5.4	5.0	5.0	4.7	4.6

Source: Crime in the United States, 1997, Federal Bureau of Investigation, 1998.

Table 12.7   Crimes per 100,000 Population in Metropolitan Areas, 1993–97

Metropolitan area	ALL SERIOUS CRIMES[2]			VIOLENT CRIMES[1]		
	1993	*1996*	*1997*	*1993*	*1996*	*1997*
Albuquerque	7,547.8	8,301.1	8,875.7	1,273.6	1,082.0	1,742.9
Atlanta	7,594.5	7,647.7	6,711.5	923.8	781.3	752.2
Austin	7,584.5	5,960.0	5,905.2	528.2	520.9	490.9
Baltimore	7,275.4	7,026.9	6,609.0	1,356.1	1,237.3	1,140.9
Bergen-Passaic, N.J.	N.A.	3,305.0	3,069.4	N.A.	322.4	293.4
Birmingham, Ala.	N.A.	5,932.0	5,639.6	N.A.	780.8	704.7
Boston	4,844.6	3,768.2	3,445.9	777.1	580.9	540.1
Buffalo	5,283.8	4,563.7	N.A.	754.7	538.8	N.A.
Charlotte	7,277.0	6,841.0	6,847.8	1,204.5	979.2	1,032.9
Columbus	6,012.8	6,332.5	6,478.2	682.2	579.6	574.5
Dallas	7,290.9	6,350.2	6,188.3	946.3	784.4	717.6
Denver	6,090.8	5,415.9	5,014.6	731.7	460.4	421.8
Detroit	N.A.	6,081.7	5,931.5	N.A.	828.9	784.7
El Paso	7,827.7	6,980.8	6,491.4	1,031.1	811.3	756.0
Fort Lauderdale	8,904.1	N.A.	7,294.7	1,005.4	N.A.	781.0
Forth Worth	6,880.9	5,865.4	5,461.3	824.6	661.9	620.4
Fresno	8,099.6	7,620.3	6,973.8	1,084.6	1,043.2	978.2
Grand Rapids, Mich.	N.A.	4,602.2	4,459.9	N.A.	489.9	461.4
Greensboro, N.C.	N.A.	6,157.5	5,941.6	N.A.	659.1	611.4
Greenville, S.C.	N.A.	6,361.9	6,004.2	N.A.	1,083.9	979.7
Hartford, Conn.	N.A.	4,224.2	3,930.6	N.A.	420.1	345.1
Honolulu	6,442.9	6,840.1	6,067.4	285.6	313.0	299.5
Houston	N.A.	5,761.0	5,518.3	N.A.	859.0	818.3
Indianapolis	N.A.	5,400.0	5,260.6	N.A.	726.5	727.4
Jacksonville, Fla.	8,598.0	N.A.	7,107.3	1,419.9	N.A.	1,133.8
Los Angeles-Long Beach, Calif.	7,049.6	5,442.4	4,744.7	1,682.5	1,278.0	1,135.5
Memphis, Tenn.	7,408.6	7,862.4	7,839.1	1,109.3	1,316.3	1,306.2
Miami, Fla.	13,500.4	N.A.	10,792.3	2,136.2	N.A.	1,691.8
Middlesex, N.J.	N.A.	2,987.2	2,956.6	N.A.	229.1	226.8
Milwaukee	5,355.8	5,206.8	4,966.5	482.1	474.6	521.1
Minneapolis	N.A.	5,346.1	5,364.5	N.A.	468.5	458.1
Monmouth-Ocean, N.J.	N.A.	3,280.8	3,107.9	N.A.	242.6	246.6
Nashville	7,331.8	7,593.9	7,510.3	1,098.6	1,149.4	1,085.0
Nassau-Suffolk, N.Y.	N.A.	2,898.5	2,701.7	N.A.	213.0	180.7
Newark, N.J.	N.A.	5,216.3	4,721.7	N.A.	869.5	748.7
New Orleans	8,511.7	8,267.7	7,408.7	1,312.7	1,326.0	1,092.9
New York City	7,532.9	4,896.6	4,606.7	1,865.6	1,191.9	1,129.5
Norfolk, Va.	N.A.	5,338.2	5,232.1	N.A.	507.2	511.5
Oakland, Calif.	7,329.6	6,250.3	6,184.3	1,137.5	871.2	850.8
Oklahoma City	7,692.7	8,252.3	7,910.7	828.2	707.8	676.9
Orange County, Calif.	N.A.	3,983.5	3,542.6	N.A.	465.3	429.1
Philadelphia	4,355.3	4,630.8	N.A.	662.2	733.2	N.A.
Phoenix	7,787.9	7,730.2	7,907.1	806.8	668.0	656.5

[1]Violent crimes are offenses of murder, forcible rape, robbery, and aggravated assault.
[2]Property crimes are offenses of burglary, larceny-theft, and motor vehicle theft. Data are not included for the property crime of arson.

(continued)

Table 12.7   Crimes per 100,000 Population in Metropolitan Areas, 1993–97 (*continued*)

Metropolitan area	ALL SERIOUS CRIMES[2]			VIOLENT CRIMES[1]		
	1993	*1996*	*1997*	*1993*	*1996*	*1997*
Pittsburgh	3,111.2	2,665.1	2,783.4	393.4	303.2	310.0
Portland, Oreg.	6,244.5	6,154.7	6,408.2	711.8	644.5	637.3
Providence, R.I.	N.A.	4,014.0	3,686.1	N.A.	353.8	341.8
Raleigh, N.C.	N.A.	6,076.4	6,295.1	N.A.	570.9	637.5
Richmond, Va.	N.A.	5,455.2	5,463.4	N.A.	596.6	606.7
Riverside, Calif.	N.A.	5,560.6	5,193.9	N.A.	814.6	757.2
Rochester, N.Y.	N.A.	4,275.3	4,187.6	N.A.	310.8	319.2
Sacramento	7,038.4	6,279.1	6,474.3	815.6	700.8	689.1
Salt Lake City	N.A.	7,037.6	7,008.9	N.A.	421.5	413.1
San Antonio	8,450.9	7,080.7	6,661.5	629.7	428.2	390.9
San Diego	6,160,5	4,623.8	4,417.1	873.8	710.0	666.4
San Francisco	6,697.5	5,381.6	4,929.2	1,088.1	801.3	688.2
San Jose, Calif.	4,640.3	4,020.3	3,777.7	524.7	562.1	578.9
Seattle	6,588.1	N.A.	6,286.9	569.8	N.A.	439.4
Syracuse, N.Y.	N.A.	3,551.3	3,515.6	N.A.	288.0	292.6
Tucson, Ariz.	9,219.9	7,853.6	7,914.4	754.2	809.2	786.1
Tulsa, Okla.	5,484.1	5,272.9	5,299.0	801.0	740.6	750.4
Washington, D.C.	5,462.4	5,450.7	4,879.2	771.4	679.7	576.5

Source: Federal Bureau of Investigation, *Uniform Crime Reports: Crime in the United States, 1997.*

INTRAURBAN VARIATIONS IN CRIME RATES

A large body of research exists on the variation in crime rates within metropolitan areas. The basic assumption that the extent and kinds of crime will differ markedly from one part of the community to another tends to be generally supported by this research. One of the earliest studies was that of Shaw (1929), who was among the first to report that delinquency rates decline from the central business district to the outlying areas of the city. He also found that the same pattern held for adult crime, and that rates of recidivism were also highest in the inner zones of the city and declined toward the peripheral areas. Shaw's original study was confined to the city of Chicago, but in a later comparative study of twenty-one cities in the United States and Canada, Shaw and McKay (1969) confirmed that reported crime and delinquency rates were similarly higher in inner zones and slums. Lander (1954) found similar results for Baltimore, as did Schmidt (1960a) for Seattle. Although Schmidt's more detailed analysis found that the central business district, skid row, and contiguous areas had the highest crime rates, it also concluded that each of these areas produced different kinds of crime. The central business district, for example, was characterized by high rates of shoplifting, check fraud, residential burglary (this is possible only in cities having a large residential population in the central business district, as was the case in Seattle), automobile theft, and attempted suicide. On the other hand, the skid row areas were characterized by high rates of fighting, robbery, nonresidential burglary, and disorderly conduct.

Mounted police officers monitoring public spaces in Washington, D.C.

In searching for explanations for the spatial patterning of crime, a number of experts have argued that the important factor is not the location or distance from the central business district but rather the social and physical characteristics of the areas in which the crime occurs, or, equally important, in which the offender resides (offenders do not always confine their illegal activities to the areas in which they live). From this perspective, such variables as poverty, unemployment, poor housing, family status, anomie, social rank, ethnic composition, and degree of urbanization have been associated in one degree or another with the incidence of crime (Butler, 1976, pp. 109–120; Boggs, 1965; Schmidt, 1960b; Schuessler, 1962; Clark and Wenninger, 1962). However, there is little agreement among studies such as these as to which of the many variables they identify best explain the tendency for higher recorded rates of crime to occur near the center of the metropolis.

Throughout the 1980s and early 1990s, drugs appeared to be associated with crime in most major cities across the nation. Increasing violence (i.e., robberies, burglaries, and felonious assaults among juveniles) led to increases in the crime rate. From 1985 to 1992, the rate of homicides committed by young people, the number of homicides committed with guns, and the arrest rate of nonwhite juveniles for drug offenses all doubled (UCR, 1997). Although many of the national trends have remained relatively stable, there has been some dramatic change in violent crime committed by young people. A resurgence of juvenile and adult gang activity in several major cities contributed to increases in homicides and other violent crimes. The mechanisms responsible for high homicide rates included the availability and use of handguns, gang wars, and drug trafficking. According to the UCR, the rates of violent crime in most of the nation's cities began to climb in the late 1960s. The prevalent theory is that many urban centers, abandoned by white populations after racial unrest and urban riots unsettled the nation's cities, declined economically, politically, and socially. A substantial proportion of the increasing incidence of crime was attributable to urban neighborhoods where unemployment, transient populations, and physical deterioration were commonplace. As a result of "white flight," many inner cities are increasingly black or Hispanic. These communities are characterized by poverty, economic dependency, family instability, and high rates of crime.

The crime index rate is highest in metropolitan areas where there have been increases in violent crime (i.e., homicide, assault, forcible rape, and robbery). Suburban and rural areas also reported significant increases in violent crimes. Despite an increase in suburban violence in recent years, crimes of violence continue to be higher in the metropolitan centers than in the suburbs or rural areas.

Although more pervasive in urban America, violent crime is also growing in rural communities. Regardless of offense, urban crime rates are generally higher than rural crimes rates. The only exception occurs in the burglary category where the rural crime rate has surpassed the urban crime rate. Where most Americans live, all crimes except auto thefts have decreased since 1980.

Urban crime and the inability of the criminal justice system to deal with it is a continuing focus of public attention in the United States. Since the early 1960s, Americans have focused on crime and violence in general. Violence is in our homes, neighborhoods, schools, and places of employment. Americans have reported increasingly fearful attitudes toward crime. Despite the prevalence of data showing a decrease in violent crimes, there is a growing public demand for a more punitive criminal justice system. For the most part, public and private responses to urban crime in U.S. society have been relatively reactive. These approaches are often riddled with emotional and political biases that deny the real dimensions of the crime problem.

Attitudes toward drugs and rising public awareness of the relationship between drugs and crime during the 1970s and 1980s has led to national strategies for reducing and controlling urban crime and violence. The strategy reflected a coordinated plan involving the criminal justice system and a collection of education, workplace, and public awareness institutions/organizations. This approach has had limited impact on the nation's perception and fear of crime despite political rhetoric about getting tough on crime, locking up offenders and "throwing away the key."

THE URBAN CRIMINAL JUSTICE SYSTEM

The police are the front-line component of the criminal justice system, which also includes prosecutors, courts, juries, and correctional institutions, such as jails, prisons, and probation agencies. However, to conceive of the combination of these components as a "system" in the literal sense is somewhat misleading, because they do not always interact in harmonious or anticipated ways. The expected sequence of procedures handled by the various agents who administer the work of criminal justice is fraught with many inconsistencies, conflicts, and strains, which render the so-called criminal justice system less effective, efficient, or fair than ideally desired (Gold, 1982, p. 305).

The work of the police would be greatly simplified if they were completely free to collect evidence, apprehend suspects, and obtain confessions according to the necessities of efficient law enforcement only. However, the courts also have a keen interest in their law-enforcement procedures of acquisition of evidence, interrogation, arrest, conviction, and detention. These procedures must conform to the rules of law and the principles of civil rights guaranteed by the Constitution or law. If this were not so, the spector of a police state would undoubtedly become apparent. The work of the police and the courts is often at cross purposes. But the courts, in turn, breed their own discrepancies between what is considered ideal and the practical realities of law enforcement in a democratic society. One major problem is that the greater population concentration and increased reliance on formal legal controls in modern urban society have imposed a greater workload on the courts and have aggravated perennial problems of delay, disparities in sentencing, or disposition of cases, and in differential justice for different classes of defendants (see Scarpitti and Andersen, 1989, p. 51).

Court dockets become so clogged that trials may be delayed for many years, while the jails are overcrowded with persons awaiting the disposition of their cases. One expediency adopted by the court system in response to these conditions is disposition without trial, to reduce the workload through more rapid processing of cases and to divert offenders from correction facilities. It has been estimated that somewhere between one-third and one-half of all cases initiated by arrests are dismissed by the police, prosecutor, or judge (Curran and Renzetti, 1996, pp. 394–395).

There are many reasons why the police have been widely perceived as a rather weak link in the chain of institutional arrangements that constitutes the urban criminal justice

Gated communities or barred windows represent one attempted form of urban crime control

system. Law enforcement carries stresses for the police because their duties may produce role conflicts in such situations as crowd control, gang fights, tavern brawls, disorderly street behavior, quarrels between neighbors, and family disputes. In these kinds of situations, one or another of the parties involved is likely to feel harassed, outraged, or neglected, and the police officer—who quite frequently has no clear legal standard to apply—must devise a solution based almost entirely on his of her own discretion and judgment, which may please none of the involved parties (Gold, 1982).

More importantly, the democratic emphasis on civil rights also places the police in an awkward position when they are under strong pressure from many groups to suppress crime at all costs. They are expected to maintain order in the dynamic and complex environment of urban streets and neighborhoods and to enforce the law as the gatekeepers of the urban criminal justice system. The identification of the police with strong demands to maintain "law and order" makes them favorite targets of criticism whenever the real or perceived incidence of crime and lawlessness exceeds tolerable limits. At the same time, the police may be viewed with hostility and suspicion or as unfair, brutal, or suppressive by members of minorities, nonconforming lifestyle groups, or political protest groups whenever they have been targeted as the objects of police operations.

In many of the big city police departments, police officers have been recruited from those segments of the community that have had little direct day-to-day experience with the minority or nonconformist groups they are expected to "keep the line" (Gold, 1982). For example, young police officers with limited formal education who are recruited from white working-class communities and are assigned to a minority "ghetto" community may have grown up without any significant contact with that minority and may experience "cultural shock" when brought into contact with what to them may be an "alien" way of life. Their latently negative attitudes thus may be reinforced by what to them appears to be the aggressive and sometimes militant hostility that greets them, even when they are attempting to perform, to the best of their knowledge, a community service or order maintenance function when they attempt to apprehend a suspected criminal in a minority community. It is under these kinds of circumstances that acts of police brutality or unjustified acts of police violence are likely to occur. Although they do not happen often, such acts tend to become highly visible through the mass media, and counterhostility and violent reactions from the offended minority community are provoked. (Curran and Renzetti, 1996, p. 387, cite the brutal police beating of Rodney King in Los Angeles as one well-publicized example; the unjustified killing of Malice Green by Detroit police officers was another.) For these and similar reasons, the urban police may be faced not only with inconsistent public expectations and public reactions, but also with inner conflict growing out of the interaction between their values or background and their intimate experience of what they perceive to be the "criminal element" of the population. The police live on the grinding edge of social conflict in urban settings without a well-defined understanding of what they are supposed to be doing. They often occupy what they perceive as a "damned if they do, damned if they don't" status in the eyes of the public. This often leads to a state of frustration and low morale among police officers, which, in turn, lowers the efficiency and fairness of the urban law enforcement process. According to Curran and Renzetti (1996, p. 388), "When a community views the police as a positive force that contributes to the stability of the neighborhood, police self-conceptions have been found to be positive, and interaction with the public is upbeat. All too often, this is not the case, however, and the public sees the police as oppressors. This situation is particularly prevalent in urban areas with a high concentration of minorities, and it is here that the police are most socially isolated." (See the following chapter on race and ethnic relations in urban America.)

THE SEARCH FOR SOLUTIONS
TO THE URBAN CRIME PROBLEM

For decades, hundreds of policies and proposals have been suggested to reduce crime in American cities and to reduce the impact of the image of the city as dangerous or unsafe. Listed below is a brief summary of some of the most common recommendations:

1. Decriminalize victimless crimes such as marijuana possession, prostitution, or gambling, while providing information and treatment programs for drug addicts. Many experts believe that this revision in the criminal law would reduce crime more than any other single remedy.
2. Institute a full-employment policy and a higher minimum wage to lessen the appeal of crime as a way of making a living.
3. Promote tough gun control legislation with mandatory punishment for the gun possession.
4. Improve police-community relations. Create community policing, in which there is a strong partnership and working relationship between the police and the community.
5. Recruit more minorities for police forces, to make sure the police are more representative of the communities that are policed.
6. Reform police departments to eliminate corruption.
7. Retrain police to function as ombudsmen, counselors, and quasi-social workers operating out of neighborhood precinct offices. This, of course, would require much better educated police officers, who were also more knowledgeable in law, political science, anthropology, psychology, and sociology. A minimum of a college degree would be an appropriate goal.
8. Establish a system of early screening and treatment of potential juvenile criminals, along with foster homes where necessary, and more community-based facilities.
9. Establish stiff, mandatory, equalized, and more certain sentences for violent crimes.
10. Redesign building construction and site planning in urban redevelopment areas to minimize opportunities for crime: better lighting, fewer blind areas, and better opportunities for street surveillance. (See chapter 14 on urban planning.)
11. Disperse or co-opt juvenile gangs.
12. Issue grants or permits to neighborhoods and block associations to employ their own security guards.

Although some of the above recommendations seem more promising than others, and although some have already been undertaken in some American cities, it is highly unlikely that the actual incidence of crime can ever be reduced without drastically overhauling some of the major values and structural characteristics of American society, which would require major sacrifices on the part of nearly everyone (Gold, 1982). Also, no consensus yet exists as to the basic causes of crime, the methods best suited to reduce crime, the target groups against whom efforts at crime iradication should be directed, or who should pay the enormous social and economic costs of a radically revamped criminal justice system. For these reasons, it is fair to conclude that some form of urban crime will be with us for the foreseeable future.

SELECTED BIBLIOGRAPHY

BELL, DANIEL. *The End of Ideology.* New York: Free Press, 1960.

BOGGS, SARA."Urban crime patterns," *American Sociological Review* 30 (1965): 899–908.

BUTLER, EDGAR. *Urban sociology.* New York: Harper & Row, 1976.

———. *The Urban Crisis: Problems and Prospects in America.* Santa Monica, CA: Goodyear, 1977.

CHAMPION, DEAN J. *Dictionary of American Criminal Justice.* Chicago: Fitzroy Dearborn Publishers, 1998.

CHIRICOS, THEODORE, et al. "Racial Composition of Neighborhood Fear of Crime," *Criminology* 35 (1997): 107–129.

CLARK, J., and E. WENNINGER. "Socio-Economic Correlates of Illegal Behavior among Juveniles," *American Sociological Review* 27 (1962): 826–834.

CRUTCHFIELD, ROBERT, et al. *Crime-Readings,* 2nd ed. Thousand Oaks, CA: Pine Forge Press, 2000.

CURRAN, DANIEL J., and CLAIRE M. RENZETTI. *Social Problems: Society in Crisis.* Boston: Allyn and Bacon, 1996.

Detroit Police Department. 1999. 135th Annual Report.

Federal Bureau of Investigation. *Crime in the United States, 1993.* Washington, DC: U.S. Government Printing Office, 1994.

Federal Bureau of Investigation. *Crime in the United States, 1994.* Washington, DC: U.S. Government Printing Office, 1995.

Federal Bureau of Investigation. *Crime in the United States, 1997.* Washington, DC: U.S. Government Printing Office, 1998.

Federal Bureau of Investigation. *UCR Handbook,* NIBRS Edition. Washington, DC: U.S. Department of Justice, 1998.

GIST, NOEL, and SYLVIA FAVA. *Urban Society,* 6th ed. New York: Thomas Y. Crowell, 1974.

GOLD, HARRY. *The Sociology of Urban Life.* Englewood, NJ: Prentice-Hall, 1982.

HORTON, PAUL, and GERALD LESLIE. *The Sociology of Social Problems,* 5th ed. Englewood Cliffs, NJ: Prentice-Hall, 1974.

INCIARDI, JAMES A. *Elements of Criminal Justice.* New York: Harcourt College Publishers, 1997.

———. *Elements of Criminal Justice,* 2nd ed. New York: Harcourt College Publishers, 2000.

LANDER, BERNARD. *Toward an Understanding of Juvenile Delinquency.* New York: Columbia University Press, 1954.

LIVINGSTON, JAY. *Crime and Criminology.* Englewood Cliffs, NJ: Prentice-Hall, 1992.

MEIER, ROBERT. *Crime and Society.* Boston: Allyn and Bacon, 1989.

MOKHIBER, RUSSELL. *Corporate Crime and Violence: Big business power and the abuse of the public trust.* San Francisco, CA: Sierra Club Books, 1988.

PACE, DAVID. *Concepts of Vice, Narcotics, and Organized Crime,* 3rd ed. Englewood Cliffs, NJ: Prentice Hall, 1991.

PALEN, J. JOHN. *The Urban World.* New York: McGraw-Hill, 1992.

PONTELL, HENRY, and KITTY CALAVITA. "White-Collar crime in the savings and loan scandal," *Annals of the American Academy of Political and Social Science* vol. 525 (1993): 31–45.

RUSSELL, CHERYL. "True Crime." *American Demographics,* August, 1995, pp. 22–31.

SCARPITTI, FRANK, and MARGARET ANDERSON. *Social Problems.* New York: Harper and Row, 1989.

SCHMIDT, CALVIN. "Urban Crime Areas: Part I," *American Sociological Review* 25 (1960a): 555–578.

———. "Urban Crime Areas: Part II," *American Sociological Review* 25 (1960b): 655–678.

SCHUESSLER, KARL F. "Components of Variations in City Crime Rates," *Social Problems* 314–323, 1962.

SHAW, CLIFFORD R. *Delinquency Areas.* Chicago: University of Chicago Press, 1929.

SHAW, CLIFFORD R., and HENRY D. McKAY. *Juvenile Delinquency and Urban Areas.* Chicago: University of Chicago Press, 1969.

SUTHERLAND, EDWIN H. *White Collar Crime.* New York: Dryden Press, 1949.

WOLFGANG, MARVIN E. "Crime in Urban America." In the 1967–68 E. Paul Dupont Lectures, *The threat of crime in America.* Newark: University of Delaware Press, 1969.

13

PROBLEMS OF RACIAL AND ETHNIC MINORITIES IN URBAN AMERICA

The problems of race and ethnic relations in the United States may be identified and defined in a number of ways. They may be viewed as aspects of a far more general tendency for all humans to separate themselves into groups in which members are linked to one another by feelings of solidarity and a common identity. Such groups, which may vary in size from a single family to an entire community, have been labeled "in-groups" by sociologists. In turn, such groups almost universally tend to develop unfavorable prejudices against "out-groups" consisting perhaps of all groups other than their own. This tendency, which applies to groups of all types, whenever they are differentiated by religion, race, ethnicity, economic status, or any other significant cultural differences, has also been referred to as *ethnocentrism* by social scientists (Gold, 1982, p. 310).

Another very general way to define the problems of race and ethnic relations is in reference to relationships between dominant and minority groups in a given society, such as the tendency for the majority groups in many societies to control or restrict the behavior of minority groups within these societies in discriminatory ways. In the case of some societies, such as South Africa of the recent past or other previously feudal or colonial societies, a minority group may dominate a subjected majority.

American cities have always been characterized by a wide range of ethnic, religious, and cultural diversity as waves and waves of immigrants have poured into them in search of new opportunities. A traditional American myth is that these groups easily assimilated into a single, united American way of life, as the population "melting pot" hypothesis has suggested. But, with few exceptions, the successive waves of immigrants that have infused American cities have tended to establish their own ethnically homogeneous neighborhoods and social institutions adjacent to those already established by other groups. For the most part, the melting has been restricted to those ethnic groups already having the social and cultural characteristics most similar to those of the dominant established groups, which have been primarily of white Protestant Anglo-Saxon origins.

In turn, the tendency for established majorities to control or restrict the behavior of minority groups in discriminatory ways has often become a source of tension and hostility. In American urban centers, relations between the white Protestant majority and racial, ethnic, and religious minorities, such as blacks, Native Americans, Hispanics, Jews, Poles, Asians, Catholics, Irish, French Canadians, and almost every other ethnic group have been characterized at various times by in-group/out-group hostilities ranging in intensity from verbal insults and prejudice to systematic discrimination, and, in some instances, to more overt physical attacks and violence, including riots, bombings, lynchings, and other kinds of hate crimes. Of course, such conflict has not been limited to relations between dominant groups and subjected minorities, but has occurred from time to time between competing minority groups as well.

It is also possible to characterize ethnic and racial diversity as a positive aspect of urban living, as did Wirth (1938) much earlier, who saw such diversity as an essential characteristic of cities. He saw unlike groups drawn to one another because they were useful to one another, and he saw ethnic pluralism as contributing to the "spice of life" in urban communities. To a certain extent, cities and metropolitan areas can be described as ethnic "mosaics," which implies an almost esthetic quality to the spatial patterning of ethnic and racial settlements within a metropolitan complex. As Dentler (1977, p. 274) so aptly put it, two or more ethnic or racial groups do not automatically experience conflict when their members meet along a new frontier. They may cooperate or compete in some ways and merge or assimilate in others, or they may make contact, but for a time might remain wholly independent of one another. Dentler qualifies this more optimistic assessment by reminding us that conflict is most likely to become the outcome of the relationships between ethnic or racial groups when one of the contacting groups is dominant in size, technology, or resources and when the subordinate groups have something that is coveted by the dominant group.

While recognizing the positive aspects of ethnic and racial diversity, this chapter focuses on those aspects that have proven to be problematic both in the past and present. We focus primarily on problems of black-white relationships, primarily because blacks are by far the largest minority group in the United States to which the more extreme manifestations of prejudice have been consistently directed. It is also the majority-minority group relationship problem that is the most widely recognized as having the greatest consequences for the country as a whole and about which there is the greatest concern or uncertainty about its implications for the future. Secondary emphasis will be given to Hispanic Americans who are members of what is the currently fastest growing ethnic group in America (*Statistical Abstract of the United States,* 1999). These emphases are not intended to minimize the seriousness of the problems faced by other minority groups in urban settings, such as Asian Americans, Native Americans, white ethnics of European descent, Muslims of Middle Eastern descent, or any other distinct ethnic groups, but merely represent the practical limitations of this chapter.

THE URBAN TRANSFORMATION
OF BLACK AMERICANS

Prejudice and hostility directed against blacks has been a cruel fact throughout much of American history, but this is not to say that its particular manifestations and intensity have not significantly varied from time to time and from region to region. Perhaps the most consistent pattern of racial discrimination in the United States was the dual system of racism and caste that dominated the Deep South during the period beginning roughly in the last decade of the nineteenth century and lasting until just after World War II. When racism comes to dominate a culture to the extent that it generates a rigid system of racial segregation, such a system is commonly referred to by social scientists as a *caste* system. A well-developed caste system does not permit any degree of social equality between the races, nor does it permit economic or political equality. In effect, a caste system keeps subjugated racial groups "in their place" by an elaborate network of laws, rituals, and customs, usually maintained by a constant threat of violence toward those who violate the norms of the system. Thus, in a pure caste system, there is no open biological mixing of the separate races, and there is no mobility from one racial stratum to another (Gold and Scarpitti, 1967). Actually there have been very few examples of pure caste systems in the history of the world: perhaps Hindu dominated India; Nazi Germany and the Union of South Africa, all of the recent past; and the southern United States during the period discussed are the closest approximations (Merton and Nisbet, 1976, pp. 438–449; Myrdal, 1944). Although slavery was legally abolished following the end of the Civil War, the foundation for the emergence of the racial caste system had already been established. It seems almost paradoxical that it dominated the South only after it could no longer be justified along the strict economic grounds of slavery. The worse aspects of the caste system reached their peak around 1900. For blacks, it was then that segregation was most complete, violence outside the courts and mistreatment in the courts most extreme, voting privileges for blacks most nonexistent, occupational restriction most stringent, and public facilities least available (Rose, 1956).

One important result of these conditions was that racism and the resulting patterns of prejudice and discrimination were introduced into other regions of the United States, where slavery or a racial caste system had not previously materialized. Today, various expressions of racial prejudice and discrimination are still found throughout the United States, but their full extent is difficult to measure, because its intensity and content vary so greatly from region to region, city to city, group to group, and person to person. Nevertheless, it has been obvious that for the last half of the twentieth century the old caste system of the South had been crumbling and that many of the racial barriers denying blacks equal rights and opportunities in other regions was also being gradually torn down. We now turn to the twentieth-century history of the migration of black Americans out of rural southern areas into the cities of the urban-industrial north that is most directly pertinent to the theme of this chapter.

In 1910, 91 percent of the nation's black population still lived in the South. They were predominantly rural, with 73 percent living in rural areas or in villages or small towns of less than twenty-five hundred persons. But by 1999, the proportion of blacks living in the South had dropped to about 55 percent, and about 55 percent of all blacks in the United States now lived in the central cities of large metropolitan areas in all regions of the country (*New York Times Almanac, 2000,* p. 284). Table 13.1 provides a list of the twenty U.S. cities with the largest black populations.

A relatively slow but steady out-migration of blacks from the South occurred during the first three decades of the twentieth century, with some acceleration during World War I, when floods and boll weevils hurt farming in the South, and the thousands of new jobs for unskilled workers in the northern cities created by the industrial demands of the war were a strong pull factor (Gold, 1982, p. 312). Escape from the worse aspects of the Southern caste system into the freer North, of course, must have also been a strong motivating factor for this migration. The out-migration reached its peak between 1940 and 1960, when approximately 3 million blacks migrated from the South to the North. World War II and the postwar reconstruction industrial boom were accelerating factors during this period, as was the fact that many poor and rural Southern black males who served in the military during World War II had been able to see other parts of the United States, or parts of the rest of the world, for the first time and had developed a taste for living, working, or getting formal education elsewhere, and the postwar GI Bill provided some of the economic means. By 1970 nearly one-half of the entire black population of the United

TABLE 13.1   Twenty U.S. Cities with Largest Black Populations, 1990

BLACK RANK	OVERALL RANK	CITY, STATE	TOTAL POPULATION (000s)	BLACK POPULATION (000s)	PERCENT BLACK
1	1	New York, N.Y.	7,322.6	2,102.5	29%
2	3	Chicago, Ill.	2,783.7	1,087.7	39
3	7	Detroit, Mich.	1,028.0	777.9	76
4	5	Philadelphia, Pa.	1,585.6	631.9	40
5	2	Los Angeles, Calif.	3,485.4	487.7	14
6	4	Houston, Tex.	1,630.6	458.0	28
7	13	Baltimore, Md.	736.0	435.8	59
8	19	Washington, D.C.	606.9	399.6	66
9	18	Memphis, Tenn.	610.3	334.7	55
10	25	New Orleans, La.	496.9	307.7	62
11	8	Dallas, Tex.	1,006.9	297.0	30
12	36	Atlanta, Ga.	394.0	264.3	67
13	24	Cleveland, Ohio	505.6	235.4	47
14	17	Milwaukee, Wis.	628.1	191.3	31
15	34	St. Louis, Mo.	396.7	188.4	48
16	60	Birmingham, Ala.	266.0	168.3	63
17	12	Indianapolis, Ind.	742.0	165.6	22
18	15	Jacksonville, Fla.	673.0	163.9	24
19	39	Oakland, Calif.	372.2	163.3	44
20	56	Newark, N.J.	275.2	160.9	59

Source: Populations Reference Bureau, "African Americans in the 1990s" (1991), based on unpublished data from 1990 census.

States was concentrated in the central cities of the nation's fifteen largest metropolitan areas. Six of these cities had black majorities, and another eight already had populations that were nearly 50 percent black by 1970. Less than one-third of all black Americans continued to live in the five states of the Deep South, most of them still in rural areas (although the trend in the South was also one of rural to urban migration. By this time more blacks lived in the Chicago Metropolitan area than in Mississippi, and more blacks resided in the New York Metropolitan area than in any of the Southern States (Pettigrew, 1971, p. 3). During the 1970s black migration from Southern areas to Northern cities had all but ended. Since then northern black populations have been increasing because of natural growth (more births than deaths) rather than rural to urban migration. The period of massive migration of blacks from the South to the North has now become history (Taeuber, 1975). In fact, since then, there has been a trickle of reverse migration by some blacks, from North to South, and most of this has been to growing Southern Metropolitan areas, such as Atlanta, Georgia; Houston, Texas; Memphis, Tennessee; or New Orleans. (see Table 13.1)

THE RESIDENTIAL SEGREGATION OF URBAN BLACKS

The early pattern of black settlement within each metropolitan area followed that of earlier white immigrant groups. The white migrants had converged on the older sections of the central cities because the lowest cost housing was there, the jobs were there, and the older neighborhoods often had good public transportation. Friends and relatives were also more likely to be there, and the neighborhoods also offered ethnic-oriented churches, businesses, voluntary associations, and service institutions that could provide support in times of need and could serve as a comforting bulwark against the impersonal forces of the larger urban world. As the earlier white immigrants were eventually absorbed by the larger society, many left their predominantly ethnic neighborhoods and moved to outlying areas to obtain newer housing and better schools. Some scattered randomly over the suburban areas, and others established new ethnic clusters in the suburbs. For these largely white ethnic European groups, living in ethnic or assimilated neighborhoods, either in the cities or the suburbs, is now largely a question of personal choice.

The later phases of black settlement patterns in metropolitan areas have diverged sharply from those typical of the earlier white ethnic groups. Nowhere has the expansion of America's black metropolitan population followed the patterns of dispersal open to the earlier white immigrants. Many black families have attained incomes, living standards, and cultural levels matching or surpassing those of many whites who have "assimilated" (Gold, 1982, p. 313). Yet most black families have remained within predominantly black neighborhoods primarily because they have been effectively excluded from white residential areas.

Their exclusion has been accomplished through various discriminatory practices, some obvious and overt, others hidden by subtle "gentlemen's" agreements. Deliberate efforts have often been made to discourage black families from purchasing or renting homes or apartments in all-white neighborhoods. Intimidation and threats of violence have ranged from throwing garbage on lawns, making threatening phone calls in the middle of the night, burning crosses on lawns, and even bombing or setting fire to properties purchased by blacks (Farley and Frey, 1994; Gold, 1982; see *Report of the National Advisory Commission on Civil Disorders,* 1968, p. 244, for some earlier examples). Of course, many whites did not approve of such tactics and were probably shocked and angered by the level of prejudice and hate that were demonstrated. Such actions do not require the participation of a majority of whites to effectively discourage black families from seeking housing in all-white neighborhoods.

More often, real estate agents simply refused to show houses or apartments in all-white neighborhoods to potential black purchasers or renters. (Although such practices were outlawed by the federal government in the Civil Rights Act of 1968, their continuing use now constitutes current examples of "white-collar" crime, referred to in the previous chapter.) Similarly, many banks and mortgage loan agencies have "redlined" neighborhoods through various mortgage allocation and approval procedures that effectively denied mortgage loans to many blacks who wished to purchase homes in predominantly or all-white neighborhoods (Farley and Frey, 1994).

All these practices helped to create an atmosphere in which it was not worth the psychological or sociological efforts or costs to try to move into white neighborhoods for many blacks who could economically afford to do so.

White flight from racially changing neighborhoods, or from cities containing high proportions of blacks, was another condition faced uniquely by black Americans. Racial transition in central cities of metropolitan areas has been at least one reason that millions of whites have moved out of the cities into all-white suburban areas. Although by no means were all such moves from cities to suburbs racially inspired, the results were nevertheless the same, that is, an increase in the pattern of residential segregation that has existed for decades.

A study by Taeuber and Taeuber (1965) had demonstrated early on that this pattern of racial segregation characterized virtually every large city in America. To measure this pattern of residential segregation, the authors had devised what they called an "index of dissimilarity." The index indicated for each city the percentage of blacks who would have to move from the blocks where they currently resided to other blocks in order to provide perfectly proportional, unsegregated distribution of the population. According to their findings at that time, the average segregation index for 207 of the largest U.S. cities was 86.2. This meant that an average of over 86 percent of all blacks would have had to move to a different block to create an unsegregated population distribution.

The 1970 U.S. Census showed that blacks were becoming more suburbanized, but this was misleading and should not be construed to mean that they were becoming less segregated. Taeuber (1975), for example, pointed out that for the most part, suburbanizing blacks moved into predominantly black suburban areas that were just as segregated as the central cities areas from which they moved. Also they were moving into older suburban areas with declining neighborhoods and deteriorating housing much like that available to them in the central cities. (See Kramer, 1972, for a discussion of early low-income black suburbs.)

Comparing data from the 1980 and 1990 censuses, Farley and Frey (1994) have shown there are very few or no signs of any significant reduction of the residential segre-

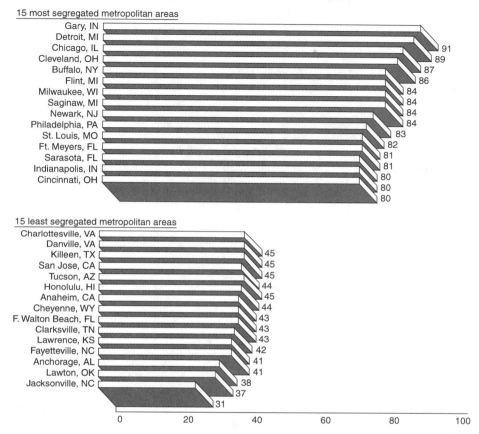

Figure 13.1   Residential Segregation of African-Americans in the United States Is Greatest in Older Cities in the North, and Lowest in Cities in the South and West. (Adapted from R. Farley and W. H. Frey, 1994, "Changes in the segregation of white from blacks during the 1980s: Small steps toward a more integrated society," *American Sociological Review* 59:23–45; Table 1). *Note:* Segregation score is measured as the percent of African-Americans in the metropolitan area who would have to move to another census block in order to achieve residential balance by race throughout the metropolitan area.

gation of blacks, at least in the "Rustbelt" cities of the industrial North and Midwest. Figure 13.1 identifies the fifteen most segregated and the fifteen least segregated metropolitan areas in the United States as of 1990. For example, according to Figure 13.1, Detroit, Chicago, and Cleveland seem to be about as segregated as they ever have been since these kinds of measurements were first made in the early 1960s, and these three metropolitan areas remain among the most highly segregated in the United States. However, Farley and Frey, using measures similar to those of Taeuber and Taeuber (1965) to measure changes in segregation scores between 1980 and 1990, have also concluded that there have been some measurable decreases in residential segregation, but that these have largely tended to be in the smaller metropolitan areas of the South and West, such as Charlottsville,

Virginia; Lawton, Oklahoma; or Cheyenne, Wyoming (see Figure 13.1; also see Weeks, 1996, pp. 415–417).

POVERTY AND UNEMPLOYMENT IN THE BLACK GHETTO

Residential segregation and the resulting de facto school segregation in urban areas are still major barriers to full equality for blacks (Marger, 1999, p. 280), and blacks are still about two and one-half times more likely to suffer from poverty than whites (U.S. Bureau of the Census, *Poverty in the United States*, 1997). The changing nature of the American economy has made it far more difficult for blacks to escape from the insecurities of poverty and unemployment than for the European immigrants before them. When the European immigrants were arriving in large numbers, America was in the process of becoming an urban-industrial society. To build its major cities, the country needed great pools of unskilled labor. The immigrants provided the labor, gained an economic foothold, and thereby enabled their children and grandchildren the opportunities to move up to skilled, white-collar, and professional employment (Gold, 1982, pp. 314–315).

The blacks, who migrated to the urban centers much later, for the most part arrived with skills comparable to those of the earlier European immigrants of the late nineteenth and early twentieth centuries. But by this time, unskilled labor was far less essential than before, and unskilled blue-collar jobs of all kinds were decreasing in numbers and importance as a source of new employment opportunities (see chapter 7). Thus, the black migrants, unlike the earlier European migrants before them, found much fewer employment

Abandoned and boarded up apartment building in a deteriorating ethnic neighborhood

opportunities in the cities. They had arrived too late, and the unskilled labor that they had to offer was no longer in great demand.

Compounding the problems of black employment opportunities was that whatever industrial growth and development that had occurred in the last three or four decades of the twentieth century had not taken place in the cities in which blacks had settled. These, including many industrial cities, such as Detroit, Cleveland, or Pittsburgh, were already leveling off or declining in economic growth (see Bluestone and Harrison, 1982). Most of the economic growth during this period had largely occurred in the outlying parts of the suburban belts surrounding the older cities. Therefore, the many kinds of new jobs that had been created as a result of the growth and dispersal of industry and commerce to the suburbs were often beyond the geographic reach of low-income inner city workers (see Wilson, 1987, 1996). The lack of effective or low cost public transportation between many central cities and their outlying areas, or the high costs of private automobile transportation, made it virtually impossible for low-income inner-city residents to seek work and to commute to the areas in which jobs potentially would have been more available. The rapidly growing entry of married women into the labor force (see chapter 10) had also compounded the employment problems for blacks because many more women were now competing for jobs with both teenage and adult black workers (see chapter 10).

As a result of these factors, along with the persistence of some of the traditional forms of racial prejudice and discrimination, urban blacks continue to experience higher unemployment rates than do white Americans. In 1998, the official unemployment rate for blacks was 7.3 percent of the civilian labor force, slightly more than twice the 3.5 percent unemployment rate of whites, and this difference has persisted throughout most of the 1990s (*Statistical Abstract of the United States,* 1999, p. 432). For black teenagers in search of work, the problem is much greater. In 1998 the unemployment rate for blacks aged sixteen to nineteen years of age was 27.6 percent, more than double the rate for white teenagers and more than six times the national unemployment rate of 4.5 percent. Similar gaps in black and white teenage unemployment have persisted for decades, whether the overall state of the economy was good or poor, and many employment experts believe that the actual unemployment rate for young blacks in urban ghettos is even higher. Official unemployment statistics only include those who actively have been seeking work for a given period of time. But many black teenagers, even those not in school full time, have lost hope of finding work in their neighborhoods and have given up the search. This group is not included in official labor force statistics and therefore is not included among the "officially" unemployed. This condition is a source of continuous frustration and unrest among many young unemployed urban blacks, and the resulting potential for crime, drug dealing, or violence has been referred to some observers as "social dynamite."

THE GROWING BLACK MIDDLE CLASS

To focus entirely on poor and underemployed blacks is somewhat misleading, for as Marger (1999, p. 281) and others suggest, at least two somewhat separate and distinct social classes now exist within the urban black community. One of these is the one described earlier, which has the grim potential of getting locked in as a semi-permanent "underclass." The other is one that is becoming increasingly middle class by most conventional standards. Some changes have been taking place as the result of the civil rights revolution of the recent past that has meant positive social and economic gains for the middle-class segment of the black minority. Also some measurable differences between blacks and whites reflecting past restriction imposed by racial discrimination have begun to diminish, such as differences in income, education, occupation, life expectancy, and levels of political participation. For example, the median income for black households was only 61 percent of that of white households in 1970, but by 1997, it had increased slightly to 64 percent of that of white households. Likewise, the percentage of black households earning $75,000 per year or over increased by more than 260 percent between 1970 and 1997, whereas the percentage of white households earning this amount or over merely doubled during this same period (see *Statistical Abstract of the United States,* 1999, Table Nos. 742 and 743).

Gains for middle-class blacks can also be seen in the occupational arena. The most prestigious and often the best paying occupations in the U.S. labor force are in managerial and professional categories. Managerial specialties include occupations, such as executives, administrators, officials, managers, accountants and auditors, whereas some of the professional specialties include architects, engineers, mathematical and computer scientists, physicians, dentists, college and university teachers, lawyers, judges, editors, reporters, and the like. Between 1983 and 1998, blacks became a larger percentage of the total number of workers in every one of the occupations listed above (*Statistical Abstract of the United States,* 1999, Table 675). This was also true for a large variety of technical, sales, and clerical positions which are also among the more desirable white-collar occupations. For example, blacks went from constituting only 7.5 percent of all statistical clerks in 1983 to 19.4 percent in 1998 (U.S. Bureau of Labor Statistics, *Employment and Earnings,* January 1999).

Many of these economic and occupational gains were highly related to educational gains for blacks over the past several decades, as attained education level differences between blacks and whites have also begun to diminish. In 1960, only 20.1 percent of blacks had completed four years or more of high school, but by 1998, 76 percent had attained this educational level. Only 3.1 percent of blacks had completed four years of college or more in 1960 and the percent reaching this level of educational attainment grew to 14.7 percent in 1998 (*Statistical Abstract of the United States,* 1999, No. 263). An increasing portion of urban blacks now complete postgraduate professional training and advanced degrees, and the attained education levels for some portions of the black middle class has become higher than for the comparable white population. For example, many black female professional workers had attained a higher educational level than many comparable white female professional workers (Gold, 1982, p. 317).

Within the central cities of U.S. metropolitan areas, some residential stratification between lower income and middle-class blacks had begun to occur by the beginning of the 1980s, with middle-class blacks moving into new, formerly white neighborhoods on the periphery of the city, while the lower "underclasses" remained in the older portions of the inner city (Gold, 1982). This should not obscure the fact that even most middle-class blacks still remain largely segregated from their white suburban counterparts. Thus, economic gains for middle-class blacks have not meant assimilation into larger middle-class white society. In this area, various forms of racial prejudice and more subtle forms of social discrimination still persist.

As a result, when many responsible whites and blacks of similar social status attempt to interact socially in today's changing but uncertain racial climate, a great deal of mutual distrust, suspicion, and misunderstanding still occurs. This conclusion is well documented with convincing anecdotal evidence reported by Ellis Cose (1993), a prominent newspaper editor and investigative reporter, in a book aptly entitled *A Rage of a Privileged Class.* He identifies a wide range of pejorative snubs, slurs, insults, indignities, and condescending remarks routinely suffered by well-educated, middle-class black professionals in their routine daily encounters with the white middle-class majority. Thus it would appear that not too much has really changed regarding attitudes toward black-white relationships during the past several decades, since when in 1977, an unpublished study by Reynolds Farley indicated that a large majority of white respondents and a smaller but still significant minority of blacks would feel "uncomfortable" living in a racially balanced community that was 50 percent white and 50 percent black (*Detroit Free Press,* December 15, 1977).

BLACK POLITICAL REPRESENTATION AND COMMUNITY CONTROL

During the peak of the civil rights revolution in the late 1960s and early 1970s, one of the most persuasive and justified grievances within the black community was the lack of adequate political representation and influence. The concept of "black power" had become a significant and widely repeated symbol of this concern during that period.

With respect to community power and control, the experience of blacks in the urban ghettos has also been different from that of the earlier European ethnic minorities. *The Report of the National Advisory Commission on Civil Disorders* (1968, pp. 279–280) suggests that this difference is one important factor in explaining why blacks had been unable to escape from poverty and the lack of opportunity to the same extent as the white ethnic groups before them. The white immigrants had settled for the most part in rapidly growing cities that had at the time powerful and expanding political machines, which gave them economic favors in exchange for political support. The political machines were decentralized among the various ethnic wards of the cities, and ward-level grievance machinery enabled the immigrants to make their voices heard and their power felt. The immigrants were also able to enter politics directly by joining the machines as ward "heelers" and in other positions. Because the local political machines exercised considerable influence over the construction of public buildings, roads, bridges, subways, parks, or other public endeavors, they were able to provide lots of employment opportunities for their white immigrant voters. White ethnic groups as public employees thus often came to dominate municipal services, such as police and fire departments, municipal welfare departments, pubic transportation and sanitation departments, and, eventually, public school systems as well (Gold 1982, pp. 318–319).

By the time the blacks had arrived, the situation had altered dramatically. The large wave of municipal construction projects had greatly diminished, and the political machines were no longer so powerful and so well equipped or willing to provide jobs, political appointments, or other favors. In many cities the political machines succumbed to reform movements that in many ways provided needed improvements in the political management of cities. The reform groups promised greater efficiency; elimination of the "spoils" system that had fostered nepotism, cronyism, graft, and corruption; and cleaner and more fair elections. The reform groups also may have been nominally more liberal on race issues, but in actuality they often were dominated by middle-class, professional, and church groups that were unskilled or uncomfortable with minorities and believed that coalitions with any low-income groups, white or black, were too "unsavory" and "unbecoming" to their reform objectives (Gold 1982, p. 319; see also chapter 8). As a result, blacks were effectively excluded from patronage jobs and political appointments based on recognition of blacks as a legitimate interest group, and were strongly underrepresented on city councils or on the governing boards of vital city agencies.

Interestingly, cities such as Chicago and New York, with some form of political machines with strong links to neighborhoods still persisting into the late 1960s, were able to avoid the civil disturbances and riots that had occurred in the black ghettoes of many other large American cities. Although there are many other valid explanations for this complex phenomenon, it is fair to conclude that the political officials in these two cities were probably better informed about conditions in the ghettos because of better links to them through the ward structures of the local political machines. Thus they were probably more responsive in foreseeing and dealing with the kinds of grievances, unrest, and provocative incidents associated with the riots and heading them off, than cities without such machines, such as Detroit, Cincinnati, or Tampa (see *Report of the National Advisory Commission on Civil Disorders,* 1968, pp. 42–52, and 84–108; see also chapter 8).

The last several decades have seen the gradual movement of blacks into municipal jobs and into key decision-making positions in local government. For example, cities such as Atlanta; Detroit; Washington, DC; Philadelphia; Baltimore; San Fransisco; Newark, NJ; and Gary, Indiana now have black mayors at the time of this writing; also so have had New York City, Los Angeles, and Cleveland less recently. Many cities now have strong black representation on city councils and on the governing boards of many vital community service agencies. Detroit, for example, now has not only a black mayor (a former associate justice on the Michigan Supreme Court), but also a strong black majority on the city council, a black school superintendent, a black-dominated school board, a black police commissioner, and many black judges. Much of this change, which now often goes far beyond the mere "tokenism" of the past, has come about as a result of the increasing proportion of blacks in big city populations. It is also a result of blacks' greater political awareness, sophistication, and participation, as well as improved black political organization at the local level. At the national level during the past several decades, there have been at least two black U.S. senators, a "Black Caucus" which includes at least forty representatives of the House of Representatives who are black, and as of the year 2000, a sprinkling of blacks were in top federally appointed positions, including one Supreme Court justice (the first black Supreme Court justice, Thurgood Marshall, had recently passed away), a number of other black federal judges, and blacks who are now serving, or have recently served, in such federal positions as surgeon general of the United States, chairman of the Joint Chiefs of Staff, U.S. ambassador to the United Nations, chairman of the Federal Communications Commission, solicitor general of the United States, and a member of the Federal Reserve Board. Finally, there are, or have been, a variety of black cabinet secretaries in the Executive Branch of the U.S. Government, including a present or former secretary of commerce, deputy secretary of the Department of Justice, secretary of housing and urban development, secretary of labor, secretary of veterans affairs, and a secretary of transportation, among others. By the end of the twentieth century, the black population had become a potentially strong force in American political life at local, state, and national levels, and at least some politicians and lawmakers at all levels of government have become increasingly sensitive to black interests. This has helped to increase dignity and self-respect among many black groups, as well as rising hopes for further social, economic, and political gains in the twenty-first century.

SOME POLICY ALTERNATIVES FOR BLACK AMERICA

Although recent trends indicate that blacks are gaining in jobs, education, and local political influence, they have by no means achieved parity with whites. It is also apparent, as already suggested, that for the most part they have remained residentially and socially separated from most of white American society. In 1968, a basic conclusion of the National Advisory Commission on Civil Disorders was that "our nation is moving toward two societies, one Black, one White—separate and unequal." A year later, the Urban Coalition and Urban America, Inc., jointly published a study entitled *One Year After,* which concluded that "we are a year closer to being two societies, black and White, increasingly separate and unequal" (*New York Times,* March 2, 1969). Much more recently, residential segregation of blacks has been called an "American apartheid system" by Massey and Denton (1993), and many others have similarly concluded that this pattern appears to be largely the result of discrimination on the part of Whites (see Feagin and Feagin, 1997; Alba and Logan, 1991; Weeks, 1996; Hacker, 1992).

Racial segregation (separation) continues to remain a very real prospect for the foreseeable future in the United States. Pluralism or integration (assimilation) are alternatives advocated by many social scientists and civil right proponents as potential solutions to the current problems of poor race relations in the United States. Some of the possible prospects and consequences for each of these three alternatives are considered below:

Segregation

Segregation or involuntary separatism is, of course, the alternative that has long been favored by white segregationists, including extremist white supremacist groups, such as various Ku Klux Klan, neo-Nazi, skinhead, or white Aryan resistance groups, many of whom advocate violence as the ultimate means for keeping "white Aryans" from racial "contamination." Studies reported by Feagin and Feagin (1997, p. 234) estimate that there were about twenty thousand active members of such groups in the early 1990s, with perhaps another one hundred eighty thousand less active supporters "who read their literature or come to gatherings." The efficacy of such groups, depends, of course, on the degree to which their goals, if not their tactics, are supported, tolerated, ignored, or rejected by the larger white community.

Separatism has also been advocated in different forms by some black groups. The late Marcus Garvey, for example, led a back-to-Africa movement that had thousands of black followers in the 1920s (Scarpitti and Andersen, 1989, p. 241). In the 1970s, some groups of young black nationalists and supporters of the Black Power Movement strongly argued that a separate state for blacks should be created within the boundaries of the continental United States (Gold, 1982, p. 320). But most blacks have rejected racial separatism as a real solution to America's racial problems, as have a large majority of America's social scientists. Horton et al. (1997, pp. 289–290) argue that segregation maintains undesirable social distance, channeling the races into the kinds of contact that create and reinforce prejudice, while at the same time preventing the sorts of contacts between them that reduce prejudice. Segregation, they further argue, has failed in its primary objective of preventing racial conflicts, "at least in a society in which democratic values make segregation frustrating to blacks and embarrassing to whites." Others have suggested that under segregation, whites increasingly learn about blacks, and blacks only learn about whites from the mass media, because they have little direct contact with each other, and this contributes to suspicion, mistrust, and misunderstanding. To the extent that residential segregation also leads to continuing segregation within the public schools (in spite of failed past efforts to desegregate the schools through busing), many educators see school segregation as "socially dangerous and politically harmful to all students, regardless of their race" (Wilkerson, 1991). This is because young people would not have learned to live cooperatively in an increasingly diversified world (Curran and Renzetti, 1996, pp. 280–281). In the 1990s, sporadic episodes of racial tensions, prejudice, and acts of violence on college campuses between white and black students who never previously had opportunities to interact cooperatively clearly illustrate this point. Racially segregated public schools are probably not the best settings in which to teach racial understanding, harmony, and cooperation.

Pluralism

Pluralism is a more subtle and complex alternative that has increasingly been endorsed by some social scientists (see Henslin, 1996, pp. 307–308; Curry, Jiobu, and Schwirian, 1999). Pluralism is a condition wherein each ethnic or racial group maintains its distinctive identification and a degree of autonomy. Such autonomy implies that ethnic and racial groups also would choose to live in ethnically homogeneous neighborhoods and maintain distinctive ethnic cultural patterns. A key element of pluralism is the idea of choice, for pluralists differ from segregationists in that they advocate voluntary rather than involuntary patterns of ethnic and racial distinctiveness (Gold, 1982, p. 321) They sometimes further argue that pluralism need not produce inequality in the status of or the relationships between various majority and minority ethnic and racial groupings.

The pluralistic alternative has been romantically attractive to a variety of American ethnics, particularly those who are seeing to establishing a positive sense of their ethnic "roots." Whitney M. Young Jr., a former influential black leader, had previously articulated this ideal, as it would apply to blacks: "In the contest of positive pluralism Black people would enter the dominant white society with a sense of roots. By now, we ought to see the fatal flaw of the old melting-pot theory, which sought to strip people of culture and traditions in order to transform everyone into middle-class, white Anglo-Saxons" (Young, 1969, p. 152). Andrew Greeley (1971, pp. 15–16), a social scientist who writes from a white ethnic Catholic perspective, had previously stated the ideal of pluralism for white ethnic groups in a similar way, but he rightly qualified his support for pluralism by raising the realistic possibilities that the tensions and diversities of pluralism could lead to a "narrow, frightened and suspicious society" rather than to a "richer, fuller human society" if pluralism is not properly directed. Stark (1998, pp. 275–277) further clarifies some of the ambiguities, contradictions, and dilemmas regarding the possible outcomes of cultural pluralism by identifying some of them: *assimilation, accommodation, extermination, expulsion,* or the emergence of a *caste system.* The history of the New World contains all of these methods of resolving issues generated by pluralism, both negative and positive, according to Stark.

Integration

Integration, or assimilation, is the alternative that is closest to the American ideals of equality of opportunity and fairness, if not the current American reality. It is the alternative most often advocated by civil rights proponents, and most social scientists would also probably support it, if they believed it to be at all possible to achieve under present or foreseeable circumstances. The main areas of disagreement among those who advocate racial integration have been about how fast the process of integration should proceed, how complete the integration should be, the degree to which it should be facilitated by planned social change, and the degree to which it should be required by legislation and/or direct governmental intervention.

For example, one of the most comprehensive proposals for increasing racial integration and decreasing residential segregation was by political scientist, Morton Grodzins. His proposal included (1) controlled migration of blacks into white neighborhoods; (2) returning white populations to central cities; (3) the suburbanization of blacks; and (4) moving blacks out of big cities into smaller cities, where they were underrepresented (Grodzins, 1967, pp. 141–151). But Grodzins did not sufficiently identify the mechanism through which such massive redistribution of both black and white populations could be accomplished, nor did he suggest specific ways in which much expected bitter opposition to such measures could be placated. And, of course, such policies have never materialized or have ever really been attempted at anywhere near the scale of Grodzins's proposals.

Pettigrew (1971, pp. 325–328) had strongly supported a course of action directed toward more complete integration, as advocated by Grodzins and many others, but he also had recognized that, given the magnitude of the problems and the degree of likely resistance, such an alternative, even if it were eventually successful, could not happen quickly enough to alleviate the long standing problems of the then existing large urban ghettoes. Therefore, in addition to maintaining a major effort toward racial integration, he also advocated a simultaneous effort to "enrich" the existing ghettoes. Such proposed enrichment efforts included restructuring the economics of the ghetto, especially, by developing urban cooperatives. Effective job training programs and some reordering of big city public school systems so that blacks would have a greater input into their programs and policies were also among the enrichment programs that Pettigrew recommended.

It seems remarkable that twenty-five years later, a quarter of a century after Pettigrew made his proposals, sociologist William Julius Wilson (1996, chapter 8) has found it necessary to make essentially the same set of proposals as those by Pettigrew (1971) for enriching poor inner city neighborhoods with greater economic, educational, and training opportunities. Wilson recognized the same kinds of barriers to economic success for residents of these socioeconomically and racially segregated inner city areas, as had Pettigrew and many others before both of them, namely, racial prejudice and discrimination, and the flight of white residents, economic enterprises, and, most importantly, jobs and work opportunities, away from the inner city areas into largely white enclaves in the suburbs.

Wilson, like Pettigrew, had recognized the negative effects of residential segregation as well, by asserting that living in segregated ghettos creates barriers to employment and adequate employment preparation. Wilson does not express any expectation of future residential desegregation or integration, nor does he advocate such a policy. As he put it, " 'a federal policy of rapid desegregation in housing is a political and practical impossibility.' As long as there are areas to which whites can retreat, it will be difficult to reduce the overall level of segregation. Blacks move in, Whites move out" (Wilson, 1996, p. 200). Where Pettigrew differed in 1971 was that he still held out hope for future integration by cautioning that enrichment programs in the racially segregated black ghettos must contain safeguards to ensure that they would not become counterproductive and hinder later residential dispersal and integration. The prospect that such hope is justified has certainly dimmed in the now approximately thirty years since it was expressed by Pettigrew, but only the future will tell if it was just a dream, or, as they say in show business, still has "legs."

As it now stands, according to a recent *New York Times* national survey, "most Americans do not live, work or worship with those of other races." Eighty-three percent of the whites polled said they worked with only a few blacks or not at all. Ninety percent of whites who attend religious services at least once a month said that none or only a few of their fellow churchgoers were black, while 73 percent of blacks said that almost all of their fellow congregants were black. Two-thirds of blacks also said that "politicians talked too little about race," and thought that improving race relations was one of the most important challenges facing the country. Only one-fourth of whites said it was one of the most important challenges. Whites were also more than three times as likely as blacks to say that "too much had been made in recent years of the problems facing black people" (Sack and Elder, 2000, pp. A1, A23).

HISPANIC AMERICANS

The Hispanic population is one of the fastest growing segments of the United States. Between 1970 and 1999, the number of Hispanics nearly tripled from 10.6 million to 31.2 million (*New York Times Almanac,* 2000). By the year 2010, the U.S. Census Bureau projects that the Hispanic population will become the largest minority in the United States at

41.1 million people, surpassing the projected 37.4 million blacks by that time (*Statistical Abstract of the United States,* 1999). The rapid rates of growth, both past and projected into the future, are due to higher migration and fertility rates than for non-Hispanic populations.

The term Hispanic refers broadly to people of Spanish or Spanish-American origins, and a majority of American Hispanics trace their roots to Mexico, Puerto Rico, or Cuba; many others come from other Central and South American countries as well. They also vary significantly, according to social class, urban or rural backgrounds, and vast cultural differences, Thus, they do not comprise a uniform or cohesive population group. The largest group of U.S. Hispanics is of Mexican origin and contains over 63 percent of all Hispanic Americans. The second largest group is Puerto Rican and constitutes about 10.6 percent of the U.S. Hispanic population, and Cubans or Cuban Americans are the third largest segment of the U.S. Hispanic population at 4.2 percent of the total.

Table 13.2   Hispanic Population of Metropolitan Areas, 1980–90

RANK/METROPOLITAN AREA	1980	1990	POPULATION CHANGE, 1980–90	
			Number	*Percent*
1. Los Angeles-Anaheim-Riverside, Calif. CMSA	2,755,914	4,779,118	2,023,204	73.4%
2. New York-Northern New Jersey-Long Island, N.Y.-N.J.-Conn. CMSA	2,050,998	2,777,951	726,953	35.4
3. Miami-Fort Lauderdale, Fla. CMSA	621,309	1,061,846	440,537	70.9
4. San Francisco-Oakland, San Jose, Calif. CMSA	660,190	970,403	310,213	47.0
5. Chicago-Gary-Lake County, Ill.-Ind.-Wis. CMSA	632,443	893,422	260,979	41.3
6. Houston-Galveston-Brazoria, Tex. CMSA	448,460	772,295	323,835	72.2
7. San Antonio, Tex. MSA	481,511	620,290	138,779	28.8
8. Dallas-Fort Worth, Tex. CMSA	247,823	518,917	271,094	109.4
9. San Diego, Calif. MSA	275,177	510,781	235,604	85.6
10. El Paso, Tex. MSA	297,001	411,619	114,618	38.6
11. Phoenix, Ariz. MSA	199,003	345,498	146,495	73.6
12. McAllen-Edinburg-Mission, Tex. MSA	230,212	326,972	96,760	42.0
13. Fresno, Calif. MSA	150,790	236,634	85,844	56.9
14. Denver-Boulder, Colo. CMSA	173,687	226,200	52,513	30.2
15. Philadelphia-Wilmington-Trenton, Pa.-N.J.-Del.-Md. CMSA	147,902	225,868	77,966	52.7
16. Washington, D.C.-Md.-Va. MSA	94,968	224,786	129,818	136.7
17. Brownsville-Harlingen, Tex. MSA	161,654	212,995	51,341	31.8
18. Boston-Lawrence-Salem, Mass.-N.H. CMSA	92,463	193,199	100,736	108.9
19. Corpus Christi, Tex. MSA	158,119	181,860	23,741	15.0
20. Albuquerque, N. Mex. MSA	154,620	178,310	23,690	15.3
21. Sacramento, Calif. MSA	105,665	172,374	66,709	63.1
22. Tucson, Ariz. MSA	111,418	163,262	51,844	46.5
23. Austin, Tex. MSA	94,367	159,942	65,575	69.5
24. Bakersfield, Calif. MSA	87,026	151,995	64,969	74.7
25. Tampa-St. Petersburg-Clearwater, Fla. MSA	80,265	139,248	58,983	73.5

Source: U.S. Bureau of the Census.

Other Hispanics in the United States come from Nicaragua, El Salvador, Guatemala, and other Spanish-speaking countries of Central and South America. Since the U.S. Census Bureau first began recognizing Central and South American immigrants to the United States as a distinct population category in 1982, their numbers have been growing, and by 1997, they numbered 4.3 million people, or 14.4 percent of the total U.S. Hispanic population (*New York Times Almanac,* 2000). Because the urban experiences of each of the three largest Hispanic groups in the United States differ markedly, each is discussed separately.

Mexican Americans

Labeling for this group has varied extensively, including terms such as "Latino," "Latin American," "Chicano," "Tehanos," or "Hispanos." The lack of agreement on an appropriate label is indicative of the unresolved struggles within this group for an acceptable common identity. The term "Mexican American" is used here for consistency. The large concentration of Mexican Americans in the southwestern states derives from a complex history that began more than four centuries ago, when Texas, California, and other states of the region were territories that were colonized by Spain via Mexico. Through frequent military conflict throughout the nineteenth century, the region was ultimately acquired and dominated by the United States. There was a rapid influx of Anglo-American (non-Mexican) settlers during this period, and by 1900, Anglos were a majority in every southwestern state except New Mexico, where Mexican Americans remained a majority until about 1950 (Gold, 1982).

Mexican Americans had continued to migrate to the United States throughout the twentieth century, for a variety of reasons. For example, the Mexican Revolution, which began in 1909, forced hundreds of thousands of peons from agricultural lands to seek employment elsewhere. At the same time, agriculture was expanding rapidly in the U.S. border states, where a large labor force was now needed. Massive Mexican immigration to the southwestern states was thus triggered, and much of the Mexican-American population today is derived from this early twentieth-century movement.

The Great Depression of the 1930s and World War II, which followed, hit Mexican Americans especially hard, and many more than ever before were driven to the cities in search of better opportunities. After the war, migration to the cities continued to accelerate, and by 1997, there were over 6 million Mexican Americans living in the Los Angeles Consolidated Metropolitan Statistical Area, where they comprised 38.5 percent of the total population (*Statistical Abstract of the United States,* 1999). San Francisco, San Diego, San Antonio, Houston, Austin, Albuquerque, Phoenix, and Tucson are all further examples of large metropolitan areas of the southwest now containing the largest concentrations of Mexican American residents. It has been estimated that the Los Angeles metropolitan area alone probably contains in its *barrios* (a Spanish word for "neighborhood") more people of Mexican ancestry than any Mexican city, except Mexico City and Guadalajara (Gold, 1982). In all, there were about 19.8 million Mexican Americans living in the United States by 1998 (*Statistical Abstract of the United States,* 1999).

Generalizations about the urban living conditions of Mexican Americans are made hazardous by the group's diversity and by the fact that the U.S. Census does not always make distinctions between Hispanics of Mexican origin from other Hispanics in data on such vital characteristics, such as employment, occupation, and income. But other sources do reveal that Mexican American workers tend to be concentrated in low-skilled, poorly paid work and are socioeconomically near the bottom of the U.S. income scale. They tend to earn more money with less education than do blacks throughout the Southwest, but because of a preponderance of young, large families with high birthrates, the income per person tends to be below that of blacks. They earn about 70 percent of what whites earn, and almost one-third live in poverty (Curry, Jiobu, and Schwirian, 1999, p. 209).

In 1998, Mexican Americans still had the lowest levels of educational attainment than of any other major Hispanic groups, and still lower levels than that of blacks or whites. For example, only 48.3 percent of Mexican Americans twenty-five years of age or older had completed four or more years of high school, compared with 55.5 percent for all Hispanics, 76 percent for blacks, and 83.7 percent for whites. Also only 7.5 percent of Mexican Americans had completed four more years of college, compared with 11 percent for all Hispanics, 14.7 percent for blacks, and 25 percent for whites (*Statistical Abstract of the United States,* 1999, Table No. 263). At least some of the above kinds of inequality comes from the high levels of prejudice and discrimination faced by Mexican Americans. Like African Americans, they have been subject to segregation and discrimination in housing, schools, and public facilities (Curran and Renzetti, 1996, p.147). These problems include public education that is often segregated, inferior, and culturally intolerant of Mexican Americans. Although not as spatially or socially segregated as blacks, some deliberate patterns of past housing discrimination directed against Mexican Americans have been documented (see Gold, 1982, p. 324).

It has been argued that many Mexican Americans have long occupied a marginal position in American society for the following reasons: (1) the great diversity of the group across region, age, and social class; (2) the accessibility of the U.S.–Mexican Border, which allows new immigrants to move easily back and forth between Mexican and U.S. society; (3) the recency and extent of the group's massive migration to the cities; (4) the history of bruising encounters with the Border Patrol, Immigration and Naturalization Service, Texas Rangers, and local police; (5) being the largest minority in the United States with an actively maintained world language (Spanish) other than English; and finally (6) the continuous conflict between assimilating in an Anglo-dominated society while trying to retain a distinctive culture (Pettigrew, 1976).

Yet there is growing ethnic awareness, consciousness, and pride among Mexican Americans, which is reflected in various ways. The land protests in New Mexico, the farm labor protests and efforts to organize farm labor unions in California, and the student-inspired Chicano movement were all efforts to solve problems of marginality and to produce positive social and economic gains through collective action, cultural pride, or greater militancy (Gold, 1982, p. 325). Like blacks, Mexican Americans have become more sophisticated and active in the political area. An increasing number have been elected to political office at the local, state, and nation levels, including some members of the U.S. House of Representatives; at least three had been appointed to President Clinton's administration as Cabinet officers; one has served as the U.S. ambassador to the United Nations; and both the Democratic and Republican political parties were aggressively seeking Mexican American support during the year 2000 national elections. These developments indicate the probable future direction of the Mexican American minority in its efforts to win more complete acceptance in American society on its own cultural terms.

Puerto Ricans

Puerto Ricans are the second largest Hispanic community in urban America. With about 3.2 million people, they constitute 10.6 percent of all Hispanic Americans (*New York Times Almanac,* 2000, p. 287). More than half of all Puerto Ricans in the United States are found within the New York metropolitan region, with large concentrations in East Harlem ("Spanish Harlem"), the South Bronx, Bedford Stuyvesant, and Brownsville. But urban Puerto Ricans have been residentially mobile, and movements to other cities, such as Philadelphia, Boston, or Chicago have become increasingly more common. Puerto Ricans have been socioeconomically worse off as a group than other Hispanic groups, as reflected in lower median family incomes and in higher poverty rates (U.S. Bureau of the Census, 1995). They also fall behind in levels of educational attainment at both the secondary and college levels (*Statistical Abstract of the United States,* 1999, No. 263). This may, in part, be due to the fact that as U.S. citizens, Puerto Ricans are able to move back and forth freely and frequently between their home island of Puerto Rico and the mainland of the United States. Thus, migration from New York to Puerto Rico has become commonplace in recent decades, but this has tended to create a problem for the Puerto Rican communities in New York and other large cities, because it is the professionally, technically, and managerially trained "elite" members of the community who produce a loss of leadership potential and a "brain drain" by their disproportionate representation among the out-migrants. On the other hand, the in-migrants are more likely to come from among the most impoverished, inexperienced, and undereducated segments of the Puerto Rican population, and these characteristics tend to keep average measures of economic or educational gains lower than they otherwise would be. Further, because a large percentage of Puerto Ricans are dark skinned, they are much more likely to suffer from the same kinds of prejudices and levels of discrimination experienced by blacks and are similarly more likely to be segregated from whites than members of other Hispanic groups (Macionis and Parrillo, 1998).

Because they share many of the same kinds of disadvantages as blacks, one might have expected more joint efforts between Puerto Ricans and blacks in the struggle to improve their common lot. In some instances, Puerto Ricans have joined in common endeavors with black political and community organizations. But these Puerto Rican-Black coalitions have been based for the most part on single issues and have been generally short lived (Padilla, 1972). Puerto Ricans tend to identify strongly with their Spanish heritage, a condition that overrides racial considerations. Also, they have an expressed preference for "looking white" and have greater opportunities for bypassing racial oppression and achieving social mobility, factors that may serve to limit stronger associations with activist black groups (Gold, 1982). However, urban Puerto Ricans, like blacks and many other disadvantaged minorities, began in the 1960s to express more conscious dissatisfaction and unrest and to develop a much stronger sense of political identity. Since then they

Volunteers tending a display at a Miami street fair for a Cuban American civic organization

have more aggressively entered the political arena of the cities and states in which they reside in large numbers to make demands for greater justice and better treatment. These political efforts have now begun to reach the national levels of Congress and the federal bureaucracy.

Cuban Americans

This group numbered about 1.3 million people in 1998 and constituted 4.2 percent of the total number of Hispanics in the United States. (*New York Times Almanac,* 2000). Because it is so highly concentrated in the south Florida communities of Miami, Dade County, and the Miami–Fort Lauderdale Consolidated Metropolitan Statistical Area and is virtually nonexistent in most other parts of the United States (except for a visible enclave in New Jersey), it was a group that was hardly known to most Americans—that is, until the winter and spring of 2000, when it became highly visible because of the vast amount of mass media attention given to the saga of Elian Gonzalez. The attention to the conflict between Elian's father and his Miami relatives, and their Cuban American supporters in Miami, over whether Elian should be returned to Cuba with his father or should be granted asylum to remain in Miami in the custody of his great uncle and cousins, also alerted many Americans to the existence of a metropolitan community that had become socially, economically, politically, and demographically dominated by a well-organized and cohesive Cuban American ethnic majority, most of whose members had not arrived in the United States until after 1960. Sometimes referred to as "Little Havana," Miami has been described in a news report as having been ethnically "fractured" by the divisiveness of this issue between its Cuban subcommunity and its non-Cuban white, racial, and ethnic minorities. In the same news report, Max Castro, a sociologist at the University of Miami, has further described the daily demonstrations over the custody of Elian Gonzalez as "the most emotionally divisive issue in this community" (*Detroit News,* July 2, 2000, p. 11A). A brief discussion of the history of Cuban migration to Miami may help to clarify the basis for the current racial, ethnic, and political tensions in that city.

Cubans began to come to the United States in significant numbers in the 1960s, following the revolutionary rise to power of Fidel Castro. Because this revolution imposed a socialist regime in Cuba, the power and wealth of the more socioeconomically successful middle and upper classes became severely threatened. These groups, therefore, became political refugees who migrated to the United States for what they hoped would be a temporary stay until political conditions in Cuba changed to their benefit (Portes et al., 1977). The largest increase in the number of Cubans in the United States came in 1961 during the Cuban airlift and again in 1980 during the Mariel boat lift (*New York Times Almanac,* 2000). These two waves of migration were aided by American immigration policies that basically permitted the entry of the Cuban refugees into the United States without the usual restrictions (Marger, 1999, p. 264). Cuba, by this time, had become a basic element in the Cold War with the communist world, including Cuba under Castro, and, accordingly, the refugees were enthusiastically welcomed. They were provided with educational and financial assistance by the U.S. government, which enabled many of them to establish profitable businesses and professions in the United States.

Because they had been better educated and more economically successful before emigrating, the Cubans fared much better in the United States along these lines, than have Mexican Americans and Puerto Ricans (*Statistical Abstract of the United States,* 1999). In turn, the economic success of many of the earlier migrants enabled them to offer jobs and other forms of assistance to those who came later (Portes and Manning, 1986). In the process, Cuban Americans came to control hundreds of businesses in the Miami area, as well as radio stations, newspapers, churches, private social services, and other ethnically based community institutions. Cuban Americans were also racially perceived as "white" and were therefore not exposed to the added handicap of racial discrimination in the labor or residential marketplace (Marger, 1999, p. 264).

Such success, however, has not been viewed without a certain level of resentment from other minority groups in the Miami area, such as the black groups that were there before them or the more recently arrived Haitian refugees. To these other groups, the Cubans were seen as having unfairly been given favorable treatment, over the less favorable treatment they perceived that they themselves had received as disadvantaged minorities. A major case in point was the extremely vocal and militant demand by a large majority of the Cuban American community that Elian Gonzalez be granted asylum status in the United States, and not returned to Cuba, a demand that was intensified by the continuingly powerful and virulent levels of anti-Castroism (anticommunism) within that group. But, as is often the case, the emotional issues that serve to unite and mobilize an ethnic or racial group toward greater militancy on behalf of its perceived interests may also help to create a backlash among neighboring or competing ethnic or racial groups, who may feel threatened or disadvantaged by such actions. And, according to the *Detroit News* report cited earlier, this represents the current state of affairs in Miami at the time of this writing.

CONTINUING PATTERNS OF ETHNIC DIVERSITY IN URBAN AMERICA

Changing patterns of immigration have continued through most of American history, and almost all of them have had an impact on the racial and ethnic diversity of American cities and metropolitan areas. Patterns of nineteenth-century immigration from a diversity of European societies and cultures into American cities were discussed in some detail in chapter 3, and since then, most of these groups have assimilated into American urban culture and society, or, as a matter of choice, some have chosen to remain in distinct ethnic clusters. For these groups, where and with whom they live is now a matter of their own preferences. This chapter has focused on some of the problems of the more recent urbanization of blacks and Hispanic groups and the difficulties most of them still experience as a result of various forms of prejudice and discrimination. But the story does not end here, because, at the beginning of the twenty-first century, immigration still continues to expand the range of nationalities, races, languages, and cultures represented in the changing mosaic of urban America. For example, the *New York Times* (July 4, 2000, p. A1) reported that by July 2001, California will have become the first large state in which non-Hispanic whites are officially no longer a majority, and that California will become by far the largest proving ground for what it may eventually be like to live in a United States in which no one racial or ethnic group predominates. California's midyear 2000 population included 17.4 million non-Hispanic whites, 10.7 million Hispanics, 3.9 million Asians or

The growing racial and ethnic diversity in Los Angeles is illustrated by teenagers at this stand selling taquitos during a street fair

Pacific Islanders, and 2.3 million blacks. In Los Angeles, where this demographic transition has already occurred, one can find miles of streets in many neighborhoods where signs are printed in "every language but English." New York City's non-Hispanic white population will have declined to only 35 percent of its total population by 2001, and its schools already accommodate children of 196 different nationalities (*New York Times,* November 8, 1999, p. A24). Los Angeles has the largest population of Koreans outside Korea and the largest concentration of Iranians in the Western world (*New York Times,* July 4, 2000, p. A12). Likewise, the Detroit metropolitan area now has the largest Arabic population outside of the Middle East and the largest Russian population outside of the former Soviet Union.

The *New York Times Almanac,* 2000, estimates that at the end of the twentieth-century approximately 750,000 new legal immigrants are arriving in the United States annually and that well over half of these come from Hispanic or Asian backgrounds. Aside from the Hispanic populations already discussed in this chapter, the rank order of the top twenty countries of birth for U.S. immigrants in 1997 include the Philippines, mainland China, Vietnam, India, Russia, the Ukraine, Korea, Pakistan, Poland, Canada, the former Yugoslavia, and the United Kingdom (U.S. Department of Justice, *1997 Statistical Yearbook of the Immigration and Naturalization Service,* 1999). In all, there were over 21 million foreign-born people residing in the United States in 1990, with nearly 24 percent coming from Europe and the Soviet Union, 25 percent from Asia, approximately 39 percent from other North American countries, slightly more than 5 percent from South America, nearly 2 percent from Africa, and 0.6 percent from Oceana (*New York Times Almanac,* 2000). Of course, virtually all of these immigrants head toward large metropolitan areas as their intended areas of residence, with the largest numbers going to New York City and Los Angeles.

Marger (1999, p. 268) argues that the most serious issue that the non-English-speaking immigrants face is that of language, and disputes arise over the use of non-English ballots in elections, language proficiency standards for citizenship, and the use of languages other than English in the workplace. In the schools, the issue revolves around what should be the proper language of instruction for non-English-speaking students. In New York City, according to Marger, classes are taught to foreign-born students in Spanish, Chinese, Haitian Creole, Russian, Korean, Arabic, Vietnamese, Polish, Bengali, and French. Of course, not all American urban schools have been as accommodating as those in New York City, and there have been continuing controversies about teaching in languages other than English in the public schools. For example, in 1998 a referendum was passed in California striking down bilingual classrooms, and more than twenty states had already passed laws making English the "official" language of education and/or public services and activities by 1995.

Marger aptly observes that the absorption of immigrants has always been a persistent issue in American society. The door has always been open to immigrants seeking political refuge or economic opportunity, but the acceptance of new groups has also been countered by repeated efforts to limit or exclude newcomers for both economic and ethnocentric motives (Marger, 1999, p. 269). One can only hope that as America's urban population continues to become more ethnically and racially diversified in a rapidly changing urban world, more cosmopolitan attitudes and responses will eventually prevail.

SELECTED BIBLIOGRAPHY

ALBA, RICHARD, and JOHN LOGAN. "Variations on Two Themes: Racial and Ethnic Patterns and the Attainment of Suburban Residence." *Demography.* 28 (1991): 431–453.

BLUESTONE, BARRY, and BENNETT HARRISON. *The Deindustrialization of America.* New York: Basic Books, 1982.

COSE, ELLIS. *The Rage of a Privileged Class.* New York: Harper Collins, 1993.

CURRAN, DANIEL J., and CLAIRE M. RENZETTI. *Social Problems: Society in Crises,* 4th ed. Boston: Allyn and Bacon, 1996.

CURRY, TIM, ROBERT JIOBU, and KENT SCHWIRIAN. *Sociology for the 21st Century,* 2d. ed. Upper Saddle River, NJ: Prentice-Hall, 1999.

DENTLER, ROBERT A. *Urban Problems: Perspectives and Conclusions.* Skokie, IL: Rand McNally, 1977.

FARLEY, REYNOLDS, and WILLIAM H. FREY. "Changes in the Segregation of Whites from Blacks during the 1980s: Small Steps toward a More Integrated Society." *American Sociological Review.* 1 (February 1994): 23–45.

FEAGIN, JOE R., and CLAIRECE BOOHER FEAGIN. *Social Problems: A Critical Power-Conflict Perspective,* 5th ed. Upper Saddle River, NJ: Prentice-Hall, 1997.

GOLD, HARRY. *The Sociology of Urban Life.* Englewood Cliffs, NJ: Prentice-Hall, 1982.

———, and FRANK R. SCARPITTI, eds. *Combatting Social Problems: Techniques of Intervention.* New York: Holt, Rinehart and Winston, 1967.

GREELEY, ANDREW M. *Why Can't They Be Like Us?* New York: Dutton, 1971.

GRODZINS, MORTON. "The Metropolitan Area as a Racial Problem." In *Combatting Social Problems: Techniques of Intervention,* Harry Gold and Frank R. Scarpitti (eds.). New York: Holt, Rinehart and Winston, 1967.

HACKER, ANDREW. *Two Nations:Black and White, Separate, Hostile, and Unequal.* New York: Scribner's, 1992.

HENSLIN, JAMES M. *Social Problems,* 4th ed. Upper Saddle River, NJ: Prentice-Hall, 1996.

HORTON, PAUL B. et al. *The Sociology of Social Problems,* 12th ed. Upper Saddle River, NJ: Prentice-Hall, 1997.

KRAMER, JOHN (ed.). *North American Suburbs: Politics, Diversity, and Change.* Berkeley, CA: Glendessary Press, 1972.

MACIONIS, JOHN J., and VINCENT N. PARRILLO. *Cities and Urban Life.* Upper Saddle River, NJ: Prentice-Hall, 1998.

MARGER, MARTIN N. *Social Inequality: Patterns and Processes.* Mountain View, CA: Mayfield, 1999.

MASSEY, DOUGLAS S., and NANCY A. DENTON. *American Apartheid: Segregation and the Making of the Underclass.* Cambridge: Harvard University Press, 1993.

MERTON, ROBERT K., and ROBERT NISBET. *Contemporary Social Problems,* 4th ed. New York: Harcourt, Brace, Jovanovich, 1976.

MYRDAL, GUNNAR. *An American Dilemma.* New York: Harper and Row, 1944.

New York Times 2000 Almanac. New York: Penguin Reference Books, 1999.

PADILLA, ELENA. "Race Relations: A Puerto Rican View." In *The City in the Seventies,* Robert K. Yin (ed.). Itasca, IL: F. E. Peacock, 1972.

PETTIGREW, THOMAS. *Racially Separate or Together?* New York: McGraw Hill, 1971.

———. "Race and Inter Group Relations." In *Contemporary Social Problems,* 4th ed., Robert K. Merton and Robert Nisbet (eds.). New York: Harcourt, Brace, Jovanovich, 1976.

PORTES, A., J. M. CLARK, and R. L. BACH. "The New Wave: A Statistical Profile of Recent Cuban Exiles to the United States." *Estudios Cubanos/Cuban Studies.* 7 (1977): 1–32.

PORTES, A., and R. D. MANNING. "The Immigrant Enclave: Theory and Emperical Examples." In *Competitive Ethnic Relations,* S. Olzac (ed.). New York: Academic Press, 1986.

Report of the National Advisory Commission on Civil Disorders. New York: Bantam Books, 1968.

ROSE, ARNOLD. *The Negro in America.* Boston: Beacon Press, 1956.

SACK, KEVIN, and JANET ELDER. "Poll Finds Optimistic Outlook but Enduring Racial Divisions." *New York Times,* July 11, 2000, pp. A1, A23.

SCARPITTI, FRANK R., and MARGARET L. ANDERSEN. *Social Problems.* New York; Harper & Row, 1989.

STARK, RODNEY. *Sociology,* 7th ed. Belmont, CA: Wadsworth, 1998.

Statistical Abstract of the United States: The National Data Book, 119th ed. Washington, DC: U.S. Department of Commerce, October 1999.

TAEUBER, KARL E. "Racial Segregation: The Persisting Dilemma." *The Annals.* 23–45, (November 1975).

———, and ALMA TAEUBER. *Negroes in Cities.* Chicago: Aldine, 1965.

WEEKS, JOHN R. *Population: An Introduction to Concepts and Issues,* 6th ed. Belmont, CA: Wadsworth, 1996.

WILKERSON, I. "Separate Proms Reveal an Unspanned Racial Divide." *New York Times,* September 30, 1991, pp. A1 and A10.

WILSON, WILLIAM JULIUS. *The Truly Disadvantaged: The Inner City, the Underclass, and Public Policy.* Chicago: University of Chicago Press, 1987.

———. *When Work Disappears: The World of the New Urban Poor.* New York: Alfred Knopf, 1996.

WIRTH, LOUIS. "Urbanism as a Way of Life," *American Journal of Sociology* 44 (July 1938), 3–24.

YOUNG, WHITNEY M. JR. *Beyond Racism: Building an Open Society.* New York: McGraw Hill. 1969.

Part V

URBAN PLANNING, SOCIAL POLICY, AND THE URBAN FUTURE

14

URBAN PLANNING AND DEVELOPMENT

The planning of cities is regarded variously as an ivory-tower vision, a practical and necessary program for development, or an undesirable interference with the citizen's freedom to do as he wishes with his own property. Some citizens see planning as a dictatorial force compelling people to do as the government directs. Planners see themselves as servants of the people who are trying to make the city a better place in which to live but who are circumscribed by legal and political restrictions. The truth lies somewhere between these extremes.

— Ralph Thomlinson, 1969

The sociologist David Riesman has earlier (1956) described the city planner hopefully, as a new Renaissance man who ultimately would have great positive influence in shaping the quality of life in modern urban society. But Jane Jacobs (1961) has sharply criticized urban planning in her popular book, *The Death and Decline of American Cities,* which opens with the sentence, "This book is an attack on current city planning and rebuilding." As these opposing images suggest, urban planning is a very controversial and complex field. Many of the recent controversies and debates revolving around urban planning have arisen because it has emerged as a potential source for producing visible and significant changes in the physical, economic, and social structure of modern urban communities.

In general, urban planning is primarily concerned with the most direct physical, social, and economic consequences of urban growth and development as reflected in the general patterns and character of land use, the location of physical structures and facilities, the design of street, transit and other transportation systems, and the nature and distribution of other physical facilities and services considered necessary or desirable for the economic betterment, comfort, convenience and the general welfare of life in urban communities. Taken by themselves, the issues associated with urban planning and related patterns of urban development are of sufficient magnitude and complexity to warrant separate consideration in this chapter.

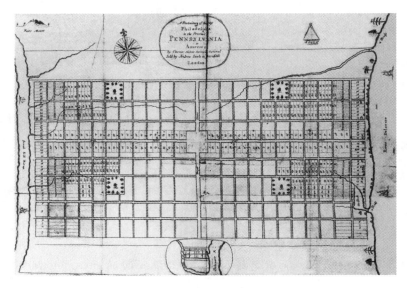

William Penn's master plan for Philadelphia, drawn in 1682.

THE EMERGENCE AND EARLY DEVELOPMENT OF URBAN PLANNING

Planning cities is not a new development, of course, and there are examples of planned cities that go back more than several thousand years (see examples in chapter 2). In the United States, planned cities were a part of its early history: Peter Stuyvesant produced a grid street plan for the early Dutch settlement on the isle of Manhattan; William Penn laid out a planned street system for Philadelphia in 1682; the original plan for Washington, DC, was prepared in 1802; and a plan was made for the fire-swept city of Detroit in 1807. Nevertheless, these were examples of fragmentary, isolated efforts and did not in themselves represent a full-scale movement toward the planned development of American cities. Rather, the emergence of urban planning in the United States can best be understood in the context of a series of at least three historically related and intertwined developments: (1) the emergence of planning as a social movement; (2) the emergence of planning as a legitimate and continuing function of local government; and (3) the emergence of urban planners as a distinct occupational skill group that attempts to apply in practice a specified body of knowledge and techniques, and that occupies a more or less specific set of role positions in the structure of local government.

The origins of city planning as a modern social movement can most accurately be traced back to the demands for social reform in both England and the United States near the middle of the nineteenth century. These demands were a response to some of the conditions associated with the industrial revolution, which brought extremely large numbers of people to the cities and helped create urban slums and blight, overcrowding, and a variety of related health and sanitation problems. The concentration of large numbers of people in relatively small land areas made itself felt in intolerable living conditions and in repeated epidemics of major proportions (see chapter 3). As early as 1834, a sanitary report from New York City called attention to bad housing as a cause of disease, and a second report, submitted in 1842, was even more detailed and insistent in pointing to the relation between the two. The first tangible result of these studies and of agitation for improvement was the creation of a New York City Health Department in 1866 and the passage of the first tenement house law in 1867. In 1879 a law was passed prohibiting the building of rooms without windows, and in the latter part of the nineteenth century, New York and many other large cities began making adequate provision for the disposal of sewage (Gold, 1965, 1976).

A more indirect and somewhat separate attack on the emerging problems of urban overcrowding and congestion was the *recreation movement of* the latter part of the nineteenth century, which concerned itself with the development of large urban parks, the preservation of scenic resources in and around the larger cities, and the development of playgrounds in the more congested urban areas. Under the direction of leading figures of this movement, such as Frederick Law Olmsted, the city of New York laid out Central Park in 1857, and before 1900 park plans had been prepared for many of the larger cities. Many of the early parks were landscape developments designed primarily to preserve natural scenery and provide passive relaxation. But the need for more active recreation was soon recognized, and a demand rose for a comprehensive park system that would supplement large parks with readily accessible neighborhood recreation areas. In 1893 a study of Boston's park requirements stressed the need for such a program and led to legislation creating the Metropolitan Park Commission. This and the similar park program being carried to completion by Kansas City about the same time set a new pattern of comprehensive park planning (Walker, 1950).

However, the fragmentary and isolated efforts being made to ameliorate problems of urban congestion, poor housing, inadequate facilities for transportation, sanitation, and a host of other needed services and developments were inadequate, and around the end of the nineteenth century, recognition grew that a more comprehensive approach to solving these problems was needed. Those interested in these needs began to realize that most of the problems were highly interrelated. It has been suggested that this realization, along with a growing awareness of the necessity of mapping long-range programs and of anticipating future needs and developments, as contrasted with piecemeal corrective measures, produced the mainspring of modern urban planning (Gold, 1965; Scott, 1969).

In England, the same kinds of concerns gave rise to the town planning or the "garden city" movement. Envisaged originally by Ebenezer Howard (1902) and led by such men as Patrick Geddes, this movement called for the creation of new self-sufficient and self-contained new towns or garden cities decentralized from the existing urban centers. It was based for the most part on utopian concepts envisaging a return to the less complex organization and physical appearance of smaller, self-contained, preindustrial communities of the past (Mairet, 1957; Leggitt, 1964).

The new town or garden city movement was influential in the development of numerous experimental communities in England, Europe, and the United States in the early part of the twentieth century. It was not particularly influential in the later development of urban planning in the United States, where the planning of new cities has been limited to a few notable examples, some of which are discussed later in this chapter. For the most part, U.S. planning activities have been focused on replanning and redeveloping existing communities that have already been built (Gold, 1982). Thus, the main experience has been a distinct departure from earlier examples of planned cities and the garden city movement.

Another important aspect of the early phases of the modern city planning movement in the United States was the growing concern by certain civic improvement associations with improving the physical appearance of their communities. Beginning in the last part of the nineteenth century and lasting roughly until World War I, this phase has been identified as the "City Beautiful" movement (Gold, 1976). Partially inspired by the garden city movement, the major emphasis was on the aesthetic appearance of the city, as reflected in civic centers, parks, streets, and urban landscapes. Much of the inspiration for this movement was drawn from the Chicago World's Fair of 1893. Impressed by the architectural splendor of the exhibits, civic leaders returning to their own cities stimulated popular interest in civic aesthetics in many other cities around the country, and new monumental civic centers, municipal libraries, courthouses, and other public buildings were among the visible products of this movement. Real estate boards, private builders, and bankers were among the private civic groups influencing this phase of the planning movement, and although they may have viewed the ugliness, crowding, and the lack of public facilities as among the worst features of urbanization, they were probably also seeking symbols of their own status and achievements through the creation of urban "monuments" to enhance the physical image of their own cities (Perloff, 1957).

One of the first major results of this movement was the appointment in 1900 of a committee consisting of three architects and a sculptor, all of whom had been associated with the Chicago Fair, to restudy the plan of Washington, DC. This was the first of a long series of similar plan reports and city plans, each prepared as a unit by professional consultants drawn from the fields of architecture, landscape architecture, and from the earlier developed field of park planning. With few notable exceptions, the plans advocated and prepared by these earlier protagonist of city planning received no official or legal status and usually were never implemented. Most of them have been characterized as little more than broad outlines of future possibilities designed to arouse public enthusiasm (Walker, 1950). Also, the actual producers of the plans, usually architects or landscape architects hired by the private civic groups on a consultant basis, usually had no official affiliation with the municipalities their plans involved.

The next phase of the city planning movement began to focus on the efficient functioning of cities and the rational coordination of municipal services. This phase of the planning movement has been labeled "The City Practical" (Gold, 1965; Scott, 1969; Gold, 1976). Dating roughly from the Burnham plan for the city of Chicago of 1909 to the late 1920s, the city practical movement provided a set of goals that could be more easily incorporated into the ongoing process of city governments, such as zoning and subdivision controls, public works, and other activities that could be justified on the basis of sound engineering and financial considerations. Also, the preservation and increase of property values associated with sound zoning practices were more certainly predominant factors in the early promotion of land-use zoning as a necessary function of local government (Gold, 1982). During the 1920s, the rapid acceptance and the use of the automobile increased the importance of traffic control and the development of efficient street plans as major goals of the city practical movement, and the economic boom of the twenties also greatly expanded the construction of mass housing, which in turn increased the concern for building, safety, and environmental standards.

In 1907, some decades after the emergence of city planning as a social movement, the first official planning commission in the United States was created in Hartford, Connecticut. The major functions of the first planning commissions included the preparation of zoning ordinances and long-range "master plans" for community development. Initially, the planning commissions had little or no formal authority, and they functioned primarily as separate advisory boards to the executive and legislative branches of local government, to be consulted largely at the discretion of the mayors or city councils. In theory, the planning commissions were supposed to represent a broad cross section of community interests, but in practice their members were heavily overrepresented by realtors, architects, engineers, and lawyers. This was often defended on the grounds that appropriate technical knowledge or professional training constituted the most desirable qualifications for membership on a planning commission (Webster, 1958). Such disproportionate representation continues to the present, now more of a carryover of an earlier pattern rather than a functionally sound prerequisite. At any rate, the particular occupational composition of the earlier planning commissions was crucial in spelling out their activities and technical focus until a distinct planning occupational skill group, with its alleged own body of knowledge and techniques, actually emerged.

The breadth and limitations of the technical scope of planning in its early days as a new function for local government can be best illustrated by a summary of the contents of the major plans of that period. An extended survey of plans prepared in the late 1920s reported that they typically were restricted to the following range of topics:

> A commonly used classification divides a comprehensive city plan into six main elements: zoning, streets, transit, transportation (rail, water, and air), public recreation, and civic art or civic appearance. Taken together, street planning, land subdivision regulations, and zoning are counted on to motivate the types of land development and housing which the city plan aims to secure, so that in many plans, housing does not appear as a separate element. (Gold, 1982, p. 339)

During the depression era of the 1930s, expenditures were somewhat cut back for many local physical improvement programs with which city planners were closely identified, which was a minor setback in the development of city planning programs and agencies at the local level. Instead, federal agencies such as the Works Progress Administration, National Recovery Act, Federal Housing Authority, and the newly created National Planning Board were created and made funds available for dealing with a wide range of economic and social problems on a national scale. During the 1930s, the planning movement saw continuing broadening of the scope of its goals and activities into a more comprehensive attack on urban problems. The disorganizing effects of the depression were instrumental in focusing heightened attention on such economic and social problems as slums, poverty, inadequate housing, disease, and others that had been glossed over in many of the architectural or engineering oriented activities of the planning movement during the 1920s.

The 1930s also were characterized by the planning movement's increased interest in the administration and organization of planning as an integral part of local government (Walker, 1950). Closely related was the growing concern with intergovernmental relations and with planning for a wider variety of geographic and governmental units, such as townships, counties, metropolitan areas, regions, and states, leaving the boundaries of the units for which planning is done open to almost all possibilities.

The latter trend probably lead to the use of the more generic term "urban" planning to describe the movement instead of the more restrictive term of "city" planning, although these terms now tend to be used interchangeably. In fact, *city planning, urban planning, regional planning, town planning, comprehensive planning, physical planning,* and *land-use planning* are now among the labels intermittently used by the agencies and professionals involved in planning for the orderly growth and development of urban communities.

Despite some of the advances in its technical scope and its acceptance as a legitimate function of local government, urban planning, overall, had not made a significantly visible impact on the urban scene in the United States before World War II. Planning activities were few, planning commissions had little or no power to effect changes in the structure and processes of urban areas, and the movement itself was little more than a handful of individuals attempting to advance the cause of planning, while at the same time accomplishing little more than preparing master plans, which were often ignored, discarded, or filed away for some indefinite or vaguely defined future use.

Since the end of the war, however, the picture had changed markedly. The postwar population explosion, the boom in housing and transportation, the rapidly growing suburbs, the declining central cities, the increased social and geographic mobility of the population, and the resultant demands for higher standards in all phases of urban living led to the dramatic postwar expansion of the planning field. Many of the current debates and controversies surrounding planning efforts in such areas as urban renewal and slum clearance, mass transit and highway construction, housing, suburban growth and sprawl, urban environmental concerns, and historic preservation of urban landmarks and other public resources and facilities now frequently arise because urban planning has come to be recognized as a visible agent of change on the current urban scene. In more general terms, the current acceptance of planning in the United States as an integral and ongoing function of local government is illustrated by the fact that ever since the early 1960s, over 96 percent of all cities with populations over ten thousand people have had official planning commissions or boards, and approximately one-third of these employ their own full-time planning staffs. Some of the largest cities employ as many or more than fifty full-time professional city planners, whereas cities under fifty thousand people rarely employ more than two or three full-time professional planners, although more than one-half of them also employ the services of outside planning consultants.

THE ROLE AND SCOPE OF THE PLANNING FUNCTION IN URBAN COMMUNITIES

The current scope of urban planning is so broad and varied that at times it seems to defy description. Some observers, for example, suggest that the scope of urban planning is almost as broad as the entire range of municipal activities. The determination of planning goals and objectives is probably the most important part of the planning process, and these can be summarized as follows:

- **Economic Objectives:** efficiency of land use and circulation patterns; preservation or enhancement of the economic base of the community
- **Social Objectives:** adequate provision for human needs; work, home, play; maximum choices of living environments; congenial social contacts; educational and cultural opportunities within easy reach
- **Physical Objectives:** sound land-use planning (types, quantities, and relationships; proper distribution and density of population [present and projected]; efficient circulation and services; preservation of scenic and historic areas and other amenities)

The range of techniques required to achieve these goals includes two- and three-dimensional physical design, social and economic analysis, research techniques and survey methods, and the varied techniques of law and public administration. In addition, urban planning has continued to extend its range from its already broad technical base by borrowing from a wide variety of new techniques, which themselves have been expanding at a rapidly accelerated place in other fields: mathematics and systems analysis, electronic data processing and computerized graphic design, aerial photography, photogrammetry, geographic information systems (GIS), and community development or community organization.

In larger cities, a staff of many persons with many different specializations is usually required, and these specialized skills are often organized into as few as six or more than twenty functionally separate divisions within the planning agencies. Until the early 1950s, planning offices were staffed primarily by engineers, draftsmen, and architects, and the nucleus of the planning agency staff was the "planning engineer." More recently economists, sociologists, social workers, statisticians, geographers, computer programmers, and people trained as public administrators have been employed by planning agencies in increasing numbers. But more and more, planning agencies are coming to be staffed by those who have been professionally trained and certified as urban planners. A master's degree in city, regional, or urban planning, usually requiring two years of specialized study beyond the baccalaureate, has increasingly become the recommended ticket of entry to the planning profession, and Ph.D. programs in the field are also becoming more common.

In occupational guidance literature for urban planning, it has been suggested that a successful and satisfying career in urban planning is a realistic possibility for one "who possesses foresight; social consciousness; ability to analyze broad situations, and to synthesize multitudinous details in order to grasp common elements; the broadest sort of imagination and interests; and the ability to engage in constructive and creative efforts involving relationships between the problems and factors of modern living" (Gold, 1982, p. 343).

Comprehensive Planning

Comprehensive urban planning has as its objective the unified development and arrangements of land uses for entire urban communities, whether they be cities, counties, or metropolitan areas. Goals of unified development are usually expressed through the determination of the desired comprehensive arrangement of land use and presented in a document variously referred to as a *master plan, general plan, comprehensive plan,* or other terminology as determined by local practices and local enabling legislation. Such plans present proposals for long-range unified developments of the entire area of its political jurisdiction. The master plans ordinarily take into account the individual functional elements of the community and the basic interrelations among them, for example, the relationships of highways and mass transit facilities to traffic generators such as places of work in commercial and industrial centers, which in turn, must be functionally linked to the residential areas which contain their customers and workers. The process of locating schools and growing residential areas so that children would not have to cross traffic hazards to and from school would also involve considerations of the relationships between residential areas, the schools, and the transportation system.

The comprehensive plan is usually based on analyses of current conditions and projections of expected population changes, land-use capabilities and activities, transportation, geographic features, and governmental and political factors as potential influences on future urban development. These analyses attempt to indicate what the possible developmental alternative might be, and which of these might be the most realistic and desirable. In their final preparations, the comprehensive plans might include maps, diagrams, charts, and design sketches. The plans usually include recommendations for density, space, and location standards for private development, programs of public improvements, and public policies necessary to achieve a coordinated development of community forms and processes. The purpose of these plans is to present general policy proposals for what the planners view as desirable future objectives for the entire community.

The Attitudes and Values of Urban Planners

The diversity of backgrounds of people traditionally engaged in urban planning would suggest that there is no common professional frame of reference among them. Thus, the goals of the various occupations that have been represented on the staffs of planning agencies tend to resemble their own previously existing professional job territories, as follows:

A planner with a civil engineering background tends to emphasize drainage, sewer and water extensions, street-widening, elimination of grade crossings and the like; a planner with an architectural background tends to emphasize monumental buildings, civic centers, harmonious exteriors and quality of design; a planner with a landscape architectural background emphasizes scenic vistas; a planner with a background in geography tends to emphasize topography, climate, weather, water resources, soil conditions, and land forms; a planner with a background in sociology tends to emphasize family and communal relationships, social and symbolic interaction, physical influences on group and individual behavior and the social effects of planned versus unplanned environments; the planner with a background in public administration tends to emphasize the management functions of the chief executive, capital budget programming, smoother relationships with the planning commission, the city council chain of command, and interdepartmental relationships; the planner with a background in law tends to. . . . (Gold, 1982, pp. 343–344)

Most urban planners stress the ideal of planning as a continuous process rather than as an activity with definitely fixed outcomes, and they would therefore argue that the planning process does not necessarily ensure that planners engaged in the process will necessarily share the same planning goals and objectives. Nevertheless, there are certain broad planning objectives and goals which tend to be among the values shared by most members of the urban planning profession, and they can be approximately summarized as follows:

1. Planners generally view the highly decentralized, dispersed, or scattered patterns of development around existing metropolitan centers as inherently undesirable. Such scatterization supposedly reduces open space; leads to longer and more energy consuming journeys to work; minimizes the efficiency of providing community wide facilities; reduces choices in housing types and residential location, shopping, and access to community facilities; uses far more land than is necessary for urban growth; usurps land that should be retained for agriculture; destroys the countryside; and is therefore somehow "undemocractic."

2. Planners traditionally favor the maintenance of a strong central business district and the preservation of the density patterns of past cities. They assume that the city must have a high-density core, containing a large proportion of the cities' shopping, banking, commercial, managerial, civic, public, educational, and cultural functions. Because central business districts have in the past also provided for a large proportion of the tax base for large cities, planners tend to believe that they must continue to do so in the future.

3. A seemingly contradictory bias of many urban planners is one in favor of the preservation of open space. This view is derived mostly from the middle-class suburban background of many urban planners, who do not necessarily prefer rural or country life to that in the cities or suburbs—rather, they are probably reacting to the never-ending "sprawl" that is threatening to consume much of the open land still available on the outskirts of many large metropolitan areas.

4. Planners often feel strongly that the journey to work, whether in cities or suburbs, should be reduced by shortening the distance between places of residence and places of work. They assume that most working people desire to economize in daily travel time, distance, and cost. They also tend to support various forms of mass transit to relieve the ever-increasing levels of traffic congestion on the highways or freeways built through or around most large U.S. metropolitan areas.

5. Jane Jacobs (1961) has previously argued that planners have been traditionally biased toward rigid separation of housing, commercial, and other mixed land uses by zoning such diverse activities into spatially distinct and separate areas. However, she may have been mistaken in this judgment, because many planners do in fact support her own preferences for more diversified, mixed land-use areas, particularly those in more densely concentrated big city neighborhoods, such as are characterized by Jacobs's favorite example: New York's Greenwich Village, in which she has previously lived (Mumford, 1962; Gold, 1965). Professional urban planners' values would also probably dictate that the development of new mixed-use and diversified projects should be creative, well planned, and well executed. At any rate, it is fair to suggest that most of the suburban zoning legislation designed to protect residential areas from commercial or other mixed land-use "intrusions" comes as much from the interest of suburban residents, local business and real estate interests, and local elected officials as it does from the recommendations of professional urban planners.

If these values are, in fact, truly representative of American urban planners, they appear not to have been particularly successful in achieving most of the goals discussed, because most recent patterns of urban growth and development in the past few decades have been in a contrary direction. Metropolitan communities for the most part actually have become more dispersed and decentralized (see chapter 4); open space within the metropolitan areas does tend to become developed; the central business districts of many metropolitan centers have been declining in density and economic activity; and the journey to work may be increasing for many more workers, as the network of freeways emanating around and outward from the central cities makes this greater commuting distance much more likely.

Many critics of urban planning suggest that these trends represent the preference of the general public as they participate in the free marketplace, and that it would be arrogant and undemocratic for "elitist" planners to interfere with "natural" economic and social processes. Many planners would argue in response that the public has not been sufficiently informed or provided with other alternatives, and that urban planners should at least provide knowledge of such alternatives to the public for their consideration (Scott, 1969, p. 640). Whatever the merits of these opposing positions (which are considered further in the next chapter), many of the goals and objectives of urban planners remain more as future possibilities than actually realized accomplishments.

One important point that tends to be overlooked in most discussions of the successes or failures of urban planning in meeting its goals or objectives is that most professional planners work in positions that are generally subservient to the formal authority structure of local government, which places them under the controls of a previously existing power structure, usually consisting of the mayor, city manager, city council, and/or the politically appointed planning commission. The view of many urban planners is that at its highest levels, planning is essentially a policy formulation process, which often brings it into direct conflict with the elected political structure. Most of the technical decisions that are made in planning, in contrast to those common to many other professions, are by their nature closely tied to and affected by public policy. For example, zoning decisions affecting land use, population projections based on controlled density standards, and long-range transportation, facility, and capital budget programming are all part of the professional planner's technical work role. It is impossible, however, to perform these tasks without regard to public policy. In such cases the professional planners often view the "politicians" as major sources of obstructionism in blocking the achievement of planning goals which they have recommended. Part of the frustration that results is also due to the fact that the large-scale and complex communitywide changes that are so often a part of the urban planners' objectives may take a good many years before they get underway or show results (Gold, 1976, pp. 848–849). And just as often, planning proposals may be rejected by the public, or, on the other hand, elected officials may choose to pursue programs and policies that the planning staff would not have approved or supported (Scott, 1969, p. 645). In either case the result may be especially frustrating or discouraging to the public policy oriented planner. In many of the cases cited below, for example, urban planners sometimes get criticized or blamed for decisions they themselves may not have made or even supported.

SOME URBAN PLANNING EFFORTS IN THE REAL WORLD

People have long dreamed of creating the ideal city. The forms of their conceptions of the ideal have varied from century to century. In the fourteenth century, for example, the English statesman and writer Sir Thomas More envisaged an ideal society, which he called *UTOPIA* in a major book of the same title. More presented a vision of a community where all sociopolitical ills had been eliminated and the entire social order was rationally reformed to benefit the community as a whole. Since the initial success of this work, the label *utopia* has been applied to all kinds of portrayals of the problem-free ideal community, no matter how impractical and fantasized such projections may seem. But since utopian visions of potential future cities have not to date been realized as a practical matter in the real world, our discussion of such utopian and other speculative projections about the urban future are contained in the next chapter of this book. Here some of the most significant planning efforts of the last half of the twentieth century in America are identified, and their successes or failures are critically assessed.

The 1950s and 1960s saw widespread recognition of many of the problems of American cities and the burgeoning suburbs, as discussed in this and many previous chapters. Many initiatives were undertaken at local, regional, and national levels to alleviate these problems through a variety of urban planning and public policy efforts. Although many of the problems and proposals were controversial, urban planners and public officials were optimistic that urban problems could be minimized or alleviated through the concerted and cooperative efforts of various levels of government, the private economy, and civic groups. But by the late 1970s many of these efforts had been seriously cut back or abandoned as apparent failures, or set aside for some vague future considerations. To their supporters, they were cut short before they were given sufficient opportunity to demonstrate their effectiveness or were blocked from implementation as too controversial, costly, or intrusive by organized interest groups or by "ill-informed" public opinion. It is also true that the political climate for massive public intervention in the affairs of American cities has rapidly fluctuated in favor of or against such efforts during the last half of the twentieth century. At this time the possibility of large-scale planning efforts in large American cities and metropolitan areas seems too cloudy to predict for the immediate future. But because the quality of life in urban America is of continuing concern, and because at least the possibility does exist for a renewal of interest in public or private investment efforts to improve the urban environment, it is useful to examine some of the most significant urban planning efforts of the recent past for the insights they might provide for early twenty-first century prospects.

Urban Renewal, Enterprise Zones, Empowerment Zones

The political, legal, and financial impetus for federally sponsored urban renewal programs in American cities was the Housing Act of 1949, as amended in 1954. Under this legislation, local communities were empowered to condemn, buy, clear, and redevelop inner city land that was considered substandard or was underused with respect to its potential value. The program was aimed at the clearance of areas designated as slums, or likely to become slums, in the near future. A major goal was the redevelopment by private developers of such land for new residential, commercial, or industrial uses that would be expected to enhance the value and desirability of the land, presumably for the benefits of the entire community. Financing of the program involved matching funds from the local community and the federal government, with two-thirds of the cost to be born by the federal government. Control of the urban renewal projects was to remain in local hands, provided that certain federal criteria were met.

Ultimately, urban renewal became one of the most controversial and misunderstood aspects of planned urban redevelopment. Technically speaking, urban renewal was not necessarily an integral part of long-range comprehensive planning, as described in earlier sections of this chapter, because many comprehensive community master plans did not contain specific provisions for urban renewal, and because some local urban renewal projects were undertaken without reference to the guiding framework of a comprehensive community plan. In many communities, planning agencies and urban renewal agencies were independent, autonomous, and sometimes competing departments of local government.

The most relevant criticisms of those urban renewal projects that had actually been undertaken and completed had to do with their impact on low-income neighborhoods and their residents. Contrary to the original goals of the federally sponsored urban renewal program, many critics maintained that urban renewal projects had materially reduced the supply of housing available to low-income groups in American cities by replacing bulldozed "slum" housing with new luxury housing for higher-income groups or replacing housing with more economically profitable nonresidential commercial or industrial development, from which the investors and other commercially oriented groups had profited. Sociologists and psychologists had criticized urban renewal for the negative emotional burdens placed on low income groups by involuntary relocation from their established and sometimes stable neighborhoods and severing their strong bonds to neighbors, churches, and other comforting local institutions (Gans, 1968, pp. 260–265). Boston's West End has become a widely cited example. The West End, which was a stable and relatively cohesive working-class Italian neighborhood, had been designated as a slum for urban renewal purposes, and its residents were uprooted and relocated in a random fashion all over the city. Marc Fried (1963), a clinical psychologist who studied the former West Enders before and after they were relocated, reported that 46 percent of the women and 38 percent of the men gave evidence of a "fairly severe grief reaction or worse" after being forced to leave their tight-knit community. Far from easily adjusting to this traumatic separation from the West End, 26 percent of the women still remained sad or depressed two years after they had been displaced from their homes and neighborhood. Similar findings have been reported about people involuntarily displaced from stable ethnic subcommunities by redevelopment projects in other cities: for example, the later massive destruction of *Poletown,* and the removal of the residents from this established Polish neighborhood in the City of Detroit, which was condemned by the city government and torn down to make room for the construction of a plant to build Cadillacs by the General Motors Corporation.

Much criticism also pointed out that urban renewal had not always adequately compensated the relocated groups for their losses and that it had not necessarily provided them with better housing or neighborhood facilities than those from which they had been evicted (Greer, 1965). Of course, these were not so much a criticism of the general concept of urban renewal itself, as it was of the particular purposes to which urban renewal had been put. Many such critics would have supported urban renewal if it had been used to provide more and better low-cost housing for low-income groups, and if relocation problems would have been minimized or handled in more helpful and humane ways than it had been done in most instances (see Gans, 1968; Frieden and Morris, 1968; and Downs, 1976, for extensive discussions of this latter point). For a variety of related economic, political, and social reasons, federally sponsored urban renewal programs fell from favor and were discontinued by the 1970s, and the decade was primarily one of neglect of urban redevelopment policies and projects. At the same time, it was still recognized that efforts to improve the economic vitality of cities through the redevelopment of commercial, industrial, and residential areas remained legitimate goals, if cities were expected to provide adequate occupational opportunities for their residents or to provide them with adequate levels of public services.

Beginning with the conservative "Reagan Revolution" of the 1980s, there were extensive cutbacks in all sorts of programs providing development projects or development funds for the cities. During the Reagan and Bush presidencies, for example, federal funds for urban housing fell by 70 percent (Dreier, 1992, p. 21), federal housing assistance for low and moderate income families was cut by 85 percent (Feagin and Parker, 1990), and federal money for low and moderate income families fell by an even larger percentage (Eitzen and Baca Zinn, 1997, p. 162). These cuts reduced the supply of housing available to low or moderate income families in cities to a level even lower than that produced by the urban renewal programs of the 1950s and 1960s. But one of the few new development programs introduced during the 1980s and continued through the 1990s, consisted of *enterprise zones,* or *empowerment zones*, as they were labeled in the Clinton years. These were based on a conservative philosophy of market-based development to stimulate economic growth and generate employment opportunities in inner city areas of the large and older cities defined as economically depressed, by providing subsidies and other economic incentives to businesses that agree to locate in such areas (O'Brien, 1992; Wartzman and Harwood, 1992). Supporters of enterprise zones, usually business groups, have been enthusiastic about them and claim that thousands of new jobs have been created, but skeptics suggest that if any new jobs have been formed, they are few in number and costly to the public. Some critics do not believe that what are now called empowerment zones will ever really work (Lemann, 1994). Palen (1997, pp. 347–348) supports the pessimistic view of empowerment zones as follows:

> [B]usinesses that do locate in empowerment zones tend to be marginal firms and tend not to make long term contributions to the community. Commonly they are highly mobile operations that use the subsidies to employ locals at minimal wages and provide minimal job training. When the subsidies are gone, they are gone. Empowerment zones sound good, but what they best provide is an expensive government business subsidy. They do little for inner city residents.

Smaller Scale Redevelopment Efforts at the Local Level

Although federal urban renewal efforts and empowerment zones have been largely abandoned or have been ineffective in improving the overall quality of urban life, most American urban communities, whether cities or suburbs, continually change over time through a series of local smaller scale rebuilding or redesign projects. These are sometimes initiated at the local level by private builders and developers, and sometimes they are promoted by local government or planning groups, but mostly they come about through private-public cooperative "partnerships." In the latter cases, professional urban planners are often engaged to do special studies of specific small areas within a larger containing community to determine their influence on other adjacent small areas within the community. These planning studies, when properly designed, are extensions of comprehensive community wide planning concepts into smaller areas. In studies of smaller areas, the planner's function is to investigate the general character of the area in relationship to overall community considerations and to help produce a design or program for improvement of the area. This can be both a test of, and an implementation of, elements in the comprehensive plan. However, although professional urban planners still attempt to deal with the concept of the small project area in terms of overall community form and function and not merely with plans for specific buildings or construction projects, the latter are still usually the responsibility of the private developers.

Suburban Downtowns.   A recent trend has been the renewal of the downtown areas of traditional small towns that had once existed as free-standing communities near large cities but were now enveloped by encroaching suburban development and have become indistinguishable from them. The centers of these towns had been losing some of their commercial, recreational, and civic functions in recent decades in competition with the newer suburban shopping malls and edge cities (see chapter 4). But many suburban residents have become jaded with the sameness and uniformity of much mall development and have rediscovered the diversity, variety, freshness, and "small town feel" of these old downtown areas. In turn, developers and public officials have recognized the potential resurgence of these areas and have been sprucing them up with new sidewalks, seating areas, street lighting, new storefronts, off-street parking areas, restaurants, theaters, coffee shops, street vendors, and other new businesses. Added to this mix are regularly scheduled parades, street festivals, fairs, and outdoor concerts. In the suburbs of metropolitan Detroit, for example, revival of old downtown areas in Birmingham, Royal Oak, Rochester, Ferndale, Plymouth, and Mount Clemens have been successful in attracting such large numbers of people to their streets, businesses, and public areas, that they now have begun to match some of the local malls in the volume of foot traffic. Further, the demand for housing within walking distance of most of these rejuvenated downtowns has increased tremendously, and the resultant increases in neighboring property values have been much larger than in other residential areas. One of the interesting responses to these successful developments are the current plans to develop totally new "old-fashioned main street" downtowns, modeled after the traditional types described earlier, in newer suburban Detroit communities, such as Macomb Township and Novi, which never did have their own traditional downtown areas (*Detroit Free Press,* June 6, 2000. p. 1B). The revitalization projects of older suburban downtowns, such as Alexandria, Virginia, or Cambridge, Massachusetts, have, in addition, emphasized the preservation and restoration of many historic buildings and sites.

Inner City Redevelopment

In contrast to the earlier Urban Renewal program or the Empowerment Zone policies discussed previously, many redevelopment projects in or near the centers of large cities have been undertaken in recent decades by private developers and investors with some assistance by local governments and planning agencies in the form of feasibility studies, zoning changes, condemnation proceedings, infrastructure improvements, and the like. The World Trade Center and the Broadway district of Manhattan, the Embarcadero Center in San Francisco, Chicago's Water Tower Place and North Loop Theater District, and Cleveland's Flats area are all examples of this kind of urban regeneration.

Built on a somewhat larger scale are the Inner Harbor development in Baltimore, the South Street Seaport complex in New York City, and Boston's Faneuil Hall complex. All of these projects were creations of the developer, James Rouse, who was also the initial developer of the new town, Columbia, Maryland. Macionis and Parrillo (1998) correctly point out that Rouse developments in Baltimore, New York, and Boston represent the "middle ground" of urban redevelopment. That is, they are larger in scale than the small projects described previously, but they are less comprehensive and all encompassing than new towns like Columbia. All three of these midsize redevelopment projects have been financially successful, and they have been attractive destinations for tourists, as well as local residents. Overall they seemed to live up to the developer's hope "that cities can be beautiful, humane, and truly responsive to the needs and yearning of our people" (Demarest, 1981, pp. 37–39). Reclaimed from a run-down and dilapidated area of largely abandoned dwellings and warehouses that once was at old Boston's city center, Faneuil Hall nicely illustrates how such an area can be transformed by the vision (and investments) of a creative developer such as Rouse and can serve as a model for similar projects elsewhere. As a brief description puts it:

> The old warehouses have been outwardly maintained, but the inner cores have been thoroughly modernized. Faneuil Hall has been revamped in the same manner. Inside, food shops run its football-field length. On either side of the hall are pedestrian areas

"Boston's Fanueil Hall seems to live up to the developers hope 'that cities can be beautiful, humane, and truly responsive to the needs and yearning of our people'"

with benches, outdoor eating areas, and places where street musicians play. The refurbished old warehouses on either side are now the place of business of high quality shops. On any summer day, the place is teeming with people—locals, tourists, visitors from the suburbs . . . the new buildings mimic or harmoniously blend with the old buildings of the area. (Macionis and Parrillo, 1998, p. 395)

New Towns

The idea of building entirely new cities from scratch is a very old one going back many centuries (see chapter 2). The modern new town or garden city movement really began in the later part of the nineteenth century with the ideas of Ebenezer Howard, and the first examples were built in England in the very first decade of the twentieth century (Hall, 1998). The original conceptions underlying this movement called for the creation of new self-sufficient and self-contained towns decentralized from existing urban centers. The new towns were to differ sharply from the more conventional patterns of urban sprawl in that they were to provide much more in the way of city amenities than was commonly associated with "bedroom" or "commuting suburbs" or subdivisions that were primarily limited to residential functions. The new towns were envisaged by their advocates as providing a balanced mix of economic, commercial, employment, civic, educational, and recreational functions which were adequate to meet the daily needs of their residents. Estimates of the minimum population size needed to support this relatively full range of urban functions have varied anywhere from 30,000 to 100,000 inhabitants, with some estimates running up to a maximum of approximately 250,000 people. The new towns would attempt to avoid the worse aspects of existing urban centers by rational planning and would be kept separated from these existing centers by rural "green belts." The green belts would maximize a desirable balance between city and countryside and preserve the natural and agricultural amenities directly accessible to the residents of the new towns for their convenience and enjoyment. Another fairly common element of new town planning is that a series of them would be developed in a ring pattern around large central cities, such as London or Stockholm. At a distance not too far from the central cities, they would be connected by mass transit systems emanating outward in a radial pattern. The new towns would provide a heterogeneous variety of housing types to accommodate people of various socioeconomic levels or at various stages of their life cycles, and they would decrease the pressures on the overcrowded cities by absorbing some of their surplus populations (Gold, 1982, pp. 348–349).

Even though the objectives of the new town movement have never been fully realized, the most visible and perhaps most successful examples of completed new towns are to be found in England, Sweden, and, to a lesser extent, France, Holland, and Spain. In England the New Towns Act of 1946 was an initiative of a new Labour Party government, which had come into power just after the end of World War II. This legislation called for the development of a ring of new towns to be built around London, separated from the city by "green belts" and connected to the city by a system of mass transit lines. The first wave of new towns actually constructed consisted mostly of single-family rental homes owned and managed by the government in communities of approximately thirty thousand residents. Although they also provided some industrial developments to provide employment opportunities to their residents, they fell short of meeting this goal, and it was concluded by the government planners that they were too small to meet the objectives for which they were intended.

Thus, when a second wave of new towns was developed in the 1950s and 1960s, they were planned for populations of up to eighty thousand people. These came a little closer to the original concept of new town planning, in the sense that they had larger and more centralized commercial and shopping districts and were somewhat more self-sufficient in meeting the daily needs of their residents than the earlier efforts. Still later efforts produced new towns planned for populations of up to two hundred fifty thousand people. But by 1979, when a new conservative political regime came to power under the leadership of Margaret Thatcher, the idea of central planning controlled almost entirely by government had lost favor by many as too inflexible and rigid. During the Thatcher–John Major era of the 1980s and most of the 1990s, most redevelopment efforts were left to the free play of the marketplace, and much of the government-owned new town housing developments were sold off to private investors. Although the redevelopment efforts during this period were aimed primarily at large commercial and industrial areas, almost all new housing since then has been privately developed, owned, and controlled. Urbanologist Sir Peter Hall (1998, pp. 903–931) has described London and its surrounding areas during this period as "The City of Capitalism Rampant." By the late 1990s, the Labour Party had once again assumed political power under the leadership of Tony Blair, although under a more "centrist" political agenda than that of previous Labour governments. And at the beginning of the twenty-first century, it was not clear that the building of more new towns would be part of this agenda.

Post–World War II new town planning in Sweden was inspired by the early British examples, but differed from them in several important aspects. First, it was recognized that any new housing or commercial development outside the existing city of Stockholm had to be preceded by the building of a full-scale subway system rather than to follow it, because at the time the subways were proposed in 1945, there were only nine cars per one thousand people in Stockholm. Even as late as 1971 after the first significant new towns were completed, 60 percent of all journeys to and from work in Greater Stockholm, and 70 percent in the city, were still by public transit (Popenoe, 1977; Hall, 1998, p. 863). Second, it was recognized that stations in the subway system should generate enough traffic to make them self-supporting and economically feasible. Therefore, the population size and density in each new satellite community had to be large enough to provide such support. Third, there was a decision to decentralize some employment and civic or commercial activities, along a three-part concept of "workplace, dwelling, center" (Hall, 1998, pp. 863). They should be self-contained and socially balanced communities for living, working, and shopping or civic activities.

The best examples of new towns that have been developed according to these principles were Vallingby and Farsta, completed by the early 1960s. Combined, the two towns contained around thirteen residential districts, each housing a population of eight thousand to sixteen thousand people. Vallingby was distinctively dominated by nine-to-twelve-story tower blocks which surround the center, and very long three- to six-story slab blocks, all found within fifteen hundred feet of either the main or a local center. The complete development consisted of six city districts within a two-mile radius of Vallingby Centre. The center combined facilities for shopping, health care, child care, medical, dental, and surgical resources, a pharmacy, theaters, and a post office, all of which were within walking distance for about twenty thousand to twenty-five thousand residents. Although there have been criticisms of the Swedish new towns as "unattractive," "drab," or "sterile" (Macionis and Parillo, 1998, p. 383), one Swedish critic has described at least Vallingby as "far from oppressive" and that it "maintains a pleasant balance between built and open spaces; the houses are sufficiently close to one another to create spatial coherence and a certain atmosphere of 'town,' and yet they are scattered enough to retain something of the original topography and natural landscape" (Thomas Hall, 1991, p. 220). Farsta, which was developed very shortly after Vallingby, was similar to it in many respects. For example, in both, approximately 13 percent of their residents lived in fifteen-story tower blocks, 19 percent lived in eight-story slab blocks, 45 percent lived in three-story buildings, and 23 percent lived in single-family houses (Pass, 1973). The main difference was that the town center was much larger in Farsta, with more private chain stores serving a population of 150,000–200,000 customers over a much larger sales area of some 21,000 square miles (Hall, 1998).

The building of additional, new, townlike developments in Sweden thereafter fluctuated in size, design, and density, according to periodic changes in the state of the

Swedish economy and political climate. In the 1970s, during a period of economic recession, but with a huge, pent-up demand for new housing, the new developments used industrialized methods of construction, with a much higher density and a general lack of feeling or imagination, giving rise to a sense of rigid uniformity. These projects proved to be unattractive not only to critics but also to their prospective residents, and they had very high vacancy and turnover rates (Hall, 1998, p. 173). By the 1980s the Swedish economy had improved, more people owned cars, and they were beginning to demand more spacious single-family homes. Those that were built were "often monotonous, with closely packed houses in unimaginative uniform rows, reminiscent of the worst kind of American suburbia" (Heclo and Madsen, 1987, pp. 215–225). By the 1990s, according to Hall (1998, pp. 875–876), the Swedish Social Democratic efforts to provide equitable housing resources to all residents in carefully planned and well-regulated new towns had come to an end, and the Swedish urban landscape had become "a vast linear Edge City of business parks and hotels and out of town shopping centres stretching along the E4 highway, for twelve miles or more. . . . It is almost indistinguishable from its counter parts in California and Texas."

New Towns in the United States

In the United States, the federal government experimented with a program of new towns in the depression years of the early 1930s. Three such new towns, or "garden cities," actually were built: Greenbelt, Maryland; Greendale, Wisconsin; and Green Mills, Ohio. However, they were never fully completed, as the federal government eventually withdrew support because of a shortage of funds and the intrusion of World War II. These experiments did produce what are still considered attractive commuter suburbs, but the new town vision of supplying jobs to its residents through the development of self-sufficient local industries was never realized. Also, the green belts that were supposed to surround these towns gradually succumbed to other uses, as nearby cities extended their suburban development radius. Thus, these experimental new towns have become nearly indistinguishable from the sprawling suburban subdivisions now surrounding them (Gold, 1982, pp. 349–350).

After World War II, interest in the new town movement revived; this time most of the interest and sponsorship came from private investors. In the 1960s President Johnson called new towns the communities of the future. To many urban planners and architects, they were a blueprint for easing the ills of the inner cities and the growing sprawl of the suburbs. According to their vision, the new towns would be carefully planned to meet the housing, recreational, and commercial needs of millions of people, rich and poor, black and white. There would be lakes and parks, town houses and high rises. Shoppers would be able to walk to malls in town centers, and workers would be able to walk to jobs in beautifully landscaped industrial parks. The federal government, through the newly created Department of Housing and Urban Development, was to assist by helping some of the developers secure government-guaranteed loans or subsidies. In all, approximately sixty-four new communities were undertaken or completed between World War II and 1970 (*Newsweek,* November 29, 1976). Whether any of these actually met the conception or criteria of a new town, as specified in this chapter, is doubtful, because most of them were primarily large-scale residential tracts or retirement communities for the elderly.

The best known and successful American new towns, which come closest to their original expectations and to the new town concept, include Park Forest South, near Chicago; Reston, Virginia, about twenty-five miles from Washington, DC; and Columbia, Maryland, also within the daily commuting range of the District of Columbia. The newest of these is Park Forest South, which may best illustrate the objectives of new town planning, in the sense that it has attracted a branch of a new state university, built an industrial park that provided a ratio of one job for every housing unit, achieved a population level of at least 25,000 people, and had successfully integrated a minority population of 25 percent (Gold, 1982, p. 350). Columbia, with an estimated 1999 population of 94,000 people (*Rand McNally Road Atlas,* 2000) is the largest American new town to date and is projected to grow still larger. As originally conceived by its developer, James Rouse, who was mentioned earlier, it was planned to offer a variety of housing styles for a broad range of income levels, which it has done by including a number of subsidized housing units for lower income groups. These have thoughtfully been scattered throughout the various neighborhoods within Columbia to try to avoid segregating the poorest residents into ghettolike subcommunities. Likewise, according to its original goal, the community is racially integrated, with blacks making up about a third of its population. Columbia is divided into a series of distinct neighborhoods, each with about eight or nine hundred homes, and each with its own elementary school, neighborhood center, convenience store, and recreation facilities. In turn, groups of neighborhoods are combined into larger "villages," containing middle schools, supermarkets, and other shopping facilities at their centers. Serving all of Columbia is one larger town center, containing office buildings, medical facilities, department stores, and a community college.

Columbia is located about halfway between Baltimore and the District of Columbia, and its growth was partially assured by its close access to both of these densely populated cities. Reston, on the other hand, is located in a more affluent suburban area west of Washington and is within four or five miles of Dulles International Airport. This may partially help explain why Reston did not turn out quite as close to the original vision of its developer, as did Columbia. Robert E. Simon intended Reston (a name based on his initials) to become an economically and racially diversified self-sufficient community, along the same idea as Columbia. But Reston was initially slower in attracting such residents, and because of its slow growth, it was taken over by the Gulf Oil Co. in the late 1960s. Since then, it has attracted mainly upper middle income groups or higher, although it does contain some subsidized units, and about 17 percent of its residents are racial minorities, less than originally intended. Overall, Reston has itself become an affluent community, with the prices of some homes rising to over $1 million. Reston contains a number of corporate office buildings, and its physically attractive housing mix includes condominiums, town houses, and single-family homes, some of which face lakes or golf courses, whereas others back up to nature trails and forests. The estimated 1999 population of Reston was approximately 54,000 (*Rand McNally Road Atlas,* 2000).

The fact that private developers and nongovernmental agencies or planning commissions had developed successful new towns, such as Columbia and Reston, should not obscure the fact that these projects had been inspired by the long-range vision of urban planners who helped lay the groundwork for these projects and made them possible. For example, one of the most significant plans was *A Policies Plan for the Year 2000* issued by the National Capital Planning Commissions and the National Capital Regional Planning Council in 1961 and later endorsed by President Kennedy (Scott, 1969, p. 573). The plan foresaw the possibility of saving the open countryside near Washington as a recreational and scenic resource. More central to this discussion, however, was the possibility raised by this plan of channeling projected future growth into well-planned new towns. The plan reviewed several alternative design schemes to illustrate how such new towns might be shaped, and the new towns of Columbia and Reston turned out not too much unlike some of the alternatives proposed by this plan (see Scott, 1969, pp. 576–578). Supporting this plan and complementary to it were planning projections and reports by the National Capital Transportation Agency and The Maryland-National Capital Park and Planning Commission, which also jointly proposed a more comprehensive highway and mass transit plan for the Washington metropolitan area, part of which has been realized by the now famous (or infamous!) beltway surrounding the region and the partially completed subway system now connecting Washington to some of its Virginia and Maryland suburbs.

Although several hundred thousand people now live (apparently happily) in new towns around the country, and several of these have drawn praise for their beauty and amenities, nearly all of them were financial flops for their developers. The new towns were inherently risky financial ventures for their backers from the start. Before they could attract paying residents, the developers spent very heavily on "front end costs" to clear zoning requirements and other land-use regulations, assemble the land and install the facilities, while paying taxes and interest at the same time. To plan and develop a new town completely can easily take twenty years or more, and even the most successful of the new towns had not earned their developers a profit within this time frame. As a result, none of the developers of existing new towns have indicated they will build any more of them, and additional new investors are not in sight for the near future. Just about everyone who was involved in developing new towns agreed that about the only way to cushion the heavy start-up costs would have to involve large governmental subsidies or investments of one sort or another, and at the time of this writing no such prospect appears to be in sight.

"New Urbanism" Developments

Although more new towns no longer appear to be realistic alternatives in the United States for the foreseeable future, a newer approach, commonly referred to as the "New Urbanism" by its advocates, has emerged, which holds some promise and has received a great deal of attention. It has also attracted some serious criticism as well. Because this approach has been applied to attempts to redesign and restore the vitality of older cities, as well as attempts to add more urbanized forms of social interaction and public life into new developments in the sprawling suburbs, both kinds of efforts are considered separately in this section.

New Urbanism developments that have been created in new or previously developed suburban areas are on a much smaller scale and are far less comprehensive than the new towns previously discussed, but at the same time, they are not merely duplicates of the more standard kinds of residential subdivisions that dominated the suburban landscape during most of the last half of the twentieth century. They are based on the idea by their proponents that the traditional suburban subdivisions are overly "privatized" and are not conducive of a high level of interaction between residents, or a real sense of community, because the public infrastructure that dominates the suburbs is not one of parks and sidewalks, but rather one of highways, collector roads, and cul-de-sacs. The suburbs have been designed for the movement of cars but not for the congregation of people. Also, the rigid zoning controls in suburbs keep residential and commercial uses apart and thus sap some of the vibrant street life, civility and vitality found in the more public realm of cities. According to boosters of the New Urbanism, the traditional suburb is "tawdry and stressful and full of banality and hostility . . . life seems less satisfying to most Americans . . . in the ubiquitous middle class suburbs, where a sprawling, repetitive and forgettable landscape has replaced the original promise of suburban life with hollow imitation." What is needed instead, they argue, is a new kind of subdivision that includes "public parks; civic buildings on important sites; commercial, office and residential buildings nearby and a carefully thought-out network of streets and thoroughfares that encourage walking." (Bradley, 2000, pp. 47–48) Keeping various destinations, whether residential or commercial, within a five-minute walk is a key design of principal supporters and developers of the New Urbanism concept, and they see it as a new combination of the traditional virtues of small town life with some of the energy, creativity, and sense of public responsibility that they suggest is derived from the "hustle and bustle" of an active street life that is ideally characteristic of cities (see Duany, Plater-Zyberk, and Beck, 2000, and Bradley, 2000, pp. 46–49 for more extended discussions of New Urbanism philosophy).

Seaside, Florida, was one of the earliest examples of a New Urbanism community, developed by Duany Plater-Zyberk & Co. (DPZ), a leading force in this movement. It has streets that are deliberately narrow to discourage car traffic, all houses are required to have front porches close to the sidewalks (which are also required) so that their residents can easily chat with walking bypassers as they sit on their front porches, and there are close by corner stores throughout the community that serve the same kinds of social gathering functions that were supposedly common to the small town general stores of bygone days. Palen (1997, p. 369), in fact, refers to Seaside and other similar suburban communities developed by the New Urbanists as "neotraditional" because of their nineteenth-century styled architecture and their deliberately planned, old-fashioned small town look and feel.

Celebration, Florida, is the best known and most thoroughly studied example of the New Urbanism approach to date. Architecturally and design wise, it is very similar to Seaside, except that it is larger and has a more fully developed downtown. This includes an area in which shops, restaurants, entertainment facilities, a post office, and other commercial buildings are arranged in a semicircle around a plaza and facing an artificial lake (Macionis and Parillo, 1998, p. 386). Celebration was a project of the Walt Disney Corporation and was originally designed to eventually house approximately 20,000 people in 8,000 home sites by the year 2015, but prepublicity created such a large demand that nearly 5,000 purchasers showed up at its opening in 1995 and all of the projected dwellings had already been sold and occupied by 1999.

Among the early residents were Douglas Frantz, a national correspondent for the *New York Times,* and his wife Catherine Collins, a freelance writer, and their two children. Together, Frantz and Collins (1999) wrote *Celebration, U.S.A.*, a book that amounts to a firsthand investigative report on life in this Central Florida community. The family had moved into a midprice home in Celebration in mid-1997 and had spent the next sixteen months as "pioneers, caught up in the struggle to make friends, find a place to buy a hammer and nails, and generally reconcile dreams with reality." Andrew Ross (1999), author of *The Celebration Chronicles,* is an American studies professor at New York University who also had moved to Celebration around the same time to conduct his own research on this neotraditional community, and he ultimately reached conclusions that were in many ways similar to those of Frantz and Collins.

Both authors described Celebration as a "dream" of the Walt Disney Corporation, as well as a dream of the "pioneers" who were the town's first settlers. Built from scratch on virgin land, it is further described as an international showcase for technology, education, and medicine, and a macroconstruction challenge that "only a company with deep pockets, booming profit margins and a financial need to expand and diversify would take on." The various famous architects who designed Celebration drew up an elaborate plan which established "correct proportions for everything from massing and setbacks to the height and opacity of fences . . . the depths of porches and the recommended facade material and color" for each of the six traditional house styles: Coastal, Classical, Colonial Revival, French Normandy, Mediterranean, and Victorian. Both authors felt that the houses were overpriced for the market and of somewhat shoddy construction.

Their greatest complaints were of what they felt to be overregimentation and control by the developers of this minutely planned town. As to the residents, for example, "their lives would be regulated in intimate detail, down to the ratio of grass, trees and shrubs on their property and the color of the curtains (white) they could hang in their windows. They would be surveyed as regularly as the Nielson families: those who accepted the lure of a free computer and cell phone would live with a 'Zeus Box' that monitored every telephone call they made and every Web site they visited." Frantz and Collins add that "there was an insularity in Celebration that was troubling, a sense that the problems of the real world, whether domestic violence or poverty, didn't intrude. There is a fine line between harmony and conformity, and too often . . . the residents of Celebration had come down on the side of conformity" (*Washington Post National Weekly Edition,* October 4, 1999, p. 33). Both authors comment favorably on the sense of community or the friendliness they felt among the residents, but they also decried the deliberate lack of affordable housing and the corresponding lack of socioeconomic or cultural diversity. As Frantz and Collins also put it, the community is "too middle-class and too white."

They further note that the community lacked such amenities as a library, a book store, and had only a "boutique" grocery rather than a supermarket. Both books dealt extensively with fierce and disruptive conflicts growing out of the problems with the "progressive" policies of the local school, which were designed by the Disney organization with the help of outside educational "experts," but which were out of tune with the more traditional educational expectations of the parents with school-age children. This led some parents to actively organize to force Disney to modify the school curriculum to a more conventional grade-based format, and some families moved out of Celebration during these political battles over the control and direction of the school.

However, at least one reviewer of these two books does find in them probably their most significant positive conclusions: mainly the best thing about Celebration was its frontier spirit embodied in the determination of the people who came there in search of community, and who actually managed to create one, against the odds of doing so. The same reviewer concludes that a further lesson of these books, with potentially larger implications for the near future, was that "middle class Americans want something different from the gated communities and the anonymous suburbs that contractors usually supplied. They are hungry for Lake Wobegon with nice front porches, big kitchens and a decent hardware store within walking distance . . . and A's and B's on the children's report cards" (*New York Times,* September 6, 1999, p. B9).

Similar New Urbanism developments at Kentlands in Gaithersburg, Maryland; Mashpee on Cape Cod; Riverplace in Portland, Oregon; an as yet unamed project planned for Novi, Michigan; and numerous other neotraditional-traditional subdivisions planned or currently under construction in many parts of the country do tend to support the belief that the New Urbanism is an idea whose time may have come, at least for a small portion of middle-class Americans who are seeking alternative places to live, different from those to which they have been, not too satisfyingly, accustomed. Whether these developments will still be as attractive to their residents after their novelty has worn off and they become "old hat" still remains to be seen.

Macionis and Parrillo (1998, pp. 281–284) correctly point out the New Urbanism concepts have been successfully applied as replacements for obsolete and worn-out public housing and other no longer workable housing developments in low-income inner city neighborhoods. As large superblocks of high-rise public housing projects have been torn down, some of them have been replaced by town houses and other low-rise housing units that don't look like the old projects they have replaced. According to Macionis and Parillo, a number of these projects, in cities such as Boston, Newark, Atlanta, and Chicago, have tried to incorporate several key objectives of the New Urbanism movement—namely, they do not try to isolate the poor from contacts with other kinds of neighbors, but instead they try to create socioeconomically mixed housing units to integrate various income levels in the same developments. They also try to create a physically attractive environment that facilitates walking and social interaction. As suggested earlier, the New Urbanists believe that this will promote a sense of community among residents and give them a sense of control over their environment.

Macionis and Parrillo (1998) cite one negative example of such a development in San Francisco, which did not transform the neighborhood social structure and the social characteristics and behavior of its poor residents in the hoped for direction of more middle-class–like lifestyles, as a failure of the kind of physical planning associated with the New Urbanism. It was also correctly recognized by these two sociologists that it is too much to hope that pleasing architecture and physical planning alone can provide such a transformation of social behavior, and they suggest that other drastic, difficult, and costly remedies would be required to produce the desired changes. The larger question still remains whether such housing alternatives should be offered to the "undeserving" poor or the homeless as a matter of right or humane public policy, whether or not this has any significant impact on their personal attributes or behavior. This more general issue has been discussed more properly and fully in other parts of this book.

Regional Planning and Regional Government

Large metropolitan regions in the United States are characterized by their extreme fragmentation into many separate and autonomous local political units (see chapters 4 and 8). By 1997, for example, there were over 87,000 separate units of government (*Statistical Abstract of the United States,* 1999). This political fragmentation seems to occur because the technological advances in transportation and communications have permitted and encouraged the decentralization and dispersion of large cities into increasingly larger geographic areas, which are physically and economically integrated with the central cities. Such integration has not been accompanied by any real increase in the integration or unification of the many separate governmental units within these metropolitan areas. The populations moving outward from the central cities have resisted annexation and have incorporated themselves into smaller residential enclaves, such as townships, bouroughs, villages, or suburban cities.

This lack of fit between ecological and political boundaries has important consequences for the decision-making structure of entire metropolitan regions. It means that no unified local government decisions applying to all parts of the metropolitan areas are possible. Yet many of the social problems of urban areas can only be effectively controlled by an areawide political system. As many public officials note, air or water pollution does not recognize existing boundaries, nor does traffic congestion, crime, urban blight, poverty, or epidemics. Governmental fragmentation, if it has not actually caused these problems, has nevertheless served to make their solution more difficult. Complicating this "crazy quilt" of local governments is a large number of special districts, usually set up to serve single purposes, such as school districts, sewage treatment districts, fire protection districts, hospital service districts, and so on, and their numbers keep growing. As of 1997, there were 34,683 single function districts, not including school districts, in the United States (*Statistical Abstract of the United States,* 1999). Directors of special districts are not accountable to city or country government officials because special districts are totally separate legal entities, and their boundaries do not always conform to those of any other local governmental units (Phillips, 1996). Perhaps the complexity of multiple jurisdictions and the deadlocks it often produces helps to explain growing interest in the need for some sort of areawide regional planning function or regional government.

Actually there are a relatively large number of regional planning commissions or boards in existence which are set up on a multijurisdictional or metropolitan areawide basis. Most of these are not an integral part of any of the local official governmental entities. Instead they just serve advisory, educational, or promotional functions. Thus, they have little or no power to affect local government programs or policies, such as zoning, land-use controls, transportation, housing or subdivision planning, density or construction standards, environmental controls, long-range master planning, or the like.

An alternative form of intraregional cooperation among adjacent political units is a Council of Governments (COG). This is a voluntary association of local governments which can provide an indirect means of integrating the planning functions more closely with the adjacent governmental units. Supporters of COGs see such agencies as playing an "adjunctive" role in which they would serve as brokers among interdependent decision-making organizations, act as a regional lobby or a "catalyst for action," and help in mobilizing resources to achieve the appropriate regional goals. This view assumes that harmony would be achieved by bringing the realities of urban development and its accompanying problems into proper focus, and by providing a framework within which local governments can cooperate with their neighbors while at the same time pursuing their own individual goals. Skeptics note that COGs operate on goodwill only, and that "sometimes good will runs smack into a fiscal crunch or serious political disagreement" (Phillips, 1996, pp. 345–346), and to date, "most have been little more than intergovernmental talk shows: Views are expressed, but nothing much happens—unless the going gets rough. Then, cities and other local governments walk out."

Other critics go further, arguing that nothing short of the complete integration of regional planning into the framework of a strong regional government will make such planning an effective force for sound regional development (see Gold, 1982). According to them, too much detachment is a serious weakness because it divorces planning from the decision-making processes of an ongoing public body with legal implementing powers. Weiher (1991, p.195) believes that the present system of fragmented local government is antidemocratic, because the current system of jurisdictional boundaries "sponsors segregation of many kinds: Whites from Blacks, lower income groups from the middle class, religious groups from one another." However rational broad-based regional government may seem to some, it does not appear to be politically acceptable in most parts of the United States, and many conservative opponents believe that small local governments are more responsive to citizens' preferences than large bureaucratic ones and that, therefore, fragmented local governments are preferable to centralized ones (Phillips, 1996, p. 346). Thus, examples of metropolitan government are still rare in North America, where resistance to the surrender of autonomy by local municipalities is still great.

One notable exception is Toronto, Canada. which has created a metropolitan planning board as a component unit of a government which has jurisdiction over an impressive array of areawide functions. For example, Toronto's two-tier consolidated metropolitan government consists of a first tier called *Metro,* which is governed by representatives from the preexisting governments, including Toronto, plus twelve suburban governments. Metro has jurisdiction over the entire metropolitan area, including first-tier vital functions such as property assessment, mass transit, health services, law enforcement, parks, public housing, redevelopment and planning, arterial roads, sewage disposal, and water pumping and reservoir functions (Phillips, 1996, p. 347). Remaining or second-tier functions are retained by the local government, including the distribution of water to the homes of their local residents. All indications are that this system works well and is supported by the metropolitan area population.

There is no such broad-based regional government in the United States. The closest approximations include Portland, Oregon's Metropolitan Services District, which has effective land use controls that have significantly restricted unregulated suburban sprawl; and the Metropolitan Council of the Twin Cities, Minneapolis–St. Paul area, which is essentially an areawide planning and coordinating agency that does have some areawide governing and planning powers (Bollens and Schmandt, 1982, p. 373). Also falling a little short of the metropolitan regional governmental ideal is a model based on consolidating governmental and planning functions at the county level, usually including jurisdiction over all cities, suburbs, and rural or undeveloped area within county boundaries. Key working examples of this relatively rare kind of city-county consolidation in the United States are Jacksonville–Duval County, Florida; Nashville–Davidson County, Tennessee; and Indianapolis–Marion County, Indiana.

A variation of this model exists in Dade County–Miami, Florida, the only difference being that this is a two-tier system, which reserves some governmental functions and powers exclusive to the city of Miami. Nevertheless, this system gives the county a powerful and integrating role over an area of 2,054 square miles and twenty-seven municipalities (Phillips, 1996, pp. 347–349). The county government is authorized to promote the entire area's economy, own and operate mass transit systems, construct roads and highways, provide uniform health and welfare services, and maintains central intelligence functions for fire and police protection (Metro–Dade County Planning Department, 1994). However, this consolidation was not accomplished without some continuing power struggles between the two levels of county and city government. This struggle was partially illustrated by the often contradictory and conflicting mass media messages coming separately from county and Miami city officials concerning how crowd control and law enforcement efforts would be handled during the Elian Gonzales episode during winter and spring 2000.

SELECTED BIBLIOGRAPHY

BOLLENS, JOHN C., and HENRY J. SCHMANDT. *The Metropolis,* 4th. ed. New York: Harper & Row, 1982.

BRADLEY, JENNIFER. "Private Suburbs, Public Cities." *The American Prospect.* (May 2000): pp. 46–49.

DEMAREST, MICHAEL, "He Digs Downtown." *Time.* August 24, 1981, pp. 36–43.

DOWNS, ANTHONY. *Urban Problems and Prospects,* 2d ed. Skokie, IL: Rand McNally, 1976.

DREIER, PETER "Bush to Cities: Drop Dead." *The Progressive.* 56 (July 1992): 20–23.

DUANY, ANDRES, ELIZABETH PLATER-ZYBERK, and JEFF BECK. *The Rise of Sprawl and the Decline of the American Dream.* New York: North Point Press, 2000.

EITZEN, D. STANLEY, and MAXINE BACA ZINN. *Social Problems,* 7th ed. Boston: Allyn & Bacon, 1997.

FEAGIN, JOE R., and ROBERT PARKER. *Rebuilding American Cities: The Urban Real Estate Game,* 2d ed. Englewood Cliffs, NJ: Prentice-Hall, 1990.

FRANTZ, DOUGLAS, and CATHERINE COLLINS. *Celebration U.S.A.: Living in Disney's Brave New Town.* New York: Henry Holt, 1999.

FRIED, MARC. "Grieving for a Lost Home." In *The Urban Condition,* Leonard J. Duhl (ed.). New York: Basic Books, 1963.

FRIEDEN, BERNARD J., and ROBERT MORRIS, eds. *Urban Planning and Social Policy.* New York: Basic Books, 1968.

GANS, HERBERT J. *People and Plans: Essays on Urban Problems and Solutions.* New York: Basic Books, 1968.

GOLD, HARRY. *The Professionalization of Urban Planning.* Ann Arbor: University of Michigan Microfilms, 1965.

_____. "The Dynamics of Professionalization: The Case of Urban Planning." In *Social Change: Explorations, Diagnoses, and Conjectures,* George K. Zollschan and Walter Hirsch (eds.). New York: John Wiley and Sons, 1976.

_____. *The Sociology of Urban Life.* Englewood Cliffs, NJ: Prentice-Hall, 1982.

GREER, SCOTT. *Urban Renewal and American Cities.* Indianapolis: Bobbs-Merrill, 1965.

HALL, PETER. *Cities in Civilization.* New York: Pantheon Books (Random House), 1998.

HALL, THOMAS. "Urban Planning in Sweden." In *Planning and Urban Growth in the Nordic Countries,* Thomas Hall (ed.). London: Spon, 1991.

HECLO, H., and H. MADSEN. *Policy and Pollitics in Sweden: Principled Pragmatism.* Philadelphia: Temple University Press, 1987.

HOWARD, EBENEZER. *Garden Cities of Tomorrow.* London: Faber and Faber, 1902.

JACOBS, JANE. *The Death and Decline of American Cities.* New York: Random House, 1961.

LEGGITTT, CAROL. *Social Values and Urban Form.* New Brunswick, NJ: Urban Studies Center, Rutgers University, 1964.

LEMANN, NICHOLAS. "The Myth of Community Development." *The New York Times Magazine,* January 9, 1994.

MACIONIS, JOHN J., and VINCENT N. PARRILLO. *Cities and Urban Life.* Upper Saddle River, NJ: Prentice-Hall, 1998.

MAIRET, PHILLIP. *Pioneer of Sociology.* London: Lund Humphries, 1957.

MUMFORD, LEWIS. "The Skyline: Mother Jacobs Home Remedies." *The New Yorker.* 38(1962): 168.

O'BRIEN, TIMOTHY J. "Bush Proposal for Enterprise Zones Draws Skepticism." *Wall Street Journal,* June 4, 1992, p. B2.

PALEN, J. JOHN. *The Urban World,* 5th ed. New York: Mc-Graw-Hill, 1997.

PASS, D. *Vallingby and Farstas—From Ideas to Reality: The New Community Development Process in Stockholm.* Cambridge: MIT Press, 1973.

PERLOFF, HARVEY S. *Education for Planning: City, State, Regional.* Baltimore, MD: Johns Hopkins University Press, 1957.

PHILLIPS, BARBARA E. *City Lights: Urban-Suburban Life in the Global Society.* New York: Oxford University Press, 1996.

POPENOE, DAVID. *The Suburban Environment: Sweden and the United States.* Chicago: University of Chicago Press, 1977.

RIESMAN, DAVID. *The Lonely Crowd.* New York: Doubleday, 1956.

ROSS, ANDREW. *The Celebration Chronicles: Life, Liberty, and the Pursuit of Property Values in Disney's New Town.* New York: Ballantine Books, 1999.

SCOTT, MEL. *American City Planning since 1890.* Berkeley: University of California Press, 1969.

THOMLINSON, RALPH. *Urban Structure.* New York: Random House, 1969.

WALKER, ROBERT A. *The Planning Function in Local Government.* Chicago: University of Chicago Press, 1950.

WARTZMAN, RICK, and JOHN HARWOOD. "Congress, Bush Back Enterprise Zones for Inner Cities." *Wall Street Journal.* May 13, 1992, p. A3.

WEBSTER, DONALD H. *Urban Planning and Municipal Public Policy.* New York: Harper & Row, 1958.

WEIHER, GREGORY R. *The Fractured Metropolis: Political Fragmentation and Metropolitan Segregation.* Albany: State University of New York Press. 1991.

15

THE FUTURE OF AMERICAN URBAN LIFE AND URBAN SOCIAL POLICY

Throughout this book, the focus has been primarily on past and current trends in the process of urbanization. Much of what has been said here about urban life suggests that it is a complex and ever-changing phenomenon. By the time we have begun to understand some of the forces that have been shaping the urban present, the even less well understood forces, which will shape the urban future, are already underway. Predictions about the urban future by social scientists, urban planners, philosophers, futurologists, science fiction writers, and ordinary citizens abound, ranging all the way from optimistic projections of a utopian or problem-free brave new urban world to the most pessimistic prophesies of doom for urban civilization as we now know it. Of course, nothing is absolutely certain about the direction of the urban future. But because current human activity is to a large extent based on anticipation of the future, it is important to look at some of the social, economic, technological, environmental, and political trends of the present that seem most likely to extend into and shape the future, thus providing the key contexts in which the opportunities and problems of urban communities and urban living are likely to unfold in the decades ahead. This chapter speculates on the future of urban America. The following chapter on world urbanization also more broadly considers the urban future in a global context.

FUTURE STUDIES

Actually the study of the future is old in many ways. Since ancient times people have speculated about the future and have tried to visualize what was ahead. These early speculations were more imaginative and fanciful than scientific, and they were usually designed by philosophers who were concerned with the "good community" or "ideal state." Later science fiction provided a more realistic note to future dreams, particularly when scientifically minded thinkers or artists, such as Leonardo da Vinci, tried to imagine flying machines and other future technological possibilities. Some of the best science fiction of the past few decades has presented brilliant glimpses of the future. As one prominent writer has noted: "One of the functions of science fiction is to serve as early warning system. In fact, the very act of description may prevent some futures, by a kind of exclusion principle. Far from predicting the future, science fiction often exorcises it. At the very least, it makes us ask ourselves: What kind of future do we really want? No other type of literature poses such fundamental questions, at any rate explicitly" (Clarke, 1977). Artistic expressions of the urban future may also be found in abstract painting and sculpture which may also conceive of the world of tomorrow subjectively interpreted by the artist.

Social scientists have approached the study of the future with different methods, using empirical and logical techniques of analysis rather than original speculation. The study of social change, for example, has been at the heart of sociology since its inception, although what was traditionally and basically examined was the history of changes in social arrangements that had already taken place or were in the process. However, in the past several decades a branch of social science known as *futurology* has grown in importance. Futurologists are concerned with examining the future systematically, either by projecting current trends into the future or by projecting alternative future scenarios developed from contemporary situations (see Hall, 1998, pp. 943–989; Weeks, 1996, pp. 269–270; Popenoe, 1993, pp. 557–559; Naisbitt and Aburdene, 1990).

The principle futurist argument is that the future is contained within a domain of alternative possibilities that may be specified by logical means and laid out in balance sheets that facilitate rational selection among the alternatives. Once this is done, policies to bring about the desired alternatives may then be more effectively formulated. In recent decades, the methods for forecasting the future have expanded almost immeasurable in many different directions, and it has become much clearer that the particular vision of the future that is achieved will differ according to the method used. For example, the following is a list of forecasting methods that have appeared in futurist literature over the years:

1. Trend extrapolation: the concept that the most recent historical changes and forces will continue into at least the near future.
2. Modeling and simulation techniques: conceptual images depicting the interrelationships of several parameters involved in a particular process or subsystem.
3. Historical analogy: the study of historical events and circumstances surrounding certain periods of change in an effort to generalize about what might happen under similar circumstances in the future.
4. Morphological analysis: all of the variables of particular problems are defined and combined in all possible ways. The less promising combinations are weeded out, and the goals or potential courses of action are selected from among the remaining alternatives.
5. Scenario writing: a process that demonstrates the possibility of future developments by exhibiting a chain of events that might lead to them, and the interaction of complex factors in this chain.

(See Berry and Kasarda, 1977, p. 426; Gold, 1982, pp. 356–357; Kornblum, 1997, p. 277; Weeks, 1996, p. 561.)

The study of the urban future has spurred the collection of data in many different contexts: many sociologists, geographers, urban planners, social policy analysts, and scholars in all of the fields concerned with urbanism and urbanization have become interested in projecting aspects of the urban future that seem both plausible and probable, if particular conditions are present. There is general agreement that the future for the United States and for most of the world (see chapter 16) will be an urban one, because the historical processes contributing to the growth of urban societies are not likely to reverse the process in the foreseeable future. Further, most projections of future population growth trends suggest that the demands for shelter, food, and other basic essentials of living will require the kinds of complex social, economic, and political organization that are characteristic of urban societies. However, within the broad range of these generalizations, there is far less agreement of the particulars of future urban societies and urban living (Gold, 1982, p. 358–359).

SOME HAZARDS OF FORECASTING THE FUTURE

Projecting the future has become a more risky task than it has been through most of history. Until several centuries ago, the rates of social change were more gradual and slower than they are today. Technology then did not yet have as powerful a grasp upon the daily lives of people, and the kinds of rapid technological transformations implied in terms such as the "industrial revolution," the "urban revolution," or the communications and information revolution so apparent at the beginning of the twenty-first century had not yet occurred. In today's urban world, in contrast, the rates of change have so accelerated and their consequences have become so significant that current developments now often outrun our awareness or understanding of what has actually been happening. The attempts to accurately anticipate the future are further complicated by the now more fully recognized fact that the goals and interests of individuals, groups, and communities—whether they are clearly articulated or consciously pursued—will most certainly have an impact on crucial future developments. After nearly two centuries of rapid technological change and a growing sophistication about the ways in which social policies may influence and promote the direction of urban growth and development, appreciation for the powerful role of human purposed in shaping the future has been growing.

In addition to an ever-accelerating rate of change and to the growing realization that human purposes affect what areas of change will develop and grow, another complexity is produced by humanity's intellectual development and its capacity to foresee the future in a growing variety of ways. For example, sociologists have produced a competing number of theories of social change. One prominent sociological perspective concerning social change is the *structural-functional* perspective, in which social systems are viewed as having a strong tendency to reach a state of "equilibrium" between the different parts of the social system. According to this perspective, if change occurs in one part of the system, it places strains on all the other parts, causing the system to develop a mechanism that will lead to equilibrium. But *conflict* theory has also emerged as a competing theoretical perspective regarding social change. This perspective argues that social conflict is a permanent condition of all human societies, and that one can find a constant struggle between different groups in a society, each trying to maximize their relative positions of wealth, prestige, or power. This last perspective, in fact, is an integral part of the new urban sociology (political-economy) approach introduced and discussed in earlier parts of this book (see chapters 1, 7, and 8 for the most direct applications). Relationships to the means of production or to the prevailing hierarchy of power and authority are among the alternative bases for social change, and social change inevitably is the result of social conflict.

The debates among the proponents of the various theories of social change have not been resolved, although a good deal of historical analysis has been employed in the attempt (see Dahrendorf, 1959; Zollschan and Hirsch, 1976; Kourvetaris, 1997). The main point being made here, however, is that projections of what the urban future may hold in store tend to be highly dependent on the intellectual perspective of the prognosticator, as well as his or her degree of optimism or pessimism, with respect to the likely causes and consequences of social change. Of course, the vested interests of those promoting certain kinds of social, economic, political, or technological changes may also shape the images of the future expounded by some prognosticators, and this kind of motivation needs to be considered as well.

The final hazard of forecasting the future is that most, even well-planned, efforts at social change have not turned out as expected or hoped for because of unintended or unanticipated social consequences. One only has to look at previous efforts to predict future events, most of which have turned out to bear scant resemblance to what was actually forecast. For example, the year 2000 had loomed large in the human imagination through most of the twentieth century, and endless predictions were made about what life would be like by the beginning of the twenty-first century—most of them assuming that amazing advances and changes would transform the world and ease its daily burdens.

A number of the more interesting twentieth-century predictions for 2000 that failed the test of time have been cited by Suzan Levine (2000, p. 11), and some of these deserve repeating here. An article in the December 1900 issue of the *Ladies Home Journal,* for example, predicted that by 2000, America's large cities would be pleasant, uncongested metropolises with nearly all traffic routed underground or high above ground. Traffic "will be confined to broad subways or tunnels, well lighted and well ventilated, or to high trestles with 'moving-sidewalk' stairways leading to the top. . . . Cities, therefore, will be free from all noises." The same article also predicted that the English alphabet would have by then shedded C, X, and Q as unnecessary and that English would become a language of "condensed words expressing condensed ideas." In a 1967 speech, Noble laureate Glenn Seaborg, then head of the U.S. Atomic Energy Commission, promoted a device that would be programmed for the needs of housewives of 2000. It would, he said, be capable of simultaneously sweeping, vacuuming, dusting, washing, and "picking up your husband's clothing." In the same year, then Vice President Hubert Humphrey was wrongly too optimistic when he predicted manned trips to Mars and the elimination of bacterial and viral diseases by the year 2000. In 1961, according to Levine, the National Capital Planning Commission report for the Washington, DC, region speculated that "family helicopters for leisure time use along controlled airways" were a possibility for 2000. Finally, a Xerox Corporation report of several decades ago concluded that because of a "greater understanding of the learning process and the use of technology, students would be able to finish an education in four years which previously had taken twelve years." Referring to educational materials that need to be learned, the Xerox report urged, "Simply wire them into a computer . . . and download away! . . . No messy keyboarding. . . . Just put on your Electro Encephalogram cap (make sure electrodes are firmly attached) and quiz the machine for the desired knowledge, even while you are sleeping." (I'm sure most students reading this book are still waiting for this last one, as is this author!)

Although all of the above illustrations were far too optimistic about social and technological "progress," it is equally possible to be much too pessimistic about the possibilities of future change, as illustrated by this quote: "In 1877 the Chief Engineer of the British Post Office was asked if the newly invented telephone would be of any practical value. He replied, 'No sir, the Americans have need of the telephone, but we do not. We have plenty of messenger boys'" (Gold, 1982, p. 359). Levine (2000, p. 11) has suggested that the precision of a prediction is often less important than the human need to make such predictions, whatever their accuracy, as a "comforting way of asserting a sense of control." In this respect, she cites the supporting view of sociologist Amitai Etzioni, who believes that society has a psychological need to speculate about future events and further argues that "the more our world is coming apart, the more anxious we are about what tomorrow holds." Nevertheless, Etzioni himself remains skeptical of the value or accuracy of long-range predictions and advises us that "anyone who tells us they can predict for 20 years out, I tell them to predict three months." With these kinds of forecasting hazards in mind, we now move ahead to review some of the major kinds of forecasts that have been made about the urban future. These involve some utopian as well as some decidedly nonutopian views.

SOME UTOPIAN VISIONS OF THE URBAN FUTURE

People have long searched for the ideal city, although their conceptions of the ideal have varied from century to century. In the fourteenth century, for example, the English statesman and writer Sir Thomas More envisaged an ideal society, which he called *Utopia* in a book of the same name. More presented a vision of a community where all sociopolitical ills had been eliminated, and the entire social order was rationally reformed to benefit the community as a whole. Since the initial success of this work, the label *utopia* has been applied to all kinds of portrayals of the ideal problem-free community, no matter how impractical and fantasized such projections may seem. From the rational scientific perspectives that have dominated the twentieth century, utopian visions of future cities usually have been described as fantasies too grandiose and unreal for a practical world and as representative of the abandonment of all reason (Gold, 1982, p. 361).

Yet utopian thinking regarding the city has been defended by at least some responsible social scientists as a useful tool for anticipating or planning the urban future. Meyerson (1961) had much earlier suggested that planners ought to recognize the value of utopian formulations in the depicting of future communities as they might be seen through alternative normative lenses, while Dahl and Lindblom had also suggested earlier that as models, utopias indicate directions in which alternatives to existing realities might be looked for, help people to focus on long range goals, and could also serve as aids to motivation (see Gold, 1982, p. 361). Some of the most serious and widely cited examples of utopian visions of the hypothetical urban future are summarized below:

A. Megastructures or minicities. These are commonly represented by Paolo Soleri's concept for giant supraterrestrial human "hives" housing up to hundreds of thousands of persons, or by Moshe Safdie's design for a "plug in, clip on" megastructure, which he called *Habitat,* and which was on display at Expo 1967 at Montreal. These concepts involved miniaturizing cities and building them so that they can be compactly arranged within a single, giant, enclosed megastructure, or within a close web of physically interconnected structures (Gold, 1982, p. 362). Called *arcologies* (architectural ecologies) by Soleri, such cities would supposedly reduce time and space obstacles to human activity and would be the means for bringing "beauty, harmony, efficiency, and spaciousness" to cities. About 30 years ago, Soleri attempted to develop a self-contained prototype city designed to house about seven thousand residents in a desert area near Phoenix, to demonstrate his arcology concept. But as of 1997, it housed only about seventy residents (Macionis and Parrillo, 1998, p. 398), and has served more as an educational tool for visitors than as a totally realized new kind of city.

Going a step further, Dantzig and Saaty (1973) had prepared a detailed plan for a compact city that incorporated the ideas of the influential architect Le Corbusier and the city planning critic Jane Jacobs, as well as those of Soleri. Their city would include a population base of two hundred fifty thousand people residing in a compact area of approximately 2.2 square miles. The city would have a circular radius of three thousand feet, and

Earthquake damage to roads, bridges, and automobiles following a San Francisco earthquake in the 1990s

would be exactly eighteen times its height. Its core would contain shops, churches, and hotels. Its core edge would serve as a parking area and would contain ramps for ascending and descending to various levels, as well as a promenade with small parks and recreation areas. The city would also have an inner residential area, a midplaza, and an outer residential area. Each part of the city would be interconnected by roadways featuring electrically powered automobiles, but only a very limited number of such vehicles would be necessary because of the compactness of the city. Most movement of people would be on foot. While governor of New York State, Nelson Rockefeller proposed a similar type of megastructure development for the lower tip of Manhattan. It was to consist of massive towers, high connecting bridges, and dozens of high-rise apartment houses with an elevated pedestrian mall surrounded by other physically interconnected dwellings housing thousands of people (Gold, 1982, pp. 361–362). The entire project, which was never undertaken, was to be developed as a large land fill totaling approximately ninety acres.

B. Water cities. These involve large scale "futurist" designs for enormous activity nodes standing on stilts in shallow coastal waters. They would include Buckminster Fuller's concept of floating communities of thirty thousand persons in up to twenty-story high structures sitting on reinforced concrete platforms, which could be built in shipyards and towed to usable places just offshore of existing coastal cities and anchored in water up to twenty or thirty feet in depth. There have been similar proposals for Tokyo Bay and for Baltimore Harbor, and some advocates had concluded that floating settlements on the oceans would be considerably less costly than settlements on difficult to develop land formations, such as mountains, swamps, deserts, or frozen soil.

B. Underground, underwater, or space cities. Jacques Cousteau had collaborated in the design of a floating island in which "more comfortable dwelling quarters may be floating stably a hundred feet or so below the surface where any wave motion is so damped as to be unnoticeable" (Eldredge, 1974). Huge salt mine caverns have been proposed for underground experimental cities that could have community temperature and atmospheric controls, which might be especially desirable in desert or subarctic regions. All these kinds of proposals have been widely illustrated in countless science fiction novels and films, and not uncommon, of course, are the science fiction–like proposals to ease the environmental burden of the planet earth by developing extraterrestrial space communities and opening up the solar system to human development.

D. Communes. These are one of the most concrete expressions of utopian goals, and they were discussed in chapter 10 as real alternatives to traditional forms of family and/or religious living. They are experimental attempts to create new and appealing lifestyles as alternatives to the traditional features of modern urban-industrial life (Gold, 1982, p. 362). Generally seeking "spirituality," "freedom," "love," or "escape," thousands of groups have sought to create such innovative communities in the United States during the past two centuries. Some of the better known early efforts included the celibate New England Shakers; the Owenites at New Harmony, Indiana; and the Oneida community of New York State. More recently, the counterculture of the so-called hippie youth movements and various religious-political cults had created a wide diversity of experimental communelike alternative lifestyles (see Shepherd and Shepherd, 2000; Stark, 1998). Eldredge (1974) argued that, despite the murderous results of a very small number of these innovative communities, "such efforts must not be crushed. . . . The affluent West affords millions of the idle rich, non-producing youngsters, idling oldsters and millions of unemployed; it most certainly can afford a few tens of thousands of experimenters seeking a better life on earth. They might even have something!"

The list of utopian designs for the urban future could go on and on. But a major criticism is the oversimplicity of many of the alternatives represented here. Although they are imaginative, usually in terms of a reordered physical or technological environment, most of them do not involve the complex social, economic, or political dimensions essential for dealing with a new kind of urban world. Sociologists and anthropologists, aware of the complexity of contemporary social arrangements and recognizing that everyday realities in all communities rest upon a complicated web of assumptions, values, and adaptive behaviors, are acutely aware of how limited is our understanding of such future large-scale urban entities (Gold, 1982) Likewise, political scientists and economists are equally aware of the dangers of projecting the kind of technological determinism that is often reflected in the physical designs for proposed utopian communities. With these precautions in mind, several nonutopian visions of the urban future are reviewed below. They are more limited in scope and more tied to an empirical assessment of the realistic constraints that make it highly unlikely that perfection is ever achievable in the social and physical arrangements of human communities. Nevertheless, as Macionis and Parrillo (1998, p. 391) have correctly pointed out: "[I]n the final analysis, society needs utopian thinkers. They are, by their work, natural consciousness raisers. They challenge our thinking about cities, point to obvious problems, and prod us to consider visionary solutions that we 'on the street' barely understand." And in a few instances, some utopian predictions may, in fact, eventually come to be at least partially realized.

SOME NONUTOPIAN VISIONS OF THE URBAN FUTURE

Some of the most common types of forecasts of the urban future by social scientists are based on the extrapolation of trends that are currently underway and extended into the near future. Chinoy (1972), for example, had forecasted continued metropolitan growth, greater growth in the suburbs than in the cities, continued white migration out of central cities, central cities becoming proportionately more black in population composition, less densely populated cities, fewer jobs available in cities for their residents and more unplanned growth. Cohen (1976) had listed some of the problems areas that he predicted would remain difficult to manage, if the urban future would continue in the direction of "more of the same." He thus predicted:

1. the continuing growth of metropolitan areas
2. the increasing bureaucratization and professionalization of municipal services
3. the growing distance between centralized urban decision making and the points of impact
4. the explosion in public demands and expectations
5. the growing complexities of federal-state-local interdependencies
6. the increasing breakdown of formal political machinery at the local level

7. changes in the scale and character of future migration patterns
8. the greater interdependencies involved in urban living
9. the metropolitanization of urban problems
10. the inability to adequately renew older sections of the cities
11. more generally the pervasive mood of alienation and powerlessness alleged to be characteristic of urban life.

These projections tended to imply a continued drift in the existence of already recognized urban social problems and a growing dissatisfaction with the quality of urban living. They also anticipate that there will be little motivation or initiative to make the radical changes required to redesign the urban future, so that, almost by default, a continuation of current social arrangements is likely to characterize the urban future. At the time of this writing, approximately a quarter of a century after the discussed projections were made, it would be hard to argue that their prognosticators were very much off the mark of current urban social realities, as they have been described so far in this book.

One problem with such forecasts is that they tend to ramble over a diversity of unrelated issues in somewhat of a "shotgun" approach. A potentially more coherent framework for anticipating the urban future in a more orderly way is the ecosystem approach mentioned in the introductory chapter and implied, if not explicitly articulated, in many parts of this book. Using the ecosystem components of *population, technology, environment,* and *social structure,* the following discussion speculates on some possible future developments in each of these ecosystem components.

POPULATION

To determine future population size, assumptions must be made along three dimensions: (1) fertility—how many children each woman will bear; (2) mortality—how many people will die, and at what age; and (3) migration—will people move, and if so, how many, and to what new locations? Uncertainty about future trends in immigration and mortality exists, and making responsible assumptions about the future course of fertility in projecting the future population of the United States is even more difficult. The total population of the United States for the year 2000 has been projected to be 274,634,000 by the U.S. Census Bureau, based on a middle series of estimates (*Statistical Abstract of the United States,* 1999). By 2050, the middle-range projection forecasts a U.S. population of 393,931,000 people. The middle-range projections probably represent the best estimate, but based on alternative low and high assumptions developed by the Census Bureau, the projected 2050 population could range any where between 282,524,000 and 518,903,000 people (*Statistical Abstract of the United States,* 1999). These estimates assume that migration to the United States will remain at its current levels, so that most of the increase in population size would then be due to natural increase—a surplus of births over deaths. At any rate, the most plausible middle series of these estimates forecast sizable and continuing population growth for the United States in the near future.

Just where the expected increased population will live is a major issue that must still be confronted. If massive migration from rural areas has just about leveled off, and no unexpected massive migration occurs from urban areas to rural areas (although a slight change in this latter direction has been detected in the late 1990s), most of the population increases will take place in the existing metropolitan areas of the United States, or within daily commuting distance of these areas (see chapter 4). This probably means continuing urban sprawl, with all its perceived advantages and disadvantages. By the late 1990s, such sprawl had begun to produce distinct no growth or controlled growth movements in opposition to unlimited urban sprawl and had become a controversial political issue for the 2000 national and local elections (*New York Times,* March 3, 2000, p. A25 and April 13, 1999, p. A 29; *Detroit News,* October 24, 1999, p. 9C; *Detroit Free Press,* October 11, 1999, p. 4B). Antisprawl groups see longer commuter trips, greater traffic congestion, depletion of fossil fuel reserves and undeveloped land, destruction of the natural environment and wildlife, the greater costs of road development and maintenance, and the loss of any "sense of community" as among the undesirable consequences of urban sprawl, whereas proponents of continuous decentralization of suburban development emphasize the freedom of choice for people to live wherever they want, unrestricted by "excessive" land-use controls. This controversy, of course, raises the issue of government planning versus the free play of the marketplace, which is discussed in more detail later in this chapter. Although it is difficult to predict the outcome of this controversy, proponents of the political economy approach to urban sociology would most likely see free market forces of "urban growth machines" determining the direction of the outcome, and this would suggest at least some continuing urban sprawl for the foreseeable future (see chapter 8).

What is even less certain is how the future metropolitan populations will be distributed among their central cities and suburban belts. If current trends continue, the large central cities will continue at their present population levels or would continue to lose population to the suburbs. If, on the other hand, a newer trend toward people moving back to the cities from the suburbs, which is now relatively small, significantly accelerates, the cities might begin to regain parity with the suburbs in their relative population size. A number of observers have suggested that *gentrification* would be the best hope for the regeneration and revitalization of city populations (see Frankfort-Nachmias and Palen, 1993; Hudson, 1984; DiGiovanni, 1984). Gentrification generally refers to the return of more affluent suburbanites back into older, previously declining areas of the central cities. The future of gentrification depends on the attractions that living in the cities hold for future returnees. It also depends on the responses of those displaced by gentrification, mainly the low-income residents of such areas and the local merchants who serve their poor customer's daily needs. Status conflicts between the new more affluent residents and the remaining poor residents can produce social class, lifestyle, and behavioral clashes that may be threatening and discourage some of the newcomers from remaining (Kornblum, 1997). Estimates of the impact of gentrification vary widely. Although Macionis and Parrillo (1998, p. 278) estimate that virtually every major city in the United States is experiencing some gentrification, Palen (1997, p. 314) concludes that it "as yet encompasses only a few new neighborhoods in any one city," and that "its importance lies not so much in its size but in its reversal of long-term patterns and in its potential for shaping future housing needs."

Whatever the prospects for central city population growth, versus anticipated continuing population growth in the suburbs, each of these sets of possible circumstances would pose different consequences for urban society. Political reapportionment and changes in the relative political power of cities and suburbs, and the resultant priorities of the federal and state governments in aiding either cities or suburbs in spending and tax policies, would be among the areas expected to be affected by changes in the relative distribution of the future U.S. population among cities, suburbs, and their surrounding regions.

The changing age structure of the U.S. population is another major factor to be considered in assessing the urban future. In recent decades, due to declining fertility rates and improvements in life expectancy and longevity, the population has been aging rather rapidly, with larger proportions of elderly and retired people. For example, although only about 8 percent of the U.S. population was age 65 or older in 1950, the percentage increased to 12.8 percent by 1996. In actual numbers the population 65 or older increased from slightly over 12 million people in 1950 to nearly 34 million people in 1996. By the year 2030, the population age 65 and older will have increased to 20 percent of the U.S. population and will number over 69 million people, according to recent U.S. Census Bureau projections (*New York Times 2000 Almanac,* 1999, p. 290). Likewise, the population age 85 and older is also expected to grow in numbers, and as a proportion of the total U.S. population, over the same time period. Past aging of the population has been reflected in the changing priorities and expenditures of local, state, and federal governments in various income, health, and housing programs for the elderly. In 1969, the elderly were getting about 23 percent of the national budget in federal programs and benefits. In fiscal year 1979, they got about 40 percent of the national budget, which was more in dollars than the entire 1969 federal budget (Gold, 1982, p. 365)!

If these projections of the elderly population are correct, it is more than likely that the elderly population will receive more than half of all federal domestic expenditures by 2030. As the elderly population becomes an even more potent political force in demanding services and expenditures from the federal and other levels of government, this would quite likely cause a squeeze or cutbacks in other needed programs not directly related to their own real and perceived needs, such as schools, day care centers, and the like. If the elderly choose to reside primarily in cities, this can mean pressure for additional government aid and appropriations to the cities, but if they choose to live elsewhere, such as in suburbs or small towns, the cities would most likely be bypassed in favor of those suburban or small town communities with more pressing priorities created by a growing elderly population.

A growing population is also expected to increase the costs of land for housing as the available homesites in and around the major metropolitan centers are gradually used up. The increased costs of housing in the 1990s has made single-family home ownership increasingly difficult or impossible for a growing portion of the American population, and nothing is now in sight that is likely to alleviate this trend in the foreseeable future. This could have a significant impact on the future standards of living and lifestyles in the United States.

If the U.S. population continues to consume energy, raw materials, and manufactured goods at its current per capita levels or higher, then the projected future population growth will most certainly create additional demands against the finite or limited supply of these resources. If new and cheaper sources of energy and raw materials are not found or developed, the rising costs and shortages expected are very likely to force consumption rates down, thus potentially lowering the American material standard of living. In antici-pation of these potential developments, the country has been attempting to develop energy policies that will bring about these changes more gradually and predictably, to somewhat ease the burden, but little visible progress has been made in this direction. Related future environmental problems are further discussed in a following section on the environment component of the ecosystem.

TECHNOLOGY

Americans have always had a high degree of faith that science and technology could be used effectively to solve critical problems and to enhance the quality of life. Technology undoubtedly has contributed in many ways to the relatively high general health levels of the nation and to much material comfort for the average individual than in prescientific eras. Many urban and social planners anticipate future advances in communications and transportation as principle technological arenas for future attempts to improve the worka-bility of urban communities.

Communications

In 1974, H. Wentworth Eldredge made a prediction of a wired city that was cited in Gold (1982, pp. 362–363) as an example of an "extreme utopian vision of the possible urban future." The wired city would become a nonterritorial, high-intensity, participatory community fitted to a national cable/microwave grid of metropolitan multinational net-works, reinforced or supplanted by satellite connections and lasers. Computers serving both as storage facilities and as analysts with display capabilities would be at the center of this technology, based on the infinite possibilities of mutichannel electronic communica-tions and interaction. "In the wired city, every dwelling would have a typewriter like key-board with print out capabilities and a display screen located in a home recreation, information, or business center." Today this projection is no longer a utopian dream, and although it has not yet been perfectly realized, it now is more than just a very realistic possibility for the near future.

Newer developments have already surpassed this projection, with newer technolo-gies based on the Internet and on the broadband channels that support it. They are begin-ning to provide a critical mass of pervasive digital communications available to most offices and homes around the world, coupled with the ability to store and manipulate many different forms of information in a common digital form, and with very small yet very powerful devices for processing, display, and communications (Hall, 1998, p. 949). In addition, many new formats of wireless communication have already emerged, and, as Bill Gates had previously described it, the personal computer would soon be a wallet PC containing electronic money and keys, as well as acting as a communications center (Gates, 1995). Related breakthroughs already available are the lightweight electronic book, and e-mail, which will be accessible through wallet, PC, or television sets. Palmtop PCs have already demonstrated these possibilities.

The applications of these new technologies are virtually endless. They include "tele-medicine and tele-health care; tele-education and tele-learning; on-line information services; electronic publishing; financial services, trading and brokering; teleshopping; all kinds of entertainment; electronic sports; security and surveillance monitoring; environmental monitoring and control; digital imaging and photography; and data searching and processing" (GB Office of Science and Technology, 1995; Hall, 1998, p. 950). Castells (1989, p. 32, and 1996) has characterized most of these types of applications as not central to knowledge and information per se, but rather as "the application of such knowledge and information to knowledge generation and information processing communication devices, in a cumulative feedback loop between innovation and the uses of innovation."

One of the critical questions is, What effect will the revolution in communications now underway have on the urban future? For example, will the new forms of communication become a substitute for outmoded and costly transportation systems, which would become less necessary, and will distance become almost irrelevant in determining the shape and form of cities and metropolitan areas? An interesting concept is what Francis Cairncross (1995) called *The Death of Distance*. As he put it, "the death of distance will mean that any activity that relies on a screen or telephone can be carried out anywhere in the world," regardless of location. According to this view, the death of distance will at least equalize the locational advantages of all places in the world, allowing almost infinite decentralization from one location to another, transferring activities to wherever people happen to be (Hall, 1998, p. 957). Bill Gates has defended this potential impact of modern communications technology on locational restrictions, as follows: "There will be a day, not far distant, when you will be able to conduct business, study, explore the world and its cultures, call up any great entertainment, make friends, attend neighborhood markets, and show pictures to distant relatives—without leaving your desk or armchair. You won't leave your network connection behind at the office or in the classroom. It will be more than an object you carry an appliance you purchase" (Gates, 1995; Hall, 1998, p. 957). Many activities, ranging from routine clerical work to higher education to shopping, can now in whole or in part be conducted remotely, in the home or in local workstations, by Internet.

William. J. Mitchell (1995) goes further than most prognosticators of the technological future in predicting the demise of the city, as we now know it, in his book *City of Bits*. He predicts the city of bits "will be a city unrooted to any definite spot of the surface of the earth, shaped by connectivity and bandwidth constraints, rather than by accessibility," and he further argues that the new technology will dissolve the glue that holds cities together, allowing entire chunks to break away and reform in new ways and new places in cyberspace.

Peter Hall, upon whose work this section of this chapter is strongly based, is in fundamental agreement with most of the prophesies of the technological revolution in communications and information systems summarized earlier. However, he does draw the line with respect to the demise or death of traditional cities. He persuasively argues that although technological change will bring about a general reshaping of the urban map, it almost certainly would not bring about a general dispersal from existing metropolitan centers, such as New York and San Francisco and other technologically advanced metropolitan centers. Although such centers will continue to grow and decentralize, even the most innovative and technolog-ically advanced activities in these centers will continue to need a great deal of face-to-face contact. Some form of agglomeration, or clustering of interdependent and interrelated activi-ties that are central to many of the new (as well as old) technologies, have required, and will require, a great deal of social networking (see chapter 5) in the development of innovative products and services. Hall mentions art, culture, entertainment, education, medicine and health care, financial and business services, architecture, engineering, and, more generally, most forms of management, as among those urban activities that routinely require face-to-face interaction, as well as those involved in communications technology. And Hall also tellingly reminds us that, although Bill Gates may have wooed his wife on the Internet, "many would find that an inadequate substitute for real life; similarly with all manner of eat-ing, drinking, and variegated schmoozing" (see Hall, 1998, pp. 956–965, for an excellent ex-tended discussion on the future of cities in the new technological and information age).

Transportation

The increases in metropolitan sprawl in recent decades have been accompanied by increased reliance on the automobile, as more people have been living and working in metropolitan areas. The World Resources Institute reports car ownership in the United States at 561 per 1,000 residents, the highest in the world (Word Resources, 1996, p 82). Fifty-eight percent of U.S. residents own two or more cars, and 20 percent own three or more. As the metropolitan area populations continue to grow even more in the future, more people and more goods will be making more trips in urban areas, often over longer distances. How America's metropolitan areas cope with this burgeoning demand for urban travel has long run implications for the environment, economic well-being, and liv-ability of these areas.

Unlike communications, however, there have as yet been no major technological revolutions or panaceas to solve urban transportation problems. Growing private automo-bile use has created a greater propensity for travel and a demand for more roads and free-ways. Adding to this demand are increasing business and industrial activities, which place more service vehicles and heavy duty freight hauling trucks on urban roads and highways. Ever more dispersed urban sprawl has also resulted in a demand for more roads, which translates into longer journeys, more congestion, and yet more fuel consumption and air pollution. As more roads are built to reduce traffic congestion, even these soon begin to exceed their capacity. A case in point is Atlanta, Georgia. So many people have been moving to Atlanta, that ever-widening rings of rural counties around the city are finding their roads clogged with daily commuters. The region, which has doubled its population in the last three decades, to 3.1 million people, had recently become ineligible for federal highway funds for new road projects because its ozone level had become one of the worst in the country (*New York Times,* March 25, 1999, p. A18). This pattern of growing high-way and road congestion is widespread in growing metropolitan areas throughout the country. A study by the Texas Transportation Institution, for example, found that the average driver in the 35 most traffic congested urban areas in the United States wasted 4 tanks of gasoline a year sitting in congested traffic jams, and that the average driver spends 34 hours a year trapped in snarled traffic jams in the nation's 68 largest metropolitan areas. Los Angeles leads the nation with the dubious distinction of an average of 84 hours (approximately 3 1/2 days) a year per driver in traffic tie-ups, with Washington, DC, a close second with 76 hours of traffic tie-ups per year for the average commuter (*Detroit Free Press,* November 17, 1999, p. 11A; see Table 15.1 for a list of cities with the greatest amount of time spent in traffic tie-ups).

One of the major factors contributing to urban transportation problems is that people do not pay for the full cost of automobile travel. Motorists rarely pay enough taxes to support the investments needed to construct and repair the additional roads that are needed (World Resources, 1996, p. 88). Nor do car or gasoline prices reflect less tangible costs such as the negative health effects of automotive air pollution or productive losses incurred by traffic delays, such as those mentioned earlier. Another problem related to the heavy reliance on private auto transportation in the United States is the social inequity that is created by the limited access to jobs by the urban poor, as well as by proportionately higher transportation costs. As already pointed out in earlier chapters, suburban flight has left the urban poor concentrated in city centers far from jobs and services that have also dispersed to the suburbs. Unable to afford cars, many poorer city dwellers must rely on public transportation that only rarely adequately serves the suburbs. This has played an important role in limiting job and income opportunities (World Resources, 1996, p. 87). In Detroit, for example, about 40 percent of the central city population does not have a car, yet most of the new jobs in the region are in outlying suburbs not directly accessible by public transportation (Mast, 1994, p. 4).

Table 15.1   Tops in Tie-Ups

The most-congested urban areas, as measured by the hours the average driver spends in snarled traffic in a year:

Los Angeles	82 hours
Washington, D.C.	76
Seattle-Everett, Wash.	69
Atlanta	68
Boston	66
Detroit	62
Dallas	58
Houston	58
San Francisco-Oakland, Calif.	58
Miami-Hialeah, Fla.	57
Austin, Texas	53
Indianapolis	52
Portland, Ore.-Vancouver, Wash.	52
St. Louis	52
Baltimore	47
San Bernardino-Riverside, Calif.	47
Average in 68 areas nationwide	34

Source: Texas Transportation Institute, 1999.

Gazing into the urban future does not provide any easy technological solutions to problems of urban transportation like those identified earlier. For example, it would require integrating future land-use planning with transportation-planning strategies into one seamless web to increase the accessibility of jobs, stores, housing, and other facilities without increasing the need to travel by car. Although this has been done relatively successfully in some European cities, such as Paris (Hall, 1998, pp. 970–971), by providing radial mass transit commuting to and from the central city, it has failed to provide adequate means for similarly commuting from suburb to suburb. In the United States, the already greater distances and sprawl of suburban decentralization, along with the greater degree of public resistance to the amount of centralized planning that would be necessary, makes this partial solution highly unlikely in most large metropolitan areas. Portland, Oregon, is often cited for its relatively successful integrated transportation and land-use strategy in an attempt to head off the problems of sprawl and inner-city decay typical of many American metropolitan communities, but Portland is the exception, rather than the rule (see World Resources, 1996; Macionis and Parrillo, 1998; Palen, 1997).

Some other developments in transportation technology designed to ease the problems of traffic congestion involve the integration of information technology into highway and automobile systems, for example, electronic highway signals that give increasing sophisticated information about traffic conditions and traffic hazards, in some cases even suggesting alternative routes, as well as, automatic guidance systems of specially equipped automobiles for such driving functions as acceleration, braking, and spacing the distance between cars on dedicated highway lanes, allowing hands-off driving in some cases. Other potential developments aimed at conserving fuel and/or reducing pollution include electrically powered autos, hybrid electric/gasoline engines, and fuel-cell propulsion. Working prototypes of these alternatives to the internal combustion engines are already in limited use or test programs, but it is way too soon to determine to what extent these alternatives will prove to be practical, affordable, or acceptable on a massive scale, or whether they will contribute in any significant way to a reduction of traffic congestion in large metropolitan areas.

Adherents of advanced technology believe that it will eventually be able to provide an unlimited supply of energy from fuel cells, nuclear power, solar conversion, water, wind or geothermal power, or from still other as yet undiscovered sources. According to them, science and technology can be relied upon to control the growth of the population, to solve problems of food shortages by increasing the food supply, and even to control climatic extremes. But technology may have its limits. Not all observers are so optimistic about the role of technology in shaping urban life and values. It can be argued that technology-driven societies would essentially be enslaving, limiting human existence to one narrow dimension. As technology introduces itself into more and more spheres of daily living, it will likely produce profound changes in the values and institutional structures of modern urban society. Many people have become increasingly aware of the finite limitations on their ability to engineer social change, and that many pressing problems tend to defy technological solutions.

Also, many well-intentioned technological improvements may yield as yet unanticipated negative consequences that may far outweigh their benefits. As a result, many "watch dog" groups have appeared which seek to monitor the potential hazards of technological innovations and to resist those that rightly or wrongly are perceived to threaten the quality of urban life. Well-organized resistance to the deployment of nuclear power generating facilities in many regions of the country is one good case in point. Current resistance by some groups to genetic engineering or universal DNA screening is another good example, as is the increasingly active role of the federal Food and Drug Administration in monitoring new drugs and medical procedures. The monitoring of air pollution, the ozone level, and global warming are, of course, more directly associated by many people as probable consequences of some of the technologies discussed in this section. It is not certain whether Americans will continue to as blindly subscribe to technological solutions to urban problems in the future as they have in the past. More certainly, no major technological panacea for the more general problems of urban living is in sight for the foreseeable future.

ENVIRONMENT

In early 1978, the Midwestern region of the United States was digging out of one of the worst snowstorms in many decades. The entire transportation system was brought to almost a complete standstill, as major highways, local roads, local transit systems, railroads, and most airports were closed by the storm. Many deaths and injuries were attributable to the storm, and most business, governmental, educational, and social activities were severely curtailed for days. In summer 2000, a severe heat wave and drought had created major forest fires in many of the Western states and drove up the demands for electric power in California to the brink of a shutdown of the electric power grid in several of the state's largest cities. A combination of the extreme heat and smoke from the fires also created unacceptably high levels of air pollution in the same cities (*New York Times,* August 2, 2000, p. A21 and August 3, 2000, p. A1). These events serve as useful reminders that weather and climatic conditions are still capable of severely disrupting the daily rhythm of urban life, no matter how extensively technology has been employed to minimize such disruptions. Floods, droughts, hurricanes, tornadoes, earthquakes, landslides, forest fires, sand storms, heat waves, and other natural disasters also continue to occur often enough to remind us that human beings have not completely mastered the natural environment, even in the most technically advanced urban centers. Any reasonable prognosis suggests that natural environmental conditions will continue to intrude into the lives of both urban and rural dwellers in the foreseeable future.

In the United States, there has been an aggregate movement of people in the last several decades from the Northeast and Midwest to the South and the West. The movement is from the interior of the country to the peripheral coastal regions. This has partly been based on the desire of many people and industries to relocate in the more moderate climate of the coastal regions and the sunbelt. At the same time, the almost universal adaptation of central air conditioning has somewhat neutralized some of the more unpleasant aspects of the hot and/or humid summers of some of the southern areas now enjoying relatively high rates of industrialization and immigration. But, according to Kornblum (1997, p. 39), some of the most desirable locations for cities, such as seacoasts, mountain slopes, or river floodplains, are risky places for human settlement because they are prone to natural disasters like earthquakes, erosion, floods, landslides, or the like. Los Angeles and San Francisco, for example, both experienced major earthquakes in the 1990s. Yet, in spite of the continued risks of future natural disasters along the fault lines that run through both of these cities, the damaged areas of both these metropolitan areas have been restored to at least their previous densities. Some environmental disasters in urban areas, of course, are also due to human negligence, greed, or combinations of both (Erickson, 1994). These may be the result of gasoline, oil or other toxic spills, toxic land-fills, nuclear accidents, lead, arsenic, or mercury poisoning, dumping of industrial wastes, use of urban water sources for dumping sewage, and the like. Erickson and other sociologists who study social and man-made disasters hope that there will be more safeguards against negligence and more emphasis on anticipating future risks of natural and man-made environmental disasters. However, Erickson fears that in the short run, the balance of power is shifting toward corporations and other powerful interest groups, to the disadvantage of the victims or potential victims of disasters most likely to effect urban communities (Erickson, 1994; C. Kornblum, 1997, p. 268).

Perhaps the most difficult environmental problems of all will be ensuring adequate fresh water supplies for metropolitan areas. In a survey of a variety of metropolitan crises during the 1960s, Meier (1974) found that problems of maintaining an adequate supply of clean water surpassed other natural disasters, energy failures, accidents, and even revolution, rebellion, or war as the crisis potentially most disturbing to large metropolitan areas

A futuristic apartment complex at Habitat in Montreal, Canada, designed by Moishe Safdie

over one million in population. The severe restrictions on water usage due to periodic droughts in areas of California is a good illustration (Gold, 1982, p. 368). More recently California has had to rely on water from the Colorado River, in competition with six other Western states for that increasingly scarce resource. In a recent pact between these states, the U.S. secretary of the interior issued "stern" warnings that California will have to learn to live with a drastically reduced supply of water from the Colorado River during the next fifteen years, as its water allotments are gradually reduced. Explosive growth in other cities dependent on the same source of water, such as Phoenix and Las Vegas, helps create the need for this drastic move (Purdom, 2000, p. A18).

In general, the future well-being of urban centers will rely extensively on the degree to which they can be brought in better balance with environmental and physical considerations. Nevertheless, these have been among the dimensions of urbanization most neglected by urban sociologists.

SOCIAL STRUCTURE

In the introductory chapter, urban social structure was described as a complex web of relationships among social units of increasing size and complexity. These units include individuals, primary groups, neighborhoods, social networks, voluntary associations, bureaucracies, and, finally, at the largest and most abstract levels, major urban social institutions. Many of these units have been reviewed here in the context of the territorially based local urban community, but it has also been recognized that the larger and more complex units of social structure have also taken on national and global forms and no longer are limited to the boundaries of the local community.

Many observers of the new urban sociology or political economy persuasion have projected this trend into the future by suggesting that we are passing through a revolution that is unhitching the social processes of urbanization for the geographically fixed local city or region, to a scale of organization that is at least as wide as national urban society and, in fact, has already become worldwide in scope (Wallerstein, 1979; Castells and Hall, 1994; Feagin, 1988; Sassen, 1991; Webber, 1968). Many of these observers have characterized the movement toward nationalization and globalization as allegedly destructive of local community social structure. For example, Webber (1968) referred to the movement "from ancestral localism toward the unbounded realms of the cosmopolites" as an inevitable form of urban social structure he called *high-scale society,* whereas Coleman (1976) further suggested that local communities were becoming less and less the building blocks of which societies are composed. This greater freeing of individuals from local community bonds, these critics have concluded, is a trend that destroys local community social structure.

Another long-term trend allegedly destructive of community organization is the growth of the mass media and the consequent invasion of the local community by values, norms, and attractions from the outside world of national and global society. Coupled with these changes have been the transition from local decision making and attentiveness to problems of the local community to more centralized decisions that override local community self-determination efforts. This trend is very likely to continue, decreasing the capability of local cities to develop and maintain strong and stable local institutions. All these kinds of changes have important implications for the treatment of urban social problems, which allegedly then could no longer be understood or treated in a local community context alone. Thus, problems such as crime, poverty, unemployment, broken families, drug addiction, mental illness, and community unrest or violence would no longer be seen as having their roots in the local communities in which they occur but would then be seen as national or international in origin. As Webber (1968, p. 1091) put it earlier, "We cannot hope to invent local treatments for conditions whose origins are not local in character, nor can we expect territorially defined governments to deal effectively with problems whose causes are unrelated to territory or geography."

The focus on urban nationalization and globalization should not obscure the fact that it is in the local community that most people live. Although there is no doubt that the United States has become a national urban society, and that much of modern urban life can increasingly best be understood at this national or global scale of size and complexity, it has also correctly been pointed out by those who are more cautious that this does not necessarily mean that the smaller social units at the local community level have disappeared or can be safely ignored. As Palen (1997, p. 287) had earlier put it,

> The city may indeed be finished . . . but someone apparently forgot to tell the inhabitants. For over fifty years sociologists have been predicting the imminent disappearance of localized ethnic and racial urban communities. . . . But the working-class ethnics and minorities who live in these neighborhoods have not yet heard that their life-styles represent a pre-industrial past and thus must inevitably fade away. The significance and strength of territoriality and ethnicity tend to be consistently underestimated.

More recently, Lofland (1998, pp. xi–xii) has reiterated a similar reservation in more global terms:

> No matter how great the impact of "world systems" on local events, no matter how far the tendrils of political and economic machinations reach into the everyday experiences of women and men, no matter how effective the modern technologies of information collection and dispersal may be in manufacturing the "global village," . . . the fact of the matter is that a person standing on the streets of Chicago or Hong Kong or Moscow or Buenos Aires is in a very different social and psychological environment than a person standing in the middle of a village in North Dakota or Morocco or Nicaragua or Tibet.

Social institutions were described in the introductory chapter as representing groping trial and error adjustments to the complexities of urban living. It was further asserted that the survival and well-being of modern urban civilizations are to a large extent dependent on how successfully urban social institutions respond to the challenges confronting them. Throughout the book challenges currently facing such institutions as the economy, family, organized religion, social welfare, education, urban planning, or local government have been discussed, along with some of the prospects for these institutions in the near future. Increasingly social observers and social planners emphasize the strategic importance of viewing these institutions on a national scale and as amenable to rational guidance.

Here again our working definition of social institutions (see chapter 1) involves a complex web of relationships from relatively small and simple forms to relatively large and complex social units, many of which continue to manifest themselves at local or territorial levels of urban social structure. Thus, to assume that basic social institutions can be easily or directly modified by centralized social planning would be a mistake. It is far more likely that social institutions will continue to change from the bottom and middle levels, as well as from the top, largely as a result of grassroots changes in the values and lifestyles of their participants. These more or less spontaneous changes cannot be easily foreseen, anticipated, or guided by agents of planned social change. The urban way of life is so intricate in its design and interdependencies that it will be extremely resistant and, in some respects, immune to frontal efforts to attempts to plan and order future social life. Ylvisaker (Gold, 1982), for example, forecasted that "urban culture, like amoebae, will be capable of infinite reproduction and will spread on its own volition."

Yet keeping abreast of institutional change and proliferation may provide at least some opportunities for directing these changes toward socially useful purposes. *Alternative* social institutions, for example, may be creative efforts to bring people together in ways that are more psychologically satisfying. According to Kanter (1972), the goals of alternative institutions are to "make work more meaningful, integrate life activities, distribute power more equitably, offer experiences of community and shared ownership, and replace stale myths with concepts that revitalized spiritual life." She adds that new values are continually being developed that challenge traditional views of life, and she describes alternative institutions as potentially bringing a new sense of institutional boundaries that are more open and subject to modification than traditionally established institutions. Recent psychological investigations of personal coping mechanisms, the effects of stress upon health and well-being, and the impact of changing natural and man-made environments on personal development could probably provide some of the directions for building such new alternative institutions (see chapter 6). Of course, the likelihood of such institutional innovation will depend on the degree to which people are dissatisfied with traditional institutions and want them modified in any serious way.

Underlying the concerns about future problems facing American urban social structure are the following critical factors: (1) the increased organizational complexity expected to be brought about by population increases, the expansion of urban areas, expanded demand for human support services, the need to ease tensions caused by economic and racial inequalities (see chapters 11 and 13), a dramatic increase in the number of events that will likely occur, and an increase in the amount of available information and knowledge; (2) the increased turmoil likely to be brought about by inevitable malfunctions in the social and physical environment, accidents, and incomplete or faulty information; and (3) scarcities of all kinds, including not only physical resources, but also scarcities of time and skill as well. It is highly uncertain whether the technological ability or the will to change the urban future will be up to the task of anticipating and dealing with challenges to the physical and social well-being of future urban society. The implications for future urban policy making and implementation, of course, pose some enormous issues and challenges that will be most difficult to resolve.

SOME MAJOR URBAN POLICY CONSIDERATIONS

There are several fundamental issues to address in any serious consideration of future urban social policies. On the surface the need to do more long-range planning is a truism, but because urban planning in the United States is controversial, one very basic issue is whether to do long-range planning at all. If so, how much planning is acceptable? For example, are plans to be as complete as former Soviet Union five-year plans, or are they to be more loosely defined guidelines to be considered when making choices? Most of the urban past was not a result of rational and deliberate planning, but rather the results of many separate factors occurring more or less spontaneously. The few occasions when either physical designs shaped development programs or concrete social policies actively directed social change in predictable directions are probably the exception rather than the rule. Also, there are those who strongly believe in a laissez faire system in which the best results are those that are left to the free play of the marketplace. To the extent that planning disrupts these "natural" forces, it is seen by such critics of planning as highly undesirable. But such critics often overlook the amount of long-range planning within the private sector by segments such as large and powerful multinational corporations. Thus, the opposition may not be so much to the concept of planning per se as it is to the idea of government doing the planning. Some advocates of urban planning in a public or governmental context often argue that inclusive and strictly defined public plans are necessary to make it possible to impose predictability and order on future urban change and development: others caution that strict urban and social planning requirements might not be flexible enough to incorporate new ideas, or might be too frozen to permit necessary adaptation to unanticipated circumstances.

If there is some agreement that planning should occur, one major issue would be who would do the planning, and for what time periods should plans be made? Should there be ways to "veto" plans by dissident groups, and what, if anything, should be done to encourage active participation in the planning process by interest groups and the public at large? It has often been alleged that too often in the past, planning has consisted of technical or physical schemes designed by technological elites, implemented by a narrow power structure, and imposed on the powerless masses (Marger, 1999; Dye, 1995; also see chapter 8). But broad citizen participation, on the other hand, has not been easy to establish. Numerous experiments in community development projects have demonstrated how difficult it has been to obtain participation by a majority of the affected population. To combine democratic values of citizen participation with the kinds of expertise required to anticipate and plan for complex future urban environments is, indeed, a formidable task.

Another important planning related issue is, Within what boundaries or political jurisdictions should planning take place? Should it be done at the national, state, regional, or strictly local levels? One of the main difficulties is the lack of fit between ecological, political, and social communities that make up American urban society. This lack of fit has important consequences for the decision-making structure of the urban community, particularly for metropolitan regions. It means that no local government decisions applying to all parts of the metropolitan or regional area are possible because of the social and political fragmentation into many autonomous, competing units. Yet, many of the social problems of large urban areas can only be controlled by an areawide political system, which would need the support of the many diverse groups of people scattered throughout such areas (see chapters 8 and 14).

If governmental and social fragmentation have not actually caused such problems as traffic congestion, pollution, and urban blight, it has nevertheless made solving these kinds of problems much more difficult. Perhaps, at least in part, this helps to explain the increasing involvement of the federal government in the many problems of metropolitan areas. But national urban planning is expected to remain highly controversial in the United States and is strongly resisted by those who argue for stronger local self-sufficiency and social control. Because of its history and tradition of states' rights and local autonomy, the United States has had more difficulty in resolving this issue than most of the other technologically advanced countries of the World (see Hall, 1998; World Resources, 1996; Gold, 1982).

If conditions are established to deal with these problems, the next series of issues revolves around values and priorities. For example, by what criteria will alternative policies be established? What are the most important and least important goals for future urban development? Because values will determine the priorities established for future policies, it is essential to make clear what these values are and to assess how widely they are shared. Throughout this book, for example, there have been numerous references to the growing gap between the rich and the poor in American metropolitan communities (see Wilson, 1996; Danziger and Gottschalk, 1995), and to the fact that such gaps are reflected in patterns of residential segregation in metropolitan areas. Still at issue, however, is to what extent is there consensus that these existing gaps between the rich and poor be reduced or eliminated, and to what extent should future social policy ensure that at least a minimum standard of living and quality of life be made available to all, regardless of their ability to pay?

Gans (1973) has argued for a detailed policy for redistributing wealth and political power, to produce not only equality of opportunity, but also what might be termed equality of results. He advocated new policies to promote greater equality in the areas of income distribution, political power, education, and the social and economic worth of jobs. To Gans's goals of equality, one could easily add proposals to provide greater economic parity between cities and suburbs. If, for example, the mix of low-, middle-, and high-income groups were the same for both cities and suburbs, regardless of individual differences in the distribution of wealth, individuals and families would have greater freedom to choose between city and suburban living. Likewise, if cities and suburbs contained similar mixes of socioeconomic groupings, some of the current strains and conflicts between cities and suburbs conceivably could be minimized. With greater equity, Gans (1973, p. 23) has more generally argued that internal political antagonisms would decline because "conflicts can best be compromised fairly if the society is more egalitarian, and if differences of self-interest that result from sharp inequality of income and power can be reduced."

There are a number of reasons why egalitarian goals are extremely difficult to achieve in American Society. First, the vested interests that profit from the status quo are highly likely to resist any policies that threaten their present advantages (see chapter 11). Moreover, the individualistic ethic and the striving for individual economic advancement in competition with others are deeply ingrained in the American value system. More generally, any conscious effort to produce major changes in the institutional structure of the society, including changes in the current system for distributing economic rewards, must contend not only with consciously organized opposition, but also with institutional inertia as well. For these reasons, the possibility of a smooth transition to a system of greater equality, no matter how desirable, would be extremely difficult and highly unlikely. But such a goal should be considered or confronted in any serious attempt to establish desirable urban policies for the future.

Finally, how can urban policies be part of comprehensive planning for the future, and yet be so constituted that they may be changed with relative speed and ease when it is prudent to make such changes? In summary, how can there be the desirable combinations of order and flexibility, long-range visions and short-range strategies, freedom and social control, elaborated futures and open-ended tomorrows? These largely unanswered questions illustrate just a few of the fundamental difficulties faced by policy makers and social planners as a prelude to the pursuit of any given future urban policy.

The obvious difficulty of the above task, however, does not mean that it is impossible. As has been earlier noted: "The improvement of society is not a forlorn hope—because many societies have deliberately improved before; nor is it an apocalyptic triumph to be accomplished once and for all—human nature being what it is. But it is not a matter out of our control, since modernization can proceed under a variety of institutional arrangements, and seems to be compatible with both despotism and freedom" (Caplow, 1975). At any rate, any reasonable prospects for controlling the urban future would have to at least include a relatively common model for the policy-making process, which would likely include the following steps:

1. an accurate description of the existing condition it would be desirable to change
2. a careful and honest description of the end condition to be achieved
3. a division of the project or plan into successive stages, and a description of the conditions to be achieved at each stage
4. practical methods for getting from each stage to the next
5. estimates of the time, personnel, material resources, and information required to get from each stage to the next
6. procedures for measuring goal attainment at each stage
7. procedures for detecting unanticipated results at each stage

It goes without saying, of course, that large-scale public support would be absolutely necessary if such an approach to planning the urban future has even the dimmest hope of ever being even partially realized. And, as William Shakespeare wrote in *Hamlet*, "therein lies the rub."

THE FUTURE OF URBAN SOCIOLOGY

Serious students of urban sociology sometimes ask what future lies ahead for this challenging field of study. It thus seems appropriate to close this chapter with some reflection on this topic. First, it is clear that urban sociology will continue to change and to broaden its scope. As it already stands, there is no "standard" textbook in the field, and each of the existing texts provides a different sense of what constitutes the core concepts or ideas of the field, and the boundaries of the field have always been very loosely defined. According to a teaching resource manual by Olson and Stone (1997), there are approximately twenty-four or twenty-five textbooks on the field, each of which has a somewhat different focus than the others. Thus, there is no "standard" body of subject matter to which all urban sociologists subscribe. Areas of interest in the field run from *macrosociological* topics, such as global urbanization or world urban systems theory, all the way to *microsociological* topics, such as person-to-person encounters in urban settings, and to every level of abstraction in between these two extremes. Some urban sociologists prefer quantitative approaches and others prefer qualitative or humanistic approaches, and the units of analysis also vary greatly, including subtopics, such as community and economic development, ethnicity, gangs, homelessness, housing, poverty, cities, suburbs, metropolitanism, and urban theory (Olson and Stone, 1997). Other divisions within the field are among those who prefer scientific or strictly academic disciplinary approaches, whereas others work as activists with social problem solving or social policy orientations. In a somewhat playful and delightful "finale" to her urban sociology book, Barbara Phillips creates an imaginary discussion between members of a group of social scientists with an interest in urban-suburban life in the global society. Among the conclusions reached by members of this group after listening to each participant state his or her interests and perspectives were:

> Each approach has its merits—and limitations. The trouble is, they don't seem to lend themselves to synthesis. . . . No doubt some of us will continue to dissect small pieces of the urban scene. . . . some will focus on substantive issues—urban transport, terrorism, pollution, and so on. . . . some will explore particular parts of urban culture. Others will try to make the connections between the small pieces and the theoretical issues. Still others will try to merge theory and practice, applying their knowledge to improve the quality of urban life. . . . We must have respect for both our plumbers and our philosophers, or neither our pipes nor our theories will hold water. (Phillips, 1996, pp. 574–577)

In a related manner, it is important to point out that urban sociology has become part of a larger interdisciplinary effort, commonly referred to as *Urban Studies*. All of the social sciences, for example are central to the examination of urban structure and processes. History, economics, political science, anthropology, and psychology, as well as sociology, all have made and will continue to make important contributions to our understanding of the many human dimensions of urban society. Physical sciences of all kinds— biology, chemistry, physics, zoology, geology, and geography—are becoming increasingly concerned with the interrelationships between social and physical structure and are likely to become involved in more collaborative research efforts with social scientists. Engineering, architecture, and landscape architecture have long focused on improving the urban physical environment and have continuously expanded their horizons to incorporate knowledge and ideas acquired from both the social and physical sciences. Urban planning, social work, journalism, and public administration are among some of the newer practicing professions that focus on dealing with some of the social problems associated with urbanization, and these applied fields and the social sciences will continue to instruct one another. Psychiatry and law are among the better established practicing professions that have expanded their focus to include urban concerns.

In short, the study of urban societies will require much more comprehensive and intensive disciplinary research, and will at the same time require academic specialists to work closely together with scholars from other disciplines and to keep abreast of information being developed across an expanding number of fields. Both of these ends will be greatly facilitated in the future by more frequent use of advanced computer technologies and new methods of information retrieval and data manipulation, by more rapid dissemination of information through new means of communication, and by new forms of academic organization that encourage more direct interaction and exchanges between scholars among the various participating disciplines.

Second, urban sociology and urban studies can flourish only if sufficient funds are available to support and encourage research and scholarship. In the past, much urban research was characterized by small-scale and narrowly defined problem areas, uncoordinated projects and unrelated topics, and sporadic funding. Without a serious investment of money, skill, and energy, the field cannot grow as rapidly or rapidly as desired. Many urban scholars, on the other hand, must find new modes of adapting to political demands for assistance in attacking well-recognized social problems and for contributing directly to the design of social policies. More and more, professionally trained sociologists and other scholars are finding employment on the staffs of various public and private agencies directly involved in developing and applying social policies to the solutions of real problems. But this may be extremely difficult to do without compromising research integrity or scholarly independence, and young scholars employed by policy-making agencies outside academia are forced to create new occupation self-images or mixed-role orientations in efforts to avoid the traumas of intense role conflict.

The relationship between disciplinary and policy research must be better defined. It must be understood that policy research is significantly different from disciplinary research in at least the following respects:

> Its object is to provide information immediately useful to policy makers in grappling with the problems they face. It begins outside a discipline with a social problem defined by a decision maker. The pace of the research is forced by the policy maker's need to make a decision dictated by non-disciplinary imperatives. The intended audience is the decision maker, to whom it must be made intelligible and convincing if it is to be useful. Generally, little time is available to collect new data or to engage in prolonged analysis. (Berry and Kasarda, 1977, p. 427)

Third, it will become increasingly important in the near future to pay a considerable amount of attention to translating for various audiences what sociologist and other scholars have learned about urban life and urban communities to date. The social policies and alternative futures considered for urban communities will affect virtually everyone, so it has become important to raise the level of knowledge and sophistication of the ordinary person high enough so that he or she can appreciate the consequences of the choices that will have to be made. Too often, popular discussions of urbanization are short-sighted, overly dramatic, or sensational, lack historical perspective, or oversimplify very complex factors. Even more important is the general purpose of providing a better understanding of the urban world in which most of us live and must function, as a tool for a more satisfactory adaptation to the many daily demands and opportunities of urban living.

For these reasons, it is essential that well-written, interesting, and clearly presented syntheses of urban processes be available for many more people than those seriously committed to becoming urban scholars or professional practitioners, and it was partially with this goal in mind that the present volume has been prepared.

Finally, ethical concerns will become critical considerations in undertaking urban sociology or urban studies. This does not necessarily mean continuing the kind of "do good" attitude that has often triggered past urban reform movements, with both beneficial and negative results, but rather creating a greater commitment to examine urban conditions with an overall concern for enhancing the quality of urban life, rather than a concern with manipulation or social control. The destructive impact of the atomic bomb over half a century ago has demolished previous myths of scientific purity and isolation. It is now much clearer that knowledge may indeed be a source of power and can be put to both constructive and destructive political uses. Although social scientists, as well as other scientists, have a common commitment to work as objectively as possible, the essence of humanity guarantees that one can never be totally objective or value free, so that no human being can forever escape making ethical choices. Many of the ethical issues in urban sociology will be difficult, painful, and confusing. Those who professionally continue the examination or control of urbanization in the years ahead may well find this task the most overwhelming of all.

SELECTED BIBLIOGRAPHY

BERRY, BRIAN J. L., and JOHN D. KASARDA. *Contemporary Urban Ecology.* New York: Macmillan, 1977.

CAIRNCROSS, FRANCIS. "The Death of Distance: A Survey of Telecommunications." *The Economist.* September 30, 1995.

CAPLOW, THEODORE. *Toward Social Hope.* New York: Basic Books, 1975.

CASTELLS, MANUEL. *The Informational City: Information, Technology, Economic Restructuring and the Urban-Regional Process.* Oxford: Blackwell, 1989.

———. *The Information Age: Economy, Society, and Culture 1: The Rise of the Network Society.* Oxford: Blackwell, 1996.

———, and PETER HALL. *Technopoles of the World: The Making of 21st Century Industrial Complexes.* London: Routledge, 1994.

CHINOY, ELI, ed. *The Urban Future.* New York: Leiber-Atherton, 1972.

CLARKE, ARTHUR. "Communications in the Second Century of the Telephone." In *The Telephone's First Century and Beyond,* A. Bolger (ed.). New York: Thomas Crowell, 1977.

COHEN, HENRY. "Governing Megacentropolis: The Constraints." In *Urbanism, Urbanization and Change: Comparative Persectives,* 2nd ed., Paul Meadows and Ephriam Mizruchi (eds.). Reading, MA: Addison-Wesley, 1976.

COLEMAN, JAMES S. "Community Disorganization and Community Problems." In *Contemporary Social Problems,* 4th ed., R. K. Merton and R. Nisbet (eds.). New York: Harcourt Brace Jovanovich, 1976.

DAHRENDORF, RALF. *Class and Class Conflict in Industrial Society.* Stanford, CA: Stanford University Press, 1959.

DANTZIG, GEORGE B., and THOMAS L. SAATY. *Compact City: A Plan for a Livable Urban Environment.* San Francisco, CA: W. H. Freeman, 1973.

DANZIGER, SHELDON H., and PETER GOTTSCHALK. *America Unequal.* Cambridge: Harvard University Press, 1995.

DiGIOVANNI, FRANK F. "An Examination of Selected Consequences of Revitalization in Six U.S. Cities." *Urban Studies.* 21 (1984): 245–259.

DYE, THOMAS R. *Who's Running America: The Clinton Years,* 6th ed. Englewood Cliffs, NJ: Prentice-Hall, 1995.

ELDREDGE, H. WENTWORTH. "Alternative Possible Futures." *Futures.* February 1974.

ERICKSON, KAI T. *A New Species of Trouble.* New York: Norton, 1994.

FEAGIN, JOE. *The Free Enterprise City.* New Brunswick, NJ: Rutgers University Press, 1988.

FRANKFORT-NACHMIAS, CHAVA, and J. JOHN PALEN. "Neighborhood Revitalization and the Community Question." *Journal of the Community Development Society.* 24 (1993): 1–14.

GANS, HERBERT. *More Equality.* New York: Random House, 1973.

GATES, WILLIAM. *The Road Ahead.* London: Viking, 1995.

GB Office of Science and Technology, London: HMSO, 1995.

GOLD, HARRY. *The Sociology of Urban Life.* Englewood Cliffs, NJ: Prentice-Hall, 1982.

HALL, PETER. *Cities in Civilization.* New York: Pantheon Books, 1998.

HUDSON, JAMES R. "SoHo, A Study of Residential Invasion of a Commercial and Industrial Area." *Urban Affairs Quarterly.* 20 (September 1984): 46–63.

KANTER, ROSABETH M. *Committment and Community.* Cambridge: Harvard University Press, 1972.

KORNBLUM, WILLIAM. *Sociology in a Changing World.* Fort Worth, TX: Harcourt Brace, 1997.

KOURVETARIS, GEORGE A. *Political Sociology: Structure and Process.* Boston: Allyn and Bacon, 1997.

LEVINE, SUZAN. "The Future That Wasn't." *Washington Post National Weekly Edition,* January 3, 2000.

LOFLAND, LYN H. *The Public Realm: Exploring the City's Quintessential Social Territory.* New York: Aldine de Gruyter, 1998.

MACIONIS, JOHN J. and VINCENT N. PARRILLO. *Cities and Urban Life.* Upper Saddle River, NJ: Prentice-Hall, 1998.

MARGER, MARTIN N. *Social Inequality: Patterns and Processes.* Mountain View, CA: Mayfield, 1999.

MAST, ROBERT H., ed. *Detroit Lives.* Philadelphia: Temple University Press, 1994.

MEIER, RICHARD. *Planning for the Urban World.* Boston: MIT Press, 1974.

MEYERSON, MARTIN. "Utopian Predictions and the Planning of Cities." *Daedalus* 90 (Winter 1961): 180–193.

MITCHELL, WILLIAM J. *The City of Bits: Space, Place, and the Infobahn.* Cambridge: MIT Press, 1995.

NAISBITT, J., AND P. ABURDENE. *Megatrends 2000.* New York: Morrow, 1990.

New York Times 2000 Almanac, 1999.

OLSON, PHILIP, and JENNIFER STONE. *Urban Sociology: A Teaching Resource Manual.* Washington, DC: American Sociological Association, 1997.

PALEN, J. JOHN. *The Urban World,* 5th ed. New York: McGraw-Hill, 1997.

PHILLIPS, BARBARA E. *City Lights: Urban-Suburban Life in the Global Society,* 2d ed. New York: Oxford University Press, 1996.

POPENOE, DAVID. *Sociology.* 9th ed. Englewood Cliffs, NJ: Prentice-Hall, 1993.

PURDOM, TODD. "States in West Reach Outline of Agreement on Water Use." *New York Times.* July 28, 2000, p. A18.

SASSEN, SASKIA. *The Global City: New York, Tokyo and London.* Princeton, NJ: Princeton University Press, 1991.

SHEPHERD, GORDON, and GARY SHEPHERD. "The Moral Career of a New Religious Movement." *Oakland University Journal.* 1, (spring, 2000).

STARK, RODNEY. *Sociology,* 7th ed. Belmont, CA: Wadsworth, 1998.

Statistical Abstract of the United States, 119th ed. Washington, DC, 1999.

WALLERSTEIN, IMMANUEL. *The Modern World System,* Vol. 1. New York: Academic Press, 1979.

WEBBER, MELVIN M. "The Post-City Age." *Daedalus* 97 (Fall 1968): 1091–1110.

WEEKS, JOHN R. *Population: An Introduction to Concepts and Issues,* 6th ed. Belmont, CA: Wadsworth, 1996.

WILSON, WILLIAM JULIUS. *When Work Disappears: The World of the New Urban Poor.* New York: Alfred Knopf, 1996.

World Resources: The Urban Environment: 1996–1997. New York: The World Resources Institute, 1996.

ZOLLSCHAN, GEORGE K., and WALTER HIRSCH, eds. *Social Change: Explorations, Diagnosis, and Conjectures.* New York: John Wiley, 1976.

16

WORLD URBANIZATION AND GLOBALIZATION

Except for the early chapters on the origins and history of urbanization, this book has focused mainly on North American urbanization and urban life. This focus should not obscure the fact that urbanization is indeed a worldwide phenomenon, which does have an important bearing on the present and future development and well-being of American urban society. The modern capitalist global economy, along with modern transportation and communications technology, makes the world's cities closer and more interdependent than ever before. As a result of globalization, American cities such as New York, Los Angeles, Chicago, or Washington, DC, in many ways may be more directly affected by what happens in London, Tokyo, Beijing, or Teheran than what may be taking place at the same time in Omaha, St. Louis, or Tucson. The volume of commuters and messages traveling between New York and London or San Francisco and Tokyo at any given time, may in fact, greatly exceed that between various pairing of American cities. As a result of the new global economy, it is common to think of these interdependencies in terms of trade and commerce, but world peace and stability may also be affected by the outcome of transactions between the world's principal cities. Moreover, accelerating and uncontrolled urban growth in other parts of the world may have such a potentially significant impact on the entire world's future environment and natural resource base that no nation could remain unaffected.

It is also true, that from an academic perspective, the theoretical frames of reference for the study of urbanization that have been used here for the North American urban experience may not be useful or valid for the analysis of urbanization in other parts of the world. There has been not just one but several paths that have been taken by modern urbanization in various parts of the world, and both the causes and consequences differ along these separate paths (Berry, 1973). Therefore, it is fitting to close this book with a brief glance at major urban trends in other parts of the world. Because of space limitations, attention is mainly focused on population and metropolitan growth trends, resultant urban social problems, and efforts to contain these problems through urban and social planning policies.

WORLD POPULATION GROWTH

Any discussion of world urbanization must be seen in the context of unprecedented growth in the size of the world populations in recent centuries and especially in recent decades. At the time reliable estimates of world population first began to be available, around 1650 A.D., the world population was about 500 million people. Assuming that the first human beings appeared well over a million years ago, it took all of this time in human history to achieve a population of that size. Ehrlich and Ehrlich (1972) estimated that it took at least 1,500 years for the size of the population to double during the nearly 10,000-year period from about 8000 B.C. to 1650 A.D. But during the next 200 years—1650 to 1850—the world population doubled again to 1 billion people. This was just the beginning of a revolutionary increase in growth. In the 80 years between 1850 and 1930, the population again doubled to a total of about 2 billion people. Between 1930 and 1975, a period of only 45 years, it doubled still again to about 4 billion people, and by the late 1970s, the time required to double the world population had shrunk to just over 35 years (Gold, 1982, p. 380).

By late 1999, the population of the world exceeded 6 billion people and was still growing by about 79 million people per year (*New York Times 2000 Almanac,* 1999). It is projected to reach 8 billion by 2026 and 9 billion by 2043 (see Table 16.1). The reasons for this unprecedented growth in the world population are relatively straightforward. Only three demographic factors can produce population changes: fertility, mortality, and migration. Although migration may significantly affect growth rates in various countries or continents, it is not a factor for the world as a whole. Therefore, only fertility and mortality need to be considered in explaining the past and present world population trends. Historically, industrialization, modernization, and urbanization have produced a gradual decline in birthrates in those parts of the world where these processes have occurred. But the same processes, along with resultant improvements in public health and curative medicine, agriculture, and transportation, have raised the standard of living—better diets, clothing, housing, cleaner sanitary conditions, and so on—and have produced even more rapid and dramatic drops in mortality rates, yielding a large surplus of births over deaths. As these demographic processes have spread to most parts of the world, they have produced a rapid explosion of the world population as an inevitable result.

Demographers (see Weeks, 1996; Freedman and Berelson, 1974) have argued that the rate of growth that characterized the recent population revolution was just a temporary deviation from the annual growth rates that prevailed during most of human history. This perception is incorporated in the concept of the "demographic transition" which had taken place in the industrialized regions of the world during the past several centuries. In these regions, the first phase of the demographic transition was characterized by high birthrates plus high death rates, which, together, produced low growth rates. The next phase was characterized by slowly declining birthrates, plus very rapidly declining death rates, which produced high growth rates. The final stage is characterized by both low birth and death rates, which then again produce low growth rates. But as Weeks (1996, p. 36) further explains, as a population increases its overall size, the same or lower rates of growth can still produce a larger absolute increase in population size from year to year. Thus the projections of the huge expected increase in the world population from now through the 2040s, as cited in Table 16.1, will take place in spite of the fact that the *rate* of population increase will be actually decreasing during the next three or four decades, as the world as a whole enters the third phase of the demographic transition (see *Statistical Abstract of the United States,* 1999, p. 831).

Some social scientists predict that the major crises most likely to effect the world during the early part of the twenty-first century are directly related to problems of the growth and distribution of the world population. These crises include severe food shortages, deterioration of the biosphere, materials and energy shortages, the risk of nuclear war, and imbalances in the worldwide distribution of wealth. According to Eitzen and Baca Zinn (1997, chapter 3), the issue is one of human survival because the world population is growing faster than its ability to produce food. Increased numbers are damaging the ecological system and absorbing resources at an ever-quickening pace. The gap between the rich and the poor nations continues to widen, and the consequences of population growth create social unrest and economic and political upheaval. These increase the possibility of nuclear warfare, not because of ideologies but more likely because of desperation brought on by the exhaustion of a nation's capacity to supply its people with the resources for their survival. This latter concern has been partially reflected in political debates in the United States during the 2000 presidential election campaign season over the need to develop a nuclear missile defense system to ward off the possibility of nuclear missile attacks by desperate "rogue" nations.

MORE DEVELOPED AND LESS DEVELOPED COUNTRIES

World population problems are compounded because the distribution of the world population, as well as its rates of growth, vary considerably from country to country, region to region, and continent to continent. The sharpest distinctions can be made between *more developed* countries, such as the United States, Sweden, the United Kingdom, Germany, or Japan, on the one hand, and such *less developed* countries as Ethiopia, Somalia, Nigeria, Pakistan, Vietnam, or Zaire, on the other. More developed countries are defined by the United Nations as those that are industrialized and have a high Gross National Product (GNP), a high per capita GNP, and advanced science and technology. Approximately forty-five countries, including those in Europe, North America, Japan, Australia, and New Zealand, are considered more developed countries. On the other hand, less developed nations are those that have been defined by the UN as having populations much poorer than in a more developed country, low GNPs, economies based on agriculture rather than industry, and lacking in advanced science and technologies (*New York Times 2000 Almanac,* 1999, p. 486). Approximately seventy-seven countries, mostly in Africa, Latin America, the Caribbean, Asia (except Japan), and regions of Melanesia, Micronesia, and Polynesia, are among those that are considered less developed. Still one more category defined by the United Nations is the *least developed* countries with the world's poorest living standards. The UN counted forty-eight countries, most of them landlocked, among this least developed part of the world.

Another significant characteristic of less developed countries is that their current rates of population growth are much greater than in developed countries, and the process of urbanization has significantly differed from that in the developed countries in terms of speed, form, and consequences. This last distinction is, of course most central to this chapter on world urbanization and is considered in more detail. For now it can be summarized that cities in less developed areas are growing at faster rates than are cities anywhere else in the world and at rates that rival those in nineteenth-and twentiety-century industrial cities.

In 1998, only 19.8 percent of the world's population lived in more developed countries, and 80.2 percent lived in less developed countries. By 2020, it is projected that the portion in less developed countries will increase to 83.6 percent, and the portion in the more developed countries will shrink to 16.4 percent (U.S. Bureau of the Census, International Data Base, 1999). In 1998, 90 percent of the world's births, but only 77 percent of the deaths, took place in less developed countries. This means that 96 percent of the natural increase in population took place in the less developed countries of Africa, Asia, and Latin America. In the same year, 56.7 percent of the world's population lived in Asia, and over half of that continent's population increase for the year was in India and China, the world's two largest nations. With a combined 1998 population of over 2 billion people, these two less developed countries contained over one-third of the population of the world. But Africa is and will continue to be the fastest-growing region of the world. It contained an estimated population of 867 million in 2000, and it is projected to reach 1.582 billion in 2025, and 2.265 billion in 2050. At 12.2 percent of the world population in 2000, Africa will contain approximately 23 percent of the population of the world by 2050 (*New York Times 2000 Almanac,* 1999, pp. 482–483). Europe, the home of many of the world's most developed countries, on the other hand, is projected to slowly lose population during the first half of the twenty-first century and to continue to decline even more thereafter.

WORLD URBANIZATION

Human beings are now urbanized on a scale unprecedented in human history. In 1996, 45 percent of the world's population lived in urban areas. Seventy-five percent of the people in more developed countries now live in urban areas, whereas 37 percent of the people in less developed regions now live in cities, as well (*New York Times 2000 Almanac,* 1999). One-third of the people in Africa and Asia live in cities, but Asia by the year 2000 now contained ten of the fifteen largest cities in the world (see Table 16.1). In Europe, North America, Latin America, and the Caribbean nations, 70 percent of the population is urban. Because of anticipated future urban growth, at least half of the world population will live in urban areas for the first time in the history of the world by 2005, and by 2025, over 60 percent of the world's population will be urban.

The world's largest cities changed dramatically over the last half of the twentieth century. In 1950, only New York had a population of over 10 million people. But according to United Nations projections, the number of world cities with 10 million or more people had grown to twenty-one by 2000, and by 2015, that number will have grown to at least twenty-six. (Table 16.1 contains a list of the world's thirty largest cities, as of 2000, and as projected to 2015.) By 2015, seven cities will exceed 20 million people. Tokyo will be the world's largest, with 28.7 million people, followed by Bombay, Lagos, Shanghai, Jakarta, Sao Paulo, and Karachi. Of the largest fifteen cities, thirteen are in the less developed countries and only two, Tokyo and New York, are in the more developed nations. It is also interesting to note that by 2015, according to data in Table 16.1, no cities in the United States or Europe, once considered the models of modern urban-industrial civilization, will be among the ten largest urban areas of the world.

Table 16.1 The World's 30 Largest Urban Areas, Ranked by 2000 Population[1]

2000 RANK; URBAN AREA	POPULATION (MILLIONS)					RANK	
	1950	1970	1990	2000[1]	2015[1]	1950	2015[1]
1. Tokyo, Japan	6.9	16.5	25.0	27.9	28.7	3	1
2. Bombay, India	2.9	5.8	12.2	18.1	27.4	15	2
3. São Paulo, Brazil	2.4	8.1	14.8	17.8	20.8	18	6
4. Shanghai, China	5.3	11.2	13.5	17.2	23.4	6	4
5. New York, U.S.	12.3	16.2	16.1	16.6	17.6	1	11
6. Mexico City, Mexico	3.1	9.1	15.1	16.4	18.8	13	10
7. Beijing, China	3.9	8.1	10.9	14.2	19.4	12	8
8. Jakarta, Indonesia	N.A.	3.9	9.3	14.1	21.2	N.A.	5
9. Lagos, Nigeria	N.A.	N.A.	7.7	13.5	24.4	N.A.	3
10. Los Angeles, U.S.	4.0	8.4	11.5	13.1	14.3	11	17
11. Calcutta, India	4.4	6.9	10.7	12.7	17.6	9	12
12. Tianjin, China	2.4	5.2	9.3	12.4	17.0	17	14
13. Seoul, South Korea	N.A.	5.3	10.6	12.3	13.1	N.A.	18
14. Karachi, Pakistan	N.A.	N.A.	8.0	12.1	20.6	N.A.	7
15. Delhi, India	N.A.	3.5	8.2	11.7	17.6	N.A.	13
16. Buenos Aires, Argentina	5.0	8.4	10.6	11.4	12.4	7	19
17. Metro Manila, Philippines	N.A.	3.5	8.0	10.8	14.7	N.A.	15
18. Cairo, Egypt	2.4	5.3	8.6	10.7	14.5	16	16
19. Osaka, Japan	4.1	9.4	10.5	10.6	10.6	10	23
20. Rio de Janeiro, Brazil	2.9	7.0	9.5	10.2	11.6	14	21
21. Dhaka, Bangladesh	N.A.	N.A.	5.9	10.2	19.0	N.A.	9
22. Paris, France	5.4	8.5	9.3	9.6	9.6	5	27
23. Istanbul, Turkey	N.A.	N.A.	6.5	9.3	12.3	N.A.	20
24. Moscow, Russia	5.4	7.1	9.0	9.3	N.A.	4	N.A.
25. Lima, Peru	N.A.	N.A.	6.5	8.4	10.5	N.A.	25
26. Teheran, Iran	N.A.	N.A.	6.4	7.3	10.2	N.A.	26
27. London, U.K.	8.7	8.6	7.3	7.3	N.A.	2	N.A.
28. Bangkok, Thailand	N.A.	N.A.	5.9	7.3	10.6	N.A.	24
29. Chicago, U.S.	4.9	6.7	6.8	7.0	N.A.	8	N.A.
30. Hyderabad, India	N.A.	N.A.	N.A.	6.7	10.7	N.A.	22

Note: An urban area is a central city or central cities, and the surrounding urbanized areas, also called a metropolitan area.
[1]Projected.
Source: United Nations Department for Economic and Social Information and Policy Analysis, Population Division, *World Urbanization Prospects: The 1994 Revision* (1995).

Although world population growth and urban growth are related phenomena, to assume that one is solely the cause of the other would be a mistake. Rather, each is more likely a consequence of still other factors, such as industrialization, capitalism, or colonialism and the like. Of course relatively large cities had emerged in the ancient and medieval worlds without these factors in play. But there has been a far more direct relationship between these kinds of factors and urbanization at least since the eighteenth century. In chapter 3, the relationships between industrialization, capitalism, and colonialism were described as directly linked in the case of Great Britain and the United States. As Hawley (1971, p. 282) put it much earlier, the economics of large-scale industrial production presuppose the various complementary services and the quick communications that only urban areas can supply. These depend in turn on the markets represented by large aggregates of consumers who earn their living from nonagricultural activities. Thus, there is a mutually stimulating interaction between industrialization and urbanization. Hawley further suggests an interactive relationship between population increase and industrialization. In the first stages of industrialization, there are significant advances of scientific knowledge and its applications to industrial productivity. These help to raise the standard of living, which, in turn, tends to release the forces of population increase (through rapidly decreased death rates, etc.). Population increases then can become a stimulant to further industrial development through the increased labor supply of young adaptable workers and the enlarged numbers of consumers of industrial products that such population increases create. Of course these are developments that tend to be concentrated in urban centers, which grow accordingly (Table 16.2).

Urban sociologists of the more recent new urban sociology—or political economy—approach would add to or modify Hawley's essentially ecological approach to world urbanization by emphasizing the idea that world urban growth needs to be understood "in the context of an evolving world system of economic interdependence that places nations in a global hierarchy." This hierarchy consists of the "core" of highly developed countries, the "semiperiphery" of lesser developed countries, and the "periphery" of the least developed countries" (see chapters 1 and 7; see also Macionis and Parrillo, 1998, p. 211; Smith and Timberlake, 1997; Castells and Hall, 1994; Wallerstein, 1984). Within this hier-

Table 16.2 Years to Reach Population Milestones

POPULATION MILESTONE	YEAR REACHED	YEARS TO REACH
1 billion	1804	N.A.
2 billion	1927	123
3 billion	1960	33
4 billion	1974	14
5 billion	1987	13
6 billion	1999	12
7 billion	2012	13
8 billion	2026	14
9 billion	2043	17

Source: U.S. Census Bureau, World Population Profile: 1998 (1999).

archy, decision makers in the principal cities of core countries, such as New York, Tokyo, and London, indirectly control the flow of resources, and the economic, political, and social arrangements within the cities of the lesser and least developed nations, thus effecting their growth, shape, and form (Sassen, 1991).

OVERURBANIZATION IN THE LESS DEVELOPED WORLD

Just as the less developed parts of the world can be described as overpopulated with respect to the capacity of their economic and political institutions to accommodate burgeoning numbers of people, so can they be described as *overurbanized* with respect to their "premature" concentrations of population in cities. While the cities of the less developed countries have been growing at an unprecedented rate, so also have been their rural populations. Also such countries attempting to industrialize are faced with the dilemma of trying to raise agricultural productivity and to reduce the number of agricultural workers needed in the countryside, while at the same time trying to stimulate industrial productivity in the large urban centers. Within this framework, large numbers of people are dislocated from rural areas and forced into the cities. At the same time, the resources of the cities, already strained by the Herculean tasks of industrialization, are not adequate to the demands of their rapidly growing populations.

Thus, one can find huge settlements of *squatters* residing in newly created slums on the periphery of many cities in less developed parts of Asia, Africa, and Latin America, such as Lima, Mexico City, Ankara, Calcutta, Jakarta, Bangkok, and Rangoon. In these newly created urban squatter settlements, hunger, poor housing, overcrowding, pollution, poor sanitation, and disease are rampant, as are extensive poverty, unemployment, and underemployment. Floods of migrants displaced from rural areas gravitate to the major cities in search of employment, only to find that their numbers are too great to be absorbed by the local urban economies. Large surpluses of workers begin to appear in administrative and service industries, as well as in overcrowded manufacturing enterprises. Even some of the more marginal occupational groups, such as peddlers, street solicitors, street entertainers, beggars, and "hangers-on" of various sorts, become overfilled and unable to accommodate additional workers.

This pattern of accommodating new immigrants in squatter slums on the periphery or outskirts of existing cities creates a spatial settlement pattern just opposite that found in most U.S. industrial cities, where so-called slum areas are most likely to be found in the inner city areas rather than at the outskirts (see chapter 4). The explanation for these differences is not to be found in the local application of traditional "natural laws" of ecological development, but rather in the specific series of historical events associated with the population, industrial, and urban growth of each of the world regions. Differences in existing systems of technology, transportation, communications, and housing, as well as cultural patterns that are in place at the time that urban growth is taking place, can also be seen as contributing to distinctive differences between the spatial and ecological patterning of cities in the more developed countries and those in the less developed countries of the "Third World" (Gold, 1982, p. 389).

PRIMATE CITIES

Overurbanization in the less developed countries also tends to be associated with the development of *primate* cities. A primate pattern is one whereby a single, extremely large city dominates the urban pattern of an entire nation, in terms of size, concentration of economic wealth, or political and administrative power. A primate city may be from as much as three to fifteen times larger that the second largest city in countries where primate cities dominate. For example, Lima is approximately thirteen times larger than the second largest city of Peru, and Teheran is about six and a half times larger than the second largest city in Iran.

The emergence of primate cities in developing societies is primarily a product of the mechanisms for the filtering or "trickling down" of urban growth from the existing urban centers outward into the smaller towns and cities. Once large cities have developed in such countries, urban growth tends to remain concentrated there rather than dispersed in a more decentralized urban pattern. One of the principal reasons for the dominant position of primate cities in developing nations appears to have been the past colonial practices of the occupying European powers, which had used these cities as administrative and commercial centers. For colonial powers to extend and consolidate their authority in "alien" social and geographic territories, cities had to be the base of action for those powers. British rule in India, for example, centered on capital and provincial cities both for maintaining an integrated and authoritarian administrative structure and for securing the economic base of its power, namely, the collection of taxes and control over the export of raw materials and the importation of British manufactured goods (Berry and Kasarda, 1977, pp. 397–398).

Partially because of this colonial legacy, the continued domination of some less developed nations through the influence of their primate cities has been described as a "malignancy" by some critics. For example, primate cities have been said to have had "paralytic" effects on the development of smaller urban places and to be "parasitic" in relationship to the remainder of local economies. They are parasitic, according to this view, because they rob the countryside of valuable labor, consume all available investment funds, and dominate the cultural pattern of a society in such a way as to lead to the breakdown of the traditional culture. They also tend to have high rates of consumption, as opposed to production (Gold, 1982, p. 390).

Not all experts agree that domination by primate cities is necessarily a bad thing for developing nations. Some argue that they may serve some very desirable, or at the very least, some necessary functions. Palen (1997, p. 384), for example, has argued that it does not necessarily follow that primate cities are parasitic on the countryside, and that primate cities contribute more than their share to the overall economies of the countries of which they are a part. Further, he argues, there frequently is no realistic alternative to the primate cities. Still other theorists conclude that the best or perhaps the only way to prevent the overgrowth of primate cities is to strictly limit the population growth in them and to build new and smaller cities in order to drain off some of their surplus populations (Kasarda and Crenshaw, 1991). Of course this latter alternative is much easier said than done, and defenders of primate cities, such as Palen, do not offer much hope that such alternatives are realistic for smaller, less developed countries. Finally, some supporters argue that primate cities are "helpful to a region's urban development. They speed up the evolution of a modern urban facility, which, in time, makes possible the 'trickling down' of advanced urban technology and economic vitality" to smaller cities and to the societies in which they are located (Macionis and Parrillo, 1998, p. 303).

Of course, whether primate cities should be allowed to continue their dominant roles in less developed countries or should be constrained by radical national policies of population and economic decentralization are questions that are not just academic exercises, because they are at the heart of national planning controversies among the leaders of the less developed countries. It is thus still too soon to evaluate in a generalized way the full implications of and future prospects for primate cities versus alternative patterns of urbanization in less developed countries as a whole. The following parts of this chapter briefly cite a number of specific urban growth patterns, problems, and planning policies in a number of specific more developed and less developed countries in various parts of the urban world. Although it is impossible in the remaining pages to do full justice to all of the essential characteristics of all of the world's major cities or metropolitan areas, this discussion tries to be selective of examples that best relate to the main themes that this chapter has already identified.

LATIN AMERICA

Latin America is characterized by a high rate of population growth as a result of moderately high fertility rates and low mortality rates. During the last half of the twentieth century, the Latin American population more than tripled, from about 166 million people to over 500 million people, about 9 percent of the world's total population (*National Geographic Desk Reference,* 1999). Mexico and Brazil together contain more than half of the region's population. The Latin American share of the world population continues to increase, in spite of recent declines in fertility rates, because the momentum for growth was already built into the population base. However, if fertility rates continue to significantly decrease and encompass the larger populated countries of the region, Latin America could exhibit a reduction of overall growth in the near future.

Urbanization, however, has been extremely rapid in Latin America in recent decades and grew from about 30 percent in 1950 to about 76 percent urban by the late 1990s. As the result of this rapid urban growth, it has now been transformed into one of the most urbanized regions of the world. As late as 1930, only one Latin American city, Buenos Aires, had over 1 million people: twenty-six cities had reached or exceeded that size by 1980 (Gold, 1982, p. 393). By 2000, four Latin American cities had estimated populations of 10 million or more people. One of them, Sao Paulo, had become the third largest city in the world, and five of them—Sao Paulo, Mexico City, Buenos Aires, Rio de Janeiro, and Lima—were among the thirty largest world cities (*New York Times 2000 Almanac,* p. 487).

Mexico City is the second largest and second fastest growing city in all of Latin America. Its population grew more than fivefold from 3.1 million people in 1950 to approximately 16.4 million people by 2000, at which time it became the sixth largest city in the world at almost the identical size of New York City. By 2015, Mexico City will have grown larger than New York, with 18.8 million people, according to United Nations projections (1995). Although Mexico City has many of the characteristics of a primate city, Mexico actually had thirty-six cities of over one hundred thousand people by the beginning of the 1970s. Such growth was due not only to natural increase but also to large streams of migration that flowed toward the cities and their immediate hinterlands. Thus, not only Mexico City, but Guadalajara, Monterey, and Tijuana and other cities along the U.S. border, as well as the various state capitals and smaller industrial and commercial centers like Chihuahua, Guernavaca, Pueblo, Leon, and Acapulco have been among the major destination points of migrants from rural areas. Because of the large natural increases in the size of the rural population, as well as overurbanization of the cities, there has been a sizable outflow of migrants, both legally and illegally, across the border into the United States (as was extensively discussed in chapter 13).

The Mexican economy has had impressive rates of industrialization in recent years, partially due to the movement of many manufacturing operations from the United States and other more industrialized nations to Mexico, and this has been partially facilitated and accelerated by the recent North American Free Trade Agreement (NAFTA) and other more liberalized world and regional trade agreements. This transformation of the Mexican economy is illustrated by the large number of automobiles now manufactured in Mexico by international automobile corporations headquartered in the United States, Europe, and Japan, and sold in the world marketplace. A large but still not fully utilized natural resource base, including potentially vast petroleum reserves, is also expected to help continue the future momentum of Mexico toward status as a more developed nation. For example, 74 percent of Mexico is now urbanized, well approaching the degree of urbanization in more developed countries, and its 90 percent literacy rate is also beginning to narrow the gap between Mexico and more developed countries.

Presidential Palace facing the main square at the Historical Center in Mexico City

Mexico City, like many other large Latin American cities, was an outgrowth of Spanish colonization, beginning in the sixteenth century and lasting well into the nineteenth century. The Spanish colonial cities were generally well planned, and because of their common origins, they tended to develop similar physical patterns. Generally, they were laid out around a central plaza, usually surrounded by ceremonial buildings, such as cathedrals and government offices. Housing sites were often of uniform shape, and the streets were laid out in a grid pattern with rectangular blocks. This pattern offered considerable flexibility for growth, as the boundaries of the city could be readily expanded as more room was needed.

Mexico City, like other Spanish colonial cities, was rigidly stratified along social class lines, and this pattern persists to the present. Elites and higher socioeconomic groups usually occupy the most pleasant and convenient areas at the center of the city rather than in the suburbs, and the lowest income groups occupy peripheral areas. The poorest newcomers settle in the shantytowns around the outskirts of the city, where they live mostly in overcrowded and undersized dwellings, usually without utilities, adequate sanitation, or clean water supplies. In spite of its industrial and economic gains, Mexico City has not been able to keep pace with the even more rapid growth in population and urbanization, and large inequities exist in the distribution of wealth, overcrowded housing, poor distribution of health care and other services, underemployment, and absolute poverty. Political unrest was magnified in many regions of Mexico in the 1990s, and the year 2000 general elections led to the defeat of the PRI, the political party that had been in power for approximately seventy years. It was replaced with new leaders who promised major reforms in the political, economic, and social structure of Mexico.

However, it should be pointed out that, with the advent of industrialization and modern transportation systems, including Mexico City's subway system, there have been some improvements in the quality of life for at least some of the city's residents over the past few decades. For example, as high rise office and commercial buildings have expanded at the center of Mexico city, a "zone of transition" has developed around the city center, and many wealthy and middle-class families have moved into revitalized or "gentrified neighborhoods" at the northern and southwestern edges of the city. Thus, industrialization and modernization may be shifting the spacial pattern of Mexico City in the direction of that found in many major urban centers in the United States (see chapters 14 and 15).

As part of a 1978 National Urban Development Plan to control population growth in Mexico's overcrowded cities, the government planned to transfer 400,000 federal jobs out of Mexico City to smaller cities. Under the plan, the government built nineteen industrial parks to create employment outside the cities and planned to give the private sector and foreign businesses tax incentives and energy discounts of up to 20 percent to encourage them to invest in the countryside rather than in the largest cities. The plan also foresaw the construction of hundreds of regional service centers throughout the countryside. These were settlements of 10,000 people or more, containing most of the basic services in an attempt to lure migrants away from the large cities (Gold, 1982, pp. 394–395; UPI, November 8, 1979). But by no means is this transformation complete, nor has it yet had a significant impact in improving the quality of life in the outlying shantytowns, where burgeoning population growth continues to create demands for housing, jobs, services, and health care or other needs that exceed the current capacity of Mexico City's social, economic, and political institutions to meet in a timely manner.

Brazil has produced an urban pattern that does not fit the generalizations applicable to the other countries of Latin America, partially because of its Portuguese rather than Spanish colonial heritage. For example, Brazil is not dominated by a single primate city, but instead contains Rio de Janeiro, with over 10 million people, as well as Sao Paulo, the world's third largest city, with nearly 18 million people, according to estimates for the year 2000 (*New York Times 2000 Almanac,* 1999). Brazil also contains two other large cities, Belo Horizonte and Salvador, each with more than 2 million residents.

The economic base of Sao Paulo is more typical of the large metropolises of Europe and the United States than of other metropolitan areas of Latin America. Within its confines are thousands of industrial plants and factories employing the highest paid labor force in Latin America. It is served by a modern international airport, more than twenty newspapers, dozens of radio and television stations, and by such cultural facilities as at least three universities, many legitimate theaters, and an excellent symphony orchestra. Many of its more than thirty suburban municipalities are industrial satellites, and public services and facilities in Sao Paulo are among the best in Latin America. Utilities, sanitation, and the school systems are reasonably well developed (Bollens and Schmandt, 1975, pp. 354–357). But even an economically well-developed metropolis such as Sao Paulo has serious problems keeping pace with its rapid growth, and it has serious housing shortages, clean water and sanitation problems, and a great deal of traffic congestion, as well as a host of administrative and political problems growing out of its rapid growth. Squatter settlements are also still found around the city's periphery, but they are less extensive than in other Latin American cities, including Rio de Janeiro. Sao Paulo's population is expected to continue to grow rather rapidly in the foreseeable future, reaching approximately 21 million people by 2015 (United Nations, 1995).

AFRICA

Africa's population is currently expanding the fastest of any of the world's continents, nearly quadrupling from 222 million people in 1950, to a projected 867 million people in 2000. By 2050, it is projected to grow to nearly 2.3 billion people by 2050 (*New York Times 2000 Almanac,* 1999). This extremely rapid current and projected growth is caused by a unique combination of a very high fertility level, with only a moderately high mortality level, and an age structure in which 46 percent of the entire African population is under age fifteen.

In spite of this high growth rate, Africa is only 34 percent urban, making it the least urbanized of all the continents. Yet there is a strong trend toward urbanization, which is one of the outstanding characteristics of its present-day life. But the degree of urbanization varies drastically from country to country, varying from as low as 2 percent urban in the Democratic Republic of Congo, to 86 percent urban in Libya (United Nations Population Fund, 1998). At the far south is the relatively wealthy and industrialized South Africa, with relatively large cities, such as Capetown and Johannesberg, and a population that was over 50 percent urban in 1998. North of the Sahara Desert are countries with ancient but disparate civilizations, such as Egypt and Ethiopia. While Ethiopia is only 13 percent urban, Egypt, with its large primate city of Cairo, is 45 percent urban.

Below the Sahara region are the new nations of the continent that have most recently been liberated as former colonies of the European powers. This vast mosaic of emerging nations is interlaced with a multiplicity of customs, languages, religions, ethnic backgrounds, and political institutions that defy generalization. Rapid transition and the thrust of modernization have intensified the problems of nation building and in the process have precipitated political instability and unrest, civil wars and military takeovers. "The number of simultaneous multiple crises facing Africa right now is unprecedented," according to the director of African studies at the Center for Strategic and International Studies, and "Africa is in worse condition than ever before. And it's only going to get worse over the next generation" (*Detroit News,* August 27, 2000, p. 4A). Militarily, about half the nations in sub-Sahara Africa are either engaged in open conflict or heated disputes, some with internal factions and some with neighboring states. Ethnic and religious strife is rampant, producing some patterns of genocide, particularly in Central and East Africa. Much of the continent has resumed a long slide into poverty, war, and disease, and these conditions have held back much of the region from the rapid free-market growth occurring in other parts of the developing world (*New York Times,* August 27, 2000, p. wk 1 & 5; *Detroit News,* August 27, 2000, p. 4A).

Because of the rapid rates of migration into the growing cities of Central and East Africa, such cities are commonly characterized by an explosive expansion of the urban population, without a corresponding increase in available city housing. As a result, large squatter slums have emerged on the outskirts of most of the larger cities. In some regions, these are called *bidonvilles,* or "tin can" cities. The inability of many African governments to expand the housing supply at the same rate at which their city populations have been growing has led many observers to the conclusion that shantytowns with homes made of scrap metal, packing crates, or such will continue to be part of the African urban experience for some time to come. In addition to housing problems, the squatter slums experience a lack of adequate services and facilities, such as adequate schools and sanitation or sewer facilities.

Nigeria is the most populated country of Africa, with a 1998 population of 121.8 million people; it is ranked as the tenth most populated country in the world. Growing very rapidly, its population is expected to double by 2025. Its largest city is Lagos. With a 2000 population of 13.5 million people, it is the ninth largest urban area in the world (Table 16.1). It will gain nearly 11 million more people by 2015, making it by then the sixth largest world city. Although Nigeria, and its principle city Lagos, is relatively affluent because of its rich natural resource base (it is a major supplier of oil to the United States), this has not protected Lagos from the same kinds of problems faced by other overurbanized cities in other parts of the less developed world. For example, it faces almost unmanageable traffic congestion, it cannot keep up with the demands for adequate housing, its political and governmental institutions are inadequate and too unstable for the growing needs of the local population, and "the open street drains continue to overflow, refuse collection is erratic, and big, overloaded trucks continue to tear up colonial-era roads" (Palen, 1997, p. 426).

Nigeria's second largest city, Ibadan, is an exception to the general African city pattern of squatter or slum development at its periphery. Although a large city with a population of nearly 1.3 million people, and a British colonial tradition similar to that of many other African cities, Ibadan's spatial structure is quite different from that just described. In the core of the oldest part of the city, density is remarkably high, open space is virtually nonexistent, roads are few, and access to many of the dwellings is still by means of footpaths. Virtually all of the houses in the central area are constructed of mud and are roofed with corrugated iron. Sanitary facilities are lacking, and the water supply is obtained from communal taps (Gold, 1982, p. 392). The surrounding suburban or peripheral areas house the more affluent members of the community, including the Europeans who began to enter the city after the British assumed control. At the periphery of Ibadan, the housing is better, the residential sites are more spacious, and the density is much lower. On the other hand, the poorer and less well-educated Africans, both established residents and migrants, must seek homes in the crowded districts of the city center. Thus, even though the spatial settlement pattern is more like that of the urban-industrial cities of the United States, Ibadan still is poorly equipped to absorb large numbers of newcomers, particularly those of poorer status. Although it is relatively large, Ibadan still retains some of the social, economic, and political characteristics of a village. That is, it is difficult for the local institutions to cope with the highly pluralist nature of a large city with its many competing interest groups and diverse loyalties.

ASIA

Asia contains societies as disparate as Israel, Turkey, India, Japan, and China. Each major region of Asia differs markedly in its population size and growth and in its rates of urban and industrial growth. Even though Asia contains most of the largest urban conglomerations in the world and at least ten of the fifteen largest metropolitan areas in the world (see Table 16.1), vast differences exist between such Asian cities as Tokyo, Calcutta, Beijing, Shanghai, Osaka, or Seoul. Likewise, there are significant differences between the societies and regions of which these and other large cities of Asia are a part. For example, although all the whole of Asia is 35 percent urban, Asian countries vary from 14 percent urban in Nepal to 81 percent urban in South Korea. Even more atypical is the city-state of Singapore, which is 100 percent urban, according to a United Nations (1998) estimate. Because it is impossible to adequately consider all of Asia in the available space, this discussion is limited to a brief description of some of the principal cities in three of the highly populated countries of Asia with the largest cities: Japan, India, and mainland China.

Japan

Japan is by far the most industrialized country in Asia and is in the same class as the more developed nations of Europe and North America in this characteristic. With 78 percent of its population living in urban areas, Japan's degree of urbanization is slightly greater than that of the United States, which is 76 percent urban, and it successfully com-

Pedestrians cross a busy street in the Ginza district of Tokyo, Japan

petes with the United States in world markets for its manufactured goods. Its largest city, Tokyo, is often ranked with New York and London as among the three most influential global cities in the world economy (Sassen, 1991). Tokyo was the largest urban area in the world in 2000, with a projected population of 27.9 million people, and it is expected to remain the largest urban area at least through 2015, according to United Nations projections. Yokohama, with a population of over 3 million people, is technically Japan's second largest city, but it also is part of the Tokyo metropolitan area, and its population is included in the Tokyo total. Also included in metropolitan Tokyo is the city of Kawasaki and the prefectures of Nanawaga, Saitama, and Chiba.

Hall (1998, p. 455) describes this conglomeration, which sprawls thirty or forty miles in every direction, as "the greatest urban sprawl in the world," and as "the greatest innovative high-technology industrial area on the entire globe." Its factories produce a disproportionate share of the world's output of television sets, VCRs, camcorders, electronic cameras, laptop computers, fax machines, CD players, music synthesizers, and every imaginable electronic device. It is "Silicon Valley's great global rival," but unlike Silicon Valley, with its low-rise campuslike buildings amidst sprawling green spaces, Hall further describes Tokyo's electronic industrial base, in physical terms, as consisting of "densely packed buildings crammed higgledy-piggledy amid houses and railroad tracks and elevated expressways," and most likely housed in ten-story high-rise towers. In the final analysis, Hall attributes Japan's impressive economic success to a unique combination of governmental vision and guidance, along with the innovations of market-driven private initiative (Hall, 1998, p. 482).

Such population and economic growth has not come without a price. The Tokyo area is one of the world's most congested and polluted. Because of traffic congestion and inadequate roads, long commutes and excessive traffic tie-ups are a part of the daily routine, even with a modern commuter rail and subway transit system. The trains are always overcrowded during rush hour traffic, and commuters are packed tightly into them by pushers. A popular transportation alternative is the bicycle, and there are nearly 6 million of them in Tokyo. However, parking spaces are inadequate even for those using bicycles! Housing is scarce and very expensive, and living quarters are very small, relative to American standards. People are tightly crowded together, mostly without the luxury of parks or open spaces. Sewage and sanitation systems are simply inadequate for serving the needs of the large and growing population, as are other public services.

It seems paradoxical that such a highly developed nation, with many advanced technological and economic resources at its disposal, has not been able to control the rapid growth of Tokyo or to plan its growth in such a way as to minimize problems such as those described. Major efforts had been undertaken earlier, including a 1950s Capital Regional Development Law, which would have provided a ring of new satellite towns and a surrounding green belt at a radius of seventeen to forty-five miles from central Tokyo (Hall, 1977). But the plan failed to realize the rate at which Tokyo was growing, and it has now become clear that this plan really had no hope of realization. For example, areas earmarked for preservation as a green belt (see chapter 14) became developed for industrial and residential purposes, partially because the powers to prevent this from happening were simply lacking (Gold, 1982). Hall (1977, 1998) has attributed the failure of planning in the Tokyo region to the strong laissez faire economic values and policies of both the central and the regional government, which believed that city and regional land-use planning should take a backseat to industrial and technological expansion, which, in the case of Japan, has long been of top priority. Whatever major planning efforts that have been made to decentralize the population of metropolitan Tokyo to date have either failed or have never materialized. For example, a new town of 100,000 near Kobe was built on a landfill in Kobe harbor, but a major earthquake in Kobe in 1995 illustrated the unwise folly of building on such an unstable landfill in an earthquake prone area (Palen, 1997). Other large cities in Japan include Osaka, with nearly 2.5 million residents; Nagoya, with approximately 2 million people; and Sapporo, with a population just over 1.7 million people.

India

With a population of approximately 1 billion people (1999 estimate), India is the second largest country in the world. But it contrasts sharply with Japan in its degree of urbanization and industrialization. Only 27 percent of its population lives in urban areas, and it is clearly an economically underdeveloped country. It is probably the poorest large country in the world, with 40 percent of its total population suffering from absolute poverty (World Resources, 1999). Its per capita gross national product (GNP) is only 370 U.S. dollars per year (World Bank, 1999), and although approximately 70 percent of its population is involved in agriculture, food production is not sufficient to feed the exploding Indian population, and malnutrition in India is relatively widespread.

The largest of the Indian cities, Bombay, Calcutta, and Delhi, have a British Colonial history, which had an important part in impeding their earlier industrial and economic development, although these cites, taken together, account for about half of all of India's industrial production. By 1990, Bombay had overtaken Calcutta as India's largest city, due to its extremely rapid growth rate. Its population more than tripled between 1970 and 2000, making it the second largest urban area in the world, with a population of 18.1 million people. It is also projected to increase by a little more than another 9 million people by 2015 and to remain as the world's second largest urban area (*New York Times 2000 Almanac,* 1999).

Bombay's impressive growth is partially due to significant changes in India's economic policies during the early 1990s, when it moved from being a mostly state-controlled economy to one more tied to capitalistic free market principles. Its industrial production rapidly increased, and there was a tremendous building boom, as more and more people came to the city seeking employment opportunities. But such uncontrollable population increases, of course, lead to overurbanization, which has been described earlier as a condition in which urban areas cannot adequately cope with all of the needs or demands of a burgeoning population. Housing supply, streets and transportation systems, water supplies, sanitation and sewage systems, health care, and other necessary services and institutions are overtaxed. As one sociological observer put it, "Bombay has more growth than it can handle and is showing signs of coming apart at the seams. . . . Bombay's social fabric threatens to unravel" (Palen, 1997, pp. 392–394). Because of its thriving economy, much new wealth has been created, but this has not been evenly distributed. Thus, the gap between the growing number of rich residents and the poor has been rapidly increasing, and the living conditions of the poor have been growing more intolerable as more and more poor people became homeless because of the shrinking and increasingly expensive housing supply. Palen (1997, p. 394) has observed that Bombay was a city that "could handle 5 million people reasonably well, and even cope with 8 million—but it has 13 million, and the 13 million are straining the municipality beyond its limits." But at the 18 plus million population in the year 2000, and still growing, the future well-being of the city is even more ominous than it seemed just a few years earlier. It is most likely that the growing patterns of social unrest and political instability that have been sweeping India during the last part of the twentieth century and the beginning of the twenty-first century are primarily reflective of the turmoil facing its burgeoning urban centers (see *New York Times 2000 Almanac,* 1999, pp. 591–594). The ruling Congress party was defeated in a 1996 election, after ruling India for many decades, because it was deemed by the electorate to be ineffective in dealing with many of India's unresolved problems. To date, it is still not clear the rather weak political coalitions governing India since then will be any more effective in governing India or dealing with the many problems caused by its overpopulation and overurbanization (*New York Times 2000 Almanac,* 1999, pp. 593–594)

With a year 2000 estimated population of 12.7 million people, Calcutta is now India's second largest urban area. It was once India's largest city, with a vibrant economy and one of the world's busiest ports, but its economy and growth have been in decline in recent decades. Of all the world cities discussed in this chapter, Calcutta suffers some of the worse consequences of overurbanization. Calcutta has long been known as an overcrowded and noxious city, and Rudyard Kipling once described it as "chance-erected, chance directed, because its growth had long been uncontrolled and without plan." (c.f. Gold, 1982, p. 399). Its mid-twentieth-century history, including the aftereffects of World War II when Calcutta was a military supply base, the Bengal famine of 1945, and the partition of the country in 1947, which produced a large influx of displaced persons from

East Pakistan, had contributed to population expansion much greater than expected. This wave of growth has now tapered off, but the most troublesome aspects of its earlier uncontrolled growth still remain to perpetuate its current image of an urban "basket case." Since at least 1990, over 70 percent of its population has lived in dire poverty, and there is little or no hope that this condition will improve in the foreseeable future. Palen (1997, p. 394) has aptly described Calcutta's international image as "one of decay, misery, and disaster."

Calcutta has long had acute shortages of open space and mass transit, and its road system has not even begun to keep pace with needs. The environmental problems of water, sewerage, and drainage have produced major health problems. The World Resources Institute (1996) and the United Nations Environmental Programme (1997), for example, have both reported that the city's poor water and sanitation conditions were undoubted causes for the continued prevalence of cholera and many other epidemic diseases.

Even more acute are the tremendous housing shortages in Calcutta. Over 75 percent of the city's population lives in overcrowded tenements and squatter slums, and more than half of all the city's families live in dwellings of no more than a single room. At least several types of slum housing areas exist. These include the *Bustees,* which are subcommunities made up primarily of one-story huts containing approximately eight little cubicles, each of which in turn may be rented to an entire family. Even worse are the *Pucca* slums, which consist of brick multistoried tenement buildings, in an area of at least a quarter million people. They lack the light and air of the bustees, and their confined nature often makes conditions malodorous and unbearable, especially when sanitary facilities break down, which is often the case. More ominous is the fact that many of these buildings are unsafe, because they are in an advanced state of decay due to their age and because of a lack of adequate maintenance. As poor as the living conditions are in these two types of slums, they are still worse for the many people living in the streets, who have no shelter at all. There is no accurate estimate of the numbers of these homeless people, but it probably is in the range of tens of thousands or more. The combined problems of extreme poverty and squalid or no housing have produced periods of unrest, disorder, and riots in Calcutta, in spite of a number of ineffective reform polices that were introduced by the central government over the years. In many ways the problems of Calcutta and other Indian urban areas, compounded as they are by extreme poverty, high birthrates, high illiteracy, overcrowding, and political instability, appear to be even more insurmountable than in the overurbanized areas of other less developed parts of the world such as Africa or Latin America.

China

Mainland China has by far the largest population on earth. Its population numbered approximately 1.26 billion people in 1998 (United Nations, 1998). Although its rate of growth in recent decades has been less than in most other less developed countries, partially due to strict birth control policies, its large population base makes yearly population increments impressive in actual numbers. For example, it is projected to reach about 1.52 billion people by 2050, representing an anticipated increase in actual numbers almost as large as the entire U.S. population of 1998 (*New York Times 2000 Almanac,* 1999, p. 483); in other words, it is growing by about 5 million people a year.

China, as of 2000, has three of the fifteen largest urban areas in the world: Shanghai, with 17.2 million people is the fourth largest; Beijing, with 14.2 million people is the seventh largest; and Tainjin, with 12.4 million people, is the twelfth largest urban area on earth. It is interesting to note, for comparative purposes, that Tainjin, China's third largest metropolis, is now only slightly smaller than Los Angeles, but will have almost 3 million more people than Los Angeles by 2015 (Table 16.1). It is equally important to note that in spite of its several extremely large and growing urban areas, China as a whole is still only 30 percent urban, far less than that of any of the world's more developed nations (*National Geographic Desk Reference,* 1999).

One cannot understand modern China's urbanization without taking into account recent Chinese political, economic, and social history since the Chinese communist state was established in 1949. Ever since then, there have been several dramatic twists and turns of Chinese urban policy, and thus, there has been no consistently straight line of urban growth or development during the past half century. During the new government's initial five-year plan put into effect in the early 1950s, there was a large investment in heavy industry and capital construction, most of which was centered in the cities. As a result, China initially experienced a rate of economic growth and an expansion of employment opportunities in cities, and this led to significant urban growth and higher urban living standards, along with a return to political stability and social order after a century of political turmoil and social unrest (Tang and Parish, 2000, pp. 19–20).

In urban areas, virtually everyone was mobilized to participate in industrial production, and urban workers were granted many privileges and benefits not available to nonurban segments of the population. At the same time, people's communes were established in the countryside, where rural peasants lived and worked collectively, but under much different political, economic, and social conditions than urban residents. These waves of massive, but separate, forms of mobilization of urban workers on the one hand, and rural peasants on the other, were the result of rapid policy changes and political and social upheavals during the periods of *The Great Leap Forward* and *The Cultural Revolution* (roughly 1957 to 1976).

What soon evolved was a distinct bifurcation of the conditions of urban living from those in the rural areas of China, and this unique pattern is not duplicated anywhere else in the urban world (see Dutton, 1998). What had happened was that in order to prevent turmoil and to ensure peace and order among the urban working classes, they were provided with government guaranteed benefits such as housing, health care, retirement and unemployment benefits, and a variety of staple goods, such as food and clothing. To pay for these benefits, agricultural regions were stripped of resources, and this produced a distinct gulf between rural and urban living standards. The inevitable result was a large movement of rural people into the cities in the late 1950s (Tang and Parish, 2000, p. 24). The government was not prepared for this movement and made every effort to keep the peasants from settling in the cities. The newcomers were denied the benefits available to the established urban population by laws that were established to create a sturdy "bamboo wall" between the two new *castes.* If one was born on the privileged urban side of the bamboo wall, one became a member of a labor "aristocracy" and was entitled to a host of urban benefits, including attending urban schools, being part of the virtually guaranteed urban job assignment process, subsidized housing, and a host of other government guaranteed benefits. Those born to rural parents were denied such benefits and job security and were left to fend for themselves. Laws were also passed to control urban growth through severe restrictions on rural-to-urban migration.

As a result, growth in city populations actually leveled off during the 1960s and most of the 1970s, but many people of rural origin did remain in the cities in large numbers, and migration to the cities remained heavy (Tang and Parish, 2000, p. 25). According to Dutton (1998), most of the people of rural origins remained poor, in something akin to a "floating" underclass of street people, living by their wits as peddlers, street merchants, trash collectors, beggars, petty thieves, hooligans, hustlers, and the like. More significant than unequal economic opportunities or privileges for the urban poor of rural origins was the symbolic caste distinction between being an urban "insider" or a nonurban "outsider." To be a nonurban outsider in a Chinese city in some ways would be analogous to being an untouchable in India. In other words, according to Dutton, these two distinct side-by-side statuses have been more important in the modern urban Chinese cultural belief system that separates these two groups, than are the hierarchical rankings of statuses usually associated with systems of social stratification in the more developed urban world (see chapter 11). And ironically and perhaps unwittingly, a Chinese government ostensibly committed to eliminating class distinctions had contributed to this bifurcated caste system by its recent policy of restricting and stigmatizing rural to urban migration.

Under the attempts to maintain tight controls over migration to the cities, an urban social and economic structure emerged whereby urban neighborhoods were organized into neighborhood committees, or more commonly called *work units*. Work units typically contained approximately 20,000 people in 3,000 to 5,000 extended families or households. By 1990, China had over 5,000 work units in 447 cities (Tang and Parish, 2000, p. 27). The work units were all-encompassing elements in most people's lives. They provided employment and income, medical insurance, labor protection, pensions, decent housing, and direct subsidies. They not only provided food and clothing, but also granted permission to get married, divorced, or to have children. They were governed by neighborhood committees of approximately 50 members and 15 to 25 residents' councils each. Their purpose was to distribute resources and benefits, manage work activities, and resolve conflicts. Their political purpose was to see to it that government policy was implemented, loyalty to the governing party was ensured, and "appropriate" programs of political mobilization were carried out. Being a member of a work unit provided security, status, and a sense of purpose and belonging: privileges that were not available to the stigmatized and ineligible rural migrants (see Dutton, 1998, and Tang and Parish, 2000, for more detailed analysis of the nature and consequences of work units in Chinese cities).

By the late 1970s, a new set of reform policies were again put in place that has produced profound changes in the Chinese economy, social structure, and urban life throughout the rest of the twentieth century: First, the economy was opened to free market forces to a degree unprecedented since the Communist Revolution. Private investment in industry and commerce drastically increased, and consumer products became more diversified and widely available, as more and more international corporations entered the Chinese marketplace, and as China, with its huge population of potential consumers, became a more integral part of the global economy. Second, Hong Kong, blessed with a vibrant economy tied to the global economy, became a major urban asset when it was returned to Chinese control in 1997. Third, internal migration controls had been lifted, and the growth of the urban population has accelerated, as more rural people left the countryside for the cities; and fourth, the policies of the more developed urbanized nations, including the United States, have been significantly effected by liberalized economic and trade policies in China, as the industrialized countries compete for the rewards and risks of participation in the freer Chinese industrial and commercial marketplace. As a result, many previous economic sanctions against China for its poor human rights record have been lifted, China will likely be admitted into the World Trade Organization (WTO), and the United States has granted permanent trade status to China in its recent global trade policies (*New York Times 2000 Almanac,* 1999, pp. 557–558).

By the 1990s, rampant consumerism and extensive mass media exposure, particularly television, became new dimensions to Chinese urban life. Increasingly commonplace were commercial billboards and commercials in place of official political slogans. Cars and private apartments have now become highly desirable incentives for marriage, and fancy supermarkets, theme parks, disco dancing, miniskirts, Coca-Cola, and Budweiser T-shirts are among the newly acquired tastes (Tang and Parish, 2000). Dishwashers, washing machines, and refrigerators have also become common household items. Although media and publishing are still controlled by the government, newspaper, magazine, and book publication has increased rapidly. Newsstands in Beijing's subway stations now sell over forty different kinds of newspapers and magazines, as compared with three or four just fifteen years earlier. Cellular phone sales have exploded, as have VCRs, video CDs, and home computers (Tang and Parish, 2000, p. 44).

One consequence of the rapid spread of consumerism that has been troubling to the Chinese government, however, is that expectations may have grown so great that it might prove to be difficult or impossible to meet the new demands. Free markets, however desirable, tend to distribute their rewards unequally and to generate or to threaten unrest. There are many signs that this has been happening in Chinese cities, as evidenced by various forms of protest, demonstrations, and the formations of new kinds of interest groups in recent decades. Many of the dilemmas and inconsistencies of a socialist economy being transformed into market economy have created uncertainties and ambiguities regarding China's future development policies that have not been fully resolved.

For example, urban housing is one area of great shortages unintentionally created by the boom in the private market economy and rapid urban population increases. A recent government administered public housing survey in forty cities revealed that more people were dissatisfied with the current housing system than were satisfied with it. Among the sources of dissatisfaction were corruption in housing assignments, inferior housing, lack of housing choices, and unfair and irrational distribution of available housing. This high-level dissatisfaction persisted despite massive investment in urban housing which helped China recover from years of neglect in this area (Tang and Parish, 2000, pp. 37–38). Much of the new housing, except for some of the traditional protected areas of Beijing, has been provided in massive high-rise apartment developments, often replacing traditional Chinese one-story housing compounds. Architecturally, the new high rises are similar to the bland "international" style high-rise developments found in most regions of the urban world. From my perspective, most of them physically resemble the former Pruitt-Igoe public housing project in St. Louis or the former Cabrini-Green public housing units in Chicago, both of which have been torn down and replaced in recent years, because this type of massive and impersonal high-rise public housing has lost favor. Other Chinese attempts to relieve housing problems include selling off public housing units to individuals in an emerging private real estate market and in raising publicly subsidized rents to "market" levels.

Nevertheless, Dutton (1998, p. 12) estimates there are over a million homeless transients on the streets of Beijing, and there are only about 5,000 beds available for them in hotels or other specially designated places. Thus, most of the transients must live as floaters and sleep on the streets. The number of people in Shanghai living in similar dire conditions is probably closer to 2 million. Dutton attributes rising levels of crime and delinquency in both cities, as well as in other Chinese urban areas, to this high level of homelessness and transiency. Both Beijing and Shanghai also suffer from relatively high levels of air pollution and traffic congestion, in spite of the fact that most residents still use bicycles, buses, or the subway for daily commuting. How well and in what direction China copes with its urban problems in the foreseeable future as it more fully enters the global economy remains an open question.

RUSSIA

Russia is an enigma when it comes to analyzing its recent urban history. First, it is both a European and an Asian country, spreading from the Baltic and Scandinavian countries at its western borders all the way across Northern Asia to the Bering Sea. Second, it has gone through several major revolutionary political upheavals during the twentieth century, moving from being a czarist Russian state to a communist state during the early part of the century, to its collapse as a vast Communist Empire, and turning back into a smaller Russian state, of a not fully formed and uncertain character, in the last part of the twentieth century. It is in this context that Russian urbanization is discussed, particularly in terms of the comparison between the state planned urban developments in the Soviet Union before its collapse, and the more chaotic thrusts toward free market reforms after the creation of the nominally democratic new Russian Federation in 1991.

The former Soviet Union had been characterized by steady urban growth ever since the inception of the communist state. It was 32 percent urban in 1939, 48 percent urban in 1959, and 62 percent urban in 1979. Under Soviet rule, more than one-half of the urban growth was caused by resettlement of former farm and village dwellers in the cities, rather than by natural increase. In the twenty years between 1950 and 1970, the urban population increased at a rate three times greater than that of the total population (Wilson and Schulz, 1978). By 1998, 76 percent of its population lived in urban areas, a proportion similar to that in the United States, according to the latest estimate available since the inception of the new Russian state.

The Soviet Union had always made persistent efforts to constrain and direct urban expansion by attempting to limit the growth of its largest cities and dispersing urban populations throughout a multiplicity of decentralized regional urban centers. These decentralization policies included the development of new towns and industrial satellites as well as the expansion of existing urban centers in outlying regions outside of Russia proper. The policies governing these developments were administered by a highly centralized State Economic Planning Commission, without evidence of any kind of interference or intervention by free market forces.

Soviet urban planning policies had been described in their purest socialist form by Jack C. Fisher (1967; 1976) , and they consisted of the following basic elements:

A. Standardization of Housing. Housing construction in the Soviet Union was standardized through prefabrication of housing units manufactured in factories and delivered to building sites. Housing units were relatively uniform with respect to size, quality, and design. The standardization of housing was planned not only to relieve tremendous housing shortages in the Soviet Union and to maximize efficiencies, but also to achieve greater socioeconomic uniformity among the residents, keeping in tune with even more basic socialist objectives.

B. Optimum City Size. Soviet planners were convinced that large cities must be contained to their present size to avoid the "inhumane" or "evil" conditions they believed to be characteristic of bigness, especially the bigness of large American or Western European Cities. The critical element in determining the size of any particular urban center was to be based on the size of its labor force, relative to the desirable size of the total population of the community. A series of dependent satellite communities should be built around existing large cities into which surplus population in the central cities should be dispersed.

C. City Centers. Soviet Planners argued that the center of a city should serve political, administrative, and cultural functions, rather than the commercial and retail functions associated with city centers in capitalistic economies. According to Soviet communist thought, the city center is the vital core necessary to coordinate the entire urban complex, and it should receive priority in city planning. The center should provide room for "parading troops and for throngs of people on holidays," as well as providing a setting for principal public buildings and monuments. A hotel for tourists, a single state-run department store, and perhaps a restaurant or coffee shop were perceived as the only kinds of commercial activities permitted at the city center.

D. Neighborhood Units. Soviet planners supported the idea of an elaborate division of each city into self-contained neighborhoods, each of which would maintain it own decision-making, administrative, service, and facilities structure. The goal was that the residents of each neighborhood would become a sociologically cohesive group and would become relatively self-sufficient in meeting their own economic and social needs (not unlike the work units in cities in Communist China, as described in the previous section, which were probably designed in the manner of this Soviet model). Thus, in Soviet city planning, elements such as the location of housing, schools, parks and recreation centers, stores, restaurants, clinics, repair shops, and meeting places were to be spatially located according to the boundaries of the neighborhood unit.

More recent reports suggest that Soviet city planners had not fully realized their planning objectives, probably because of the extremely high costs of removing and restoring the devastation of principal Soviet cities in World War II, the rigidity of the Soviet political system, a lack of knowledge of modern construction techniques and architecture, the regime's higher priorities for military, industrial, and agricultural development, and, of course, because of the ultimate collapse of the Soviet Union. Nevertheless it still can be argued that in spite of these limitations, some well-planned cities with relatively attractive and comfortable residential units had been built during the Soviet period (Gold, 1982, p. 404).

At the beginning of the twenty-first century, free market forces have now taken root, but in a much more haphazard, unplanned, and unregulated way than in China, as reported in the previous section of this chapter. The distribution of consumer goods and economic opportunity is uneven, with large gaps between the winners and losers of economic competition, which is a system still not fully embraced or appreciated by many Russian citizens, who felt more secure under the old Soviet system. Because market mechanisms have not yet ensured a reliable and fair distribution of consumer goods, and political leadership appears to be weak or not sufficiently in control of the economy, there is an active and growing black market for the products that people want and need, and organized crime has grown to the point where it is sometimes referred to by many as a Russian "Mafia." Thus, many foreign investors are leery of participating in the Russian economy because of too much uncertainty about its political and economic stability.

Despite previous Soviet efforts to constrain and disperse urban growth, Moscow's population had increased from 5.4 million people in 1950 to an estimated 9.3 million people in 2000. But it has slipped from being the fourth largest city in the world to being the twenty-fourth largest over the same time period (Table 16 .1). Nevertheless, with all of the satellite cities and new towns within a forty-mile radius included, the population of the Moscow urban region includes approximately 13 million people, making it one of the largest urban complexes in continental Europe. Because so much of the administrative and political power of Russia is concentrated in Moscow, as are cultural, trade, and communications facilities, the Moscow urban area has many of the characteristics and functions of the primate cities in less developed countries discussed earlier in this chapter, although Russia differs markedly from these countries in its current rates of industrialization, urban growth, and geopolitical history.

We conclude this discussion of Russian urbanization with some of the best balanced, salient, and most recently available firsthand observations about current conditions in Moscow from a newspaper article by Michael Dobbs, a former Moscow bureau chief of the *Washington Post* between 1988 and 1993, who revisited Moscow in the summer of 2000. Sections of his article most relevant to this chapter are quoted in detail, as follows:

> I am amazed by the gleaming new face of Moscow: the American-style supermarkets and shopping malls, the repainted facades, the gentrification of crumbling tenement buildings, the bustling highways and beltways that are the pride and joy of Mayor Your Luzhkov. . . . At the same time, I am saddened by the vulgarity of the new rich, the sight of beggars being splattered with mud . . . the seemingly all-pervasive corruption, the stunning gap between haves and have nots. . . .
>
> Despite the fancy restaurants and luxury automobile dealerships that have sprung up almost overnight in big cities like Moscow . . . it seems undeniable that most people are worse off than they were in 1991, at the dawn of the new free-market era. Factories have closed, prices have gone through the roof, and old economic ties

have been destroyed. "There are no jobs" was a recurring refrain everywhere I went. In some places, unemployment is as high as 50 or 60 percent. . . .

And yet there are shards of hope. The brightest, it seems to me is the release of huge amounts of energy. . . . Russia is becoming a nation of hustlers. . . . The most visible evidence of this energy is the number of gleaming new buildings going up all over Moscow. If architecture is the sign of the vigor of a civilization, then the new Russia—or at least the new Moscow—is gaining daily in self confidence. Entire areas of the city are being ripped apart and remodeled. Churches are springing up like mushrooms after a storm. . . . Just as Stalinist architecture was the physical expression of Soviet power, so are these gleaming new skyscrapers, beltways and churches the perfect reflection of the new area of crony capitalism. In exchange for the privilege of doing business in Moscow, they are required to hand over a portion of their profits, to be spent on the mayor's favorite projects. . . .

Like Russia itself, the new Architecture is a bizarre mishmash of resurgent nationalism and crass commercialism. The symbols of Czarist Russia . . . jostle for attention with a forest of billboards advertising everything from toothpaste to . . . the occasional red star or hammer and sickle left over from the Soviet period. The overall effect is jarring, but also breathtaking in its scale and ambition. . . . As to where this country of bewildering contradictions is headed, it is difficult even to hazard a guess. (Dobbs, 2000, p. 21)

NORTHERN AND WESTERN EUROPE

The urban-industrial revolution, of course, first emerged in northern and western Europe (see chapter 3), and it was there that the great urban-industrial cities first developed. But now the region is not only highly developed, it has matured to the extent that its population growth has virtually stopped. If zero population growth is a desirable goal, Europe comes closer to meeting this goal than any other region in the world. What little growth there is, mostly in northern European countries, is offset by declining population in other countries. For example, Italy, Spain, Germany, Portugal, and many of the European countries of the former Soviet Union are all expected to have declining populations through 2025 (United Nations, 1998). Urban growth rates in Europe, which accelerated most rapidly in the eighteenth, nineteenth, and early parts of the twentieth century, have slowed drastically in this region during the middle and latter parts of the twentieth century. London, for example, which was the largest city in the world at the beginning of the twentieth century and was the second largest by 1950, was only the twentieth-largest city in the world at the end of the century.

Yet the countries of northern and western Europe have been and still remain among the most urbanized on earth. The populations of France, Spain, and Norway are more than 70 percent urban; those of Denmark, Germany, the Netherlands, and Sweden are more than 80 percent urban, and the United Kingdom and Belgium both have populations that are 90 percent or more urban. The relative economic, political, and social stability of these countries since the end of World War II is in part a product of the well-maintained balance between population growth, urban growth, and industrial or technological growth achieved by these societies during the postwar period.

A characteristic that the countries of northern and western Europe also have in common is a high commitment to city and regional planning and to intensive land-use controls. In most cases, such planning is a highly centralized function of the national governments, which anticipate and attempt to guide urban growth and redistribution trends into the foreseeable future. Nevertheless, there are countless variations in the approaches to urban planning from country to country and from city to city. Furthermore, different countries have reacted to more recent free market and globalization trends in different ways. A brief discussion of two principal European cities—London and Paris—illustrate some of the similarities and differences.

London

England has been one of the world's most urbanized countries for many decades, with many major cities, such as Birmingham, Leeds, Sheffield, Bradford, Liverpool, Manchester, Bristol, and, of course, London. Yet, even with its many urban centers, British life is still highly dominated by London. It has a widely recognized dual function, because not only is it the political, economic, and cultural capital of the nation, it is also a principal world city, because it is at the center of world finance, banking, and commerce. In terms of world systems theory, it is one of the "core" cities of the world, along with New York and Tokyo (Sassen, 1991; Hall, 1998). Aside from economics, London, in the 1960s, became the international capital for the fashion, design, and music of a new generation of young people: "the Swinging London of Carnaby Street, jeans, and mini-skirts, where teenagers had money to spend. In this new affluent, permissive, and still largely racially homogeneous metropolis . . . the future could still look bright—and certainly very much better than in the past" (Sheppard, 1998, pp. 341–342).

By the 1970s, London's middle classes were moving to the suburbs, leaving mainly the very rich and the very poor living in the city. The economy was in a recession, and large sections of the city, residential and commercial alike, were being neglected or abandoned. In particular, the port of London, with its many docks, suffered from a decline in shipping activities, and there was a loss of approximately twenty-five thousand jobs in the dock areas. Manufacturing industries in Greater London also declined between 1971 and 1981, and the unemployment rate almost doubled from 4.6 percent to 9.0 percent during this period.

While many areas of the economy declined and the middle classes were leaving the city, there were countertrends as well. First, new kinds of technological advances were beginning to replace industries and commercial entities with obsolete and failing methods of manufacturing and doing business. Second, many banking and financial institutions were being replaced or absorbed by international corporations interested in global trade, banking, and finance. And third, some of the population losses were being replenished, mainly by a large stream of migrants from former British colonies, such as India, Pakistan, and other previous colonies in Asia, Africa, and the Middle East. According to Sheppard (1998), the changed ethnic composition of its population has been the most significant single change in the makeup of London since World War II. There has been a mixed reaction to the greater ethnic heterogeneity, with many instances of tension and hostility on the one hand, and much welcoming receptivity to the greater degree of cosmopolitanism, cultural vitality, and new economic opportunities, on the other. Another countertrend has been the gradual gentrification and upgrading of older housing in the inner areas of the city by relatively affluent "yuppies," not unlike similar past trends in New York, San Francisco, or Boston.

By the last decade of the twentieth century, London's economy had revived, mainly on the basis of its role as a prime broker of the global economy, and during the last five years of the century, its economy had grown faster than the rest of England. Peter Hall (1977, 1998), who has long been a keen observer of London's changing social, economic, political, and physical structure, now refers to London as the "City of Capitalism Rampant," even though it has had a Labour government since the late 1990s. There has been new, large-scale commercial building development and "slum" clearance in the Dockland areas of Greater London and a tremendous growth in high-rise office towers in further reclaimed and redeveloped land along the banks of the Thames River (Hall, 1998). Its current economic success has been achieved mainly through its acceptance of a substantial measure of globalization. Many of London's factories, commercial buildings, banks, newspaper and television interests, hotels, and department stores (including the world famous Harrods) are now owned by international interests (Sheppard, 1998). Such outside investments have improved British prospects in the short term, but there is the risk that such gains may in the long run come at the cost of highly valued local and national autonomy.

Whatever the future consequences of globalization, the metropolitan green belt surrounding the city and the accompanying ring of new towns are among the "most enduring elements of the post-war planning of London and (now greatly enlarged), for a variety of reasons, still command strong public support" (Sheppard, 1998, p. 341). The goal of the green belt and the new towns was to provide controlled decentralization of people from the overcrowded city of London into small satellite new towns beyond the green belt and to provide a more equitable balance between town and country life, while at the same time preserving the amenities of both these alternatives. Another important goal of the new towns was that they should be relatively self-sufficient and should contain centers of employment for local residents to minimize the need for commuting. Each new town was to be made up of neighborhood units, each containing its own schools, shops, and other local facilities. Also, all social classes were to be represented in each neighborhood unit in a "well-balanced mixture" (Gold, 1982, p. 407).

Most observers agree that on the whole, new town and green belt planning in the London region has been eminently successful it achieving its goals. As outstanding examples of comprehensive and humanistic planning, the London area new towns have attracted admiring visitors from all over the world, and, as this and earlier chapters (see chapter 14) have already suggested, they have been widely imitated in other parts of the world. However, in the case of London, the new towns were not accomplished without some negative consequences. For example, the loss of central city middle-class residents to the new towns, robbing the city of some of its socioeconomic balance, has already been mentioned. But the new towns also were not successful in attracting lower-income groups, who remained trapped in poor housing in the city. Also, new town populations "overspilled" still farther out from the city than originally planned or anticipated. Thus, although daily commutes to the city were anticipated to be no more than an average of 15 to 25 miles from (or to) London, those in housing decentralized beyond the new town boundaries now face daily commutes of forty to fifty miles to the city center. More recent development plans for London focus on efforts to stabilize both population and employment in the central area and to supply a quality of life that persuades Londoners to remain in the city (Sheppard, 1998; Hall, 1998). It appears that this is already beginning to happen.

Paris

Paris is known the world over for its wide boulevards, handsome architecture, scenic streets, parks, museums, monuments, theaters, concert halls, and night spots. In the world's imagination, the city remains unique, "a city of style, beauty and love with more familiar monuments and heart-stopping second-hand memories than anywhere else" (Fenby, 1999). Much of the physical beauty of Paris is associated with the work of Baron Georges Haussman, who was given extraordinary, almost dictatorial, power in the decades of the 1850s and 1860s by the emperor Napoleon III to revitalize the city by virtually tearing the existing city apart and then rebuilding it anew. According to Hall (1998), "No one in the entire history of urbanism . . . ever transformed a city so profoundly during such a short period of time." As others have stated, it was arguably "the biggest urban renewal project the world has ever seen" (Sutcliffe, 1993, p. 83). In quantitative terms, Haussman's accomplishments have been summarized as follows:

> Between 1852 and 1869, 71 miles of new roads were built in Paris, and the average width of roads in the City . . . were doubled. Over 400 hundred miles of pavements were laid. The number of trees lining the streets was doubled and approached 100,000. Two hundred and sixty miles of sewers were laid and all but 9 of the original 92 miles were laid. . . . Four new bridges were built and 10 reconstructed, against 27,500 houses demolished in the department of the Seine, over 102,500 were built or rebuilt. In addition, 13 new churches, 2 synagogues, 5 town halls, 6 barracks, 5 theaters, and very many new markets . . . and schools, together with expansion and reconstruction in all these fields throughout the old and new Paris. (Sutcliffe, 1993, p. 83)

The beauty and romance of Paris have remained, but by the middle of the twentieth century, the city had grown rapidly and became one of the most overcrowded, congested, and poorly housed cities in Europe. During the decade from 1965 to 1975, officials of the French government and of the Paris region built five new towns and expanded six older suburbs within a twenty-mile radius of Paris. These efforts were designed to provide badly needed housing and to redistribute surplus populations outward from the central city. By minimizing some of the overcrowding, the officials also hoped that existing Parisian neighborhoods could be renewed and modernized (Hall, 1998).

A 1960s Master Plan for the Paris region had established construction areas, open space standards, and a communications network. Development was encouraged east of Paris to counter the existing drift to the west. Two new types of communities were created: those to be built on virgin land and those to be built on the base of an existing suburb (Gold, 1982). Each of the new units was designed for an eventual population of two hundred to three hundred thousand people. In turn, each of these was designed to be served by the appropriate political, economic, cultural, and recreational agencies, as well as by a service infrastructure, schools, universities, art galleries, and a "lively mix of urban activities." These new towns were also designed to be served by a newly planned network of roads and rails to connect them to central Paris, although zones of industry and commerce were also planned for the new towns to make them reasonably self-sufficient and to make their residents free from the need to commute daily to city jobs (Huxtable, 1978).

To a certain extent, the new towns of the Paris region have served the functions for which they were intended. They have been made both accessible and affordable for a worker population no longer able to afford the rising costs of central Paris. The housing in the new towns has been able to absorb persons forced out of the older Paris neighborhoods that had been going through the process of gentrification. Gentrification had turned historic "slums" into costly, chic neighborhoods that the former residents could no longer afford (Fenby, 1999).

The new towns offered the virtues of central heating and running water and open green spaces—amenities that were not always available to the residents in their former city dwellings. The many kinds of services and facilities just described were also available, but most of the housing available in the new towns is contained in uniformly designed, modernistic, high-rise apartment buildings that were a sharp break from their traditionally loved Paris neighborhoods and their lively streetscapes. The traditional neighborhoods had always been considered attractive and exciting because they were filled with a life of constant use and activities (these qualities are discussed in more detail in chapter 6; see also Lofland, 1998).

According to Fenby (1999, pp. 288–290), the popular spirit that was once an essential element in the lifeblood of Paris has been dampened in many ways by gentrification, and many of the diversified kinds of people who made the reputation of Paris as a bustling, irreverent people's city have now moved to the suburbs. The city center, according to Fenby's view, has become an upper middle-class place, and Paris, the capital of France, is "becoming nothing more than a splendid showplace, from which the mass of people grow increasingly alienated." Fenby further reports that the French themselves say they would rather live in many of the other cities in France, rather than Paris. He points out that the newspaper, *Le Figaro,* has judged Paris to now be "a joyless, overcrowded metropolis where neighbourhoods have lost their individual character to bargain basement conformity." This has also been the view of some architectural and city planning critics, who had earlier decried the loss of the "traditional scale, character, easy functional and social mix, and elegant and sophisticated architecture of Paris, which may be the most beautiful and urban city in the world" (Huxtable, 1978, p. 167). But although the new towns and the transformation of many of the neighborhoods of Paris are still highly controversial, they had at least begun to fill a widely recognized need to relieve some of the congestion and overcrowding of Paris. However, it still remains to be seen whether, in the long run, their residents will be able to re-create a more traditional pattern of social interaction and lifestyles which they seem to miss, or will eventually invent even more satisfactory new social patterns in the physical environment of the new towns and neighborhoods, in spite of the critics' lack of enthusiasm for these developments.

POSTSCRIPT

On September 6, 2000, approximately 150 heads of state of the world's countries gathered together at the United Nations headquarters in New York, the largest such group ever assembled, for a three-day "millennium summit." The purpose was to look ahead at what kind of a global society the leaders hoped to achieve in the centuries ahead (*New York Times,* September 6, 2000, p. A13). Many of the world's leaders spoke of many of the problems identified earlier in this chapter, including overpopulation, the uneven costs and benefits of economic globalization, and the growing gap between the have and the have not nations of the world. Also discussed by many were the worldwide "Malthusian" problems of war, famine, and disease, as well as poverty, squalor, and environmental degradation on a world scale. As the secretary general of the United Nations put it, "Protests at the World Trade Organization meeting in Seattle last November showed that many people are unhappy about globalization, or at least about the way it is being handled. They feel too much attention is paid to commercial interests, not enough to social, cultural or environmental ones" (*Detroit Free Press,* September 7, 2000, p. 19A). The prime minister of Ireland added, "The statistics of poverty and inequality in our world are shocking and shameful. Half the world's population struggling on less than $2 dollars a day, over half a billion on less than $1. A quarter of a billion children of 14 and under working, sometimes in terrible conditions."

The summit concluded with a United Nations Millennium Declaration from the UN General Assembly. Some relevant excerpts from that declaration are as follows:

> We believe that the central challenge we face today is to ensure that globalization becomes a positive force for all the world's people. For while globalization offers great opportunities, at present its benefits are very unevenly shared, while its costs are unevenly distributed. We recognize that developing countries and countries with economies in transition face special difficulties in responding to this central challenge. Thus, only through broad and sustained efforts to create a shared future, based upon our common humanity in all its diversity, can globalization be made fully inclusive and equitable. These efforts must include policies and measures, at the global level, which correspond to the needs of developing countries and economies in transition, and are formulated and implemented with their effective participation. We consider certain fundamental values to be essential to international relations in the twenty-first century. These include:
>
> **Freedom.**   Men and women have the right to live their lives and raise their children in dignity, free from hunger and from the fear of violence, oppression or injustice. Democratic and participatory governance based on the will of the people insure these rights. . . .
>
> **Equality.**   No individual and no nation must be denied the opportunity to benefit from development. The equal rights and opportunities of women and men must be assured.
>
> **Solidarity.**   Global challenges must be managed in a way that distributes the costs and burdens fairly in accordance with basic principles of equity and social justice. Those who suffer, or who benefit the least, deserve help from those who benefit most.

Tolerance.   Human beings must respect each other, in all their diversity of belief, culture, and language. Differences within and between societies should neither be feared or repressed, but cherished as a precious asset of humanity. A culture of peace and dialogue among all civilizations should be actively promoted.

Respect for Nature.   Prudence must be shown in the management of all living species and natural resources, in accordance with the precepts of sustainable development. Only in this way can the immeasurable riches provided to us by nature be preserved and passed on to our descendants. The current unsustainable patterns of production and consumption must be changed, in the interest of our future welfare and that of our descendants.

Shared Responsibility.   Responsibility for managing worldwide economic and social development, as well as threats to international peace and security, must be shared among the nations of the world and should be exercised multilaterally. As the most universal and most representative organization in the world, the United Nations must play the central role. (*New York Times,* September 9, 2000, p. A4)

The United Nations also recognized that in order to achieve these objectives, it would need to develop stronger partnerships with both the private sector, and with organizations representing "civil" society. This latter idea has been more fully developed in a recent article by Benjamin R. Barber (September 11, 2000). He argues that as a first step toward democratically governing or regulating economic globalism, there is another form of internationalism, which is still in an emergent stage but which is beginning to grow and to become more visible on the world stage. What he is talking about is the surprising gains being made by non-governmental organizations (NGOs). These are made up of people who care about public forms of well-being and who are working to create on a global scale the normal civic balance that exists within democratic nations. He includes among such groups the multiplying coalitions of workers, environmentalists, students, and anarchists who use the Internet to "fashion a decentralized, non-ideological resistance to the International Monetary Fund (IMF) and the World Trade Organization (WTO), effectively capturing media attention by taking to the streets in Seattle, Washington DC, and London." Other examples include citizen groups who use "Good Housekeeping seal" methods to underwrite safe fisheries and rug manufacturers without child labor; university students who initiate movements to ensure that campus sports apparel is not manufactured in child-exploiting sweatshops; and global Internet communication among groups facilitated by organizations producing Web sites, such as oneworld.org and Globalvision's new mediachannel.org supersite. Such civic organizations attempt to divert new telecommunications from pure commerce to the public interests of global civic society (Barber, 2000).

Barber lists many more examples of newly formed civic groups that now attempt to influence the global strategies of international corporations. His main point is that there needs to be a counterforce to the current collusion between the multinational corporations and many of the sovereign nations which act in concert to protect free markets from any kind of government surveillance or control, even if these would be in the public interest. This counterforce, in effect, would be the newly emerging international civil society, which would potentially be capable of "opposing, subduing, and civilizing the anarchic forces" of the global economy. Civil groups, as so envisaged, would continue to work toward such control within the confines of national governments, much as they already do in the civil life of democratic societies, even though their goals are aimed toward a more democratized and responsive world economy. This would be necessary, because sovereign nations remain the domain of democratic societies, and they are the only organized entities powerful enough to regulate or control the global economy, that is, if they are sufficiently motivated by the demands of their citizens and if they are able to act in concert with other nations with similar internal demands (Barber, 2000).

For the moment, at least at the time of this writing, it appears that nothing short of a worldwide economic slowdown or crash could seriously curb the current momentum toward continued economic globalization and virtually unrestricted free market penetration of virtually all of the regions of the urban world. At the political level in the United States, serious organized opposition to increased globalization and free trade at this time comes primarily from Ralph Nader of the Green Party and Pat Buchanan, who now represents the Reform Party. Together, these two candidates for president in the 2000 election had the acknowledged support of only about 4 or 5 percent of the electorate, according to several public opinion poll results reported at the time of writing (Inside Politics, CNN, September 9, 2000). Some opposition also comes from organized labor, but the forces producing economic globalization are currently way too powerful to be resticted in any serious way by any existing or potential organized opposition in the foreseeable future. The full benefits and/or negative consequences for the urban world resulting from the economic globalization need to be more fully understood and evaluated by the citizens of the world's urban and urbanizing countries most directly affected by the changing world economy than is currently the case.

SELECTED BIBLIOGRAPHY

BARBER, BENJAMIN R. "Globalizing Democracy." *The American Prospect*. (September 11, 2000): 16–19.

BERRY, BRIAN J. L. *The Human Consequences of Urbanization*. New York: St. Martins Press, 1973.

———, and JOHN D. KASARDA. *Contemporary Urban Ecology*. New York: Macmillan, 1977.

BOLLENS, JOHN C., and HENRY J. SCHMANDT. *The Metropolis, Its People, Politics, and Economic Life,* 3d ed. New York: Harper and Row, 1975.

CASTELLS, MANUEL, and PETER HALL. *Technopoles of the World: The Making of Twenty-first Century Industrial Complexes*. London: Routledge, 1994.

DOBBS, MICHAEL. "Were the Bad Old Days Better?; Capitalism Has Brought Russia Greed, Corruption, and Nostalgia." *Washington Post National Weekly Edition*. August 21, 2000, p. 21.

DUTTON MICHAEL. *Streetlife China*. Cambridge: Cambridge University Press, 1998.

EHRLICH, PAUL R., and ANNE H. EHRLICH. *Population Resources; Environment: Issues in Human Ecology,* 2d ed. San Francisco: W. H. Freeman, 1972.

EITZEN, D. STANLEY, and MAXINE BACA ZINN. *Social Problems,* 7th ed. Boston: Allyn and Bacon, 1997.

FENBY, JONATHAN. *France on the Brink: A Great Civilization Faces the New Century*. New York: Arcade, 1999.

FISHER, JACK C. "Urban Planning in the Soviet Union and Eastern Europe." In *Taming Metropolis: How to Manage an Urbanized World,* Vol. II, H. Wentworth Eldredge (ed.). New York: Praeger, 1967.

———, Z. PIORO, and M. SAVIC. "Socialist City Planning: A Reexamination." In *Urbanism, Urbanization and Change: Comparative Perspectives,* 2d ed., Paul Medows and Ephraim H. Misruchi (eds.). Reading, MA: Addison-Wesley, 1967.

FREEDMAN, RONALD, and BERNARD BERELSON. "The Human Population." In *Scientific American: The Human Population*. New York: W. H. Freeman, 1974.

GOLD, HARRY. *The Sociology of Urban Life*. Englewood Cliffs, NJ.: Prentice-Hall, 1982.

HALL, PETER. *The World Cities*. New York: McGraw Hill, 1977.

———. *Cities and Civilization*. New York: Pantheon Books, 1998.

HAWLEY, AMOS. *Urban Society: An Ecological Approach*. New York: Ronald Press, 1971.

HUXTABLE, ADA LOUISE. "Cold Comfort: The New French Towns." *New York Times Magazine*, November 19, 1978.

KASARDA, JOHN D., and EDWARD CRENSHAW. "Third World Urbanization: Dimensions, Theories, and Determinants." *Annual Review of Sociology*. 17(1991):467–501.

LOFLAND, LYN H. *The Public Realm: Exploring the City's Quintessential Social Territory*. New York: Aldine de Gruyter, 1998.

MACIONIS, JOHN J., and VINCENT N. PARRILLO. *Cities and Urban Life*. Upper Saddle River, NJ: Prentice-Hall, 1998.

National Geographic Desk Reference. Washington, DC: National Geographic Society, 1999.

New York Times 2000 Almanac. New York: Penguin References, 1999.

PALEN, J. JOHN. *The Urban World*, 5th ed. New York: McGraw Hill, 1997

SASSEN, SASKIA. *The Global City: New York, Tokyo, and London*. Princeton, NJ: Princeton University Press, 1991.

SHEPPARD, FRANCIS. *London: A History*. Oxford: Oxford University Press, 1998.

SMITH, DAVID A., and MICHAEL F. TIMBERLAKE. "Urban Political Economy," In *The Urban World*, 5th ed., J. John Palen (ed.). New York: McGraw Hill, 1997.

Statistical Abstract of the United States: The National Data Book, 119th ed. Washington DC: U.S. Bureau of the Census, 1999.

SUTCLIFFE, A. *Paris: An Architectural History*. New Haven: Yale University Press, 1993.

TANG, WENFANG, and WILLIAM L. PARISH. *Chinese Urban Life under Reform: The Changing Social Contract*. Cambridge: Cambridge University Press, 2000.

United Nations Environmental Programme. *Global Environment Outlook*. New York: Oxford University Press, 1997.

U.S. Bureau of the Census. International Data Base, 1999. Washington, DC: U.S. Bureau of the Census, 1999.

WALLERSTEIN, IMMANUEL. *The Politics of the World Economy: The States, the Movements, and the Civilization*. Cambridge: Cambridge University Press, 1984.

WEEKS, JOHN R. *Population: An Introduction to Concepts and Issues*, 6th ed. Belmont, CA: Wadsworth, 1996.

WILSON, ROBERT A. and DAVID A. SCHULZ. *Urban Sociology*. Englewood Cliffs, NJ: Prentice Hall, 1978.

World Resources Institute. *A Guide to the Global Environment: The Urban Environment*. New York: Oxford University Press, 1996.

NAME INDEX

SUBJECT INDEX